TRIUMPHS AND TRAGEDY

A HISTORY OF THE MEXICAN PEOPLE

BOOKS BY RAMÓN EDUARDO RUIZ

The Great Rebellion

Cuba: The Making of a Revolution

The People of Sonora and Yankee Capitalists

Labor and the Ambivalent Revolutionaries: Mexico, 1911–1923

Mexico: The Challenge of Poverty and Illiteracy

In Spanish

La gran rebelión: México, 1905–1924

Cuba: Génesis de un revolución

El pueblo de Sonora y los capitalistas yanquis

La Revolución mexicana y el movimiento obrero

México, 1920–1958: El reto de la pobreza y del analfabetismo

Edited Works

The Mexican War: Was It Manifest Destiny?

An American in Maximilian's Mexico, 1865–1866: The Diaries of William Marshall Anderson

Interpreting Latin American History

With Robert Detweiler, *Liberation in the Americas: Comparative Aspects of the Independence Movements in Mexico and the United State*

Edited Works in Spanish

Historia general de Sonora. V Historia contemporanea de Sonora: 1929–1984

TRIUMPHS AND TRAGEDY

A HISTORY OF THE MEXICAN PEOPLE

Ramón Eduardo Ruiz

W·W·NORTON & COMPANY New York London

Printed in the United States of America.

The text of this book is composed in Janson Alternate,
with the display set in Augustea.
Composition and manufacturing by the Haddon Craftsmen, Inc.
Book design by Jack Meserole.

Library of Congress Cataloging in Publication Data
Ruiz, Ramón Eduardo.
Triumphs and tragedy : a history of the Mexican people / by Ramón Eduardo Ruiz.
p. cm.
Includes index.
1. Mexico—History. I. Title
IN PROCESS (ONLINE) 91-13136

ISBN 0-393-03023-7

W.W. Norton & Company, Inc., 500 Fifth Avenue, New York, N.Y. 10110

W.W. Norton & Company, Ltd., 10 Coptic Street, London WC1A 1PU

2 3 4 5 6 7 8 9 0

Devuelvo al pueblo mexicano
lo que de la herencia histórica de
sus antepasados pude rescatar.

Why must we be eternally on our knees before the Kants and Hugos? All praise to the masters indeed, but we too could produce a Kant or a Hugo. We too could wrest iron from the bowels of the earth and fashion it into ships and machines. We could raise prodigious cities and create nations, and explore the universe. Was it not from a mixture of two races that the Titans sprang?

—José Clemente Orozco

CONTENTS

FOREWORD

"Nothing is as it was," insisted Ramón del Valle Inclán, the Spanish intellectual, "merely as it is remembered." What Valle Inclán meant was that history is what actually occurs, but something else when historians recall it. Valle Inclán's wisdom, which I deem indisputable, flies in the face of Leopold von Ranke's hoary cry for objective history, the need, as he put it, to "simply show how it really was," a call to arms answered by three generations of German, British, and French historians of the nineteenth century and, also true, by a legion of American scholars and not a few Mexicans.

But, from the hindsight of today, that aphorism looks profoundly shallow if not downright impossible because what historians refer to as "facts" are a strange phenomenon. The empirical theory of knowledge to the contrary, there is no complete separation between subject and object. "Facts," to quote Edward Hallett Carr, one of the fine historians of our age, "like sense-impressions, impinge on the observer from outside, and are independent of his consciousness." For better or worse, written "history consists of a corpus of ascertained facts." The historian, after he has pieced them together, "takes them home, and cooks and serves them in whatever style appeals to him." Facts never speak for themselves, but "only when the historian calls on them; it is he who decides to which facts to give the floor, and in what order or context." That a core of "historical facts" lies "objectively and independently of the interpretation of the historian is a preposterous fallacy" because the "historian is neither the humble slave, nor the tyrannical master, of his facts." When Carr writes that the "function of the historian is neither to love the past nor to emancipate himself from the past, but to master it and understand it as the key to the understanding of the present," I am in total agreement with him. That, in a nutshell, is what underlines my interpretation of Mexico's history. I have endeavored to be "objective," but, I must confess, I have a point of view which has colored my assessment of the "facts."

This interpretation of Mexican history has two themes, as different in scope as the mastodonic figures and Homeric themes of José Clemente Orozco, one of the Promethean Mexican muralists, are from the delicate blue fishes of the Russian Marc Chagall. The triumphs of the Mexican people in the arts and literature and, from time to time, in the realm of the social conscience are numerous and wonderful. How many people, to quote chapter and verse, can lay claim to a Lázaro Cárdenas, the radical reformer and doer of the 1930s, or to a Benito Juárez, a politico from a tiny Indian pueblo in Oaxaca who, against overwhelming odds, held his country together at the middle of the nineteenth century against the perfidy of disloyal Mexicans and the military fury of French imperialist troops? Then there is Emiliano Zapata, a dirt farmer from Anenecuilco, a hamlet in Morelos, who, notwithstanding bribes of sundry sorts tendered to him to lay down his arms, died defending the rights of campesinos to a parcel of land and the plea of industrial workers for a decent wage.

Despite this parade of triumphs—and they are mighty indeed—the history of Mexico, if the happiness and welfare of the underdogs is our barometer for judgment, is mostly a tragedy. From the Spanish Conquest on, when the cross and the sword of the Europeans bent ancient Anáhuac to their will, the poor, usually bronze of skin and racially more Indian than Spanish, have carried the burdens of Mexico, victims of man's inhumanity to man. Thus, the title, the triumphs of some juxtaposed to the never-ending tragedy, the dogged struggle to keep body and soul alive. Warts and all, just the same, it is an epic saga, of a mestizo people, partly Spanish and partly Indian, trying to forge a culture and a nationality, made all the more difficult by the omnipotent presence of the United States, the neighbor next door.

I am indebted to multitudes of scholars, writers, and travelers, whose books and articles did the spadework for me. I am grateful especially to William B. Taylor, who read the entire manuscript. Andrés Lira, in particular, but also Carlos Herrejón and Heriberto Moreno helped, as did Enrique Semo, Luis González, and Enrique Florescano. I thank, too, the wonderful staff of the Library of the Colegio de Michoacán, ready always to find what I was looking for, and Miguel Monteon and David Ringrose, who read chapters of the manuscript, as did my daughter, Olivia Teresa Ruiz, an anthropologist who believes in the importance of history. Above all, I thank Natalia, my wife of more than four decades, who helped me put my garbled typing into sensible form on the computer, supposedly our century's gift to authors.

Rancho Santa Fe
California

TRIUMPHS AND TRAGEDY

A HISTORY OF THE MEXICAN PEOPLE

1

THE FOREFATHERS

I

Long, long ago, in the New World and Europe, the story of Mexico's people began to unfold. Mexicans, generally speaking, trace their family tree back to both pre-Columbian and medieval Spanish societies. In the early years of the sixteenth century, when Hernán Cortés and his band of plunderers overwhelmed Tenochtitlán, the capital of the Aztecs, crossbreeding got going. That miscegenation was more than just racial. Though the Spaniards imposed their will on the Indians, as Christopher Columbus mistakenly baptized the natives of the New World, their customs, food, and beliefs, often to a surprising degree, weathered the gale storms of Conquest. For Mexico, therefore, the shape of the future starts with two "races" and cultures literally an ocean apart.

Because Mexicans are the offspring of Europeans and native Americans, their meeting, from the start, led to a confrontation of remarkable consequences. The two "races," the icon used loosely, were, after all, dissimilar. The Spaniards, say some anthropologists, had stumbled upon an "archaic" civilization, in diverse ways perhaps living in an earlier evolutionary stage whose technical accoutrements, by Western standards, were modest. Cultural and social anthropology, as a matter of fact, made its reputation as a discipline from the study of non-Western peoples, of what the Spaniards encountered in the New World. Bronislaw Malinowski and his school of anthropologists, who closed their eyes to all but isolated societies, would have crowed like roosters over the natives discovered by the Spaniards.

What draws attention to this confrontation, obviously, is how and why it came to pass and, of course, its results. The themes for analysis are endless, beginning with alienation by subjugation, which implies, to cite the wisdom of Karl Marx, loss of the means of production. The ancients lost, no one disputes, control over the land, the foundation of their independence. Alienation also included the Spanish assault on family kinship ties, the glue that held together the pre-Hispanic community, and, most significantly, on the pagan religion, for, to cite Elsie Clews Parsons's study of Mitla, a town with ancient roots, when "the ceremonial life of a highly ceremonialized community is suppressed," much "of its general culture goes by the board." During the sixteenth century, moreover, Spanish colonists and the Catholic clergy made only sporadic efforts to teach the natives the Spanish language, preferring to learn the Indian tongues in order to communicate with them. The few Indians who mastered Spanish usually did so not to teach their neighbors but, to the contrary, to interpret for the labor of Conquest beyond the Valley of Mexico and for the administration of colonial affairs. "Every colonized people," writes Frantz Fanon, "finds itself face to face with the language of the civilizing country," which is "used to convey the master's orders." The irreducible and stubborn fact is that for the natives of the New World, there was merely marginal acculturation because the Spaniards offered no olive branch. Actually, the term *acculturation,* as defined by anthropologists, has meaning only for the mestizo, the progeny of Spaniard and Indian. Yet, regardless of the nature of the Conquest, the morphogeny of the society which emerged from the momentous meeting of these two diverse populations surely is one of the most fascinating episodes in the annals of human history.

But, preoccupations of anthropologists aside, we must get on with the story. Where to begin or, to put the question succinctly, which of the two societies must we give priority? I have chosen to tell first the story of the pre-Columbians, for they were the original inhabitants of Mexico and, biologically at least, absorbed the few Spaniards who ventured forth into the New World in the course of three centuries of colonial tutelage. As a consequence, Mexicans, to underline again, embody the heritage of two civilizations, albeit one, that of the Europeans, seemingly destroyed the native one.

II

Men and women, be they Europeans or natives of a world an ocean apart, do not live in a vacuum; they inhabit a physical environment, a land which, in turn, helps to mold their way of life and that of their community, particularly if they are an "archaic" people who, because of the absence of technology and machinery, are subservient to the whims of an all-powerful Mother Nature. We must, therefore, get under way our study of pre-Hispanic societies with the geographical domain on which they built their civilizations and which, conversely, influenced the parameters of Spanish colonial society.

When Charles I asked, "What is the land like?" an envoy sent by Cortés picked up a sheet of paper and crumpled it into a ball. Then, opening his hand, he let the paper unfold in his palm, saying, "It's like this, Sire." That twisted and wrinkled land helped set historical contours. Though cast in the form of a cornucopia, it was, more often than not, an empty horn of plenty.

Pre-Columbians inhabited a topsy-turvy land. The Valley of Mexico, which sat atop the Mesa Central, or plateau, was fertile. Referred to as Anáhuac by its native inhabitants, it encompassed the present Basin of Mexico but included lands to the east, known as Tlateputzco by the early dwellers. It was a much coveted and beautiful land, at its core lakes, among them Texcoco, the largest, fed by waters from the melted snow of the surrounding mountains. Beyond them lay sierras and lowlands, heat and cold, and tropical jungle. North of Anáhuac were arid expanses where cactus and thickets of mesquites thrived, an austere and endless steppe country, according to the ancients of Anáhuac, a "place of dry rocks . . . of death from thirst and . . . starvation." Along both coasts were gigantic mountain ranges, stretching from the current borders of the United States south to the Isthmus of Tehuantepec, where they disappeared to rise again in Chiapas in a forest of mountains and hills. Nestled between the ranges was the Mesa Central, rising from 4,000 feet at Ciudad Juárez, gateway to the North American Southwest, to over 8,000 feet in the south. The volcanic peaks of Popocatéptl, Iztaccíhuatl, and Orizaba towered dramatically over the coastal ranges and split the central plateau into dissimilar pieces. Lesser volcanoes encircled them, while giant ravines swept inland for hundreds of miles from both coasts. Just 8 percent of the land was level, and much of the flat country lay in soil-impoverished Yucatán or the arid north. Mountains occupied two-thirds of Mexico's total area, about one-fifth that of the continental United States.

Because of the mountains, altitude and not latitude set the life of ancient Mexicans, who spoke of going up or down, not of traveling south or north. There were three distinct levels. From sea level to 3,000 feet lay the *tierra caliente,* or the hot lands, usually tropical but arid in the northwest. Above them to 6,000 feet was the *tierra templada,* or temperate zone, much of it desert. The *tierra fría,* the cold lands, rose still higher, often barren and inhospitable. At the heart of Mexico was the Mesa Central, a plateau favored by nature. The north was an extension of the mesa but arid except for occasional rains. On the west was the Pacific slope, rich but cut off from the mesa by unconquerable mountain ranges; on the east lay the Gulf slope, fertile but unhealthy. Present-day Michoacán, Guerrero, Oaxaca, and Chiapas formed the mountainous region of the south. Jutting into the Gulf of Mexico was the peninsula of Yucatán. Completing the geographic picture was the arid arm of Lower California, isolated by the Gulf of California and the deserts of Sonora.

From Ciudad Juárez to the Guatemalan border, Tláloc, the ancient god of rain, ruled with grim humor. He made the north a desert; rainfall averaged seven and a half inches a year. On the southern and coastal lowlands of the Gulf of Mexico—Veracruz, Campeche, Tabasco, and the Isthmus of Tehuantepec—he dumped four to ten feet of water annually. The rain leached the land of its plant food and turned it into a green desert. Only from Aguascalientes to Mexico City did Tláloc give his people the water they craved. These were the facts of the water supply. Two-thirds of Mexico's arable land suffered from scarce seasonal rainfall; crops survived only during the rainy season. A bare 6 percent of the arable land did not require irrigation. Navigable rivers were conspicuous by their absence, and only a handful of lakes dotted the landscape. Outside of the Mesa Central, generally speaking, this land was niggardly for human life.

Despite that, human beings had made it their habitat. From remote antiquity, maybe as many as four hundred varieties of maize, or corn, made possible sedentary civilization, probably from as early as 5000 B.C. The primitive system of agriculture, of cutting down trees and burning them and the grass underneath in order to plant corn, known as slash and burn, originated some two thousand years later, most likely among the Maya of Yucatán. The inhabitants of the Mesa Central called their corn patch a "milpa." In time, corn became the lifeblood of society.

Beans and squash were other staples of the diet. The people of Anáhuac cultivated over fifty types of beans, cooking them with chili peppers of multiple varieties and eating them with tortillas, flat, round cakes made of ground corn. Pumpkins, onions, and tomatoes were grown, as well as the maguey, from which pulque, an alcoholic drink, was fermented. Eaten sparingly, meat was largely game. Among the fibers, cotton and henequen were cultivated.

III

From these advances derives the ebb and flow of civilizations. Archaeologists have gradually pieced together their story, but, to quote one of them, "because there are many controversial points in the ancient history and culture of Mexico, and too little information, all data must be interpreted." Naturally interpretations abound, and some are diametricaly opposed to others. Traditionally, to complicate matters, most of us have been taught that all European cultures stood head and shoulders above the indigenous cultures of pre-Hispanic America. That is an ethnocentric view which stems from our European heritage and cultural preferences. Europe undoubtedly had mechanical superiority, but in the fine arts and practical crafts as well as in social and ethical values the New World was on a par with Europe. As one writer points out, millions of Indians were killed "to prove that Europeans were more civilized."

The first of these civilizations was that of the Olmecs, who, living in western Tabasco and Veracruz, flourished between 800 and 400 B.C. One of the mother cultures of ancient Mexico, the Olmecs made La Venta their principal city and opened the stage for the drama of the Classic era, the years from approximately 150 B.C. to about A.D. 900, occasionally an era of peace, when people devoted their talents to creative pursuits. At the apogee of the Classic age, the cultures of the inhabitants of ancient Anáhuac were on a level with those of Europe. During these centuries, the great cities of Teotihuacán, Palenque, Yaxchilán, Monte Albán, Xochicalco, and Tajín took form, offspring of the genius of Maya, Totonac, Huaxtec, Zapotec, and Teotihuacano. The cities, almost always religious shrines, document the importance of religion, ceremony, and ritual. An omnipotent theocracy ruled over each of them, dictating dogma and behavior. The priests were the intelligentsia, the scientists, and the cultural standard-bearers, spokesmen for a pantheon of gods.

Learning was a hallmark of this Classic world. The Olmecs, perhaps, and surely the Maya, had mastered the concept of the zero. Astronomy, while not as advanced, did not lag far behind. The pre-Hispanic calendar, more accurate than the European, had 365 days. With a keen sense of history, the ancients developed a system of hieroglyphics, setting down their thoughts in picture books and codices. Cortés discovered in the towns of Veracruz "books made of . . . paper, doubled in folds, like the cloth of Castilla." Unfortunately, in their fanatical rush to wipe out the old, the Spaniards burned priceless manuscripts. Typical of them was Bishop Diego de Landa of Yucatán, who destroyed countless native chronicles because "they contained nothing but superstition and lies of devils."

The arts, too, thrived. Sculpture set the pace, linked closely to religion and expressing, in figures carved from stone, the mysteries of rites and gods. Painting, especially murals, was popular, as the splendid Maya drawings at Bonampak testify. Mural art, like sculpture, complemented architecture, its themes dealing mostly with religion and history. Yet at Teotihuacán and at Maya shrines artists painted scenes of daily life. Though lacking the potter's wheel, artisans turned out elegant bowls and dishes. The useful and the beautiful were one and the same, though purely functional pottery, simple and crude, was produced. In pre-Hispanic Mexico, pottery was a major industry, the work of specialists, often living in one village, where fathers passed on the craft to their sons. Music, song, and dance flourished. There were flutes, rattles, and drums galore and, maybe, trumpets of wood. Dances held in the town square could, on occasion, prove erotic, with "phallic rites and sexual orgies." The *danza de los voladores,* where dancers hanging from ropes fly around a pole a hundred feet high, started at this time.

Two dominant cultures flourished during the Classic era. First was that of Teotihuacán, lord in the Valley of Mexico by 200 B.C. With 100,000 inhabitants, the city of Teotihuacán, just outside present-day Mexico City, was twelve miles square. A ceremonial city, it sat astride an empire reaching from

Guanajuato to Oaxaca. At one end of its central square rose the Pyramid of the Sun, 215 feet tall and resting on a base over 700 feet long on all four sides; facing it stood the Pyramid of the Moon. This place of the gods, over which Quetzalcóatl, the Feathered Serpent, presided, fell into ruins about A.D. 650. Side by side with Teotihuacán were Cholula, a commercial hub and holy city; Xochicalco, a cultural oasis in the sierra of Morelos; and Monte Albán, a Zapotec sanctuary in Oaxaca which, infiltrated by the Mixtecs, eventually lost its dominance.

The greatest of the Classic civilizations, the golden age of the pre-Hispanic world, was that of the Maya, who occupied the lands of Yucatán, Campeche, Tabasco, eastern Chiapas, and Quintana Roo and northern Guatemala. Of their ceremonial sites, Tikal, in the Petén of Guatemala, served as the vanguard, while Uaxactún, the oldest of the Maya centers, lay just north of it. Palenque in Chiapas was small by comparison but a cultural jewel, the "Athens of the Maya world." These sites lay abandoned for centuries, until John L. Stephens's marvelous account *Incidents of Travel in Central America and Chiapas and Yucatan,* written in the 1840s, rescued them from oblivion. The Maya, whom archaeologists dub the Greeks of the New World, excelled in science and learning, their writing verging on the phonetic. A sort of bible was the *Popul vuh,* the book of the Cakchiquel Maya, rewritten after the Conquest in Quiché by a Maya in Guatemala.

IV

About A.D. 900, the Classic period began to fade out. Still, the Valley of Mexico continued to shelter vigorous civilizations, this time the Toltecs from Tula, dynamic builders and warriors but less advanced than their Classic ancestors. The Toltecs, one of the northern tribes known as Chichimecas, established their control over much of Anáhuac on the ruins of Teotihuacán. At about the same time, the Zapotecs, who had abandoned Monte Albán, built Mitla. From Zaachila, their capital city, the influence of the Zapotecs spread to Puebla, Guerrero, and western Oaxaca. But, again, the Mixtecs compelled the Zapotecs to forsake Mitla or to live alongside of them. The Mixtecs, their ranks swollen by refugees from Tula and wayward Olmecs, forged a Mixteca-Puebla culture.

Meanwhile, a post-Classic Maya culture, strongly influenced by the Toltecs, appeared in Yucatán, on a flat limestone shelf barren of rivers. The Maya-Toltecs established their base at Chichén Itzá, a ceremonial site in the image of Tula, governing through an alliance with the Maya cities of Uxmal and Mayapán. The post-Classic Maya, perhaps because of the Toltec influence, looked to warriors for political leadership. Quetzalcóatl, introduced by the Toltecs, became a deity of the Maya, for whom he was Kukulcán, his worship transformed into a cult of human sacrifice. The Maya, the evidence shows, had adopted the religious symbols of the Toltecs. However, a century before the coming of the Spaniards, the Maya cities were merely ruins. In the *Libros de Chilam Balam,* the Maya left for posterity their version of history.

After the collapse of the Toltecs' Tula, savage Chichimecas invaded the Valley of Mexico, fighting with bows and arrows, a military innovation for that time. The lords of the Chichimeca tribes were the Aztecs, also referred to as the Mexica. No one, it seems, knew their place of birth. They spoke Nahuatl and worshiped Huitzilopochtli. Over the course of time, these savages adopted the more refined ways of their neighbors and became civilized. From 1250 to 1298, they lived in Chapultepec; but they were poor neighbors, stealing the wives of others and horrifying everyone with their repugnant rites of human sacrifice. Their next stop was near Tizapán, from where they fled to uninhabited islands in Lake Texcoco. On these swampy lands, hemmed in by Texcoco, Atzcapotzalco, and Culhuacán, rival tribal towns, the Aztecs in 1325 laid the cornerstones of Tenochtitlán, capital of their world. Later, joining hands with Tlacopan (Tacuba) and Texcoco, Tenochtitlán, under the able guidance of Itzcóatl, one of the early chieftains, broke Atzcapotzalco's hegemony in the Valley of Mexico. Thereafter, this triple alliance had the final say.

Led by Itzcóatl and his successors—Moctezuma I, Axayácatl, and Moctezuma II—the Aztecs built an empire. When the Spaniards arrived in 1519, Moctezuma II had under his sway lands extending from the Pacific to the Gulf of Mexico and from Guatemala north to Querétaro. Only a few states escaped the Aztecs' net, notably Tlaxcala and the Tarascans of Michoacán. The Tlaxcalans, a fiercely independent people, stayed free by being vigilant, providing victims for Aztec sacrifice, and offering battle when necessary. In just over a century, the Aztecs, the crude barbarians of recent times, had become "flower-smelling connoisseurs of gracious living," the masters of a society exalting piety and religion while making killing and warfare common practice. Their society was both brutal and just, a society of laws ably administered by rulers of high ideals. Not yet on a par with that of the Classic Maya, Aztec civilization, for all that, was on the march.

Some demographers estimate that as many as twenty-five million people inhabited central Mexico in 1521. Dwelling in different towns and paying homage to diverse kings, the people of Anáhuac had a common language, civil codes, and religious beliefs. Although part of a triple alliance, Tenochtitlán had usurped the authority of both Tlacopan and Texcoco by 1500. The Aztecs, nonetheless, were never able to destroy tribal diversity in the Valley. Tenochtitlán was the shining star of Anáhuac, but each of the principal tribes, fiefdoms bowing before Aztec wishes, had cities and towns of their own—Tenayuca, Tacuba, Chalco, Atzcapotzalco, Ixtapalapa, Xochimilco, and Culhuacán among them.

Tenochtitlán was a metropolis of vast stone pyramids and stucco walls of bright colors glistening in the sun. The temples of Huitzilopochtli and Tláloc, both standing on top of pyramids, looked out over the city. Buildings to store grain or serve as treasuries and arsenals occupied strategic locations and, occasionally, stone sculptures of deities, some of impressive size, added grandeur to the city. Botanical gardens interspersed among the pyramids and buildings and an abundance of trees and flowers gave Tenochtitlán a feeling of gaiety and light. Merchants, artisans, and farmers sold their wares at the *mercado* of Tlatelolco, the biggest and most famous of the marketplaces. Sitting astride Lake Texcoco, the city was connected to the mainland by causeways, at intervals cut by canals with drawbridges over them. The homes of the nobility, many two stories tall and some with fifty or more rooms, ringed the inner city. The common people lived on the fringes, in huts, jacales of mud and bamboo. Out in the hinterland, dirt farmers, who fed the city, made their homes in hamlets, from where they went out to till their milpas.

Society and the common welfare, not the good of the individual, was the rule. As individuals, men and women counted for little. "Simpler" societies, after all, are more uniform, providing opportunities for a far smaller diversity of individual occupations than more complex ones. Individual rights mattered not a bit. Everyone had a place in society and duties to perform and obligations to fulfill. No one questioned the established order, "knowing perfectly," to quote one scholar, "his status in relation to his family, his clan, his community and his gods." Happy were they who did what they were asked and did not question their status.

For Aztec society, essentially in the tribal stage, the calpulli, a clan united by blood and family ties, was the cornerstone, conferring life on its institutions and dictating property concepts. Each calpulli owned lands of its own, divided among the heads of families, who tilled them and paid tribute. The farmer had merely the right of usufruct so long as he complied with his duties and obligations. However, there was also private property. Owned by a nobility, these lands, called *pillali,* were passed from father to son. (Among the Mixtecs and Zapotecs of Oaxaca, moreover, land was held by the "divine right" of the lord.) *Mayeques,* usually conquered people bound to the soil like the serfs of medieval Europe, tilled the lands for the benefit of their owners. There were lands bestowed as a reward for a meritorious deed—valor in war, for example, to a *tectecuhtzin,* or lord; peasants, referred to as *teccallec,* tilled them. By the sixteenth century, the owners of these lands formed a powerful landed nobility. There were also public lands, set aside for the monarch and farmed by *mayeques,* as well as lands to support officials, including priests, judges, teachers, and the military. These lands, along with those of the pillali and *tectecuhtzin,* were the most fertile. The large and growing population of central Mexico, moreover, had begun to place agricultural lands at a premium; the problem of land scarcity was a fact of life.

To provide labor was the duty of the common folk who, as *macehuales*, planted the lands of the calpulli. Labor to build or to repair public buildings, bridges, temples, or streets was demanded of everyone not of the nobility, the clergy, or the military. At the bottom of the labor picture were the slaves, men and women in bondage, recalled a Spanish soldier of the Conquest, sold in the marketplaces "tied to long poles with collars around their necks so they couldn't escape." Yet children of slaves were born free, and slaves had certain rights, among them the right to marry women of their choice, own slaves, and buy their freedom. Slavery, no matter how benign, attested to the existence of a hierarchical society and to the wide gap separating rich from poor.

The economy was not simply an agricultural one, because commerce, too, was important. *Pochtecas*, traveling merchants, carried on a lively trade between towns hundreds of miles apart, going everywhere in search of business. When the Spaniards saw the *mercado* of Tlatelolco, the biggest of its time, they were astonished "at the number of people and the quantity of merchandise." Business was conducted by barter, goods being exchanged for goods. Gold, too, apparently served as currency, though the Aztecs referred to it as the "excrement of the gods."

In the Aztec universe, democracy, as Westerners know it, was nowhere to be found. As in bygone civilizations, a hierarchy of priests shaped politics; their presence was felt even in military affairs. At the pinnacle of the theocracy stood the monarch, both priest and warrior. A committee of notables chose him from the royal family, the throne passing from brother to brother until no kin survived. The monarch was chief priest, chief general, and chief judge. Over the years, he ruled more and more as an absolute despot and presided over a larger and larger nobility. Once in a while, offices rotated, giving a select few an opportunity to share the responsibilities of public administration, in which the Aztecs excelled.

The Aztec empire consisted of subject states. However, unlike the European masters of empires, the Aztecs neither colonized, annexed alien territories, nor imposed their political system on their vassals. They did collect tribute, more so with the growth of population in the Valley of Anáhuac. To thrive, Tenochtitlán, Texcoco, and Tlacopan required increasingly more food and raw materials, all beyond the capacity of the Valley to produce. While compelled to pay tribute, the vassals of the Aztecs kept their language, customs, religion, and, paradoxically, rulers. Rarely were they controlled directly by the Aztecs, though their tax collectors were never absent. This panoply of tribute-paying states seethed with discontent, a fact the Spaniards put to good use.

Laws and courts of justice were the anchors of Aztec life. Named by the monarch and chosen for their integrity, judges wielded great authority, empowered to order the arrest of even dignitaries. The nobility, nevertheless, could be tried only in special courts. Each town had its own judges, with the emperor serving as the final court of appeals. Aztec law was rigid and harsh. Failure to obey superiors and violations of tribal customs stood at the top of the list of crimes. Land disputes occupied much of the agenda of the courts; to destroy or remove boundary markers meant death, a fate that befell persons who robbed four or more ears of corn. Hanging awaited homosexuals as well as adulterers when they belonged to the nobility. Lying and cheating drew the wrath of the law, while striking a parent could lead to loss of inheritance or life.

The Aztecs believed that they dwelt in a tempestuous and hostile universe presided over by capricious deities who must be placated. Religion stressed the worship of natural objects and phenomena such as clouds, fire, earth, and forests. The sun and moon, the stars and planets, day and night, water and rain, as well as earthquakes made up a pantheon of gods, identified with special days, months, and years and with towns and cities. The Aztecs identified Huitzilopochtli, their tribal god, with the sun; a god of fertility and learning, Quetzalcóatl, was revered, while Tezcatlipoca, patron of Texcoco and of night, inspired fear. Tláloc, the rain god, had a legion of admirers, as did Coatlicue, the goddess of fertility. Hell was briefly for the dead, and immortality awaited everyone. Aztecs confessed to priests and won forgiveness for their sins, a rite associated with the goddess Tlazoltéotl, the Eater of Filth. But the gods did not punish sin, at least as the Aztecs defined it.

To learn what the gods wanted was the responsibility of priests. Living austere lives, they did the bidding of the gods, performing penance and teaching. As a reward for their selflessness, the state fed, clothed, and housed them, often in sumptuous palaces. Usually the sons of prominent families, the priests "wore a dark habit like a cassock and robes reaching to their feet," recalled a Spanish soldier. They never cut their hair, so it "was long, reaching to their belts" and, occasionally, to their feet. Men filled the ranks of the priesthood, but female priestesses, titled Cihuateopizques, catered to the whim of the earth goddess, Cihuacuacuilli.

Seeking to please their gods, the Aztecs made offerings to them. The highest act of piety was the sacrifice of human life, for Huitzilopochtli relished human hearts wrenched from the living. The practice, not unique to the Aztecs, began about 1450 when, in the midst of a prolonged drought, the Aztecs, thinking that Huitzilopochtli was angry at them, set out to placate him. When the weather improved and the corn flourished, the Aztecs, in gratitude, sacrificed more victims. As Huitzilopochtli helped the Aztecs to expand their empire, imperial success led to wars in search of victims to sacrifice in order to expand more. No wonder, therefore, as the Spaniards discovered, that the walls and altars of the temples "were bloody with the hearts of victims."

The Aztecs, like most societies on this earth, glorified warfare. People, after all, will fight, writes one historian, for "any conceivable motive or combination of motives," including "for fun and profit, for . . . land, for glory and freedom, for honors and plunder." A bellicose people, the Aztecs believed aggression to be the best defense. From the time they could walk, boys were taught how to fight, what their forebears had done since they had invaded the Valley of Mexico. No less militant, women went along on military expeditions, to cook, take care of their soldiers, and carry supplies. Military victories added tribute to the empire and, concomitantly, made the Aztecs more parasitic, as they increasingly lived off the tribute of the vanquished.

Aztec women, like their males, lived in a two-tiered society. The wives, mothers, and daughters of the nobility dwelt at the top of the hierarchical pyramid; the females of the *macehuales,* the great majority, at its base. Yet elite women, the *pilli,* though sheltered from childhood on and taught to weave, embroider, and sew, were excluded from political, military, and most clerical posts. Meanwhile, the *macehualtines,* the poor, not only did the cooking, cleaning, and caring for children of the home but, in addition, labored in the fields, made ceramic pots, wove cloth, and cooked tortillas and tamales for sale in the marketplace.

But Aztec males, whatever their status in society, employed a double standard. The men, according to one anthropologist, wanted their woman "tied to her *metate,* the *comal,* and the preparation of the tortilla." It was the duty of women to bear children, to care for them, and, most important, to transmit Aztec culture and traditions to them. Men frowned upon talkative women, desiring, one Spanish chronicler remarked, both their "ears and nose stopped up." At mealtime, women fed their men and did not talk; at other times, they stayed in the houses men had built. Only marriages between brothers and sisters or between fathers and daughters were frowned upon. Men of the elite prized virginity in their women, equating it with honor, but were polygamists; Moctezuma II, for example, had two wives and a household of concubines, the daughters of nobles. While elite males often chose their wives on political or economic grounds, love or erotic fantasies, the evidence seems to show, played a more significant part in how *macehuales* picked their partners. Women wore makeup and decorated themselves with tattoos. Diego Rivera, the noted Mexican painter, later captured beautifully this use of cosmetics in his mural of the women of Tlatelolco, where he depicted a tall prostitute wearing a white cotton tunic and displaying shapely legs covered with tattoos.

The Aztecs placed schooling on a pedestal, declaring it public and obligatory. All children from the age of six had to attend. Coeducation, however, was unknown; the sexes were segregated. Social status determined what schools boys attended, the sons of the nobility enrolling in the *calmécac* and those of plebeians in the *telpochcalli.* Boys from well-off families were prepared for high political office and to lead troops; the sons of the common folk learned moral citizenship and got ready to be foot soldiers. In both *telpochcalli* and *calmécac,* soldier-priests made up the faculty. The schools for girls, run by priestesses, taught the domestic arts and offered religious training. Daughters of the elite who did not marry, a tiny handful, were the priestesses.

The Aztecs were hardly artistically innovative. They were imitators, but still painted splendid murals and codices. They left a resplendent legacy of stone sculpturing, of huge figures grotesque in character but carved with skill and imagination. As the terrifying Coatlicue, a thing of skeletal heads and protruding tusks, demonstrates, art served as the instrument of religion, voicing the Aztecs' preoccupation with death and gods. The Aztecs also built stone temples, maybe forty thousand of them. Music, like art, was the handmaiden of religion.

The pre-Hispanic world, in retrospect, appears both old and complex. Diverse cultures, from the Olmecs on, had their day in the sun. Tongues spoken by Mazatecs, Mixe, Chinantecs, Yaquis, and Tarahumaras, to name just a few, added linguistic diversity. The habit of obedience to priests and military lords, as well as religious orthodoxy and social distinctions, was deeply ingrained in ancient Anáhuac. The Aztecs, although one of the principal tribes, created merely one of many cultures. It is also clear, however, that the Spaniards did not introduce civilization to the New World; it was there already and, even measured by European standards of the time, culturally alive and well.

V

The history of our nation, believed José Vasconcelos, the eminent Mexican thinker, begins with "with the discovery and Conquest of the New World; before the coming of the Spaniards, Mexico did not exist. We entered the halls of civilization under the royal tiara of Castilla." Vasconcelos, a Hispanist first and foremost, exaggerated but did not entirely distort the truth. As a young Mexican student, after visiting the "mother country" for the first time, discovered, "the footprints of Spain are present everywhere in our culture; we are so much alike."

Like the inhabitants of the New World, the European ancestors of the Mexicans, inhabitants of a similar and remarkably varied geographical terrain, which embraced the oak forests of the Pyrenees, the bare, high plains and cliffs of Galicia, the untilled wastes of Aragón, and the deserts of Almería, were also bearers of a rich and diverse cultural baggage, strikingly different yet, at one and the same time, comparable here and there to what they found in old Anáhuac. Interestingly, it seems that, on occasion, their mutual embrace, rather than enhance the society that emerged, tended to countenance and perhaps magnify common Achilles' heels. Two that come to mind are religion and politics.

Iberians and Celts arrived early in Spain, followed by Phoenicians, Greeks, and then, about 200 B.C., the Romans, who left behind Latin, mother of the Spanish language, Roman law, the essence of Spanish statutes, the Catholic faith, and a legacy of latifundia. After the Visigoths, successors to the Romans, Moslems from North Africa made their bow and stayed for seven centuries. The Moslems or Moors instilled fresh vigor in Greek and Roman culture, spurred science and mathematics, and introduced an ornate architecture of mosques, cupolas, and richly colored *azulejos,* or tiles. Under their tutelage, the economy, both commerce and agriculture, took a turn for the better. Quarrels among the Moslems opened the door to the Reconquista, the Christian crusade to purge Spain of the infidels, which went on until 1492, when Granada, the last Moorish bastion, capitulated.

However, before the Reconquista triumphed, Spaniards had also adopted Moorish customs, including machismo. Women were kept apart from men and secluded from worldly affairs, a formula which the Reconquista, and the failure to modernize, hardened. Earlier, when Spaniards were struggling to unite Spain, women had enjoyed certain liberties, including the right to participate in municipal affairs, which they had often exercised. In time, nonetheless, women had fallen more and more under the sway of the church while men had placed them on pedestals, worshiping them for their "beauty, honor, and loyalty" but denying them schooling beyond prayer books. Women were "educated" for matrimony: to be clean of body, discreet, humble, and, when of the elite, to sing a bit and play a musical instrument. This tradition arrived with the Spaniards in the New World.

The Reconquista reshaped the Iberian Peninsula. Under Ferdinand and Isabella, the Catholic kings of Aragón and Castilla linked by marriage, a united Spain emerged. Spanish was now the common language, but diluted by countless words of Arabic origin, such as *arroz* (rice), *azúcar,* (sugar) and *aceitunas* (olives). The Catholic faith, the battle flag of the Christian crusaders, bound Spaniards together.

Just the same, the Reconquista passed on an ambivalent inheritance. To oust the Moors, the Catholic kings, requiring popular backing for their effort, gave certain rights to the peasants and granted charters to cities. However, ridding the country of the infidel, especially in Castilla, required the aid of the nobility, which was rewarded with huge grants of land, thus strengthening a latifundia system dating from the Romans. On the other hand, the new wool trade spurred commerce along the Cantabrian coast, transforming Burgos and sister northern towns into thriving entrepôts while promoting the growth of shipping. But sheep ranching on the central highlands, which made possible the wool industry, also helped to nourish the latifundia.

When Isabella and Ferdinand joined the two crowns, Spain had five major provinces: Castilla, Aragón, Navarra, Granada, and Portugal. Castilla, the largest, controlled about two-thirds of the Iberian peninsula. Some five to six million people lived there, while Aragón had but one million and Navarra fewer. After 1640, Portugal went its own way. The kingdom of Castilla of Isabel la Católica was a land of vast estates in the hands of a backward aristocracy, especially in Andalucía, the land of birth of a majority of those who settled in Mexico. Less than 3 percent of the population owned 97 percent of the lands of Castilla; a tiny group of families, relying on the practice of *mayorazgo,* or entail, controlled more than half of them. The nascent *burguesía* (bourgeoisie) of the northern cities could not challenge the hidalgos of the south, the gentlemen who never soiled their hands with labor or business affairs. By contrast, the peasantry, perhaps 80 percent of Spain's population, fared less and less well. By the second half of the sixteenth century, there were more peasants and fewer public lands, *tierras baldías,* to occupy; population growth had outstripped land supply. As this occurred, a horde of *mendigos,* beggars, began to wander about the country. Castilla obviously sat on rickety agrarian foundations.

Castilla, warts and all, was still the more dynamic of the Spanish kingdoms, thanks mainly to its wool trade and its textile industry, centered in the towns of Segovia, Avila, and Cuenca. Until the fifteenth century, the tiny kingdom of Aragón, the royal home of Ferdinand, which embraced Cataluña and Valencia (the Levantine States), had flirted with glory. Cataluña had led the outburst of overseas trade, and Aragón enjoyed a lucrative commerce based on the exports of textiles. Merchants from Cataluña competed with their rivals from Venice and Genoa for the spice trade from the Orient, shipped Catalan iron to buyers from abroad, and sold their textiles in Sicily and Africa.

Trade and commerce encouraged the rise of a dynamic *burguesía* in Aragón. The rural nobility, far less powerful, had to take a backseat to the nascent capitalists of the cities who exacted from the crown a constitutional system, including a cortes, a sort of parliament, that voiced their hopes and aspirations. The merchants and shipping magnates of Aragón, along with the clergy of Castilla, casting about for heathens to baptize, cajoled Isabella and Ferdinand into supporting the scheme of Christopher Columbus to sail westward to reach the Indies. The capitalists of the port cities saw opportunities for profit in the blueprints of the Genoese captain. By sailing westward, Columbus would reopen the trade with the Indies, shut down almost completely when the Turks captured Constantinople. Unfortunately, it was too late. Already, Aragón's fortunes had fallen on evil days. As early as the middle of the fourteenth century, trade and commerce had declined and the textile industry of both Castilla and Aragón stopped growing, while the bubonic plague and Turkish disruptions of the Mediterranean trade had blunted the prosperity of the port cities. Ferdinand, who assumed the throne of Aragón in 1479, inherited a troubled kingdom.

The Catholic kings left Spain, now controlled by Castilla, to Charles I, monarch from 1515 to 1558, who ruled Spain for nearly forty years but spent less than sixteen of them at home. The Conquest of ancient Mexico, and that of almost the entire New World, occurred in his lifetime. It was to Charles I that Hernán Cortés wrote his famous *Cartas.* But Charles I of Spain was also Charles V, emperor of the Holy Roman Empire, which took in Germany and Austria. The first of the Hapsburgs, Charles was only partly Spanish, being German by birth and speaking a rudimentary Spanish. He wasted much of his reign trying to keep Europe and the conquistadores in the New World under his control. Unlike the earlier Spanish kings, he faced outward, plotting a costly imperialism that put much of the Western world in Spanish hands.

Philip II, the son of Charles, governed Spain until 1598, dying a feeble old man. Legend says that Charles I led his soldiers into battle; Philip, by contrast, loved sedentary life and spent his days "surrounded by piles of documents," a fitting commentary on the passage of Spain from the epoch of the conquistadores to the days of the civil servant. Philip's penchant for record keeping plunged public officials into an ocean of paperwork. The chief bureaucrat, the title best suited for Philip, had eventually an army of clerks at his beck and call. Philip, however, kept alive the imperialism of his father, mainly with silver pilfered from the New World, precipitating conflicts in the Netherlands, intervening in France, and dispatching the Glorious Armada to punish England for meddling in Holland and relying on pirates to rob Spain of its New World loot.

But imperialism requires vast sums of money to finance. Unable to promote his foreign policy on taxes culled from Spaniards, Charles I had, ultimately, to borrow from foreign bankers. His reliance on credit bankrupted the economy of Castilla and placed the financial burden on the classes least able to carry it. Despite the flow of silver from the New World, Philip, too, had to turn to foreigners to pay for his imperialism. Even so, the Spanish crown went bankrupt in 1557, in 1575, and again in 1596.

Charles I and Philip II brought to a successful close the struggle to unify Spain. But in doing so, they converted the crown into a despotic master, a transformation that had its roots in the battle for supremacy between the landed nobility and the *burguesía* of the commercial cities of the late fifteenth century, above all in Aragón. Wanting national blueprints more to their liking, merchants, traders, and bankers asked the king for help. For its part, the crown had long waged a struggle against the privileges of the nobility, including the freedom from paying royal tribute. With the Battle of Olmedo (1467), where the crown prevailed over the nobility, the king, particularly in Castilla, had things more or less his own way. Faced with growing royal power, nobles, dukes, and counts sided with the king, thus tilting the scales against the *burguesía.* By becoming courtiers at the court of the king, members of the nobility saved for themselves many of their economic and social advantages. Although they lost their political independence, they kept their lands and all that land implied. The crown, plainly, emerged the victor in this contest between feudal lords and nascent capitalists of towns and cities. So was born the absolute monarchy of sixteenth-century Spain, mother of colonial Mexico.

Kingly supremacy had fatal consequences for popular government. Almost from the start, Ferdinand and Isabella had done what they could to undermine the autonomy of the cortes. Their decline started in Castilla, where the crown limited their functions, undercut their taxing powers, found ways to circumvent their opinions, and failed increasingly to call them into session. During his thirty-five-year reign (1665–1700), Charles II never once convoked the cortes of Castilla.

A similar fate awaited local government. In the kingdom of Aragón, the more liberal of medieval Spain, an open council had made political decisions in the municipalities. An assembly of heads of families, the council had evolved in the villages, then been adopted by the cities. With the growth of the cities, the open council proved unworkable; there were simply too many heads of families. Not all families, said the more powerful, were equal, hence not worthy of an equal voice in public affairs. From this turn of events appeared the municipal council, later called the ayuntamiento or cabildo; it placed local authority in the hands of a small group of elected officials, prominent citizens usually. The ayuntamiento, of course, lent itself more readily to the abuse of authority and transformed public office into an opportunity for personal profit. More and more, members of the ayuntamientos were handpicked by royal dictate *(designados por dedo).* These changes, initiated ironically in the more progressive kingdom of Aragón, aborted the growth of municipal autonomy and, of dramatic significance for the future, the political importance of the *burguesía,* the voice of capitalist ideals.

The rise of the Spanish despot, benevolent or otherwise, had repercussions in the New World. Charles I, to cite one historical anecdote, seldom failed to have at hand a copy of Machiavelli's *The Prince,* which extolled the virtues of absolute monarchy, applying its lessons to the New World. He seldom failed to impress on the conquistadores that he was boss, never permitting them to sever their ties to the crown or hesitating to remove them when they tried. Even Cortés, the popular leader of the conquistadores of Mexico, tasted defeat when he challenged the monarch.

Another ideal of the Reconquista was religious orthodoxy, to transform

Spain into a haven for the Catholic faith and purge it of Moslems and Jews as well as of freethinkers. Along the way, the goals of the Reconquista became dogma, a religious fanaticism transported to colonial Mexico by devout friars and conquistadores. Christianity had reached Spain in the days of the Romans. Among the first to preach Christianity, say Spaniards, was Saint Paul. In A.D. 400, the Council of Toledo declared the Nicene Creed to be the official Catholic one. The Catholic kings, practical politicians, employed the Catholic faith to heal regional and class differences. For this, they relied on the clergy, the builders of a powerful and *españolizada* (Hispanized) church. In this endeavor, they had the enthusiastic backing of Francisco Ximénez de Cisneros, archbishop of Toledo and later a cardinal of the church. A militant believer in both faith and crown, he put the church at the service of Ferdinand and Isabella, whose marriage he helped arrange, over the opposition of the Castilian nobility.

Intolerance, the ultimate characteristic of the Reconquista, however, arrived tardily. During the thirteenth century, Castilla enjoyed a cultural awakening in an atmosphere of religious tolerance and political tranquillity. Despite the battles with Moslems, Castilla opened its arms to contemporary European currents. The fabulous Gothic cathedrals of León, Burgos, and Toledo were built, while Valencia, Salamanca, and Valladolid saw universities established amid a climate of free intellectual inquiry, respectful of modern and old ideas as well as of Christian and Moslem beliefs. The University of Salamanca, of high standing in Europe, offered initially no course in theology, unlike others of its day. Unhappily, all of that perished, swept aside by the depression of the late thirteenth century, the fixation of Castilla on the capture of Granada, a stagnating agriculture, the expansion of the latifundia, and, by the middle of the next century, the specter of the black plague. As a result, intolerance replaced open inquiry.

The church, meanwhile, acquired enormous wealth, including huge estates, property held in mortmain and free of taxation. Not infrequently, it was the biggest landlord in the region; Christian and Moorish serfs labored on its lands or as servants in convents and monasteries. The monks of the richest monasteries had social standing as well, power akin to that of nobles over people within their domains. The *fueros* (privileges), such as the right to hold property in mortmain, were granted to the clergy by the crown, eager to have allies in its battle with dukes, counts, and knights and the *burguesía.* Innocent VIII, by a papal bull of 1486, bestowed on the crown the power of patronage, the right to appoint bishops and other high clergy and to collect ecclesiastical benefices in Granada, on the verge of falling into the lap of Christians. Ferdinand and Isabella, the pope's beneficiaries, used the papal bull to bring the church under the sway of the crown. The church in colonial Mexico labored under its jurisdiction.

One generation after the Reconquista, Catholic Spain confronted a challenge it had not counted on. In distant Germany, Martin Luther, a wayward Catholic priest, nailed his ninety-five theses on the door of a church. Luther and his disciples called themselves Protestants, and their heresy spread to Sweden and France. Not long afterward, the Frenchman John Calvin, another dissident, broke with the pope and the Catholic church, giving Protestantism a foothold in Holland and Scotland. A bit later, the opportunistic Henry VIII severed England's ties with Rome and established the Anglican church, an ally of the Protestants on the Continent. The Protestant Reformation had started.

With the blessings of Rome, Charles I, a fanatical believer, declared Spain the defender of the true faith. Spain became the cradle of the Counter-Reformation, the Catholic response to the Protestant challenge. Charles as well as Philip II seldom failed to employ force to stem the tide of heretical doctrines. The wars against the infidels were joined together with imperialistic adventures on the Continent and against the Turks. From the Council of Trent there emerged a revitalized church, ready for battle with the disbelievers, more than ever convinced that God was on its side, and, increasingly, intolerant of dissident views. Earlier, in 1536, Ignatius Loyola had organized the Jesuits, a militant order and axis of the Counter-Reformation. At a time when Protestants decried the pope, Loyola and his Jesuits swore absolute submission to him, vowing to fight heresy everywhere. Spain's leaders adopted additional measures to stamp out heresy, which virtually shut Spain's doors to humanist influences and foreign ideas. One was the revival of the Inquisition.

Often employed by Protestant scholars and theologians to vilify Spain's past, the Inquisition, or Holy Office, dated from thirteenth-century Castilla. Among its top villains were Archbishop Ximénez de Cisneros, confidant of Isabella, and Fray Tomás de Torquemada, whose name historians made synonymous with it. The Catholic kings used the Inquisition, as one writer phrased it, not merely to "homogenize" Spain's population but also to control a restless *burguesía* in the commercial cities. More than Moslems, this goal had in mind the Jews, key elements in the commercial and financial sectors, rivals of the landed nobility. Relying on the Inquisition, the Catholic kings drove the Jews out of Spain.

Religious orthodoxy had more-pernicious consequences, also linked to the Jewish issue. For many Spaniards, purity of faith required a purity of race or blood. By the middle of the sixteenth century, the doctrine of *limpieza de sangre* had gained wide popular appeal. At this time, official policy started to exclude conversos, Jews who embraced Catholicism, from public and church office. One could not trust conversos, because, despite their public subservience to Christianity, they remained Jews. In 1520, moreover, the revolt of the townspeople, or *comuneros,* in Castilla, at first confined largely to the urban centers, had brought to the fore a hatred of foreigners and their ways. Artisan guilds, for instance, began asking for proof of *limpieza de sangre* as a condition for membership, closing their doors not only to Jews and conversos but to Moors as well. In 1609, the Moriscos, officially Christian Spaniards of Arabic culture, suffered the fate of the Jews; 275,000 Moriscos fled Spain. Their expulsion, like the earlier ban on Jews, hurt Spain; Moriscos were not only a key element in agriculture but bastions of the wool industry of Toledo and Sevilla.

At about the same time, furthermore, a Spanish play by Andrés de Claramonte, *El valiente negro en Flandres,* was harping on the racial inferiority of the Negro. A contemporary of Lope de Vega, Claramonte, in describing the character of the Negro Juan de Mérida, wrote, "only because of the color of his skin he could not be a man of gentle blood," while Mérida laments the "disgrace" to be "black in this world." For "that outrage I will denounce fate, my times, heaven, and all those who made me black. O curse of color." This play makes clear that color prejudice, the Spanish variety, had old roots on the Iberian Peninsula; claims to the contrary, it was not an invention of the 1800s.

Sixteenth-century Spain became the champion of orthodoxy. Trifling with tradition was not permitted, in the realms of either faith, ideas, or politics. By the end of the century, the relative freedom to think for oneself was merely a historical anecdote. Heterodoxy, the spirit of the Renaissance, enjoyed scant welcome in Spain, while scholasticism, a discredited formula in much of Europe, dictated learning in schools and universities. Given this lugubrious atmosphere, only the daring and unorthodox risked the wrath of church and state to stay abreast of learning.

For a while, the influx of silver and gold from Mexico and Peru hid the ills of Spain from public scrutiny, but not for long. By 1600, the signs of decay were self-evident; at the close of the next century, the downfall of imperial Spain was public knowledge. Corruption and graft beset the regime of Charles I, who looked the other way when his sycophants stole from royal revenues and walked off with public properties. His chancellor, Juan de Sauvage, made a profit of two million ducats in just two months off royal rights to the African slave trade. Philip II sold public offices to the highest bidders and failed to stop the corruption of his father's time. At his death, Spain suffered from an inflated and graft-ridden bureaucracy.

The church traveled down the same path. Ritual and ceremony, rather than dedication and compassion, were often its hallmarks, while corruption seduced much of the clergy. The efforts of Ferdinand and Isabella to clean up the morality of the clergy had mostly failed. Priests, like lay sinners, took concubines and fathered offspring. The high clergy, rich by any standard, enjoyed the life of the nobility, a reflection of society, where great wealth and dire poverty lived side by side; the rich, the few; the poor, the many. "Our condition," wrote a Spanish sage of that time, "is one in which we have the rich who loll at ease, or the poor who beg." To Miguel de Cervantes, Spain had become a country of the "haves and the have-nots." As the century ended, no middle class of any significance existed.

By the middle of the seventeenth century, Spain had lost its hegemony over Europe, and Castilla no longer wielded it at home. With the appearance of the pronunciamiento, or military coup, Castilla's politics assumed the characteristics of a comic opera, its rulers losing the respect of Europe. Philip II bequeathed his throne to his son, Philip III, a man of learning who could never make up his mind. Philip IV, his successor, tasted defeat at the hands of the French and lost valuable slices of the Spanish Empire to Englishmen and the Dutch. His son, the feebleminded Charles II, allowed the greedy and powerful to plunder Spain. When the childless king, the last of the Hapsburgs, died, the French Bourbons took over. Eager to restore Spain to its old glory, they committed the mistake of reinstating the hegemony of Castilla when it no longer sat atop the pyramid. At this juncture, scholars maintain, Spain had "lost its sense of national purpose." Nearly a century earlier, *Don Quixote,* Cervantes's masterpiece, with its "parable of a nation which had set out on a crusade only to learn that it was tilting at windmills," had aptly captured the gist of what was taking place. Why had this occurred?

A national bourgeoisie, a powerful class in England and France, had failed to develop. The capitalist orders of Aragón were never able to expand and thrive. Until late in the eighteenth century, Castilla, a semifeudal kingdom presided over by an absolute monarch and beset by a decadent nobility, controlled events. That nobility, an ally of its counterpart in the kingdom of Aragón, kept the nascent commercial class of the northern cities of Castilla and of the ports on the Mediterranean on the periphery of power. The imperialist adventures of Charles I and Philip II, as may be expected, squandered the wealth of Mexico and Peru on foolish wars and intrigues. The expulsion of the Jews, which set back capitalist development, was a victory for the retrograde nobility of Castilla, a mortal enemy of the coastal cities.

The silver and gold of the New World, ironically, nailed shut the coffin. As the riches of the New World flowed into Castilla, the recipient of the conquistador's labors, its lords saw no need to modernize its economic structure. Precious ores from the Americas nurtured the feudal edifice. What Castilla did not produce, it imported from England, France, and the Low Countries. The Conquest of the New World, according to one savant, "provided Spanish feudalism, almost on its death bed, with a fresh burst of oxygen" and, at the same time, suffocated "the nascent capitalism of the Iberian peninsula." Moreover, by making the New World a Castilian preserve, Queen Isabella and her successors excluded from the benefits of the Conquest the merchants, traders, and bankers of Aragón, León, and Valencia, the heart of the Spanish *burguesía.* That policy dealt them a mortal blow. Similarly, the Conquest drained Castilla of some of its most enterprising young men, who, had they stayed home, might have injected fresh vigor into its feudal body.

Under the dominance of Castilla, Mother Spain, the wealth of Mexico and Peru notwithstanding, ended up being a dependent country, without an industry of its own and forced to import foreign goods. To supply its domestic market and its colonies overseas, Spain looked to the manufacturers of England, France, Italy, and Germany, often for articles once produced in Segovia, Toledo, Valladolid, Barcelona, and Valencia. During the days of Philip II, the raw materials taken from the New World found their way into the hands of merchants and manufacturers of western Europe. Some of them came back to Spain in the form of finished articles for home consumption or for shipment to the New World. A dependent Spain, itself a colony of the "developing" countries of Europe, set the stage for the tragedy of Mexican history.

VI

For two centuries, all the same, Spain basked in the sunlight of an artistic and intellectual awakening. Castilla, where the spirit of the Reconquista, an outpouring of religious and nationalistic zeal, discovered a home, gave it birth. With the defeat of the Moslems, the Conquest in the New World, and the triumph of Spanish arms in Europe, God, Spaniards were convinced, had designated them the children of destiny. Before subsiding, the Spanish awakening embraced literature, art, theology, international law, medicine, and chemistry; at the same time, the chronicles of the Conquest added luster to Spain's historical guild.

The Golden Age, as the two centuries are known, elevated Spanish authors to the pinnacle of European literature. Their forte was the novel, its pioneer *La Celestina,* a story with a woman as its chief protagonist. A moving portrayal of the humanist concept of life, *La Celestina* had universal appeal, the forerunner of the picaresque novel *Lazarillo de Tormes* (1554) and, to the delight of colonial Mexicans, Mateo Alemán's *Guzmán de Alfarache* (1599), the memoirs of picaro who becomes a converted sinner. It remained for Cervantes (1547–1616), nonetheless, to crown Spanish letters. His *Don Quixote,* a masterly study of the human psyche, portrayed succinctly the rise and fall of imperial Spain. Among the dramatists of the day, Lope de Vega earned fame as the father of the Spanish theater, which, in the opinion of one critic, "most perfectly, perhaps, reflected the Baroque Spirit," a signpost of the Golden Age. Both he and his eloquent successor Pedro Calderón de la Barca had enthusiastic audiences in colonial Mexico. No less towering among playwrights were

Tirso de Molina, Alarcón, and Moreto and, among writers of ballads, Lope de Vega, Francisco de Quevedo, and Luis de Góngora, an author notorious for his ornate and complicated syntax.

Spanish painters, among the finest of Europe, labored alongside these authors. A Spanish school thrived, portrait painters mainly, shaped by the religious temper of the times and probably the most authentic symbols of the Reconquista. They walked in step with the Flemish, Dutch, and Italian masters of their day: Rubens, Rembrandt, Michelangelo, Titian, and Raphael. The Spanish painters also drew inspiration from their own, the talented artists of the fifteenth century: the Catalan Luis Dalmau and Bartolomé Bermejo, a Cordobés and the first painter on the peninsula to use oils, and Pedro Berruguete, called "the most Spanish painter of this time."

In this era of masterful art, four giants emerged. El Greco, a Greek by birth but Spanish by adoption and spirit, left behind monumental works, among them the haunting *Burial of Count Orgaz,* which enshrined religious dogma. José de Ribera, a mystic, exalted Spanish piety and dealt with human passion, handling his figures, *The Boy with the Clubfoot* for one, with shocking realism. His style had a powerful impact on the art of José Clemente Orozco, the Mexican muralist. Francisco de Zurbarán, master of a barren asceticism, painted about death and the saintly who carried the Christian gospel to the infidels. Diego Velázquez, a devout Catholic by conviction and the giant among giants, painted religious themes. As an artist at the court of Philip IV, he passed on to history portraits depicting graphically the mental decay of the Hapsburgs. A fine painter was Bartolomé Esteban Murillo, whose pictures reveal a richness of color and a vivid imagination.

Spain transferred to Mexico a monumental architectural legacy, as old as Roman times, but principally from the Gothic and Moslem era. The Alcazar at Toledo, the Alhambra of Granada, and the Mezquita at Córdoba testify to the prowess of Moorish architects. During the Reconquista, architecture, now essentially Spanish, prospered; the great cathedrals of Salamanca, Burgos, and Valencia, which incorporated both Gothic and Romanesque elements, stand as witnesses to that. This architecture, basically a combination of Arabic and Gothic styles, was known for its magnificent cupolas, horseshoe arches, and glazed *azulejos.* Made possible by the abundant silver from Mexico and Peru, the architecture, rich in ornamentation, won fame under the name Plateresque. The Colegio de San Gregorio, a sample of this architecture, dates from the reign of the Catholic kings. Ultimately labeled Baroque art, this architecture symbolized the Catholic Counter-Reformation in Spain. With it came an admirable sculpture, more often than not religious statuary but also sculpture in relief for ornate doors for churches and their elaborate façades. Burgos, Toledo, Sevilla, and León boasted some of its finest examples.

Fittingly, the agony of death befell the Golden Age during the rule of the imbecile Charles II. Velázquez, the greatest of the painters, died in 1660; Zurbarán four years later. In 1681, his mourners buried Calderón de la Barca, the last of the luminaries. With his demise, a pall descended upon Spanish letters and the arts. The Spanish encyclopedists of the eighteenth century, who exemplified the brief flurry of intellectual vitality under the Bourbon kings, rarely matched the talents of the Golden Age.

VII

This Spain, with Castilla at its helm, was the patriarch of colonial Mexico. What it stood for, it conferred on its offspring: the Golden Age, with all of its grandeur and the spirit of the Reconquista, a crusade for God and country enhanced by religious intoxication and nationalistic fervor. Along with the artistic and the grandiloquent architecture, absolute monarchy arrived, as well as corruption and malfeasance in public office. The church, too, its spirits enhanced initially by dedicated apostles, betrayed eventually its mission, victim of its sins and those of its countrymen. Capitalism, the promise of a powerful commercial bourgeoisie, languished. From the start, Castilla, home of a retrograde landed nobility, closed the door to harbingers of middle-class ideals. Worse still, it conferred on its offspring in the New World a skewed society. Colonial Mexico, an offshoot of a pre-Columbian civilization under the sway of a military and priestly caste, and hardly democratic, and of Spanish medieval society, inherited the sins and virtues of both.

Whatever their blessings, Spain and the New World are the forefathers, to repeat, of Mexicans, but not in identical ways. Although Mexican culture is "derivative," to quote the philosopher Samuel Ramos, it is essentially Spanish; "through our veins flows the blood of Europeans who brought their own culture with them to America." A part of the European blended with the American, but one must not forget that in the mestizo, the progeny of Spaniard and Indian, little of the native cultures endured. "The Indian rock," wrote Aldous Huxley, "was a very large one, but the [Spanish] hammer, though small, was wielded with terrific force. Under its quick reiterated blows, the strangely sculptured monolith of American civilization broke into fragments." "The bits are still there," he concluded, "indestructible," but no longer a "shapely whole." Ever since the colonial era, therefore, Mexican life has tended to conform to cultural molds imported from Europe. Nonetheless, something of the native endured, obviously in the genes or, to put it in the vernacular, the "blood," as well as in a bit of its psychology and way of life. Equally important, the memory of an Indian past, eventually almost an ideal, never died.

2

THE CONQUEST OF TENOCHTITLÁN

I

Terrible omens, telling of dangers ahead, the old chronicles say, beset ancient Anáhuac by 1519. Strange comets belching fire raced through the heavens; for forty days, a bright light was seen to the east; and at night the cries of a woman weeping could be heard, warning her children that they must flee. More factual were other omens. A *macehual* from the shores of Veracruz reported seeing "towers or mountains floating on the sea, carrying strange beings, white of skin, with long beards and hair hanging down to the ears." In Tenochtitlán, fear and dread gripped the superstitious Moctezuma. What the *macehual* had seen, of course, were the sails of ships of the early Spanish expeditions. The Aztecs did not yet know it, but their universe was about to go up in flames. From then on, Miguel de Cervantes would write, they could "expect nothing but labor for their pains."

II

The Conquest, underlines a distinguished anthropologist, "is a series of events which will remain forever" shrouded in mystery because, as he explains, "no amount of inference from the meager facts recorded can ever establish" the full truth. European commentators left behind scores of accounts but, he emphasizes, what the natives thought "about what was happening to them" was never adequately taken down. From the beginning, there were virtually no native versions of their reactions to the invaders. True, occasionally, the words of some native leaders were set down, but, even then, the recording was done by Europeans, which gives them a European slant. "Again and again, what purports to be a record of the native viewpoint is actually what the European writers thought the natives were thinking."

Rare was the Spanish chronicler, furthermore, who was equipped to report objectively on what was taking place. Even when sympathetic, as the observations of the some of the early friars certainly were, their versions display "the inevitable bias of writers from one culture looking through the barriers of language and cultural differences at the members of another." Nothing can be done to eliminate this prejudice. Even after long contact with Indians, moreover, Spaniards only infrequently altered their views. One Jesuit missionary, for example, even after half a century among the Tarahumaras of Chihuahua, could still write that they were "by nature and disposition a sly and crafty folk from whom sincerity is not to be expected." He labeled them "accomplished hypocrites." His bias was not unique. It would be foolhardy to take seriously this unqualified indictment of a conquered people. Surely, if this Jesuit had made contact with the Indians as one human being to another, he would have offered a more balanced appraisal. Historians of the Spanish Conquest of Mexico, therefore, must never close their eyes to this distortion.

As in similar feats of usurpation, the thirst for profit largely explains the Spanish Conquest of Tenochtitlán. That Queen Isabella sold her jewels to finance Christopher Columbus's voyage in 1492 is simply a lovely myth. From the start, the crown of Spain gave carte blanche to a legion of freebooters, asking only for a share of their plunder. The lust for personal gain, whether of soldiers of fortune or royal despots, poured the foundations of colonial Mexico. The lure of adventure and the crusade to Christianize pagans, of course, played important roles; yet, after all is said and done, the dream of striking it rich drove Spaniards to gamble their lives on risky New World enterprises.

For Spaniards of that epoch, profit meant gold and silver. The hunger for land and Indians to till it came later, not until virtually the next generation of Spaniards. From the days of Hernán Cortés, it was the lust for precious metals that drove Spaniards. At the age of eighty-four, when he completed his legendary *Historia verdadera de la conquista de la Nueva España,* Bernal Díaz del Castillo, a soldier in that undertaking, recalled vividly gifts of gold sent Cortés by Moctezuma, emperor of the Aztecs. "It was a wonderful thing to see," he wrote of a "gold disk representing the sun and as large as a cartwheel . . . worth, we learned later . . . over ten thousand pesos."

All the same, when Cortés stepped ashore in 1521, two Catholic friars accompanied him—Bartolomé de Olmedo, remembered as the "First Apostle of New Spain," and Juan Díaz. This was shortly after the Reconquista, when Catholic Spain believed itself entrusted with a holy mission; it was a time to save the souls of pagans in the New World. "The Conquest," accordingly, "was the last crusade," an enterprise both military and religious. The bearer of the sword, Cortés made certain that a cross accompany it, as his actions at Cempoala, a Totonac village just off the Gulf coast, illustrate. Cortés, tired of watching its inhabitants sacrifice slaves to their gods, ordered his soldiers to destroy the idols in the temple, replacing them with an image of the Virgin and putting flowers at her feet, recalled Díaz del Castillo. Fray Olmedo said mass the next morning. Cortés and the other conquistadores, occasionally religious zealots themselves, repeated that performance time and time again.

Hernán Cortés's famous *Cartas de relación,* letters he wrote Charles I describing his accomplishments, and the book by Díaz del Castillo form part of the epic literature of the Conquest. Much of what is known of the fall of Tenochtitlán stems from the account written by Díaz del Castillo to refute the official version of the *Historia general de las Indias,* whose author, Francisco López de Gómara, never saw the New World. Born in Spain about 1492, Díaz del Castillo took up arms in 1514, arriving in Cuba from the Isthmus of Panama in time to join Francisco Hernández de Córdoba and Juan de Grijalva on their voyages of exploration. Díaz de Castillo personified the conquistadores. An adventurer, he was an ambitious man, unhappy with his lot in society, and a prototype of the men who, after giving up fighting Indians, spent the rest of their lives looking for ways to get their share of the plunder from the crown, first gold and jewels and then land and Indians to exploit. An *encomendero* (a man given Indians for labor) in both Mexico and Guatemala, he wrote his account partly to justify his thirst for more spoils.

The Aztecs, too, bequeathed to posterity truncated versions of the Conquest. Studied alongside of Díaz's *True History,* they provide a fuller account of what actually occurred. But the canticles, written by Aztec poets, date from 1523, after their authors learned to use the alphabet. Of later vintage, and written in Nahuatl but using the Spanish alphabet, is the famous *Manuscrito 22*, written by natives of Tlatelolco about 1528. *Unos anales históricos de la nación Mexicana* narrates the destruction of Aztec society. In 1555, under the direction of Fray Bernardino de Sahagún, a Spanish monk, more Aztecs put together the *Código florentino,* the most complete "native" portrayal of the Conquest. Pictorial drawings of the Conquest in native glyphs also survive; they tell the story by means of the ancient form of writing, partly ideographic. One is the *Lienzo de Tlaxcala* (painting on linen cloth) of the mid-sixteenth century. Additional sources are the old native codices (manuscripts) of Azcatitlán, Mexicanus, Aubin, and Ramírez. Unlike Bernal Díaz, the Aztecs mourn the death of a way of life.

III

Of an old and fairly respectable family, Hernán Cortés, a native of Medellín, a city in Extremadura, was born, so to speak, with the sword of the soldier in hand, for his father was a captain in the Spanish infantry. But Don Martín and his wife, Doña Catalina Pizarro Altamirano, parents of lofty pretensions, wanted Hernán to become a lawyer and not a soldier. When he was fourteen, they sent him to study law at the University of Salamanca, but Cortes stayed only long enough to learn to write decent prose, a skill he later put to good use in his *Cartas de relación.*

In 1504, after a life of idleness, Cortés set sail for the Americas, on a ship bound for Española, where he acquired land, and became an encomendero and mayor of Santiago del Puerto. In 1511, fortune smiled on Cortés, when Diego Velázquez, under whom Cortés had soldiered, was asked to subdue the neighboring island of Cuba; Cortés joined the expedition as an aide to its treasurer. The campaign over, he settled down in Cuba as a *granjero* (gentleman farmer), cultivating grapes, raising cows and horses, and, occasionally, digging for gold and engaging in commerce. Cortés, a veteran of multiple amorous affairs, eventually took a wife, Catalina Suárez, the daughter of Spanish colonists. At this juncture, Cortés was hardly wealthy; a minor landlord, he owned Indian slaves, some mines, and a small business. He spent much of what he earned on the good life and was in debt.

In the meantime, Velázquez had been designated governor of Cuba. A veteran of the Italian campaigns, he had arrived in the New World with Columbus, then on his second voyage, in 1493. An ambitious politico, Velázquez earned the backing of Juan Rodríguez de Fonseca, bishop of Burgos and later head of the Council of the Indies, which set policy in the New World. To explore the mainland, Velázquez dispatched two expeditions: that of Hernández de Córdoba in 1517 and that of Grijalva a year afterward. Córdoba landed on Yucatán and traveled to Bahía de Campeche, while Grijalva sighted Yucatán, sailed past Campeche, and discovered the Río Tabasco (now Río Grijalva), where the Spaniards first heard of the Aztec empire. Determined to push ahead with exploration on the mainland, Velázquez picked Cortés to lead it, a decision he lived to regret. To outfit the expedition, Cortés mortgaged his estate, borrowed money from wealthy merchants, purchased what he could on credit, and begged from friends.

Named captain general, Cortés started to dress the part. His demeanor as well as his attitude led Velázquez to question the wisdom of calling upon Cortés, but he decided to replace him too late. Warned that Velázquez intended to name a rival, Cortés set sail abruptly on his historic adventure. When he lifted anchor in Havana harbor, on February 10, 1519, he had eleven ships, 508 soldiers, and sixteen horses. Among his chief lieutenants were Pedro de Alvarado, Cristóbal de Olid, and Gonzalo de Sandoval, names the Conquest enshrined.

The Cortés who departed Cuba was short of height, thickly set, strong and robust of body. Light of skin with "eyes mild and grave," he sported a black beard, the color of his hair. Of broad chest and shoulders, he had legs bowed from years in the saddle. A scar partly hidden by his beard testified to a scuffle with the suitor of a woman on one of his amorous affairs. Gambler by instinct, he loved to play cards and dice. A born leader, he knew how to command. He preferred flattery or intrigue but could be ruthless, employing sword and cannon without mercy. Yet he avoided battle if victory could be achieved by peaceful means. When Alvarado, a freebooter, plundered the homes of natives on Cozumel (Yucatán), Cortés told him angrily to give back what he had stolen. You could not pacify the country, he explained to Alvarado, by stealing from natives. A Catholic but no fanatic, he paid homage to his monks, erected crosses, and tore down pagan idols; but he seldom permitted religion or clerics to interfere with his plans.

Cortés had not risked life and limb merely for adventure or to convert heathens. The rich life and power and status in society drove him. His adventures would make him wealthy, the dream of every conquistador. To obtain gold was the goal. On the approach to Tenochtitlán, one native chronicle recalls, the Aztecs sent gifts to the Spaniards, "flags of gold . . . collars of gold." Like "monkeys," the Spaniards played with the gold pieces, examining them with care, all the while displaying their joy, as though "gold renovated and brightened their hearts." Upon his triumphant return to Spain in 1529, Cortés, who became the marqués del Valle de Oaxaca, was the richest man in the New World. Yet the natives who built his home in Coyoacán complained that "Cortés had not paid them for their labors."

The good life to Cortés and his companions also meant women. Like Arab potentates, the conquistadores, on their march from the Gulf to Tenochtitlán, acquired harems. For his own, Cortés took Marina, a native acquired in Cozumel; Isabel, daughter of Moctezuma and one of the wives of Cuauhtémoc, last of the Aztec emperors; Francisca, sister of Coanacoch, another chieftain; and Inéz, about whom nothing is known. Additionally, he had two Spanish concubines: Leonor Pizarro and Antonia Hermosillo; both vanished when Catalina Suárez, Cortés's wife, landed in New Spain. During her brief sojourn in New Spain, Catalina lived surrounded by servants and adorned with jewels. When Cortés died in 1547, he left a heterogeneous lot of offspring: Martín and his sisters María, Juana, Catalina, and one more, by his second wife; two sons born out of wedlock, one by Doña Marina, and three daughters fathered in identical manner, one to a Cuban woman and the others to natives of New Spain.

Cortés's companions did not lag behind him when it came to taking women for their own. For this, Bernal Díaz provides abundant evidence. The girls were baptized, he wrote, and the daughter of Xicoténcatl "was named Dona Luisa, and Cortés took her by the hand and gave her to Pedro de Alvarado." She bore him a son. A daughter of another chieftain, baptized Elvira, went to Juan Velázquez de León. On the long march to Tenochtitlán, Cortés had girls he captured branded as slaves, then put them up for sale, the "good-looking ones" for a higher price—but not until he had sampled his share of the delights, recalled Díaz. These native women proved loyal companions during the battle for Tenochtitlán. When the city fell, they got drunk with the Spaniards and danced on tables. They also bore the Spaniards mestizo offspring, the first Mexicans.

But Cortés, the son of a devout mother, also carried the banners of the Reconquista. A Catholic by birth, he bequeathed the faith to the New World. The heathens, he lectured his companions, "must see that we have . . . God on our side." Like many of his captains, Cortés was a pragmatist, though a Catholic. By and large, he personified the attitude of his men, even of Fray Olmedo, never one to risk his neck for the sake of church doctrine. Catholics they were, nevertheless, intent on saving pagans and raising aloft the ensigns of Spain over the conquered lands. "Your cause," Cortés told his men before departing from Cuba, "is . . . just, since you are to fight under the banner of the Cross."

But, to fall back on an aphorism, "neither man nor angel can discern hypocrisy, the only evil that walks invisible." Cortés's claim aside, devotion to the faith was not necessarily a Spanish trademark. Blasphemy, for one, was a characteristic of Spanish culture. Religiosity notwithstanding, the Spaniard was hot tempered, foul in his choice of words when angry, and passionate when it came to gambling. Nothing moved him more to ejaculations and profanity than the vicissitudes of cards and dice. Many a conquistador took his faith in vain. Rodrigo Rangel, one of those who cast his lot with Cortés and later alcalde of Veracruz and Pánuco and regidor of Mexico City, for example, was known for his apostasy. Church authorities accused him of denying the virginity of Mary and of saying she was a *puta,* a whore. Rangel was not unique. Spanish religiosity must be taken with a pinch of salt.

At Cozumel, the first stop after leaving Cuba, Cortés reviewed his forces, the men who would conquer one of the biggest native empires in the New World. They were armed with the weaponry of Europe: crossbows, muskets, bronze cannons, and "much powder and ball." Of herculean advantage were the horses, sixteen of them, which Bernal Díaz remembered by name, breed, and color. At first, the frightened natives thought horse and rider one and the same.

The Conquest was the labor of bold young men. Cortés, among the eldest, was just thirty-six; Alvarado, a key lieutenant, thirty-four; Gonzalo de Sandoval, a favorite of Cortés, a mere twenty-two. Alvarado, typical of one group among the conquistadores, won fame for his daring and cruelty; the Aztecs nicknamed him Tonatiuh (the sun) for his haughty bearing and blond hair. A good horseman, he loved to dress up and wore a gold chain around his neck and a diamond ring on his finger. One intrepid black man accompanied the Spaniards, recalled Díaz, and, "like the horses, [was] worth his weight in gold." Later, five young women from Castilla joined Cortés; one of them,

María Estrada, survived the debacle of the Noche Triste, a terrible defeat at the hands of the Aztecs. Ironically, with notable exceptions, the conquistadores died poor. At first, a spectacular rise from anonymity to prominence by way of wealth, maybe marriage to a woman of better class, then misfortune and poverty in old age—this, more often than not, was the fate of the conquistador. Cortés, who died wealthy, was an exception to the rule.

At Cozumel, Cortés had a bit of luck. Until then, natives and Spaniards had communicated by sign language. Two Spaniards, Cortés learned at Cozumel, had survived an earlier shipwreck, but Gonzálo Guerrero, who had acquired a native wife, had no wish to return to Spain; Jerónimo de Aguilar, a native of Ecija, wanted to be rescued. Aguilar, who had studied for the priesthood in Spain, had learned Maya during his captivity. At Tabasco, the next stop for Cortés, the native caciques, in the manner of a peace offering, gave the Spaniards twenty girls, among them Malintzin, a slave. The daughter of a Náhua cacique, she knew Nahuatl, the language of the Aztecs, as well as Maya. The Spaniards baptized her Marina. Since she and Aguilar could communicate with each other, Aguilar translated the Nahuatl spoken by the Aztecs.

Doña Marina, as history refers to her, proved an invaluable ally of the Spaniards. She never failed them. "One of our women," tell the Indian chronicles of Fray Sahagún, had come with them; "she speaks Nahuatl. Her name is Malintzin." Able and attractive, she became the companion of Cortés, "his shadow," according to a Mexican intellectual. Baptized a Christian, for the Spaniards seldom slept with "pagan" women, Doña Marina eventually became the concubine of Alonzo Hernández Puertocarrero. When he returned to Spain, Cortés took her back and had a son, Martín, by her. With the arrival of Cortés's wife, Doña Marina became the companion of Juan Jaramillo, whom she married. A man of low moral character, Jaramillo was drunk during the wedding.

This remarkable woman, the helpmate of Spaniards, is a legend in Mexico; the name Malinche, which the Indians gave to her, is synonymous with betrayal. No figure in Mexican history, not even Antonio López de Santa Anna, who lost Texas and half of Mexico to the United States, writes Fernando Benítez, a noted author, epitomizes more eloquently the willingness of Mexicans to prostrate themselves before foreigners. By the mid-nineteenth century, this mistress of Cortés was the symbol of "the perfect judas." Soon after her death, popular opinion made her into La Llorona, the "official ghost" of Mexico. With hair flying in the wind and her dress in disarray, La Llorona wandered about at night grieving for her lost children, the Indians she had betrayed.

IV

At a site he called Veracruz, Cortés established a town; its ayuntamiento, or town council, which he appointed, gave him an independent base for his operations. Legally, he was rid of Governor Velázquez. Under Spanish law, he was free to go his own way. Veracruz was the first city of New Spain. At Cempoala, a Totonac town near Veracruz, the Spaniards met Aztec emissaries, who greeted them warmly, bringing them game, fruits, vegetables, and cooked dishes; whetting Spanish appetites more were gold trinkets. The emissaries reported the presence of the Spaniards to Moctezuma, informed of their movements since their landings at Yucatán and Tabasco. Cortés told the Aztecs of his desire to visit Moctezuma in his palace at Tenochtitlán. Trying to persuade the Spaniards to return home, Moctezuma committed the mistake of sending them two disks of solid gold and silver. With his gifts Moctezuma assured his downfall.

From the Totonacs, Cortés had learned of Indian dissension. Their chief had spoken bitterly of Moctezuma, who demanded tribute—women to be concubines and men to sacrifice to Huitzilopochtli. Not only did the Aztecs have enemies, but their rivals fought with each other. This disunity would aid the Spaniards, who, under the leadership of Cortés, played off one Indian group against the other. When Cortés began his march, leaving behind a small garrison at Veracruz, four hundred Totonacs accompanied him as porters. It was August 19, 1519.

When the Spaniards made their next stop, they were on the other side of the steep mountains that separate the heat and mosquitoes of coastal Veracruz from the cool and verdant Mesa Central, the domain of the Tlaxcalans. Fiercely independent, they were mortal enemies of the Aztecs. To defend themselves from their haughty neighbors, they built a stone wall more than two leagues long, nine feet tall, and twenty feet thick with parapets at the top. Behind this wall, the Tlaxcalans refused adamantly to pay homage to the Aztecs; this led to interminable wars between the two people. The Aztecs, wealthier and more numerous, inflicted a heavy penalty on their indomitable neighbors, capturing them for human sacrifice and cutting them off from the salt, cacao, and cotton of the coast.

Having monitored the advance of the Spaniards, the Tlaxcalans were of two minds on how to handle them. One element, thinking the Spaniards likely allies against the Aztecs, wanted to allow them entrance to the kingdom. The faction led by the old chieftain Xicoténcatl believed that the Spaniards could not be trusted. His views prevailed; it was decided that an army of Tlaxcalans would confront the invaders. Cortés had to fight his way into Tlaxcala, once battling thirty thousand warriors. The Tlaxcalans wounded and killed Spaniards as well as their horses, but, ultimately, lances and crossbows prevailed, aided by volleys of musket fire, which inflicted staggering losses on the enemy. The bows and arrows, slings and javelins of the Tlaxcalans were no match. Despite the misgivings of Xicoténcatl, the Tlaxcalans made their peace with the Spaniards. Thereafter, Spaniards and Tlaxcalans were allies; without them, Cortés and his tiny band could not have defeated the Aztecs.

While peace negotiations were still under way with the Tlaxcalans, more of Moctezuma's envoys arrived in the Spanish camp. They bore more gifts: "three thousand ounces of gold" in multiple forms. Moctezuma, they declared, congratulated Cortés on his victory but regretted he could not receive him in Tenochtitlán. Cortés rejected that advice. After a stay in the capital of Tlaxcala, a city Cortés compared to Granada, the Spaniards moved on, but not before erecting a cross and converting to Christianity a bevy of daughters of the native caciques. When he was offered them as gifts, Cortés had replied that he could not accept them unless they became Christians.

The route chosen by Cortés took the Spaniards to Tenochtitlán through Cholula. Just prior to departing from Tlaxcala, Aztec envoys had again arrived in the Spanish camp, saying that their emperor had changed his mind. He would, after all, receive Cortés in Tenochtitlán and invited him to travel by way of the city of Cholula. Its people, the emperor promised, had been told to offer the Spaniards hospitality. The Tlaxcalans, old enemies of Cholula, urged Cortés not to pay heed. Cholula, they said, was a nest of hypocrites, willing tools of Moctezuma. Believing that Spaniards could show neither fear nor weakness, Cortés ignored the warning.

The city of Cholula, with a population of about sixteen thousand, lay some twenty leagues southeast of Tenochtitlán. From Cholula, Cortés could see the mighty Popocatéptl and Iztaccíhuatl, guardians of the entrance to Tenochtitlán. Far richer and more cultured than the Tlaxcalans, the inhabitants of Cholula were under the sway of the Aztecs. In this sacred city, surrounded by fields planted to corn, chilies, and cactus, a conspiracy, according to the Spaniards, broke out. Moctezuma, so goes the story, had ordered his vassals to kill the unsuspecting Spaniards. Without their Tlaxcalan allies, whom Cortés had left outside the city, the Spaniards would be easy prey. To their good fortune, the Spaniards discovered the plot. Doña Marina, it seems, had befriended a wife of one of the local caciques, who, in gratitude, revealed the intrigue, putting the blame on Moctezuma.

To forestall the treachery, Cortés summoned the caciques of Cholula to appear before him, rebuked them for their perfidy, and asked them to provide two thousand men to carry the guns and supplies of the Spaniards, assuring them that he would depart the next morning. When they arrived with more porters than requested, Cortés, who awaited them in the great court of the city where he had posted his men, ordered the slaughter of the defenseless natives. Every musket and crossbow claimed victims, and those who escaped were killed by sword-wielding Spaniards. The Tlaxcalans, meanwhile, attacked Cholula from the rear, taking a frightful toll of human life. When the butchery was over, more than three thousand natives had perished and Cholula was no more.

The Spanish interpretation, however, fails to convince. The native version, for one, casts doubt on the tale of the conspiracy. Caught in Cholula among people known to be vassals of the Aztecs, Cortés either lost his nerve or, using the supposed conspiracy as a pretext, decided to frighten Moctezuma and his allies. According to another native view, the culprits were the Tlaxcalan soldiers of the Spaniards. Old foes of Cholula, they got their revenge when the Spaniards gave them free rein. Whatever the truth, the Spaniards and their allies butchered defenseless people, including women and children. With the "massacre at Cholula," the natives baptized the Spaniards *popolucas,* barbarians.

A fortnight later, Cortés set out from Cholula for Tenochtitlán. Before leaving, the Spaniards erected a huge cross on the pyramid of the temple of Quetzalcóatl, the Christian symbol towering over the scene of the recent massacre. The route from Cholula went over the majestic Popocatépetl, at its base a pine forest, and then through a pass to the Valley of Anáhuac, planted to maguey as far as the eye could see. As they approached, the Spaniards saw ahead of them the lakes of Anáhuac, their shores settled with villages and towns and, like the head of a giant sea squid, the pyramids of Tenochtitlán and, in the distance, Texcoco, a sister city. Amid the stately cypresses of Tenochtitlán loomed Chapultepec, the hill with the temple of the Aztec monarchs.

When first sighted, Tenochtitlán stood about five miles distant. As the Spaniards approached its ramparts, they passed by Lakes Chalco and Xochimilco, traveling alongside of patches of cultivated lands, floating gardens, and hamlets. The scenes traversed by the Spaniards reminded Bernal Díaz of "the enchantments told about in the book of Amadis of Gaul because of the high towers, cues and other buildings, all of masonry, which rose from the water." Then the Spaniards entered Ixtapalapa, famous for its gardens, orchards, and houses of stone, where Cuitláhuac, brother of Moctezuma, awaited them. At his invitation, Cortés and his men dined royally and took up quarters for the night. With the dawn, the Spaniards marched out, Cortés and his cavalry in the advanced guard, on their heels the infantry, and, defending the rear of the column, the Tlaxcalans. At Xoloc, the caciques of Tacuba, Texcoco, Coyoacán, and Ixtapalapa greeted the Spaniards. Wearing fanciful dress, they were the advance guard for Moctezuma. On the causeway which the Spaniards followed into Tenochtitlán, Moctezuma and his retinue of nobles could be seen on the opposite side of a drawbridge. Crossing it, the gateway to a city surrounded by the water of the lakes, placed the Spaniards at Moctezuma's mercy. Once they were inside, there was no going back.

That "bold and lucky entrance," recalled Bernal Díaz, occurred "on November 8, in the year of Our Savior Jesus Christ 1519." The city itself, as Cortés described it to Charles V, was "as large as Sevilla or Cordoba," with markets everywhere displaying goods of diverse types. One market (Tlatelolco), Cortés testified, was "twice as large as that of Salamanca." The city, Cortés went on, "contained many mosques, or houses for idols, very beautiful edifices situated in the different precincts." The priests of the religious orders lived in the biggest ones. Such was the city Cortés had come to conquer, where he now confronted the lordly Moctezuma.

V

Moctezuma, successor to Ahuítzotl, climbed to the Aztec throne in 1502. A gentle person, courteous and kind in dealing with others, he suffered from excessive pride and was superstitious. The strength of the Aztecs, the harsh realism with which they had built their empire, was not ingrained deeply in the soul of Moctezuma. If we can believe accounts recorded years after the fact, the magical rites of divination, prophecies, and the art of interpreting dreams meant more to him. He prostrated himself before his gods, feared the prophecies of their priests, and worshiped Huitzilopochtli. About forty years of age, of medium height, and slender, Moctezuma was not too dark of skin. His black hair, more short than long, barely covered his ears. Only a few whiskers sprouted from his face, a bit long but not unpleasant.

This Moctezuma, a vacillating but proud ruler, confronted Cortés, a man of the Reconquista, hungry for gold and adventure and willing to die for them. When Moctezuma descended from his litter, his principal chiefs supporting him with their arms, he appeared frail and weak. A "rich canopy of green feathers, worked with gold and silver pearls," and borne aloft by his chiefs, shielded him from the sun. He wore sandals, "with soles of gold covered with precious stones," and was richly dressed. Lesser lords walked ahead, sweeping the ground and placing mats for him to step on. When Cortés tried to embrace Moctezuma, they stopped him.

By invitation of Moctezuma, Cortés and his soldiers spent a week, more or less, in one of the palaces. With princely courtesy, Moctezuma ordered that they be well attended and, from time to time, paid them courtesy calls. As guests of the Aztec monarch, the Spaniards ate the best of food and enjoyed the best of care. But, from their entrance into the city, they knew that they were but a step away from being Moctezuma's hostages. They were in hostile territory, where thousands of Aztecs watched their every move. Were the

Aztecs to fall upon them, the jittery Spaniards feared they would be hard pressed to escape. Thus, when news arrived from Veracruz of the death of two Spaniards at the hands of natives—at the instigation of Moctezuma, it was rumored—Cortés, after consulting with his lieutenants, decided to kidnap the emperor. Moctezuma was told to accompany the Spaniards to their quarters or be killed. A weeping Moctezuma, according to Spanish accounts, complied; on the way to the lodgings of the Spaniards, he kept hostile Aztecs, who watched sullenly the degradation of their emperor, from attacking his captors. Once in his quarters, Cortés put Moctezuma in chains.

For six months, Cortés, behind the façade of Moctezuma, attempted to govern Tenochtitlán. According to the Spaniards, Moctezuma did what he was told willingly; his subjects, accustomed to obeying their chieftains, did the bidding of the captive emperor. Meanwhile, the Spaniards took advantage of this interval to loot Aztec treasures, to hunt for gold mines, and to explore the territory. After setting aside a fifth of the treasure for the crown and a fifth for himself, Cortés split what was left among his men. Moctezuma watched this without protest, devoting himself to the business of administration, granting audiences to his subjects, and even playing games with Cortés. All the same, Moctezuma refused to embrace Christianity; no matter what the Spaniards said, he remained faithful to Huitzilopochtli. Plainly, the native peoples encountered by Cortés, if Bernal Díaz's account is truthful, accepted his rule more readily than the idea of religious conversion, though the Spaniards hoisted the image of the Virgin atop the tallest pyramid of Tenochtitlán, toppled its idols, and had Father Olmedo celebrate a mass.

Not all Aztecs accepted the state of affairs as readily as their emperor did. Resentment at and dissatisfaction with Moctezuma's obsequious behavior ran rampant. One angry chieftain was Cacama, nephew of Moctezuma and lord of Texcoco. No more than twenty-five years of age, Cacama disdained the behavior of his uncle. With the backing of neighboring caciques, among them Moctezuma's brother, the chief of Ixtapalapa, Cacama plotted the rescue of his uncle and the downfall of the Spaniards. Unfortunately for him, Cortés learned of the plan and, with the connivance of Moctezuma, captured Cacama and his fellow plotters and put them in chains. Cacama's plot was but one manifestation of the resentment; the more the Spaniards bent Moctezuma to their will, the greater the discontent among the Aztecs, especially after the Spaniards attempted to substitute their faith for the ancient creeds. At this juncture, Moctezuma, after conferring with his chieftains, told the Spaniards to leave or face an uprising of his people.

VI

For the Spaniards, the future looked bleak, more so because there arrived from Veracruz at this moment news of the landing of Pánfilo de Narváez and his men, dispatched by Governor Velázquez from Cuba to depose Cortés and ship him back to Spain in irons. Narváez had a fleet of fifteen ships and nine hundred men. To Cortés's good fortune, Gonzalo de Sandoval, the lieutenant in charge of the garrison at Veracruz, captured two of Narváez's men and sent them to Cortés, their hands and feet bound together, on the backs of Totonac porters. The astute Cortés set them free, gave them a tour of fabulous Tenochtitlán, loaded them with gifts, and returned them to their companions at Cempoala; but, not before offering them a share of the spoils if they joined in the battle against the Aztecs. Meanwhile, Cortés, with half of his men, departed for the coast and, during a night of heavy rains, fell upon Narváez, routed his men, and took him prisoner. Repeating his earlier promise, he offered Narváez's men a part of the loot if they would return with him. Such was Cortés's power of persuasion that most of them chose to join the enterprise. Narváez, to his unhappiness, stayed behind as a captive in Veracruz.

Just as Cortés seemed to have everything under control, terrible tidings arrived from Tenochtitlán. The Aztecs were attacking the Spaniards. Determined to hold on to Tenochtitlán, Cortés returned immediately. Again, the Tlaxcalans received him with hospitality and the offer of two thousand soldiers. When Cortés and his allies once more entered Tenochtitlán, only sullen faces could be seen. Pedro de Alvarado, whom Cortés left in charge of the garrison, had blundered. When the Aztecs had gathered together in the big courtyard of Tenochtitlán for the May festival in honor of Huitzilopochtli, Alvarado had his men attack them. The angry Aztecs drove the Spaniards back to their quarters. For all intents and purposes, they were prisoners of the Aztecs, now unwilling to listen to Moctezuma.

Alvarado and his soldiers had inflicted terrible losses on the Aztecs. It was, according to Aztec accounts, a bloodbath. While they celebrated, dancing and singing, the Spaniards, swords in hand, had sealed off the entrances to the courtyard and started to kill Aztecs. They cut off hands and arms of some and decapitated others; some Aztecs died from knife wounds in their backs. When they attempted to flee, their intestines hanging out, their feet became entangled in them. On the floor of the Gran Teocalli (main temple), the blood of the Aztecs "ran like water." This slaughter convinced the Aztecs that the Spaniards, far from being gods, were just *popolucas* who wanted to plunder and destroy their city.

The Aztecs, having allowed Cortés and his men to enter the city, closed their ring around them, intending to starve the Spaniards and, when their resistance weakened, to storm their battlements and kill them. Trying to break the siege, Cortés released Cuitláhuac, the brother of Moctezuma, taken prisoner earlier for his part in the plot hatched in Texcoco, believing he would persuade the Aztecs to surrender and provide the Spaniards with food and water. Instead, Cuitláhuac made himself their leader and ordered an attack on the Spaniards. Soon the entire city was up in arms. Thousands of warriors crowded rooftops, streets, and causeways where the Spaniards had barricaded themselves. After a week of heavy fighting and mounting Spanish casualties, Cortés prevailed upon Moctezuma to appeal to his subjects to permit the Spaniards to leave Tenochtitlán. After some hesitation, Moctezuma, hoping probably to end the killing of his people, consented. However, when he climbed a rooftop, he was struck dead by a shower of stones and arrows; his former subjects, according to the Spanish tale, killed their pusillanimous lord. The Indian account, usually ignored by the storytellers, says that the Spaniards, aware that a Moctezuma bereft of his authority was of no use to them, murdered him.

Once out of food and water, the Spaniards could do nothing but try to escape. On a rainy night, the Spaniards, attempting to catch the Aztecs off guard, began to leave their quarters, but not before taking what they could of the gold and silver. Narváez's men, the greediest, took everything they could carry, which cost them dearly because heavily loaded they fell easy prey to the Aztecs. To get across the open canals in the causeway, Cortés had a portable bridge built to transport them from breach to breach until the mainland was reached. Just as the Spaniards were putting down the portable bridge at the first breach, Aztec sentinels sounded the alarm and hordes of warriors, yelling for the blood of their enemies, fell upon them. A hailstorm of arrows and stones followed them, from both land and water since the lakes were filled with Aztec canoes. When the portable bridge stuck, the plight of the Spaniards knew no limits; every Spaniard had to ford the breaches in the causeway as best he could.

Fewer than half of the Spaniards survived that night. Much of the gold and silver jewelry sank to the bottom of the lakes, along with its bearers. Among the 869 Spaniards killed or sacrificed by the Aztecs were 5 Spanish women who had accompanied Narváez, their nude bodies flung into the lakes. Only Doña Marina and 2 others escaped. Over 1,200 of the Tlaxcalans perished. Also lost were weapons, cannon, and horses. When it was all over, legend has it, Cortés sat under a huge cypress and wept. It was June 30, 1520, the famous Noche Triste (Sad Night). The road of the retreat led to Tlaxcala, where, Cortes prayed, his old allies might still offer him refuge and time to heal wounds. The Tlaxcalans, to the joy of the Spaniards, received them as friends.

Even when everything appeared lost, the stubborn Cortés refused to accept defeat, swearing to return and capture Tenochtitlán. Happily for the

Spaniards, Dame Fortune smiled on them. Spanish ships from Cuba, Haiti, and Jamaica had dropped anchor in Veracruz, bringing soldiers, horses, and guns. By persuasion and the use of gold, Spaniards loyal to Cortés at Veracruz got the new arrivals to join hands for the campaign ahead. At Tlaxcala, Cortés regrouped his forces and set about subduing the towns lying between the coast and Tenochtitlán. When their inhabitants proved recalcitrant, or shielded Aztec garrisons, Cortés's soldiers, with the help of their Tlaxcalan allies, killed them. The women, as well as the gold, went to the Spaniards; Cortés and his captains, wrote Bernal Díaz, kept the beautiful ones. At this point, moreover, the Spaniards acquired a new ally: smallpox. The disease, it appears, arrived with one of Narváez's men, killing thousands of Aztecs just as the Spaniards made their entrance at Texcoco. Among the dead was Cuitláhuac. "The Indian," the old accounts tell, "had never had such a disease."

For his siege of Tenochtitlán, Cortés counted on some eighty thousand men. Of that number, fewer than six hundred were Spaniards, forty of them cavalry. The foot soldiers were armed with swords, lances, and crossbows. Cannon totaled nine, but their effectiveness was limited by the short supply of gunpowder. Tlaxcala, as well as Cholula and Tepeaca, furnished most of the native warriors, who wielded bows and arrows and long pikes. Cortés also counted on thirteen brigantines, small vessels built by the Spaniards for an attack by water on Tenochtitlán. The brigantines rid the lakes of Aztec canoes.

Texcoco was the first of the cities to succumb, betrayed by its nobles and abandoned by its inhabitants. Then the Spaniards captured and sacked Ixtapalapa, beating its defenders, who fought with courage. Chalco fell next, but only after a bloody battle. As the Aztecs retreated, more and more of their subjects went over to the Spaniards. Cortés then occupied Tacuba, one more key city, after a furious resistance by its guardians. By this process, the Spaniards isolated Tenochtitlán, with Alvarado, Gonzalo de Sandoval, and Cristóbal de Olid, the Spanish captains, advancing from Tacuba, Tepeyac, and Coyoacán.

The Aztecs endured the siege of their city for three months. Once the Spaniards had made the lakes their own, the Aztecs had to eat worms, insects, and the bark of trees. Until the final hour, they fought valiantly, once capturing sixty-two Spaniards, whom they sacrificed on the alters of Huitzilopochtli in full view of Cortés and his men. Nonetheless, Aztec valor proved inferior to Spanish arms and military tactics. Yet the Aztecs never surrendered; to occupy their city, Cortés had to ravage it. No temple, palace, or idol survived the Spanish assault, their remains becoming, one Mexican author notes, the stones for the foundations of Spanish buildings.

When the Aztecs could no longer defend Tenochtitlán, Cortés sent in a detachment of his men. "We found the houses filled with dead," wrote Bernal

Díaz; "the discharge from their bodies was the kind of filth evacuated by pigs that have nothing to eat but grass." The entire city "had been dug up for roots," which its inhabitants "had cooked and eaten. . . . We found no fresh water, only salt. . . ." Defeat, say the Aztec accounts, produced a profound trauma. The end was dramatic and tragic.

> Sob, my friends,
> For with this defeat
> We have lost the Mexican nation.

The Aztecs, who called themselves the "children of the sun," had been beaten. With their gods destroyed, their rule shattered, and their glory lost, writes a Mexican historian, the memory of defeat embedded itself in the soul of the vanquished.

When the resistance ended, a canoe left Tenochtitlán, which fell prey to a Spanish brigantine. On board was Cuauhtémoc, the last of the Aztec emperors. A "young man of about twenty-five, and very much a gentleman . . . he was married to a daughter of Moctezuma." A brave leader, "he had made himself so feared that all his people trembled before him." Cuauhtémoc did not long survive his capture. According to records of the Chontales of Tabasco, his death occurred in the region of Acalan, on the Gulf of Mexico. On his trip to Honduras, Cortés took Cuauhtémoc with him. During the march, the Spaniards claimed, Cuauhtémoc attempted to foment an Indian uprising against Cortés, who, alerted, killed him. However, the Chontal version differs. The Spaniards put Cuauhtémoc in chains and, "on the third day, after having baptized him, cut off his head, and stuck it on a tree standing in front of the temple of the god of the people of Yaxzam."

3

A NEW SPAIN

I

By the 1550s, the Spaniards had put in place the building blocks for three centuries of colonial rule. Like conquerors the world over, they wanted, as the name New Spain testifies, to rekindle the ashes of what they had forsaken in the *patria.* "There is so much similarity between this country and Spain," Cortés informed Charles I, "that it seemed to me the most suitable name . . . and thus . . . Your Majesty I have christened it." Until 1821, Spaniards celebrated the Conquest of New Spain. Its establishment, for the most part, hardly brought a heaven on earth for its ancient inhabitants, who, unable to stand sentinel, watched Spaniards plunder their land.

II

From the Conquest, a New Spain appeared on the stage, the foundation for the Mexico to follow. Spaniard and Indian, each in his own way, bestowed life on this society and, as José Vasconcelos, a litigious intellectual, boasted, on a "cosmic race," referring to the universe of the mestizo, partly Indian and partly Spaniard. Since Spaniards, who never doubted their racial superiority, rarely married Indians, their sons and daughters saw the light of day as bastards. Cortés and his mistress Doña Marina, the first of a long line of Indian collaborators, conceived one of the first mestizos. Cortés called him Martín. When he had a son by his Spanish wife, in the eyes of the church his legitimate heir, Cortés baptized him Martín too. This Martín, born of Spanish parents in the New World, went on to become a founding father of the criollos, or creoles, of New Spain, rivals of their Spanish parents.

The Spaniard did not arrive empty-handed; he brought baggage, introducing, to start, 170 varieties of fruits, grains, and vegetables, including rice, wheat, and sugarcane, as well as oranges, lemons, and limes and, beyond that, apples, peaches, pears, and apricots. Despite the coming of wheat, corn (or maize) more than held its own, remaining not merely the staple of the Indian diet but, in the shape of the tortilla, the bread of Spaniards and mestizos. Horses, cows, sheep, pigs, goats, chickens, and donkeys, novelties in ancient Anáhuac, accompanied the Spaniards. With astonishing enthusiasm, the Indian adopted donkey and chickens, making them virtually the hallmark of his life. Cattle, meanwhile, multiplied with alacrity, invading lands of central and southern Mexico and, as time went by, the arid north, home to hostile Chichimecas.

From the Spanish contribution originated the justly famous and unique "Mexican cuisine," a concoction of indigenous dishes made tastier by the infusion of pork, chicken, beef, and lamb. Until the arrival of the Europeans, the Indians had eaten merely venison, rabbit, and a small dog called *xoloitzcuintli* by the Aztecs and *kik-bil* by the Maya. The Spanish ingredients added flavor and *buen gusto* to the tamale, enchilada, and tostada and paved the way for mole, the piquant dark chili sauce from Puebla.

The Conquest and its aftermath brought a technical revolution of untold importance. The dawn of the iron age, as well as the introduction of the wheel, added a profound dimension to the changes that befell the Indian community. While the iron tools of sixteenth-century Europeans had scarcely changed for centuries, they transformed the ways of the Indian, who took to the wheel and tools of iron like a duck to water. When describing how the Indians adopted European techniques, Jerónimo de Mendieta, the scholarly friar, likened them to "monkeys who imitated everything done by the Spaniards in their shops." So facile were the Indians at learning that Spanish craftsmen had second thoughts about teaching their skills. Reliance on European technology, to employ a favorite term of anthropologists, helped "acculturate" the Indian to the Spanish way of life. Whether he knew it or not, the Indian, when he learned to use European technology, fell out of step with ancient society.

III

Settlement, the nuts and bolts of conquest, was left to private enterprise. Both unable and unwilling to shoulder the task, the crown entrusted it to individuals. They came to the New World, to quote a wag, "to serve God, his Majesty and to earn wealth and fame." Or, as Miguel de Cervantes said, "the New World became a refuge and haven for all the poor devils of Spain." That statement carried, above all for the first three decades of the sixteenth century, dire implications for the people of Anáhuac and their neighbors. Regardless of the rhetoric of allegiance to God and king, the Conquest was a fortune hunt.

In 1521, when Tenochtitlán succumbed, the soldiers of Cortés had not earned a penny in almost three years. Most of the plunder had been shipped home to the crown or lost in the bloody Noche Triste. Early explorations uncovered no hidden deposits of gold or silver. The Spaniards, of course, continued their feverish hunt for precious metals; in the meantime, the land was apparently the sole source of wealth. But without men to work it, it had little value, so the Indian became the sine qua non of Spanish welfare. Only by exploiting the land, which required Indian labor, could the Spanish colony flourish. Thus began the rape of the Indian, especially brutal between 1521 and 1550. The pillage of the Indian community included the taking of women, "the most beautiful and the virgins," according to the natives of Santo Tomás Ajusco; the Spaniards "were never satisfied."

The hunt for labor and tribute, which Spaniards exacted from the Indian, helps explains the never-ending expeditions to explore, pacify, and enlarge the boundaries of New Spain. Even before the dust had settled on Tenochtitlán, Cortés dispatched expeditions to the four winds. Before long, Spanish soldiers had seized all of Mexico, marched into Central America and braved the arid region lying between the Californias and New Mexico. In this adventure, Spaniards faced untold dangers, beginning with the vast expanses of uncharted lands.

The subjugation of the Maya of Yucatán, actually never truly completed until the middle of the nineteenth century, lasted for a decade and a half, from 1527 to 1542. The mastery of Yucatán was entrusted to Francisco de Montejo, a companion of Juan de Grijalva on his expedition to Yucatán and later of Cortés. With the blessings of the crown, which named him an *adelantado* (the head of an expedition), Montejo sailed from Spain in 1527 with four hundred men. In 1540, with the pacification of Yucatán still unfinished, an old and exhausted Montejo delegated the subjugation of the Maya to his son. Montejo El Mozo (the Young One) completed what his father had set out to do, founding Mérida, the capital city of Yucatán, in 1542.

The pacification of southern Mexico started in 1521, when Cortés sent Gonzalo de Sandoval to Coatzalcoalcos (Puerto México). Luis Marín went off to impose Spanish control on the Zapotecs of Oaxaca and, to do so, pushed south into Chiapas, where he established a town. Chiapas resisted the Spaniards until 1527, when Diego de Mazariegos subdued its inhabitants. When Cristóbal de Olid, ordered to Honduras about 1523, succumbed to the entreaties of Diego de Velázquez, Cortés, determined to punish his erstwhile companion, followed him. On this march, unnecessary because his allies had already beheaded Olid, Cortés spent nineteen months trekking through Tabasco, Campeche, and Yucatán. The natives of southern Mexico, unlike their ancient neighbors to the north, weathered these expeditions because they had the good fortune, says one scholar, to inhabit a region bereft of gold and silver "that held little potential for commercial profit by Spanish standards and hence little attraction for Spanish settlers."

Pacification of northwest Mexico began under Beltrán Nuño de Guzmán, a corrupt and sanctimonious lawyer of noble family with friends in high places. Head of the first audiencia in New Spain, a court of appeals, Guzmán set off for Michoacán in 1529, acquiring almost immediately a reputation for cruelty. The natives knew him as the *señor de la horca y cuchillo,* the man who relied on noose and knife to kill. Among his wanton acts one stood out: the hanging of six Indian chieftains simply because they failed to sweep the path over which he would walk. For six years, this sadistic Spaniard pillaged Michoacán, southern Zacatecas, Jalisco, and Culiacán, a region baptized Nueva Galicia. One of Guzmán's lieutenants, Cristóbal de Oñate, founded Guadalajara in 1542. An ally of Governor Velázquez of Cuba and an enemy of Cortés, Guzmán, to the delight of his sundry foes, ultimately paid for his dastardly deeds. Tried in Mexico for his misbehavior, he was shipped back to Spain in 1538, spending the last decades of his life as a prisoner of the royal court.

In 1540, Francisco Vázquez de Coronado marched off to explore the far north, the present-day southwest of the United States. Stories of the Seven Cities of Cíbola lured him. Alvar Núñez Cabeza de Vaca and his African slave, Esteban, who survived the shipwrecked expedition of Pánfilo de Narváez, were responsible for Coronado's expedition. For years, Cabeza de Vaca, Esteban, and two other Spaniards had wandered over the southwest, traveling from Texas to Culiacán, where they heard of the fabled Seven Cities, reportedly rich in gold. Marcos de Niza, a Franciscan friar and head of a subsequent expedition, confirmed the news but saw the "cities" only from afar. With a force of over three hundred Spaniards and Indian allies, Coronado retraced Marcos de Niza's footsteps, traveled north as far as Kansas, but found no cities or gold. His travels had taken Coronado into New Mexico, where in 1609 Juan de Oñate, son of the founder of Guadalajara, laid the foundations for Santa Fe.

Elsewhere, Juan Rodríguez de Cabrillo charted the California coast in 1542. Four years later, the Spaniards reached Zacatecas, while Diego de Ibarra spent twenty years marching up and down Nueva Vizcaya, the territories of Sonora, Chihuahua, Sinaloa, and Durango. In the flatlands of Chihuahua and Durango, the Spaniards established cattle ranches stocked with offspring of animals brought north by Coronado. During the middle of the sixteenth century, Luis de Carbajal undertook the settlement of Nuevo León, establishing the town of Monterrey in 1548.

This tide of Spanish expansion did not always flow evenly. At times, it foundered on the shoals of Indian hostility. Unlike the Aztecs in central Mexico, who seemingly became docile once their hierarchical order collapsed, their neighbors on the periphery danced the war dance time and time again. Without a tradition of obedience to one emperor, they could not be conquered simply by killing their leader. The Spaniard had to stamp out resistance, not just in one city or by defeating one tribe.

The Indian, even so, did not always stay conquered. The biggest of his battles to remain free broke out in 1541. The Mixtón War, as it was labeled, set aflame the territory lying between Jalisco and Zacatecas. A few years before, Nuño de Guzmán had inflicted his brand of civilization on it, killing and enslaving at will. His legacy of cruelty was kept alive by Spanish encomenderos. The war, which lasted two years, erupted on the edges of Zacatecas, where the Caxcanes, a sedentary farming people, blocked the northward Spanish march. Its leaders, native priests mostly, gave the war a profoundly religious, anti-Christian character. The Indians burned churches, destroyed monasteries, and cut down crosses. If they triumphed, so their banners proclaimed, they would extirpate all Christian vestiges, restore the ancient religions, revive old customs, and rid the land of Spaniards. The defeat of the Indians in the Mixtón War opened the way for the Spanish occupation of Zacatecas. The war brought death to Pedro de Alvarado, who, fleeing from the Indians, had a horse fall upon him.

Fighting broke out again when the Spaniards advanced beyond Zacatecas. The War of the Chichimecas, an on-and-off conflict of some forty years, cost the Spaniards sundry lives and considerable property because the Indians, in the Spanish manner, rode horses and carried firearms. By the 1580s the Spaniards had rid the north of Chichimeca warriors but not of opposition, because in 1617 the Tepehuanes, natives of the sierra of Durango, took up arms against the invaders.

To the south, the saga had a familiar ring. In 1547, the Zapotecs of Titiquipa rebelled, driven, like the warriors of the Mixtón War, by a fervent desire to wipe out all traces of the Conquest. Native priests led the uprising. At about the same time, the Maya made one last effort to cast off the Spanish yoke. Between 1546 and 1547, their war, with headquarters in the towns of Cupul, Cochuah, and Sotuta, ravaged Yucatán from Mérida to Campeche. Like that of the other conflicts, the goal was to cleanse the Maya world of Christianity. With much cruelty, the Maya, who took orders from their priests, killed Spaniards, put to death horses, cows, pigs, and other animals not native to Yucatán, and uprooted plants and grains of European origin.

The pacification of New Spain was accomplished in the face of fierce Indian opposition. As may be expected, the vanquished Indian compiled his version of it. Akin to the lament of the Aztecs, the book *Chilam Balam de Chumayel,* of the Maya, tells of strangers called *dzules,* men of fair skin who destroyed "what had been good before." Until the Spaniards arrived,

There was no sin . . .
No illness afflicted man,
Aches did not hurt the bones,
Fevers were unknown,
There was no smallpox . . .
All that ended with the *dzules*
They taught fear. . . .

The Maya and, undoubtedly Indians everywhere in New Spain, labeled the Spaniards hypocrites, because what they preached stood at odds with what they practiced.

IV

Encomiendas, grants of Indian labor to Spaniards, had Old World origins. In medieval Castilla, though, they were land grants on a temporary basis to the military, usually in territory taken from the Moors. The New World encomiendas, which dated from the days of the Spaniards on Hispaniola (Española), entrusted Indians but not lands to the Spaniards. Himself the possessor of an encomienda, Cortés was the first to grant them, mostly as a reward to his freebooting soldiers, who, penniless despite risking their lives, wanted compensation. The beneficiaries of encomiendas became encomenderos, some of whom, by fiat of Cortés, received as many as 20,000 Indians. The crown, incidentally, rewarded Cortés with an encomienda of 23,000 Indians, which he increased covertly to 50,000. Pedro de Alvarado, who staked out Xochimilco for himself, enjoyed an encomienda of 20,000 Indians. The smallest encomienda, that of Tequistlán, had 450 Indians. In 1528, encomiendas were limited to 300 Indians. With the fall of Tenochtitlán, Cortés also acquired the Aztec rolls of tribute-paying towns, which numbered nearly four hundred. Cortés distributed these towns among his soldiers, granting the best and largest of them to his lieutenants.

Charles I, however, had misgivings about the encomienda, not wanting to unlock the gates to a hereditary feudal aristocracy in New Spain. He had no wish to repeat the experience of Castilla and Andalucía, where a nobility ready to defy the crown sank roots with the grants of land and towns made for service in the wars against the Moslems. The New World encomienda was therefore a compromise, a concession by the crown to the men who conquered a New World for Spain. The conquerors got Indian towns, and the right to exploit their labor force, but not their lands. The encomenderos, who profited from the labor of their vassals, were, in theory, not "lords of the land."

The encomienda, at first glance, appeared to benefit crown, encomendero, and, not unimportant, the religious goal of the Conquest. The encomendero, the principal beneficiary, received the labor of the Indians, who worked without pay of any kind. He was entrusted with the care of the Indians; he saw to their welfare and maintained order in the villages and, at the same time, helped Christianize them. In return, he had first claim on the tribute of his vassals: a share of their corn and beans, some of the fish they caught, and part of their eggs and chickens. The encomienda, the law stipulated, could not be passed from father to son; at the death of the encomendero, it reverted back to the crown, to be reassigned or abolished.

During the early years, the encomienda served as a mechanism for colonization, as well as for the acquisition of wealth by Spaniards. Theoretically, the encomendero protected and controlled the Indian for the crown, while his labor helped Spaniards settle the land. From the vantage point of Cortés and his men, everyone profited from this arrangement. Even the mendicant friars, originally hostile, viewed favorably the encomiendas when they acquired their own; so did town dwellers, especially when Cortés put Indians to work rebuilding Tenochtitlán (now called Mexico City) and, ultimately, mineowners who coveted unpaid labor.

From the start, nevertheless, the encomendero exploited his vassals. The Indian was compelled to work for Spaniards unwilling to till the land, forced to supply parasitical men with food, clothing, and shelter. So began the exploitation of the "bronze" man by the white, the subjugation of one race by another, the New World by the Old. Ironically, the law judged encomienda Indians "free men" because they were not slaves. Theory and fact stood at opposite poles. Intent notwithstanding, crown legislation conferred sanction on encomenderos waiting to transform themselves into a colonial aristocracy. Not a few of them succeeded. Lacking the responsibilities of the feudal lord, the encomendero dealt heavy-handedly with his workers, not merely exploiting them but inflicting cruelty and even death. The encomienda, in actuality, headed the list of Spanish institutions responsible for the fast decline of the Indian population, a tragic occurrence of the sixteenth century.

Its evils were endless. Encomenderos, first off, had their pick of the Indian women, whether with husband or not. They used them as domestics and as concubines and, when they were no longer useful, drove them away. On the sugar plantations, the encomenderos "married" them off to their slaves. Some beat their Indians to death; others buried them alive; the less cruel killed them with guns. When they fled from his grasp, the encomendero pursued them with bloodhounds. Cortés and fellow encomenderos earned money by selling their Indians into slavery. Juan Ponce de León, one of these encomenderos, beat his Indians so badly that the authorities arrested him for crimes. The best of the encomenderos drove their Indians from dawn to dusk, while the heartless robbed them of their goods. All of the early encomenderos, writes a noted scholar, looked upon the encomienda as a license to exploit, not excluding robbing villages of their lands. The crown ultimately corrected the worst of these ills but failed to eliminate them entirely; they survived to corrupt even mestizo encomenderos such as Gonzalo Cano, son of Isabel Moctezuma and a Spanish father, a tyrant in Tacuba legendary for his cruelty to Indians.

Nor did the crown prevent the encomendero from becoming a lord of the land. At first, the land had little appeal; without tools and oxen to plow it or without markets, it was useless. Slowly, however, encomenderos began to find buyers for agricultural products in the nearby Spanish towns, which gave value to the land. Encomenderos, therefore, were the first to buy land, when they could not steal it. Eventually, the encomienda, divorced from the ownership of land by Spanish law, had nonetheless planted the seeds for the big estates, precisely what the crown did not want. Troubled by these developments, the crown abolished the encomienda. The New Laws of 1542 declared that no encomienda would survive its holder and that henceforth no more would be granted. The laws freed Indians unjustly enslaved, and the crown sent Francisco Tello de Sandoval to enforce them.

His arrival in New Spain caused an uproar. Business came to a virtual halt, six hundred Spaniards announced they were returning home, and encomenderos asked Spanish officials to suspend the legislation. Even the bishop of New Spain, himself an encomendero, insisted that the abolition of the encomienda would merely worsen the exploitation of the Indian. Deeming wisdom the better part of valor, Tello de Sandoval and colonial authorities declared the New Laws unenforceable. Bowing before this opinion, the crown set aside the legislation, though it did not abandon the idea of curtailing the powers of the encomendero, declaring in 1549 that they could exact tribute from the Indian but no longer his free labor. Charles I, just the same, ruled that encomiendas could be passed on to a son and, after 1555, to a grandson.

With most of the old encomenderos gone to their grave, Philip II decided again to abolish encomiendas, thinking their criollo owners more tractable than their conquistador fathers. Philip misjudged them. They were just as bellicose in the 1560s, when Philip published his intentions, as their fathers had been twenty years earlier. The threatened loss of their Indian tribute enraged the encomenderos and encouraged a few of them to plot the independence of New Spain. Their leader was Alonso de Avila, the son of a famous conquistador. The conspiracy aborted, mainly because Martín Cortés, a wealthy encomendero and the fatuous son of the conqueror, could not make up his mind. Supposedly offered the crown of New Spain by Avila and his allies, Martín could say neither yes nor no. Local authorities caught wind of the plot, beheaded Alonso and his brother, and displayed their heads on the end of pikes as a reminder to all not to tamper with the king's will. For his role, Martín was shipped back to Spain, there to be tried and acquitted. The plot to topple Spanish rule, at least as the crown saw it, rang down the curtain on the barbarous encomienda, though it survived, in somewhat modified form, into the eighteenth century. In Yucatán, for instance, encomiendas were not abolished until 1786. By the time of their demise, in the eighteenth century, of the 934 original encomiendas, a mere handful existed outside of Yucatán.

V

What the crown feared most in the New World was the rise of powerful individuals or representative institutions ready to defy its power. Come what may, the king and not a local nobility would dictate affairs. Cortés and his lieutenants might capture a New World, but only the king would rule it. The duty of the colonial Spaniard was to obey.

Still, reality had to be faced. That meant, initially, dealing with Cortés, at a time when rebellious nobles in Spain challenged the authority of the crown. For all his apprehension that Cortés might emulate his nobles at home, Charles I named him governor and captain general of New Spain. Charles had little choice, since Cortés commanded the loyalty of the men who controlled New Spain. Yet Charles hardly wanted adventurers in distant New Spain, by sea three months away, acquiring power and prestige. He lost no time, therefore, dispatching royal officials to watch over the crown's share of the booty.

Unwittingly, Cortés helped the cause of the crown. When he marched off to Honduras, a rival faction in Mexico City deposed his subordinates, started to take encomiendas away from his followers, and spread rumors of his death. These rivals even sent letters to Charles accusing Cortés of stealing a share of the royal tribute and of disloyalty to the king. Cortés came back to Mexico City to oust his rivals, but failed to convince Charles of his loyalty. Cortés, it appears in retrospect, proved a faithful governor, exploring the land for the crown, searching for mines, and promoting trade and commerce.

But he had enemies at the royal court in Spain. On their advice, Charles, who needed no prodding, sent officials to New Spain to circumvent Cortés's authority. In 1528, to allay royal suspicions and prove his loyalty, Cortés sailed for Spain bearing gifts for his monarch and accompanied by Indian nobles. A grateful Charles confirmed Cortés as captain general of New Spain and told him to select the villages and towns he coveted for his encomiendas. Since Cortés had already appropriated them, the crown's grants confirmed mainly what he owned. Given the title of marqués del Valle, Cortés became the master of Oaxaca. Charles, however, did not restore to Cortés the governorship of New Spain. From that time on, Cortés was free to enjoy his immense wealth but not political power.

In 1540, Cortés returned once more to Spain, this time to complain of ill treatment by the viceroy and fellow royal officials. Again, he went to see Charles. The monarch was not at home, and the bureaucrats at the royal court looked unfavorably on his complaints. In 1547, shortly before his departure for New Spain, he died near Sevilla; he was sixty-three years of age. Buried in Spain, he was later reburied in Texcoco. All told, Cortés was buried at least nine times. The eighth burial, in 1823, was done out of fear that the people of Mexico City, inflamed with nationalist zeal and hatred for the Spaniard, might dig up his bones and destroy them.

Even before Cortés's death, the crown had begun to organize a government for its New World empire. The Casa de Contratación, a legacy of Isabel la Católica, dated from 1503. It handled Spanish trade, commerce, and colonization in the West Indies, while the bishop of Burgos, Juan Rodríguez de Fonseca, determined policy. With the acquisition of New Spain and, shortly thereafter, Central America, Spanish authorities set up the Council of the Indies, which advised the king and, in his name, watched over the empire. Earlier, to administer justice in the Indies, there was established in Santo Domingo a court of appeals, or audiencia, which could rule as well as legislate in the Indies. In 1527, a year before Cortés traveled to Spain for his initial visit, an audiencia of three judges was established in Mexico City.

The audiencia under Nuño de Guzmán, its chief justice, proved inept. Government in New Spain had gotten off on the wrong foot, as tax evasion and bureaucratic corruption sank their claws into society. Spanish authorities replaced Guzmán with another audiencia, this one staffed by able *oidores,* as its justices were called. One of them, Vasco de Quiroga, a Franciscan friar, went on to win renown for his work with the Indians. Under Sebastian Rodríguez de Fueleal, a man of integrity and ability and its chief justice, the audiencia handled wisely and effectively a host of knotty problems. One of them had to do with Cortés, ready always to multiply the Indians on his encomienda, to add to his property, and to defend his privileges.

Wishing to tighten its grip, the crown appointed a viceroy for New Spain as its personal representative. This viceregal system did not just appear out of thin air, because Fernando el Católico had employed viceroys to govern Aragón, Cataluña, and Valencia. The viceroy was a man of noble lineage known for his loyalty to the king and held to be both competent and wise. The post fell to Antonio de Mendoza, a Castilian nobleman related to the royal family and Spain's ambassador to Rome. Appointed in 1530, Mendoza made a delayed entrance into Mexico City after five years of "negotiating salary" with the crown. His perquisites included a palace, a good salary, and an honor guard. An executive with legislative and judicial authority, Mendoza had to look out for the colony's welfare, defend it from foreign attack, watch over the Indians, enlarge crown revenues, and, as a faithful Catholic, be a patron of the church. The audiencia, over which the viceroy could preside, kept judicial affairs in its own hands.

Mendoza served his king ably. With a deft hand on the public pulse, he was both a good viceroy and a wise governor. He ended the Mixtón War, imposed order and discipline on the rowdy conquistadores, collaborated with the audiencia, and, to the applause of encomenderos, neglected to enforce the New Laws. When he left office in 1550, after almost fifteen years in New Spain, he could look back on the beauty of Mexico City, take pride in its hospitals and schools, and point to its prosperity. Compassion, by the same token, was not his forte, nor was financial integrity, because he acquired a small fortune from dealings of marginal legality. Mendoza was the first official in New Spain to profit from public office but not the last.

During this formative period, the crown, urged on by the friars of the Conquest, started to bring the Indian under its direct control. Spaniards were ordered to stay out of Indian communities, and cattle ranching was barred from their lands. Spaniards had to settle in Spanish towns, lands empty of Indian communities, leaving the Indian free to live alone. Scattered and sparsely populated Indian hamlets were joined together with their parent towns; up to eight towns, along with their attendant hamlets, were consolidated into one large settlement, labeled a *congregación,* an Indian pueblo. After they were gathered together as *congregaciones,* they were referred to as *repúblicas de indios.* The pueblos were given ejidos (communal lands) to cultivate, along with pastures and forests. So long as the Indian tilled his lands, they were his, but he was not free to move about. These *repúblicas de indios* were entrusted to the care of Spanish corregidores responsible to the crown. This, however, was not always so; in Yucatán, to cite one case, no corregidores were ever appointed, the Maya being left to the supervision of encomenderos and clergy, while in parts of Oaxaca the hostility of Mixtecs and Zapotecs to the *congregaciones* barred their establishment.

What the crown wanted was to place its vassals under its wings and, equally important, to profit from their tribute. By eliminating the encomendero, it fattened its coffers. With its demands for tribute, the crown had started off dealing with the Indians in the pattern of the old Aztec monarchs. Like Moctezuma, it demanded tribute but, unlike him, controlled its vassals. The tribute, which the Indian paid originally in goods (corn, squash, and beans, to name three), evolved, as time went by, to approximately two pesos annually per adult. That tax, which is what the tribute signified, was an awesome burden on the Indian. By way of compensation, the crown exempted him from paying the *alcabala,* a sales tax, and the *diezmo,* money demanded by the church. The crown, moreover, took steps to protect the property of Indian communities from avaricious Spaniards. Laws enacted between 1523 and 1532 ordered Spaniards to leave communal property; a law passed in 1535 told them, when they disobeyed, to return what they had stolen.

Defenders of Spanish colonialism label these measures social justice. For all that, they were self-seeking. The crown wanted to protect the Indian because he paid tribute; Indians despoiled of their property could not pay it. The defense of communal property and demands for tribute were opposite sides of the same coin. The crown protected the Indian community so as to be able to tax it. The success of Spanish colonization rested on the labor of the Indian as well as on the food he produced. When Spaniards robbed the Indian of his lands, he fled into the hills, depriving the crown of both labor and food. Social justice, the Spanish brand, barred Indians from bearing arms, owning a horse, or wearing European dress. They could acquire private property only under certain conditions and could not sell their communal lands, join urban guilds, or abandon their communities.

The crown, for all that, left partly intact the hierarchical pyramid of ancient Anáhuac. During the first decades, the former nobility preserved its authority since the Spaniard, to rule his subjects, relied on it. (In Yucatán, this Indian nobility survived, more or less, until the early eighteenth century.) The Spaniards called them *caciques,* using an Arawak word they adopted during their days in the Antilles. The collapse of Aztec sovereignty, especially the downfall of the pagan priesthood and the military chieftains, shattered the old ruling elite. While Indian nobles held on to a bit of power and wealth, they were the exceptions. To establish their colonial bastion, the Spaniards, however, built a new ruling elite of Indians from what remained of the old, but joined by fresh adherents. A few former political power brokers stayed on while ambitious commoners elbowed their way into the circle of caciques. Whether old or new, these caciques, with the exception of those in Yucatán, did what they could to separate themselves from the Indian masses, adopting, writes one historian, "Spanish culture . . . and seeking to conform to the Spanish image of the gentleman and hidalgo," erecting elaborate houses for themselves that dwarfed the humble adobe huts of other natives. They put on airs, winning the right to wear European clothing, to carry swords and muskets, to "ride horseback with saddle and spurs," and to appropriate Spanish names for themselves. The Indian caciques "who could trace their lineage back to pre-Conquest" aristocracy, according to this historian, "indulged in a taste for genealogy comparable to that of any Spanish hidalgo."

During the sixteenth century, some of these caciques, by Spanish fiat, became *gobernadores,* heads of Indian communities that, with the help of Indian alcaldes and regidores, who were in theory elected, ran the Indian pueblos, supervised their communal lands, kept order, managed the labor gangs of encomenderos and clergy, organized repartimientos (the labor system which replaced the encomienda), and saw to it that Indians paid the royal tribute. Their underlings often flogged wrongdoers and enforced church attendance. As a reward, the Indian caciques acquired land and vassals of their own.

Ordinary Indians had little use for this elite, making up perhaps one-tenth of the Indian population; they viewed it as corrupt, tyrannical, and a toady. Its day in the sun, outside of regions such as Yucatán and Oaxaca, barely survived the sixteenth century, its demise brought on by the sharp decline of the Indian population and because the bulk of Indian workers, through the appearance of the system of wage labor, passed into the employ of Spaniards.

VI

The church, in the meantime, reserved for itself a prime role in pacification and settlement. No other institution had more impact on the shaping of colonial society, because the church had the responsibility for converting the Indian into a good Christian and a loyal subject. The pope, moreover, had placed the church under royal tutelage. By the *patronato real,* Spanish kings, designated heads of the Catholic church, collected the *diezmo* and appointed archbishops and bishops in their colonies, while the crown assumed responsibility for the welfare of the church, which henceforth obeyed the state. Linked arm and arm, the church and state set about molding New Spain into a Spanish and very Catholic colony.

The first man of the cloak stepped ashore with Cortés. Father Bartolomé de Olmedo, upon whom Cortés relied for advice, shared with the conquistadores the sorrow of the Noche Triste as well as the thrill of victory. In 1523, the Franciscans, the initial missionary order and eventually the largest, arrived; Pedro de Gante, famous later for his schools, was one of three; in the following year, more came, not the least of them Toribio de Benavente, referred to as Motolinía by the Indians, and part of the "twelve apostles." Barefoot, they walked from Veracruz to Mexico City. Cortés, the consummate politician, made their entrance into Tenochtitlán a drama of the first order, kneeling, before the startled Indians to kiss the hands of the friars. The Franciscans, an order founded by Francis of Assisi in 1215, lived by a vow of poverty; only the poor, they believed, passed through the gates of heaven. Next were the Black Friars, the Dominicans, known for their intellectual bent and their legal proclivities. The Augustinians, with reputations as architects and builders and the last of the early orders, entered Mexico in 1533. Much, much later, the Jesuits, champions of the pope and sympathizers of the Counter-Reformation, made their bow. By mid-sixteenth century, over eight hundred friars were in New Spain.

Not far behind were the nuns of the convents, adjuncts initially of the regular orders. The first of them, La Concepción, an offshoot of the Franciscans, made its debut in 1540, established by four nuns of the convent of Santa Isabel in Salamanca, Spain. As the convents multiplied, the colonial rich became their patrons, encomenderos, mineowners, merchants, and, later, hacendados. Most of their nuns were Spaniards and criollos, daughters of conquistadores and colonists. So popular did the convents become as havens for the daughters of the well-to-do that by the end of the seventeenth century the number of nuns had alarmed royal authorities. At the rear of this entourage trod the seculars, the priests to staff parishes for Spaniards, criollos, and other non-Indians, bringing along their panoply of bishops and archbishops. By the 1560s, their numbers were multiplying rapidly, leading inevitably to a clash with the regular orders.

The Franciscans set the tone for the evangelical crusade. The twelve apostles established themselves in the principal Indian communities; the crown, likewise, appointed the Franciscan Juan de Zumárraga bishop of New Spain and later its first archbishop. These early friars, true believers, identified with the Indian. They dressed poorly, went barefoot, ate the food offered them, and made their homes among the poor. They were mendicants, members of begging fraternities, for whom the evangelization of the Indian was the goal of Conquest. They, too, wanted Spaniards barred from the Indian pueblos, and the Indian segregated under their care, isolated from Old World corruption and immorality. The Indians they likened to "baby birds," with wings not yet ready for flight. Indians, as children, must be shielded from harm. This belief, wise as well as mistaken, shaped paternalistic legislation for the Indian. The views of the friars, nevertheless, did not always tally. Significant differences split them. The Franciscans, the most paternalistic, refused the Indian the sacraments of Communion and Extreme Unction. The Augustianians, on the contrary, exalted his moral capacity, conceding him the sacraments. In their view, the Indian was predisposed spiritually to accept Christianity and required only a brief tutelage. The Indian's soul resembled that of Spaniards; to the Franciscans, it needed molding.

Whatever their opinion, leaders of the missionary orders were familiar with the religious and social ideas of their epoch. They walked arm in arm with the spiritual avant-garde of European thought, a belated arrival in New Spain. Erasmus's interpretation of Christ and Sir Thomas More's *Utopia* lay at the heart of Zumárraga's philosophy, outlined in his *Doctrina cristiana* and *La doctrina breve.* With patience and guidance, the Indian's simple society, "soft wax" molded easily, affirmed Jerónimo de Mendieta, could become the basis for the perfect Christian community. Zumárraga, a moral stalwart in the flabby age of Charles I, upheld the teachings of More on labor, believing no one to be naturally lazy.

One of the best salesmen for Christian humanism was the Franciscan Vasco de Quiroga, bishop of Michoacán and also a disciple of Thomas More. Among the Tarascans of Pátzcuaro, a town in Michoacán, he founded *repúblicas y hospitales de Santa Fe,* communities of Indians on the idea of More's *Utopia,* where he banned private property and made the community the sole owner of the lands and goods and, in the manner of Spanish legislation, the lands inalienable. The social structure of the community rested on the family, which, collaborating with its neighbors, did the work of field and shops. The fruits of labor were distributed according to need, the surplus set aside for the poor and for charity. On these *repúblicas,* no one was exempt from work, while administrators were elected by secret ballot. Other friars endeavored to protect the Indian, but only Don Vasco considered him ideal material for the perfect human model, the goals of humanism and primitive communism.

Bartolomé de las Casas, author of the famous *Breve relación de la destrucción de las Indias,* also devoted his life to defending the Indian. With forty other Dominicans, he had come as bishop of Chiapas to Christianize and save. An enemy of the encomienda, he fought tooth and nail to get it abolished, having known its ills firsthand for, on the island of Hispaniola, Las Casas, before taking his vows, had been an encomendero. Legend has it that he became a friar shocked by Spanish exploitation of the Indian. His tireless demands for social justice earned him the sobriquet Apostle of the Indians.

First and foremost, the friars came to convert, to make Christians out of pagans. God had willed it, else why had he entrusted to Spaniards the discovery and subjugation of a New World? It was, they believed, by divine intervention. Until the New World fell into the Spanish lap, the Christian world was but a tiny fraction of the whole; with the addition of the converts, Christianity could become the universal religion. Indeed, the Catholic faith did profit, if the claims of missionaries are believable. Motolinía, for one, wrote that nine million Indians were baptized by 1537. If only half correct, that number added millions to Catholic rolls.

To convert heathens, the good friars, majestically intolerant of conflicting beliefs, initially employed love and persuasion. They inveigled the Indians into embracing Christianity, but, not infrequently, charm yielded poor results. Convinced that the ends justified the means, the friars reverted to force. Zumárraga, one of the most fanatical of them, believed that they must discipline Indian heretics. As apostolic inquisitor, he brought before him some nineteen Indian "sinners," one being Don Carlos Chichimecatecuhtli, whose notorious trial in Texcoco in 1539 ended with his burning at the stake. In Michoacán, an Augustinian zealot had four Indian heretics tied to a pole in the town plaza, laid quantities of wood at their feet, and then lit a fire, which the wind supposedly blew out of control. Whatever the friar's intent, two of the Indians were burned alive and the others scarred for life. Another friar in Michoacán had an Indian tortured in order to compel him to confess his sins. On the next day, when the jailer came to his cell, he found that he had hanged himself to escape further torture. Similar accounts besmirched the reputation of the Franciscans in Yucatán, where they kept a tight rein for over two centuries. Beatings were common, as well as reliance on church jails to woo the unconvinced. At church masses, the absent were noted and, when caught, whipped. Asked to justify their behavior, the Franciscans not infrequently insisted that the Indians "wanted to be punished." The whippings, they pointed out, were, more often than not, administered by Indian caciques, not by Spaniards. Until 1571, furthermore, Indians were subject to the jurisdiction of the apostolic inquisitors, who investigated idolatry, superstition, and like sins.

Unknown Indians, ironically, spurred the conversion to Catholicism. In 1531, according to one story, the Virgin appeared miraculously atop Tepeyac, a hill just north of Mexico City, the old site of the temple of Tonantzin, the Aztec mother of gods. An Indian named Marcos, historians say, later painted her image, dark of skin and of native features. Almost overnight the cult of the Virgen de Guadalupe, as she was titled, blossomed. Identified with Tonantzin, the Virgin won disciples quickly among the Indians.

The worship of the Virgen de Guadalupe sank deep roots into the soil of Anáhuac. By the middle of the next century, altars in her name were everywhere. In the beginning, the holy friars looked skeptically at the Virgin, labeling idolatrous a cult that claimed as a miracle an image painted by an Indian. However, Spanish colonial society eventually came to terms with it, accepting it as part of the faith. Yet the worship of the Virgen de Guadalupe, part and parcel of the most salient religious ceremonies in New Spain, remained essentially Indian, though it came to challenge the supremacy of the Virgen de los Remedios, the patron of Spaniards.

The Indian did not always take kindly to the Spanish version of the universe. According to *El libro de los coloquios,* compiled in Nahuatl by the early Franciscans, Indian wise men defended their religion steadfastly. During one encounter, after listening to friars condemn the ancient beliefs, the Indians, "with courtesy and urbanity," made manifest their unhappiness for this "attack on the customs and beliefs of their ancestors." Before the arrival of the Spaniards, they reminded the friars, "there had been no hunger, no disease, no poverty." One story, taken from the Indian chronicles, captures this sentiment succinctly. When Ixtlilxochitl, lord of Texcoco, was baptized a Christian, he went to tell his mother, Yacotzin, the good news, adding "that he had come for her so that she too might be baptized." "You are out of your mind," she replied. "How could you permit a handful of barbaric Christians to brainwash you so quickly?"

Conversion to Christianity, in reality, often proved fleeting. Indian relapses into paganism were commonplace, for instance among the Mixtecs of the region of Yanhuitlán. On October 14, 1544, the dean of the cathedral of Oaxaca City, Pedro Gómez de Maraver, told Francisco Tello de Sandoval, successor to Zumárraga as apostolic inquisitor, of the heretical behavior of the Indian caciques of Yanhuitlán. Don Francisco, the *gobernador,* and Don Juan Xual, along with other dignitaries, consistently "performed idolatry and made sacrifices, including human ones," bestowing offerings "of their own blood and hair, and of birds and slaves." Christianized Indians were the victims. That same year, the priest Pedro de Olmos reported seeing the practice of human sacrifice near Coatlán, a village just two days from Oaxaca City, telling of a sacrificial site with a large stone idol drenched in blood, the heart of a recently killed child in its mouth. Some sixteen human skulls littered the ground around it. The cacique of Teutalco, according to another report, held sacrificial ceremonies to the rain god, disdained going to confession, ate meat on Fridays, and compelled his servants to work on the Sabbath. In many villages, Indians shot arrows at the friars who arrived to preach and remove hidden idols.

For the time being, the Indian clung to his polytheistic universe, regarding himself as a good Christian but never fully grasping the Christian abstractions of sin or virtue. The community of saints, intermediaries between God and man for Christians, the Indian accepted as a pantheon of manlike deities. He paid homage to the symbol of the crucifixion, but saw it as an act of sacrifice. God was powerful but neither omnipotent nor exclusory. The Indian thought of heaven and hell as places, while ascribing souls to animals and inanimate objects. Human sacrifice ended, but not all pagan rituals when practiced dissemblingly. The transition proved none too harsh, for Aztec religion included Christian rituals such as matrimony, penitence, baptism, fasting, and offerings. The Indian, therefore, embraced Catholicism but in his own fashion.

If total success escaped the friars, it was not for lack of effort. Education, the indoctrination of Indians, started early. Wherever they went, the Franciscans established schools, to teach the rudiments of language, Spanish values, and Christian doctrines. The students of the friars were the sons of the Indian nobility, destined, in the Spanish colonial blueprint, to help rule their own people. Pedro de Gante built the model school, the Colegio de San Juan de Letrán, in Mexico City. At the Franciscan Colegio de Santa Cruz in Tlatelolco, an Indian elite studied European traditions; the teaching of the Spanish language made up the core of the curriculum, along with Christian theology. Upon learning Spanish, the pedagogues insisted, the Indian became a good Spaniard.

To subjugate, church and crown endeavored to destroy the beliefs, customs, and traditions of the past. The conqueror bestowed Spanish names on rivers, mountains, bays, oceans, and forests, thus claiming them for himself. The Indian lost out because they were no longer his. True, the Spaniard made concessions, adding to villages and towns his own names but also keeping the old. Teotihuacán, in this manner, became San Juan Teotihuacán; Tlatelolco, Santiago Tlatelolco; and so on. Beyond that, the Spaniards banned the songs and dances of old, thinking they kept alive memories of pagan idols. They disrupted pre-Hispanic community activities, supplanting them with European ones, placing the emphasis on individual performance.

The Spaniards brought their music and, more significant, their instruments, particularly the stringed ones; the guitar, now a Mexican standby, evolved from one of them. Spanish music made its debut with Cortés, among whose soldiers Benito Bejel, Cristóbal Rodríguez Dávalos, Sebastián Rodríguez, and Diego Martín played the trumpet, kettledrum, and drums. One soldier, nicknamed Canillas because he was so thin, played the fife. Some of them became teachers of music after the Conquest; Bejel, for example, founded a studio of music and dance in Mexico City. But playing for solitary enjoyment made no sense to the Indian. Sales to Indians of stringed instruments, as one anthropologist points out, measured necessarily "the breakdown of communal aspects of native music." Happily, the friars ignored native crafts; no missionary bothered to teach ceramics to Indians. As a result, the ancient art of pottery making survived, as did things largely Indian, because Spaniards had no use for them, among them the *metate,* a curved stone for grinding corn for the tortilla.

VII

With the razing of Tenochtitlán, a distinct architecture replaced the old temples, palaces, and abodes of the nobility. Influenced by the Moorish, the imported blueprints introduced remnants of medieval Spain to the New World. To cite Manuel Toussaint, a venerable Mexican art authority, it was the Spanish world, "the last gasp of the Gothic style" and of the Middle Ages. The Franciscan monastery of Tepeaca, built between 1530 and 1580, a prototype of edifices on the horizon, wrote Toussaint, was exclusively of the Middle Ages. Yet its design, paradoxically, was largely homegrown. Few, if any, blueprints arrived from Spain, although surely the memories of temples left behind inspired local designs.

The Franciscan style of the early sixteenth century, a conglomerate of angles and straight lines, came to be known as the fortress church, where strategic considerations superseded priestly needs. Solitary towers rising above the wilderness, these forts, religious shrines by function and aggressively masculine, were majestic yet simple, with walls topped by parapets, where soldiers might take cover when under attack. Utility rather than aesthetics took precedence. They were massive, with thick walls of stone, these monasteries, convents, and churches, designed to last ages and to withstand, among other dangers, the earthquakes of the Valley of Mexico.

The Franciscans were the pioneer architects, at Tepeaca, Tula, Texcoco, Tlaxcala, Tlatelolco, and Atlixco. Not limited by the vow of poverty, the benchmark of the Franciscans, the Augustinians erected more-sumptuous temples, at Actopan and Acolman, to name two. The Dominicans, who built in southern Mexico, put up grandiose buildings, among the finest in New

Spain, aided by the Mixtecs, a people with a long history of working in stone. As the Dominican monasteries of Oaxtepec and Oaxaca City demonstrate, the technical ability of the local Indian population, as well as its resources, controlled the design for buildings, whether they were simple or elaborate. The richer the Indian community and the more numerous its masons and carpenters, the bigger and more elaborate the building. Whatever the level of his skills, the Indian built the fortress churches, as well as the palace of Cortés in Cuernavaca and other lay structures. In places such as Mexico City, skilled Spaniards helped, often by directing the labor of Indians. All the same, in the peripheral world it was the Indian masons and carpenters; when skilled, they did the work immediately; when not, the friars taught them how to do it.

Labor requested, needless to say, was labor demanded. If the Indian failed to offer his services, he was made to do so. In the early years, it was mostly forced labor. Encomiendas, additionally, were sometimes transferred by the crown to the clergy; the Indians of Texcoco, when Cortés lost control of them, to cite a specific case, were given to the Augustinians. Later, the church received repartimientos, forced paid labor, and funds from the crown to build the cathedral, the palace of the Inquisition, the temples of La Concepción, Santa Clara, and La Santa Veracruz, all in Mexico City, and, quixotically, the temple of Our Lady of Guadalupe, the Indians' Virgen. In the small towns, Indian converts to Christianity built the temples. Beyond that, Indians served the friars and, afterward, the urban priests as cooks, maids, gardeners, acolytes, musicians, and, in the absence of pack animals, beasts of burden.

Once built, the friars were convinced, temples required decorating, the painting of religious scenes with saints, angels, and heavens. In general, Spanish artists did the notable works, but, again, Indian artists lent a hand. Indians alone painted some of the early murals in convents, monasteries, and temples, such as those at Ixmiquilpan and Culhuacán.

Painting, however, maintained its Spanish character. In no way was it a fusion of European and Indian; as an artist, the Indian accepted European tutelage. Spaniards taught him to paint—for instance, at Gante's famous school—but the art, as the friars visualized it, was for a religious purpose. From this blend of Spanish religious design and the labor of Indian artist evolved a "Christian-Indian" school of painting. It was Christian because of its religious goals; Indian because the artist, a neophyte, left his ingenuousness or candor stamped on it.

The Indian sculptor proved less malleable, more independent. It was he, more than the painter, who wove his unique trademark into the fabric of his work. Monasteries required not merely murals but sculptures, both in relief and in the round, art forms the Indian had mastered long since. Because of their nature, the similarity of materials used as well as his technical skills, the Indian shaped to his liking the sculptures he carved. The total design might well be entirely European, but, here and there, both technique and ornamental motif were Indian, such as the spires on the dome of the church at Acolman—a design utterly European but, because of its native floral motif, difficult to catalog as European.

VIII

During these tempestuous decades, the years after the fall of Tenochtitlán, Spaniards set about to make New Spain their colony. Their success, which laid the foundations of colonial Mexico, cost the natives dearly. Yet out of the exploitation of Indians by Spaniards, there emerged a new people, the Mexicans, and with them a distinct way of life.

4

MIRACLES OF SILVER

I

One chance find, the culmination of the hunt for riches which Hernán Cortés began at Vera Cruz, laid the cornerstone for New Spain's society. Until almost the mid-sixteenth century, the frantic chase, despite discoveries of silver in Pachuca, Sultepec, Tlalpujahua, and Taxco, none too distant from Mexico City, yielded middling gifts. Then, quite by accident, in September 1546, Spaniards stumbled upon a windfall in Zacatecas. On the eighth of that month, Juan de Tolosa, the commander of a detachment of Spanish soldiers, established camp at the foot of a mountain baptized La Bufa by neighboring Indians. Almost immediately, Tolosa made friends with them; grateful for his behavior, they escorted him to a site with "live rocks" they thought might be of interest to Spaniards. The rocks, it turned out, were silver. Tolosa went on to become a millionaire.

La Bufa unlocked the treasure chest. Soon after, Sombrerete and Fresnillo, also in Zacatecas, bore additional pay dirt, followed by the discovery of the hidden ores of Guanajuato and, far to the north, Santa Barbara in Chihuahua. In 1631, more silver was unearthed in Parral, just over the hill from Santa Barbara, and, later, at Alamos, in the rugged mountains of Sonora. These mines came to form some of the biggest mining operations in the world of that time. By 1600, shipments of silver ore and, afterward, sales of minted coins to Spain and the Far East totaled 80 percent of New Spain's exports.

For Zacatecas, the brightest of the emporiums, silver symbolized halcyon days. With its advent, some Spaniards and criollos could wallow in wealth. Mining gave birth to cities—to Zacatecas and Guanajuato, bastions of elegant colonial architecture, and to Pachuca and Parral, less ostentatious. Adventurous men rushed to the mining camps, converting them into towns and cities. To haul the silver out and to bring food into the camps, the Spaniards opened routes which became channels for commerce with neighboring towns and far-off Mexico City. Spain made up deficits in its balance of payments by shipping silver bullion to England, France, and Holland, which supplied the Spanish colonies with most of the goods they imported. Mining conferred on New Spain its initial centers of capitalist enterprise.

Of notable importance, wageworkers made their debut in the northern mining camps. Initially, Aztecs, Tlaxcalans, and other natives traveled north, lured by the prospect of good pay in the mines; a multiracial lot of Indians, mestizos, Africans (imported slaves), and mulattoes composed the labor gangs. Whatever their origins, these northern miners, relatively well paid and notorious for their spendthrift proclivities, were an "aristocracy of labor."

Silver paid for the upkeep of Spanish bureaucrats in New Spain: the viceroys, the judges of the audiencia, the legions of clerks, and the friars and parish priests. Silver reimbursed the crown for the cost of the naval escorts of the flotillas on their journeys to and from Spain. Thanks partly to the "white metal," the crown brought the Spanish nobility to heel without falling into the hands of a merchant bourgeoisie, the fate of the English kings, despite governing in a time of profound social transformations.

Here and there, however, the crown had to share its treasures. The subsoil belonged exclusively to it. Yet, unable itself to haul out the silver ores, the crown ceded the rights to individuals so that Spaniards were free to roam the land to prospect for silver and gold and to profit from what they discovered. The crown received merely one-fifth of its value, the *quinto* (later one-tenth for silver). In the mining towns and cities, wealthy mineowners, at times criollos, managed to control politics. For example, in Zacatecas, a Spanish stronghold, mineowners were alcaldes (mayors) and regidores (councilmen) because officials were selected from among the respected and prosperous of the community. Happily for the crown, hereditary rights to political office never materialized.

The mining towns, exploding with people hungry for food, opened up vast hinterlands to the plow. The Bajío, the region between Mexico City and Guadalajara, and the province of Michoacán became granaries for the miners of Zacatecas and Guanajuato. Hacendados, the masters of the land, planted corn and wheat, while cattle made their appearance, their beef and hides earmarked for mining camps. The growth and prosperity of the Bajío was tied directly to the mining boom, that of Zacatecas primarily. Miners in Parral, days off by horse, ate oranges imported from Guadalajara and Valladolid and, more astonishingly, from Culiacán, a town on the Pacific rim, and wore clothing of coarse woolen cloth manufactured in distant cities.

II

Much transpired during the age of silver. Earlier, conquistadores turned encomenderos, evangelical friars, and Indians had performed on center stage; now, miners, hacendados, and merchants did, along with the secular clergy and royal officials. For the elite of New Spain, more and more criollo, these were splendid years. For a while, the colony enjoyed a relatively self-sufficient economy, similar to the incipient capitalist ones of Europe. New Spain shipped its silver across the Atlantic, which kept the Spanish economy afloat and supplied most of its own needs. That circumstance endured only briefly. On the model of the mother country, New Spain's economy bogged down in the mire of dependency.

Until 1568, local industry was, relatively speaking, free to call its own tune. Colonial entrepreneurs produced silks, taffeta, and velvet equal in quality with Spanish imports. Others manufactured wool and cotton cloth in quantities sufficient to meet the needs of the entire working population of New Spain and for export to Peru. However, textile barons and merchants in Sevilla persuaded Spanish authorities to bar colonial enterprise, and, consequently, manufacturing in New Spain received a severe setback. Textile manufacturing on a small scale lived on mainly because the Spaniards sold premium cloth, made more expensive by import duties. Only the wealthy of New Spain could afford to buy it. Furthermore, because of its European conflicts, Spain failed to supply its colonies, compelling their inhabitants to manufacture their own cloth. Local industry, mostly *obrajes,* sweatshops making coarse cloth, survived on cheap labor. Guilds controlled price and quality and set aside the jobs of masters for Spaniards and criollos.

Relying on the Casa de Contratación, authorities watched over commerce. Their goal was to aid Spanish merchants, whose goods arrived by way of a fleet sailing annually from Sevilla, carrying wines and perfumes as well as steel, iron tools, hats, and the like for the well-off. The royal treasury taxed almost everything sold in New Spain; one tax, the *alcabala,* grew rapidly over the years. These policies stifled commerce and industry, driving prices up and encouraging colonials, again and again, to buy contraband goods.

Under these conditions, a rickety infrastructure emerged. The Spaniards, unlike their Roman conquerors, built poor roads or none at all, the best of them between Mexico City and Veracruz, and north to the mines of Zacatecas and Guanajuato. During the dry season, when the roads were passable, heavy wagons required from three to four months to travel from Santa Barbara and Parral, mining towns in Chihuahua, to Mexico City. Inns at stopovers served food badly prepared and provided skimpy lodgings. Wharves and warehouses at Veracruz and Acapulco, the principal ports, barely met the needs of ships and sailors. A tiny clique of wealthy men monopolized the capital available for investment.

III

The dramatic decline of its native population also recast the society of New Spain. The death of millions of Indians, as well as the fickleness of mining, shaped the silver age. According to some scholars, of the twenty-five million people who dwelt in central Mexico in 1519, just slightly over one million survived a century later. Even when the original figure is cut in half, as dissenting sages urge, and the number of survivors is doubled, the loss of Indian life is still breathtaking. Not until the mid-seventeenth century did the decline come to an end. No other European conquest had such devastating repercussions. The question is, Why?

European disease, unknown to the Indian, explains much of this loss of human life. Plagues, which during the fourteenth century devastated cities in the Old World, killed millions in the lands of Anáhuac who, because of a lack of immunity and the high density of population, resisted feebly. Before the arrival of the Spaniards, population growth had already reduced much of Indian society to a subsistence economy. From 1454 to 1457 and again from 1504 to 1506, hunger killed off hundreds of thousands. Smallpox, the first of the European maladies, struck with devastating fury, especially from 1532 to 1538. In the town of Usila, to illustrate, the disease left only four hundred alive out of a population of sixteen thousand. Measles, a nuisance for Europeans, claimed the lives of millions, particularly in 1563 and 1564, as did a strange disease the natives baptized *cocolixtli* between 1543 and 1548. The "great pestilence," which lasted from 1578 to 1581, snuffed out thousands of others. To exacerbate the Indians' plight, famines swept the countryside in 1538, 1543–44, again in 1550–52, 1563–65, 1573, and once more in 1579–81. Entire towns lost half or more of their inhabitants, and some disappeared from the face of the earth. When the young and able died, the land lay untilled and there was less food to feed the living.

Illness alone did not kill the Indians. The black legend of a ruthless Spain was no myth. The Spaniard was directly responsible for the death of millions of native peoples. The Spaniards, after all, came to get rich, if not with gold and silver, off the labor of the Indian. Spaniards, it seemed, could do almost nothing for themselves, testified Francisco Carletti, an Italian visitor of the late sixteenth century who traveled with Spaniards from Acapulco to Mexico City. The "bad treatment" given the Indians, he emphasized, was "the cause of their dying off." His Spanish companions used the Indian like a beast of burden. When "they reached some hamlet . . . they wanted every one of their needs served and taken care of," summoning "the chief Indian of the village" to wait on them hand and foot. "And he appears with great speed and submissiveness, and punctually does whatever is commanded, which is to bring food for the men and their mounts." Frightened of the Spaniards, the chief "sees that this is done, ordering from among his Indians here one thing and there another—that is, you or someone bring the bread, the wine, you the meat, you the straw, and you the oats." But, "when the accounts are figured, instead of giving the Indians money in payment," the Spaniards "give evil words and worse deeds."

The conquistadores, writes a historian, "were undoubtedly harsh and very greedy," demanding frequently work beyond the Indian's physical capacity. For the first decades of the Conquest, it was forced labor, and then harsh, paid labor in the mines and in the planting and harvesting of sugarcane. Always, there was the tribute to pay, initially in labor and then in money, so the Indian had to work no matter how long the hours, how poor the pay, or how atrocious the conditions on the job. The ravages of disease cannot be appreciated unless one takes into account the appalling conditions introduced by the Conquest. Economic exploitation lay at the base of the demographic disaster, so terrible for some of the subjugated that, unable to cope with the shock, testified a Spaniard, they preferred to die.

The culprits, however, were not simply European diseases and the cruelty of conquistadores. Not exempt from blame were the missionaries, often the same friars who defended the Indian. Determined to erect temples, convents, and monasteries, they demanded labor of their neophytes and settled them on mission lands, where European maladies spread like wildfires. Every one of the Catholic shrines, usually edifices for the use of a few friars and staffed with a raft of Indian servants, arose at the expense of the Indian's way of life. The clergy and their secular allies, furthermore, disturbed the ratio of food to man by reducing the numbers of dirt farmers while multiplying the ranks of townsfolk who must be fed. The policy of congregating Indians in pueblos, which exposed them to European diseases, exacerbated their plight. Spaniards, also, upset the ecological balance, cutting down the forests and using the wood for their buildings or for fuel. Within a century, vast stretches of land lay barren of trees. The iron plow cut deep into the soil, often on unprotected slopes; when the rains came, they carried the topsoil away, leaving ravines and gullies. Cattle roamed freely, stripping the earth of its grass cover and adding to its woes in time of rain, or, more than once, wandered into the fields of corn and squash tilled by Indians, destroying crops and endangering their food supply. Colonial records are replete with Indian complaints of damage done by cattle.

The pivotal injury done to the Indian, maybe the clue to his demise, only students of the human psyche can measure. By intent and by accident, Spaniards altered drastically the native cultures. Conquest was a traumatic experience because the Spaniards made no effort to reach a cultural compromise. The Indians, recalled Bernardino de Sahagún, were so "trampled underfoot that not a vestige remained of what they had been." Sahagún exaggerated, but none of the major Indian groups, the Aztecs included, weathered the Conquest; only groups of marginal importance to the Spaniards, the Maya for one, survived. Still, even in Yucatán, the Conquest was a terrible episode. The arrival of the Spaniards reduced Maya society essentially to one class, converting even the native elite, which lost all but a few of its privileges, to milpa farmers. Eventually, there were no native soldiers, no full-time craftsmen, no shopkeepers or millers of flour, occupations reserved for non-Indians. On top of that, the decline of the Indian population in the aftermath of the Conquest, when a large proportion of adults died, hurt kinship ties, the strength of the Indian community.

Subjugation transformed other aspects of native life. Before the arrival of the European, Indians ate raw food and vegetables in abundance and drank alcohol sparingly. The Europeans changed that. Among the Maya, for example, a people who drank sparingly before the Conquest, alcoholism became a major vice and the drinking of aguardiente, a raw, white rum, commonplace. The quality of the diet, most of the evidence shows, dropped as the use of alcohol rose; when this occurred, Indians died earlier. Indians were also told to change their ancestral way of dress, to give up their loincloth for *zaraguelles,* white cotton trousers, standard wear by the end of the sixteenth century. Women of the humbler families, accustomed to leaving their bosoms naked, were shamed into covering them with the huipil, before long their "traditional" blouse.

The imposition of European culture, say scholars, disturbed the sex life of the Indian, making men and women less active. Spanish domination, the enslavement of the Indian, yielded contradictory results. Some Indian women, the evidence shows, wanted, after their menfolk had fallen, to cohabit with Spaniards; the Tlaxcalan allies of the Spaniards may have encouraged such unions, hoping, to quote one expert, to gain "nephews and grandsons of valor and strength equal to that of the Spaniards"; they "were eager to have children by them." The archives also bear witness that Indian women aborted or killed their newborn. Here and there, they refused to bear children, a practice widespread among the Mixes and Chontales of the south. In some parts of western New Spain, tribal rulings barred them from having children, while, on their own, women shunned sex with their men. These tribes, it was said, did not want to live on their knees.

Population decline was linked to changes in work patterns. Before the Conquest, anthropologists insist, the Indian may have worked more, but he did so for himself and for his community. Later, he worked almost entirely for others. The concept of work had undergone a transformation: earlier, work and religious ritual were one and the same; afterward, work was solely for the economic benefit of the employer. While the friars attempted to camouflage this transformation under an elaborate Catholic ritual, they fooled no one. No matter what the church might pontificate, Indians labored for individual Spaniards, who, not uncommonly, took advantage of them.

IV

The death of millions of Indians turned upside down patterns of landownership. "I did not come," Cortés once said, "to till the land like a peasant." Without doubt, that opinion mirrored the aspirations of most of the Spanish adventurers, who expected to get rich off the labor of others. Yet tilling the land became the principal occupation of New Spain. Rural dwellers, the majority, tilled their own lands or, increasingly, those of others. For multiple reasons, more and more of the land fell into the hands of an elite of landlords. First and foremost, the death of millions of Indians had left unoccupied huge expanses of land. Until their death, Indians had tilled a part of it and used the rest to hunt game and to gather wood for their hearths. When entire villages disappeared, Spaniards and criollos, usually with the blessings of crown officials, claimed their lands. If the lands lay near water, or on the outskirts of towns, they were facile prey of Spaniards, who bought them for ridiculously low prices or simply occupied them.

With the demise of the Indian, farming became more profitable. The growth of mining towns required a steady supply of grains and other foods. When the towns were small, Indian farmers had supplied them; now others had to do it. With the rise in demand for food, farming paid better dividends. Similarly, the crown, which at first kept a close eye on the theft of Indian lands, relented, permitting Spaniards to acquire them. Profits from agriculture turned gold-hungry Spaniards into farmers but, it must not be overlooked, of a peculiar kind. Instead of tillers of the land, they became hacendados, the masters of vast estates.

These Spaniards were of many types. Initially on the scene were the encomenderos, who found ways to get their hands on the lands of their Indians. More pernicious were the bureaucrats, mining moguls, merchants, and owners of *obrajes* who became hacendados. Public officials started early to gobble up the lands, whether held by Indians or not, although colonial legislation prohibited it. Viceroys, *oidores,* or judges of audiencias, *visitadores* (the spies sent to watch over public officials), corregidores, alcaldes, and regidores became landlords. Antonio de Mendoza, the first viceroy, set the pattern, affixing his name to haciendas and a sugar mill. Numerous *oidores* got rich off their lands. Bureaucrats, notoriously poorly paid, used public offices to acquire lands. When laws barred their way, they relied on *hombres de paja,* front men.

From these early landlords emerged the colonial latifundio, grain haciendas, and sugar plantations primarily. Hacendados, too, were mineowners and merchants. Whatever the relationship, a small elite monopolized haciendas, mines, and commerce.

North of Zacatecas, obstacles rarely blocked the spread of the latifundio. Open country lay ahead, inhabited usually by nomadic and warlike Chichimecas. For a century or so, law and order were honored more in the breach than in the practice; legal obstacles, prevalent in central New Spain, were circumvented easily. Only Indian resistance slowed the northward advance of the latifundio, for instance in the Mayo and Yaqui valleys of Sonora. In addition, colonization laws awarded land to individuals ready to gamble life and limb on the pacification of the north. Among them were wealthy mineowners and, later, merchants, above all in Chihuahua. Crown incentives converted the north into a region of powerful men and giant haciendas.

Whether grain, sugar, or cattle hacendados or *pulqueros,* who sold pulque from their maguey plants, they made their presence felt in the countryside. They were the influential men, which included an array of mayordomos (supervisors), capataces (field bosses), and administrators. In the local community, their word was law. More often than not, they ill used their Indian workers, a tyranny checked occasionally only by the priest, when he was not an ally of the hacendado. In the provincial cities and towns, the landed gentry sat in the ayuntamientos alongside of wealthy merchants and mineowners.

Land came to confer social status; upon it rested the hierarchical structure. To the socially pretentious, land and family standing were one and the same. Land passed from father to eldest son preserved the family name and gave life to a rural aristocracy. The *mayorazgo,* or law of primogeniture, held sway until the end of the colonial era. "Lands divided among the children," went a current saying, "were lands lost." In the hands of the eldest son, lands and family remained together. The *mayorazgo,* not illogically, led to the search for titles, that of a *marqués* or *conde,* for instance. By this method, wealthy men of dubious origin, mostly criollos, joined the nobility. Increasingly, moreover, criollos were the landlords of the seventeenth century.

Whoever the hacendados, whether criollos or Spaniards and, eventually, a mestizo or two, the Indian suffered the most from them. If he withstood disease and misuse, he could still lose his lands. Not all, of course, did; countless Indian pueblos, especially in Oaxaca and Yucatán, thanks to poor soil, the absence of water, or their own vigilance, perhaps in that order, saved their lands. When deprived of his lands, the Indian lost his means of production for, essentially, he lived off the land. Without it, he became a wageworker, either tilling the land of the hacendado or wandering off to dig ore in a mine. The ownership of land bound together the Indian village and conferred meaning on family and individual. So long as it had lands, the village maintained its traditions and customs. Once it lost them, life disintegrated and the Indian ceased being Indian. The Indian's struggle for his lands, a constant theme of the colonial centuries, signified not just a battle for land but, more important, his survival as an Indian.

The hacienda, increasingly the kingpin of agriculture, evolved in response to the needs of mining camps, then to local and regional markets. Generally, the haciendas relied on commercial crops, either wheat, corn, sugarcane, or maguey. By law, crops which competed with those grown in Spain could not be cultivated—wine grapes and olive trees, to cite two. In practice, colonial farmers usually ignored these prohibitions. Most haciendas had vast amounts of land, enough to be planted and to lie fallow. They sold their produce on the market and bought little from the outside; for the most part, they were self-sufficient. Hacendados raised cattle and planted chili, beans, and squash for their own needs.

Still, it was a commercial agriculture. The big, successful haciendas developed on the fringes of the cities, becoming part of the fertile, agricultural zones. Just outside of Mexico City, Chalco was one, serving as its granary. Some fifty haciendas, both large and small, produced the corn consumed by the inhabitants of the metropolis. What was true of Chalco appeared again and again in the hinterlands around Guadalajara, Guanajuato, Zacatecas, and other cities. From the start, too, an agriculture for export took hold. Cochineal, a red dye made from a bug on the maguey plant of Oaxaca and produced on Indian lands, found markets in the textile industry of Europe, as did a blue dye from the indigo plant. The cacao bean, the essence of chocolate, rewarded its planters handsomely, as did the sale of vanilla. Sugar, too, was sold abroad, although most of it stayed home.

Cattle and sheep ranching went hand in glove with the hacienda. Cattle multiplied rapidly, first on the central plateau but, more and more, in the north. The plains of Durango, Chihuahua, Coahuila, and Sonora had grass for cattle to feed on. Huge herds developed, some with as many as 150,000 head, while sheep by the millions grazed on the grassy stubble of Zacatecas. As in Castilla, the Mesta, an organization of stockmen, wielded power and influence. Out of this activity evolved the ranching world of *charreadas* (rodeos), charros (gentlemen horsemen), and vaqueros (cowboys), who, along with miners and missionaries, colonized the north.

The precipitous decline of the native population, according to one interpretation, distorted the economy of the seventeenth century. For lack of labor, New Spain suffered a "century of depression," as the colonial economy stopped expanding both as a market and as a producer of goods. Indeed, a depression did strike, despite massive importations of African slaves to fill labor demands, primarily for sugar plantations and mines. The "century of depression," all the same, was hardly that; New Spain basked in prosperity until 1630, and again after 1670. Depression, moreover, had multiple causes, principally the woes of mining. The economy, true enough, revived only after the growth of the laboring population, still mainly Indian, but also with the recovery of mining, above all as a result of the use of mercury to separate silver ore from the chaff.

V

From antiquity, Spaniards had dwelt in towns and cities, and that is what they did in New Spain. "Ever since I came to this country," Cortés said, "I have tried to find a harbor on the coast where I might establish a settlement"; Cortés meant a town, where Spaniards could replant a way of life, as much for security as for cultural reasons. Cities, therefore, became the cornerstones of New Spain, where Spaniards established two types of them, one on the ruins of the old Indian sites (Mexico City comes to mind) and others as commercial hubs to supply the mining enclaves. As a rule of thumb, Spaniards dwelt in the cities; Indians, in pueblos in the countryside. The ruling class of city and countryside, nonetheless, was one and the same: mine moguls, hacendados, merchants, and bureaucrats.

Cities were an amazingly successful transplant of Iberian society to the New World, reflecting faithfully the Spanish model. As in Europe, the rights and privileges of a town depended on a royal charter, the trademark of municipal government in medieval Castilla. The urban designs of the Old World, above all Andalucía, dictated the blueprints of cities in New Spain. Around their main plaza stood the municipal buildings, the main temple, the monasteries and convents, and, always, the homes of the well-heeled. On their fringes lay the Indian ghettoes, called barrios by the Spaniards.

Mexico City, the capital of New Spain, led the parade, followed by Puebla, Querétaro, Valladolid, and, a bit later, Guadalajara. Whatever the attractions of the latecomers, they were no match for Mexico City, which was, by the early seventeenth century, testified a visiting Spaniard, "the Athens of America," a "literary metropolis . . . famed for its schools, the sophistication of its citizens and for the meticulous Spanish spoken." Thomas Gage, an English friar who saw Mexico City in 1625, compared it to Venice, different merely because "Venice sits upon the sea water and Mexico upon a lake." Travelers entered via causeways linked to a grid of streets each wide enough for three or more carriages to drive abreast. The Plaza Mayor, or Zócalo, lay at the heart of the city, while the government buildings, among them the palace of the viceroy and the cathedral, fronted it. Around and in back of the Zócalo were the other buildings of church and state. Squat houses built of stone enclosing verdant gardens fronted on the principal avenues, the abodes of the distinguished families. To Bernardo de Balbuena, a lyric bard, "a thousand lovely canals, teeming with long, narrow boats, veritable mine-hoards of supplies, goods, and singular articles for the shops, twist[ing] and turn[ing] delightfully like crystalline serpents through spacious streets," bestowed color and glamor on Mexico City.

The biggest city in the Western Hemisphere, Mexico City had over 200,000 inhabitants, who formed a kaleidoscope of skin colors. Europeans, mostly Spaniards, numbered 72,000, fewer than half of them women. Over a third of the Europeans in New Spain lived in Mexico City. Indians totaled 80,000, and Africans and mulattoes, both slave and free, 10,000. Mestizos, who ran the gamut of skin colors, made up the rest. The richest families of New Spain made their homes in Mexico City, just a short distance away from the hovels of indigent Indians, blacks, and mestizos. While upper-class women "ate dirt in order to stay thin and pale of skin," down the street foul-smelling "dens of iniquity" dispensed pulque to the besotted. Every quarter, every street, had a pulqueria. No one worried about the gap between the rich and the impecunious, while a middle class, then emerging in western Europe, was wanting.

Founded in 1532, Puebla City ranked next in importance. Lying at the heart of one of the richest agricultural zones, Puebla flourished until well into the next century. From the start, it was a Spanish city, the offspring of the second audiencia, which gave Spanish vagabonds, then very numerous in New Spain, small plots of land; they transformed the Puebla region into a granary for Mexico City.

Established in 1541, Guadalajara developed as an assemblage of flat, adobe houses sitting on a less than fertile plain. Set apart from other cities by the absence of roads, Guadalajara thrived as a commercial and administrative entrepôt, but was known also for its fine schools. No gold or silver was discovered nearby, although as the capital of the province of Nueva Galicia it profited from the mines of Guanajuato and Zacatecas. Guadalajara's neighbors Valladolid as well as Querétaro, in the Bajío, began as commercial hubs.

Veracruz, the oldest city and the chief port of New Spain, lay on the Gulf of Mexico. Hot and muggy most of the year, it came alive when the fleet from Spain dropped anchor in its harbor, when merchants from Mexico City arrived with money to spend. Incoming viceroys, archbishops, and diverse royal dignitaries made their entrance into New Spain by way of Veracruz, often before reception committees from Mexico City.

VI

Like its capital, New Spain was a potpourri of peoples. With its disparate cultures, its peculiar Catholicism, and its isolation from Europe, it was hardly just a reincarnation of Western civilization. Racially, it was, by all accounts, "one of the most diverse and complicated societies the world had yet seen."

True, Spaniards settled New Spain, but they were always a minority. In 1570, for instance, there were merely seven thousand Spaniards alongside of three and a half million Indians. In Yucatán, moreover, Indians made up 90 percent of the population until the early eighteenth century, a statistic probably duplicated by Oaxaca and Chiapas. During three centuries of colonial rule, perhaps no more than three hundred thousand Spaniards arrived in New Spain.

From the days of Hernán Cortés, Spaniards were the elite. Above all, they claimed *limpieza de sangre,* the mythical purity of blood so venerated by Spaniards of the Reconquista. Color of skin was one of their major preoccupations. Writing in 1570, to illustrate, Juan López de Velasco pontificated in his *Geografía y descripción de las Indias* that Spanish Americans were darker in color than Europeans; ultimately, he warned, they would be "indistinguishable from Indians," even though they avoided cohabitation with them. Ironically, hidalgos settled rarely in New Spain. Most of the conquistadores were cobblers, masons, seamen, carpenters, or soldiers, some barely literate. Immigrants of a different sort followed them. In the eyes of the sons of the conquistadores, they were *gachupines,* a pejorative term, or *peninsulares.* High royal officials and church prelates, *gachupines* to the core, were generally men of learning, lawyers, and professionals. They had little good to say about the rough-hewn colonists and, with this opinion, gave birth to the clash between criollos, Spaniards born in the New World, and *peninsulares.* Labeled latecomers by the criollos, the *peninsulares* monopolized quickly the best jobs in government, the church, and commerce. They were "kings of the hill." When they married a criollo woman, no matter how wealthy her family, the *peninsular,* simply by being born in Spain, bestowed social distinction upon her.

Not all Spaniards prospered in New Spain. Self-proclaimed hidalgos were numerous; most, however, had neither fortune nor social credentials. But as hidalgos they held manual labor in low esteem, refusing to learn a trade or some other useful occupation. Scorning hard work, they became vagabonds, roaming the byways of New Spain, "loafers, ne'er-do-wells, pickpockets, and the like on the streets and squares of the larger towns and cities." These picaros, as they were called, supported themselves by preying on Indians and poor mestizos. They had a knack for reporting to Spanish officials "unused lands" of Indian pueblos, in this way earning a fee for their endeavors. The "vacant" lands, of course, were sold to Spaniards.

A step down from the *gachupines* were the criollos, at the start sons and daughters of conquistadores. Whereas the early Spaniards arrived mostly alone, some eventually brought wives, daughters, mothers, and sisters who shared the rigors of colonial settlement and sired offspring of Spanish descent. The criollo held an ambiguous place on the social scale. Fair of skin, he could not be lumped with Indians and the *castas,* the mestizos and mulattoes. Law, medicine, and theology were open to him. As a lawyer or simply as a man of means, he could hold office in the church or the bureaucracy. During the age of silver, criollos ruled the secular clergy; of the orders, only the Jesuits were predominantly Spaniards. Two criollos became archbishops, and others were bishops of Mexico, Puebla, Michoacán, Guadalajara, and, more frequently, Oaxaca, Chiapas, Yucatán, and Nueva Vizcaya. They sat on the ayuntamientos. Some were hacendados, mineowners, or cattlemen. Socially, their status took a turn for the better during the lean years of the seventeenth century when the crown, short of cash, began selling jobs in the bureaucracy and the clergy to wealthy criollos, who sent their sons abroad for schooling, married their daughters to Spaniards, and dwelt in splendid homes staffed by servants. Obviously, not all criollos reached the top; some were out and out failures. Thomas Gage thought of them as a particularly obnoxious and parasitic lot.

Offspring born in the New World, no matter how pure of blood, did not sit well with Spaniards. To their way of thinking, place of birth mattered deeply. The criollo, simply by being born away from home, was inferior. Climate and the shape of things in New Spain debilitated human beings, rendering them lazy, irresponsible, and morally degenerate. To cite López de Velasco, in the physical and climatic conditions of the New World, brain and mind went to pot, making the criollo "progressively more barbarous and stupid." Born an ocean apart, the criollo could not be trusted to carry out the duties of crown, nor "to run," one famous Jesuit proclaimed, "even a hen-pen." The Spanish clergy—Jerónimo de Mendieta, for one—believed that criollo priests sided with the interests of the colonists, thus betraying the goals of the *patria.*

The criollo, for his part, resented this attitude, especially when it cost him appointments in the bureaucracy or elevated above him *peninsulares.* It galled criollos, at times descendants of conquistadores, to see Spaniards discriminate against them. Gage believed that both groups "hated" each other. Fortunately for the criollo, this attitude, if it did not undergo a metamorphosis, began to change in the seventeenth century, when some Spaniards even came to think well of him. Altruism, however, was not always the spark plug. The growing criollo population, larger and often far richer than that of the Spaniards, had to be reckoned with. In his *Política indiana,* Juan de Solórzano, to demonstrate, saw criollos as "genuine and authentic Spaniards." Despite that, the prejudice against criollos survived in the souls of many Spaniards.

The epoch of silver was also the stage for a more powerful drama. Numerically, the mestizo, some 150,000 strong by 1650, was making his bow. Initially, the Spaniards did not know what to do with him. For a while, unbelievably, they failed to count him as a distinct category. When offspring of wealthy Spaniards, mestizos were classified as criollos; if not, they were labeled mulattoes. The better labor guilds, the sword makers, for instance, barred them; lesser ones accepted them. Mestizo sons and daughters, initially of Spanish and Indian parents, were sired increasingly by mestizo fathers and mothers. The mixture of native and European blood produced a bewildering array of physical types, from very Indian to very Spanish. Skin color ranged from fair to dark, frequently in the same family. Such was the ethnic universe of the mestizo.

Mestizaje, the blending of the two races, began early, probably on the day the Spaniards landed. They came to get rich, said Cortés, but they also had sex on their minds. One of the first mestizos, mentioned earlier, was Martín, the son of Hernán Cortés and Doña Marina, the Indian translator. Taken to Spain by his father, Martín, a Knight of the Order of Santiago, battled Spain's enemies in Algeria and Germany, dying at the hands of Moors in Granada. The daughter of Pedro de Alvarado, born of an Indian woman, had the good fortune to marry the cousin of the duke of Albuquerque. On occasion, mestizo offspring of other conquistadores were lucky, too. Some mestizos, clearly, enjoyed illustrious birthrights; the fortunate, however, were a minority. The Spaniards, whatever their virtues, suffered from the common vices of Europeans. On questions of race and skin color, they were more bigoted than tolerant. What they established in the New World was a pigmentocracy, a social order based, all too often, on the color of one's skin.

Racial prejudice to the contrary, Spaniards seduced Indian women. Only a handful of Spanish women accompanied Cortés, while during the early years they generally stayed home either out of preference or, equally likely, because their husbands, fathers, or brothers did not want them in New Spain. Before 1540, just 6 percent of the Spaniards in New Spain were women. But Spaniards, like males the world over, could not live without women, and so they fornicated with Indian females and sired mestizos. It was the Indian mother who raised the children, who nursed them and taught them language, culture, and beliefs. More often than not, the mestizo grew up in the home of an absentee father who symbolized the conqueror while the Indian mother, who took care of him, symbolized the defeated, and less able. Spanish women rarely if ever went to bed with Indians, and only a few married mestizos, and then only if they were wealthy or powerful.

Seldom did Spaniards marry their Indian concubines. Some who did had wives in Spain; they were, in the eyes of Western jurisprudence, bigamists. Many conquistadores and early colonists, moreover, never married or lived apart from their Spanish wives, whom they had left at home. Some married mestizas, if they were pretty, light of skin and "Spanish looking," and, above all, of wealthy families. Marriage, it was asserted, bestowed stability on the colony. If encomenderos failed to marry within three years, for example, they lost their Indians; so some took their Indian mistresses for wives, not a few of them the daughters of the old Aztec nobility. Eventually, Spaniards brought their wives and other Spanish women, usually relatives. These women, plus the growing number of light-skinned mestizas, dubbed "Spanish girls," some fairer than Spaniards from Castilla, put a stop to marriages between Spaniards and Indian women. Henceforth, Spanish and criollo men married fair mestizas or, more likely, simply went to bed with them. For their part, mestizos, more and more, slept with each other and married, producing second, third, fourth, and so on generations of mestizos. Before long, miscegenation made highly improbable claims to "purity" of blood.

Mestizos shared the poverty of Indian and other castes. A few made it to the top, especially if fair of skin or the child of a Spanish father who legitimized them and sent them to school. Most mestizos had limited social mobility. Still, they were better off than the Indian and, ultimately, the *castas* of black ancestry. In mining towns, *obrajes,* haciendas, and the cities, they made up the core of the work force. Urbanization multiplied their numbers. Only in the south, especially in Yucatán, Puebla, Oaxaca, and Chiapas, did Indians make up the majority of the population, although rural New Spain, generally, remained heavily Indian. Numerically, as the years took their toll of the Indian, mestizos, more dark than fair of skin, became the majority in the north, in the Bajío, and in the cities of the west and central plateau. They went into the trades and crafts, usually as journeymen, and bore arms, an honored profession in New Spain; soldiering was a hallmark of the mestizo macho, the he-man of society. It was the mestizo soldier, both as officer and as enlisted man, who staffed the presidios, from California to Texas.

Compared with the life of most Spaniards, that of the Indian meant poverty and hardship. During the colonial centuries, Indians, as in pre-Columbian days, neither slept in beds or hammocks nor ate from tables or chairs. They used mats, sat on the floor, and lived in huts lacking windows or doors. Indian came to signify poor, above all rural poor. Whatever Bartolomé de Las Casas, Vasco de Quiroga, and Motolinía may have preached, the Indian, in the eyes of Spaniards, was inferior. When he would not do their bidding, they labeled him lazy, untrustworthy, and a drunkard, a man prone to vice. Indians were not *gente de razón,* people with the ability to think. The *gente decente,* another way of saying it, were Spaniards and criollos and, perhaps, mestizos.

When they lived in the barrios of the cities, on big plantations, or on haciendas, Indians were integrated into Spanish society—"espanolized," that is—arrogating for themselves the ways of their mestizo, African, and mulatto neighbors. They lost their language, learned Spanish, wore European dress, slept in simple beds, and ate rice, wheat bread (when they could afford it) as well as tortillas, and, once in a while, meat, the food of Spaniards. If inhabitants of barrios, they quenched their thirst at squalid pulquerias. After a generation or two, they ceased being Indian, becoming just poor, dark-skinned residents of the cities or haciendas. The loss of their lands to Spaniards or criollos drew more and more Indians to the cities and towns.

In the countryside, life for the Indian was a different story. Separated from Spaniards, criollos, and mestizos, he lived in Indian pueblos, kept the nuclear family together, usually three generations of it, and preserved his language, one of over four hundred, if one includes dialects. While the major groups, such as the Aztecs, lost their group identity, marginal ones did not. Maya, Mixtecs, and Zapotecs, to name three, remained cultural and linguistic units and never forgot to think of themselves as a people. When native kinship ties broke down, the Indian adopted the Spanish compadrazgo, the custom of the godfather, which helped keep alive the nuclear family. Spanish prejudice and discrimination, oddly, helped preserve Indian culture. After all, if there were no incentives to change, why do so? Why adopt European culture if it would not improve one's economic lot? Indians in the pueblos, therefore, rarely learned to speak Spanish or adopted European customs. Corn, beans, squash, and chili made up their diet, just as in pre-Hispanic days. The lucky tilled their communal plots of land and worked, when occasion demanded, on the lands of their hacendado neighbor. The priest who visited on certain days to confer the sacraments, an occasional royal official, and the mayordomo of the hacendado were their contacts with the outside world. On Catholicism, which Indians embraced, they conferred a peculiar imprint, molding it to their manner of thinking.

Cortés also introduced the first African slaves to New Spain. Most of them were of the Islamic faith, hailing from the western Sudan, the Congo, and the Gulf of Guinea. Spanish slavery had antecedents harking back to the eighth century, when Christians and Moors enslaved their captives in the interminable wars they waged against one another. The practice endured throughout the Middle Ages, reaching its apogee during the early part of the fifteenth century, when the cities of Aragón and Cataluña prospered from the slave trade. The Spaniards had first enslaved the Indian, at times placing him in chains, as had Nuño de Guzmán in Nueva Galicia. In the Pánuco region of the Gulf of Mexico, they sold into slavery 15,000 Indians, shipping them to the sugar plantations of the Caribbean. Spaniards held as many as 200,000 Indian slaves in 1542, the date of the New Laws, which, theoretically, abolished slavery.

With the decline of the Indian population, Africans were imported for labor. By 1650, about 120,000 of them were in New Spain, and maybe 130,000 more by the close of the colonial years. Yet, at most, they were but 2 percent of the population. Because African men outnumbered their women by two to one, many of them took Indians for their wives. Their offspring were labeled zambos; they, as well as mulattoes, the children of Spanish fathers and African mothers, exceeded Africans eventually. By the end of the colony, mulattoes and diverse African *castas* formed 10 percent of the total population, most of them free.

Originally imported for labor on the sugar plantations and mines, most Africans, and later mulattoes, with exceptions such as those in the fertile valley of Zamora, in Michoacán, made their homes along the tropical coasts of the Gulf of Mexico and on the Pacific south from Acapulco, where sugar plantations prospered. Their cane was planted and cut by African slaves. But Africans also worked in the mines of Zacatecas and in the *obrajes* of the cities. In 1621, to document, five hundred African slaves, and an equal number of free Africans and mulattoes, lived in Guadalajara. Slavery, for all that, proved a poor substitute for Indian labor; by the close of the colonial period, there were just six thousand slaves in New Spain, a far cry from their numbers in English North America.

Life for Africans and mulattoes was harsh. Like the Indians and most mestizos, they filled the ranks of the destitute. In the mining camps, Africans did the hard labor, though they rarely worked underground. So highly prized were they as workers that the sale of African slaves in Zacatecas provided the principal revenue of its ayuntamiento. Africans labored long hours in the *obrajes,* whose owners, like the planters, relied on the whip. Africans did not take kindly to this mistreatment, more than once rebelling; one of their protests, in the Córdoba region of Veracruz in 1735, had to be put down with rifles. A handful of Africans and mulattoes fared better. Physically strong and usually adaptable, they were employed occasionally as the labor bosses of Indian workers in mines, *obrajes,* and haciendas. In this role, they were as cruel as their Spanish masters. Some Africans found their way into crafts and trades. Africans also enriched the culture of New Spain, especially its music and dance. The marimba, a musical instrument so much a part of Veracruz and Chiapas, was African, as were the jarabe and the sones, now traditional Mexican dances.

VII

To govern its colony, the crown established an elaborate political structure. At its top was the viceroy. Don Antonio de Mendoza ruled until 1550, when the crown sent him to Peru to repair matters there. His successor, Don Luis de Velasco, a splendid proconsul of His Majesty, served with distinction, "combining sagacity and humanity with a rigid sense of duty and dignity." More than anyone, he set the tone for the political edifice. Like his king, Philip II, Velasco ruled with an iron fist and an eye out for corruption, already becoming a nasty sore on society. Although a stern disciplinarian, he believed paternalism the proper formula for handling the Indians, even attempting to enforce the New Laws of 1542. For this effort, he earned the sobriquet Father of the Indians. In exemplary fashion, Velasco died poor and in debt, unlike Mendoza, who made private gain synonymous with public office.

In New Spain, Don Antonio and Don Luis wore the robes of the king. Their successors, sixty of them, more or less able public servants, did the same. At first, they enjoyed a considerable degree of independence, being empowered to make decisions on their own. Fleets from Spain bound for Veracruz sailed only once a year; royal orders arrived tardily; consultation on every detail would have halted the daily operations of government. However, the Hapsburg kings slowly transformed the viceroys into puppet rulers, bureaucrats who served on bended knee. The king and the Council of the Indies demanded subservience. Not a few of these bureaucrats placed pocketbook ahead of personal integrity; a number of them spent time and money on frivolous things. Fray García Guerra, archbishop and viceroy in 1611, loved bullfights so much that he had a bullring built on the palace grounds and found time to visit a nearby Dominican convent, where he spent hours with a nun.

The king or the Council of the Indies appointed the viceroy; but they rarely trusted him. So they established a system of checks and balances, ordering authorities in New Spain to spy on each other, reports of misbehavior bestowing rewards on the informer. The viceroy wielded the scepter, but the judges of the audiencia, legally under him, reported to Spain. The crown also dispatched royal spies, known as *visitadores,* to check up on his performance. The review or trial was called a *juicio de residencia* since most *visitadores* were lawyers or judges. The checks and balances, perhaps wise in theory, hardly encouraged bureaucrats to speak their mind. Viceroys, judges of the audiencia, and corregidores had to heed, if they wanted to govern effectively, the views of the powerful in the community. Royal officials were thus caught, so goes the cliché, between a rock and a hard place. Next in the hierarchy were the *oidores* of the audiencia. That of Mexico City had ten while that of Nueva Galicia, established in 1548, had five. Most of them were lawyers who sat as judges, for the audiencia was essentially a court of review that helped the viceroy run the affairs of New Spain. Like the viceroys, most of the *oidores* served ably, although often profiting from office.

Each geographical subdivision of the viceroyalty had its officials. These districts, called generally *corregimientos,* were run by corregidores (also named alcaldes, *mayores,* or *gobernadores*) appointed in Spain, who took orders from the viceroy. The conquistadores, more often than not the ones without encomiendas, served as the initial corregidores; officeholders of another type replaced them. *Corregidores de indios* administered the Indian pueblos.

Municipal government ranked at the bottom of the political edifice. The first town council, or ayuntamiento, dated from the founding of Veracruz in 1519. Cortés appointed its members and those of other early settlements. In time, the regidores, who made up the ayuntamiento, were elected from among the wealthy of the town. Democracy had a narrow base. An alcalde, His

Honor the mayor, presided over the ayuntamiento, which did what municipal bodies usually do: hire and pay police, keep garbage off the streets, bring water into town, and fill the granary. The corregidor, who managed political affairs in the district, saw to it that ayuntamientos toed the line.

Whatever the intent, rot managed to seep into the design. The best jobs were reserved for court favorites, hangers-on of the king and his clique, while the colonial bureaucracy multiplied, partly in response to the appetites of *peninsulares* and criollos for public jobs. A retinue of job-hungry relatives and friends accompanied every viceroy who landed at Veracruz. Royal appointments, despite prestigious titles, paid little, encouraging the view of public office as an avenue for private gain, a practice that developed long tentacles during the seventeenth century. From Mendoza on, viceroys filled their private coffers; one of them, by the name of Albuquerque, sold *alcaldías* and *corregimientos* to the highest bidders. Not uncommonly, the Hapsburgs filled public offices with adventurers eager to line their pockets. Judges of the law courts, often with large families to support and wives with social pretensions, sold their favors.

The worst and most corrupt of these officials were the *corregidores de indios,* a remedy supposedly for the evils of the encomendero, whose obligations they assumed. They were to aid in the Christianization of the Indian, to defend him from abuse by Spaniards, to see to it that he got fair prices for his goods, and to collect the crown's tribute from him. The corregidor was also a judge entrusted with the adjudication of Indian complaints; he was admonished not to steal land from the Indian, own cattle, or engage in commerce. Practice, all the same, was something else. Most corregidores took advantage of the Indian, enriching themselves at his expense. They employed Indians to build their homes and to plow their fields and jailed them on a whim. As middlemen, they fixed the price of cotton, cacao, and cochineal and peddled liquor at exorbitant prices because they controlled its distribution. With monopolies over the sale of salt, seeds, and tools, they charged whatever the traffic would bear. When compensated properly, they provided Indians for little or no pay to hacendados or labor contractors. Their petty despotism paved the way for the *caciquismo* that desolated the countryside after Independence.

5

BAROQUE YEARS

I

Silver was the bedrock for what became known as the Baroque Era, the seventeenth century and much of the next. Once a term applied to a style of architecture and plastic arts, *Baroque,* implying "ornate" or "arabesque," now defines a way of life of a historical epoch. The flow of silver from the New World, which filled the coffers of Europeans, ignited in Spain, to employ the eloquence of one savant, "a pyrotechnic display of artistic genius." Some of this Golden Age rubbed off on New Spain. The Baroque centuries, likewise, witnessed the ascent of the criollo, who transformed New Spain into his universe, rich, pompous, and florid, a society "eminently aristocratic" but an "aristocracy of money," lauding the glossy and trivial. Linked with the Counter-Reformation, the Baroque combined, oddly, medieval ideas with the spirit of the Renaissance.

II

Nothing captures better the pith and nub of the Baroque than its luxuriant architecture, which rapidly displaced the vogue of the austere fortress church. The clergy and wealthy colonials, most of them miners who had struck it rich, erected a plethora of buildings, each vying with the others for ornate design and grandiose size. Vast fortunes were spent on them, occasionally as penance for sins. When private entrepreneurs financed their construction, styles varied according to the latest fads. A blend of Romanesque, Gothic, Mudejar, and Renaissance, at times modified by the labors of anonymous Indian craftsmen, architecture begot scores of regional genres, the florid *poblano* of Puebla among them. Churches of similar design towered over the towns and cities of Oaxaca and Jalisco. A lusty and opulent church, completed in 1713, loomed above Durango while another, of approximately identical vintage, looked out on the rooftops of Chihuahua.

The silver age gave birth to the majestic cathedral, the loftiest symbol of the Baroque. Foundations for the huge churches were laid during the latter half of the sixteenth century in Tlaxcala, Oaxaca, Michoacán, Yucatán, Chiapas, and Guadalajara. Along with them, the celebrated cathedrals of Mexico City and Puebla began to rise. The original cathedral of Mexico City, the biggest in the world, dated from 1573, when masons put down the first stones. Rebuilt again and again, the Catedral fronted the Zócalo, rising on the ruins of the Gran Teocalli. The most beautiful of the cathedrals stood in Morelia, the heartland of Michoacán. Begun in 1640, it was completed a century later.

Native craftsmen, meanwhile, left their imprint on the buildings, above all on the decorative designs of the façades of church doorways, towers, cupolas, and ceilings. The arched entrance was encircled with statuary, raised work, and engraved decorations which occupied the space on the side of the tower. Figures of the apostles watched from both sides of the doorway, and on top of them was a picture carved in relief of some divine occurence, with the patron saint displayed prominently alongside of sundry saints who worshiped the Holy Trinity. Angels and celestial cherubs, peering out from their niches, completed the scene.

The Mudejar or Moorish influence shaped Baroque architecture, which, aside from its ornate artistry, combined two striking features. The cupola, a cylindrical vault forming part of the ceiling or roof, a symbol of the Arab Renaissance, was one. New Spain ripened as "the country of the cupola," found on churches and public buildings alike in a dazzling display, each boasting its own design and unique decoration. The *azulejo,* polychrome tile, was the other characteristic of Baroque architecture, especially of the popular *poblana,* or Puebla, style. Also a gift of the Arabs, the *azulejo* was a trademark of colonial architecture, used extensively on the surfaces of cupolas and church towers.

In the era of ornate churches and majestic cathedrals, the design of public buildings and private homes lagged. The early colonial years produced just a sprinkling of notable lay architecture; one exception was the palace of Cortés, in Mexico City, which lacked a patio or inner courtyard, a hallmark of colonial blueprints. Yet the Spaniards, like the Romans, were builders, and, as time went on, they left ample evidence of their genius in the homes of the colonial elite, often sumptuous, multistoried stone mansions, with thick walls, built around a patio, a design inherited from the Moors. Many stood in Mexico City, but some also in Guadalajara, Guanajuato, Oaxaca, Querétaro, Zacatecas, and San Luis Potosí. Exemplary public buildings of the Baroque age included the palace of the viceroys, built on the site of Moctezuma's, where the Palacio Nacional now stands. It occupied one entire side of the Plaza de

Armas or Zócalo. In Mexico City, too, were the monumental Palacio del Ayuntamiento and the solemn edifice of the Real y Pontificia Universidad.

Blueprints for what might be called a colonial "middle-class" home also date from the seventeenth century. This was the single house of the *burgués* (burgess) who, though he owned merely a small lot, enjoyed sufficient income to allow himself comforts. The house, of adobe or stone, was literally two, both fronting on one wall or, in some instances, a kitchen. A square or rectangular patio, cut in half by the wall, served both sides of the double house. Living quarters for servants, the kitchen and pantry, and the stables and storehouses formed one side of the house; the other, with a large entrance called a zaguán, was made up of the bedrooms and the sala, the quarters for the owner and his family. This house survived, more or less, until the 1920s, when the North American model began to displace it.

The poor, if lucky, had simple homes. In the cities, they inhabited *viviendas,* tenements, one or two stories tall. Built of adobe, the rows of apartments, comprising two rooms usually and a kitchen, faced a long, dark, and narrow patio or, if just a single row, a high wall. Each apartment had but one entrance, the doorway facing the patio or wall. Housing in the provincial cities was of identical mold, but not always. In the city of Zacatecas, struggling storekeepers and their like, a kind of "upper-class poor," lived on the outskirts in adobe houses with a bedroom, sala, kitchen, and pantry. In the backyard, at times, they had a corral. The very poor, whether rural or urban, Indian or mestizo, inhabited tiny, one-room adobe huts or, in the tropics, round or square shelters of sticks under a thatched roof.

Baroque meant religiously inspired art, scenes of angels, of saints and virgins, and of devout believers ascending to heaven, where God the Father, Christ, and the Holy Ghost awaited. Replete with mystical emotions, it was an art of the Counter-Reformation. The church, for practical reasons, prompted much of it, chiefly to build a large, powerful, and emotional base from which to combat the appeal of the Protestant Reformation. It was an art that no longer reflected the certainty of the sixteenth century, supremely confident that history was moving toward a universal Christian kingdom. The church was not its sole sponsor; the feudal aristocracy employed it to defend the status quo. Believe, accept the inevitable, do not question, and you will go to heaven—that was the message the elite wanted the poor to swallow. Conversely, the poor, probably in awe, looked to this art entrapped in religious themes to compensate for their misery and suffering on earth.

Art, whether Baroque or not, speaks eloquently of the attitudes of a social class and, obviously, of theological and philosophical convictions reflecting the social and political reality of a people at a precise time in its history. Given this interpretation, the whys and wherefores of Baroque painting, which appeared just when medieval man's faith in God and his view of the universe were being shaken by unanticipated discoveries, are clear. This was especially so in the cities, where the commercial revolution, urban growth, the discovery of the New World, Renaissance ideas, and the emergence of modern science turned topsy-turvy ancient theological beliefs. The English, the Germans, and the French had, on more than one occasion, embraced heretical Protestantism. Even in Spain, Luther and Calvin had listeners. The prevailing attitude was to question, to doubt, and to assert that man did not know the ultimate truth.

Faced with this challenge, the church mounted a counteroffensive, assigning art a pivotal role. By playing on the emotions, art had to hold the loyalty of the faithful and win over the skeptical. That, say savants, lay at the heart of Baroque painting. The rhetorical character of the Baroque reveals that art no longer stalked beauty for itself but, on the contrary, to keep Spaniards loyal to church and king. To be effective, it must be a popular art, understandable at first glance, as Diego Rivera would say three hundred years later, a stimulant to the visual senses and directed at the common folk. Art with a message made its bow to serve the goals of the church.

Baroque painting flourished everywhere. Generally speaking, artists belonged to two schools. Easel painters, a popular one, used oils on canvas, wood, and copper. Muralists, artists who painted on walls, formed another school; their labors covered walls and altars of churches, convents, and monasteries. Examples of their art date from the sixteenth century, at the Franciscan monastery in Cholula, where anonymous painters depicted the life of Saint Francis; on the walls of the fortress church of Acolman; and the convent of Oaxtepec in Morelos. On walls left unpainted, other artists hung portraits of bishops, archbishops, and saints galore.

Of the pioneer painters, the two Alonzos, Vázquez and López de Herrera, stand out. Vázquez's murals in the chapels of the viceregal palace and the university earned him praise; López de Herrera's paintings included one of García Guerra, the flamboyant viceroy and archbishop. Quality took a turn for the better upon the arrival of Simón Pereyns, a native of Amberes, who came to the New World by way of Toledo, where he painted alongside famous Spanish artists. Mostly a court painter, Pereyns left a plethora of portraits and religious pictures. Equally noteworthy, he established a school of distinguished painters, which included Francisco Zumayo, Francisco Morales, Andrés de Concha, and Juan de Arrue, the best known of them. It was at this time that Rodrigo de Cifuentes painted the famous portrait of Hernán Cortés.

One of the colonial masters was Baltazar de Echave Orio, nicknamed El Viejo (the Old One) to distinguish him from El Mozo, his grandson, also a fine painter. Some of his work, critics believe, matches in quality the Golden Age painting in Spain. His two sons, Baltazar and Manuel, along with his disciple

Luis Juárez, excelled, too. An artist remembered for his *Saint Theresa* and the *Apparition of the Child Jesus before Saint Anthony,* Juárez frequently repeated religious themes. Sebastián López de Arteaga, born in Sevilla but residing in Mexico City by 1643, achieved dubious fame of sorts for his portraits of judges of the Inquisition. His *Incredulity of Saint Thomas,* a painting in the mold of Francisco de Zurbarán's work, introduced Baroque art to the New World.

Toward the end of the seventeenth century, a gaudy, elaborate style of painting surfaced, identified with the swelling elegance of Baroque architecture. Highly decorative, it exalted color, for the most part blues and reds, displayed a superficial brilliance, and attached less importance to the human figure. The titles of its religious paintings dealt with themes such as *The Child Jesus, The Healing of the Cripple by Saint Peter, The Cadaver of Christ,* and so forth.

Artists of reputation could be found in every corner of New Spain, but primarily in Mexico City and Puebla, a cultural bastion. Juan Correa, a mulatto, and Cristóbal de Villalpando, as well as the two Rodríguez Juárez, Juan and Nicolás, were among the painters of note. Correa's paintings hung on the walls of the vestry of the cathedral of Mexico City, while his *Expulsion of Adam and Eve from Paradise* won him the accolades of art admirers. José Juárez may have been the top painter; the son of Luis Juárez and identified with Zurbarán, he painted the splendid *San Alejo* and *The Death of Saint Francis,* foremost of colonial works. Like the much copied Zurbarán's, his paintings exude a religious mysticism. Baltazar de Echave y Rioja was the fourth of the prolific clan of painters.

III

Schooling and learning, too, weather vanes of cultural vitality, won garlands. About 1550, Mexico City welcomed a printing press, the first in the Western Hemisphere and a century before the publication of a book in the thirteen English colonies. Within a decade of the Conquest, the Jesuits established the Colegio de San Ildefonso, a seminary teaching at the level of a university; after Independence, it became the Escuela Nacional Preparatoria, the country's initial upper school. Over and above that, Viceroy Don Luis de Velasco founded, in 1551, the Real y Pontificia Universidad, the first of its kind in the Americas. Not all learning matched this impressive start.

For two hundred years, scholasticism, a medieval form of learning, held sway. Essentially ecclesiastical, it carried over to the secular the methods and attitudes of theology. To the scholastics, God sat at the apex of the truth. In his wisdom, he delegated that truth or a part of it to chosen individuals. Their writings, because they "revealed" the truth, were the source of learning and the final authority. They were the church fathers, who, rather than human reason, knew the truth. This interpretation looked upon memory as more important than rational thought. Experiments and the laboratory, the tools of modern science, were ignored. Aristotle and the Bible, as interpreted by Vatican authorities, had the final say in secular philosophy. Dogma and verbal expression, not subtlety of thought, enjoyed prestige and recognition.

What scholastics left unharmed, the influence of Luis de Góngora, a poet of note in Spain, undermined more. Poetry, the principal form of colonial literature, succumbed to his nefarious style. Once a bard of clarity and lyric charm, Góngora took it upon himself to compose metrical writing only he could understand. The cult of artificiality, upside-down metaphors and syntax gone awry, swept literature in New Spain with lightning speed. Gongorism, as the fad was baptized, marched hand in glove with the Baroque love of the ornate in architecture.

Poets and men of learning, for all that, partly circumvented the ills of *gongorismo* and scholastic dullness. Bernardo de Balbuena (1561–1627?) was one of them. Born in Spain, he grew up in Guadalajara, attended the Real y Pontificia Universidad in Mexico City, and became a priest. His *Grandeza mexicana,* a lyrical poem, exalted the beauty and glitter of Mexico City while portraying vividly its women, the theater, and intellectuals. Mateo Alemán, author of *Guzmán de Alfarache,* retired to New Spain in 1608; his famous novel, along with Cervantes's *Quixote,* helped bury the romances of chivalry so popular until then. Written in the picaresque style, *Guzmán de Alfarache* trod the path of *Lazarillo de Tormes,* the pioneer of the genre. *Sucesos de Fray García Guerra,* Alemán's last story, relates the life of the resplendent clerical bureaucrat, with whom he arrived in New Spain in 1608.

Regardless of the laurels of Balbuena and Alemán, one of the premier authors of the seventeenth century was Juan Ruiz de Alarcón, a criollo hunchback with an inferiority complex who, early on, moved to Spain, lived there most of his life, and despised his colonial birth. His writings rank with the finest of the Spanish Golden Age. Gifted with a mastery of the Spanish language, he wrote plays, comedies, and commentaries on manners; *La verdad sospechosa* (Truth Suspect) is his best-known work. The plots of his plays rediculed the vices of gossip, deceit, selfishness, and ingratitude, common, Ruiz asserted, in the Madrid of his times.

In this age of men, women occasionally made their voices heard. That, however, should not come as too much of a surprise, because, in the opinion of straitlaced Spaniards, criollo men gave their "respectable" women excessive freedom, allowing them, to cite one particular shocking custom, to "play cards and dice in mixed company." One of them, Dona María de Peralta, the widow of a distinguished lawyer, had even been accused of blasphemy by the Holy Office. Another freethinker, Elena de la Cruz, a nun and daughter of Don Juan Gutiérrez Altamirano, attorney for Cortés, had also a brush with the Inquisition, accused of "discoursing . . . on the powers of the papacy, the binding nature of the decrees of the Council of Trent, and the character of sin." Supposedly, she doubted the authority of the pope and Archbishop Alonso de Montúfar, successor to Zumárraga, to grant pardons or indulgences for violations of divine law.

Students of colonial letters place one woman at the head of the literary scene, alongside of Ruiz de Alarcón, who, after all, rarely called New Spain his home. Sor Juana Inés de la Cruz, a beautiful and talented criolla, was the first outstanding poet of America. An illegitimate child, she was born in Nepantla in 1648, arriving at eight years of age in Mexico City, where, eventually, her talents caught the attention of the viceroy's wife, who brought her to the palace. For inexplicable reasons, perhaps a love affair that turned sour, Juana forsook the glamour of the viceregal court for the vows of the Jeronymite nuns and devoted her life to books and learning. She wrote love lyrics, morality plays, and dramatic comedies. Of keen mind with a passion for inquiry, Sor Juana, although prone occasionally to embrace *gongorismo,* towered above scholastic authors. Her *Hombres necios,* a poetic critique of men's hypocrisy, and, especially, the *Respuesta a Sor Filotea,* an essay defending her right to learning as a woman, stamp her as the first feminist of the New World. Unexpectedly, she abandoned her books and died unhappy and forlorn in 1695.

Mestizo intellectuals also made their appearance on the eve of the Baroque Age, specifically Diego Muñoz Camargo and Juan Bautista Pomar, like Fernando de Alva Ixtlilxóchitl authors of pre-Hispanic histories. Alva Ixtlilxóchitl's *Historia de la nación Chichimeca* stamped him as the better known. Unfortunately, these mestizo authors, thoroughly *malinchistas,* thought in Spanish, wrote in Spanish, and judged Indians by Spanish values. They were, in actuality, court historians, employing history to justify events. Alva Ixtlilxóchitl even infused pre-Hispanic religious thought with Christian concepts of the Bible: Noah's ark, to give one example. He described Cuauhtémoc as "white of skin and bearded," a look-alike for the Spaniard.

By the end of the sixteenth century, the seeds of a criollo nationality, distinct from that of the Spaniard, had started to germinate. Before the mestizo saw himself as Mexican, the criollo sensed that his New World birth blessed him with a culture of his own. He spoke Spanish with a softer accent, not the guttural sound of his parents, and employed a more delicate yet more bombastic vocabulary to voice unique sentiments. In 1590 or thereabouts, Juan de Cárdenas, ironically a young *peninsular* enamored of the New World, expressed this sentiment for the first time. In his *Problemas y secretos maravillosos de las Indias,* he spoke of "my land," showing how New World inhabitants differed from those of the Old. Yet he was not referring to the Indian, whom he described as "filthy and obscene," but to the criollo, whom Cárdenas believed superior to the *peninsular.*

On his heels appeared Juan de Torquemada, a Franciscan friar, whose *Monarquía indiana* was a history of old Anhuac based mainly on sources collected by Motolinía, Bernardino de Sahagún, and Jerónimo de Mendieta. He believed that Francisco López de Gómara and Antonio de Herrera, the Spanish historians, had presented a distorted version of the ancient peoples. Unlike the official chroniclers, Torquemada wrote glowingly of pre-Hispanic Indians, insisting that they were on the verge of civilization and comparing Moctezuma with Alexander the Great. He pioneered the use of pre-Hispanic Indians to justify the criollo's search for an authentic culture. But, he was ambivalent, too, believing the ancient religions to be the work of the devil and seeing the Conquest as a means of redemption from paganism. The real founders of New Spain were the twelve apostles, the Franciscans who arrived in 1524, not Cortés. Because of their inordinate religious bias, Torquemada's views proved unacceptable to the broader criollo search for nationalist foundations.

More than the others, Don Carlos de Sigüenza y Góngora, a friend of Sor Juana Inés de la Cruz, helped plant the seeds of criollo nationality. A scientist, mathematician, historian, and church scholar, he embodied the transition from the orthodoxy of the seventeenth century to the more heterodox thinking. For his astronomy, one of his hobbies, he relied on Kepler, Galileo, and Copernicus and doubted the wisdom of Aristotle, the priest of the Baroque Age. A nephew of the poet Luis de Góngora, he was a Jesuit originally and, after his expulsion from the order in 1688, a secular priest with a penchant for writing history.

What fascinated him most was "Mexico," a name more and more popular. He never tired of collecting "Mexican antiquities" and drew the first map of New Spain. In his studies, he endeavored to learn what he could about pre-Hispanic Mexico but, unlike Sahagún and the friars who explored the past in order to better convert, Sigüenza y Góngora simply thirsted for knowledge of what he titled *mi patria,* my motherland. He believed that "Mexico was no mere adjunct of Spain but a country with a rich heritage of its own," anchoring his criollo identity in the Indian past, which he envisaged as a counterweight to the European, comparing its accomplishments to Rome's. Without negating the importance of Europe, Sigüenza y Góngora discovered the unity of New Spain in Spaniards, criollos, mestizos, Indians, and *castas.* Cortés and Cuauhtémoc were two sides of the identical coin: to accept one did not deny the other. Moreover, the Spanish conqueror, the truth required saying, dealt harshly with the Indian.

For all his rhetoric, Sigüenza y Góngora did not worship the contemporary Indian. When the hungry Indians of Mexico City rioted and burned buildings in June 1692, Don Carlos experienced a metamorphosis. A brave man, he rescued his precious documents from the archives, which rioters and fires threatened. Still, he felt no pity for the Indians, blaming them for the disturbances and, for good measure, the ones of 1537, 1549, and 1624. He believed they had no business living among Spaniards, urging that they be excluded from Mexico City, and located in barrios of their own, a remedy guaranteed to ensure peace and order. From then on, Don Carlos had little good to say about Indians, a prejudice amply revealed in his account of the native uprising and Spanish reconquest of New Mexico. He was, nonetheless, a precursor of creole nationality.

It remained for Francisco Javier Clavijero, a criollo from Veracruz and a Jesuit, to imbue that identity with life and meaning. In Mexico City, he had taught at the Colegio de San Gregorio, in whose fine library he stumbled upon accounts of the pre-Hispanic civilizations. Fascinated, he studied them and did fieldwork. Clavijero was not alone, for the late eighteenth century witnessed a revival of curiosity in the ancient peoples. An interest in archaeology led to the study of ruins; those at Palenque, for instance, were rediscovered and excavations begun.

Knowledge of the pre-Hispanic past persuaded Clavijero to reject the Enlightenment version of the Indian as a savage, noble or otherwise. To him, the "ancient Mexicans" had conceived wonders: laws, justice, government, education, the arts, and a Nahuatl language equal in quality to the European ones. They had welded together, in Clavijero's opinion, a model to emulate. Exiled from Spain in 1767, Clavijero wrote his famous *Historia antigua de México* in Italy—to quote its author, "a history of Mexico written by a Mexican."

Indians and Spaniards were heirs of wonderful legacies, Clavijero postulated; the blending of the races had yielded good results. Yet Clavijero was no radical; he was referring to the union of Spaniards and the women of the old Aztec nobility, between "blood untainted" and not "besotted and degraded by servitude." Intolerant at heart, Clavijero revealed his prejudices by boasting of the "many light-skinned women" *(blancas)* in the New World. How much better off would New Spain be, pondered Clavijero, if Spaniards, instead of bringing women over from Spain or importing Africans, had just gone to bed with the Indian nobility and, afterward, with the offspring of that union.

Trying to forge a nationality, the criollo of the Baroque Age took one more step. He invented a Virgin, although not an entirely new one, adopting, in reality, the Virgen de Guadalupe for his own. That usurpation began in 1648 when Miguel Sánchez, a criollo priest, published *Imagen de la Virgen María de Dios de Guadalupe,* which told of Juan Diego, the Indian before whom the Virgin appeared. Sánchez did not invent the story but took it from Indian tales that circulated in New Spain. The Virgin, according to the Sánchez version, revealed herself to Diego on the hill of Tepeyac, declaring that she was the Mother of God and asking that a temple be erected in her honor.

Not until she appeared five times, nevertheless, did the Virgin, speaking through Diego, manage to convince Bishop Juan de Zumárraga. On this last journey from Tepeyac to Mexico City, Diego carried the image of the Virgin stamped on his tunic and roses in its fold. When the Virgin, dark of skin like the Indian, confronted Juan Diego, she stood on a nopal (prickly cactus), a symbol of the ancient Mexicans.

The cult of the Virgin swept over New Spain, where temples were erected in her honor while pope and crown, believers in miracles, baptized her the patroness of the colony. By implication, the popular cult carried a special meaning: the apparition of the Virgin conferred on New Spain's church an autonomous status. Christianity had arrived not through the efforts of the friars but with the Mother of God. The Conquest occurred because God in his infinite wisdom chose New Spain for the appearance of the Virgin. The Conquest, therefore, had a higher purpose, beyond the mundane needs of the crown.

The story, as told by Sánchez, combined religious traditions of European origin with the mythical and idolatrous superstitions of Indian piety. Her worship united every ethnic group in New Spain, not the least the Indian, who, whatever the criollo may have wanted, held on to his "brown" Virgin. New Spain, as the feats of the Virgin testified, had given birth to a distinct nationality. She became, eventually, the emblem of the *patria criolla.*

IV

But there were the nuts and bolts of economics, too. Labor needs, to begin, were a prime worry, more so after the pool of Indian workers began to shrivel up. True, Spaniards migrated to the New World; but only a handfull of dirt farmers, men willing to work under the hot sun, abandoned the mother country. Given the nature of colonial reality, Indians had to labor to build New Spain. For this task, the Spaniards invented the repartimiento, having, theoretically, ruled out slavery and the encomienda. Under this unsavory form of compulsory labor, Spaniards had to pay Indians to plow their fields and toil in the mines. The formula was wage labor. However, since Indians saw scant merit in toiling for Spaniards, no matter what the monetary reward, they had to be made to do it.

Indian men, drafted for work by their native caciques, labored forty-five days of every year for the Spaniards. The Indian was paid, and, the legislation stipulated, his employer had to deal justly with him. Only so many Indians could be taken from a village at any one time, and heads of families had to be allowed time to plant and harvest their own crops. Crown policy was both patriarchal and despotic. No longer a slave of the encomendero, the Indian was free; but in a catch-22 dilemma, he had to toil for the Spaniard, particularly in the mines, where, despite the importation of African slaves, he did most of the labor. Repartimientos, forced-labor drafts, were also employed to build the cities, to do the heavy construction work of streets, aqueducts, jails, and parks. The Indians, moreover, were not exempted from the labor required by the clergy for churches, cathedrals, monasteries, and convents.

As before, Spanish law and practice stood poles apart. Under the repartimiento, the Indian made out poorly. Not uncommonly, Spaniards, wanting to bleed white their repartimientos, used their workers from sunup to sundown, beat them, failed to pay them, or took their clothes away so that they would not run off. Under the guise of the repartimiento, the owners of *obrajes* in Puebla, sweatshops producing cheap cloth which dated from the late sixteenth century, relied on thugs to ensnare Indians to work for them. Once shut up in *obrajes,* the Indians, to quote one scholar, "had about as much chance of escaping as from prison." Not a few *obraje* moguls locked up their Indians at night under the watchful eye of their hired goons. The ill treatment boomeranged; Indians did their best to avoid the repartimiento, apparently quite successfully because crown authorities intensified their "recruiting" efforts, ordering local officials and caciques to provide Indians or face punishment. In 1587, to give an illustration, the viceroy threatened to jail the corregidor and alcalde of Cimapán if they failed to corral Indians for the mines of Pachuca. On another occasion, authorities ruled that constables who could not get Indians to work would have to do it themselves. For all that, the crown, in 1633, abolished the repartimiento except in the mining industry, deeming the extraction of silver too important to leave to volunteers. Nor did the repartimiento die completely elsewhere, lingering on until the next century in the backward regions of New Spain.

Eventually, wage labor, mostly Indian, held sway; only here and there did unpaid work survive, ironically mostly on public projects. Wage labor, more likely than not, won out primarily because of the scarcity of Indians, the consequence of the population decline, the bonanza of mining, and, to a lesser extent, the needs of the *obrajes.* The mining boom depended on an army of workers, whatever their nature. When slavery, both African and Indian, as well as the repartimiento proved inadequate, mineowners, who were reaping fabulous profits, started to pay higher wages and, by doing that, attracted Indian workers; for instance, at Zacatecas, good wages, the best in New Spain, drew Aztecs, Tlaxcalans, Cholultecans, Otomis, and Tarascans, producing a migration that lasted until the end of its mining bonanza.

Given the growing shortage of Indian workers, part and parcel of the decline of the native population, systems of agricultural labor also started to change. Eventually, hacendados had to pay their field hands. One offshoot of that necessity was debt peonage *(peones acasillados),* a system common to regions of acute labor shortages, notably central Mexico. Debt peonage took form during the late sixteenth century. For many a hacendado, it was the answer to his labor problems: how to guarantee the availability of Indian workers during the planting and harvest seasons. Mineowners in Zacatecas, too, relied briefly on debt peonage, as did the *obrajes.* But it was on the hacienda that it took root, especially with the rising demand for grains in the mining towns and cities. By ending the repartimiento, the crown conferred tacit approval on debt peonage. By this system, the Indian bound himself to his employer by going into debt to him. The hacendado lent him money, often an advance on his wages, or sold him goods on credit, on the condition that he work off what he owed. The peons, as the workers were named, and their families resided on hacienda lands, living in humble huts not far from the master's house, which, during the seventeenth century, evolved into a palatial mansion.

Debt peonage benefited mainly the big hacendados, who, with capital at hand, were able to entice Indians to their estates by offering to pay them. The peons were given small plots on which to plant corn, beans, and squash. With workers at their disposal, the hacendados could then, by acquiring additional land, expand their plantings, multiply their harvests, and monopolize local and regional markets. Relying on debt peonage, the big haciendas became the lords of the countryside of central Mexico. They were, in essence, units of production endowed with enough land to plant and to let lie fallow, granaries to store the harvest, houses for hacendados and mayordomos, huts for workers, buildings for blacksmiths, and sheds to keep farm implements in. Debt peonage, on the other hand, hurt small planters, who, capital poor, either had to rely on the labor of their sons or become *aparceros,* sharecroppers on the big estates.

Difficult as it may be to believe, debt peonage partly saved the Indian from his worst enemies. When he moved himself onto a hacienda, his lot could improve. By joining the hacendado, the Indian, who had lost his lands or never owned any, gained a measure of protection—a job and a home for his family. The hacendado, if wise, became the defender of his Indians, looking after them in emergencies. He kept at bay voracious labor contractors and saw to it that his workers had food, clothing, shelter, and a priest to baptize their young, marry their offspring, and bury their dead. Not to do so meant risking the loss of his workers by death or by flight. Even when heavily in debt, it must be remembered, the Indian, by and large, could leave the hacienda; he stayed on because he had a job and a bit of security. Few rebellions of *peones acasillados* were recorded during the colonial period. All the same, wageworkers from neighboring villages harvested most of the crops on the haciendas.

Not all hacendados, unfortunately, proved wise. Some worked their peons to the bone, beat them, and, the evidence reveals, stole the virginity of their daughters. The sale of a hacienda, not infrequently, included its peons in the price, sold like buildings and land to the buyer. Hacendados hungry for more lands dispatched armed goons to invade the lands of nearby villages, or bribed authorities to shut their eyes while they made off with them. Countless villages lost their lands. Despicable behavior of this kind spawned the story of selfish and cruel hacendados, slavemasters in disguise.

Debt peonage and wage labor underline the transformation of the colonial economy during the seventeenth century. Capitalist institutions had surfaced—the commercial hacienda, for one—and gradually won a bigger role to play, not just in agriculture but in mining and the *obrajes*, which relied exclusively on manual labor and were never mechanized. Spaniards and criollos, and the lucky mestizo, were living off the profits of their individual enterprise. It was no longer simply a subsistence economy.

V

The Indian had to adapt to more than just changes in the labor system. Spanish colonialism, as was explained earlier, placed in jeopardy ethnic and tribal ties and reduced Indian society to one class. For a brief respite, the Spaniards had allowed the old nobility to survive, employing it to rule the conquered natives. The nobility became the lackey of crown, church, and encomendero. However, outside of Yucatán and Oaxaca, most of the Indian caciques, the last of the old nobility, vanished from the scene. With their demise, Spanish colonialism dictated that Indians be poor and members of the lower class. Being poor and being Indian, more likely than not, meant the same thing.

For the Indian, Baroque splendor spelled trouble. The economics of the time, upheld by crown legislation, confined him increasingly to the toil of agriculture, especially when mestizos replaced him in the mines. Spaniards and criollos monopolized the trades, commerce, mining, and what passed for manufacturing. Similarly, most rural dwellers were Indian campesinos, men who tilled their ejidos or the lands of a hacendado. When the hacienda, about the end of the sixteenth century, became the principal supplier of food for the Spanish towns, the agriculture of the Indian suffered. From that point on, the Indian was generally a subsistence farmer; when he had land of his own, he cultivated it to feed himself and his family, having only marginal ties to the capitalist markets of the Spanish towns. His farming techniques remained primitive; his tool was the planting stick of his ancestors, and he domesticated no more than chickens. When the Indian disposed of his products on the marketplace, he sold them cheaply; in contrast, he paid dearly for Spanish goods. Indian craftsmen had difficulty selling their wares in the Spanish towns; their competitors, whether Spaniards, criollos, or, more and more, mestizos, saw to that.

Nothing depicts better their fate than what befell Indian women. Many of them, orphaned or widowed by the wars of the Conquest or the epidemics of disease, found themselves left to fend for themselves, increasingly, if residing in the Spanish towns, as domestics or to labor in mines or *obrajes,* thirty-six of them by the middle of the century. When they had jobs as servants in Spanish or criollo households, they worked for little more than board and room, as well as for the chance to care for their children, at times the bastard offspring of the master. If not domestics, they carried the produce of countryside to the town or city for sale at the *tianguis,* the marketplace, learning Spanish, it was said, in order to sell their wares to Spaniards, criollos, and mestizos. Colonial legislation and the church, meanwhile, dictated that Indian men discard their polygamous habits, which meant that they could no longer openly maintain their harems. In pre-Columbian times, however, polygamous men had been responsible for the welfare of all of their women; after the Spaniards banned the practice, they turned to clandestine affairs, but shed the burden of taking care of their illegitimate offspring.

Oddly, at first glance, Indians appeared to be free; they were not slaves. As individuals, they were, more or less, at liberty to do what they wished; but, the pueblos to which they belonged were not, being victimized by the omnipotent Spanish town. This exploitation of one community by another, the latter always more powerful, Mexican scholars title "internal colonialism"; with a flair for words, Marx labeled it the "Asiatic mode of production."

The Indian, as his behavior revealed, knew he was not free. So, like the Maya in Yucatán, he took to drinking more. On this point, most scholars concur. Few "people in history drank more than the Indian" of New Spain. Again and again, the Indian relied on pulque to mitigate the hardships of colonial rule. Men, particularly, drowned their sorrows; women drank "mostly at fiestas." A wife, according to the shared wisdom, "should not drink while her husband is drunk." Every village or family fiesta, whether the wife drank or not, ended in a drunken orgy.

To feed the habit, a pulque industry developed and flourished. Entire regions, Puebla principally, were known for their maguey fields. Because of his poverty, the Indian never took to distilled liquor, the beverage of Spaniards; he was faithful to his pulque, the drink of his ancestors. Hacendados of central Mexico planted more of the maguey, the mother of the pulque sap. Formerly set aside for corn, village milpas even grew the maguey. The plant came to occupy some of the most fertile lands of the Valley of Mexico. Like their menfolk, women had a hand in the pulque traffic, carting on burros the family's output to market, where they sold it from stalls. In the villages, women usually sold the pulque from the doorways of their adobe huts.

Nor did the Indian stop being defiant. He knew what most Spaniards said of him and, in retaliation, he thought of them in like manner. "The monkey even dressed in silk," declared a Spanish neighbor of an Indian village, "is still a monkey. Whoever speaks of Indians speaks of shit because the Indian is like the monkey." In reply, the Indian tagged the Spaniards "dog" and "pig." Occasionally, he refused to work for them, preferring to be labeled "lazy" and thus avoid the harsh labor in mines and *obrajes.* At the same time, the Indian, belying the claim of his stupidity, turned Spanish law against the Spaniard. His legal battles in defense of village property against hacendados and their ilk dragged on for centuries. Nor, contrary to what is believed, did the Indian always lose these legal squabbles.

The Indian was hardly docile or apathetic; the death of pre-Hispanic society did not end Indian resistance. During the dark days of population decline, the Indian, holding Spaniards responsible for the death of his companions, attempted, more than once, to contaminate their food and water supply. He threw rotting bodies into their wells and mixed the dough of their bread with the blood of the dying. Reports exist of Indians who compelled Spanish prisoners "to hear pagan services." Indians, it was said, forced Spanish women to marry them—in native ceremonies presided over by native priests. Supposedly docile Indians in Oaxaca killed hacienda mayordomos, while others made corregidores and priests bow before village elders.

Beyond that, riots broke out time and again. During the seventeenth century, two erupted in Mexico City, one in 1624. The high price of corn stoked the fury. During the uprising of 1692, as Spaniards labeled it, mobs of Indians burned the viceregal palace, the office of the ayuntamiento, and the jail, while making a shambles of the Zócalo, the public square. The viceroy barely escaped with his life. In Sonora, the "rim of Christendom," Apaches, Janos, and Jacomes, Father Eusebio Kino wrote, "robbed, damaged property and killed" Spaniards; 1696 was a terrible year for Kino and his brethren.

VI

Religious beliefs, mortality, and the values of the Catholic church were the glue that bound together the polyglot peoples of Baroque New Spain. Catholicism wrought a miracle, uniting Spaniards, criollos, Indians, mestizos, and Africans under one roof. The secular and the religious were cut from the same cloth, all the more so in the cities. Political as well as religious shrines, the cities sheltered the offices of the bishop, the convents, most of the monasteries, the best Catholic schools, and the universities, where medieval scholasticism and traditional church teachings reigned. The church set the tone for the art, music, theater, poetry, and, most assuredly, architecture, the essence of the Baroque Age. Given this bewildering ubiquity, the church, to the glee of believers, thrived, becoming powerful and wealthy. Theoretically subservient, the church, in reality, challenged state authority. Fat and content, the clergy, more and more, identified with cities and urban culture and cooled its moral ardor.

Church wealth flowed from diverse sources. With the blessings of the crown, the church collected a startling number of duties, donations, and legacies from last wills and testaments paid by Spaniards and criollos and by cofradias (community savings) of Indians and *castas*. The church had the *diezmo,* a tax of 10 percent; only Indians, who paid tribute to the crown, were exempt. Of *diezmo* funds, the church kept all but a tiny fraction. Nearly all of them stayed in the cathedrals; parish priests, the poor clergy, received less than a quarter of them. *Capellanías,* the privilege of the well-off, brought additional funds to church coffers. Fearing for their souls, the rich and not-so-rich entrusted money to the church so that priests might say masses for them after death. The censo added more funds, a sort of quitrent payable to the church for its services—for example, on a loan of money by a convent to a landlord in exchange for a mortgage on his property. The borrower then paid the censo, about 5 percent on the mortgage. The church, its coffers bulging, had turned banker, lending money not merely to hacendados but to merchants and mine-owners, too.

Early on, moreover, the church, on its own, had acquired haciendas, sugar mills, cattle ranches, urban real estate, and *obrajes.* The orders, particularly, displayed a passion for owning real estate. The church spent part of its profits on the building of temples, convents, and so forth, investing the rest in properties paying dividends, despite laws that barred the clergy from acquiring property. The orders relied on *hombres de paja,* front men willing to do their bidding. Of the missionaries, the Jesuits ran the most efficient haciendas, while the Franciscans, forgetting conveniently their vows of poverty, were famous for the size of their haciendas. The Dominicans, thirsty for land from the start, built sugar mills, the best-known at Cuautla-Amilpas, worked by African slaves during the sixteenth century. The Jesuits justified their extensive real estate holdings by spending income from them on their schools and missions. Among the ablest of gentlemen farmers, the sons of Loyola cultivated the soil with up-to-date techniques, understood the importance of fertilizers, and employed both *peones acasillados* and wageworkers. In the cities, the orders owned houses and buildings which they rented out. Aside from its monopoly of schooling, the church ran the hospitals, asylums for the insane, and the orphanage.

The orders, moreover, had not slept; they were busily expanding their domains in the north. For the conquest and settlement of Sinaloa, Sonora, and Baja California, the Jesuits led the way; the Franciscans answered the challenge in New Mexico and California, erecting missions in such far-off places as Santa Fe, San Diego, Los Angeles, and Monterey. In Sonora, a striking chapter in this drama, Eusebio Francisco Kino, a Jesuit missionary born in the

Austrian Tyrol, headed the effort. Schooled in Europe, with a gift for languages and widely read, Kino turned down a professorship at the University of Ingolstadt to explore the wastelands of the Pimería Alta. Arriving in 1687, he explored, built missions, baptized Indians, and established schools. His memoirs, *Favores celestiales*, which covered life in northwest New Spain until 1706, told of his adventures, of Manuel González, a friar who "suffered from hemorrhoids" but gave the clothes off his back to the heathen and dropped to his knees to face the arrows of hostile Indians, dying with the crucifix in his embrace.

Along with property, the church enjoyed special privileges. With its own courts, the clergy escaped trial by royal judges; that was a matter for ecclesiastical authorities. In the realm of law, the church, if not above the state, was certainly its equal. By the right of mortmain, its wealth could not be taxed, the possessor of property held in perpetuity. Critics referred to it as the "dead hand" of the church. "What went in," they said, "never came out."

The Baroque Age welcomed the secular church. From the time of Isabel, the crown had relied on it to teach obedience, to label dissent a sin. This fitted in nicely with the views of the prelates, imbued equally with the hierarchical ideal, who employed bishops to ensure loyalty to the clerical apparatus. Crown and secular clergy distrusted the regulars, semifeudal orders with ties to the Vatican. Not to be forgotten, the sons of Spanish nobles, commonly, held the best jobs in the clerical panoply. Along with the nobility, they formed the establishment. From the days of Don Luis de Velasco, therefore, the crown sided with the priests who wanted to secularize the missions. By 1600, the seculars, who had opened their doors to mestizo priests, were on their way to winning the upper hand, breaking the hold of the friars on the Indian communities and compelling them to travel north to baptize heathens on the "rim of Christendom" or to stay in Yucatán, where the Franciscans held on until the eighteenth century.

In time, priests largely replaced friars in the Indian pueblos. Tiny hamlets had visiting priests who said mass, but pueblos of any size supported one of their own. After the alcalde, the priest was the highest authority in the pueblo. What he said carried the weight of church and crown. Also, the big haciendas had priests who, if they wanted to stay, did mostly the bidding of the hacendado. The size of the mining operation determined the number of priests in the *reales de minas.* The plight of the orders, nevertheless, merited no tears. In 1611, when Fray García Guerra governed New Spain, the Franciscans alone had 172 monasteries, the Augustinians 90, and the Dominicans 69. Their huge numbers, as well as the religious houses of the rest of the orders, led Pope Paul V to order the closing of every one with fewer than eight monks. No one heeded his command. The "glory years of the orders," recalled Jerónimo de Mendieta, were between 1524 and 1564. After that, a decline in apostolic ardor set in. Soon, the friars were asking to return home; few bothered to learn an Indian language. Doctrinal differences, jurisdictional disputes, and, undoubtedly, the pursuit of personal gain had dampened the crusading spirit, while the secular clergy had undertaken to fatten its pocketbook. Bishops and archbishops led the way, but parish priests, on occasion, did not lag far behind. Ultimately, priests, monks, and nuns, their numbers swollen out of proportion to the spiritual needs of their flocks, became a burden on New Spain.

Corruption, to the despair of the devout, went beyond money grabbing. Equally blatant was the moral laxity of much of the clergy. Profits from business made possible a hedonistic life-style for much of the clergy. Sundry priests and monks, cloistered supposedly behind walls, lived a double life, more than once with concubines and families or soliciting women in the confessional. They drank hard liquor and gambled—as Thomas Gage, the English friar, testified—and fornicated freely. As in the outside world, Spaniards and criollos, whether priests or monks, quarreled over jurisidictional rights. The unmarried daughters of the rich became nuns, "brides of Christ," but demanded frilly cells where servants and slaves waited on them hand and foot.

That was not the entire sordid picture either. Superstition and fanaticism bred neurotic behavior. Frenetic monks and nuns, praying for salvation, flagellated themselves, beating or starving themselves to death. In *Paraíso occidental,* Carlos de Sigüenza y Góngora, himself a priest, set forth the distraught acts of mortification of the nuns of the convent of Jesús María, describing how Sister Francisca de San Lorenzo splattered the floors and walls of a cell with her blood, begged to be whipped, and rewarded handsomely the servant who did it best. Tomasina de San Francisco, the mother superior, bound her body with chains and drove wooden splinters into her feet, and one nun branded her own forehead with the inscription "Slave of the Saintly Sacrament." Outside of the walls of convent and monastery, the misery and ignorance of the poor rendered them easy prey of quacks, sorcerers, and witch doctors. Nor were Spaniards and criollos, usually the upper class, beyond the appeal of the occult.

To punish "bad examples of Christianity" and bar heretics, Philip II had, in 1569, dispatched the Holy Office of the Inquisition to New Spain. Run by the church, it functioned as "censor, detective, jail warden, and informer," assuming the guilt of the accused until they were proven innocent. However, the Holy Office, at least in the sixteenth century, was not viewed as a repressive tribunal by most colonists; to the contrary, they looked upon it as a "benign and popular institution . . . protecting religion and . . . society from traitors." Still, between 1571, when it assumed its vigilance, and 1601, it delivered thirteen "sinners" to secular authorities for burning at the stake. That attitude was also typical of Protestants, no less intolerant. In nearly three centuries of Spanish rule in the Americas, the Inquisition probably sentenced to the stake no more than ninety "sinners," while in Tudor England victims of religious persecution exceeded five hundred.

Especially unwelcomed in New Spain were "crypto-Jews," conversos suspected of not embracing Catholic dogma fully. In one famous trial, the Inquisition convicted Don Luis de Carvajal, a converso and the conqueror of Nuevo León, of sheltering Jewish relatives, some of whom it burned at the stake. Indians, classified as children by Spanish law, were, after 1571, excluded mercifully from judgment. Crimes against "good morals," as defined by the holy fathers, mostly occupied the Inquisition: bigamy, sexual perversion, "solicitation in the confessional" (a common occurrence), blasphemy, quackery, and superstition.

Under the Baroque church, Indians, by and large, did not fare well. Less than a century after the arrival of the friars, there were churches, boasted Jerónimo de Mendieta, in the four hundred convent towns of New Spain, and an equal number in the secular parishes and chapels in the pueblos, all built by Indians, who also did the backbreaking labor for the construction of the sumptuous convents, monasteries, and cathedrals. To cite a letter of Archbishop Alonso de Montúfar of 1556, "Indians in gangs of five hundred, six hundred, or a thousand" were brought in from a "distance of four, six, or twelve leagues, without paying them any wages or even giving them a crust of bread." Once settled in their quarters, friars, nuns, and priests asked Indians to be "gardeners, servants, cooks, sacristans, messengers, all without a cent of wages." The "cost of . . . the rich and superfluous oranaments" in the churches was met by assessing them. In theory, the giving of alms was voluntary; by the early seventeenth century, it had become compulsory.

Not illogically, Indians often distrusted friars and priests. This attitude had early origins. By 1550, attendance at mass by Indians had declined drastically, especially among men. Even in regions thought safely Christian, few natives visited the church. Near Bacanuche, on the desolate frontier of Sonora, Indians told Father Kino why they neither wanted to be Christianized nor welcomed missionaries. The fathers, they complained, killed people, stole the fertile land, permitted their cattle to dry up watering holes, and, more telling, "deceived with false promises."

That notwithstanding, in the provincial towns, the church was, more often than not, the center of social life. The myriad religious festivals of the ecclesiastical calendar offered plentiful opportunities for well-deserved social get-togethers, a time to rest from arduous labors. In the mining towns, work came to a halt during the holidays, at Santa Eulalia, a forlorn mining town in northern Chihuahua, to give one example, to hail San José, its patron, and later San Francisco, San Felipe, and San Andrés and to celebrate Corpus Christi. Many of these festivals took place on the square before the church in neighboring Chihuahua City, where priests and public officials in their Sunday best paraded, holding aloft the images of the saints being honored, joined by horsemen who waved banners and flags. The ayuntamiento, for its part, set up benches and tables where food and drink were served. According to archival documents, a merry time was had by all.

Beyond that, in spite of the misdeeds of some, the early clergy left a valuable legacy, not only a record of piety and decency and a crusade for social justice but, additionally, a written record of the Conquest of New Spain. Toribio de Benavente (Motolinía), Jerónimo de Mendieta, José de Acosta, Diego Durán, Juan de Tovar, and Andrés Olmos rescued from oblivion the pictographs and oral traditions of the pre-Hispanic peoples. They wrote grammars and compiled vocabularies of their languages and, to ensure that posterity remembered, the first ethnographic and historical texts of the inhabitants of Mesoamerica. Who can forget Fray Bernardino de Sahagún's monumental *Historia general de las cosas de la Nueva España,* the story of Aztec life compiled with the aid of native writers? Without the endeavors of these men, much of what Mexicans know today about their past would be lost.

6

FINAL DAYS

I

The contours of the eighteenth century, the pinnacle of colonial rule, were striking. But, as Miguel de Cervantes once said, "It seldom happens that any felicity comes so pure as not to be tempered and allayed by some mixture of sorrow." And so it was in New Spain, where opulence and learning existed side by side with poverty and ignorance. New Spain had clasped to its bosom the Enlightenment (Ilustración), the most recent wave of European thought, but it was a cautious embrace. Spaniards, both at home and abroad Catholic and traditionalists, exhibited no wish to discard old ideals simply because the French and English believed them outdated. A few did, nevertheless, and by doing so revamped ideas, mostly against the wishes of prelates and, at times, the crown, neither being eager to abdicate its cherishesd berth in the hierarchy.

II

The Age of Reason upset hallowed concepts of scholastic thought. Colonial savants, clerics among them, read Voltaire, Descartes, and Leibniz, pondered the lessons of Galileo. Bacon, and Newton and debated the relative merits of Malebranche and Gassendi. Here and there, the scientific method of the sciences, what western Europe was embracing, slowly shunted aside syllogistic reasoning. Experimentation and the laboratory, the principal actors in the unfolding scientific drama, challenged the universality of traditional doctrine. The emergent philosophy, exemplified by *Elementos de la filosofía moderna,* of Juan Benítez de Gamarra, a book published in 1774, drew the sword against scholasticism. Voicing the spirit of the Ilustración, Benítez de Gamarra questioned the role of church, crown, and, heartwarming to criollos, *peninsulares.*

Marching alongside Benítez de Gamarra, scores of scientific thinkers surfaced, scholars such as Velázquez, Gama, and Alzate, as well as the literary critics Uribe, Cerrato, and Bravo. Of them, José Antonio Alzate stood out. A clergyman like most intellectuals, Alzate edited two leading journals of Mexico City, *Gaceta de Literatura* and *Diario de México,* and was committed to the ideas of the Ilustración, an advocate of science who worshiped reason, believing it to be a tool for the transformation of man and society. What he saw or read set astir his mind; nothing was intellectually too remote. A Renaissance man, he studied nature, drew up plans to protect the lakes around Mexico City, explored the pre-Hispanic ruins at Tajín and Xochicalco, and read deeply into the nature of syphilis and yellow fever. Miguel Constanzo, Juan Crespi, and Junípero Serra, a Franciscan friar, explored by land and sea the Californias, winding their way north to San Francisco. The coastline from Acapulco to Alaska lured expeditions such as that of Alejandro Malaspina, who kept records of the flora, fauna, and geography along his journey.

Reflecting the shift to the scientific, professors at the Colegio de Minería taught physics, mathematics, chemistry, and mineralogy. Built in the Neoclassical style, the design of the School of Mines sealed the doom of Baroque architecture, a trademark of the scholastic era. Earlier, in 1768, the Real Escuela de Cirugía, a college of medicine, enrolled its first students; independent of the university, which was still under the tutelage of the church, it specialized in practical medicine and medical science.

The intellectual upheaval went beyond the simply scientific. Literature, too, enjoyed an awakening, although it spawned no giants of the stature of Sor Juana Inés de la Cruz or Carlos de Sigüenza y Góngora. Yet Alzate and his cohorts, scholars and journalists, published a wealth of fine writing. They also turned their backs on old themes; poetic heavens, the Hades of Greek mythology, nymphs, Homeric heroes, and epic sagas supplanted religious tracts. Newspapers appeared for the first time; the *Diario de México,* Alzate's brainchild, featured news of European events. The mouthpiece of enlightened criollos, it also covered national life and politics. Carlos María de Bustamante, Francisco de Verdad, and Jacobo Villarrutia, luminaries of the coming struggle for Independence, wrote for it. The *Mercurio Volante,* edited by José Ignacio Bartolache, was the initial medical journal in the Western Hemisphere.

III

The century had its twists and turns. The new clung to the old. Of the arts, Baroque lost popularity, replaced by the Churrigueresque, even more ornate. Still the Baroque survived, coexisting with the new style in both church and civil architecture. Once thought simply an offspring of the Spanish architect José Churriguera, the new style had complex origins. Churriguera bequeathed, intentionally or not, his name to the genre, which arrived in Mexico with Jerónimo de Balbas, a native of Sevilla who, in 1718, worked on the altar of the kings in the cathedral of Mexico City. The Churrigueresque spread rapidly throughout the colony, until late in the century when the Neoclassical became popular.

Originally believed merely an ornate copy of the Baroque, Churrigueresque stamped its unique trademark on the buildings of the era. Unlike the Baroque, which did not disturb traditional blueprints, Churrigueresque architecture tampered with the logic of orthodox design, altering proportion, profiles, and fundamental tenets, appearing to challenge, to cite a Mexican scholar, the laws of gravity. The Churrigueresque was not just "destructive" but, more than that, "gloried in being so." Its design replaced the habitual column of Baroque architecture with the *estipite,* or reversed pyramid, building supports of cylindrical or quadrilateral form.

The Churrigueresque achieved its most notable expression in the temples, old or newly built, and in the redesign of lay buildings and the construction of other ones. With a plethora of ornaments and decorations, the Churrigueresque covered their walls and ceilings. One of the churches of Cholula, to illustrate, featured ceilings of grotesque masks, each molded as though sculptured in relief, which assumed diverse shapes and colors. A cacophony of faces peered down on the worshiper. So intricate and so complex were Churrigueresque altars that few understand how the design was done. A sculpture in relief far more elaborate than those of the Baroque embellished the façades of doorways and bell towers.

Experts judge the Churrigueresque the most Mexican of art styles, referring to it as the symbol of Mexican nationality. In their opinion, it revived the spirit of pre-Hispanic art. The abhorrence of empty space and the rush to decorate it testified to the lingering influence of the Indian as artist and sculptor. Centuries of subjugation had failed to erase his presence.

Churrigueresque architecture reflected the prosperity of the eighteenth century, a society enjoying fully its mining bonanza. Examples of it abounded. In Mexico City were the temples of the Santísima Trinidad, San Francisco, Santa Veracruz, and Enseñanza. In Querétaro rose the majestic temples of Santa Clara and Santa Rosa, their bejeweled interiors flaunting their supremely ornate design. South of Mexico City, in Puebla, the Churrigueresque dominated the temples of San Francisco and San José. Monuments to the Churrigueresque were found elsewhere: in San Luis Potosí, the chapel of Aranzazu; in Hidalgo, the façade of the temple at Atitalaquia; Oaxaca had its temple of San Francisco; Guadalajara also a chapel of Aranzazu. On the desolate northern frontier of Coahuila, inhabitants of Saltillo, at the urging of their priest, built a sumptuous temple in the Churrigueresque manner; few buildings matched in decor and richness of ornamentation the design of its entranceway.

Civil architecture, while less impressive, also had its day in the sun. In Mexico City, both the palace of the viceroys and that of the Ayuntamiento came under the spell of the Churrigueresque, as did the Colegio de San Ignacio and Real y Pontificia Universidad. Guadalajara had its Palacio de la Audiencia de Nueva Galicia; Aguascalientes, its building for the ayuntamiento; and Michoacán, the Colegio de Pátzcuaro. During the century, every hospital of New Spain was rebuilt from the ground up in the grand style of the Churrigueresque. Two stood out: the Hospital de San Pedro in Puebla and the Hospital de Belén in Guadalajara.

Prominent criollos, some with titles, also wanted to display their affluence. The façades of their homes, to use a metaphor, announced figuratively to visitors that they were in the presence of an important family. The houses had huge patios surrounded by massive pillars holding up the roof. Private chapels graced their interiors, as well as long dining rooms for scores of guests. In Mexico City, about forty homes were in this category. Alexander von Humboldt, the observant German traveler, baptized it the City of the Palaces, having in mind, no doubt, the Casa del Conde de Miravalle, the Casa del Marqués de Santa Fe de Guardiola, the Casa del Conde del Valle de Orizaba, and, of course, the Casa de Don José de la Borda, the mining magnate. On a lesser scale, similar residences could be found in Puebla (the Casa de Alfeñique), Querétaro, Oaxaca, San Luis Potosí, Guanajuato, Guadalajara, and, because of its mercantile importance, Veracruz.

Just when the Churrigueresque loomed undisputed monarch, a rival style made its entrance. The Bourbons, of certified French stock, wanted to modernize Spain, to bring it into the Western mold. The Neoclassical found its way to Mexico City when the Real Academia de San Carlos, the national art school, accepted its first students, in 1781. Its patron, Jerónimo Antonio Gil, a Spaniard of Neoclassical bent, modeled its building after the Academia de San Fernando in Madrid and the Academia de San Carlos in Valencia. Teachers from Spain taught classes in painting, sculpting, and architectural design. Their secular art shattered the church's grip on painting, the cornerstone of the Baroque and Churrigueresque, and transformed architectural design. Both state and church buildings were influenced by the Neoclassical. To critics nostalgic for the old, the Neoclassical, rather than establish an architecture of note, introduced imitations of the European, seldom matching the grandeur of the Churrigueresque.

Enduring just forty years, Neoclassical architecture bequeathed monuments of its own. One was the Colegio de Minería, the genius of Manuel Tolsá, who also drew up the blueprints for the church of Bishop Juan Cruz Ruiz in Guadalajara, later the Hospicio de Cabañas, where José Clemente

Orozco, the twentieth-century muralist, painted. Another stalwart of architecture was Miguel de Costanzo, born in Barcelona and remembered for his mapping expeditions to California. Two criollo architects made significant contributions: José Damián de Ortiz, born in Jalapa, and Eduardo de Tresguerras from Celaya, a town in the Bajío.

Neoclassical painting, however, rarely partook of the triumphs of architecture. Admiration for Descartes and his companions encouraged a rejection of the Baroque and a fancy for Neoclassical art, destined to dictate tastes until the mid-1850s. This art frowned on the wild imagery of the Baroque, distrusted emotion and passion, and demanded obedience to form. The painting of Francisco Goya and his realistic school influenced strongly the artists of this time in New Spain. Lamentably, imitation spawned a feeble art, lacking the spontaneity and ingenuousness of the Baroque, cold, seemingly done by prescription.

Still, portrait art won acclaim during the eighteenth century, relegating religious art to the ashcan of history. Anonymous artists left countless pictures of viceroys and church dignitaries and of rich criollos, while the Academia de San Carlos conferred official stature on this art. The art of the anonymous portrait painter survived the colony, becoming the gist of its popular successor of the nineteenth century. Among the painters of imagination were Miguel Cabrera, famous for his portrait of Sor Juana Inés de la Cruz; Patricio Morlete Ruiz, who painted the Viceroys Amarillas, Cajigal, and Croix; José de la Paz, noted for his *Jueces de la Acordada;* and José Ibarra and José Alcibar, both of whom did religious scenes. A stalwart of this era was Rafael Ximeno, praised for his portraits of Manuel Tolsá and Jerónimo Gil; both appear solemn and majestic, dressed in elegant finery. Ximeno, who also did saints and angels, painted the murals in the dome of the cathedral of Mexico City. The best of the artists, say critics, dwelt in Mexico City; yet painters of equal talents worked in Puebla, Valladolid, Guadalajara, Tlaxcala, and Oaxaca.

With its emphasis on form and the human body, the Neoclassical breathed fresh life into the labors of the sculptor. One exponent, the architect Manuel Tolsá, who arrived in Mexico City to teach at the Academia de San Carlos, was not merely the best of the day but the giant of his century. Born in Spain, he raised the art of the sculptor to the levels of pre-Hispanic days. His statue of Charles IV, standing in the heart of Mexico City, embodied the flavor of the Roman era. Sitting proudly on a prancing stallion, Charles wears a Roman toga, and his regal manner recalls Alexander the Great.

Popular music and dance, too, enjoyed a turnabout, which imbued them with a hearty and sensuous savoriness. Once molded by church dictates and puritanical mores, they assumed a secular and worldly air. For the poor and middling sectors of society, the sones, fandangos, jarabes, seguidillas, tiranas, and boleros, the popular dances, bespoke sensuality. Their music was in identical taste, while those who danced to its seductive rhythms wore colorful and provocative dresses. Never again were the dances or music of New Spain the same.

IV

Beneath the glitter lay the reality of colonialism. New Spain was a dependent society; foreign masters wielded the baton. Inside the structure of dependency was a social pyramid determined by both class and caste. At its top was a pampered elite, whose tastes were out of kilter with the rest of society, but not with the nature of New Spain, dubbed the "richest" country in the world by Humboldt. Only there was "a rich man truly a millionaire." At the other extreme lay a sprawling lower class, literally almost a caste. The elite was mainly fair of skin; the bottom, mostly dark. For the poor and the dark of skin, it was virtually impossible to climb the ladder.

New Spain was a country of inequality. Nowhere, admitted Humboldt, had he found such disparities in the "distribution of wealth . . . and levels of civilization." A minuscule elite possessed the good things in life; everyone else, far less. The very rich lived alongside of the very poor. Race and color of skin, not always one and the same, split society further. *Blancos* (whites) were better off than *morenos,* the dark of skin.

For the highborn, priggish behavior, stylized etiquette, and fancy clothes were a hallmark of society, especially in Mexico City, the hub of the good life for the "beautiful" people. In the countryside, the landed gentry, hacendados of Brahmin cast, put on airs on their baronial estates. Ostentatious displays of wealth were the norm. To baptize a godchild, one mining magnate in Dolores, a small town in Guanajuato, lavished 36,000 pesos; a rich tycoon hired a hundred coaches drawn by thoroughbred horses for the christening of his daughter; the funeral of a wealthy dignitary cost a lordly 89,000 pesos. When the daughter of a rich family took her final vows as a nun, she wore a velvet gown bedecked with dazzling jewels while a crown of flowers rested on her head.

Three types of people, by and large, made up society. *Peninsulares* and criollos ruled the roost; next followed the *castas,* primarily mestizos but also mulattoes; Indians (and blacks) sat at the bottom of the social scale. At baptism, an infant was placed into one of these categories. However, since racial miscegenation had cut a swath for three centuries, the dictators of social custom could not adopt an inflexible attitude toward race. After all, unless a recent immigrant from Spain, few could prove racial purity. Many Spaniards and criollos turned out to be mestizos, fair of skin and usually well-off, while mestizos and Indians, depending on their jobs and income, were confused. Mulattoes entered into this category; the less *negro* or *moreno,* the more acceptable. The rich and snobbish liked to divide people into just two categories: *la gente de razón,* the Hispanic community, as they titled themselves, and, on the other side, *los indios,* the poor and downtrodden.

Wealth of person or family, skin color, as well as ancestry decided place in society. Color, plainly, played a major role; whiteness of skin was a key to social status. But money "whitened" the skin, confirming one's *limpieza de sangre.* A hierarchical pyramid existed everywhere: for Spaniards, for criollos, for mestizos, and, as the experience of Yucatán demonstrates, for Indians. Spaniards, however, never overlooked class. Money, family tree, and color of skin dictated one's social pedigree. Not everyone in the elite was "lily white"; light-skinned mestizos, Spanish in appearance, and even mulattoes equally "passable," could be found at the top if they had money. The Spaniards, to underline once more, had established a pigmentocracy, with status based, to a large extent, on appearance. To be light of skin, a European characteristic, was a mark of honor and prestige; to be dark of skin, or *moreno,* was not.

Whites, whether *peninsulares,* criollos, or fair-skinned mestizos, were the "happy few." Without a close examination of racial pedigrees, they made up, at best, no more than one-fifth of the population. Of New Spain's 6.1 million inhabitants in 1810, just over 1 million were of the "white race." According to current estimates, New Spain had between 11,000 and 14,000 *peninsulares* and approximately 1 million criollos, dwelling mostly in Mexico City, Guadalajara, Valladolid, and Puebla.

Given these statistics, and the value attached to being of Spanish descent, one's racial classification acquired major importance. Everyone wanted to be white. In this classification charade, church and crown connived. The parish priest who kept the baptismal record had a special role to play because he decided one's family ancestry, a matter of life and death for citizens of New Spain. For a mestizo to be labeled Indian was the kiss of death, just as criollos dreaded being judged mestizos. What the priest decided was crucial since, at one stroke, he affirmed racial lineage as well as future social status. The wealthy and not-so-rich, therefore, relied on a judicious bribe or on friendship to guarantee that the priest ruled in the correct manner. Only moving to a distant town, where no one knew you, overcame the stigma of being born in the wrong category. With this attitude, many a person claiming Spanish descent was, undoubtedly, born of mestizo parents blessed with good social standing in their community and fair skin. Even Spanish authorities had caught on, employing, by 1800, legitimacy and status of family to classify race.

Strange phenomena sallied forth from this twisted and contorted universe. Here and there, mestizos infiltrated the ranks of the nobility. After 1750, the crown, in response to bountiful gifts, had bestowed titles of nobility upon their donors. All told, about fifty titles fell to the very wealthy of New Spain, usually that of *conde,* less frequently that of *marqués.* No fewer than ten mestizos possessed a noble title. They were, moreover, quite noble, alleging descent on their Indian side from Aztec emperors. One was the conde del Valle de Orizaba who inherited, he claimed, one of Moctezuma's fiefs. Of the others, thirty were criollos and twelve were Spaniards. At the same time, the bureaucrats who landed in Veracruz, appointees of the Bourbons, brought their Gallic airs, French servants, hairstylists, cooks, and valets, who introduced French bread, the custom of sipping coffee in sidewalk cafés, and Continental dress fashions.

A small clique of families, a de facto aristocracy, presided over the social pyramid. More criollo than not, it traced its origins to the sixteenth and seventeenth centuries. Entail, the passing on of property from family patriarch to eldest son, facilitated it. The laws of primogeniture bestowed preference on men, but women could inherit their father's property and titles of nobility. Of the Mexican peeresses, mostly criollas, five were unmarried, but the rest had married at least once. By the right of entail, women enjoyed full control of their property; only they could sell it. In 1800, the crown abrogated the right of entail, which had spawned this spurious colonial aristocracy.

The rich, allowing for an exception or two, were plutocrats, new millionaires. The marqués de Inguanzo, emblematic of the lot, landed in Veracruz late in the eighteenth century with 250,000 pesos in his pocketbook, not a trifling sum but neither monumental. He wooed and won the daughter of a Basque mineowner and became a millionaire with investments in cacao, cotton, cochineal, and the Manila Galleon. With their newfangled millions, these plutocrats purchased haciendas, which bestowed social éclat on them. For some, the expulsion of the Jesuits proved to be a gold mine. The conde de Regla, for one, acquired 20 of the 119 Jesuit haciendas sold by crown edict.

This highly stratified society had experienced a population explosion, increasing, between 1742 and 1810, from 4.5 million to over 6.1 million. Indians and mestizos, the bottom rung of the ladder, had multiplied the most. Mestizos, including other *castas,* numbered 1.3 million, the second-largest group in New Spain, and increasingly numerous in Nuevo Santander, Durango, Coahuila, Zacatecas, Sonora, and New Mexico. Except in the south, they were the principal source of labor in the cities and countryside. Indians, the biggest category, numbered approximately 3 million, nearly half of New Spain's inhabitants. Overwhelmingly numerous in Yucatán, Chiapas, and Oaxaca, they were the majority in Puebla, Veracruz, Tlaxcala, and Mexico.

Mulattoes, including a tiny band of *negros,* stood, more or less, apart. Although like Spaniards, criollos and mestizos labeled *gente de razón,* they had to pay tribute to the crown. Black "blood," as it was popularly referred to, still bore the stigma of slavery. Mulattoes could not aspire to municipal office or, theoretically, take clerical vows. *Negros* and *mulatos* inhabited mostly the coastal belts of Veracruz and Guerrero, where the labor of sugar plantations settled them. But they were also inland, tilling the soil of sugar plantations about La Barca, in Jalisco, and in Michoacán, specifically in Zamora, Jacona, and San Juan Guaracha, a big sugar plantation on the road to Jiquilpan, where they were known as *guaracheños.* Some lived in the cities or in the northern mining towns.

Along with demographic change appeared an urban explosion. The colonies of Spain were highly urbanized; nowhere else had cities and towns grown so rapidly. In 1810, the Spanish colonies had forty-one cities of over twenty thousand inhabitants, eight of them in New Spain. With Guanajuato, León, and Querétaro, the Bajío was overflowing with people, the most urban of the regions. New Spain, nevertheless, was still predominantly rural; less than one-tenth of its population resided in cities and towns. However, nearly all of the urban growth had come from rural flight to the cities.

Urbanization notwithstanding, the status of women had changed little since earlier days. As before, life for women revolved around marriage and the family. The social order was patriarchal, the father controlling all material goods and seeing to it that his family upheld his honor and social status, which required that women not bring shame upon him. Until the age of twenty-five, for instance, daughters and sons could not marry without parental permission. Spanish legislation, by the same token, looked upon women as minors, legally and economically dependent on father or husband. Not all women, though, fell into this trap, as the story of Juana López, a native of Santa Fe, New Mexico, illustrates vividly. Accused of adultery by her husband, a mortal sin in the eyes of colonial men, she told the judge "it was her ass, she controlled it, and she would give it to whomever she wanted."

Women, moreover, were entering the labor force. Yet, for women of the better-off families, work outside of the home was a taboo, even doing domestic chores, which were best left to Indian servant girls. This was the world eulogized by José Joaquín Fernández de Lizardi, author of the justly famous *El periquillo sarniento,* a story about the society of the times. For Fernández de Lizardi and like-minded males, a woman's place was in the home, where she had to do man's bidding. Some urban women, all the same, were receiving more schooling. If young and single women of families of middling status had a job, they were usually teachers. This, nonetheless, was not the norm among campesinas, who, as formerly, did the work of home and field, nor among the urban poor, where women, more and more, found jobs in *obrajes* turning out textiles, cigarettes, and cigars. For its part, the crown, seeking to encourage the employment of women, had abolished guild restrictions against them late in the eighteenth century. Another ruling stipulated that guilds could not prevent women from being "taught all those labors appropriate to their sex," a decree brought about by the widow Josefa de Celis, a native of Mexico City, who had complained to the viceroy that the Embroiderers' Guild had prevented her from selling shoe uppers, upon which she relied for her livelihood.

In courtship, criollas had a special role. Nearly all white females in New Spain were criollas, with the exception of fair-skinned mestizas, far more Spanish than Indian who were coveted as wives by criollos and *peninsulares* alike, especially if they were from well-off families. Marriage in New Spain, nonetheless, rarely broke down social barriers, as statistics bore out; seven of every ten marriages occurred within the same category of society, seldom between "classes." Spaniards and criollos usually married one another. When mixed marriages occurred, they did not stray far afield. Spaniards married mestizas; mulatto men chose Indians; and mestizos picked Spaniards, criollas, or Indians. Rarely did Spaniards choose *mulatas* for wives, while better-off *mulatos* preferred Indian women over *mulatas.* Both *peninsulares* and mestizos rated Indian women above *mulatas.* All things being equal, to marry up was to marry a fair-skinned individual.

Women, regardless of social class or pigmentation, were rarely encouraged to educate themselves. Few men put much stock in the education of women. It was enough, wrote a colonial savant, that women know how to take care of kitchen, home, and family. Rare were the schools for women. When they existed—the Colegio de las Vizcaínas, for instance—they taught their girls useful knowledge: how to manage the household. Only occasionally did schools for girls deviate from this model; in Guadalajara, the Colegio de San Juan de la Penitencia was one such institution. Its curriculum had courses in reading, writing, and arithmetic, as well as in Christian doctrine. More typical of the church schools were others in Guadalajara which taught the three R's but insisted that girls learn how to sew, weave, and embroider, skills more "useful" to them. Demanding payment of tuition, the schools, unmistakably, were for the daughters of the wealthy.

Nothing expressed better the nature of this disparate society than *El periquillo sarniento,* an immensely popular picaresque novel published in 1816. In this masterpiece of social satire, Fernández de Lizardi, a criollo, held up to the light a society corrupted by diverse maladies. He wrote of hypocrisy, of women who worshiped God but sinned in his name; of dissolute priests who stole from their parishioners; of bungling physicians; of thieving notaries, court reporters, and attorneys-at-law; and of usurious merchants. A class novel, it was written for an upper-class public, primarily criollo, to remind it of its faults: for individuals, Fernández de Lizardi believed, able to learn from his advice. The principal character, Pedro the *picaro,* boasts, according to his criollo pretensions, that he was the son of "parents of pure blood"—of Spaniards, that is—a revealing insight into the criollo's feelings of inferiority. Fernández de Lizardi saved his harshest fulminations for the indigent, usually dark of skin and of mixed blood, blaming their condition on indolence; they bathed rarely, wore dirty and tattered rags, and smelled to high heaven.

But its author, a journalist by trade, sat on the horns of a dilemma; he yearned to cure the sores of society without altering its fabric. While shocked by its ills, he exalted it, for the simple reason that, warts and all, it opened doors to the criollo. Attacking it undermined the foundation of criollo accomplishments. Instead of indulging in the fantasy of making a fortune in New Spain and retiring to the mother country, a typical pipe dream of creoles, Fernández de Lizardi wished very much for them to stay home.

V

An apple of discord dangled from the tree in this New World. Colonials lived off exports to Spain of silver and, to a lesser extent, of cochineal, indigo, sugar, and coffee, a system that rewarded handsomely those who financed their production and sale. Two groups profited. The big importers, allied to the mining moguls either by loans or by their ownership of mines, were mostly *peninsulares.* Mineowners, *peninsulares* as well as criollos, also fared well. Both groups tended to identify their welfare with the mother country. On relations with Spain, the criollo mining barons of Guanajuato, like their *peninsular* counterparts in Zacatecas, along with the powerful merchants, thought more or less the same. At the pinnacle of the economic ladder, therefore, talk of an ethnic split between criollos and *peninsulares* largely misses the mark. Much of the time, economic interests usually united criollos and *peninsulares.*

Of the millionaire families, half were criollo. At this level, marriages between Spanish men and criollo women, a fact of daily life, tended, to cite Francisco Javier Clavijero, to erode strife. Whether *peninsulares* or criollos, elites got along splendidly. In their social circle, wealth and not just place of birth counted. To quote a criollo plutocrat from Guanajuato, "these abominable distinctions between criollo and *gachupines* (Spaniards) . . . were never the rule among the noble, cultivated and distinguished families of this city." The *gachupines* married "our daughters and sisters," and, he added, "they were our good friends and we did business with them."

All was not, just the same, sweetness and light. Regardless of the testimony of the gentleman from Guanajuato, *peninsular* and criollo did not always see eye to eye. Their antagonism sprang from complex causes. Clavijero to the contrary, marriages of Spaniards to criollas, no matter how idyllic the union, failed to lessen the antagonism. Quite the opposite: they increased it. Spanish immigrants, for example, usually had first pick of the wealthiest and most beautiful criollas, to the anger of gentlemen born in the colony. Criollo nobles, most often than not, chose Spaniards for the husbands of their daughters. Of the thirty-four daughters of nobles, twenty-three married *peninsulares,* only eleven their own kind. Females of the colonial nobility preferred Spanish men; the marquesa de Aguaya, to mention one, married three; the second condesa de Cortina, two. Whether rich or impecunious, many a Spaniard titled himself *don* (squire), and made his snobbish pretensions stick.

Colonial administration was another sore point. The most prestigious jobs in colonial government, military, and church went to Spaniards. They were the viceroys, archbishops, bishops, and *gobernadores,* as well as their many hangers-on, the personal secretary and first secretary; the chief judge of the audiencia and most of the *oidores;* the attorneys general; the justices of the peace; the head of the bureau of mining; and the hospodar of *alcabalas.* From the perspective of the criollos, a European clique ran New Spain for its own benefit.

The bitterest criollos could be found in what, loosely defined, might be labeled an embryonic middle class. At this stage, a middle class, fully aware of its niche in society, had yet to form. But economic growth, the expansion of internal markets, urbanization, and the exploding bureaucracy had stimulated the development of an inchoate or runt "middle class," which included journalists, lawyers, bureaucrats, notaries, military officers, teachers, storekeepers, master craftsmen, rancheros, and large numbers of lower and middle clergy from the provinces. More recruits appeared with the trade reforms of the eighteenth century when new merchants made their debut, especially in the provincial cities and towns. They included distillers of alcoholic beverages, manufacturers of playing cards, dealers in contraband, and their ilk, all of whom carried on their business behind closed doors.

No matter how well educated, these criollos found the doors to high public office closed to them. Their education yielded limited benefits, which explains why so many of them took up the arts and the intellectual life. Still, many of them occupied minor public posts and, occasionally, even judgeships on the audiencia. In the provincial cities, they were the lesser judges and administrative clerks and occupied the smaller parishes. This incipient "middle class," essentially criollo, was a *don nadie,* a nobody, lacking real political and social clout. To cure their misfortune, its members looked to a future in which no *peninsulares* blocked their path. They aspired to be masters of their own house, to rule New Spain as they saw fit, tired of watching generations of *peninsulares* disembark at Veracruz to occupy the top rungs of politics and society.

Despite their complaints, they had no stomach for radical change, aspiring simply to replace the *peninsulares.* Social engineering of help to downtrodden Indians and mestizos frightened them. After all, everything considered, they were not badly off. Yet for ambitious criollos this was not enough. They hungered for a bigger slice of the pie, hiding their ambitions under the cloak of the Enlightenment. Behind the rhetoric, the criollo pressed for personal advantages. What criollo *letrados,* the university educated, coveted most was a job in state or church, as Melchor Talamantes, one of their priests made abundantly clear when, in 1808, he sided with the plot in Mexico City to curtail *gachupín* rule. In his often quoted *Representación en favor de los humildes* (1771), José González Castañeda, a criollo regidor of the ayuntamiento of Mexico City, phrased it well: end our exclusion from public office. Appealing to the laws of Castilla and the dictums of the Council of Trent, he demanded that criollos be given preference, asking that public posts be denied Spaniards and referring to them as foreign immigrants. For the criollo, the *peninsular,* more and more, was the adversary. In his declaration of 1810, which ignited the Wars of Independence, Father Manuel Hidalgo y Costilla, a criollo himself, accused the *peninsulares* of being "expatriates who forsook home and abandoned their fathers, brothers, sisters, and children." Why? Their motive, Hidalgo held, was "sordid avarice." Money was their "god."

Nationalism, adolescent and half-baked, burst forth from this unripe, "middle class" of criollos. Until its coalescense, nationalism was merely an esprit de corps of group or community. By the turn of the century, changing conditions had spurred the formation of a sector with common bonds, aspirations, and a dim awareness of its place in society. To shake off their subordinate status, its members concluded, New Spain must emancipate itself from outside tutelage. Overall, criollos constituted this incipient, "nationalistic middle class," the enemy of the *gachupín.*

VI

Regardless of the importance of mining, agriculture held center stage in New Spain, yielding over half of the value of colonial production. Most colonials, directly or not, tilled the soil for a living, a minority on lands of its own, and the rest as wageworkers. In Guanajuato, the richest mining province, nearly half of the labor force was in agriculture, less than one-tenth in the mines.

Not all tillers of the soil benefited. Commercial agriculture, a phenomenon of the late colonial years, received priority. By 1800, many a hacienda had undergone a transformation, becoming a commercial enterprise of, more or less, capitalist bent. Most hacendados were criollos. Along with wealthy merchants and mining barons, they were the colonial *burguesía,* a class wedded firmly to the ideal of private property. At the bottom of the ladder was subsistence farming, the *ejido* of the pueblos or the milpas of Yucatán. Wedged in between haciendas and ejidos was the rancho, usually belonging to a mestizo; the ranchero, its owner, tilled lands of modest size, marketed a part of his harvest, and raised a few horses, cows, pigs, and chickens.

Agricultural growth was uneven. The Bajío, Jalisco, and Michoacán prospered. No region challenged the Bajío, the chief granary of New Spain, for supremacy. The Bajío, Jalisco, and Michoacán had over 1,200 of the 5,000 haciendas in New Spain and 6,635 ranchos, home to a budding rural "middle class." Corn, wheat, barley, cotton, beans, chilies, and lentils headed the list of crops cultivated, while production also included aguardiente and mescal, a liquor distilled from the agave plant. Veracruz, on the Gulf of Mexico, produced grains, sugar, and vanilla, as well as beef. Except for Yucatán's sugar and henequen, more and more important, and the cochineal of Oaxaca, the principal agricultural export of New Spain, most of what southerners raised was consumed locally. Large haciendas, the property of absentee landlords, and the Indian ejido and milpa, existed side by side. Mestizo rancheros were rare.

Cattle ranching and, here and there, farming had invaded Sonora, Chihuahua, Coahuila, and Nuevo León. Beef on the hoof, but also salted, cattle hides, and wool from sheep were the principal products. The long drives of sheep from Coahuila, Durango, San Luis Potosí, and Zacatecas to Mexico City, the southern marketplace, took months, countless sheep dying on the way. Ranchos and haciendas to feed mining camps dotted fertile valleys, giving origin to such towns as Arizpe, in Sonora, and San Bartolomé (now El Valle de Allende), in Chihuahua, the breadbasket for Parral. On this frontier, life was a daily struggle with barren terrain and, time and again, hostile Indians. Sonora and Chihuahua, provinces rich in silver, lay underpopulated primarily because of the Apaches.

Almost nothing, moreover, had been done to upgrade technology. Only in the sugar belt of Morelos had hacendados made efforts to introduce modern techniques. Elsewhere, most hacendados and rancheros relied on teams of oxen to pull wooden plows, seldom constructing reservoirs to store water, digging irrigation ditches, or fertilizing the soil. On the Indian ejidos and milpas, the planting stick and slash-and-burn agriculture prevailed. As a result, agricultural productivity did not match population growth.

In addition, haciendas producing for domestic markets usually failed to show a profit. The problem lay in the nature of their markets; because of the lack of a national system of roads, the hacienda had a local or, at best, regional outlet. The hacendado limited production to nearby markets, obeying the dictates of the law of supply and demand. Confronted with small markets, he relied on cheap labor for his profits. What he feared most were years of overproduction, when his competitors, rancheros usually, harvested more than the market could consume. To circumvent this, the hacendado held his surplus grains off the market until their price rose. He had no need to make his hacienda more productive. By manipulating prices, the hacendado drove out his competitors, often buying them out. The more land he owned, the fewer rivals farmed. The fewer his competitors, the more his customers.

Economic reality dictated the hacendado's behavior. Limited markets, for instance, tell us why he left so much of his land lie fallow. Cultural traits, Spanish values, and arguments of that sort fail to explain the hacienda's fabled inefficiency. This, too, makes clear why the hacendado seemed to lack a keen business sense or, as some believe, a capitalist mentality. Fully aware of market realities, many a hacendado simply wanted to stay out of the red; so long as his budget showed a surplus, he was satisfied.

The hacendado's dilemma also helps us to understand his reliance on debt peonage. By 1810, about one-fourth of the rural population dwelt on haciendas. In the Bajío, for instance, half of the rural inhabitants called the hacienda home. The system had firm roots in the Valley of Mexico, Puebla, Tlaxcala, and, increasingly, Yucatán. At least a third of the men in rural Mexico worked part of each year for the hacendado, mostly residents of pueblos with plots of land too small for them to keep body and soul together.

Mother Nature exacerbated the food picture. Tláloc was a flighty rain god; farmers could rarely count on his benevolence, even in the Bajío. Years of crop scarcities followed on the heels of times of abundance. The consumer carried the burden. Population growth during the eighteenth century aggravated his plight; there were more mouths to feed and less food, which cost more. Cycles of poor harvests befell New Spain again and again. The "year of hunger," that of 1785–86, caused the most severe shortages of corn in history, but also dealt roughly with the harvests of beans and wheat in the Bajío. To quote one witness, "no calamity escaped the poor." Manuel Hildalgo y Costilla, the patriot priest, led efforts to mitigate the ills of hunger from his parish in the Bajío. Students of colonial history believe that the "year of hunger" upset permanently the relative parity between food prices and income. The cost of food was never normal again. The droughts of 1801–02 and 1808–10 simply worsened the situation.

Poor harvests had multiple effects. When the price of corn shot up, the poor ate less well and, because of bad diets, succumbed to epidemics that killed the weak, old, and very young. Lacking water for their crops, many campesinos sold their barnyard animals, abandoned their lands, and migrated to the cities to look for work. Without corn to feed mules, mines could not operate, a turnabout that led to their closing and to jobless miners. Inflation in the northern mining camps, far worse than anywhere else, more than quadrupled the price of corn. During the late colonial years, the poor in such places as the Bajío were jobless and hungry, while hacendados reaped a bounty selling scarce grains at exorbitant prices. Their profits were the highest on record. The resulting tensions shook society.

With the expansion of the hacienda and the growth of the population, the situation in the countryside turned ugly. Between 1750 and 1800, the numbers of rural communities multiplied by 44 percent. This population upsurge placed new pressures on the land. But, again and again, hacendados possessed more land, which they tilled increasingly themselves, thus undercutting the role of sharecroppers and tenant farmers, formerly a mainstay of agriculture. More country folk were jobless, and more vagrants wandered about.

These developments hit the Indian pueblo especially hard in central Mexico, where they represented 62.5 percent of the population. The numerical growth of mestizos exacerbated their situation. Hungry for soil to call his own, the mestizo, time and time again, encroached on Indian lands. Pressure for land, often disputes over boundaries, led to chronic violence in the countryside. Virtually "all of the lands," reported one witness, "were controlled by whites." When Indians possessed land, they cultivated tiny, waterless plots and labored seasonally for nearby hacendados. The expansion of the hacienda, the Indian knew by experience, had come at the expense of their ejidos. Conversely, for hacendados, the swelling rolls of the landless offered a plentiful supply of cheap labor.

This lopsided picture of landownership eventually drew censure. Even before the tragedy of the "year of hunger," Juan Agustín Morfi, a Franciscan, had called attention to the unequal distribution of land in Querétaro and Guanajuato, provinces of the Bajío, explaining how that hurt the Indian pueblo. The catastrophe of 1785–86 swelled the anger of dissidents, among them merchants and mineowners who blamed monopolistic hacendados for the scarcity of corn. Even the conde de Revilla Gigedo, the viceroy of New Spain, lashed out in 1791 and 1793 at the evils of monopolistic landlords, not only hacendados but clergy. In 1799, Manuel Abad y Queipo, bishop of Michoacán, claimed that a minority of Spaniards owned most of the property and wealth of New Spain. He urged legislation to curb this ill, going so far as to ask for the subdivision of public lands among landless Indians and mestizos. A man of capitalist ideals, he also wanted to subdivide communal lands into private property. Carlos María de Bustamante, editor of *El Diario,* denounced "cruel monopolists who took advantage of crop scarcities to fatten their coffers with the blood of the destitute." To Bustamante and his cohorts, the monopoly of land aggravated the problems of New Spain, creating food shortages and high prices. Like Abad y Queipo, Bustamante wanted public lands distributed among Indians, mestizos, and, interestingly, impoverished Spaniards.

None of these critics, least of all Abad y Queipo, longed for an attack on the lands of the hacienda itself; private property was sacred. Abad y Queipo and his kind yearned, primarily, to make agriculture more efficient and to eliminate the ward status of the Indians, which they believed responsible for their backwardness. They dreamed of Indians incorporated into Western civilization; the problem was the Indian and the way he thought, not the hacienda. The hacendados, however, put the blame on others, the "lazy" Indian, to start with, reserving their most strident criticism for crown policy; what ailed agriculture were tariffs, *alcabalas,* and meddling bureacrats.

VII

New Spain, additionally, had little industry. Colonial manufacturing transformed a few agricultural and pastoral products, primarily into cotton and wool cloth, leather, soap, and candles. The weaving of cloth, the chief industry, took place in *obrajes,* mainly clustered in the Valley of Mexico, the Bajío, and the Puebla-Tlaxcala basin, quasi-capitalist institutions having little in common with the mechanized textile mills of England. By 1810, the making of textiles, nonetheless, employed sixty thousand workers, while, except for the rich, at least two-thirds of the inhabitants of New Spain wore clothing of domestic cloth, some of them living as far away as Sonora and Coahuila.

Crown policy opposed the development of industries that competed with Spanish manufactures. Silk, wine, and olive oil were three of them. To cite José de Gálvez, entrusted with enforcing crown dictates, "It behooved Spain not to permit colonials to live independently of it." One of his decisions led him to establish a royal tobacco monopoly. Wise in the ways of the law, Gálvez had forgotten how colonists looked on legislation deemed foolish by them. *Obedezco pero no cumplo* (I obey but I won't do it). Restrictions on the cultivation of wine grapes, for example, were mainly ignored. In provinces such as Aguascalientes, where grapes thrived, their cultivation went on unabated. Most residents of the city of Aguascalientes, the hub of the province, either made wine or sold it. They also produced, clandestinely, of course, *chinguirito,* a grape aguardiente, its alcohol level enriched by the addition of *piloncillo de cana,* unrefined brown sugar. This activity, according to the law, was illegal. Yet, in 1784, when authorities searched households in the city of Aguascalientes, they found that even the wealthy made *chinguirito.* The chief culprits were unmarried women who sold it for money to buy food to feed themselves and their families.

Spanish failure invited foreigners, mostly the English and the Dutch, to plug the gap between colonial demand and the inadequate supply. In 1800, foreigners continued to monopolize much of the commerce with the Spanish colonies. After the War of the Spanish Succession (1713), the English, who triumphed in this imperialistic venture, had forced Spain to allow them to sell African slaves in the colonies and the goods of one merchant ship a year at the Porto Belo fair. Later, they compelled Spain to accept English commercial agents in the ports and cities of New Spain. Also, contraband trade flourished, above all between the Caribbean colonies of England, France, and Holland, on the one side, and, on the other, New Spain. The English especially reaped a bountiful harvest. When their country went to war with France and its Spanish puppet, ships from the United States transported goods to New World colonists, while Americans set themselves up as commercial agents in the leading ports and cities. In New Mexico, they ferried goods into Santa Fe and from there to Chihuahua. Spain's inability to supply its colonists, and its unwillingness to permit their industries, transformed New Spain's markets into virtual bordellos, with foreigners coming and going at their whim; the colonists, like ladies of ill fame, welcomed them with open arms.

VIII

Indians, as the picture of landownership testifies, bore the brunt of colonialism. Wherever the opportunity presented itself, the Indian was exploited ruthlessly. Authorities could jail him for failure to pay tribute or for disobeying his employer, while the expenses of religious festivals, which many clerics encouraged, kept him in debt. Indian schools, like that of the Colegio de Santa Cruz, dropped out of favor. Indians, similarly, must be "Hispanized"; now the goal was to eradicate the Indian languages, no matter what the cultural cost. Until late in the colonial era, the church even denied the Indian entrance into the priesthood. Exceptions were made merely for those able to verify descent from the native nobility, so they were never more than a handful. One or two of them scaled the ladder of clerical success. Most occupied out-of-the-way curacies or none at all. They were ordained *de idioma,* certified ready to minister in an Indian language, in the opinion of criollo priests good at languages but ignorant of theology and canon law and thus unworthy of promotion. Lamentably, too, by the time they wore the robes of a priest, they were not truly Indian, believing themselves socially superior.

Many an Indian family and community, just the same, somehow weathered much of the storm. Their resiliency astonished their exploiters, whether Spaniards, criollos, or mestizos. Fighting to protect themselves, Indians took shelter behind their customs and traditions, relying on language and isolation to bar the enemy from their doorstep. In this struggle, Indian women emerged as pillars of strength, passing on to their offspring the languages and beliefs of yesteryear. Priests baptized Indians but were unable to stop them from elaborating Spanish Catholicism in their own terms. Indians, not uncommonly, proved adept at manipulating Spanish law.

The Indian, moreover, did not accept his plight docilely. As before, he rebelled, particularly after secular authorities during the eighteenth century tried to jettison the religious rites of his community. Disciples of the Enlightenment, the Bourbons looked askance at the mixture of Christian and pagan practices of Indian communities, including Virgins that appeared miraculously on rocky hillsides. Higher clerical fees touched off all but eight of the more than thirty uprisings against priests in Oaxaca and central Mexico. By the close of the colonial era, a burial cost as much as 56 reales, marriages up to 64 reales, and a mass sung 80 reales. There were clergy who demanded money for confession. An Indian labored all day for less than a real. The Tzeltal revolt of 1712, in Cancuc, Chiapas, erupted when María de la Candelaria, a young woman, saw a Virgin who asked for her own kingdom. The local bishop, along with encomenderos and regidores of the ayuntamiento, had exploited unmercifully the Tzeltals of Cancuc. The rebellion of the Maya of Yucatán in 1761, led by Jacinto Canek, sent shivers of fear into the hearts of Spaniards. Women often played major roles in these uprisings. What José Vasconcelos labeled "the peace of the grace" hardly meant that Indians turned the other cheek.

All things considered, the fate of the non-Indian poor was not really any better. Of the slightly more than five hundred thousand city dwellers, half were wage laborers trying to make ends meet on a paltry wage. The agricultural crises of the late eighteenth century aggravated their plight. Not only did food prices climb; the workers faced growing competition for jobs from Indian and mestizo campesinos, the victims of the droughts, who flocked to the cities to look for work. Hordes of the hungry and jobless became beggars, vagrants, and léperos, the wretched of the earth. These invasions occurred especially in Guanajuato and Celaya, bastions of the Bajío, but also in Valladolid and Guadalajara. Humboldt reported seeing thousands of vagrants in Mexico City, where they slept in doorways and congregated in the plazas and sidewalks during the day. Trying to stop the influx of vagrants, the popular term for the destitute, officials banned begging in the cities of New Spain.

For most types of skilled or semiskilled labor in city or countryside, wages had stagnated, above all after 1760. In the cities, workers earned between three and nine pesos a month, with the textile industry and construction, for example, paying six pesos. By comparison, in agriculture, which employed about 80 percent of the labor force, most workers earned five pesos a month. Inflation, a blight on the colonial economy, cut real wages in half. The drop in the peso's value was most dramatic in the last quarter of the century, largely because of a rise in the cost of consumer goods; food prices, for example, had virtually doubled by 1810.

Year	*Total Population*	*Per Capita Income*
1742	3.6 million	30 pesos
1793	5.2 million	41 pesos
1806	6.1 million	28 pesos

Meanwhile, the distribution of income grew more unequal. The rich were richer, and the poor were poorer. Widespread impoverishment, the handiwork of listless wages and exploding inflation, partly explains the enthusiasm of the poor in the Bajío for the authors of Independence.

In 1789, Hipólito Villaroel, a lawyer, published his *Enfermedades políticas,* a perceptive study of what afflicted New Spain. A self-serving bigot, he showed no mercy for jobless Indians, mestizos, and mulattoes, whom he stigmatized as "repugnant and malicious," saying they should be made to work by the lash of a whip. But this man who judged the poor harshly had to acknowledge that unbridled wealth and dire misery existed side by side. Some forty thousand persons, he asserted, had flocked to Mexico City to seek work. Corruption, like "a spreading cancer," was everywhere; no segment of society escaped its consequences, hobbling clergy, public officials, police, and merchants alike.

That Villaroel spoke the truth, colonial reality corroborated. Testifying to the omnipotence of corruption, José de Iturrigaray, viceroy from 1803 to 1808, parlayed his authority over mining into a lucrative business for himself. In return for bribes (Mexicans refer to them as *mordidas*), he sold extra amounts of mercury in short supply to mineowners. Educated criollos, the *licenciados* of their day, employed public office for private gain. Similarly, the quest for a public job was a national disease.

Geographically, New Spain, in spite of three hundred years of colonial rule, was disunited; regionalism prevailed everywhere. One reason was the absence of roads. Passable ones going north from Mexico City could be found only because merchants, hacendados, mineowners, and, occasionally, ayuntamientos built them. The transport of heavy or bulky goods was costly and slow, while travelers rode horse or mule or, if poor, walked. Bandits infested the routes, making travel risky and, at times, downright dangerous, and preyed on haciendas, mines, and towns. So bad was banditry that authorities, believing stiff punishment a remedy, ordered, in 1699, that culprits caught lose a hand or foot; when that failed to stop them, a law passed in 1719 decreed the death penalty. Neither ended thievery.

7

UPSHOT OF REFORM

I

In 1774, when Edmund Burke, the conservative thinker and orator, addressed the British parliament on the eve of the rebellion of the Thirteen colonies, he urged its members to reflect on "how you are to govern a people who think they ought to be free, and think they are not." To tax the colonists, what parliament had in mind, he warned, would yield "nothing but discontent, disorder, disobedience." The Bourbon rulers of late eighteenth-century Spain would have done well to listen to Burke because they, too, aspired to transform colonial relationships in the New World. More than the British, furthermore, they had ample justification for wanting to alter them.

When the imbecile Charles II, the last of the Hapsburg monarchs, died in 1700, Spain was but a shell of its magisterial self. Wracked by foreign wars and domestic wrangling, Spain had become the laughing stock of Europe. Its treasury was bare, industry and agriculture had fallen on hard times, while foreigners, mainly English merchants, profited daily from their illegal trade with Spain's colonies. Just one third of the silver taken from the New World ended up in Spanish chests. In the meantime, a regressive tax system, parasitic corporations, and archaic attitudes crippled the colonial economy.

During the eighteenth century, the Bourbons, despots of the Age of the Enlightenment, tried valiantly, particularly between 1759 and 1788, the reign of Charles III, to turn things around. Their reforms, which initiated the shift to laissez-faire economic policies, partly restored Spain's princely grandeur, helped revive the sputtering economy and brought its colonies to heel but, just the same, left old ills undisturbed. Specifically, the Bourbon reforms, a hodgepodge of decrees, attempted to rebuild Spain's military prowess, win back colonial trade, fix anew royal supremacy over New Spain's politicos and corporations, above all the monopolistic merchants of Mexico City and Sevilla, and discipline the wealthy Church. Placing the unpredictable mining industry on more solid footing was a major goal. Success followed the reforms. By 1810, to document it, more royal taxes were being collected. However, the upshot of reform, as Burke had earlier warned his English colleagues, set afire colonial unrest.

II

The bible for the reforms was Jose del Campillo's *Nuevo sistema de gobierno economico para la America* of 1743, which condemned the low yields from the New World, contrasting them with the profits France and England obtained from their Caribbean colonies. Campillo, Felipe V's minister of the Indies, urged the adoption of a *gobierno economico,* business-like administration, Jean-Baptiste Colbert's mercantilistic French formula. For more efficient colonial administration, he urged organizing *intendencias,* political demarcations dependent directly on royal authority. Campillo's ideas, with the end of the old monopolies in mind, struck at the privileges the Hapsburgs had conferred on groups and corporations in the New World.

The reforms advocated by Campillo were entrusted to Jóse de Gálvez, one of the most remarkable Spanish officials sent over to New Spain. Intelligent and dynamic, and not one to bow before critics, Gálvez arrived in New Spain as *visitador general* in 1767, returning home in 1772 to oversee the reforms he helped implant as minister for the Indies. During his sojourn in New Spain, he helped ferret out, his apologists say, the "innumerable abuses" which had developed during "two centuries of administrative decay." Nothing, it appears, escaped his attention; for example, he even granted pardons to the Seris and Pimas, Indians of far-off Sonora, for all past offenses, assuring them of kind treatment in the future. Two able viceroys, Carlos Francisco de Croix and Antonio María de Bucareli, who overlapped with his visit, made his task less difficult.

Even before Gálvez, Spanish authorities had started to correct the old trade picture. To recover colonial commerce for Spain, its officials permitted, in 1702, two ships a year to sail from Manila, capital of the Philippine colony, to Acapulco, twice the number of former trips. Then in 1717, Cádiz, replacing Sevilla, became the port of fleets sailing westward. In 1740, authorities suspended temporarily the fleet system and, half a century afterward, discarded it, abolishing the trading monopolies of Veracruz and Acapulco. In 1790, the Casa de Contratación, the centerpiece of the old monopolies, was set aside. With these changes, Spanish merchants could ship goods to the New World whenever they felt it was profitable.

As expected, the collapse of the monopolies upset the plans of old-line merchants. The Mexico City Consulado de Comerciantes, a kind of chamber of commerce, had grown rich since 1592 collaborating with its cohorts in

Spain. The merchants of the Consulado were the only ones who could buy in quantity the articles shipped either to Veracruz or to Acapulco, being able to pay the prices at the fairs for the goods unloaded by the fleet. They purchased up to 80 percent of the articles from Europe and Asia.

The merchants, then, sold the goods either through their stores or, occasionally, to retailers in the provinces. More likely than not, the Mexico City entrepreneurs bypassed the provincial merchants, selling their wares directly in the commercial fairs of such places as San Juan de los Lagos and Saltillo, towns in Jalisco and Coahuila. What they failed to sell, they stored in warehouses in Mexico City, to await the day when demand overtook supply. The Mexico City monopolists established branches in the provinces, above all in the mining towns. No matter how they disposed of their goods, the consumer, the victim, paid through the nose. Early on, merchants had suborned corregidores and *alcalde mayores,* the bureaucrats who managed affairs in the provinces. Without a salary to speak of and, at times, having to buy their posts, the *corregidores de indios* had become agents for the distribution of goods of the monopolists in Mexico City, doing it for a share of the profits. As middlemen, they developed a stake in keeping the market to themselves. Given this state of affairs, the Indian fell victim to both corregidor and Mexico City merchant.

That was but one aspect of the commercial pyramid. Additionally, the rich merchants became, in the course of events, the chief exporters; with their money, they bought hides, tobacco, cochineal, indigo, vanilla, cacao, sugar, cotton, and silver for sale abroad. Amassing profits from the sale of imported articles and exports, the merchants, ultimately, had sufficient money to lend at interest to miners, farmers, *obrajeros* (owners of *obrajes*), artisans, and lesser merchants. As a *consulado,* or corporation, furthermore, the merchants enjoyed special privileges, one being their own tribunal.

Not content with their monopolistic business, they played Juliet to the Spanish Romeo. Allies of their associates in Spain, they saw no harm in obeying Spanish dictates in the New World. If Spanish merchants frowned on competitors, their partners in New Spain discouraged local manufacturing. During their monopolistic reign, they helped suppress the nascent silk industry, worked incessantly to block the expansion of *obrajes,* and, gleefully, declared war on merchant rivals of Sevilla and Cádiz.

The reforms of the Bourbons, their proponents predicted, would eliminate the worst of these abuses. They were only partly correct. The reforms encouraged a kind of free trade within the Spanish Empire, but with limits set on what the colonies could produce. The limited free trade sufficed to break up the monopoly of the Mexico City Consulado, spurring an economic boom and the appearance of rival merchants in the provincial cities, among them Guadalajara, which began to thrive after 1760, its population jumping from 11,000 to 35,000 by 1803. Population growth reflected the new role of Guadalajara as a commercial and political entrepôt, evident in the importance of the audiencia of Nueva Galicia. Roads to Durango, Sinaloa, and Sonora started from Guadalajara. The capital of a province famous for its wheat, hides, and leather, Guadalajara added the manufacture of cotton and woolen cloth to its assets. Its first textile *obraje* was established in 1776. In 1792, the University of Guadalajara was founded, over the objections of academics in Mexico City. The Real Consulado de Comerciantes de Guadalajara signaled the coming of age of its merchants. Partly thanks to the trade reforms, Guadalajara evolved into the commercial hub of the Bajío, drawing into its vortex the towns of San Juan de los Lagos, La Piedad, Irapuato, and Celaya, as well as the Pacific port of San Blas, from where merchant ships set sail for Sonora and California.

The end of trade restrictions, however, failed to shatter the predominance of the *peninsulares* in commerce. From the days of the Consulado, they had, so to speak, kept it in the family. Rarely did their criollo progeny follow in their footsteps, more often than not going off to study law or medicine or take the vows of a priest. Only tardily, after *consulados* had been established in Veracruz, Guadalajara, Puebla, and one more in Mexico City, did criollos start timidly to enter commerce.

Traditionally, the merchant hired a young Spaniard, probably just off the ship. Not uncommonly, he might be a nephew. If the merchant had a daughter, he tried to marry her off to the younger man. In time, the son-in-law, whether a relative or not, inherited the business. The widow of a Spanish merchant very likely married her husband's cashier. And so it went, with the result that only a scattering of criollos, and certainly no more than a handful of mestizos, became merchant kings, usually in the provincial cities. Spaniards, it appears, had commerce in their blood. As one observer remarked, they "would rather open a store or hawk wares on the streets than till the soil." Or, to quote Justo Sierra, the venerable Mexican historian, "the grocer, not the conquistador, is the real Spanish father of Mexican society, with his laughable faults and his solid virtues."

III

Mining, from the start, drew the attention of the Bourbons. In the 1750s, the industry again, as was increasingly its wont, confronted an economic crisis, the result of a world oversupply of silver, rising production costs, and, measured by its purchasing power on the international market, a decline in its value. The solution of the Bourbons was to increase mining output, in the belief that it fixed the level at which the colony could be taxed. Yet mining production accounted for less than half of the government revenue. As one scholar notes, government "taxed to stimulate more silver production" in order "to tax still more." Bourbon policy, in short, glossed over the ills of the mining industry. Still, mining in the silver bastions of Guanajuato and Zacatecas fared well (though not in the northern camps) because of the rehabilitation of old mines, reliance on the *patio* process, and indirect subsidies from government. Royal policy, for instance, lowered the price of mercury used to separate the metal from the crushed ore; until then, its high price held down production. Mineowners were also allowed to import machinery without having to pay a duty on it.

To shore up the mining interests, moreover, Gálvez organized the owners of mines into a *consulado* akin to that of the merchants, thus conferring on them more economic and political clout. Additionally, the Tribunal de Minería, which exercised jurisdiction over legal disputes in mining, had its own courts. Meanwhile, the Colegio de Minería, the first secular school in New Spain, set about training mining engineers; Lucas Alamán, the distinguished Mexican intellectual of the early 1800s, was one of them. Gálvez also reduced taxes and, briefly, supported a miners' bank. The crown, nevertheless, kept for itself ownership of the subsoil; mineowners had the right merely to exploit it. If for any reason the owner stopped operating his mine, it reverted back to the crown.

To the delight of the crown, the supply of silver ore, moreover, was apparently inexhaustible. The deposits at Bolaños, discovered by an Indian in 1736, provided one reason to think so. During its heyday, Bolaños, lying between Zacatecas and Guadalajara, grew to over sixteen thousand people in a decade or so. Of the old mines, Guanajuato's underwent a metamorphosis, transforming the province into the biggest producer of silver in the world, its mines yielding one-sixth of the precious metals of the Americas. With three thousand mines, New Spain was the world's leading supplier of silver.

Mining, unfortunately for the Spaniards, had a skittish side. Rarely did money invested in it pay off in millions. It was a gamble. However, with luck, the results were dramatic, as the story of Antonio de Obregón, a criollo prospector, documents. Using money provided by local merchants, Obregón poked about old diggings on a hill above the city of Guanajuato unworked since the sixteenth century. After risking his money in deep shafts, Obregón struck it rich. Between 1788 and 1809, La Valenciana, the name of his mine, yielded nearly thirty-one million pesos of silver, a fortune for the time, its production in 1791 alone matching the entire output of Peru and Bolivia. Profits from the mine bought Obregón the title of conde de la Valenciana. Obregón was one of the lucky ones; countless Spaniards, on the other hand, lost their shirts in mining ventures.

Bourbon legislation, at least in the opinion of the mineowners, was equally fickle, taking back with one hand what it offered with the other. Not only did they pay a tax; they had to buy their mercury and powder from the state, which alone fixed the supply and the price of these two essential commodities.

By royal fiat, all silver ore had to be sent to Mexico City, where the Real Casa de Moneda, the royal mint, turned it into coin. None of this pleased the mineowners, who, along with merchants and landowners, never tired of accusing authorities of undercutting colonial well-being. Mining, on top of that, suffered from a chronic shortage of capital, needed, experts said, to dig deeper shafts, lengthen tunnels, and enlarge reduction works. Technology in the mines, as Alexander von Humboldt, the German visitor pointed out, lagged far behind that of Europe.

Labor conditions, which disturbed Gálvez not a bit, were also far from idyllic. To haul the silver ore from the bowels of the earth, men carrying up to 150 kilos on their backs crawled on hands and knees along dark, narrow shafts. Scaffolding often broke, collapsing tunnels and burying miners alive. At other times, a false step led them to plunge to their death in bottomless pits. Silicosis, a disease of the lungs, yearly claimed its share of victims. As silver near the surface petered out, mineowners sank deeper shafts; the deeper, the hotter the bowels of the earth and the more dangerous the working conditions.

Still, miners represented an "aristocracy of labor." Although the Bourbon reforms, which endeavored to multiply mining output, encouraged employers to exploit their workers, forcing them to work harder, they were relatively well off. Most miners, despite the occasional use of debt peonage, at Santa Eulalia, in Chihuahua, for example, were wageworkers, generally mestizos and mulattoes. They were at liberty to move about, from one job to another. Labor in the mines paid approximately four reales a day, compared with one and a half to two reales in agriculture. Mineowners, moreover, had to heed workers' demands; failure to do so meant trouble. When the owner of the mines at Real del Monte, the conde de Regla, lowered wages from four to three reales, the miners walked off their jobs. Miners had enough money to get drunk, brawl, gamble, and whore. That behavior, undoubtedly, reflected the tough and dangerous nature of their toil; when they relaxed, they did so with a vengeance.

Coincidentally, the mineral wealth of Mexico, Peru, and Bolivia, the colonial mining bastions, helped finance the transformation from feudalism to capitalism in Europe. Ores taken from the Spanish colonies spurred the Industrial Revolution of England in the eighteenth century. Between 1503 and 1660, according to one estimate, 500 million pesos of gold were transported to Europe by the Spaniards alone. All told, the loot from the entire colonial world, the benefits of Spaniards, Englishmen, Frenchmen, and Dutchmen, says one scholar, surpassed in value the money invested in European industrialization before 1800. Ironically, the looting of the Americas failed to perform capitalist transformations for Spain.

IV

Change arrived in other forms. Military questions also occupied the Bourbons, who wanted to rebuild Spain's imperial glory. In 1764, two regiments of Spanish soldiers, ten thousand men in total, landed in Veracruz, the first to tread New Spain's soil since Cortés. Unwilling to shoulder the economic burden of defending the colonies, Spain passed it on to their inhabitants, who thought the idea costly and unnecessary. In 1767, the soldiers helped Spanish officials oust the Jesuits from New Spain and, more shocking to the colonists, squelched the protests that erupted in Michoacán, Puebla, and Guanajuato.

More obnoxious to inhabitants of New Spain was the order to organize a colonial militia of 22,000 men. Attempts to recruit men foundered on the rocks of apathy and distrust. When organized finally, the militias were small, poorly trained, and scantily equipped. The crown had to sell commissions to rich colonials eager to strut around in gaudy uniforms. Of the 624 officers in the militia, 338 were criollos. As an inducement to join the military, men who enlisted did not have to pay tribute to the crown. Indians, finally, had a way of circumventing the tirbute tax, bait that lured them into the royalist army.

Being an officer in the militia provided rewards, not merely splendid uniforms but titles as well. In return for money invested in commissions, the young and the young at heart had a place in parades and access to medals and the glory of military honors. Being an officer conferred the *fuero militar,* the right to special trial; no civil judge could try or punish a military man. Overnight, bored merchants or fat moguls of mining could become men about town, free to gamble, fornicate, and, for once, enjoy themselves far from wives, mothers, sisters, and the police. So was born a hankering for the military life.

To bring colonial politics more under their control, the Bourbons, adopting Gálvez's recommendations, tightened colonial administration, curtailing the power of viceroy and audiencia by organizing twelve intendencias, territorial divisions linked directly to the crown. Appointed in Spain, the intendentes wielded executive, judicial, financial, and military authority, undermining, by implication, the colonial power structure: clergy, hacendados, merchants, and mineowners. Much of the authority of the ayuntamientos went to *subdelegados,* subordinates of the intendentes and also replacements for the corrupt *corregidores de indios.* From this point on, ayuntamientos rarely made decisions without consulting the intendente. The viceroys, for all that, survived Gálvez's designs, though the intendentes established their headquarters in the major provincial cities: Arizpe, Oaxaca, Puebla, Valladolid, Guadalajara, Mérida, and so forth, becoming capitals of territorial entities, the forerunners of modern Mexican states.

Political change, part of the Bourbon reforms, raised the hackles of many a criollo. Of the intendencias, only that of Guadalajara was entrusted to them. Until the reforms, they had, after all, occupied scores of public posts, although seldom the top ones. Now they were nearly shut off. Spanish bureaucrats, young and ambitious, disembarked at Veracruz by the shipload to fill public posts, at times at the expense of older officials, some natives of New Spain. Believing *peninsulares* more loyal than criollos, the crown reserved for them two-thirds of all posts on the ayuntamientos and audiencias; by 1790, for example, just three of the eleven *oidores* of the audiencia of Mexico City were criollos. Places on the ayuntamientos, moreover, had little turnover. Once designated, regidores stayed on. The ayuntamiento of Aguascalientes was a case in point; all seven of its members were appointed for life. The alcalde, or mayor, had served on the ayuntamiento for forty-five years; the post of *depositario general,* assistant to the mayor, was held by the same individual for twenty-five years; only his death left it vacant. One regidor held office for twenty-one years. When one resigned because of ill health, his post went to his nephew, who kept it for sixteen years.

From the perspective of the criollos, the Bourbons had sabotaged their political aspirations and, by reserving important public jobs for *peninsulares,* confined them to the ones that paid poorly. The Bourbon reforms had cost them political clout and money. Yet rich criollos proved marvelously resilient; by 1810, they had reclaimed numerical if not actual control of the ayuntamientos.

For less fortunate criollos, the sins of the Bourbons were not easily atoned for. More than likely upward bound, these criollos had a corner on learning and university degrees, but no golden door beckoned. The liberal professions, what criollos educated themselves for, offered jobs only to the few. At the turn of the century, nearly half of the lawyers did not practice their trade. Making ends meet was difficult even for the fortunate ones. As one of them, Carlos María de Bustamante, said, he "hardly had enough bread for his family" despite eight years as a lawyer. A handful, he claimed, who litigated before the audiencia, grew rich; the rest survived as best they could. Physicians as well as notaries, many of them lawyers, were no better off. Denied access to bureaucratic office, the prerogative generally of *peninsulares,* criollo professionals confronted a dismal future. No wonder that they flocked to the church; of the clerics in New Spain, all but a minority were criollos.

The Bourbons also disciplined the church, an institution with eight thousand priests and an equal number of friars. The millionaire of the colonial corporations, the church collected the *diezmo* and enjoyed income from compulsory tithes. Church wealth included urban property and big haciendas. Private funds flowed into church coffers for pious works, capital or income from property entrusted to the orders for the upkeep of hospitals, orphanages, and schools. Funds from *capellanías*, established by wealthy benefactors at their death, provided funds for a *capellán* (priest) to pray for their souls on a given day of the week for so many years. Thousands of *capellanías* were established, corroborating the belief that every well-off individual left some sort of legacy to the church.

The church lent money to hacendados, mineowners, and merchants. Only a handful of them operated on their own. Church credit was the oil that kept the economy humming; two-thirds of all commercial transactions relied on it. The church, additionally, was usually the sole lender of capital, gaining, in this manner, a stake in virtually every economic enterprise.

Wishing to curtail the power of the church, the crown, its edict carried out by Gálvez and the marqués de Croix, expelled the Jesuits from New Spain in 1767, the first step on the path to clerical reform. The Jesuits, loyal adherents of the pope in Rome, were the most powerful and influential of the orders. Among the four hundred Jesuits exiled was Francisco Javier Clavijero, one of the fathers of criollo nationalism. The expulsion of the Jesuits raised the hackles of countless colonials, poor and rich alike.

The heaviest blow, no longer plotted by Gálvez, was yet to come. With its coffers empty, the crown, by the *real cédula* (decree) of 1804, ordered the church to deposit in the royal treasury capital held in pious funds and *capellanías.* The church must also sell its lands, profits to be lent to the crown. For the most part, the capital called in was tied up in mortgages which, to heed the dictates of the crown, had to be foreclosed. Debtors, among them influential criollos, had just ten years to liquidate their loans.

The results were devastating. The *real cédula* undermined the economic foundations of the church, the principal source of its political power. As Bishop Abad y Queipo charged, it was the worst blow in centuries. The *cédula* stipulated that the money be deposited in Spain, leaving colonials without capital or credit to operate their economy. The decree injured especially the hacendados, a majority of them criollos, but it also hurt rancheros, largely mestizos who, frequently, borrowed money from the church or were obligated to *capellanías.* Rich hacendados could liquidate their loans; poor rancheros could not. Hoping to forestall foreclosure, hacendados and rancheros, as advertisements in the *Diario de México* documented, put their properties up for sale; their simultaneous appearance on the market lowered the price of rural real estate, but not royal taxes on it. Even rich merchants and moguls of mining with mortgages on their haciendas had to use capital invested in productive enterprises to liquidate them. Not until 1809 was the *real cédula* revoked.

With the *real cédula,* the last of the Bourbon reforms, the crown had unintentionally united the powerful of New Spain against it. No sooner did news of it reach the colony than letters of protest began to pile up on the desks of royal authorities. Hacendados, particularly the criollos, were alarmed. Ayuntamientos, where they held sway, petitioned the viceroy not to enforce the decree.

V

In 1808, the French legions of Napoleon Bonaparte invaded Spain, in part because of the stupid diplomacy of Manuel de Godoy, Spanish prime minister and paramour to María Luisa, his ugly queen. Eventually, the citizens of New Spain learned that Charles IV, king since the death of his father in 1788, had stepped aside in favor of his son, Ferdinand VII. Unwilling to abide by that, Napoleon occupied Madrid, jailed Godoy, to whom authorities in the New World owed their appointments, and forced Ferdinand, contrite and cowardly, to abdicate. Napoleon then asked his brother Joseph, known as Pepe Botella because of his fondness for wine, to rule Spain and placed Charles and Ferdinand in custody.

A few weeks afterward, news reached Mexico City that the Madrid junta had sworn allegiance to Napoleon. The junta did not speak for most Spaniards, who, in May, rebelled against the French. In Valencia, a junta of patriots defied Napoleon in the name of "Religion, *Patria,* and Union," calling on the colonists to rally to the aid of the mother country. With his art, Goya, the colossal Spanish painter, glorified this epic struggle.

Most criollos in New Spain had no hankering to grovel at Napoleon's feet. The more daring urged the appointment of a caretaker government to run affairs until Ferdinand regained his throne. Viceroy and audiencia, however, quarreled over who should wield the baton. In the meantime, the ayuntamiento of Mexico City, a redoubt for rich criollos, declared that neither viceroy nor audiencia had any authority, since it emanated from the king, a prisoner of the French. By Spanish law and the precedent established by Hernán Cortés at Veracruz, power rested with the municipal authorities, the ayuntamiento. Having laid its cards on the table, the ayuntamiento urged the appointment of an acting junta of municipal officials to manage the colony while the king was in custody. The audiencia, mostly Spaniards, labeled the idea nonsense.

Iturrigaray, however, sided with the criollos on the ayuntamiento. When, in August 1808, he convoked a junta, Spaniards smelled a plot to separate the colony from Spain; criollos, after all, controlled the junta. Led by the audiencia and the archbishop, who opposed tampering with political arrangements, the Spaniards staged a coup, jailed Iturrigaray, and shipped him back to Spain. The first of many to follow, the coup that ousted the viceroy, interestingly, was led by rich merchants, primarily from the port of Veracruz. Gabriel Yermo, who captained it, was an affluent sugar planter; backed by armed clerks from the port's leading stores, he entered the viceregal palace and arrested Iturrigaray. The audiencia and the mining moguls of Zacatecas, Spaniards almost to the last man, applauded Yermo's valor.

In the provincial cities and towns, where criollos controlled the ayuntamientos, the mood had a different cast. Less inclined to obey the dictates of Mexico City, the criollos were a troubled lot. The chronic weakness of the interim viceroys encouraged them to take matters into their own hands. Before long, clandestine criollo societies honeycombed New Spain, debating what should be done to right the ship of state. They were titled literary clubs. In 1809, loyalists denounced one such club in Valladolid, which numbered in its constituency the usual assortment of criollos, priests, and officers of the colonial militia, as well as natives of an Indian village. The next year, other criollos started plotting in Querétaro, a city in the Bajío. Headed by Captain Ignacio Allende, the "Literary and Social Club of Querétaro" included influential criollos from as far away as Guanajuato. One of them was Miguel Hidalgo y Costilla. History remembers him as the father of Mexican Independence.

8

MUTINY OF THE CRIOLLOS

I

From Mexico City, it was a four-day ride by horseback to the Bajío, a fertile plain that stretched from Celaya to León and embraced Guanajuato. In this colonial heartland, the most progressive of New Spain, Miguel Hidalgo y Costilla, the criollo priest, unfurled the banner of rebellion in 1810. The Bajío enjoyed wide renown, not just for its agriculture and mines but, as any traveler knew, for its towns and cities, some, like San Felipe, San Miguel el Grande, and León dating from the sixteenth century. Industry, too, had a foothold. Querétaro and San Miguel el Grande made the finest wool textiles in the colony; cottons were produced in Celaya and Salamanca; León had an enviable reputation for leather goods; and silver spawned Guanajuato.

The Bajío was highly urbanized but dotted with ranchos and largely mestizo. In 1800, about one-third of the people in the intendencia of Guanajuato, the richest of the Bajío, lived in towns of over five thousand inhabitants, the majority of them mestizos. Equally true, more than one criollo, claims to *limpieza de sangre* notwithstanding, probably had a drop of Indian blood in his veins. Nearly 45 percent of the people in the Bajío were "Indians," though highly Hispanized and rapidly losing their identity. Many of their pueblos had no land of their own; Spanish authorities spoke of non-tribute-paying Indians who filled the streets of the cities as *vagos,* or vagrants.

Long before Hidalgo, the Bajío had earned something of a reputation as a trouble spot. The Bourbon reforms did not sit well with the citizens of Guanajuato. In 1767, when news of the expulsion of the Jesuits arrived, miners and *vagos* alike took to the streets. Not one to tolerate dissent, José de Gálvez, the Bourbon enforcer, squelched the protest, hanging its leaders. To guarantee order in the Bajío, he raised one of the initial colonial militias, then imposed a municipal tax on corn and flour to pay for its upkeep.

Why the mutiny? The answers—for surely no single one suffices—are complex. Obviously, the colonial legacy cannot be ignored. The exploitation of the many by the minority, which the rising cost of living intensified, provided fertile soil for the seeds of revolt. But, as Leon Trotsky was wont to argue, the downtrodden rarely rebel against their masters. The Bourbon reforms, however, had shattered the unity of crown and clergy, leaving many priests disgruntled. Events in Europe, too, served as the catalyst. What is clear is that the criollos, the least exploited, flew the flag of Independence.

The prosperity and achievements of the criollos probably explain best why they severed the umbilical cord. They had outgrown their need for the crown; on things that mattered to them, they were at loggerheads. Trade with Europe, as well as domestic questions, could be handled better by them. Always the middleman, Spain was a millstone around their neck. Whatever doubts criollos had about their relationship with the mother country were exacerbated during the interlude of European wars at the turn of the century when Spain joined France to fight England and, then, embraced John Bull to expel Napoleon. While the wars lingered on, many criollos fared well, despite a blockade of the colonies by English frigates which kept out Spanish exports. In the face of the Spanish debacle, New Spain's economy ran on. No wonder that criollos concluded that they could stand on their own feet!

Criollo dreams of power were hardly newsworthy. The plot of 1810, nonetheless, differed markedly from the others. Prematurely, the plotters had to call on Indians and mestizos to bail them out. When they did that, they lost control of the struggle for Independence, permitting it, if only momentarily, to turn into a battle for social justice. The drums of revolution beat loudly, pitting the poor against the rich and, briefly, uniting criollos and *peninsulares.*

The criollos were obviously not all of one mind on the matter of Independence. Those profiting from the colonial relationship expressed no dissatisfaction. There were many in this camp, from public officials, prelates, more than one hacendado, mine operators, and powerful merchants to militia officers. Economic as well as political ties to Spain assured their loyalty. Rebel criollos were on the outs, their aspirations, at least in their minds, thwarted by the colonial system. Well-off criollos were rarely rebels.

The Enlightenment, some say, unlocked a Pandora's box of unorthodox ideas, many in disharmony with the aims of the crown. Still, although Hidalgo and his companions in arms may have read Rousseau, Voltaire, and the Encyclopedists, one looks in vain for their wisdom in the Independence proclamation of 1810. Nor did the Inquisition, which examined his library, ever find books by the French philosophes. Only after his death did these symbols of the capitalist age appear among the insurgents. Nothing indicates that the French Revolution or the struggle of the Thirteen Colonies influenced Hidalgo or his allies. That they knew of them, as well as the facts of the slave uprising in Haiti, is certainly true. Yet when asked, at his trial in

Chihuahua, why he thought himself fit to judge the kingdom, Hidalgo replied simply: "the right of every citizen who believes the *patria* to be on the brink of disaster."

Most likely, traditional Spanish thought, if ideas were indeed important, encouraged Hidalgo to rebel, above all the writings of Francisco Suárez, a Jesuit who believed that God was the ultimate source of power. To Suárez, society was the final authority on earth; God had conferred power on the whole of it, not on any one individual. The people, by this logic, had the right to choose their rulers and the type of government they desired. God did not grant kings the right to rule, but delegated it through the people. Suárez belittled the "divine right" of kings, who, he believed, must govern for the welfare of their people; when they ignored this, they were tyrants. According to Suárez, citizens had the right to rebel in order to overthrow despots.

Titled *Defensa de la fe,* Suárez's controversial book, a synthesis actually of existing ideas, went through five printings in the seventeenth century and one more in the next. His populist views were widely known in New Spain, where, incidentally, they were branded seditious. Others restated them again and again, authors such as Fernando Castro Palao and Juan Caramuel. As a student of the Seminario Tridentino de Valladolid, Hidalgo was surely familiar with them. One of the texts read by Hidalgo had been written by Juan Bautista Gonet, a French Dominican who emphasized the concept of what he called the common good. Laws and actions, he said, must respond to it—in other words, the needs of the people.

II

Criollos of the "Literary Club of Querétaro," four of them, particularly, hatched the plot of 1810. Hidalgo's companions, the sons of newly arrived Spanish immigrants, were of the colonial militia and served on ayuntamientos. Ignacio Allende, the soul of the conspiracy and a captain in the Queen's Cavalry Regiment in Guanajuato, was a man of thirty-five or so and a fine horseman, handsome but with a lame arm, who loved women, dissolute living, and gambling. Fearless, he was never one to accept defeat easily. His father, a hacendado, ran a store on the side. Of limited schooling, Allende revealed no talent for intellectual pursuits but, always disciplined, stuck to his guns once he made up his mind.

A typical criollo, he had no love for radical ideals; the *plebe* (poor), to Allende, were an alien lot. Acquainted with Viceroy José de Iturrigaray, whom he knew from his days in the barracks of Jalapa, Allende sympathized with the aborted plot of 1808. Concocted by the ayuntamiento of Mexico City, it was a criollo scheme from start to finish. Its leaders had a simple but convoluted blueprint: remain loyal to Ferdinand VII, obey the viceroy, but pay no heed to other Spanish officials. Put differently: the criollos wanted a government for themselves but no structural changes. Until his death, Allende remained faithful to that goal. As a military man, he envisaged a war for independence fought with traditional soldiers, who wore uniforms and obeyed officers of the better class.

After Spanish authorities had abdicated, Allende wanted to appoint a *junta nacional* in Mexico City, with one representative from each province, to run the government. The viceroy would preside over the junta, for this was a curious kind of independence, one that swore allegiance to Ferdinand VII, the captive monarch. Since criollos or their allies controlled the ayuntamientos in the province, they would pick the junta and dictate its decisions, whether to the liking of the viceroy or not.

Juan Aldama, also a militia captain, was another rebel. He was born in San Miguel; his father managed an *obraje* owned by a wealthy family. Aldama thought liberty "saintly," having no use for an antireligious French version. The youngest of the Querétaro plotters was Mariano Abasolo, whose father, a man with good political connections, ran the royal tobacco monopoly in Dolores. Abasolo, too, was a captain in the militia. His wife, María Manuela Toboada, whom he had married recently, was the daughter of a rich Spanish hacendado from Chamacuero. Allende, according to historians, led Abasolo into the conspiracy against the wishes of his wife, a fervent loyalist. Abasolo had but a bit part in the insurrection of 1810.

Mexican history, however, remembers Miguel Hidalgo y Costilla, one of the Querétaro Club, as the patron saint of his country. Writing almost a century afterward, Justo Sierra described Hidalgo's status thus: "He is the father of his country, our father." Hero worship the likes of this is rare. But, this is Hidalgo's niche in Mexican history. No one did more to enshrine this Promethean figure than José Clemente Orozco, the muralist, whose Hidalgo, a balding man with shaggy white hair wearing the black frock of a priest, whom he painted on the staircase of the Palacio de Gobierno in Guadalajara, stands two stories high. His arms outstretched, he offers hope to the poor and dark of skin. This Hidalgo, regardless of the truth of the legend, undid the colonial stability of three centuries in just 120 days.

Hidalgo is a controversial hero. During his lifetime, critics lambasted him. Worse still, he failed; the Spaniards captured him, tortured and defrocked him, and, before decapitating him, made him recant. Not until 1821, a decade after Hidalgo's death, did Mexico achieve its Independence. Yet Agustín de Iturbide, the victor in 1821, was relegated quickly to the rubbish heap. To muddy the waters more, the evidence suggests that the Hidalgo of Querétaro, like Allende, had the blueprints of 1808 very much in mind. Nothing would be done unduly to disturb existing laws and practices, least of all the Catholic church. Yet when the rebellion broke out, something about Hidalgo's behavior recalled the notorious Conspiración de los Machetes (1799), when artisans, workers, and soldiers in Mexico City, in a fit of rage, attempted to rob Spaniards of their goods, kill them, and get the populace to take up arms, all in the name of the Virgen de Guadalupe.

According to the rules of the colonial game, Hidalgo passed muster easily. On his mother's side, his family had been in New Spain since the sixteenth century, having helped "pacify," as the conquistadores liked to say, Michoacán. His relatives were among the founders of Valladolid, while his father, a criollo who boasted of his *limpieza de sangre,* managed a hacienda, San Diego de Corralejo, in the vicinity of Pénjamo, and, on the side, dabbled in commerce. Judged by the standards of the day, Hidalgo belonged to what might be tagged a rural "middle class." Of his brothers, two took up farming, one commerce, and one the law, and another, like Hidalgo, joined the clergy. Eventually, Hidalgo acquired the ranchos of Jaripeo, Santa Rosa, and San Nicolás. No longer a young man, but youthful of spirit, Hidalgo fell in step with the Querétaro conspirators. For his time, he was, by age alone, a remarkable man.

Sturdy of body, slightly balding but erect of figure, Hidalgo started his schooling in Valladolid, at the Jesuit Colegio de San Nicolás. In 1774, the Real y Pontificia Universidad awarded him his *licenciatura* (bachelor's degree), and four years later he donned the robes of a priest. Almost immediately he returned to Valladolid, where, for twenty-four years, he taught and afterward served as rector of his alma mater, the Colegio de San Nicolás, one of the finest seminaries in the colony.

He had another side, unorthodox and difficult to fathom. Neither light nor dark of skin, *moreno claro,* as Mexicans describe it, Hidalgo had green, piercing eyes. He listened more than he spoke. On intellectual subjects, Hidalgo could more than hold his own. He loved to debate, and controversy stirred his spirits. He was, for all that, more a man of action than contemplative. Whatever his critics might say, he possessed a good head, as the following anecdote reveals. In 1783, José Pérez Calama, bishop of Michoacán, offered a prize for the best study on how to improve teaching in the seminaries. The winner was a paper titled "Disertación sobre el verdadero método de estudiar teología escolástica," a biting attack on a manual then used to teach theology. With high praise for its merits, the bishop bestowed the prize on Hidalgo, its author. Hidalgo read and owned a respectable library, which included books on the list of the Inquisition. He knew Manuel Abad y Queipo and Miguel Domínguez, the corregidor of Querétaro.

Steeped in Latin and Thomistic logic, Hidalgo had studied the classics. Among the Spanish giants, he had read Cervantes, Quevedo, Sor Juana Inés de la Cruz, and Carlos de Sigüenza y Góngora and, beyond that, Bacon, Regis, Descartes, Newton, Leibniz, Cicero, and Vergil. Following in the footsteps of the missionary friars, Hidalgo found time to learn Nahuatl, Mixtec, Otomí, and Tarascan. A man of independent mind, he once got into trouble with the Inquisition for questioning the "immaculate conception" of Jesus Christ. He lived by his own moral code, thinking fornication out of wedlock not a sin and, to prove his point, fathering two daughters. His passion for gambling may have cost him the rectorship of the Colegio de San Nicolás. Hidalgo was, by and large, a man of simple tastes; for social pretensions, he had no time to spare.

Hidalgo had a social conscience. In *Los pasos de López,* Jorge Ibargüengoitia caught this side of him, remarking that "he dealt with everyone, rich or poor, as equals." Hidalgo had more than just equality on his mind. Dispatched to the town of Dolores, partly as punishment for his gambling misdeeds, he made himself quickly at home with his neighbors, most of them mestizo campesinos. He taught them to grow grapes, to make wine, and to plant mulberry trees for silkworms; this against crown regulations. He showed them how to dig irrigation ditches, improve their ceramics, and make bricks, as well as how to dry and cure hides. A Catholic but modern of bent, Hidalgo spent little time in the confessional, preferring to labor alongside of his parishioners. That the poor admired him, there can be no doubt. Unlike most criollos, who aspired simply to supplant the hated gachupin, Hidalgo had love in his heart for the poor.

But Hidalgo was more than just a born-again Saint Francis. Of a strong backbone, he could be a pragmatist. What would happen, asks a conspirator in Ibargüengoitia's novel, who finds a cannon hidden poorly, if one of the neighbors sees it and tries to tell the authorities? "I hope that doesn't occur," Hidalgo replies, "because we would have to kill him." Once the insurrection started, Hidalgo would have shot anyone who stood in its way. To liberate New Spain, he knew, might mean his own death. For his cause, Hidalgo was ready to die.

What did Hidalgo seek when he rebelled in 1810? That question divides critics and eulogists, particularly since Hidalgo left almost nothing behind to explain his intentions. He did, however, when judged by his captors, say emphatically, "I was certain that Independence would benefit the kingdom," so "we had to appeal to the people who could bring it about." That, unmistakably, meant the poor who had little to lose. Yet while their defender, Hidalgo was a criollo, part of the unhappy *letrados* who looked to better days for themselves once the Spaniards departed. The Spaniards, nevertheless, would not just leave; they had to be beaten on the field of battle, which required men willing to die. To achieve this goal, Hidalgo wooed the poor, the majority of them angry. It was that "need to win a popular following in order to achieve Independence," Hidalgo confessed, that "overcame my scruples." One of them, of course, was the principle of the sanctity of private property; given his values, it was legally and morally wrong to seize it arbitrarily.

That may explain some of Hidalgo's ambivalence, but not entirely. Hidalgo, it is well to keep in mind, belonged to a conspiratorial band of criollos, none of whom gave a tinker's damn for the plight of the poor. On this score, they were no different from most Spaniards. Led by Allende, they had planned an uprising for December 8, 1810; unfortunately for them, their plot was betrayed by Mariano Galván, a postal clerk. The day was September 13. Upon learning of it, Josefa Ortiz de Domínguez, wife of the corregidor of Querétaro, sent a messenger to warn Allende, then in Dolores. It was there, in the parish house of Hidalgo, that Allende, Aldama, and Hidalgo met to discuss their alternatives.

Actually, they had but two: to flee or to take the bull by the horns and declare themselves in rebellion. To challenge Spanish power was no easy decision. The plans for the December uprising, for one thing, counted on suborning a part of the colonial militia. That, apparently, was no longer possible, although Allende and Aldama managed to persuade a sprinkling of the king's troops to follow them. For Allende and Aldama, professional soldiers of a kind, the assault on the royalists would be an orderly one, with disciplined troops fighting on both sides. Property would be safeguarded, and, once the fighting ceased, everything would return to normal, except for the departure of *peninsular* bureaucrats.

That plan had suddenly gone sour. What chance for victory existed required calling on campesinos, miners, the unemployed, vagrants, and jailbirds—the exploited and embittered. As Allende knew, that was playing with fire. Had it not been for Hidalgo, say Mexican historians, Allende and Aldama might have abandoned the struggle. Hidalgo never wavered; his allies, he declared, would be the poor. "Gentlemen," he told Allende and Aldama, "nothing is left for us but to shoot *gachupines.*" In reply, Aldama could only repeat again and again, "Sir, what have you in mind? For the love of God, take heed of what you do."

At this juncture, September 15, 1810, Hidalgo, the idol of Mexican nationalists, made his bow. Brushing aside Aldama's fears, Hidalgo climbed the tower of his parish in Dolores, rang its bells, and implored the people to follow him. His battle cry, however, rang with a tinsel sound. "Long live Ferdinand VII. Long live religion. Long live the Virgen de Guadalupe. Death to the *gachupines!*" That, Mexicans believe, is what Hidalgo said. Much of this is speculation, for no record remains of Hidalgo's declaration of independence.

What seems out of kilter in Hidalgo's defiance was his pledge of allegiance to Ferdinand VII, a prisoner of Napoleon. If one were to believe Hidalgo's rhetoric, Ferdinand was the protector of New Spain, a king above the crimes of his subjects. As history documents, that was just a pipe dream. Hidalgo either misplaced his faith in the king or, more likely, thought it unwise to declare for total independence. The criollos, to whom Hidalgo and his cohorts appealed initially, remained loyal, in theory at least, to the crown.

Whatever his intentions at this moment, Hidalgo had something else on his mind. At Valladolid, one of the first stops on his military campaign, he abolished slavery and the tribute borne by the Indian, "that shameful tax, the brand burned into the body of a slave," which "we have endured for three centuries as a symbol of tyranny." Its abrogation foretold "the collapse of the old order." The system of *castas,* where men and women were classified by birth, Hidalgo added, was a relic. In Guadalajara, Hidalgo went one step further. His decree of December 5, 1810, ordered the restitution of lands illegally taken from Indian communities. What he intended by it is debated hotly. Debate aside, the goal was not entirely novel, for both Bishops Antonio San Miguel and Manuel Abad y Queipo had urged the distribution of public lands among Indians and mestizos. But San Miguel and Abad y Queipo had not taken up arms to enforce their ideas; Hidalgo did. That, too, as the criollos knew, gave Hidalgo's rebellion the color of a social revolution, the last thing they wanted. Whether dictated by zeal for social justice or by practical politics, the need to woo the disenfranchised, the gist of the decree of Guadalajara, alienated most criollos.

Hidalgo also embellished his crusade with a religious symbol. On the road from San Miguel el Grande, as he explained, it occurred to him to adopt for his banner the Virgen de Guadalupe. Thereafter, the Guadalupana, as she was known, symbolized Hidalgo's struggle for independence. Later, his successors, Ignacio López Rayón and José María Morelos y Pavón, would do the same. More than a religious icon, the Virgin, by the date of the insurrection, had acquired a more important role. As the Virgin of criollos, mestizos, and Indians, she was the cornerstone of *mexicanidad,* the emerging Mexican nationality. Everyone could rally around her.

By raising aloft her image, Hidalgo transformed the Virgin into the protector of the insurgent cause, and this was what partly attracted Indians, campesinos, miners, and the unemployed to it. Hidalgo had merely followed precedent. During the Conspiracy of the Machetes, artisans, workers, and the poor had employed the Image of the Virgin to win supporters. Starting with Hidalgo, the insurgents saw themselves as the defenders of the true faith against heretical *gachupines* accused of succumbing to French heresies. They learned to label the Spaniards "Royalists, Jews, and enemies of God." The insurgency was a religious war, like those of Cancuc, Jacinto Canek, and Antonio Pérez in the previous century. When the "simple people" of the towns and villages of the Bajío saw Hidalgo exalt the Virgin, to quote José María Luis Mora, historian and sage, they "came running" to him. The enemy, the hated *gachupín,* threatened their faith and their Virgin.

Don Miguel was a priest, one of many of the lower clergy to rebel. Historians calculate that approximately 400 of them sided with the insurgents by 1815; royal officials put to death 125 of them. Hidalgo had set the example. He was a respected figure among the clergy of the Bajío; sundry clerics had known Hidalgo as a rector, a theologian of repute, and a kind and loving priest in Dolores. Many of them applauded his challenge to Spanish rule but, when confronted with reality, drew back. His successor, Father José María Morelos y Pavón, when asked why he joined the rebellion, replied, "Partly because of my high esteem for the priest Hidalgo."

The lower clergy, itself shunted aside by their hierarchy, voiced the popular anguish. By taking up arms and calling attention to the ancient ills, Hidalgo awakened a dormant clerical conscience, sharpened by the years of food shortages of the late eighteenth century. In the Bajío, the lower clergy had battled hunger and droughts, helping dig irrigation ditches to water the parched land and distributing money to needy campesinos to buy seeds. They had gone to the hacendados to beg for tiny plots of land so that Indians might plant corn to keep from starving. By doing this, the lower clergy of the Bajío, the most radical, cemented its ties to the campesinos and came to know intimately the conditions of the countryside. It was no mere accident of fate that the bishopric of Michoacán, one of the most afflicted, should be one of the storm centers of the insurrection.

The Hidalgo upheaval invites, inevitably, comparisons with millenarianism, a belief in the Christian prophecy and the ideal society. That article of faith tends to emerge from revolutionary movements that agitate the souls of the poor, campesinos or urban workers. Such was the Hidalgo episode, where, to quote a distinguished Mexican, "we are face to face with a mass uprising of the plebeian classes, without precedent until then in the history of the Americas and without parallel in its emancipation struggle."

The upper clergy, the hierarchy of archbishop, bishops, and well-heeled parish priests, denounced both the insurrection and its leaders. In their opinion, the devil had stirred up the trouble; Hidalgo had committed an unpardonable sin. From their pulpits, these defenders of the status quo, more than a few of them criollos, excoriated priest after priest who sided with the insurrection. The church paid a terrible price for this mischief. By failing to support a popular cause, and aligning itself with its enemies, it lost standing among nationalists and the poor. Had the church identified itself with the insurgency, a Mexican cause, it might have done better after Independence. By siding with the crown, the loser in the struggle, the church squandered its moral capital.

III

From Dolores, Hidalgo marched on San Miguel el Grande. Overnight almost, his motley army of mestizos and Indians doubled and then tripled.

Wherever he went, lamented Lucas Alamán, historian and politico of the era, he picked up disciples; he had merely to appear to win them over. After easily capturing San Miguel, Hidalgo's campesinos, miners, and the unemployed pillaged and burned it. Frightened *peninsulares* and, more and more, criollos and occasionally well-off mestizos cowered before the advancing enemy, armed with machetes, slings, and, here and there, a rusty firearm. An alarmed Allende tried to stop the looting but to no avail; only a tiny band of the king's soldiers, who gambled their lives on the rebellion, obeyed. Celaya succumbed next and, like San Miguel, suffered the rage of the mob. By now, wrote Alamán, Hidalgo had eighty thousand followers, who resembled "savage tribal hordes from the north" (he referred to the Chichimecas of the Conquest era) and addressed Hidalgo as Generalísimo.

Guanajuato, the capital of the intendencia, lay next on the line of march. As Hidalgo approached, miners and twenty thousand Indians, more often than not accompanied by their wives and children, joined up. Expecting help to arrive, Juan Antonio de Riaño, the intendente, gathered up the city's Spanish inhabitants in the Alhóndiga (granary) and decided to resist. Riaño, interestingly, had flirted with the Enlightenment, holding *tertulias* (meetings) in his house, which both Abad y Queipo and Hidalgo attended. Not surprisingly, this disciple of the nascent capitalist ideals of the Enlightenment had handled harshly the protests of miners.

Hoping to avoid the looting of Celaya and San Miguel, Hidalgo asked Riaño to surrender Guanajuato without a battle; Riaño refused. As Hidalgo's men came upon the gates of the Alhóndiga, Riano gave the order to fire; his artillery killed hundreds. Infuriated, the attackers fell upon the Alhóndiga, killing Riaño with musket shot, and, braving the fire of the Spanish artillery which decimated their ranks, set aflame the wooden gates of the Alhóndiga. When they collapsed, the army of the poor rushed in, slaying most of the Spaniards. For a day and a half, pillaging took over as Hidalgo's allies sought revenge, not just against *gachupines* but criollos and prosperous mestizos alike. Just eighteen years of age, Alamán witnessed the fury of the mob. To this scion of the elite, "the most despicable classes of society" had put the city to the torch, terrorized its inhabitants, raped women, and "drunk themselves into a stupor." Mora, the Liberal oracle, was no less caustic: "In a few hours the ruin of the city was complete, its wealth dissipated and the productivity of its mines destroyed." Some five hundred Spaniards died at Guanajuato, along with nearly two thousand of Hidalgo's sympathizers.

With the fall of the city, Hidalgo added funds and arms to his war chest and, equally important, new allies. Everywhere, it seems, people were emboldened to follow in his footsteps. By mid-October, Valladolid, Zacatecas, and San Luis Potosí had been taken and Hidalgo, fortified with cannon, rifles, and thousands of recruits, was heading for Mexico City. Its capture, which military observers predicted, would liberate New Spain from the Spanish yoke. At Monte de las Cruces, Hidalgo's forces defeated a smaller but well-equipped Spanish army. The gates to Mexico City beckoned; nothing formidable barred Hidalgo's entrance. Had Hidalgo continued on his path, the metropolis would have fallen to him.

But he did not. Instead he retreated. Some historians say that Allende wanted to march on but that Hidalgo, perhaps fearing for the safety of Mexico City's Spanish inhabitants, overruled him. The victory at Monte de las Cruces, likewise, had been costly, in both men and ammunition. With Hidalgo and Allende less and less inclined to work together, the insurgents turned back to Guadalajara, to face an army advancing from Querétaro under General Félix María Calleja. The decision to retreat from Mexico City proved a calamity for the insurgents. On the way back, desertions cut deeply into their ranks, and, although they captured Guadalajara, they were never the same again.

To prepare for Calleja's assault, Allende endeavored to instill a bit of military discipline, to organize the kind of army he had desired from the start. He cast cannon, found muskets for some of his soldiers, and organized a cavalry unit. Hidalgo's popular appeal, meanwhile, rebuilt numerically the rebel force; when Calleja got near Guadalajara with six thousand disciplined troops, Hidalgo once again had eighty thousand men, but poorly armed. At Puente de Calderón, on the Río Lerma near Guadalajara, the two armies met. For a while, the insurgents fought bravely, though sustaining heavy losses to the artillery and musket fire of Calleja's soldiers, almost all, ironically, Indians. Then a cannon shot set fire to a rebel wagon loaded with ammunition, igniting a grass fire, which panicked Hidalgo's men, who broke ranks and fled. For all intents and purposes, Hidalgo's rebellion had come to grief.

With their men in flight, Hidalgo, Allende, Aldama, and Abasolo took the road to Zacatecas, hoping to find adherents and weapons in Coahuila and Texas, where, according to rumor, flames of the revolt still burned. The march northward called to mind the last rites for the dead. With the consent of his companions, Allende stripped Hidalgo of his command, holding him in custody. Near Monclova, a small town in Coahuila, a turncoat betrayed his old allies to the Spaniards, who took them for trial to Ciudad Chihuahua, a journey of two hundred miles.

At the trials in Chihuahua, Allende and Aldama denied having ordered the killing of Spaniards, but Hidalgo accepted full blame, adding that he was also responsible for "unjustly taking private property." Hidalgo regretted, Alamán never tired of saying, "the terrible ills he had brought upon religion, customs, and the state." Before dying, he begged for pardon, "so that the Lord and Father of Mercies, who grants me death from love and pity for my sins, may bestow upon me His blessings." One foreign historian later wrote that

Hidalgo's "mea culpa" had few equals "for sheer poignancy."

Military men, Allende and Aldama were executed quickly. Abasolo, who had surrendered earlier, escaped death. Hidalgo died at the hands of a firing squad on July 31, 1811, judged guilty of treason and defrocked by the Inquisition for the sin of heresy. Soldiers then cut off their heads and stuck them on poles in front of the Alhóndiga in Guanajuato, a reminder of the penalty for treason until the Spaniards departed New Spain in 1821.

But, actually, did Hidalgo regret his actions? Was he truly a sadder and wiser man? Frankly, on this point, the evidence is ambiguous. At no time did Hidalgo reject his belief in the righteousness of Independence. What afflicted him was not the objective but the violence employed to gain it. He reproached himself for the harm done by the struggle for Independence; death and the destruction of property, for that he rued the day. "The anguish of Hidalgo," to cite a Mexican historian, "was not due to sorrow for starting the battle for Independence but" simply "remorse for the violence he failed to foresee."

From the start, the struggle of 1810 fanned discord, even among believers in the Independence cause. Mora, one of them, expressed the belief in his *México y sus revoluciones* "that no man, . . . no matter how much he might sympathize with the idea of Independence, wanted Hidalgo to enter Mexico City." Mora, however, was not totally objective. His family had suffered at the hands of the insurrection. A ranchero on the prowl for funds for Hidalgo, as Mora told the story, arrived at the home of his father, Don José, demanding 18,000 pesos. Anxious for his life, Don José gave the ranchero the money and then, worried sick that he might lose the rest of his savings, deposited 73,000 pesos in Celaya, which Hidalgo's forces captured. Overnight, the rebellion had brought ruin to the Mora family. "Many people," Mora wrote, would have supported the revolt "if not for fear that they stood to lose everything in the general disorder." On the other side of the fence, Alamán, who opposed Independence, labeled Hidalgo's uprising a crime against "the laws that govern how human beings deal with one another," referring to it as a "shocking union of religion with murder and pillage."

Abad y Queipo, bishop of Michoacán, excommunicated Hidalgo, thus using a pet tool of the Catholic hierarchy for handling insurgents, and he compared events in New Spain to the earlier, bloody episode in Haiti. Until late in the eighteenth century, Abad y Queipo swore, Haiti was a paradise, where its elite, "the richest and happiest men on earth," used their country to the fullest. Terror reigned in Haiti because "anarchy strangled whites, the French and criollos . . . leaving only *negros* and *mulatos.*" José Joaquín Fernández de Lizardi, afterward an insurgent, remembered the revolt of Hidalgo as one "of horror, crime, blood, and desolation."

Of all the insurgents, only Hidalgo suffered this bitter censure from fellow criollos. Why? The answer seems self-evident. By siding with the have-nots, the poor and the Indians, Hidalgo, who set out to win political freedom from Spain, had lit the fires of class conflict, the dark of skin against whites. In doing this, Hidalgo, in the opinion of Mora and like-minded criollos, betrayed the cause. The criollos, to cite a Mexican thinker, wanted "only so much change." Hidalgo's critics, most of whom desired Independence, trembled at the thought of social revolution. As Alamán observed astutely, Hidalgo ignited "an uprising of the proletariat against property and civilization."

IV

After the death of Hidalgo, the wand of Independence passed to two men cast in dissimilar molds. Ignacio López Rayón, a criollo and a lawyer by profession, had served as Hidalgo's personal secretary, then organized troops for the insurgents in the north. Fleeing south, he teamed up with the criollos in the Junta de Zitácuaro, a town in Michoacán. Of similar thought, they wanted either to control or, better yet, to destroy the popular movement set in motion by Hidalgo. An admirer of France, England, and the United States, López Rayón was a student of constitutional law who walked, so to speak, in the footsteps of Allende. Among the criollos at Zitácuaro were Carlos María de Bustamante, Andrés Quintana Roo, José María de Liceaga, Sixto Verduzco, and José María Cos. Mexicans remember them as the *letrados,* the erudite criollos. With them in spirit were Fernández de Lizardi and Servando Teresa de Mier.

José María Morelos y Pavón, a priest of a no-account parish in Michoacán, was Hidalgo's other heir apparent. Born in Michoacán, in the village of Tehuejo, he was a mestizo with African ancestry in the family closet and the child of indigent parents. His father was a carpenter and his mother the daughter of a schoolteacher. Not quite five feet tall, robust, chubby of face, and dark-skinned, Morelos was blessed with a regal bearing. A mule driver until thirty years of age, he took the vows of the priesthood tardily. Because of his spotty educational background, he barely made it to the Colegio de San Nicolás in Valladolid when Hidalgo was its rector. Upon completing his studies, the bishopric dispatched him to the impecunious parish of Carácuaro, the kind usually assigned to priests of limited schooling. No one coveted it, because of the grinding poverty of its inhabitants and its hot and muggy climate. At Carácuaro, Morelos learned of Hidalgo's revolt.

Poised and canny, Morelos was a born soldier; he could usually outgeneral, outmaneuver, and outflank the enemy. Although entirely bereft of military training, he was a master of battlefield tactics. Like Allende, he preferred disciplined soldiers to excitable hordes. His men earned notoriety for their use of the machete, a weapon they substituted for the sword. Aside from Indians and mestizos, Morelos recruited blacks and mulattoes from the sugar haciendas of Veracruz. Initially, Morelos fought his battles in the European manner but, out of necessity, learned guerrilla tactics, which he employed deftly against the better-equipped royal troops. By 1813, at the height of his military triumphs, Morelos had defeated the wily Calleja and virtually encircled Mexico City, bottled up the Spanish forces in the cities, and controlled the countryside. Scores of Mexican heroes earned their patriotic credentials under Morelos, including Nicolás Bravo, Vicente Guerrero, and Mariano Matamoros, the indefatigable priest.

Morelos was a man of the people. His appeal was that of the caudillo, the popular boss by natural right, prowess, and election. A populist, he wished for the abolition of all privileges, judging slavery neither just, rational, nor humane. The color of one's skin, he lectured Quintana Roo, did not "change one's heart or one's way of thinking." He thought social distinctions based on race and color evil; only the sins of vice or the power of virtue distinguished men from one another. The sons of campesinos and workers, he believed, deserved schools equal in quality to those of the rich. He envisaged a country that provided jobs for everyone and not just for *peninsulares.* On agrarian matters, Morelos was more than just abreast of his times. The land, he implied in his *Sentimientos de la nación,* belonged to those who "tilled it," urging the return of stolen lands to the Indian communities, their rightful owners. He would not lay down his arms, he warned the Spaniards, until they gave "our campesinos the fruits of their labors." Some of his followers, perhaps Morelos himself, also advocated the redistribution of the lands of haciendas of more than two leagues in order to establish small farms, thinking them the most efficient way to cultivate the land.

Of the insurgents, Morelos was the first to elevate to the status of national heroes the pre-Hispanic chieftains who battled Cortés, and the first to identify their cause with his. In his opening remarks to the Congreso de Chilpancingo, the next stop after Zitácuaro, Morelos, after referring to New Spain as Anáhuac, paid tribute to Moctezuma, Cacama, Cuauhtémoc, and Xiconténcatl, making much ado about how they lost their lives fighting tyranny. In hindsight, he appears a pioneer *indigenista,* a person who wished very much to help the Indian raise his standard of living and to incorporate him into the national mainstream.

Morelos, too, embraced the Virgen de Guadalupe, stamping her image on his banners. All of his lieutenants swore eternal fealty to the Virgin, and one of them, Manuel Félix Fernández, a future president of Mexico, adopted the name of Guadalupe. All the same, among the men of faith no one outdid Morelos himself, who asked that the constitution of 1813, a charter elaborated by criollos, be consecrated to her. A fanatical Catholic and intolerant of other faiths, Morelos looked upon those who did not worship the Virgen de Guadalupe as traitors.

Unhappily for the future, Morelos had allies. Almost from the start, he had to work with López Rayón and the criollos who fled Guadalajara. By then, many of them had soured on Hidalgo. Some were hacendados or sons of hacendados with little or no stomach for social engineering. Plans for agrarian reform, no matter how couched, shook their loyalty to the insurgency. Yet, when it came to the criollos and their views, Morelos and Hidalgo behaved in strikingly different ways. Confronted with the enthusiasm of the disenfranchised, Hidalgo veered leftward, becoming something of a social reformer. Conversely, Morelos, a man of humble origins, listened to the siren whistle of the *letrados,* doing an about-face that damaged the insurgency and cost him his life.

Why did Morelos accept the ideological tutelage of the criollos? One can merely speculate. Most likely, his background played a part in it. The son of a carpenter, of mixed racial parentage, and at heart a country bumpkin, Morelos must have felt overwhelmed by the *letrados.* Articulate and outspoken, they had read Plato and Aristotle, the French philosophes, and the English thinkers in vogue at the time. Filled with theories of the Enlightenment and bombastic rhetoric, they convinced Morelos that they knew what was good for New Spain. Tragically, he went along with them, becoming, in the process, a defrocked Solomon. By embracing their views, the caudillo shed his authority, cutting himself off from his supporters. From that point on, he was the tool of the *letrados.*

That Morelos came to rely on them, the events of the day leave little room to doubt. One of these *letrados* was Vicente de Santa María, a priest whose insurgency began with the plot at Valladolid in 1809. For that, he spent time in jail, then joined the revolt against Spain in 1812, briefly as adviser to López Rayón. An aide to the Junta de Zitácuaro, he may have urged Morelos to replace it with a *congreso* at Chilpancingo, so as to confer form and direction on the Independence movement; López Rayón, Bustamante, Cos, and Quintana Roo were among its members. Along with that, he gave Morelos a draft of a constitution; its outlines appeared in the final document.

Just twenty-six years old, Quintana Roo, one more of the influential *letrados,* was a private secretary to Morelos. Of a long face and pale forehead, he was a native of Yucatán and part of the conspiracy of 1808 in Mexico City to unseat the *peninsulares.* Son and grandson of militia officers, he attended school in Mérida, graduated from the Real y Pontificia Universidad with a degree in canonical law, and then accepted an offer from the prestigious law firm of Agustín Pomposo Fernández de Salvador, a friend of his father, but left the firm to follow Morelos. He was one of the thirteen delegates to the Congreso de Chilpancingo who, in the pattern of most *letrados,* looked upon the ills of New Spain as political and administrative. Once able criollos replaced bungling and incompetent Spanish officials, everything would be well.

Quintana Roo had an impeccable virtue: he knew how to marry well. Leona Vicario, who became his wife, was the daughter of a criollo family of Mexico City and, in her early twenties, betrothed to him. A friend of Bustamante, this woman of stout heart and mind sympathized with Hidalgo and Morelos. Without telling her family, she used her home to relay news from Mexico City to the insurgents and established a small shop to make and repair clothing for them. Discovered, she was taken to jail by the royalists but, fortunately for her, escaped to the camp of Morelos, where she was reunited with Quintana Roo. Good-looking and very Catholic, she won Morelos's esteem, serving him in Oaxaca and suffering terrible deprivations. When the royalists captured Morelos and shot him, Leona Vicario and her husband fled for their lives, frequently finding shelter in the most humble huts. Both served Nicolás Bravo, who fought on. Leona Vicario never abandoned the battle for Independence, even when Cos, Bustamante, and their companions made peace with the royalists. Captured once more in 1817, she lived to see her cause triumph, dying in 1842.

Carlos María de Bustamante, lauded and damned for his polemical *Cuadro histórico de la revolución mexicana,* belonged to the coterie of Morelos's advisers, wielding a powerful influence on him. Born and educated in Oaxaca, he was the son of a Spanish bureaucrat and a lawyer. A scion of the elite of Mexico City, he edited the *Diario de México,* the influential journal. A fiery spokesman at the Congreso de Chilpancingo, he was responsible partly for the Acta de Independencia of 1813, the formal Declaration of Independence. Along with Morelos, Bustamante echoed the admiration for the pre-Hispanic past, eulogizing Cuauhtémoc and referring to the insurgents as his heirs. Ancient Anáhuac was a time of greatness, the Conquest a black episode. The insurgents were fighting to liberate the nation from the chains of slavery; so proclaimed the rhetoric of Bustamante.

By no stretch of the imagination, however, was Bustamante a radical. A Catholic by birth and conviction, he stood up for the miraculous apparition of the Virgen de Guadalupe. Unwilling to tolerate dissident creeds, he insisted that Catholicism be declared the official faith of the Mexican people and, as a zealous defender of the Jesuits, persuaded Morelos of the need to bring them back. Nor did Bustamante display ardor for popular rule, once saying, "The people are an ungrateful and savage beast." While singing the glories of the pre-Hispanic, he explained that they had perished centuries ago. Like Francisco Javier Clavijero, the exiled Jesuit, Bustamante judged dead Indians good and wasted no sentimentality on their heirs.

Under the Junta de Zitácuaro, the *letrados* began to confer a semblance of order on the rebellion. Morelos, distrusting López Rayón, stayed on the sidelines, though he recognized the junta, thinking, conjecture has it, that it presented a united front to the enemy. The junta, meanwhile, set out to elaborate a political platform and define goals. López Rayón's *Elementos constitucionales*, a sketch of a national charter, upheld allegiance to Ferdinand VII, but, as he privately informed Morelos, this was but window dressing to ensure the loyalty of the criollos, some of whom opposed total Independence. Beyond that, the *Elementos* repeated mainly slogans from the Glorious Revolution and endorsed British political principles, with "free trade" and the "right to work" spotlighted boldly. López Rayón's draft made no mention of Morelos's agrarian ideals. Aside from that, the junta accomplished little, mainly because López Rayón quarreled with his companions.

At this juncture, Morelos convoked a *congreso* in Chilpancingo, a town in Guerrero, to write a constitution. López Rayón's rivals chose to collaborate, but he declined. Meeting in September 1813, the *congreso* turned life upside down in Chilpancingo; the hungry *letrados,* one wag reported, ate up all of the town's food and consumed "tons of paper." The delegates, their task uncompleted, had to flee when General Calleja's army broke Morelos's siege of Mexico City and started to encircle Chilpancingo. Escorted by Morelos's men, the *congreso* of *letrados* found refuge in Apatzingán, where it promulgated the Constitution of Chilpancingo, also known as the Decreto de Apatzingan. The document, which discarded the fig leaf of loyalty to Ferdinand VII, proclaimed Mexico a republic, inspired not by López Rayón's faith in the English but, instead, by the French charters of 1793 and 1795. The Constitution of 1813 established a national system of representation; executive, legislative, and judicial branches of government; and, in the manner of the Enlightenment, individual rights. The happiness of the individual, it affirmed, flowed from the enjoyment of equality before the law and, most important, guarantees for private property. Only for dire public necessity, and then only with "just compensation," could one be deprived of it. The Constitution spoke glowingly of "economic liberty" but said nary a word about the agrarian ideals of Morelos and Hidalgo. It bestowed official status on the Catholic church, trumpeting loudly that no "heretic, apostate, or non-Catholic foreigner" could become a Mexican citizen. Earlier, the same delegates in Chilpancingo had voted to invite the Jesuits to come home.

Believing they had done a praiseworthy job, the *letrados* ascribed it to their European wisdom. As Santa María, the most influential of Morelos's advisers, had urged, the "immortal Jeremy Bentham . . . should be our oracle." Santa María died on the eve of Chilpancingo, but his ideals outlived him. Ironically, Morelos, though seeing only the good points of Santa María, thought little of Bentham or the philosophical ideals of the French Revolution, deeming them out of step with reality in New Spain. Nonetheless, he went along with the rhetoric of Chilpancingo.

While the *letrados* debated among themselves and copied foreign ideals, General Calleja won victories. With each, Morelos's army dwindled in size, becoming, near its end, a ragtail guerrilla. When the Spaniards attempted to capture the Congreso de Chilpancingo, Morelos, trying to save it, fell into the hands of the Spaniards. The fateful place was the village of Temalaca; the day, November 5, 1815. His captors, both soldiers and clerics, convicted Morelos of treason, defrocked him, and then shot him in dusty and forlorn San Cristóbal Ecatepec. Had Morelos left the *letrados* to their own devices, instead of trying to save them, he might have lived on and, so too, the cause of Independence, not as envisaged by the criollos but, to the contrary, as Morelos dreamed of it originally.

Long before his capture, nevertheless, Morelos, symbolically speaking, was already dead. When he bowed to the wishes of the Congreso de Chilpancingo, the popular caudillo relinquished his authority to the *letrados,* who wanted to arrogate to themselves the mantle of power. Under the Constitution drafted by them, the tool would be a national assembly elected, above all, by the criollo ayuntamientos. Meanwhile, the rump *congreso,* which survived briefly, took command of the insurgent army away from Nicolás Bravo, the successor to Morelos. With this, the people's revolt kindled by Hidalgo was no more. Fittingly, General Manuel Mier y Terán, an insurgent aspiring to the role of caudillo, dissolved the *congreso* shortly afterward.

Unlike Hidalgo, whom most of his criollo contemporaries castigated, Morelos died a hero, as they say, with his boots on, neither repentant nor sorry for fighting for Independence. Even Alamán, conservative and Catholic, lamented his death, charging that participation of the Inquisition in this affair "helped bring about its total disrepute." For Mora, the death of Morelos in San Cristóbal Ecatepec represented "the most glorious and patriotic episode of the insurgency."

These crocodile tears of Alamán and Mora, and of countless historians since then, do not explain fully the admiration for Morelos, a leader notorious for his cruelty to Spaniards. Morelos spared no enemy. The answer must be sought elsewhere, in what Mora, in a moment of candor, wrote in his *México y sus revoluciones.* "With only skimpy knowledge of the principles of the representative system," Morelos "hastened to adopt them." Morelos's action won the plaudits of the *letrados* and of like-minded ideologues since then. For them, Morelos towers above Hidalgo because he embraced their wisdom. But, judged in hindsight, that was also his tragedy.

V

For the time being, the demise of Morelos brought to an end the insurgency of the criollos. Calleja, meanwhile, scattered their forces to the four winds, his political star rising with his victories, until he was named viceroy of New Spain, a post he held from 1813 to 1819. An able warlord, Calleja had fought in the African campaigns of Charles III before departing for the New World as a lieutenant colonel with Viceroy Revilla Gigedo. Lucky and enterprising, he married the daughter of a wealthy criollo hacendado, becoming a gentleman of elegant social graces and something of a history buff. Brave and daring, he dealt gruffly with the insurgents, winning notoriety for his cruelty. When he captured Zitácuaro, he burned it to the ground. As Justo Sierra acknowledged, Calleja was no more ruthless than Hidalgo or Morelos; neither asked for quarter. A firm believer in the efficacy of terror, Calleja converted "the insurrection into a war without mercy."

Whatever his faults, Calleja knew his criollos. Allende, for one, had served under him while on duty in San Luis Potosí. Calleja believed, perhaps rightly, that most criollos favored Independence; had the "absurd uprising of Hidalgo" not occurred, he wrote, the battle for Independence "would have faced token opposition." Given this view of criollo opinion, Calleja set out to woo them, trying, first off, to entice criollo hacendados into the Spanish camp. Additionally, he recruited an army, using money donated by the Spanish mineowners of Zacatecas and making sure that most of its officers were criollos. Antonio López de Santa Anna, Anastasio Bustamante, José Joaquín de Herrera as well as Agustín de Iturbide, criollos and prominent Mexican military figures eventually, fought on the royalist side. Criollos disciplined to take up soldiering, Calleja appointed to high public office. Despite all of that, Spanish distrust of the criollos unfolded posthaste.

Just when Calleja reckoned that he had the insurgency under control, Francisco Javier Mina, a Spaniard, briefly revived it. Not yet thirty years of age, Mina had fought against the French in Spain. After the defeat of Napoleon, Mina, imbued with ideas about freedom and equality, led an uprising in Spain to restore the liberal Constitution of 1812, which Ferdinand VII, true to his autocratic nature, had disowned once back on the throne. Vanquished, Mina fled to England, where, prodded by Servando Teresa de Mier, a priest from Nuevo León who sympathized with the insurgency, he concluded that the struggle for liberty in the mother country and New Spain were inseparable. Mier not only persuaded Mina to undertake to liberate New Spain but joined his expedition. After disembarking on the Gulf coast with a small force, Mina set off for the Bajío but was defeated, captured, and shot. Mier survived the debacle because of his family's prominence.

That Mier heavily influenced Mina should astonish no one. An eloquent speaker and writer, Mier was one of the stalwart historians of the insurgency and, perhaps, its most original ideologue. He was born into a wealthy and powerful criollo family. His Spanish grandfather, a public accountant, had settled in Monterrey in 1710; his son, Joaquín de Mier y Noriega, who climbed the political ladder, went from regidor to alcalde of Monterrey to governor of the province of Nuevo León. Born in 1763, Servando Teresa de Mier studied in the Dominican seminary in Mexico City but had to seek exile in Europe when he compared Quetzalcóatl to Saint Thomas in a public speech. He left New Spain when thirty-one and did not return for two decades. For taking part in the Mina foray, he spent three years in the prison of the Inquisition.

A man of equivocal moods, Mina was both a zealot of Independence and a conservative of aristocratic airs who took most of his ideas from Edmund Burke and Montesquieu. On the one hand, he lauded the Hidalgo uprising but, on the other, not its populist bent. With the aid of his friend and disciple Carlos María de Bustamante, he wrote a nationalist interpretation of Independence, tracing its origins to the exploitation of the sixteenth century. Consciously or not, he resurrected Bartolomé de las Casas's thesis of an evil Spanish Conquest, finding the "ancestral" rights of the criollos in it. He spelled Mexico with an *x* and not a *j*, as Spaniards commonly did. Mier's *Historia de la revolución,* which saw the light of day in 1813, justified the cause of Independence, comparing the debacle of Hidalgo to Las Casas's account of the "destruction of the Indies." Hidalgo, Moctezuma, and Cuauhtémoc had suffered alike.

With Mina out of the way, Spanish authorities had only to mop up scattered guerrillas. In the mountains of Puebla and Veracruz, Guadalupe Victoria, with two thousand ragged men, held out, as did Vicente Guerrero, who led half as many in Oaxaca. Both had earned their spurs under Morelos. Recalled to Spain, Calleja could rest easy; the insurgency of 1810 had collapsed.

VI

Elsewhere in the Western Hemisphere, however, the cause of independence, a crusade of colonials from New Spain to the viceroyalty of La Plata, at the tip of South America, had taken a turn for the better. Both Simón Bolívar, the caudillo of the criollo revolts in Venezuela and Colombia, and José de San Martín, their leader in La Plata, had the Spaniards on the run by 1820. To squash the rebellions, Ferdinand VII called on General Calleja, back in Spain, to organize an expeditionary army. Unhappily for them, a colonel by the name of Rafael Riego and his troops refused to board the ships awaiting to transport them to the New World. Instead, Riego and his men compelled the cowardly Ferdinand to swear allegiance to the Constitution of 1812, which he had disavowed, and to the reestablished Cortes.

A mildly liberal document, the charter, adopting the bourgeois values of republican France, contained a bill of rights, scolded the clergy, and spoke of popular sovereignty. The Cortes went beyond that, decreeing the end of clerical privileges, a reduction in the amount of the tithe, the sale of church property, the abolition of the Inquisition, the suppression of the monastic orders, and, for good measure, the expulsion of the Jesuits. To the higher clergy at home and in the colonies this was not merely blasphemy but a dagger aimed at the heart of the church. In New Spain, hacendados, most of whom again relied on the church for mortgages since the repeal of the *real cédula,* as well as wealthy and conservative mineowners, shared the clerical alarm. Hidalgo's upheaval had united criollo and *peninsular;* the decrees of the Cortes, as well as the return of the Constitution of 1812, split them apart again.

From the perspective of most criollos, "liberal" Spain had become a stone around their necks. Like the *letrados,* they concluded that it was better to walk alone. Searching for someone to do their bidding, they chose Agustín de Iturbide, an ambitious criollo military officer. The son of a Spanish merchant, Iturbide hailed from Valladolid (now Morelia), joining the army at fourteen. During his days in the royal military, he waged war against Hidalgo, Morelos, and whatever insurgent stood in his Royal Majesty's way. In Guanajuato, no insurgent lingered for long, because Colonel Iturbide, the local commander, handled them roughly. In 1820, when Viceroy Juan de Apodaca entrusted 2,500 soldiers to him to employ against Vicente Guerrero, Iturbide, in true Machiavellian fashion, asked the guerrilla chieftain to help him topple Spanish rule. The wary Guerrero fell in step reluctantly with Don Agustín. On July 5, 1821, Iturbide, an officer in the king's regiment, aided and abetted by Guerrero, compelled Apodaca to resign after only a skirmish or two.

The Plan de Iguala, Iturbide's declaration of Mexican Independence, ruled null and void the Constitution of 1812 and the decrees of the Cortes. For the wealthy, powerful, and conservative criollos, there were "three guarantees": independence, religion, and union. On the clergy, the plan conferred a monopoly of religion; by law, all Mexicans were Catholics. The church, by the same token, preserved its special privileges. For criollos, there were equal rights with Spaniards and, by implication, for mestizos, other *castas* and Indians. Finally, the Plan de Iguala declared Mexico a constitutional monarchy and, hard to believe, offered its crown to Ferdinand VII or, should he not want it, to another European prince. Even the *letrados* sided with Iturbide for, to quote Fernández de Lizardi, he held out guarantees to private property. Most *peninsulares* also pledged their loyalty to the Mexican monarchy.

Confronted by this reality, the Spanish crown sent Juan de O'Donoju to replace Apodaca. Wise and realistic, O'Donoju, judging the situation irredeemable, met Iturbide at Córdoba to sign the Plan de Iguala, now slightly altered by Iturbide. If no European prince coveted the throne, a Mexican could fill it. On September 28, 1821, the Ejército Trigarante entered Mexico City. Criollos as well as mestizos and Indians, whether formerly insurgents or royalists, marched triumphantly behind Iturbide, resplendent in a garish uniform and plumed hat. The residents of the city, poor and rich alike, turned out to greet their liberator, dancing in the streets and setting ablaze with lights the cathedral and National Palace, on the Zócalo. "By grace of celestial clemency," pontificated Francisco Tagle, a *letrado,* "live Religion, Union, and Independence." The three centuries of colonial rule had ended; the history of a people "born of the blood and soul of Spain," affirmed Sierra, had begun.

9

ANGUISH OF THE REPUBLIC

I

On the day of Independence, the mood of the criollos, the masters of Mexico, was euphoric. "Who then failed to foresee days of glory, of liberty and of prosperous times? Who did not anticipate an auspicious and untroubled future?" So wrote Lorenzo Zavala, whose life, full of promise, ended in death in exile, and his being branded a traitor by his countrymen. Fate, seemingly, had thought proper that Zavala and his Mexico, as the Bible says, be "born unto trouble."

II

God, the criollos fancied, had enthroned them as the chosen people. As proof of divine intervention, they pointed to the mineral treasures of their country, taking for granted, to quote Justo Sierra, a historian in love with his *patria,* that "they were the richest people on earth." Had Alexander von Humbolt in his *Essay on New Spain* not marveled at Mexico's good fortune? Under wise leadership, no clouds would darken the horizon. The believers, of course, forgot conveniently that, when researching his *Essay,* Humbolt had relied on criollo scholars who, naturally, tended to overlook shortcomings. However, the results of Independence were disasterous. The happy days never dawned. Instead, tragedy stalked the country, starting with the Mexican Empire, the first foray into self-government, which lasted less than a year. With a republic established, its presidency changed hands approximately forty times; only one chief of state completed his term in office. Politicos of one stripe or another imposed three constitutions, as though laws were the solution to the country's maladies. As one poet lamented, "Each year a new president, every month a military coup."

III

Agustín de Iturbide, Mexico's "real father," affirmed Lucas Alamán, unlocked the gates to the disaster awaiting in the wings. A criollo, he was the son of José Joaquín de Iturbide, a native of the Spanish town of Pamplona, and Dona Josefa de Aramburu, of an old and venerable family of Valladolid. By tying his destiny to a daughter of wealth, Don José got ahead. Born in 1783, Agustín, his eldest son, went to school in Valladolid but, bored by books, abandoned the halls of learning at fifteen to run his father's hacienda. Not cut out for that, he signed up as an ensign in the infantry regiment quartered in Valladolid. In 1805, he took for his wife Ana María Huarte, the daughter of a distinguished family, later acquiring haciendas on the outskirts of Maravatío and Chalco. By Ana, he sired eight offspring. Always something of a bon vivant, he made the pursuit of money a prime goal of life.

Like most criollos in the royal military, he fought against Maguel Hidalgo y Costilla, though offered a higher grade in rank by the insurgents. His initial baptism by fire was at Monte de las Cruces, where Félix Calleja's army routed Hidalgo's. Along the way, he gained for himself a reputation for cruelty, being tough on his captured foes, once putting to death María Tomasa Estévez, a woman from Irapuato. After the defeat of José María Morelos, Iturbide led a life of dissipation while stationed in Mexico City, squandering his money on women and drink. By 1820, Iturbide was dead broke and, by implication, ready for any opportunity that came his way.

The Plan de Iguala called for a provisional junta to govern the country until a national congress was elected. Iturbide chose its members mostly from conservative criollos, excluding even Vicente Guerrero, the mestizo insurgent chieftain. However, he allowed some *criollo letrados,* representatives of the provincial ayuntamientos, entrance to it. The junta, conveniently, asked Iturbide to preside over it, and then named him to a regency of five to serve as the executive until a European prince could be found to rule Mexico. One of the regency, Antonio Pérez, the bishop of Puebla, had urged Ferdinand VII to abrogate the Constitution of 1812 and opposed Independence for New Spain. The junta conferred on Iturbide the title Generalísimo de Tierra y Mar.

Soon afterward, a congress was elected, again with a preponderance of rich criollos and, like the junta, included a coterie of *letrados* from the middle clergy and licenciados (lawyers), Carlos María de Bustamante among them. Although numerically small, the *letrados,* intelligent and educated, exercised a strong voice in Congress. On the opposite side of the fence, well-off hacendados, the upper clergy, and the army, a motley bunch of *leva* soldiers (conscripts), mostly Indian campesinos and jobless workers led by criollo officers, backed Iturbide. Many of the conservative criollos in Congress, upon learning that Ferdinand VII had rejected the Mexican throne, embraced the doctrine of a centralist republic, joining hands with the *letrados,* no friends of the "real father" of Mexico. Urged on by the Masonic lodges, then getting a foothold in Mexico as advocates of republicanism, the *letrados* persuaded Congress to bar members of the regency from holding a military command and, simultaneously, to reduce the size of the bloated army. Iturbide interpreted this as a blow at him.

Almost at the same time, Pío Marche, an army sergeant quartered in Mexico City, went out into the streets shouting, "Long live Agustín I, the Emperor," gathering a mob as he made his way to Iturbide's house. From his balcony, Iturbide, at his Tartuffian best, bowed gracefully to their wishes. The next day, Pío Marche and his friends packed the halls of Congress, which had met for the first time just three months earlier. With Iturbide in attendance, the deputies *(diputados)* to Congress, intimidated by the mob, voted 70 to 15 to declare Iturbide emperor of the Mexican Empire and made the crown hereditary. To add pomp and glamour to the official coronation of June 21, 1822, as well as satisfy the lust for titles of criollo plutocrats, Iturbide, with the blessings of a majority in Congress, established the order of Knights of Guadalupe.

Among the biggest in the world, the empire stretched from California south to Central America and east to the Sabine River, the boundary of the United States. In Honduras, El Salvador, and Costa Rica, where patriots desired their independence, Mexican troops kept them in line. Glad tidings arrived in December 1822, when Washington conferred diplomatic recognition on Iturbide's empire. Commercial ambitions had led Washington to overcome its misgivings about the suitability of monarchy in the Western Hemisphere.

The empire had a short life span. Still, it left behind accomplishments, some of dubious distinction. In the fall of 1822, it abolished racial categories, ending the system of *castas.* Henceforth, everyone was simply a Mexican and equal before the law; the colonial apparatus of Indian government, including the *repúblicas de indios,* was tossed into the ashcan of history. No longer did Indians enjoy legal protection from the state, which included their communal property. The empire dismantled restrictions on trade, opened Mexican ports to the commerce of the world, cut down on the *alcabala,* reduced taxes on pulque and tobacco, and permitted mine operators and hacendados to import equipment duty free. To liquidate the national debt, it levied a forced loan on the church.

Just the same, politics went on unabated. Entrusted with the drafting of a constitution, Congress devoted more and more time to quarreling with the emperor. Hardly enthralled with the idea of monarchy, many deputies had less use for it as time went on. When newspapers supported republican views, Iturbide shut them down. In retaliation, the opposition in Congress, headed by Fray Servando Teresa de Mier and Bustamante, conspired against him. Iturbide jailed Mier, Bustamante, and thirteen more deputies. When members of Congress rallied to the defense of their jailed colleagues, Iturbide dissolved it, and when their replacements, deputies chosen by him, still balked at writing a constitution to his liking, he ruled without them. By now, both Nicolás Bravo and Vicente Guerrero, initially allies of Iturbide, had broken with him, as had Guadalupe Victoria. By his behavior, Iturbide had invited the wrath of the *letrados.* To cite a sarcastic jingle to Iturbide in the *Diario de Veracruz:*

> Bolívar you failed to imitate
> And Washington to follow,
> Liberty you oppressed
> And violated your pledge.
> Shamelessly you crowned yourself,
> Dissolved the honorable Congress,
> Jailed its *diputados*
> And now you rule alone;
> Tell us, don't you deserve
> That they cut off your head?

Antonio López de Santa Anna, a young criollo officer in the port city, accepted that advice. Then occupied in ridding San Juan de Ulúa, the fortress in the port of Veracruz, of remnants of the Spanish army, Santa Anna called for a republic and labeled Congress sovereign and its dissolution "scandalous." He placed himself at the head of a "liberating" army of *leva* soldiers, the formula now, and, not long afterward, sundry generals, among them Bravo and Guerrero, went along with the uprising against their old commander, proclaiming the Plan de Casa Mata, which enshrined Congress, dethroned Iturbide, and hailed Roman Catholicism as the national religion. With the departure of Iturbide, on March 19, 1823, Central America also went its own way. On the surface, the *letrados,* who controlled the new Congress, had captured power. Iturbide, meanwhile, banned from Mexico, made the fatal error of returning. Landing on the shores of Tamaulipas, he was taken captive and shot on the same day, just slightly over a year after his abdication.

IV

Upon the demise of Spanish power in 1821, the insurgents had split into three factions: the Borbónicos desired a Spanish prince of the house of Bourbon to rule Mexico; a second group championed Iturbide's lofty pretensions;

believers in a republican form of government composed the third. A realignment occurred with Iturbide's departure. The Borbónicos, an alliance of the richest hacendados, the clergy, and top military brass, declared themselves partisans of a Centralist republic, akin to the political structure of the old viceroyalty. Generals Nicolás Bravo and Pedro Celestino Negrete were its leaders, backed by Fray Servando Teresa de Mier, Vicente Santa María, the old ally of Morelos, and Lucas Alamán. The rival faction, headed nominally by General Vicente Guerrero, but given political direction by Lorenzo Zavala, Vicente Gómez Farías, and Miguel Ramos Arizpe, advocated a Federalist republic, a union of sovereign states, partly in imitation of the United States model. Blaming the wealthy criollos for the fall of their idol, the Iturbidistas joined this faction, which represented provincial interests. The Centralists, on the other hand, spoke for the ancient privileges of Mexico City and its hinterland. From this clash, the Federalists, briefly, emerged victorious.

Since both factions were republicans, no insurmountable obstacle seemed to block the road ahead. That hope, all the same, vanished quickly. The Federalists had shot their way to victory, threatening to secede if a Centralist republic were adopted. It was either the Federalist formula or the fragmentation of the old viceroyalty. The republicans were at odds not only over the type of organization but also over the degree of permissible popular participation. They could not agree on how much power to grant Mexicans. Both the Centralists and the provincial oligarchies beat an alarm against what they labeled demagogues, the defenders of popular rights, as they referred to *letrados* with reform on their mind. Budgetary worries, too, divided the republicans, with provincials of assorted views fretting and fuming over whether Mexico City would take the lion's share of national revenues.

The Constitution of 1824, the crowning achievement of the new Congress, took into account most of the demands of the Federalists. Mainly the work of Ramos Arizpe, a priest and theologian from Coahuila, the Constitution established a federal Republic of nineteen states and four territories; a Federal District carved out of the state of Mexico in 1826 was its capital. The charter provided for an executive, a bicameral Congress, and a judiciary, independent theoretically of each other. Every state had a governor and a legislature which, voting as a bloc, elected for four years the president and vice-president of the Republic. Federal senators were elected for four years by the state legislators and the deputies of the national chamber were elected for two years by indirect vote in the states on the basis of one deputy for every eighty thousand inhabitants. By these checks and balances, the power of the popular vote was negated severely. Judges with life tenure sat on the Supreme Court. The Constitution banned all but the Catholic faith from Mexican soil and kept intact the *fueros* of church and military. Additionally, it conferred on the president of the Republic special powers in times of emergencies, a stipulation that invited mischief.

The elections elevated Guadalupe Victoria to the National Palace and Nicolás Bravo, a rival Centralist, to the vice-presidency. A lawyer, Victoria had studied at the Colegio de San Ildefonso in Mexico City, then sided with the insurgents, doing most of his fighting in Veracruz. Madame Calderón de la Barca, the Scottish-born wife of the first Spanish minister to the Mexican Republic, described him as an "honest, plain, down-looking citizen, lame and tall, somewhat at a loss for conversation, apparently amiable and good natured." Of "undeniable bravery" and unambitious for himself, he, for all that, did not measure up in leadership. Striving to be fair, Victoria, a Federalist, invited Centralists to join his cabinet, whose members, not astonishingly, feathered their own nests.

The Congress, in compliance with the intent of the charter's drafters, became the hobbyhorse of the *letrados.* Lawyers, journalists, and priests were the only ones who, by schooling and learning, met the qualifications for serving in Congress. In that manner, the *letrados,* a "middle class" in gestation, made short shrift of the legacy of the people's caudillo, what Hidalgo and Morelos symbolized when they captained the insurgency of the have-nots. From this time on, Congress shut eyes and ears to the pleas of the lower class. The united front against the indigent scarcely meant that harmony reigned in the halls of Congress. Quite the opposite: debates over the nature of the Republic exacerbated differences of opinion among criollos. Acrimony and distrust had a field day.

To add fuel to the political fires, Freemasonry, a current fad, split up into warring camps, with Escoseses (Scottish Rite Masons), Centralists and Conservative, pitted against Yorquinos (York Rite Masons), Federalists and Liberal. The Masonic movement had infiltrated Mexico by way of Spain. The first lodges in New Spain, established in 1818, lobbied for the end of clerical control of education; from this emerged the Lancaster school in Mexico. Their Spanish equivalent had backed the revolt of Colonel Rafael Riego and the restoration of the Constitution of 1812. This occurred over the vehement objections of the Inquisition, which looked upon Freemasonry as the work of the devil. After Independence, the *letrados* took to Freemasonry like a duck to water.

The Escoseses, first on the scene, supported Iturbide, before going over to the republicans and throwing their weight behind the Plan de Casa Mata. With the arrival of Joel R. Poinsett, the United States minister to Mexico, the Yorquinos, an offshoot of the grand lodge of Pennsylvania, got a toehold. Allies of Poinsett, its founders were Zavala and José María Alpuche, a priest from Tabasco and a senator. Under President Victoria, the ranks of the Yorquinos expanded rapidly. In Mexico City, both lodges ran newspapers—the Yorquinos, *El Correo,* and the Escoceses, *El Sol*—while provincial affiliates published their own. Through their newspapers, the two lodges waged a propaganda war against each other and, consequently, whipped up conflict in the Republic. The war of words turned hot when the Escoceses, embittered by Victoria's partiality for the Yorquinos, supported an aborted uprising spearheaded by Vice-President Bravo. The rebels wanted Poinsett expelled, an end to the Yorquinos, and a cabinet housecleaning. With the failure of the rebellion, the Escoceses broke up and the Yorquinos split into quarreling factions when they could not agree on whom to support to succeed Victoria, with Zavala, joined by Poinsett, backing Vicente Guerrero. After that, Freemasonry, though still held dear by the better schooled, lost its preeminence.

Hampered by lackluster leadership, Victoria's administration confronted a host of problems, not the least of them an empty treasury. Balanced budgets were figments of the imagination. To make things worse, the Republic inherited a public debt of over 76 million pesos from the viceroyalty. Without money, not much could be done. Still, Victoria's administration weathered its term in office, won diplomatic recognition from Great Britain and most of Europe, and signed commercial treaties and a boundary agreement with the United States, which confirmed the Sabine River as the eastern limits of Texas.

Victoria's administration believed foreign capital was a solution to its difficulties. Europeans, its politicos affirmed, could revive the economy either by lending money or by investing in it. Alamán, Victoria's minister of foreign affairs, proclaimed it wise to borrow from Europeans, especially from the English, in order to identify their economic interest with Mexico's. In that manner, he explained, they would rush to Mexico's defense if threatened by the United States, a nation distrusted by Alamán. English bankers were ready to oblige. Mexico, as everyone knew, was rich in minerals; if mining were restored, the economy would prosper. In 1824, Mexico borrowed 16 million pesos from Goldshmitt & Company, a London firm and, a few months afterward, an equal amount from Barclay & Company. From these loans, the Republic received, by all accounts, only about 12 million pesos. The money was largely wasted, to quote Sierra, on "bad ships, bad guns, and war supplies," needed supposedly to stop a purported attempt at reconquest by Spain.

When elections came around, General Manuel Gómez Pedraza defeated General Vicente Guerrero, the candidate of the Federalists. A scholar of note and a Centralist, Gómez Pedraza had been minister of war in Victoria's cabinet. Courtly and absentminded, he had, it was said, forgotten the day of his wedding, so it was necessary to look for him in order for the ceremony to proceed. He triumphed by the narrowest of margins, encouraging the Federalists and General Santa Anna, as he was known, to rebel. When Gómez Pedraza purged Federalists from government posts, ousting Zavala from the governorship of Mexico State, the Federalists were up in arms. Gómez Pedraza had to abandon the National Palace when soldiers quartered at the prison of La Acordada, goaded by Zavala, sided with the Federalists.

Defeated at the polls, Guerrero had achieved victory by a cuartelazo, a military coup, the first of scores to follow. A hero of the Independence wars, Guerrero, a southerner more Indian than mestizo, was, for the most part, uneducated. Suffering from a wound inflicted by soldiers of Iturbide, Guerrero, who often appeared weary, occasionally "spit blood and splinters of bone." His vice-president was General Anastasio Bustamante, once a royalist army officer. Santa Anna, who masterminded the coup, went back to Veracruz as its governor.

The cuartelazo of the Acordada brought Lorenzo Zavala, minister of the treasury in Guerrero's cabinet, into the limelight. Until 1836, this criollo from the town of Conkal in Yucatán and a deputy to Congress in the days of Iturbide, loomed large on the political scene. A spokesman for the Federalists, he had been a champion of Independence, and had been jailed for his efforts from 1814 to 1817. Loyal to Iturbide until the end, he embraced republicanism in 1823. Of a sharp mind and boundless ambition, Zavala had politics in his blood, as well as the fever of the money speculator. During his lifetime, he studied medicine, helped organize the Yorquinos, contributed to the Constitution of 1824, and served as governor of Mexico State from 1827 to 1828 and again in 1832 and a term as deputy to Congress from Yucatán. Somehow, too, he found time to write *Ensayo político de las revoluciones,* a two-volume history of the era from 1808 to 1830.

Mexicans remember Zavala mostly for his role in the Texas rebellion of 1836. As Mexico's minister to France, he had resigned when Santa Anna became president and fled to Texas, where he owned land. Opposed bitterly to Centralist rule, which Santa Anna personified, Zavala aided the American colonists in Texas to achieve their independence. Months afterward, bitter and disillusioned, he died in Texas, at a place baptized Zavala's Point. Mexicans also think of Zavala for his role in the Cuartelazo de La Acordada, the curtain raiser for the use of soldiers by politicos hungry for public office.

Politics aside, wars soon came to occupy the attention of Mexicans. The first one was with Spain. Encouraged by Mexican internal strife, Spain decided to reconquer its former colony. In July 1829, some three thousand Spanish troops landed at Tampico, which, to their surprise, they found undefended. Though they captured the port easily, yellow fever killed countless Spanish soldiers. Weakened by the disease and lacking medical supplies and food, the Spaniards were no match for a Mexican army led by General Santa Anna, who emerged from the episode the "Hero of Tampico."

The foreign menace disposed of, the political scene went back to what was rapidly becoming a chronic state of unrest. Using as a pretext President Guerrero's refusal to surrender his emergency wartime powers, Anastasio Bustamante, the vice-president, got the army to back his coup. When Mexico City fell, Guerrero took refuge in the mountains to the south, joined by Juan Alvarez, the caudillo of Guerrero State, where they held out for nearly a year. Enticed aboard an Italian merchant ship in the harbor of Acapulco, Guerrero was betrayed by its captain to Bustamante's forces, tried for treason, and shot. Lucas Alamán, the erstwhile defender of Spanish lives in Guananjuato, was one of those who soiled their reputation in this shameful episode.

After Bustamante's triumph, Centralists, increasingly labeled Conservatives, wielded the baton. A former admirer of Iturbide, Bustamante was a man of medium height, rather stocky, and affable of personality. Frank and simple in his manners, he seldom imposed his views on others. Personally honest, he despised corruption but closed his eyes to the chicanery around him. Having fought against the insurgents, he distrusted them, thinking of them as either bandits or sinners. Earnest and disciplined, he craved order no matter what the cost, alleging that the ends justified the means. His reliance on wanton cruelty tainted his administration with the blood of his adversaries.

In his cabinet of Conservatives, Lucas Alamán, the secretary of state, loomed tall above the rest, all of criollo stock. The other kingpins were the reactionary priest Ignacio Figueroa and José Antonio Facio, an obstinate defender of the military *fuero.* Alamán was the brains and soul of Bustamante's administration. Under his tutelage, the Centralists turned back the clock, trying to conserve as much of colonial Mexico as possible, restricting the functions of Congress while giving voice to the will of property owners. They also rid themselves of Federalist governors and legislatures, relying on troops to do it in eleven states. Dissenting newspapers were shut down. Bandits, a sore on the land, had their comeuppance, smugglers no longer went unpunished, and the national treasury accumulated funds for a rainy day.

Bustamante's tough policies quickly antagonized the Federalists, more and more referred to as Liberals. Soon mutterings of discontent could be heard in the provinces, especially in the north. When General Santa Anna rebelled in Veracruz, vouching for the virtues of federalism, authorities in state after state, with *leva* troops to support them, seconded the uprising. Seeing the handwriting on the wall, Bustamante, in late 1832, fled the National Palace for exile. To cloak their cuartelazo under the mantle of legitimacy, the victorious rebels invited Gómez Pedraza to serve out his interrupted term. The next year, the elections placed Santa Anna, sporting the robes of the Federalists, in the presidential chair. From that time until 1855, this quixotic man wore the presidential sash on eleven different occasions. The elections also put Valentín

Gómez Farías, the fiery Federalist reformer, in the vice-presidency and Zavala in the governorship of Mexico State.

V

Thus began the "Age of Santa Anna," a calamity in Mexican history. No one has explained how this man, "with just enough intelligence to develop in himself . . . the faculty called astuteness," said Sierra, hoodwinked both wealthy criollos and *letrados* for so long. Crafty and treacherous, Santa Anna held himself in high esteem, believing that providence had chosen him to be the "Republic's savior," an "ambition sustained . . . by figments of Catholic superstitions." Vain and susceptible to flattery, he was a man shorn of principles, "save his own ambition," to quote Sierra. "A hero to his soldiers, he never "hesitated to take charge of any military campaign though he had no qualifications except the ability to infuse the troops with his own ardor."

In 1833, Santa Anna was just thirty-six years of age. Of medium height, more slender than fat, this criollo from Veracruz was fair of skin but of sallow complexion. Women found him "gentlemanly" and "good-looking." He could be charming, spicing his conversation with the *jarocho* accent of his native Veracruz; although neither a glutton nor a connoisseur of food, he enjoyed holding forth on the virtues of the fare on the table, discussing in detail the seasoning of a dish, how to prepare oysters, octopus, and so on. Intellectually an illiterate, for he never read, Santa Anna spoke a bastard Spanish enlivened by words foreign to it. He was a profound judge of men, with a keen insight into the human character, generally with his fingers on the public pulse. He spent "his entire political life making war, raising money and plotting." When out of office, he plotted to get in; when in office, he plotted to stay there.

Santa Anna loved to gamble, especially to play cards, and, when the occasion permitted, to woo women. He was a bit of a Don Juan: "His Excellence," remembered Madame Calderón de la Barca, "is by no means indifferent to beauty—*tout au contraire.*" Cockfights were his chief pleasure; he never neglected to care for his gamecocks at his hacienda, Manga de Clavo. At the cockfights in Mexico City, which he attended faithfully, he knew by name every fine gamecock. At these events, he was their elixir, ready to fix odds, collect bets, and wager himself, while mixing freely with the rabble. At thirty years of age, he married María Inés de la Paz García, the daughter of Spaniards, and spent his honeymoon at Manga de Clavo, where he found solace when fate betrayed him.

Whatever else he may have been, Don Antonio was a politico of his time. Adaptable, he was everything to all factions, as well as to men such as Esteban de Antuñano, the textile magnate, who once called Santa Anna the solution to Mexico's ills. A royalist officer, he embraced the insurgency and fawned on Iturbide, hailing his "sublime" imperial pretensions, then acclaimed the banners of the Republic. During the 1820s, he was a Federalist, a sympathizer of the Yorquinos and Guerrero. In 1832, after allying himself with the cuartelazo against Bustamante, he helped bring back Gómez Pedraza, before winning the presidency as a Liberal, an admirer of the Constitution. Then he swung over to the camp of its critics, became a Centralist by 1843 and a dictator the next year, only to be an ally of the apostles of "constitutionalism" by 1846, ending his political career as a dictator. Once more seeking the blessings of public applause, he offered his sword to the French invaders of Mexico in the 1860s; rejected, he swore allegiance to the Republicans, who disdained his offer.

Santa Anna's era was a fatted calf for graft and corruption. Detractors referred to Santa Anna as "Fifteen Hands," alluding to his fondness for money and his "sticky fingers." That he courted wealth, no one doubts. Corruption in public life, often identified with his name, antedated him by centuries; its origins went back to the colonial period. Santa Anna's lackeys, all the same, piled up fortunes through sleazy ventures. His age, lamented Guillermo Prieto, journalist and politico, spawned a "corrupt society." One of its notorious scandals concerned an aide of Santa Anna, a certain Colonel Yáñez, a favorite of high society who drew attention to himself by his shady friends and by how well he lived on a soldier's pay. One day, it was learned that a robbery had occurred in the capital and that Colonel Yáñez headed the gang of thieves. Thievery and graft in the days of Santa Anna, a man with the face of Caesar but the mind of a rogue, so went a popular ditty, was as Mexican as the tortilla.

Unexpectedly, the initial entry into presidential politics of this charlatan produced a memorable attempt at reform. It was, however, not of his doing. Santa Anna, who won the election of 1833 by a whopping majority, had campaigned with Gómez Farías on the Liberal ticket, by now synonymous with Federalist, promising to push reforms awaited by the nascent "middle class," heavily provincial and mostly criollo. The future looked bright for the Liberals, but shoals lay ahead. Sensing that trouble with the Conservatives was brewing, Santa Anna, disinclined to jeopardize his popularity, left the National Palace to Gómez Farías, a native of Zacatecas and a physician who had studied at the University of Guadalajara and served as a deputy in the Congress of 1824, where he did battle for federalism and the Constitution. In his ideological convictions, he stood firm, not knowing, wrote Francisco Bulnes, an iconoclastic journalist and historian, how to "lie, dissemble, be silent, hide, cede, or relent." As president of the Republic in Santa Anna's absence, Gómez Farías, supported by a Liberal Congress, pushed through a series of weighty reforms in just ten months.

This stalwart criollo spoke for young, educated, and ambitious provincials, part of the emerging "middle class." Mostly from the state capitals, they were, ideologically, ahead of their time. Their debut on the national scene testified to the passing of the *letrado* generation of the insurgency. The old heroes were dying off; Andrés Quintana Roo, his "body bent over" like that of an "old man," walked "only with difficulty," to quote Prieto, his mind rarely dwelling on the insurgency, and now a "distinguished Latin scholar who embellished his conversation with quotes from Cicero, Horace, and Virgil."

Neither was Carlos María de Bustamante any longer a firebrand. Friends remembered him as an "old man with big silver eyeglasses sitting atop his aquiline nose, defending an amalgam of diverse dogmas." In some ways, he had remained faithful to his former ideals, still believing Hidalgo and Morelos to be the true fathers of Mexican Independence. In Congress, he had fought tenaciously to celebrate the sixteenth of September, the date in 1810 of Hidalgo's Grito de Dolores, as the official birthday of the Republic. He continued to eulogize the pre-Hispanic past and the Virgen de Guadalupe, and he hated Santa Anna. But he was now a Conservative, standing up for the church, its *fueros,* and its right to own property. He belittled Gómez Farías, decried attacks on the church, and had no use for Yorquinos or for Adam Smith and free trade.

Gómez Farías, a fervent disciple of the capitalist creed sweeping western Europe, meant to extirpate, once and forever, colonial vestiges from the Mexican scene, to transform "society . . . into a lay society" and undo the authority of the church. As a Liberal, he wished very much, at one and the same time, to multiply the numbers of property owners but not to tinker with private property. Like most capitalist ideologues, he saw secular education as a panacea for society's ills, once Mexican teachers taught English, French, and German, as well as physics, chemistry, and political economy. When this schooling had reshaped the minds of the young, a bright future lay ahead for Mexico.

Gómez Farías lost no time getting reform under way. Under his prodding, Congress, also Liberal from the recent elections, enacted far-reaching reforms. It abolished the compulsory payment of the tithe; declared monks and nuns free to retract their vows; shut down the clerical University of Mexico; and, in California, closed the Franciscan missions, confiscated their funds, and set their Indians free. To teach children in the Federal District and territories, Congress established the Office of Public Instruction; education would be secular and free in its schools. Bent on curbing the power of the army, it reduced its size and deprived officers of the *fuero.*

For his ideas, Gómez Farías could thank Zavala and José María Luis Mora. Of the Liberal ideologues, none surpassed Mora in importance; he was, so to speak, the party ideologue. Born in Chamacuero, a town in Querétaro, he was a priest, theologian, and lawyer. As a teacher of Latin and the humanities at the Colegio de San Ildefonso, he offered the first course in political economy taught in Mexico. Mora established the Instituto Literario y Científico in Toluca, which both Ignacio Ramírez and Ignacio Manuel Altamirano, towering figures of the following generation, attended. In his brief political career, he was a deputy in the legislature of Mexico State, a deputy to Congress from Guanajuato, and head of the Office of Public Instruction. Rigid of mind and enamored of the rugged individual, he wrote for the educated minority, to whom he belonged. Primarily the axioms of capitalist ideologues, his ideas inspired not just the generation of Gómez Farías but the Reforma of the 1860s. His *Mexico y sus revoluciones,* written to refute Bustamante's *Cuadro histórico,* examined society during the early years of Independence. His numerous articles, published initially in newspapers and journals, appeared in *Obras sueltas.* The "right to property," he affirmed in *Mexico y sus revoluciones,* "is the foundation of all political association." A dyed-in-the-wool free trader, he welcomed foreign investment and opposed protective tariffs, ascertaining that trade with the Western world was the answer to Mexico's ills.

For Mora, the Spanish colonial past was no guide to the future. Liberal ideas symbolized progress. This was not a moment for paternalistic formulas; the Indians, one of their victims, must be set free. Bartolomé de las Casas and Vasco de Quiroga, the intellectual authors of the Laws of the Indies, had erred. All Mexicans were just Mexicans, free of racial distinctions and equal before the law. But Mora held Indians in low esteem, implying they were unambitious if not lazy. No matter how poor, he wrote, the Indian, "with one day's pay to his name, takes off the rest of the week," whether or not he had money for "food, clothing, or medical care." Anticipating social Darwinism by half a century, he took for granted the superiority of some "races," arguing that the labor of the Indian "was not just inferior to that of a German but," worse still, "to that of the weakest races" of southern Europe. Frightened by rebellious Maya, he urged officials in Mexico City to seek British aid and, a bit later, the expulsion of the Maya from Yucatán. Taking a leaf from Mora, the hacendados of Yucatán sold Maya Indians to Cuba. It was to this Mora that Gómez Farías and his Liberals turned for ideological guidance.

The apostasy of the Gómez Farías regime lasted just long enough to raise a hue and cry from church, military, and Conservatives. Before long, with army units in revolt, Santa Anna decided to cut short his absence from politics. Showering curses on Gómez Farías and his companions, "atheists" and "York Rite Masons," the recent champion of Federalist and Liberal causes cast them to the four winds, turned Conservative, and rid Mexico of its redeemers. Once in the National Palace, he discarded every law adopted by Congress. Gómez Farías, Zavala, and Mora had to find refuge in exile, Mora never again to set foot on Mexican soil.

Conservative, Centralist, and Catholic: that was the nature of the new regime. Santa Anna savored merely the triumph, not its aftermath. Repeating his previous performance, he named General Miguel Barragán interim president and retired to Manga de Clavo, emerging now and then to squash Federalist revolts in the provinces. When Zacatecas rebelled, an army led by the Hero of Tampico crushed it and sacked its capital city, then, like a scythe, cut a wide swath through Querétaro, Jalisco, and Michoacán. Meanwhile, the military brass, supported by the clerical hierarchy and wealthy criollos, dissolved Congress and elected one of their own, abrogated the Constitution of 1824, and replaced it with the Siete Leyes of 1836.

That charter transformed the states into military departments, their chieftains named from Mexico City. Presidents, elected by vote of the Senate, the Chamber of Deputies, the National Council, and the departments, served for eight years, twice as long as before. To reserve politics for the elite, *las clases pudientes* of Alamán, the Siete Leyes stipulated that officeholders be well-off. A candidate for the presidency had to have an annual income of 4,000 pesos; for the Senate, 2,500; and for the Chamber, 1,500. The rich employed the Siete Leyes to impose their rule.

During these years, tussles with foreigners again occupied the national stage. One was the secession of Texas in 1836 and another the Guerra de los Pasteles, or Pastry War, with France. At the time, General Anastasio Bustamante, after the death of Barragán, was once more in the National Palace. Early in 1838, France called upon Mexico to pay for damages to the property of its citizens, alleging that it owed 600,000 pesos, partly as recompense for harm done to a French pastry shop—thus the title of the conflict. When Mexico dragged its feet, a French fleet dropped anchor off Veracruz; more ships were added, the blackmail raised to 800,000 pesos, and diplomatic relations broken when Mexico failed to reply promptly. Confronted with this show of arms, the Mexicans agreed to negotiate, offering to pay the 600,000 pesos, but, as a precaution, ordered soldiers to San Juan de Ulúa, the fort protecting the city of Veracruz. The French ships shelled the fort and drove out its defenders.

Veracruz lay helpless before the French. Partly because he could call on no one else and because Santa Anna, of his own volition, had rushed to the port city, Bustamante put him in charge of its defense. The three thousand French soldiers found Santa Anna prepared to repel their attack. Fortunately for Mexico, Santa Anna's troops did just that, their commander losing part of his left leg in battle. From that moment on, the Hero of Tampico, and now also of Veracruz, never permitted Mexicans to forget that he had sacrificed a leg on their behalf. Back on their ships, the French, less bellicose, decided to forgo their demands for 800,000 pesos, accepting the original amount. The Mexicans had to agree to an unfavorable treaty of commerce with France, while the blockade had shut down Mexico's principal port for seven months and paralyzed its trade with the outside world. Santa Anna, who had tarnished badly his prestige in Texas, was once more a hero.

It was a Pyrrhic victory, lamented Sierra: "the period . . . was one of the darkest in our tragic history." Hampered by chronic deficits in the budget, Mexico stumbled from one financial crisis to another. Yucatán, where the Liberals held out, had abandoned the Republic, preferring to travel its own path. A revolt in San Luis Potosí by General Esteban Moctezuma had to be put down by Bustamante, who left Santa Anna in the presidency. Bustamante's troops defeated rebel armies under the Federalist generals José Antonio Mejía and José Urrea. They captured and shot Mejía, but Urrea escaped, to throw in his lot with one more Federalist plot to overthrow the government. The chaotic picture and the despair that accompanied it persuaded José Miguel Gutiérrez Estrada, a deputy from Yucatán, to advocate publicly a European monarchy for Mexico. Nothing else, he believed, would save Mexico from itself and from the United States, a danger increasingly to its territorial integrity. General Juan N. Almonte, a son of José María Morelos, spearheaded the cry of indignation and Gutiérrez Estrada had to go into hiding.

That did not prevent Santa Anna from lending a hand to a cuartelazo by Generals Mariano Paredes Arrillaga and Gabriel Valencia, the latter the commander of the troops in Mexico City. Smelling federalism in the revolt, President Bustamante, in a turnabout, called for the restoration of the Constitution of 1824. Paredes Arrillaga, the ringleader of the military coup, dubbed "the most cynical," was the caudillo of Jalisco. Short of stature and with a Roman nose, this criollo with a taste for bright uniforms, according to Prieto, might better have been employed "to collect tickets at the box office of a theater." Of monarchist sympathies and "supremely servile," he was a go-between for the clerical and military factions. Like most generals, he was barely literate though brave and upright. Admiring Lucas Alamán, he married a woman of identical views, the offspring of plutocrats from Guadalajara, and Catholic to the marrow, who went about saying that the Liberals obeyed the dictates of the devil himself. She was a social butterfly in the snobbish circles of Guadalajara. For faultfinding federalists, Paredes Arrillaga, along with Santa Anna and Valencia, had contrived a Centralist coup against a Centralist president for the simple purpose of robbing the public till, under the pretext that the Constitution needed reforming.

By the treaty ending the uprising, Santa Anna, who came out on top, was to appoint a committee to name an interim president who would call for elections for a congress to draft a charter. In the interval, the interim chief had dictatorial powers. The committee picked Santa Anna, who, once this was done, had himself elected president. However, the ayuntamientos, asked to elect the Congress of 1842, returned a majority of Federalists to Mexico City. When they set about curbing presidential authority, Santa Anna, as was his habit, left for Manga de Clavo, leaving General Bravo, a fellow Centralist, to use soldiers to disband Congress. Bravo then chose a *junta de notables* to draw up a charter. Made up of ninety-two criollo plutocrats, the junta devised the Bases Orgánicas of 1843, by which the Republic remained safely Centralist. When all was quiet again, Santa Anna departed Manga de Clavo to occupy the presidential chair.

Santa Anna did little to alleviate national ills. Adept at raising money, he forced loans on the church, to its surprise and consternation; levied higher import duties; and sold mining concessions to the British. He squandered the money on the army, adding officers and recruiting more men and buying military hardware. To entice Yucatán back into the fold, Santa Anna sent an army, which failed to reconquer it; not till 1846 did Yucatán hoist aloft the tricolor flag of the Republic. On the lighter side, when his wife died, Santa Anna married once more, a girl just sixteen years of age. Desiring to honor the leg he lost in Veracruz, he had it disinterred and buried afresh in the cathedral of Mexico City, amid much pomp and ceremony.

By 1844, some Mexicans had tired of Santa Anna. Using as a subterfuge his unwillingness to obey Congres, General Paredes Arrillaga, the perennial malcontent, rebelled in Jalisco, and, when Santa Anna sallied forth to punish him, Valencia ambushed him from behind. Caught in this untenable situation, Santa Anna's troops deserted their leader, who, fearful for his life, took flight to Veracruz, where rebellious soldiers seized him. Authorities in Mexico City spared his life but shipped him off to Cuba.

With Santa Anna out of the way, Congress named General José J. Herrera president of the Republic. Formerly the owner of a drugstore in Jalapa, he was a veteran of the Wars for Independence, having fought on the side of the insurgency. Poorly schooled, he accepted docilely the counsel of others, especially of Paredes Arrillaga and Mariano Otero, a budding Conservative politico. Their views hardened the moderate inclinations of the president but did not save him from their aspirations. In December 1845, just as he revealed his willingness to negotiate with Washington, which had recently annexed Texas, General Paredes Arrillaga, once more supported by the army, revolted, toppling Herrera. His administration had survived for one year, most of that time attempting to fend off the United States, eager to annex California.

Paredes Arrillaga then had himself designated president by an assembly he chose. At this date, an army of the United States had entered Texas and blockaded Mexican ports on the Gulf. Trying to take advantage of the terrible emergency, Paredes Arrillaga did what he could to pave the way for a monarchy, using constitutional reform as an excuse. A republican outcry in the provinces laid the scheme to rest. However, when his troops failed to halt the invasion of Mexico by the United States, the military of Guadalajara, prodded by Gómez Farías, rose up in arms, demanding the return of Santa Anna, the only man thought capable of defending Mexico. (Texas and the war with the

United States are discussed separately.) The Gudadalajara cuartelazo sealed the fate of Paredes Arrillaga. Fervent Federalists, the victorious rebels convoked a Congress, restored the Constitution of 1824, and named Santa Anna president and Gómez Farías his vice-president, the alliance of the 1830s.

The Federalists manipulated the elections and won control of Congress. With Santa Anna off in San Luis Pototsí trying to train an army for the war with the United States, Gómez Farías and his congressional allies, more and more of them orthodox Liberals, set about curtailing the power of the church. To pay for the war, Congress voted to nationalize and sell church property until 15 million pesos were raised. If the church lent the money, it would get its property back. The legislation alarmed the clergy and the faithful, most of whom denounced Gómez Farías, Congress, and the legislation or refused to bear arms against the North American invaders. Doing his usual flip-flop, Santa Anna abrogated the legislation and named, in his absence, General María Anaya interim chief of Mexico. Shortly thereafter, Santa Anna, his army vanquished by the invaders, had to resign the presidency and go off to exile, leaving Manuel Peña y Peña, the chief justice of the Supreme Court, to sign the peace.

The departure of the Americans in June 1848 left Mexico in shambles. It was up to General Herrera, once more in the presidency, to restore order, for which he could count on only the $15 million Washington paid for nearly half of Mexico's territory. He had, moreover, to deal with a rebellion of the Maya in Yucatán. On top of that, sundry uprisings broke out elsewhere, at Xichú in Guanajuato and, in Veracruz, at Misantla and the Huasteca, one or more of them encouraged perhaps by the United States. The bloated army, at the same time, had to be reduced in size, a task entrusted to General Mariano Arista, the minister of war and Herrera's successor by way of a military coup.

Arista, who assumed office in January 1851, somehow managed to stay in office for two years, though filibusters from north of the border swooped down on Mexico's frontier states; one band, composed of Americans and Mexicans, endeavored to incite Tamaulipas to declare itself a separate republic, while Apaches fell upon towns in Sonora and other Indians ravaged Durango. In Yucatán, the Maya refused to lay down their arms, converting the Caste War into a nightmare. Unwilling to tax the provinces, Congress refused to raise revenue to pay off the towering public debt. Arista's interval in office ended in the summer of 1852, when a rebellion in Guadalajara, which caught on like wildfire in the army, turned Congress against him. Plotting in the wings was the insatiable Santa Anna and, beside him, Alamán, still dreaming of yesteryear. Confronted by this sorry picture, Arista resigned, the victim of betrayal.

Off and on the political stage since the 1820s, Alamán had in 1849 finally given form and substance to the Conservative party, tainted, from the start, by its identification with monarchical designs. Alamán, its architect, was the son of a Spanish merchant who struck it rich in mining; his mother, who belonged to a distinguished criollo family of Guanajuato, traced her ancestry to the sixteenth century. In 1823, Alamán married Narcisa Castrillo, a criolla of known pedigree. Although his hair had turned completely gray by this time, Alamán was yet a handsome man, of medium height, high forehead, prominent nose, and delicate white skin. Vain about his looks, he dressed carefully and was of a regal bearing. Widely read and erudite, he prided himself in his knowledge of the classics, reading both Latin and Greek, in addition to English and Italian. An avid author, he rose at dawn to write, standing up before a tall desk and seldom polishing his original draft. A gentleman of the old school, he was polite of manner, rarely voicing controversial opinions in social gatherings. A fervent Catholic, he asked a priest to bless each meal and then, before excusing himself from the table, said an Our Father and, just as he was getting into bed, went through the rosary.

Alamán was an intelligent and complex man. Unlike most provincial criollos, he had traveled widely during his journey to Europe in 1814, visiting Spain and France, where he met Napoleon. In Germany, he studied mining technology and Greek and, thanks to letters of introduction provided by Humboldt, spent time with eminent scientists. Before coming home in 1819, he visited England and Belgium. Above all, Alamán was a man of ideas, more and more conservative ones. His *Historia de México,* a five-volume account of the years he witnessed, as well as his other works, copied much from Edmund Burke, to whom he liked to compare himself. In the mold of Burke, he saw property as the basis of society; without security for its owners, no society could exist. Though he believed in elections and liberty, he thought both impossible without order, which he said was the essence of a nation. Yet he accepted the Enlightenment myth of progress, thinking it possible to improve mankind through education. He spoke of bettering the lot of the common folk but ignored the need to transform the social structure, a kind of reform from the top down. Religion could help extirpate the terrible habits of the poor, the unwillingness to save for a rainy day, drunkenness, and being dirty.

Once an advocate of Independence, he came to see it as a tragedy, viewing the colonial years as a wonderful age. The Hidalgo episode had been a horrible aberration. Although the past could not be restored, Alamán conceded, a viable future had to respect customs and traditions. Because liberalism, the capitalist dogma of the nineteenth century, belittled the past, it was pernicious. Judged by contemporary economic criteria, Alamán was a man ahead of his time, fighting to establish industry in Mexico, pointing out that free trade, the panacea of Mora and the Liberals, would stifle Mexico's development. Fearful of the United States, he sought to promote a union of the Spanish-American republics, the dream of Simón Bolívar, whom he admired, and, while minister of foreign affairs in the 1820s, wished very much for Mexico and the republic of Colombia to rid Cuba of Spanish rule and, by so doing, thwart Washington's designs on it.

VI

The departure of General Arista led to a government by Santa Anna, lured back from exile by Alamán and the Conservatives. High clergy, wealthy hacendados, and the army chiefs looked to Santa Anna to save Mexico from ruin. "Providence," Alamán told Santa Anna, chose "you to heal the nation's ills." On April 20, 1853, Santa Anna, granted absolute authority by the "revolution," returned; Alamán, who expected to control the flamboyant caudillo, headed the cabinet but died soon afterward, which gave Santa Anna a free hand.

Titling himself Most Serene Highness, the sixty-year-old Santa Anna set about resurrecting the frills of monarchy, the order of Knights of Guadalupe for one, and "the panoply and protocol of royalty." He aspired to ape Napoleon III, refusing to crown himself only because he knew it would lead to his downfall. He rebuilt the army, in that way ensuring its loyalty to him; he gave it resplendent uniforms, colorful banners, and better pay, and shut his eyes when military grades were bought and sold. In the National Palace, Santa Anna basked in the flattery of sycophants, as graft and corruption wreaked havoc with the budget and the country's morals. Somehow, nevertheless, Miguel Lerdo de Tejada, the best of the cabinet, found money to build a highway between Mexico City and Cuernavaca, to set up telegraph lines to Veracruz and Guanajuato, and to begin the construction of the railway to Veracruz.

Santa Anna's final fling lasted only briefly. His companions, the criollos of the first republican generation, were dying off, not just Alamán but General José María Tornel, an unabashed worshiper of His Most Serene Highness. Santa Anna, missing sorely the wisdom of his cronies, handled badly the affair of Gaston de Raousset-Boulbon, a French filibusterer from California who twice engineered attempts to conquer Sonora; on his second, in 1854, he fell upon the port city of Guaymas. General José María Yáñez, who repelled the attack, committed the error, in Santa Anna's eyes, of pardoning the adventurers but executing their leader, an act that garnered for him wide, popular acclaim. Santa Anna, who had no stomach for rival heroes, was filled with envy, so he court-martialed Yáñez, to the dismay of the army and countless patriots. Then, to acquire funds to suppress a military uprising in Ayutla, a town in Guerrero, he sold the Mesilla to the United States, cutting in half the territory of Sonora for a paltry seven million pesos.

With that news, a clamor of outrage swept over Mexico, rocking badly the ship of state. The capture of Veracruz by rebels in 1855, which threatened to cut off his escape route, persuaded Santa Anna to take a hasty flight into exile. Just over a decade afterward, when he attempted to disembark at Sisal, a port in Yucatán, he was taken prisoner and tried for treason at San Juan de Ulúa. Judged too old and senile to be executed, Santa Anna was banned forever from Mexico, his regal stage for nearly forty years.

10

THE STUFF OF PIPE DREAMS

I

The criollos, palpably, had "left undone those things which," to quote the *Book of Common Prayer*, "we ought to have done; and we have done those things which we ought not to have done." Why the contretemps of the Age of Santa Anna? The calamity, most assuredly, had multiple causes, not always easy to identify. Aside from the colonial heritage, and the chaos of the Wars for Independence, the shape of the international scene warrants our close scrutiny.

II

From the decade of turmoil, beginning with the Grito de Dolores and ending with the Plan de Iguala, Mexicans inherited a formidable burden of wrack and ruin. The battles between insurgents and royalists, which devastated the country off and on, left some 600,000 dead, a majority of them workers, perhaps half of the labor force. The fighting planted bitter seeds, aptly described by José María Luis Mora's story of a royalist soldier who, rendered half mad after killing an enemy soldier who turned out to be his brother, shouted, "I have no brothers among the insurgents." In the wake of Independence, thieves of every stripe infested the cities while bands of robbers plundered at will on the Republic's roads. Whether going to or coming from Puebla or Veracruz, the Mexico City traveler expected to be robbed, a circumstance "so common," according to one witness, "that when the stage . . . arrives safely, it excites rather more sensation than when it has been stopped."

More to the point, Mexico was not yet a nation of citizens who identified their interests with each another's. While calling themselves Mexicans, they had tenuous bonds or none at all. National unity was merely a gleam in the eyes of patriots. Both Liberals and Conservatives saw property owners as the bastions of the Republic, to cite Lucas Alamán's ideal of a *gobierno de las clases pudientes* or Lorenzo de Zavala's wish to build a "respectable social class." Of those in power, few wanted government, in accordance with current ideological dogmas, to interfere in economic matters. The criollo elite, as well as the tiny band of mestizos ready to join it, believed politics should be in their hands, both fearing the participation of Indians and country folk. The power brokers had to live in a Mexico on the brink of bankruptcy, in debt to foreign bankers, and short of funds for any undertaking.

III

The mining industry, to start with, lay in shambles, partly the result of the Wars of Independence, especially in the Bajío, where many mines were flooded or wrecked, while their workers had gone off to fight, whether voluntarily or not. The damage was severest in Guanajuato, where the output of silver fell by half and water filled the shafts of the Valenciana mines. The Wars of Independence, wrote Mora, paralyzed mining, laying waste to more than half of the capital invested in it.

For all that, the mining industry had broken down under its own weight. With Napoleon's invasion of Spain, it was no longer possible to continue to subsidize the industry, while the price of mercury leaped upward. Tax exemptions and official credit also dropped off. "Mining collapsed," writes one historian, "when government disintegrated." An industry already on its deathbed in 1810, "propped up by distorted public incentives," simply fell on its face when colonial authorities could no longer provide them.

The recovery of mining, additionally, occurred in fits and spurts. For years, many a rich mine lay abandoned. Independence had spurred unrealistic expectations, inviting risky schemes, helped along by Alexander von Humboldt's tales of fantastic mineral wealth. Given the shortage of domestic capital, officials turned to foreign speculators, offering them concessions and privileges; between 1825 and 1830, the British, the favored, were given rights to half of the value of the ores dug from the subsoil. Of the English investors, the United Mexican, English Mining Company, with its operations in Pachuca, led the others. Though in Guadalupe Victoria's cabinet, Almán promoted the company, serving as president of its board of directors, a questionable relationship for a public official. At Pachuca, Englishmen held the best jobs, while most of the miners were Indians. So began the alienation of Mexico's subsoil, as well as its dependence on outside capitalists. By the date of Antonio López de Santa Anna's final foray into politics, the British, French, and Germans owned the lion's share of Mexico's mining output. While the boom lasted, Mexican mining stock sold at good prices on the London market.

Unhappily for Mexicans, the foreigners brought merely plans devised to earn a quick profit. Hopes of easy wealth lured them to Mexico, not mining expertise. Mining failures were commonplace. These neophytes, for instance, ordered heavy machinery from Europe which could not be transported to the mines, and so it lay rusting in the port of Veracruz. Bad management and a zeal for high profits brought their ruin. At just the wrong time, the boom collapsed, on the heels of the bankruptcy of the English speculators. In the meantime, the rising cost of mercury, which the English controlled, endangered the survival of small Mexican mine operators. So mining never really recovered; as time went on, the mining boom of the early eighteenth century was just a memory. The Mexicans, for their part, continued to tax mining exports because they were their principal source of revenue.

IV

Agriculture, the country's foremost industry, endured a similar fate. Except for haciendas in provinces such as Veracruz, most of them suffered from the fighting; damage, just the same, was not uniform. Some haciendas were sacked and burned to the ground, but others escaped unscathed; by 1821, some were on their way to recovery. The agricultural region hardest hit by the Wars of Independence was the Bajío, where insurgents and royalists alike plundered haciendas and ranchos, looting their stores of corn and wheat, robbing their barnyard animals, and destroying their irrigation works. Enterprising Indians, upon seeing a hacienda under attack, stole doors for their houses and churches. The collapse of mining in the Bajío wreaked havoc with agriculture; the mining towns and cities, after all, were the principal markets for the grains of hacendados. Denied its best customers, agriculture, especially grain haciendas, fell on hard times. The Bajío, however, was not alone in feeling the effects of the fighting. One of the other regions was Morelos, where insurgents and royalists engaged in battles of attrition. The valleys of Puebla and Tlaxcala were pillaged more than once by diverse bands fighting to control the route between Mexico City and Veracruz. The pulque plantations, whatever their location, endured possibly the most damage as thirsty soldiers pounced on cargos of pulque bound for market.

The wars also played favorites, inflicting heavy damage on the grain haciendas of the Bajío but leaving plantations on the fringes mostly undisturbed. Planters who cultivated cotton, vanilla, and sugar along the Gulf of Mexico were particularly fortunate, as were the cochineal exporters of Oaxaca. By 1830, this sector sat at the pinnacle of the export ladder and, conversely, reaffirmed agriculture's dependency on outside markets. The prosperous planters relied on foreign customers. Meanwhile, consumer demand for agricultural products lagged, mainly because of the small population and, as a result of widespread poverty, its minuscule purchasing power.

The decades of chaos modified the former relationship between Mexico City and the provinces. With national instability, Mexico City lost not only some of its political hegemony but its economic dominance. The countryside, on the other hand, remained relatively stable: agriculture, in contrast to mining, required no big capital outlays to speed its recovery. With Mexico City embroiled in political squabbles, hacendados were relatively free to go their own way and to expand their holdings. After Independence, moreover, debt peonage gained a legal sanction never accorded it in colonial days. From this course of events, the hacendados solidified their hold on the countryside, while the rising demand in the industrial centers of Europe for coffee, sugar, tobacco, cotton, and henequen encouraged the development of massive plantations in Veracruz, Chiapas, Coahuila, Durango, and Yucatán, tipping the scales even more in favor of the big landlords.

While the hacienda, judged by its earnings, frequently did poorly, the social prestige of its master had never been better. Hoping to climb the social scale, lawyers, engineers, and architects, some them mestizos, came to own haciendas; hacendados seldom willingly divided up their lands, preferring to pass them on to the eldest son. With or without the laws of primogeniture, the hacendado kept his lands intact. In the meantime, the states, looking about for ways to add money to their empty treasuries, began to sell off what they titled *terrenos baldíos,* or idle lands. By this duplicity, the upwardly mobile, often men holding public office or military brass, got hold of communal lands.

As in colonial times, the hacienda, with lands measured in leagues, sat atop the rural pyramid. Only on horseback could their owners oversee them. One such hacienda, the property of a criollo, lay about ninety miles from Mexico City; its manor, "a large house in a wild-looking country," stood "in solitary state, with hills behind, and rocks before it . . . surrounded by great uncultivated plains and pasture fields." For Madame Calderón de la Barca, whose husband was the Spanish ambassador, everything was "*en grande* in this domain, from a handsome chapel and sacristy" to a *plaza de toros,* or bullring. When she sat down for dinner, the table held "thirty or forty people," but, she noted, nowhere were there any books or "a feeling of equality . . . except between people of the same rank." She thought it was "more like some remains of the feudal system, where retainers sat at the same table with their chief, but below the salt."

The hacendados almost invariably paid puny wages, using chits redeemable at the *tienda de raya* (hacienda store) instead of money. They wasted no opportunity to rob the lands of adjacent villages. Driven to despair by this behavior, Indian campesinos in Morelos and Mexico State rebelled in the 1840s, frightening the governor of Mexico State, who implored the hacendados to deal more justly with their peons. The reply to his plea, signed by the biggest hacendados, both Liberals and Conservatives, not only denied his allegations but attacked him for making them. Taken aback by the rancor of their reply, the governor could only swear that he had never meant to trifle with the sacred rights of property. That did not save him from a subsequent outburst by the hacendados, who labeled the Indians an inferior race destined to disappear from the face of the globe; to heed the governor's advice would push Mexico back into the Stone Age. Among those voicing this opinion was Andrés Quintana Roo, a hacendado in Apam. Carlos María de Bustamante took a similar stance in the quarrel between hacendados and Indians in Chiapas, siding with the hacendados and referring to the dispute as a war of *castas.*

Liberals, just the same, thought property was badly distributed. Too few Mexicans had too much land, while the landless multiplied. That, said the oracle Mora, was what kept down the value of rural property. Mora dreamed of a republic of small farmers, thinking agriculture the fountain of civic virtues and happiness. What thwarted the realization of their dreams, he believed, was the hacienda. Yet, like European ideologues of his day, Mora held private property sacred. The state could merely encourage the hacendado to sell bits and pieces of his property and, if need be, buy up haciendas in order to place their lands on the market as small parcels, as Governor Francisco García had done in Zacatecas. Even Conservatives such as Lucas Alamán urged Congress to grant campesinos the right to reclaim lands taken from them by hacendados. Talk, for all that, never got beyond rhetoric.

V

Similarly, commerce faced problems of its own. A legacy of the Wars for Independence was the collapse of the financial structure. Foreigners lost confidence, to quote H. G. Ward, Britain's first minister to Mexico, in the country's financial stability, refusing to invest because of the "risk to which capitals were exposed." To rub salt into the wound, Mexicans chose the late 1820s to expel the remaining Spaniards from the Republic; Mexicans, mainly criollos, coveted their roles as merchants as well as their mines and lands. Their departure left Mexico almost bereft of its capitalists—that is, of men with money to invest. Ruinous for the country, their expulsion placed commerce and mining at the mercy of the English, French, Germans, and Americans. In Mexico City, before long, they were the importers of manufactures and the owners of stores selling foreign goods.

Mistaken policies on duties for imports and exports, the country's principal source of revenue, also hurt. Iturbide, in a style reminiscent of many politicians, had slashed them in order to win popularity, in that fashion reducing national income. Yet both Liberals and Conservatives, despite their differences on free trade, relied on money from these duties to stay in office. By doing so, more likely than not, they cut off their nose to spite their face. When duties on imports went up, people stopped buying them or, worse, looked for contraband goods. Either way, the government lost revenue, compelling it to rely on the *alcabala,* a tax harmful to commerce.

No national market existed. Mexico was an assemblage of local or regional markets, each isolated from the others. The lack of passable routes and wagons to transport heavy merchandise was an obstacle to trade, which the absence of navigable rivers exacerbated. Most goods were carried on mule back or on clumsy wagons pulled by mules driven by arrieros, men willing to brave the dangers of bandits and roads no more than trails. Partly because of transportation barriers, the high cost of Mexican goods, especially when competing with cheaper, imported ones, hampered efforts at industrialization.

The breakup of the merchant monopoly of Mexico City during the late colonial years had also planted the seeds of commercial discord. The much heralded free trade, which opened additional ports of entry to foreign goods, had encouraged commercial rivalries that undermined political stability. On the Pacific Ocean, San Blas, one of the new ports, stimulated the economy of Guadalajara's hinterland while a similar phenomenon occurred on the Gulf coast with the opening of Tampico, gateway to San Luis Potosí. Sisal and Progreso, Yucatán's ports, established nearly autonomous trade ties with the outside world, as merchants imported manufactured goods for a society dependent more and more on the sale of sugar and henequen. Unable to count on Mexico City, local authorities levied taxes on interstate commerce, including the *alcabala.* Puebla, for instance, taxed cotton and woolen cloth from the port of Veracruz, itself a veritable nest of smugglers.

The government in Mexico City did not ignore these challenges to its authority, fighting long and hard to assert itself. Part of the incessant conflict between the capital and the provinces involved the control of commerce. To enforce the will of its merchants, the central government employed the army. That explains in part the sundry military uprisings in the Bajío, including the much castigated one of General Mariano Paredes Arrillaga in 1841; as the caudillo of Guadalajara and its hinterland, he was defending the commercial interests of its merchants against the entrenched power of their rivals in Mexico City.

This tug-of-war between officials in Mexico City and the provinces helps make understandable the flourishing contraband trade of the era. As authorities imposed taxes on imported articles, their prices shot up. Unable or unwilling to pay them, Mexicans turned increasingly to contraband. The illegal trade, of course, was hardly new, having roots in the colonial era and in the Wars of Independence, when double-dealing criollo officers, known as military merchants, lined their pockets with profits from smuggled goods. Some of them acquired fortunes, purchased haciendas, and married into the criollo plutocracy. By the 1820s, two-thirds of all imported goods escaped payment of customs duties.

VI

Political stability required more than just a thriving commerce or a revival of mining and agriculture. Long-range economic growth, the mother of peace and order, called for some kind of an industrial edifice, as Alamán well knew. Yet Mexico could never erect even a skeletal one, and not simply because of its lack of capital, absence of technology, and tiny domestic market. What also blocked the way was the nature of the international scene. The advent of the Industrial Revolution, given birth in England in the 1750s, was transforming rapidly the relationship between the capitalist West and the former Spanish colonies. The industrial West was no longer just buying raw materials but, increasingly, looking for markets for its manufactures. It was this reality that Mexico confronted upon winning its Independence. Ideologues of the stripe of Mora, who called free trade a panacea, it bothered not a wit. Nor did it disturb hacendados who relied on export markets or merchants who bought foreign goods for resale at home. Mineowners, too, were birds of a feather. None of them wished to topple the colonial relationship. But to Alamán and the disciples of industrialization, this reality was an ominous portent for the future. How to lay the cornerstones of native industry while competing with cheaper and better imported goods?

When Mexico severed its ties with Spain, its markets lay at the mercy of European exporters, principally the British. An aggressive lot, they flooded Mexican markets with their wares, outselling the little manufactured locally. In no time at all, they reestablished the colonial terms of trade: manufactured articles in exchange for precious metals and agricultural goods. Laws of comparative advantage to the contrary, the terms of trade rarely favored Mexico.

Europe's Industrial Revolution disrupted Mexico's economic development. From 1790 to 1810, during England's naval blockade of Spain, local *obrajes* making cheap cotton cloth had enjoyed something of a bonanza. However, even before the conclusion of these two decades, contraband textiles of English and North American manufacture had started to outsell local cloth, a situation that worsened after Independence. Relying on hand labor, the *obrajes* could not compete with cheap cloth from Lancashire. As they shut down, jobless men started to haunt the streets of Mexico City, Puebla, and Querétaro, and with them rose a demand for tariff protection, voiced by artisans and the owners of *obrajes* which had survived the strife of Independence. In 1829, the Vicente Guerrero administration, heeding popular clamor, prohibited imports of all but the most expensive cloth.

The mining doldrums and rising unemployment help one to comprehend Alamán's dream of industrialization, essentially a textile industry. Formerly an advocate of an economy based on mining, Alamán, disturbed by its lingering maladies, became a champion of industry. Only in this fashion, he insisted, would Mexico not be a vassal of foreigners, a view shared by Esteban de Antuñano, the textile magnate. With industrialization, Alamán argued, both men and women would have jobs and vagrancy would be undercut. This required tariffs or *proteccionismo.* The Liberals, apostles of free trade, had no stomach for any of this.

Alamán had two chances to implement his plan, as a cabinet minister under Vicente Guerrero and then under Anastasio Bustamante, who approved his Banco de Avío, a development bank which called for the cooperation of government and private capital. The bank financed investors who built industrial plants. It also imported machinery, paid foreign technicians, and published technical manuals. Duties on imports provided the money for these services. As the architect of the Banco de Avío, and as chairman of the National Association of Manufacturers, Alamán labored day and night to achieve his dream. One of his final acts was to establish the Ministerio de Fomento, a cabinet post to spur economic growth.

A merchant capitalist, Antuñano, one of the first recipients of a loan from the Banco de Avío, built his textile mill just outside the city of Puebla. La Constancia Mexicana, the handiwork of this extraordinary entrepreneur, "very deaf, and obliged to use an ear-trumpet," had nearly bankrupted him. Operating with 3,840 spindles, the plant, as well as others in Puebla, employed thirty thousand workers. Taking their cue from Don Esteban and textile manufacturers in Mexico City, entrepreneurs in Jalisco organized plants of their own: La Caja de Agua and La Experiencia. By 1845, Mexico had seventy-five textile mills, many of them clustered around Mexico City and along the corridor from Puebla to Veracruz, at Nogales, Orizaba, Río Blanco, and Jalapa and, in the Bajío, at Querétaro.

The city of Puebla was the kingpin of the textile edifice, controlling half of the yarn and coarse cloth woven in the Republic and marching ahead in the production of shawls and wool fabrics. Using modern machinery, the textile plants relied on water and mules for their power. The best of the cotton mills were in Atlixco, on the outskirts of Puebla City. Of equal significance, Mexicans owned most of the cotton mills in Puebla, Veracruz, and Mexico City, among them Cocolapam, located in Orizaba and the biggest of them. Thanks to a government bank, Mexico had a textile industry before sister Spanish-American republics and, additionally, fourteen manufacturing companies with a capital of over 100,000 pesos, producing, apart from textiles, flour, paper, plows, and threshers.

These embryonic accomplishments did not go unchallenged. English merchants and, later, North Americans saw to that, introducing their wares whenever possible, legitimately or by contraband. Always in need of revenues, Mexican officials, for their part, lowered tariffs in order to collect duties, believing that high tariffs simply encouraged contraband. But imports of cheap textiles, made possible by low tariffs, hurt Mexican entrepreneurs, compelling them to compete on unequal terms. It was a vicious circle: the poverty of the Republic's exchequer sabotaged efforts to achieve a semblance of economic independence, without which national politics were subject to the whims of foreigners. The invasion of Mexico by the United States in 1846, similarly, paved the way for its merchants to sell cheap textiles, jeopardizing more the industrial edifice.

The Liberals, headed by Mora and Lorenzo Zavala and then by Melchor Ocampo, the messiah of the approaching Reforma, fought Alamán's designs tooth and nail, wanting no part of protective tariffs. Disciples of laissez-faire, they battled for a free market, claiming that Alamán's industry denied consumers the right to buy cheap foreign goods because of the desire for profits of the few. To quote Mora, "free trade . . . must determine the nature of capital investment and industry"; government meddling made no sense, it being a "pernicious" error "to want to produce everything and not buy from foreigners." Mexicans were "neither sufficiently intelligent" nor "industrious enough" to build a modern textile industry.

This clash of views, far from being merely ideological, as many historians say, had its origins in the nuts and bolts of rival economic interests. On the one side were textile workers and their employers; on the other were provincials, often Liberals, who, more likely than not, looked with favor on agriculture and mining, sectors favoring low tariffs. Many of them, such as Ocampo, were hacendados or, as lawyers and professionals, bureaucrats dependent on the public trough, which required a national exchequer sufficiently plump to pay their salaries. Provincial merchants who lived off sales of imported goods could not be expected to admire protective tariffs that stifled business.

The clash between Alamán and his opponents encouraged partisan strife. Provincial interests, especially, vowed to fight until the bitter end what they termed a return to Spanish colonial policy. The "commercial wars," as they were baptized, were part and parcel of the national disharmony. Since authorities in Mexico City proved unable to keep provincial interests in line, each region, more or less, went its own way, with key cities spawning their oligarchies, "clinging with a death grip to newly won power and Federalists through and through." This splintering took on the trappings of a states' rights movement, with the old province of Nueva Galicia, calling itself the "Sovereign State of Jalisco," leading the pack. Prodded by Nuevo León, the former Eastern Interior Province emerged as another entity. In the south,

Yucatán headed one more. *Caciquismo,* the cancer of bossism, mirrored this fragmentation of power.

The tedious cuartelazo, or barracks revolt, testified to nonconformity with the party line in Mexico City. Seen from this perspective, the cuartelazos, certainly the principal ones, represented diverse interest groups. For instance, the failed coup of 1840 engineered by Valentín Gómez Farías against Anastasio Bustamante had the backing of entrepreneurs friendly to foreign capital, prominent men such as Manuel Escandón, the textile magnate. Gómez Farías and his ally José Urrea, a native son of Sonora, swore they would abolish local duties, specifically the *alcabala,* on goods circulating within the Republic, thus ensuring domestic free trade. The cuartelazo that toppled Bustamante, which Paredes Arrillaga and Santa Anna captained the next year, counted on the support of merchants in Veracruz and Guadalajara; Generals Juan Alvarez and Nicolás Bravo, one a Liberal and the other a Conservative but both provincials, sided with the plotters. Their merchant allies depended for their goods on foreign manufacturers, primarily Englishmen. To show his support, the British envoy, a representative of his country's exporters, gave a banquet in Guadalajara for General Paredes Arrillaga, who spoke for regional mercantile interests and free trade. Conversely, Mexican industrialists defended Bustamante, whose administration enforced rigidly the collection of protective duties.

VII

National unity was simply a daydream. Mexico inherited from Spain a society split not only by class but by caste. From top to bottom of the social scale, the color of one's skin influenced personal and class relations. As before, money and education "whitened" the skin but not entirely. How much this prejudice poisoned relationships between individuals and groups in society, no one really knows; but no one doubts that it did.

By the 1850s, Mexico's heterogeneous society had approximately eight million inhabitants, over half of them persons of dark skins, largely because of Indian ancestry. A small population of mulattoes further darkened the country's complexion. Most persons "of color," as Mora referred to them, inhabited the countryside; whites, perhaps a million, dwelt in the cities. Yet *mestizaje,* the interminable blending of Indian and Spaniard—"continuous as the stars that shine"—hardly permitted the racial stereotyping indulged in by Mora. Although an oligarchy of whites ruled the roost, a mestizo universe toiled beneath it. The shaky social pyramid rested on a bronze base, with mestizos exploiting Indians and both criollos and light-skinned mestizos of the upper strata riding herd over both.

This splintered Mexican society was hardly a model to be emulated. At the pinnacle, an oligarchy of criollos, infiltrated increasingly by mestizos, quarreled and split up into factions. The day when some of the well-off worried about the less fortunate had yet to dawn. By "their selfishness and cowardice," to quote Justo Sierra, the rich "were almost wholly withdrawn from public affairs, endlessly parroting in the drawing room . . . their favorite maxim." Just below them, "bureaucrats served those who paid them, and . . . plotted with deadly, unrelenting solidarity against those who failed to pay them." The high clergy fought to preserve its privileges, and the army brass looked out for itself.

The supreme value in society was to be rich. Ostentation and pomp were the rage. In his *Memorias de mis tiempos,* Guilllermo Prieto painted a vivid portrait of this society, of its bejeweled women, of Virginia Gourgues, the fashion plate of Mexico City with a son engaged to marry the daughter of General Paredes Arrillaga. "It was told by a lady here," recalled Calderón de la Barca, "that on the death of her grandchild, he was not only enveloped in rich lace, but the diamonds of three *condesas* and four *marquesas* were collected together and put on him, necklaces, bracelets, rings, broaches, and tiaras to the value of several hundred thousand dollars." Among the trendsetters, who were annoyed frequently by "procrastinating tradesmen," the "badness of the servants . . . was an unfailing source of complaint."

Calderón de la Barca saw just one side of the coin. Most Mexican women were neither wealthy nor fashion plates. On the whole, they were an exploited lot, subject to the whims of fathers and husbands. For most women, freedom from Spain did not improve their lot. Only widows, one wag wrote, were truly free. The gains of the late eighteenth century, which had opened doors to women, had fallen largely by the wayside. The economic doldrums of the early decades hit women of poor families especially hard, driving more campesinas to look for jobs in the cities. By 1848, to illustrate, women made up nearly 60 percent of the population of Mexico City, where, perhaps, as many as one out of four never married. Unmarried women, or women who did not live with a man, along with widows, represented over half of the adult women in Mexico City.

With the growth of the textile industry, as well as the siren call of the tobacco factories, additional women had entered the work force, especially because industrialists such as Antuñano, who coveted cheap labor, welcomed them with open arms. However, he asked them to toil twelve hours a day for wages one-third those paid men. At the advent of Independence, women, 82 percent Indians or mestizas, made up one-third of the labor force of Mexico City; more than one out of four had jobs. Over half of them, nonetheless, did domestic work; jobs for women, at least in Mexico City, did not mean liberation from the drudgery of household chores.

For the Indian, the criollo oligarchy, whether rich or *letrados,* had little but disdain. In its opinion, the problem of Mexico was its Indians. One discovered "the true Mexican character among the whites," claimed Mora. To this man of bourgeois values, the Indian, even when partly educated, commonly lacked imagination. Only with European colonization, he insisted, could Mexico progress. To integrate the Indian into white society, on terms dictated by it—that was the goal. Partly to rid the country of the Indian past, the state of Mexico, the adopted home of both Mora and Lorenzo Zavala, abolished communal property in 1833, opening the way for the further alienation of village lands.

Independence was not a blessing for the Indian. Quite the reverse: his lot worsened. Shunted aside, he lived out his life in the isolated pueblo or rancheria, attempting to defend himself as best he could against his oppressors; to the Indian, they were all *blancos,* whether they were or not. Mexico, the Republic, meant nothing to him. As in the past, he rose before dawn, walked from his pueblo to his fields (if he had a parcel of land), and came home at nightfall. At nine in the morning and three in the afternoon, he ate corn tortillas flavored with chili sauce and beans and drank atole, a liquid corn gruel. Once in a lifetime, he ate meat but drank himself into a stupor with pulque or *aguardiente de caña,* a liquor distilled from sugarcane.

But the outcasts of society were not just Indians in the pueblos. The poor were ubiquitous. Designated *leperos* by the snobbish, they infested Mexico City and, to a lesser extent, the provincial capitals. In Mexico City, the multitudes of poor and hungry begged for alms, "dirty and half naked," to quote Prieto, squatting on their knees or lying down. Home was a miserable barrio, squalid and stinking, where rats, lice, and flies infested every niche and cranny. The poor dwelt in jacales (shacks), in barrios, one of them Santiago Tlatelolco, site of the famous Aztec marketplace, and in Tepito, a century later made famous by the book *The Children of Sánchez.* Squalor meant crumbling adobe walls, "mangy dogs, ulcerated sores, mummys that walked, misshapen human beings, the humpbacked," and pulque, its manufacture a source of profits for many of the wealthiest families of Mexico City.

For Indian and urban poor, politics had scant, if any, appeal. For them, political parties, the unending national charters, and vows by generals to change this or that lacked rhyme or reason. Voting was a farce. To manipulate the vote of the underdogs, on the rare occasion when it was bestowed on them, politicos resorted to every trick in the book. In Mexico City, they distributed pulque or aguardiente; in Mérida, capital of Yucatán, hot chocolate; and so it went. The donors told the recipients how to vote.

VIII

Sandwiched between the poor and the rich was a tiny, mostly urban "middle class," which aped the well-off, despised the poor, and feared that an unfortunate accident might jeopardize its standing on the social ladder. Initially criollo, mestizos were infiltrating it more and more; it was from this nebulous category that the *letrados* had come. By "race" and schooling part of the oligarchy, its members, measured by wealth and income, belonged to a lower category. This ill-defined "class" dwelt in the Republic's capital and the provincial cities, though a bare one-tenth of the population inhabited the twenty-five cities. Mexico was still predominantly rural. As in the epoch of the colony, Mexico City was the fountain of public jobs and favors, a metropolis of 250,000 inhabitants dotted with churches and convents and graced by streets lined with elms and poplars, where the weather was "lovely, the air fresh and clear," and the "sky one vast expanse of blue." Beyond the Republic's hub lay the provincial capitals, some with as many as 70,000 inhabitants. They had their distinctive features.

Some two days' ride from the capital of the Republic, Catholic Puebla, the biggest of them, resembled a convent with its inhabitants, according to a visitor, "shut up in the performance of a vow." The high society of Morelia, formerly Valladolid, lived in the past, regretting, like Mexicans of their status, the passing of better times. A magnificent *catedral*, resplendent temples, and the Colegio de San Nicolás, once administered by Maguel Hidalgo y Costilla, added luster to Morelia. To the west and north rose Guadalajara, a kingpin in its own right, and Guanajuato and Querétaro, mining and commercial entrepôts. Farther north lay Zacatecas and, beyond that, Durango, Chihuahua, Saltillo, and other capital cities of the frontier. South of Mexico City was Oaxaca, colonial and very provincial. A fort with "black and red walls" greeted ships docking at Veracruz, "a miserable, black-looking city," plagued by "hordes of large black birds called *zopilotes.*" All the same, Veracruz, a trade depot, had a sizable "middle class." Tampico resembled a New England village, with "neat, shingle palaces, with piazzas and pillars." There was nothing Spanish or colonial about the port city.

This nascent, urban "middle class" was ambitious and a thirst for gain. For this array of lawyers, physicians, engineers, accountants, and army officers of middling status, public jobs were the staff of life. Given the nature of Mexico's economy, they could not survive outside of the public bureaucracy, "that superb normal school for idleness and graft," Sierra lamented, which "educated our country's middle class." Entrance into the government, the key employer in this world of stagnant economies, kept alive hopes for a better life for self and family. Peace and order on the national scene meant that officials in Mexico City had the money to pay salaries of bureaucrats. This was made partly possible in the 1820s, the years of President Guadalupe Victoria, by borrowing money from the British. An aphorism held in Mexican politics: "When salaries are paid, revolutions fade."

The malady had colonial origins, exacerbated by the difficulties of the early national era. With mining and commerce in the doldrums, jobs dried up, so jobless lawyers and their ilk looked to the public coffers. The more the economy tottered, the more the aspirants for public posts, and the greater the determination of lucky bureaucrats to hold on to what they had. Peace and order prevailed only when officials in Mexico City met the payroll. To stay in office, an administration had to pay its bureaucrats and, in addition, find jobs for office seekers. All of this inflated the budget. Mora labeled it *empleomanía*, a hunger for public jobs.

The federal system of government may have been, to some extent, a response to *empleomanía*. At Independence, as Zavala quipped jocularly, "300,000 criollos wanted to occupy jobs held for three centuries by 70,000 Spaniards." The acute conflict pitting Yorquinos against Escoseses, the two Masonic orders, stemmed partly from this; the Yorquinos, Federalists and mostly jobless, wanted the Escoceses, Centralists and the bureaucrats, to step down. A multilayer structure of government, calling for ayuntamientos, state legislatures, a bicameral Congress, and a host of cabinet officers, was the carrot offered ambitious *letrados*.

Corruption in public life was tied intimately to this struggle to get at the national treasury. A bankrupt Mexico could rarely pay decent salaries, emboldening officeholders to sell their services—a magistrate, for example—to the highest bidder. They did this with impunity, knowing that higher-ups behaved in identical manner and, if honest, would not linger in office long enough to be able to punish malfeasance. Public graft had similar causes. These maladies debased public service in the National Palace, state government, and the ayuntamientos, in the eyes of Mexicans, making a mockery of it.

IX

The cuartelazo, the visible sore of the military cancer, was linked to the aspirations of lawyers and their ilk who, lacking firepower, could not enforce their will and, so, looked to soldiers for support, a gang with identical designs on the national exchequer. The problem of the army dated from the Wars of Independence, which multiplied many fold the sprinkling of troops dispatched to New Spain by the Bourbons, converting the military into the dominant force on the national scene by 1821. Captained generally by criollo officers, mestizos and Indians filled the ranks of the armies.

During the wars, dissident soldiers had broken with the royal army. Ignacio Allende and Juan de Aldama were just two of them. The ranks of the insurgents, furthermore, included scores of local chieftains, some of them mestizos, who formulated their own rules, seized property for themselves, and demanded blind obedience from their followers. Seldom did they gladly accept orders from above, to cite the behavior of Albino García, an insurgent boss who told the Junta de Zitácuaro that "only God was King." José Antonio Arroyo, another of them, made his soldiers refer to him as "father." They and others like them lived from plunder. Bloody and cruel, they were petty lords, the masters of their territory, where their word was law. General Félix Calleja and his armies ended this charade, but, to the sorrow of Mexico, many of the caciques joined the royalist forces, fighting with identical aplomb on the side they had formerly opposed. The cause mattered little. The public inherited this motley collection of popular caciques.

The army of *leva* soldiers constituted an autonomous political entity, more powerful than the civil authority. Its chieftains were also the presidents of the Republic; Iturbide and Santa Anna were two of them. Virtually every state in the Republic had a general overseeing it, whether as governor or as military watchdog. The army ate up 80 percent of the Republic's budget, money for ninety thousand men by 1855. Generally without firm political convictions, though more Conservative than Liberal, the officers of the army allowed ambition to determine their behavior, placing matters of pay and promotion at the head of their priorities. For the army officer, the government was no more "than a bank for its employees, a bank guarded by armed employees called the army." Nothing else mattered, as Prieto learned during his days as minister of the treasury. With the Republic on the edge of bankruptcy, Prieto reduced the federal payroll, but no sooner was the news out than key army officers demanded that the ruling be nullified and Prieto fired.

To carry out their orders, the officers relied on their soldiers. Every long military campaign transformed a military unit, giving it cohesion and converting its commander into a caudillo who, in the eyes of his soldiers, could do no wrong. Mostly Indians from rural hamlets, the soldiers could neither read nor write; their officers, according to Carlos María de Bustamante, were forced to explain battle plans by drawing lines on the ground. Though perhaps compelled initially to take up arms by a press-gang, the soldiers eventually adjusted to life in the army, forgetting they once tilled the soil or labored in the mines. They came to think soldiering an improvement over what they had before. The military promised adventure, a kind of security and freedom from hard toil, and, additionally, women could tag along, the soldaderas who "trotted on foot in the rear" of the infantry "carrying their men's boots and clothes." Still, not everyone loved being a soldier, especially since few were volunteers; so soldiers deserted, their ranks filled by the levy.

Every state had its own militia, soldiers to employ against the national authority when occasion permitted. Poorly paid and at the beck and call of the governor and his henchmen, militia soldiers were, generally, the dregs of society. Instead of protecting private citizens, they gained notoriety for their thievery and killing. They were the backbone of the provincial cuartelazos, usually the platforms of "demagogues who assaulted the exchequer in order to loot it." Yet exceptions must not be overlooked: most of the military strife occurred in the region between Guadalajara and Mexico City, the most dynamic economically, where rebels fought often to defend local interests.

The cuartelazo had the air of a *pachanga,* a carnival, an occasion for merriment. In the cities, stores closed, government offices shut their doors, and empty streets resounded with the clatter of the hooves of horses. People congregated on street corners or on rooftops to watch the fire of the artillery. Roads leading out of the cities were filled with people fleeing the turmoil, on foot, with donkey, or by coach, taking with them what they could carry: mattresses, birdcages, pictures of saints, and clothing. The entire scene had a surrealistic quality, with people singing, eating, and drinking while soldiers fired at each other.

The instigators of these affairs were rarely professional soldiers. Officers lacked discipline, bowing to orders from superiors only when it suited them, an esprit de corps being largely absent. As army units for the defense of Mexico, they were more rabble than soldiers, costly to maintain, and, to quote Mora, "entirely useless." Bandits turned guerrilla chiefs who went on to become colonels, then generals and presidential candidates, were, lamentably, all too common. On their bayonets they flew a declaration and in the wallets of their advisers, "whether priests, lawyer, or merchant," a plan guaranteed to bring more misfortune to the Mexican people. This military caste, enjoying *fueros* of its own, was the bellwether of Mexican politics.

X

No less troublesome was the role of the church. Accounts of its wealth and power were topics of conversation the length and breadth of the Republic. But the telling of tales is hardly a science, at best sheltering a grain of truth but seldom the whole of it. The church, paradoxically, was both rich and powerful but also weak. For a population of about eight million, Mexico had 3,232 priests, 88 lay brothers, and 1,295 monks, for a total of 4,616 ministers of the gospel, fewer than one for every one thousand inhabitants. Nuns numbered 1,484, with an additional 103 novices.

Of the secular clergy, bishops and canons lived handsomely off tithes and money collected on religious holidays. The archbishop of Mexico, to illustrate, lived in a palatial house in Tacubaya. Most priests lived far less well. Nonetheless, the secular clergy had property, in Mexico City valued at 1.3

million pesos, far less than the 11 million pesos of real estate of the regulars. The owners of magnificent haciendas, the Franciscans were the biggest of the orders and the Augustinians the wealthiest. Wealth varied, the Franciscans being, for example, relatively poor in property but not in capital. The nunneries were richer than the monasteries, havens for the daughters of the wealthy, who brought with them large doweries, usually mortgages on urban property. The church was the biggest property owner; just the same, the church, an ear cocked to the political winds, had started to sell off its real estate, particularly after the aborted anticlerical reforms of 1833, convinced that capital invested wisely offered more security than buildings and lands its enemies could confiscate. Tales to the contrary, church property was not always immobile; it had begun to circulate.

As during colonial days, the church was the Republic's banker, to whom hacendado, mine operator, and merchant looked for loans. Both Guadalupe Victoria, the Republic's first president, and Alamán borrowed money from the church. How much property was mortgaged to it, no one knows for a certainty. One indication was the bishopric of Mexico City, where the church held mortgages on the greater part of its real estate. In Puebla, the church owned approximately one-half of the property. Virtually every hacendado had a church loan to pay off.

Reputed church wealth invited the envy of politicos responsible for filling an empty treasury. Confronted by the specter of bankruptcy, Liberals and Conservatives alike turned to the church, asking it regularly for loans. Liberals, moreover, believed that church wealth could be put to better use. The church, for its part, though willing to lend the government money, had no intention of divesting itself of either its wealth or its influence, dabbling in politics and, like the *letrados* and their cohorts, seeking out the military for support.

Independence, clearly, altered the rules of the church-state game, though by the Plan de Iguala as well as the Constitution of 1824 the church emerged unscathed from the collapse of colonial rule, keeping its *fueros,* tithes, and property and, it believed, shaking itself free of secular control. Government thought otherwise, claiming for itself the rights of the *patronato real.* With Independence, the church attempted to regain its freedom; the state, especially in the hands of the Liberals, to maintain its control. That dispute, featuring factions of the military on both sides, lasted until the defeat of the church in the 1860s.

Whatever its defenders might say, the church, by and large, had only itself to blame. During the Wars for Independence, bishops had expelled insurgents from the bosom of the church, driving many of them to view the high clergy as their enemy. The church, according to these insurgents, had used religion for political ends. The church was not entirely guilty. Some of the responsibility for the troubles must be shared by the Liberals, adherents of a capitalist society which the church, as they saw it, blocked by its monopoly of property and education. One of the first to say that was José Joaquín Fernández de Lizardi, who proclaimed that the property of the church ought to be put into circulation. Servando Teresa de Mier, a kindred soul who wanted the primitive church of the sixteenth century restored to life, urged the clergy to rid itself of its mundane interests. A man of the Enlightenment, Mora spent a lifetime thinking up plans to divest the church of its property and influence.

Anticlericalism did not translate into anti-Catholicism. With notable allowances—Lorenzo Zavala, for one—critics of the church were Christian and Catholic, faithful disciples of Jesus of Nazareth, including Valentín Gómez Farías and Mora. They aimed their salvos at the economic and political church, not at religion, although they belittled the way the poor worshiped. Even Alamán, a fervent defender of the church, had a low opinion of popular religiosity.

The attack on the church surfaced immediately after Independence. In 1824, Jalisco attempted to control clerical revenue; Durango, in 1826, lacking funds to finance an irrigation project, confiscated clerical funds; a year afterward, the state of Mexico decided tentatively to collect tithes; in 1828, Zacatecas, hoping to establish an agricultural bank, toyed with the idea of taking over the property and savings of the pious fund; and, in 1829, Chihuahua declared itself the administrator of tithes and church property and ruled illegal the collection of compulsory parochial dues. The church, nonetheless, withstood these challenges.

On the national scene, the confrontation over whether the state had the right to appropriate church property awaited the ascent to power of Valentín Gómez Farías and his allies. As proof that it could, the Liberals pointed to the Spanish crown's use of ecclesiastical capital, its expulsion of the Jesuits and its expropriation of their property. They had also a study by Mora affirming the right of the state to the property of the church. However, Gómez Farías and his allies, who enacted the anticlerical legislation, failed to confer on the state the right to expropriate church property. Although Santa Anna abolished the legislation, the foundations for clerical reform had been laid, as well as the seeds for the struggle between church and state.

For this clash, the church was poorly prepared. Outside of the upper echelons of society and, here and there, less affluent disciples, the church had to rely on a faithful of dubious loyalty, especially in the countryside, where its clergy, which survived on the alms of its parishioners, charged exorbitant fees for the performance of the sacraments. Urban workers, too, paid these fees and, as a result, few of them married. This burden seldom endeared the clergy to its parishioners. Again to the detriment of the church, its clerics were not always in the right place. The Wars for Independence, first off, had decimated the ranks of the lower clergy, many dying or going back to Spain. While cities had a surplus of priests, the faithful in the countryside waited years for the sacraments. The church, likewise, sent its most badly trained priests to minister to the religious needs of the pueblos. Clerical morality was lax: priests courted women, feathered their own nests, and, in the countryside, often sold their services to the hacendado. All the same, the clergy had a powerful hold on the faithful.

XI

Then, to complicate the picture, along Mexico's northern border a neighbor waited impatiently for the chance to add California and Texas to its domain.

11

THE WAR OF 1847

I

The bickering criollos, moreover, had to confront the enemy next door, who, to gratify territorial dreams, threatened at any moment to "cry 'Havoc!' and let slip the dogs of war." At the Republic's birth, Servando Teresa de Mier, one of its founding fathers, had admonished his countrymen to be wary of the United States, "stronger steadily and more belligerent." He dreaded the relentless westward advance of Americans who, in their doctrine of Manifest Destiny, an omen, proclaimed blatantly that "all territory adjoining the United States" not governed effectively by Mexico "should belong" to them.

Even so, some Mexicans, Liberals mostly, looked to the United States for guidance. One of them was Lorenzo Zavala, a criollo who belittled the Spanish colonial inheritance and labeled Mexico's Indians a burden. After a visit to the United States in 1830, he returned home aglow with admiration for its inhabitants, who "work while Mexicans frolic" and save their money while Mexicans spend even what they "do not have." For Zavala, Texas was "the gateway to the land of liberty." Mier denounced such ideas as *nortemanía,* the frenzy for aping the neighbor across the border.

II

The Adams-Onís Treaty of 1819, signed by Spain and the United States, had fixed the border between them at the Sabine River, from there to the Red and Arkansas rivers and westward to the Pacific Ocean along the forty-second parallel. West of that demarcation lay New Spain, from Texas to California. After its Independence, Mexico inherited that boundary line. All the same, to cite José María Luis Mora, a witness to the events, the United States, almost immediately, made attempts to modify it, trying to encroach on Texas and gazing longingly at California. These designs, flaunted by politicians and journalists alike, frightened Mexicans, who, less numerous, less unified, and less powerful, stood in mortal dread of their Yankee neighbors.

Until the end of the eighteenth century, New Spain's northern territories were largely unsettled. Washington's acquisition of Louisiana from France in 1803, which left Spain face-to-face with the unruly Americans, drove Madrid to establish presidios in Texas, trying, in that manner, to fortify the province and to attract settlers from other parts of New Spain, particularly from Florida, gobbled up recently by the United States. Few of these colonizing schemes bore much fruit, despite an abundance of fertile lands in Texas.

One that did bequeathed Moses Austin, an American who became a Spanish citizen, a concession to settle three hundred American families in Texas, each to get approximately one thousand acres and, in addition, one hundred for every child and eighty per black slave. The settlers were exempted from paying taxes and given license to import duty-free whatever they needed. However, they had to be Catholics, settle themselves away from the coast and the border with the United States, and swear allegiance to Spain. While they could bring their slaves, they could not sell them, and, Spanish law stipulated, their children were born free. Moses Austin died before he could lead his American colonists to Texas, leaving his son, Stephen, to carry out the project; since Mexico had declared its Independence by then, he traveled to Mexico City to get Agustín de Iturbide to confirm the concession.

Given the turmoil in Mexico, its officials failed to enforce the stipulations for settlement. Taking advantage of this, the colonists, citizens of the United States, ignored openly the religious requirement and flouted the slavery restrictions. Worse still, the Federalists, who supplanted Iturbide, turned over responsibility for colonization in Texas to Coahuila, transforming Saltillo, its capital city, into a mecca for American colonists and Mexican land speculators, among them Zavala, Miguel Ramos Arizpe, and General Vicente Filisola, an intimate of Antonio López de Santa Anna. In company with José Antonio Mejía, Zavala, one of the recipients of a concession for colonization in Texas, sold vast tracts of land to American colonists.

After 1825, officials in Saltillo, more or less on their own, began to grant additional concessions, and, before long, American settlers outnumbered the Mexicans in Texas. Of its 25,000 inhabitants in 1825, slightly under 3,500 were Mexicans. Not only that, but most colonists were militant Protestants, blissfully ignorant of the Spanish language, disdainful of Mexicans, their laws and customs, and fiercely loyal to the United States. One of them, Hayden Edwards, a land speculator and patron of 800 colonists, seized Nacogdoches, a Mexican town on the Louisiana border, and flew the flag of the republic of Fredonia, a preliminary step to adoption by Uncle Sam. The Mexicans crushed the rebellion and awakened tardily to the dangers lying ahead.

Alarmed by developments in Texas, the administration of Guadalupe Victoria dispatched General Manuel Mier y Terán to investigate what was going on. In 1829, he reported that Washington had its eyes on Texas, that the American colonists were disloyal to Mexico, that the sprinkling of Mexican soldiers stationed in Texas lacked guns, ammunition, and horses, and that belligerent Indians raided towns at will. Of the American colonies, only two, Austin's and another one, were legal; the rest were trespassers. Mier urged Mexico City to establish presidios, send more soldiers and Mexican colonists, and build a string of customhouses to stop the flow of contraband entering Texas. Earlier, to reestablish Mexican control, authorities had attempted to set free all slaves brought previously into Texas, while officials in Saltillo had barred imports of more of them. Finally, in 1829, Mexico abolished slavery in the republic. So loud was the outcry of slaveholders against the decree in Texas that Mexico, in fear of an outbreak of violence, tabled temporarily its enforcement. To circumvent it, furthermore, the slave owners compelled blacks to sign fictitious work contracts, conferring on them the appearance of wage laborers.

In Mexico City, meanwhile, officials, no longer believing that American colonists could be integrated into the fabric of the republic, decided to bar them altogether. By the colonization law of April 1830, which closed off Texas to American colonists, Mexican authorities hoped to entice their own people to settle in Texas and, by so doing, regain control of it. When the American colonists learned of this, they were soon clamoring for what they called justice. On their own, however, they defied Mexican authorities, convoking a general meeting in Anáhuac, a coastal town now known by the name of Galveston, and excluding Mexican residents of Texas from attending. Under the leadership of Austin, they voted to ask Mexico City to shut down its customhouses, extend tax exemptions, issue property titles to settlers, and confer statehood on Texas, though by the terms of the Mexican Constitution it fell short of the required population. At another meeting a year afterward, the colonists drew up a state constitution and sent Austin to Mexico City to sell the idea to the authorities. When Mexico City turned thumbs down on it, Austin, still in Mexico City, wrote a letter to his companions in Texas urging them to ignore Mexican law and take the bull by the horns and organize their own town councils. The letter fell into Mexican hands, and Austin, for his troubles, had to stay in Mexico City until released in 1834. On his journey back home, he stopped in New Orleans to pick up a cargo of arms.

As this drama unfolded, Joel R. Poinsett, Washington's minister to Mexico, was telling President Guadalupe Victoria of his country's plans for its neighbor. A South Carolina planter and a gentleman of pleasing manner, Poinsett, before arriving in Mexico, had served his country in Argentina and Chile. Since he spoke Spanish, he gained entrance easily into the political circles of Zavala and his allies, applauding enthusiastically their Federalist views and helping them to organize the Yorquinos, a branch of the York Rite Masons. Also, he used his charms to stymie the designs of H. G. Ward, Britain's minister to Mexico, relying on Zavala and the Yorquinos for help. He was so successful that Mexican historians refer to the Vicente Guerrero administration, which he helped to install in power, as that of "Zavala-Poinsett."

The plans of the United States, as Poinsett revealed, entailed a treaty of friendship and commerce bestowing preferential status on it; stopping Mexico and Colombia from freeing Cuba of Spanish control, the dream of Lucas Alamán; and a trade route from St. Louis, a river hub in Missouri, to Santa Fe, New Mexico, for the transport of American goods for sale in Mexico. More telling, Poinsett said that his country was ready to buy Texas. When Alamán, a pillar of Victoria's cabinet, balked, Zavala and his allies, egged on by Poinsett, persuaded Victoria to dismiss his stubborn minister. However, Alamán's successor, to Poinsett's disappointment, proved no less inflexible. His meddling, furthermore, compelled Mexico to ask for his recall.

To Washington's chagrin, Anthony Butler, its next messenger to Mexico, had also to deal with Alamán, foreign minister under President Anastasio Bustamante. The plans Butler carried with him had not changed one whit. A southerner, too, Butler was a land speculator in Texas and a crony of Andrew Jackson. Neither polite nor soft-spoken, Butler was a redneck, a heavy drinker, and, most probably, a bigot. Like Poinsett, Butler told Mexicans that his country was eager to acquire Texas and, additionally, to move its border west of the Nueces, placing it within the territory of New Mexico. Oddly, though he failed to persuade Mexicans to sell Texas, he obtained a most-favored-nation treaty from Alamán. Butler started also to press Alamán for the payment of grossly inflated claims submitted by Americans for damage to their property in Mexico. Butler stayed in Mexico until 1835, when, because of his ties to the dissidents in Texas, he, too, was asked to pack up and leave.

In Texas, in the interval, the situation had gone from bad to worse. A law enacted in 1835 to prevent speculation in lands had the American colonists up in arms, but only briefly; Mexican soldiers had no trouble squelching the protest. All the same, the fires of rebellion had been lit and could not be doused. Determined to secede, rebel colonists began to recruit allies in New Orleans and New York, promising to reward them with fertile Texas land. While this went on, Washington feigned ignorance, though Mexican authorities, fully aware of the activities of the plotters, asked it time and time again to enforce its neutrality laws, which barred citizens of the United States from intervening in foreign wars. When Washington played deaf and dumb, Mexican officials warned that armed foreigners who "attack our territory shall be punished as pirates."

That did not dissuade William B. Travis, named governor of Texas by the rebel colonists, from capturing the presidio of Anáhuac. Then, upon his return from Mexico, Austin became commander of a Texas army, being, in turn, supplanted by Samuel Houston, a former governor of Mississippi. A crony of Jackson's, Houston stood over six feet tall and had a taste for liquor and a gift for "magniloquent oratory." For reasons unknown, he had abandoned his family to live among the Cherokee Indians, who, knowing of his fondness for liquor, referred to him as Big Drunk. Houston, who knew how to command men, had journeyed to Texas to join the rebels, redeem his reputation, and restore his depleted fortune. He made his initial foray in December 1835, when his army captured San Antonio Béxar, the biggest Mexican town, its defenders, led by General Martín Prefecto de Cos, taking refuge across the Río Bravo.

One month earlier, delegates chosen by the colonists had met at Washington-on-the-Brazos, a town east of San Antonio, to draft a declaration of independence and elect David Burnet provisional president of the Texas republic and Zavala its vice-president, who had applauded the colonists for their proclamation, driven, to quote Justo Sierra, "by his congenital affinity, as a Yucatecan, for loose federation, states' rights, and even for local autonomy and secession" and, he might have added, by an unbridled admiration for the United States. As a pretext, the colonists asserted that Santa Anna's restoration of the Centralist republic had nullified their social contract with Mexico, forgetting conveniently that Iturbide's empire, no less Centralist, had given them entry into Texas.

Back in Mexico, the criollo charlatan Santa Anna, after crushing a Federalist uprising in Zacatecas against "military despotism and the Centralized Republic" about to be given birth by the Bases Orgánicas, abandoned once again the presidency to head the military campaign against the Texas rebels. Saying he "preferred the hazards of war to the seductive life of the National Palace," he established his headquarters at San Luis Potosí, where he quartered his ragtag army of nearly six thousand men. "The government of the United States," Santa Anna told an audience of foreign and national dignitaries in San Luis Potosí, "is responsible for the disturbances" in Texas; but, he assured his listeners, "I personally will march forth to subdue the rebels and, once this is done, my cannon will establish the boundary between Mexico and the United States." Among those who heard these words was Anthony Butler, the United States minister to Mexico, who made no attempt to conceal his rage, though he surely must have known that Santa Anna, for one of the few times in his life, spoke the truth. To finance his military expedition, for the national exchequer was empty, Santa Anna mortgaged Manga de Clavo and got a loan of 400,000 pesos from a Mexican financier, guaranteed, at the point of a gun, by the states of San Luis Potosí, Zacatecas, Guanajuato, and Jalisco.

Finally, on January 2, 1836, Santa Anna started his march across the desert that stood between him and Saltillo, his destination in Coahuila. He spent a month there, which he devoted to the training of his army, as always, of conscripts; no detail, no matter how insignificant, escaped his attention, noted a soldier on the expedition who, copying Bernal Díaz del Castillo, titled his account *"Historia verdadera" de la Guerra de Texas.* Then, on February 2, Santa Anna's army set off for Texas by way of Monclova, a town in Coahuila; the winter weather was cold, and more so for Santa Anna's soldiers, nearly all of them from the warm climates of Mexico. In late February 1837, the army, such as it was, reached Texas. At El Alamo, just outside of San Antonio, it found Travis with 146 men barricaded in an old Franciscan church, determined to "win or die." Unwilling to take on Santa Anna's army, Houston and his men had retreated before the advance of the Mexicans, leaving Travis to face the music alone. On March 6, the Mexicans attacked, scaled the walls of the old church, and, fighting man to man, took it. "Travis," according to the diary of the Mexican soldier, "died bravely"; Jim Bowie, the second in command, "like a coward." Every defender perished, save for a boy of fourteen, two women, and the black slave of Travis. Mexican losses, much heavier, totaled 400 dead and countless wounded. "Another victory such as this one," the Mexican chronicler wrote, "and we will lose the war."

With the victory at El Alamo, Santa Anna divided his army into three divisions and at the head of one of them gave chase to Houston and his army of 800 men, who continued to fall back, taking with them the American colonists. At Goliad, a Texas hamlet, the division under General José Urrea captured an armed force of 365 American volunteers, a few of them colonists; Urrea urged clemency, but Santa Anna, resolved on stamping out the flame of rebellion, overruled him. To the horror of Urrea, Santa Anna ordered them shot. Don Antonio, the historical documents note, lost no sleep that night.

Santa Anna's mopping-up operation, as he labeled it, had a short life span. Fortified by men, rifles, and supplies from across the border, and Washington's blessings, Houston, now with an army of 1,500 men, felt strong enough to make a stand. In April, Santa Anna found him encamped in Lynchburg Ferry, not far from the Río San Jacinto but, instead of attacking Houston immediately, decided to rest his men. On the afternoon of April 21, to the surprise of the Hero of Tampico and Veracruz, Houston's men fell upon the Mexicans, finding them cooking their dinners and Santa Anna taking a siesta, the most costly, as it turned out, in Mexican history. Half an hour later, the rout was complete, victory falling to Houston. Of the Mexican army, 400 were dead, 200 wounded, and 700 taken prisoners. Santa Anna, who fled during the brief battle, was discovered the following day hiding in tall grass, "dressed in a blue shirt, white pants, and red carpet slippers." As a prisoner of Houston, Santa Anna, to his ultimate shame, ordered General Filisola and his principal lieutenants not to attack the enemy. News of the fiasco was received in Mexico with stupefaction but not so in Washington, which that same year recognized the Lone Star Republic.

While a prisoner, Santa Anna, fearing for his life, signed two treaties, one public and the other not. By the first, he acknowledged the end of hostilities between Mexico and the Texans; by the second, Santa Anna, in return for his freedom, swore to obtain Mexican recognition of Texan independence. Equally ignoble, Zavala sat down with Santa Anna to discuss the future of Mexico and, as he explained, that of his "new *patria.*" Distrustful of his captors, who hungered to avenge the Alamo and Goliad, Santa Anna, by letter, pleaded with Andrew Jackson to spare his life; meanwhile Houston, just elected president of the Lone Star Republic, set him free and prevailed upon him to visit Washington before returning to Mexico, where an unfriendly reception awaited him. To the misfortune of Mexico, Santa Anna returned home ultimately, to take up residence at Manga de Clavo and plot.

Rightly so, Mexico disavowed Santa Anna's cowardly behavior, refusing to recognize the Lone Star Republic. Yet with the exchequer bare and the country torn apart by internal discord, it did nothing to bring Texas back into the fold. However, the Texans, their victory at San Jacinto gone to their head, sent a raiding party to Santa Fe, the junction in New Mexico for the trade between Missouri and Chihuahua; to their embarrassment, the Mexicans captured it and, in reprisal, fell upon San Antonio while a Texas army, which invaded Tamaulipas, had to surrender, with every tenth man being shot. So matters stood until 1846.

III

American expansionists broke the truce. The hunger to annex Texas but, of far greater import, to take California, led to war between Mexico and the United States. Known as the American intervention in Mexico, the war had, as the Texas episode reveals, old roots. Already in 1842, Thomas C. Jones, the commander of the United States naval squadron anchored off the coast of California, had seized the port of Monterey, believing hostilities had erupted between the two countries. Upon learning that this was not so, the embarrassed Jones apologized, returning the port to Mexican hands. Just the same, his folly unmasked Washington's true intentions, leaving it bereft of even the proverbial fig leaf.

For ten years, northern fears in the United States that the annexation of Texas, a slave territory, would upset the balance of power in Congress, kept the Lone Star Republic waiting for the invitation to join. From the start, most Texans favored union with their American kin, and, as time went by, a majority in the United States felt that way. Manifest Destiny, the doctrine of the expansionists, had popular support, as the election of 1844 documents. Promising to annex Texas and, by implication, acquire California, James K. Polk, a southern expansionist, won the presidency easily. His election, Mexicans knew, meant war. Not to be outdone, John Tyler, a slaveholder from Virginia and the departing president, got Congress, on February 27, 1845, to annex Texas; in July, the Texans conferred their stamp of approval. That accomplished, Juan N. Almonte, the Mexican minister to Washington, asked for his passport, warning that annexation meant war. In response, Washington recalled its representative from Mexico and, arrogantly, replaced him with a diplomatic agent with financial claims against Mexico.

On the subject of Mexico's warning, American historians have been less than forthright. Alleging that Mexico's ultimatum started the war, they have been saints abroad and devils at home, employing "different criteria . . . to judge similar phenomena," to quote a Mexican scholar. While upbraiding Mexico for its "stubborn refusal to accept the Independence of Texas," they hail, at the same time, Abraham Lincoln's vow to prevent the South from seceding from the American Union. For them, the South had no right to do so. Viewed dispassionately, however, the challenges of Texas and the South ring uniformly.

Three annexationists, apostles of Manifest Destiny, sat in Polk's cabinet: James Buchanan, the future president; George Bancroft, the historian; and Robert Walker, the financial whiz. Like Polk, they wanted California, even if it meant war with Mexico. With ample cause, Mexicans believed that Polk was bent on provoking a conflict between Texas and Mexico so that the "United States would be forced to intervene." Polk, as a matter of fact, not only hungered for war but believed that a short, relatively painless one was possible, thinking that Mexico lacked the will and the military capability to fight. As he saw it, victory would come in a few months. He was almost a prophet.

Carrying out his plans, Polk ordered General Zachary Taylor, awaiting Washington's pleasure in Louisiana, to march his army into Texas, "to defend it," as he phrased it. Wanting to keep Mexican Gulf ports under surveillance, he sent a naval squadron and told John D. Sloat, in charge of the Pacific fleet, to occupy San Francisco when war broke out. Not desiring to leave anything to chance, Polk also dispatched Robert Stockton to California, with instructions for Sloat and Robert Larkin, the United States consul; once fighting started, they were to incite a local rebellion for California's independence and Sloat would disembark sailors.

Washington justified these belligerent measures as precautions against a Mexican attack. But Mexico, at that juncture in its history, had no more than thirteen hundred soldiers on the borders of Texas and a mere handful in New Mexico and California. Without any doubt, Washington knew that the soldiers were poorly armed recruits, eager to desert at the first opportunity and captained by officers with politics on their mind. Even the cavalry and artillery, once Mexico's pride, had lost their luster. Mexico, as usual, was bankrupt, lacking money for any foreign adventure and afflicted by domestic turmoil.

Almonte's departure severed Mexico's diplomatic relations with the United States. Just the same, Washington, during the fall of 1845, asked Mexico to receive a special envoy, a diplomat, the Mexicans supposed, who would do his best to restore relations between the two countries. That was not to be, because John Slidell arrived in Mexico City as minister plenipotentiary, precisely what Mexico had said it could not accept. Not only that, but he came to offer forty million dollars for the territory between the Nueces River and the Río Bravo and, additionally, northern New Mexico and California. Under these circumstances, President José Joaquín Herrera told Slidell to go home, knowing that no Mexican government could survive the sale of any of its territory. Polk, professing not to understand, declared that Mexico would pay for its intransigence.

During the interval, Herrera's administration looked about frantically for a way out of the danger, going so far as to offer to recognize the Lone Star Republic, convinced that Texas was lost irrevocably. Popular sentiment in Texas, however, favored union with the United States. More to the point, Herrera acknowledged that Mexico could not defend itself against its more powerful neighbor. That attitude led to his downfall in December 1845; General Mariano Paredes Arrillaga, who ousted him, vowed to defend Mexico to the last man.

For Polk, that was a golden opportunity, exactly what he had been waiting for. Of his cabinet members, neither Bancroft nor Buchanan, legal-minded expansionists, would vote for war unless Mexico began it. All the same, they were disinclined, as the old saying goes, to look a gift horse in the mouth, giving Polk plenty of room to maneuver. Ready to risk war, Polk, on January 13, 1846, told Taylor to cross the Río Nueces, Mexico's northern boundary, and camp on the shores of the Río Bravo. As Taylor advanced, the Mexican inhabitants of Frontón, a hamlet on the Nueces, fled southward. With "flagrant contempt for international law," Sierra wrote, an American army "invaded the territory of a nation" at peace with its neighbors, "on the pretext that Texas had always had the Nueces for boundary." Recognizing what that might entail, Polk sat down at his desk to compose his declaration of war.

On the banks of the Río Bravo, Taylor erected a fort across from the town of Matamoros, ignoring cries of alarm from the Mexicans. When General Pedro de Ampudia, the Mexican commander, demanded that he withdraw, Taylor, instead, ordered American warships to blockade the mouth of the Río Bravo, cutting off the supply route for Matamoros. "We do not have a particle of right to be here," confessed an American colonel with Taylor; "it looks as if the government sent a small force on purpose to bring on a war, as to have a pretext to take California." On April 25, the incident Polk had been praying for occurred when, during a skirmish, Mexican soldiers killed or wounded sixteen Americans. News of the encounter reached Washington on May 9, 1846, with Taylor saying the "hostilities may now be considered as commenced." With Taylor's report in hand, Polk went before Congress to deliver his message of war. To the draft he had prepared earlier, he added merely one sentence: "American blood," he declared, "has been shed on American soil."

With debate limited to two hours, Congress backed Polk quickly, but not before Abraham Lincoln, a fledgling politician, had his say. To quote Lincoln, who challenged Polk to prove his claims to the Rio Grande (Bravo), "But if he can not or will not do this—if on any pretense or no pretense he shall refuse or omit it—then I shall be fully convinced of what I more than suspect already—that he is deeply conscious of being in the wrong," adding, "that he feels the blood of this war, like the blood of Abel, is crying to Heaven against him." Lincoln had truth on his side. By the Adams-Onís Treaty of 1819, according to a distinguished American historian, Washington had accepted the Sabine River as the boundary between New Spain and Louisiana and, by signing it, John Adams noted, relinquished "a mere color of a claim." Texas, he added, was never part of the Louisiana Purchase. Over and above, Spain, in 1816, had affixed the boundary of Texas, then a province, at the Nueces, as uniformly shown on maps and atlases of the period, "extending no further westward than the Nueces." Stephen A. Austin, the "father of Texas," had acknowledged that on his maps of 1822 and 1829, as did Andrew Jackson, Martin Van Buren, and John Quincy Adams, and, in 1836, the evidence demonstrates, even the Texans were willing to accept the Nueces as their boundary. Polk, this historian concluded, knew that he was in the wrong, as did the literate, educated American public of that day.

Just the same, Polk and his disciples, protesting falsely their innocence, voted for war. From Missouri, General Stephen Kearny marched into New Mexico and California, a part of his troops capturing Ciudad Chihuahua, while Sloat's fleet occupied Monterey and San Francisco. Vanquishing a detachment of Mexican soldiers, Taylor crossed the Río Bravo and, after three days of hard fighting, took Monterrey and then Saltillo. General Winfield Scott, in the meantime, was ordered to invade Mexico by way of Veracruz.

Unbelievably, in the Mexico of the criollos it was politics as usual. The Federalists, still reeling from Paredes Arrillaga's cuartelazo, organized one of their own and ousted him from office, replacing him with Santa Anna, enticed back from exile, aided and abetted by Polk, who let him slip through the naval blockade of Mexico on Santa Anna's promise to negotiate. The Federalists named him president and Valentín Gómez Farías, the indefatigable anticlerical, vice-president. With Santa Anna off to war, Gómez Farías and Congress, to finance it, confiscated fifteen million pesos of church property.

Unwilling to give up an inch of its holding, the church, in time-honored fashion, found men willing to defend it. The revolt of the Polkos, as it was dubbed, broke out just as Scott was off the coast of Veracruz. Young men from the "best families," largely criollo dandies, the Polkos were officers in the national militia; its intellectual leaders numbered Mariano Otero and Manuel Payno, a novelist destined for fame but who, at this hour of need, selfishly put politics ahead of *patria.* For one entire month, the Polkos, rather than march to Veracruz with their men to oppose Scott's army, fought soldiers loyal to Gómez Farías. Thinking the Polkos abreast of the political currents, Santa Anna, then on his journey to battle Scott, stopped off in Mexico City to chase Gómez Farías out of the National Palace and revoke his legislation, in return for a pledge from the church to lend money for the war.

Earlier, Santa Anna, again at San Luis Potosí, had assembled an army of eighteen thousand men, mostly raw conscripts, to block Taylor's invasion. He broke camp in late January 1847, for his trek across miles of arid lands during the middle of winter, leaving with insufficient food and water for his lightly clad and poorly armed soldiers, followed by hundreds of soldaderas burdened by children they had to feed. As Santa Anna moved north, bitterly cold winds lashed his soldiers, who at night huddled around campfires trying to stay warm. By contrast, during the day, with the desert sun ablaze, the heat parched the mouths of the weary soldiers. Dead horses and oxen, broken wagons and leftover supplies, as well as the rotting carcasses of soldiers, marked the route of march of Santa Anna's army; all told, it suffered four thousand losses, made up of the dead, sick, and deserters with no stomach for fighting. Not so Santa Anna, who, on his white stallion, rode up and down the line of march, shouting words of encouragement to his soldiers, dismounting to help load gunpowder on a wagon and scolding stragglers. Santa Anna was in his glory.

The battle of La Angostura, a pass Santa Anna likened to Thermopylae, site of a heroic battle of the ancient Greeks, lasted just two days. Taylor, who heard of Santa Anna's approach on February 21, waited for his foe at the hacienda of Buena Vista, not far from Angostura. Mountains rose on both sides of the trail going north, the Mexican army's route of travel. Fighting began on February 22, with the Mexicans attempting to encircle Taylor's left flank, which he had forgotten to fortify. They almost did, but, ultimately, the heavier American artillery prevailed. While the Americans were getting ready for the next day's battle, Santa Anna, his soldiers exhausted and starving, abandoned the field of battle, leaving Taylor to claim victory. Nearly fifteen hundred Mexicans died in the encounter.

Like Napoleon's flight from Moscow, the retreat from Angostura left the dead by the roadside, to be eaten by coyotes at nightfall. When the shattered regiments of the army camped at Agua Nueva, a deserted hacienda, the suffering was terrible to behold. The wounded lay on the ground, their cries of pain heard day and night, while soldaderas, who ministered to them, washed rags in water the color of blood. Santa Anna had gone on ahead to proclaim victory, only to learn on his approach to Mexico City that news of his defeat had preceded him. Mexicans had no time to debate Santa Anna's behavior at La Angostura. Scott had landed his army at Veracruz, captured the port, and begun his march to Mexico City.

As Scott and his army marched inland, another war had broken out in Mexico, the responsibility for it largely that of the criollos. In Yucatán, the half-forgotten province, the Huits, the frontier Maya, tired of paying homage to the exploitative *dzules*, as the whites were known, who, as sugar and henequen hacendados, almost daily trampled underfoot more of their corn patches, had rebelled. By 1848, when resistance to the Yankee invaders had collapsed, the Maya had come within a hair's breadth of capturing Mérida, capital of Yucatán, and driving the *dzules* into the sea. The Caste War, as the conflict was known, outlasted the fighting with the United States and, before it was over, brought out the worst in the criollos of Yucatán, which revealed much about their leadership in general and helps to explain why Mexico's criollos signed the disgraceful treaty of 1848 with the United States.

As events demonstrated, the criollos of Yucatán were vastly more interested in defeating their Maya adversaries than in upholding the sovereignty of their country. In March, with much of the Maya population up in arms and threatening to overrun all of Yucatán, its criollos, the hacendados and merchants of the province, wrote a letter to Washington, with duplicates to Madrid and London, offering, in return for "powerful and effective help" against the Maya, complete "domination and sovereignty" over Yucatán. Justo Sierra O'Reilly, native of Yucatán and father of the future historian, was its special envoy to Washington, arriving there partly by courtesy of an American warship which had taken him from Campeche to Veracruz. In Washington, Sierra O'Reilly, on behalf of the frightened criollos of Yucatán, asked Washington to recognize Yucatán's neutrality in the war against the Republic of Mexico. Washington rejected both overtures, but Sierra O'Reilly, alarmed by news that the conflict between Mexico and the United States was coming to an end and fearful that national leaders might want to punish the perfidy of Yucatán, then sought a defensive treaty and pleaded for military aid for the fight against the Maya. In Yucatán, the inhabitants of Ciudad Carmen, with the Maya on their doorstep, begged protection from the American occupation forces; forgetting their earlier slogan "Gringos go home," they welcomed with open arms three hundred United States Marines detailed to defend them from the Maya. For their part, the criollos of Mexico City spent a part of the money "paid" by the United States for the captured territories on guns purchased from the departing American army to use on the Maya.

One story gives the gist of this tale of less than patriotic behavior. Following the end of the American War, the criollos of Yucatán recruited American volunteers to fight the Maya, soldiers from the Thirteenth Infantry Regiment mustered out at Mobile, Alabama, in the summer of 1848. Accepting an offer of eight dollars a month and 320 acres of land, 933 men of the regiment went off to kill Maya in Yucatán. This project was the brainchild of Sierra O'Reilly, who longed for white settlers to improve local bloodlines. Sailing from New Orleans, the American mercenaries ended up at Culumpich, their initial contact with the Maya warriors, where, refusing to heed the advice of the criollo military commanders, veterans of the fighting in Yucatán, they assaulted the Maya defenders frontally with fixed bayonets. The first volley of the Maya, a survivor of the debacle recalled, "caught them point-blank," and the Mexican soldiers with them "had their hands full bringing out the forty casualties." Leandro Poot, one of the Maya warriors at Culumpich, remembered, "It was easy to kill the strange white men, for they were big and fought in line, as if they were marching. . . . We hid behind trees and rocks wherever we could, that they might not see us, and so we killed them." A week of such fighting, according to one account of the Caste War, led to the resignation of many of the American officers and, significantly, the abandonment of the idea of another revolt in the Texas style of 1836, one of the goals of the American mercenaries.

In the meantime, Santa Anna, at the head of a fresh army recruited hastily, had awaited Scott's soldiers, again to taste defeat. From April to September, the Mexicans, now no longer merely hungry recruits, battled Scott's soldiers, poorly at Cerro Gordo and Puebla but ferociously after that, retreating only grudgingly. Although sustaining heavy casualties, the Americans captured Molino del Rey, watched cadets from the military college wrap themselves in the Mexican flag and leap to their death rather than surrender at Chapultepec and, then, on September 13, 1847, entered Mexico City.

If they expected a royal welcome, they were mistaken. The inhabitants of Mexico City watched the invaders sullenly. No sooner had the American soldiers dispersed to take up their quarters in the city than a hail of stones greeted them from the rooftops of buildings, hurled by angry Mexicans. One woman, by her appearance and speech clearly of the lower class, hit a soldier with a stone, and the police, trying to restore order, arrested her. As she was being led away, she told a sympathetic crowd that gathered that she was attempting to punish the invaders for killing her son, one of the soldiers who had defended Mexico City. "I wanted to kill," she sobbed, "and if I could I would kill all of them." Just the same, the Mexicans made peace with the invaders, a few young women, for example, rushing to entertain American officers at the Hotel Bella Unión, among them whores, who set up a lively trade in the upstairs bedrooms.

On his journey to Mexico City, Scott had been accompanied by Nicholas Trist, sent by Polk to negotiate peace. Its terms, Trist and Scott made clear, were harsh indeed; few conquerors had imposed more severe penalties. The Americans demanded that Mexico relinquish half of its territory, the lands from the Pacific Ocean to Texas, including Baja California. They also asked for the right of passage across the Isthmus of Tehuantepec. For accepting the treaty, Mexico would receive fifteen million dollars and, as icing on the cake, the cancellation of its debts to American citizens, their total, interestingly, reduced drastically once Washington assumed payment of their claims.

Upon learning what the victors demanded, many Mexicans balked. One of them was Melchor Ocampo, governor of Michoacán and architect of the Reforma, then looming on the historical horizon. He wanted to fight on, relying on the hit-and-run tactics of guerrilla warfare to drive out the enemy. "Give the people arms," he argued, "and they will defend themselves." Of similar opinion was Ponciano Arriaga, a journalist from Guanajuato and, like Ocampo, a future luminary of the Reforma, "tall, thin, with tiny eyes and a pock-marked face, the ravages of smallpox." In Aguascalientes, General Paredes Arrillaga, a man who shared no common ground with Ocampo and Arriaga, said that he would not lay down his arms. Opposition to American demands was best personified by José María Cuevas, a lawyer who, lying on a sickbed, had himself brought before Congress, then debating the American terms at Querétaro, where it had taken refuge. From his bed, Cuevas stood up and pleaded that Mexico not make peace.

The majority of the criollos at Querétaro, nevertheless, voted to accept the Treaty of Guadalupe, which Trist and Scott dictated to the Mexican representatives when they met on the outskirts of Mexico City. Unwilling to risk losing their dominance of Mexican society, which popular resistance to an American occupation would surely entail, they preferred to give up half of Mexico. Mexicans held on to Baja California and retained sovereignty over the Isthmus of Tehuantepec.

IV

With the blessings of Lucas Alamán, Santa Anna returned to rule Mexico one more time. His days, however, were numbered, as were those of the criollo oligarchy. The loss of half of Mexico had unveiled the magnitude of criollo incompetence. Unless Mexicans shook themselves free of the political turpitude, their country would disappear from the face of the earth, devoured by the giant next door.

Even the criollos, who had made such a mess of national life, understood this. Writing during the occupation of Mexico City by Yankee soldiers, a crestfallen Alamán lamented that "Divine Providence" had punished Mexicans for their sins. A nation once worshiped as a model by Mexicans had betrayed them in the "most unjust war in history." Of Mexico, the embittered Alamán wrote, merely "the shadow of a once noble and illustrious name" survived, while Carlos María de Bustamante, from the pages of his *Cuadro histórico de la revolución,* reminded its readers that "it dealt with the mistakes and failures of our government," dedicating one of its volumes to "the memory of a Mexican who, with unerring aim, shot and killed an American soldier as he flew the Stars and Stripes over the National Palace."

But the Liberals, too, lost face. Had they not admired the American model and attempted to transplant it to Mexico? With their desire to imitate, Mexico had been sold down the road to the disaster of Guadalupe—so said sundry Conservatives. That attitude, in all probability, helped strengthen the resolve of some Conservatives, among them Alamán, to find a European savior for Mexico. Mexicans, they believed, could not govern themselves. With the humiliation of 1848, the army, part of the criollo cabal, had also lost prestige, tempting renegades of the runt middle class to challenge it.

At this juncture, too, Mexicans, face-to-face with the incompetency of criollo army chiefs and politicos, discovered anew the glories of ancient Anáhuac. The true patriots were the ancient Mexicans, chieftains such as Cuauhtémoc, who boldly told Cortés, "Why do you hesitate to kill me? I deserve to die at your hands because I did not have the good luck to die for my country." From the sorrow of defeat, Cuauhtémoc had risen from the tomb to personify a yearning for a different and better Mexico. Not Cuauhtémoc but the Reforma, the brainchild of the nascent middle class, more and more mestizo, answered that call.

12

LA REFORMA

I

A cataclysmic triumph for the runt, provincial middle class, the Reforma was, simultaneously, a response to a changing international order. While Mexico disintegrated, the Western world, specifically Europe and the United States, was enjoying a metamorphosis, the invention of the Industrial Revolution. As the second half of the nineteenth century commenced, capitalism, a virginal word in the vocabulary, made its triumphal bow. From that time on, particularly after the aborted European "revolutions" of 1848, capitalism, both as ideology and as panacea, met more and more public approval, spawning a society convinced that competitive enterprise, primarily buying cheaply, paying labor poorly, and selling dearly engendered economic growth. The resulting economy, the handicraft of an industrious, thrifty, and intelligent bourgeoisie, unlocked the doors, its ideologues claimed, to a world with opportunity for one and all, but only if they embraced the acceptable codes of behavior. The disciples of capitalist dogma talked blithely of "progress," the sacrosanct goal, and of its "inevitability." Herbert Spencer, the English author of social Darwinism, christened it a world fit for the fittest.

For Mexican Liberals, the capitalist blueprints had the bewitchery of patristic articles of faith. One of the most conspicuous features of this bunch of copycats was the way it mesmerized itself, "like a rabbit practicing self-hypnosis in the absence of a stoat." That left just one option: to echo the Western model, to copy its institutions and, above everything, embrace its values, first off by ridding the body politic of the tyranny of colonial traditions and the supremacy of the Catholic church. Peripheral people might yet save themselves by welcoming the ideal of the nation state, adopting constitutions, safeguarding property rights, setting up representative assemblies and governments responsible to them, and permitting, "where suitable, a participation in politics of the common people," so long as it did not jeopardize the bourgeois social order.

This premise was music to the ears of Mexican Liberals, the native *burgueses*, conditioned to think in those terms by the teachings of José María Luis Mora and his disciples. These Mexicans, more and more of them mestizos, felt a "profound need," as Justo Sierra, one of their brethren, defined it, "for a stable political constitution" guaranteeing liberty and private property. That could not be accomplished unless corporate privileges were eliminated, specifically those of church and military. The Reforma was the Liberal tonic for the ills of Mexico, laid bare by the facile victory of the Yankee invaders. Sadly, as the Liberals recognized, the Mexican Republic was but a shell, "the amorphousness of an organism that could hardly be called a nation." To paraphrase Mariano Otero, once a Polko dandy, something was terribly wrong if a Yankee army could march through hundreds of miles of Mexican territory unmolested by the native population.

For these Mexicans, like their European counterparts, capitalism was the light at the end of the dark tunnel. Liberalism, a euphemism for capitalist dogma, held the key, so its ideologues must be studied carefully, acknowledged Guillermo Prieto, a kingpin of the Reforma. For him, Adam Smith kept lit the lamp of knowledge. But that wisdom drew a critic, a thinker who questioned capitalist dogma. In 1867, Karl Marx published *Das Kapital,* the principal work of capitalism's foremost censurer. In Mexico, too, dissenters made their objections known. They probably knew nothing of Marx, but they had doubts about the wisdom of laissez-faire. Scholars refer to it as social liberalism, a concoction of capitalist doctrine and a social conscience, dealing mostly with agrarian issues. It was, say those who write about it, the adaptation of classical liberalism to the conditions of Mexican underdevelopment. Unfortunately for the indigent, social liberalism was but a voice crying in the wilderness, yet one fated to eventually influence Mexican thought. Ignacio Ramírez, like the German thinker, hungered for justice for the poor, not just blueprints for the welfare of the Mexican *burguesía.*

II

The Reforma did not just burst forth on the historical scene. Quite the contrary: it had roots in the colonial past, specifically the Bourbon reforms, as well as in the post-Independence era. Ironically, the bitter years of the bungling criollo oligarchy, which nipped in the bud the expectations of the early patriot fathers, nurtured the seeds of an intellectual awakening. Alongside the sordidness of politics and the economic quagmire, "the tree of Mexican letters," said one historian, "burst into leaf," conferring life on the "spirit, even though there was no light in the country's overcast skies." Newspapers and journals made their appearance, while young authors began to publish books and essays and to write poetry, perhaps, to cite our learned historian, "to spike the guns of fratricidal wars with garlands of wit and poesy."

Heart and soul of the intellectual stirrings were the youth who, from 1836 on, met at the Academia de San Juan de Letrán, in Mexico City, which, as a *colegio,* had been dedicated to the teaching of mestizo youth by Viceroy Antonio de Mendoza during the sixteenth century; Fernando de Alva Ixtlixóchitl, who wrote about the pre-Hispanic past, was one of its luminaries. Nearly all that is known of the Academia comes from the *Memorias de mis tiempos* of Prieto, who, at age sixteen, partook of its learning. The building, he recalled, was "squat and clumsy-looking," with a coach gate for a front door; built around two patios, one floor housed the classrooms while the library, its "dusty and rickety bookshelves covered with cobwebs," stood apart.

Under the tutelage of José María Lacunza, aspiring writers and scholars started to congregate there, to read their poetry, discuss the classics, and learn about contemporary literature. Every Wednesday, Prieto and Ramírez, then in their early youth, heard Manuel Payno and José Joaquín Pesado, established luminaries, read their poetry and, best of all, ask for commentary. Andrés Quintana Roo, the aging patriot, presided over the intellectual feast. From the circle of writers at the Academia emerged a Mexican literary school, endeavoring to *mexicanizar* (to make Mexican) the written word, whether poetry, the short story, or journalism. Four poets of the Academia, disciples of Romanticism, placed their imprint on Mexican belles lettres. Aside from Pesado, there was Fernando Calderón, a Liberal politician who wrote plays; Ignacio Rodríguez Galván, a penniless poet who, in his *Profecía de Guatímoc,* mourned the injustices committed against the Indian during the Conquest; and Manuel Carpio. José María Heredia, a well-known Cuban poet, found the intellectual climate so invigorating that he stayed to become a Mexican citizen. Prieto and Payno developed the *cuadro de costumbre,* one of the initial forms Mexicans employed to write about themselves and a cornerstone of realism in Hispanic-American letters.

Whatever the merits of poets and *cuentistas* (authors of short stories), the literary revival discovered its capital expression in journalism and works of history. *El Mosaico Mexicano,* a journal of the Academia de San Juan de Letrán edited by Ignacio Cumplido, matched the best of Europe. Not far behind was *Años Nuevos,* the journal of Rodríguez Galván, as well as *Calendarios de las Señoritas Mexicanas, Miscelánea Pintoresca,* and *El Siglo XIX,* published with the idea that literature was to be read not just by connoisseurs but by the general public. Historical scholarship of quality, a cardinal pillar of the revival, included the works of Lucas Alamán and Mora and, perhaps less enduring, those of Lorenzo Zavala and Otero. The popular Francisco Zarco wrote historical fiction.

Prieto and Ramírez, additionally, played powerful roles on the historical stage. The son of a baker and a poet of note, Prieto served as minister of finance and taught economics, which, he confessed in his *Memorias,* he comprehended poorly, and military history at the Colegio Militar. As editor of the *Diario Oficial,* which supported the criollo oligarchy, he made an about-face and embraced, as chief of *El Siglo XIX,* the Liberal camp, achieving renown for his biting attacks on Antonio López de Santa Anna, for which he was in and out of jail. An orthodox apostle of capitalist theories, he admired the United States but, just the same, resented bitterly its war on Mexico.

Remembered as El Nigromante, Ignacio Ramírez was one of the first "Indians" to climb the ladder of success. His father, of Tarascan antecedents, hailed from Querétaro and his mother, supposedly an Aztec, from Tacuba. Ramírez was hardly an "Indian," because by culture, language, and values he was, for his time, as modern a Mexican as modern could be. Only by race or blood was Don Ignacio an Indian who, of vaster importance for understanding him, never suffered want, his father being vice-governor of Querétaro in 1835. He did, however, have the look of a waif about him, for he never gave a moment's thought to his appearance. When he was seventeen, his parents took him to Mexico City, where he, like so many of his contemporaries, became a lawyer.

As a Mexican Liberal, Ramírez was a bundle of contradictions. With Prieto, he helped write the Constitution of 1857 and served as minister of public instruction. He was a prolific writer, whose essays could fill twenty volumes. The foremost spokesmen for social liberalism, he called attention to the moral deficiencies of capitalism yet adhered to its basic tenets while demanding justice for the Indian and the poor. At the Academia de San Juan de Letrán, he shocked his listeners when, in an essay titled "God Does Not Exist," he declared himself an atheist. "What do you like best about Mexico?" he was asked on one occasion. "Veracruz," he replied, "because one leaves Mexico by way of Veracruz." A Jacobin at heart, he knew intimately the writings of Voltaire, the Encyclopedists, and the classics of Greece and Rome. In painting, at which he dabbled, he was an arch-conservative of orthodox tastes. While fearing the United States, he described it as a "model Republic," admiring its ideal of liberty for everyone.

Newspapers appeared in the remotest places, with Conservatives and Liberals vying for readers. *El Tiempo,* a semi–government journal, featured articles by Alamán and his cronies, while *El Siglo XIX,* which bore Prieto's trademark for a while, printed the Liberal view. Published by Ignacio Cumplido, scion of a patrician family from Guadalajara, *El Siglo XIX* had scores of distinguished persons writing for it, among them José María Iglesias, Manuel Orozco y Berra, a budding colonial historian, and Otero. Another Liberal journal was the *Monitor Republicano,* a vociferous critic of the regime of General Mariano Paredes Arrillaga.

The plastic arts, too, displayed signs of vitality. Mexican themes made their appearance in painting, once the exclusive bailiwick of Spanish art, though techniques, especially at the Academia de San Carlos, did not change. In the fine arts, a visitor commented, "there is a good deal . . . worthy of notice." As in literature, a national conscience was gestating, in art criticism primarily. One of its practitioners was Bernardo Couto, an adviser to Santa Anna, enemy of Liberals, and, in 1848, one of three Mexicans who negotiated the Treaty of Guadalupe Hidalgo. He was among the first to rediscover colonial art.

On the eve of the Reforma, for all that, Mexicans, like most former colonials, still copied European culture. Europe, to rely on the wisdom of one Mexican savant, "was where the most civilized people lived." For urbanites in Mexico City, Guadalajara, and the like, European culture meant that of England and France, reading their novels and mastering their languages, French most of all. Until Independence, few Mexicans bothered to learn French, but now, boasted one of them, it was an integral part of a good education. With the mastery of these languages, so its proponents affirmed, fresh ideas filled the mind, "ennobling and giving a delicacy to the Mexican character," said Mora. Initially, English dress for women and men, Queen Anne furniture for the home, and bland food held sway, even when they were the opposites of traditional Mexican tastes. Then arrived the French, sporting habits and customs more attuned to Mexican ways and, along with them, French goods: towels, bed sheets, and tablecloths which better-off Mexicans purchased avidly. Confronted by the French invasion, the English tide receded, bestowing on Mexican "high society" a French flavor.

Despite the European pretensions of urbanites, Mexican culture, in actuality, had not jelled. Mexico was not one culture but a miscellany of many, each with characteristics of its own, a confusing amalgam of habits, uses, and customs, by and large inspired by Mexico City, France, and England. Behind the façade lay the cultural underpinnings of three centuries of Spanish rule, tempered by the omnipresent Indian. Travelers to Mexico never failed to call attention to this contrast between the "native" culture and the foreign. European Catholics, to provide an illustration, mourned their dead on All Souls' Day, remembering tearfully the loss of dear ones; but not so in Mexico, wrote Paula Kolonitz, an Austrian visitor, where "one celebrated with frivolity and mirth." Kolonitz, her prejudice aside, had caught the difference.

That contrast could also be observed by how Mexican women of the "better families," from middle class upward, grew up pampered, handled as though they were "delicate flowers." More likely than not, at fifteen years of age or so, they were married off, to give birth to numerous progeny, as many as ten or more. As mothers and wives, they ran the household and, with husbands spending time with old friends, raised their children. However, household chores, the cleaning and cooking, were rarely theirs, but the responsibility of a bevy of servants, Indian girls usually. These women, the wives of Mexico's leaders, with idle time on their hands, not infrequently overate and, as they aged, said Kolonitz, "grew fat."

For the generation of the Reforma, schooling, like that of former times, was reserved for men. The education of women, as Madame Calderón de la Barca described it a few years before, hardly merited the term. "Generally speaking . . . Mexican Señoras and Señoritas write, read, and play a little"; but, she added, when "I say they read, I mean they know how to read; when I say they write, I do not mean that they can always spell; and when I say they play, I do not assert that they have generally a knowledge of music." When they did, they played the music of European masters on their pianos, being especially fond of Rossini, Mozart, and Bellini. Few schools worthy of the name accepted women, and no governesses were hired to teach them. Occasionally, when quite young, they were sent to school with boys but, at age twelve or so, were "considered too old to attend." Fathers, among them the "cleverest," were content if their daughters "confess regularly, attend church constantly, and can embroider and sing a little." A quarter of a century later, Kolonitz could still remark that, unless it was a prayer book, only a handful of women read a book from cover to cover in the course of a year. For them, Europe was Spain, which they saw as their birthplace; Rome, where the pope held court; and Paris, the home of their couturier.

Honor and virtue were what men sought in women, and what women had adopted for values of their own. These values were the instruments men manipulated in order to keep women in a subordinate role and to maintain their hierarchical society. Women were told by their fathers to marry men of their own class, of kindred families if possible. This kept property in the family and, under the best of circumstances, enlarged it. By insisting on marriages between men and women of fair skins and similar background, fathers limited the choice of their daughters, thus barring entrance to their social circle to men of lower class.

By the 1850s, Mexican society needed revamping. While the winds of change were sweeping the Western world, Mexico stagnated and wallowed in despair. With a mixture of resignation and fatalism, Mexicans had come to believe that in politics there were only crooks and knaves. They spoke harshly of their neighbors, accepting as truth whatever malicious tale was said of them. No one trusted anyone, with everyone accusing everyone of treason or of holding defeatist attitudes. Of the Republic and its inhabitants, they had little good to say. Mexico, one Frenchman argued, was divided into two camps, one referring to itself as "Clerical" and the other as "Liberal," both lamenting the disreputable state of affairs. Yet while "five million Indians" labored from dawn to dusk, the "Clericals wanted to safeguard their ill-gotten gains" and the "Liberals" to enrich themselves and win access to high public office.

III

At this time of despair, a rebellion flared up in Ayutla, a nondescript town in Guerrero, against Antonio López de Santa Anna, "His Most Serene Highness." The straw that broke the camel's back was the sale of the Mesilla, the so-called Gadsden Purchase of 1853. The uprising, which sought to oust Don Antonio and restore the rule of law, was the prelude to the Reforma, Mexico's second major upheaval of the nineteenth century. The inglorious defeat of Mexican arms by Yankee troops and the shameful antics of Santa Anna had united the opposition under the leadership of Juan Alvarez, the cacique of Guerrero. No longer a young man, Alvarez had been an insurgent ally of Vicente Guerrero, an admirer of Mora, and a friend of Ignacio Comonfort, a criollo dismissed recently by Santa Anna from his lucrative job of collector of customs at the port of Acapulco. Unorthodox in thought and behavior, Alvarez was the son of a hacendado and a hacendado himself, but of curious bent. In the 1840s, he had sided with the Indian attackers of Chilapa, alleging that they were trying simply to regain stolen lands. A decade or so afterward, authorities accused him of sheltering the assassins of the Spanish mayordomo of the hacienda San Vicente, on the outskirts of Cuernavaca; Alvarez declared that the sugar hacendados, who wished to establish a feudal system, robbed local pueblos of their lands. He also came to hate and distrust Santa Anna, so much so that during the American advance on Chapultepec he had refused to come to his aid, even though he commanded a contingent of ready troops. Neither an intellectual nor a politico, Alvarez was a man of simple tastes and limited ambitions.

Alvarez and Ignacio Comonfort, his chief lieutenant, captained a rebellion uncontaminated by military bedfellows. The army, knowing on what side its bread was buttered, had remained loyal to Santa Anna. The Revolution of Ayutla, so it was christened, was headed by civilians who had taken up arms for a cause, mostly provincial lawyers, small merchants, bureaucrats, rancheros of the Bajío, and, here and there, maverick hacendados, Alvarez for one and, in far-off Sonora, Ignacio Pesqueira, the leaders of a motley array of confederates, on paper no match for Santa Anna's army. Alvarez relied for advice on Liberals born after Independence, scores of them mestizos. Even the Liberals of criollo lineage were, by psychology, culture, and values, thoroughly Mexican and, judged by that, "mestizo." For them, the days of New Spain were merely history.

Despite the odds, the rebels toppled Don Antonio from his perch atop Mexican politics. Although Alvarez had to retreat into the mountains of Guerrero, Comonfort, defending Acapulco, held Santa Anna at bay while Santos Degollado, a law professor from Michoacán, organized guerrillas in Jalisco, and Manuel Doblado and Santiago Vidaurri, the caudillos of Guanajuato and Nuevo León, ragtag armies. By early 1855, northern Mexico, from Sonora to Nuevo León, had come out for the Plan de Ayutla, the banner of the rebels. Meanwhile, Melchor Ocampo and Benito Juárez, two of the famous exiles in New Orleans, had joined Alvarez. Seeing the handwriting on the wall, the Hero of Tampico and Veracruz abandoned Mexico, not to step on its soil again until 1874. Wrinkled of face, bent of shoulders, and gray of hair, he died in bed two years later, a forgotten and discredited old man.

But Mexico was not out of the woods. It was at this time that Henry A. Crabb, one more of the seemingly inexhaustible storehouse of American filibusters, marched south to conquer Sonora. With adventurers from California, Crabb, in 1856, descended upon the town of Caborca, northwest of Hermosillo, where he barricaded himself in the church. Luckily, the Mexicans defeated Crabb and his adventurers, killing nearly a hundred of them. Unbelievably, Washington later added their deaths to the list of American claims against Mexico.

The generation of Ayutla boasted a galaxy of future stars. Melchor Ocampo, named minister of relations by Alvarez, loomed over the others, far above Benito Juárez, the attorney general, or Guillermo Prieto, of the treasury, and Ponciano Arriaga, in finance. In this notable generation were José María Mata; Miguel and Sebastián Lerdo de Tejada; José María Iglesias, a prominent lawyer in Mexico City and former member of its ayuntamiento; the indefatigable Degollado; Doblado, the lord of Guanajuato who taught public law at the Colegio del Estado; Francisco Zarco, journalist, novelist; Ignacio Luis Vallarta, a lawyer with an undying faith in individual rights, private property, and liberty, the accoutrements of liberalism; and, naturally, Ignacio Ramírez. Nearly all of them hailed from the provinces, from Michoacán, Oaxaca, San Luis Potosí, Puebla, Jalisco, Veracruz, Guanajuato, Mexico, Durango, Zacatecas, and Querétaro; during the days of Valentín Gómez Farías's aborted reforms, they were mostly between thirteen and twenty-seven years of age, students in the majority of cases. It was not merely a neoteric generation but young.

Born in 1814 in Peteo, a hacienda in Michoacán, Ocampo, the patriarch of these brothers in arms, had presided over the circle of exiles at New Orleans, refugees from Santa Anna's tyranny. Brilliant, satirical, and stubborn, Ocampo, after spending his childhood in Mexico City, had returned home to study at the Colegio San Nicolás in Morelia and then gone to law school, but never obtained his degree. Always hungry for learning, Ocampo, at the age of twenty-two, cataloged the Palafoxiana Collection at Puebla of 22,536 volumes, then wrote a bibliography of the Indian languages of Mexico, an essay on cactus, and a philological study of ancient Mexico. In 1840, he traveled to France and Italy, lingering in Paris, Rome, and Florence and, upon his return home, becoming a deputy to Congress and governor of Michoacán, a post he held during the American invasion of Mexico. Exiled by Santa Anna, who feared his political influence, Ocampo joined Juárez, Arriaga, and Mata in exile in New Orleans. A disciple of Rousseau and Proudhon, he believed in "good" and thought God and Nature one and the same, rejecting the concept of a personal and transcendental God. Highly individualistic, he insisted that man determined his own fate.

At New Orleans, Ocampo and his confederates had drawn up a blueprint for reform, to be implemented once they wielded power. That blueprint, its outline inspired by Ocampo, became the basis for the Liberal Constitution of 1857, a document shaped partly by the exiles' perception of the statutory underpinnings of American progress. An apocryphal story, worth retelling despite its dubious authenticity, says this well. Watching the traffic of ships on the Mississippi River, Juárez and Mata, profoundly impressed by its magnitude, tried to explain it. The reason for it, Mata exclaimed suddenly, is liberty, that of "liberty of commerce."

The Reforma, Mexico's "bourgeois revolution," burst on the scene with the Ley Juárez, modifying the system of military and ecclesiastical *fueros.* Although failing to abolish all special courts, the cornerstone of these privileges, it restricted their authority to cases concerning canon or military law. For violations of civil or criminal law, clergy and military now had to stand trial in civil courts.

The Ley Juárez brought howls of protest. The outcry from priests and Catholics, among them Comonfort's mother, could be heard the length and breadth of the Republic. Before too long, *religión y fueros* was the banner for battle of the faithful, among them Pelagio Antonio de Labastida, bishop of Puebla. Frightened by the outcry, the Liberals split into two camps, with the *moderados* (moderates) wanting to back down and the *puros,* the true militants, urging no compromise. Unable to head off the division in Liberal ranks, Alvarez, linked with the firebrands, resigned the presidency, and took with him Ocampo.

Ignacio Comonfort, his substitute in the National Palace, was the Hamlet of Mexico, an indecisive man who always hesitated. Heavyset, swarthy of complexion and sporting a full, black beard, he was everything but the man for the job. More mediocre of intellect than not, he had been a bureaucract, deputy to Congress, and soldier, excelling in none, though never dishonorable. While he learned his politics at the feet of Gómez Farías, he was, at the same time, the son of a devout Catholic mother. Revealing little stomach for civil strife, and less for battlefields, he endeavored to pacify, to conciliate, even believing that he could win over the Conservatives. He did not hanker to lead a Liberal revolution under a Plan de Ayutla for the separation of church and state. Although acknowledging that church property had to be sold, he had no desire to strip the army of its *fueros.* Mexicans, he argued, would not tolerate radical change, what Ocampo and his Liberals advocated.

The Ley Lerdo of June 25, 1856, the second of the Reforma laws, shook the Republic to its rafters. Drafted by Miguel Lerdo de Tejada, it embodied the cardinal principle of the Liberals, that property ought to be owned by private individuals and not rest in the "dead hands" of the church. Property had to circulate. To achieve this purpose, the Liberals legislated the *desamortización* (disentailment) of corporate property, barring ecclesiastical corporations from owning or administering it. They could, nonetheless, keep their churches, monasteries, and convents. The legislation did not confiscate property but simply compelled the church to sell it to private individuals.

The *ley's* goal was hardly financial, because the public treasury, apart from a 5 percent capital gains tax on profits from the sale of the property, received not a penny. The objective was a mishmash of ideological ingredients, which rested on the assumption that *desamortización* would produce a vigorous sector of private property holders, the foundations of a healthy, liberal society. The *ley,* in actuality, was a timid step because, by 1856, capital investments of the church far surpassed its wealth in real estate and, the evidence shows, were of much more concern to the Liberals.

There was precedent for the Ley Lerdo, first of all in the expulsion of the Jesuits and the confiscation of their property by the Bourbons in the eighteenth century. Then there was the example of nineteenth-century Spain, which disentailed some church property in 1835. When in financial straits, Mexican Conservatives as well as Liberals had appropriated church property or capital as forced loans. The Liberals, moreover, counted on popular approval for the legislation, especially from the urban "middle class," most likely because much church property was in the cities. In Puebla, by way of illustration, where the faithful had preferred capture by an American army to a defense of their city, individuals of university schooling applauded the legislation, as did the owners of *talleres* (workshops) and *tiendas mixtas* (corner stores) in other provincial cities, everyone of them eager to acquire a house of his own. In the countryside, too, rancheros, sharecroppers, and tenant farmers awaited the subdivision of church lands.

The church was the target for obvious reasons. It owned much urban and rural real estate, rented out to private individuals; it collected the rents and left the tenants to run the property as they saw fit. It was also the major mortgage bank. But the church, despite its pomp and glitter, was not nearly as wealthy as was believed. In 1832, Mora had estimated its worth at 180 million pesos, an inflated figure. The church itself claimed to own and to administer no more than 50 million pesos of "productive goods." More than likely, its total worth was about 100 million pesos, which included land, buildings, jewels, and works of art; the church, in retrospect, owned from one-fifth to one-quarter of the national wealth, a far cry from the 50 percent so often asserted.

By the Ley Iglesias of January 1857, the third of the laws of the Reforma, the Liberals, again striking at the church, forbade it to charge exorbitant fees for administering the sacraments. That spark of a social conscience flickered only momentarily. The Ley Lerdo, to the sorrow of apologists for the Reforma, also took in the ejido, the communal lands of the Indian pueblos, in its definition of corporate property. The Liberals held Spanish legislation responsible for the plight of the Indians. By making them wards of the state, by isolating them in their communities, and by keeping alive their system of communal property, colonial legislation had isolated them from the progressive ideas of Western civilization. Despite their noble intent, colonial laws had made impossible the acquisition of private property, the foundation of personal independence and initiative. By leaving intact the archaic system of communal property, the colonial panaceas of love, schooling, and paternalism had come to grief. So the Liberals legislated the end of the ejido and watched as more and more Indians became peons on the haciendas or wage laborers, in the meantime urging the fusion of all races through colonization schemes, inferring that the in-migration of Europeans into Mexico would assimilate the Indian. The Caste War in Yucatán, the uprising of Manuel Lozada in Nayarit, and the burning of cane fields by campesinos in Morelos helped persuade the Liberals, often racists at heart, to plunge ahead with their plans to destroy the Indian community, which, they rightly interpreted, was the citadel of the Indian's resistance.

The soul of the Reforma was the Constitution of 1857, which included the three *leyes.* No Conservative darkened the halls of the Congress that drew it up, and neither did spokesmen for urban workers, while just Ponciano Arriaga, a lawyer by trade, defended the campesinos. As in the body that drafted the charter of 1824, the delegates were predominantly representatives of the provincial "middle class," over half of them lawyers. Differences of opinion flared between a minority of radicals and a majority of moderates, both of whom found guidance for individual liberty in the Rights of Man of the French Revolution and for the political organization of the Republic in the Constitution of the United States.

According to the charter of 1857, which was imbued with the peculiar logic of Rousseau, "man is born free" and "nature created all men equal." In Mexico "equality" reigned, a stipulation guaranteed by law. With the stroke of a pen, social classes and differences of race vanished. Guarantees of constitutional government—these were the remedies for Mexico's political ills. However, the truth was, as Emilio Rabasa, a keen student of Mexico's politics wrote, that the charter's bill of individual rights held little significance for a people unprepared for a Western-style democracy. Equally certain, as Arriaga noted, nothing was done to improve the lot of society, because a tiny minority monopolized the land and had the Republic's wealth all to itself.

Given its ideological slant, the Constitution of 1857 spoke for capitalist doctrines, free trade being one of them. Francisco Zarco, one of its framers, argued that tariffs hurt consumers; Prieto, a kindred spirit, equated his faith in liberty with free trade. Even Ignacio Ramírez, a man troubled by social inequalities, displayed no qualms in 1857, because "Mexican capitalists were not enemies of the working man." The charter's framers had not hesitated to write in guarantees for capitalists, as Ramírez explained, pointing out that nothing in it obligated the state to provide jobs, a principle enshrined just in Communist societies. Congress lacked the authority to dictate a "social revolution" and, besides that, "the country had no appetite for one." The right of labor recognized by the Constitution was "the freedom of the worker to look for a job."

Under the charter, Mexico once more became a Federalist Republic but rid itself of the Senate. Taking their cue from the Constitution of Chilpancingo, its sponsors affirmed that a strong Chamber of Deputies curbed the dictatorial proclivities of the executive. Not wishing another Santa Anna, the Liberals wanted a weak presidency, while the justices of the Supreme Court lost their tenure, freeing Congress of judicial constraints. Under the amparo, a form of habeas corpus, an individual could appeal to the Supreme Court for an injunction, making individual property rights sacrosanct. No article of the Constitution stipulated freedom of religion, though none recognized Roman Catholicism as the state church. A majority of its framers, apparently, was more Catholic than Liberal.

The charter's political edifice, whatever its rhetoric, was self-contradictory. Though Federalist, it had a Centralist slant. The Chamber of Deputies, for instance, could impeach governors, and the Supreme Court decide disputed elections in their states. Voting was indirect, with electors chosen to represent districts who cast ballots for Congress, judges of the Supreme Court, and the president; but the chief executive had the electors in his hands because many of them either held a public post, aspired to one, or depended on his benevolence for the success of their business affairs. The president of the Republic, after all, controlled the patronage, either directly or indirectly naming public officials, and had a strong voice in the awarding of government contracts.

When they spoke of their love for small property, the Liberals, furthermore, were not altogether truthful. Neither in the Ley Lerdo nor in the Constitution of 1857 did they stipulate the subdivision of the haciendas of the church. They were to be sold intact. Only the rich merchants, mine operators, and hacendados had the money to buy them. By this logic, the legislation encouraged more concentration of land in the hands of the few, exacerbating the latifundia character of Mexican agriculture. The subdivision of the ejidos provoked a similar result, but for different reasons. According to the Ley Lerdo, incorporated into the Constitution as Article 27, the pueblos had to subdivide their communal lands among the families that tilled them. The Indian, either because he lacked the money, misunderstood the intent of the legislation, or, more likely, knew that it guaranteed the breakup of his community, did not comply. When he failed to do so, rancheros and hacendados denounced the unclaimed lands to authorities in order to buy them for piddling sums of money.

As before, the Indians did not take this lying down, some of them employing arms to defend their lands. Confronted with this widespread defiance, the Liberals declared that henceforth ejido parcels would be given only to their tillers. No longer was legislative intent to be left to chance; by receiving title to his parcel of land, the Indian would become the owner of private property. That, nonetheless, failed to halt entirely the acquisition of communal lands by greedy outsiders, who found the means to circumvent the law, at times, the record shows, by giving drunken Indians mescal for their lands. How much land the Indians lost is a mystery, but that it was sizable most historians agree.

The Liberals invited Valentín Gómez Farías, their elderly patriarch, to be the first to swear allegiance to the Constitution. The old man did, on his knees, with a hand on the charter, saying proudly, "This is my last will and testament." All the same, time soon proved ephemeral the elation of Gómez Farías; as events confirmed, not for love or money could the Constitution be enforced. Before its ink was dry, Catholics and Conservatives, usually one and the same, were making elections, individual rights, and the like merely rhetoric.

IV

Upon the promulgation of the Ley Lerdo and Ley Juárez, Lázaro de Garza, the archbishop of Mexico, threatened to excommunicate Catholics who purchased ecclesiastical property and, after the Constitution was put through, levied a similar sentence on those who pledged allegiance to it. Priests who conferred the sacraments on these sinners faced suspension. From far-off Rome, the pope declared "null and void" the decrees which "scorn . . . ecclesiastical authority and the Holy See." What the church elders most objected to were the Leyes Lerdo and Juarez but also articles in the Constitution that provided for freedom of worship, lay schools, a free press, and the right of nuns and priests to forsake their vows.

Given this political climate, it was not long before a rebellion flared in Puebla, led by a wealthy criollo and former student of Lucas Alamán. Comonfort squashed it and, suspecting clerical complicity in the affair, banished Bishop Labastida from Mexico and sold church property to pay the cost of suppressing the mutiny. However, Francisco Javier Miranda, another disgruntled cleric from Puebla, was traveling about the country plotting rebellion with unhappy military chieftains. In the autumn of 1856, his plots hatched dividends; an uprising led by General Miguel Miramón and Tomás Mejía, an Indian cacique from Querétaro, captured Puebla. Brothers in arms carried the revolt to Michoacán, Tlaxcala, Veracruz, and San Luis Potosí. Yet, by the date of the promulgation of the Constitution, Comonfort had defeated the rebels and Mexico was once again at peace. This was the calm before the storm.

One reason was President Comonfort, beguiled constantly by the tears of his fanatically Catholic mother, hating civil strife, and wanting to displease neither Conservatives nor Liberals. He swore to uphold the Constitution but asked for its revision, complaining that he could not govern under a Congress more powerful than the executive, claiming he could do so only with emergency powers because of the unrest in the country and the menace of Spain, then demanding repayment of claims against Mexico by its citizens. Suspecting Comonfort of duplicity, Congress refused to concede him that authority.

Congress had good grounds for its skepticism. Comonfort was planning, along with General Félix M. Zuloaga, his friend and the commander of the garrison in Tacubaya, a cuartelazo of his own. They had the support of the governors of Veracruz, Puebla, and San Luis Potosí, perennial hotbeds of dissatisfaction. When Comonfort hesitated, Zuloaga, flying the banners of the Plan de Tacubaya, marched into Mexico City and disbanded Congress. The upper clergy cheered him on. Thinking the triumph assured, Comonfort embraced Zuloaga, ruling the Constitution void but unwilling to revoke the Ley Lerdo. Days earlier, Zuloaga had jailed Benito Juárez, the chief justice of the Supreme Court and by the terms of the Constitution of 1857 the legal successor to the president. When Comonfort, the placater, released him, Juárez fled to Querétaro to join his Liberal allies. Unwilling simply to do the bidding of Zuloaga, Comonfort attempted to regain military control of Mexico City but, failing, abandoned the Republic for exile in the United States.

As this scenario unfolded, Benito Juárez, a remarkable man of almost fifty years of age, stepped onto the national stage. Until his death in 1872, he ruled Mexico as no one had before. Standing just over five feet, a small man of small hands and feet, he was dark of skin with a coppery complexion, deep, piercing eyes, and a large scar on his face. Reserved and impassive, Juárez symbolized, as few have in the history of Mexico, the rise from rags to riches. Born in 1806 in San Pablo Guelatao, a village in the mountains of Oaxaca, he was a Zapotec Indian. An orphan at four years of age, he was raised briefly by an uncle who treated him badly. Wanting to flee both the uncle and Guelatao, Juárez, at age eleven and knowing merely a word or two of Spanish, left for the city of Oaxaca, where his sister, who worked as a cook for a family, found him a place to stay with a Franciscan lay brother and bookbinder who, in return for help around the house, enrolled him in school.

Under the tutelage of the bookbinder, Juárez learned to speak, read, and write Spanish, going on to the Seminario Conciliar de la Santa Cruz, a training school for the priesthood, where he studied Latin, philosophy, theology, and metaphysics. Not finding a priestly career to his liking, he transferred to the recently established Instituto de Ciencias y Artes, taking classes in political economy, mathematics, physics, chemistry, natural history, and modern languages and later teaching there. Like so many students of his generation, Juárez, ultimately, became a lawyer, receiving his degree in 1834.

Contemporaries of Juárez and historians have made much ado about his Indian background. Justo Sierra, just one of them, composed rhapsodies to "that Indian of porphyry and bronze," dedicating his famous biography of Juárez to "the great Indian." But for most Mexicans, who viewed the word *Indian* as a pejorative term, as Emilio Rabasa acknowledged, Juárez, though born one, was hardly an Indian. When he joined Ocampo in New Orleans, Juárez, by schooling and values and, more pertinent, by his behavior was a Mexican of his time. Speaking and writing Spanish and, as a lawyer, thinking in Spanish, he surely did not see himself as an "Indian." Nor did he side with the Indian, as governor of Oaxaca condemning the "evasion of the law by the pueblos, which threatened to plunge the nation into anarchy." His political years in Oaxaca, furthermore, witnessed the rise of haciendas and ranchos at the expense of the pueblos. When he married, he chose the daughter of a family of Italian origin, one of the wealthiest of the city of Oaxaca, for whom Juárez's sister had been a maid. She was, Sierra remembered, "white of skin and beautiful."

Not his mind but strength of character, his ability to persevere, that was Juárez's forte. Intellectually, he was far less able than either Ocampo or Miguel Lerdo de Tejada, his principal collaborators. He read little, being neither a poet nor a dreamer. Though a poor public speaker, he was a good listener, never unwilling to learn from others. Schooled imperfectly, he was of sound judgment, thoughtful and prudent. Nothing fazed him, said Ignacio Manuel Altamirano, neither danger, misfortune, nor the military prowess of foreign adversaries. He never panicked when defending the nation's honor. He could hate with a vengeance but seldom for political reasons, being able to put up with ideological opposites so long as they did not offend his own person.

However, when it came to slights against him, he was a stubborn and implacable enemy.

Whatever his limitations, Juárez was a leader, what Mexico awaited in this hour of crisis, a man of strong will and not a Comonfort. A keen politico, Juárez capitalized on this need for leadership and, little by little, extended presidential authority beyond the limits of the Constitution of 1857. He did not permit sentimentality to interfere, as one episode documents. When asked by a friend to spare the life of a rebel, Juárez replied, "You can tell him that he will not be shot," but, he added, "we who govern must never lose sight of the public welfare and discard feelings of the heart." By "shooting men who make a career of rebellions, we save the lives of countless persons," and "you who claim to respect human life should not forget it."

Juárez was primarily a moderate Liberal. Starting his political career as a Federalist and sympathizer of the presidential aspirations of Vicente Guerrero, he was, by 1830, a Liberal who advocated a government of checks and balances. He conceived of public opinion as a moral force, thinking popular suffrage useful, the more so according to the educational level of the voters. The more educated, the more logical direct elections. For Juárez, the political problem was an educational one. A disciple of free trade, he wanted liberty of commerce both at home and abroad. A Catholic who attended mass, married in the church, and baptized his daughters, Juárez was profoundly religious; priests were among his cohorts even at the height of the anticlerical Reforma. During the war of 1847, nevertheless, Juárez sided with Gómez Farías, urging the use of church funds to combat the enemy, and under his presidency an effort was made to organize a Mexican Catholic church independent of Rome.

Juárez, for all that, was a pragmatist. Beginning his political ascent in 1831 with his election to the ayuntamiento of the city of Oaxaca, he served in the state legislature, in Congress as a deputy and as secretary general of Governor Antonio León of Oaxaca, an inflexible Conservative and consort of Santa Anna. By 1846, he was back in Congress; from 1848 to 1853, he was governor of Oaxaca, where he displayed his administrative talents and defended provincial autonomy. In the midst of the turbulence and despair of the American War, Juárez somehow found funds for roads and schools. While a Liberal, he established friendly relations with the church, asking that parishioners pay their tithes. As the "model governor," the title bestowed on him by his admirers, he surrounded himself with able advisers, some far more intelligent than he, one of whom, Manuel Ruiz, wielded a strong influence on him.

As a politico, Juárez had to deal with Santa Anna, the bête noire of this era. Not astonishingly, Juárez, every now and then, hailed the glories of the Hero of Tampico and Veracruz but still had to go into exile in 1853. Once the Revolution of Ayutla was under way, Juárez returned to Mexico, joining Juan

Alvarez in Guerrero, where, according to Altamirano, he "arrived, resembling a kind of Indian priest, riding . . . a mule." Upon his triumph, Alvarez named Juárez his minister of justice and ecclesiastical affairs, in which capacity he helped draft the Ley Juárez, remaining in the cabinet even after the departure of Ocampo. Comonfort dispatched him to govern Oaxaca for a second time but recalled him as minister of *gobernación,* the political boss of the Republic. From there he became chief justice of the Supreme Court. When General Zuloaga rebelled and Comonfort took flight, Juárez, the Liberals insisted, was president of the Republic.

V

From 1858 to 1860, the Guerra de la Reforma, a horrendous civil war, painted the soil of the Republic red with the blood of its people. During these years, when the country seemed on the verge of disintegrating, it was Juárez who held it together. When Liberal armies tasted defeat, and Liberal chieftains urged a compromise, Juárez, never despairing of victory, kept them going. In the "Indian" Juárez, the provincial middle class, as well as Mexico itself, had discovered their champion. When victory arrived, Juárez was Mexico and Liberal dogma the law of the land.

The battle lines, just the same, were never drawn clearly. For the conflict ahead, Juárez and his Liberals could count for allies on provincial professionals, a host of them lawyers, but not on every one of them; they were also in the rival camp. Although usually friendly to the Conservatives, hacendados as well as merchants were partisans of the Liberals, too. No less enamored of the Ley Lerdo, many land-hungry rancheros, hostile to the hacendados, followed the Liberals. At the same time, the Bajío, a region heavily populated by rancheros, sided mostly with the Conservatives. Virtually all of the Indian pueblos, still smarting from the Liberal attack on their lands, sat out the conflict, unless they had something concrete to gain from either protagonist. The Indian, it was clear, shed no tears for Liberal doctrines. The church, certainly its hierarchy, embraced the Conservatives but not every priest, some of whom joined the Liberals. Given the Liberal goal to reduce its size, the army, by and large, fought alongside the Conservatives. Regionally, the north was Liberal, especially under the leadership of Ignacio Pesqueira of Sonora and Santiago Vidaurri of Nuevo León. Conservatives fared better in the central zone of the Republic but some Liberal commanders were natives of it, among them Degollado and Doblado. The Guerra de la Reforma pitted Mexican against Mexican, Catholic against Catholic, and, every now and then, brother against brother.

For virtually two years, the Conservatives had the better armies and the better generals. Whatever else Santa Anna had failed to accomplish, he had restored the fighting edge of the army. From the Colegio Militar, and from the practical school of civil strife, emerged a generation of army officers who replaced the veterans of the calamitous war with the United States, among them Miramón and Leonardo Márquez. Almost to a man, they went over to the Conservatives, bringing with them pride in soldiering, love of war, and a desire for the accolades of high society. They were young in 1858; this was to be a war of youthful generals. A graduate of the Colegio Militar and the most able of the Conservative generals, Miramón was but twenty-six, the son of a military officer, more short than tall, agile, and elegant of dress. Of good disposition and sense of humor, Miramón, a loyal Catholic, made the veteran army obey his will. Audacious, skillful, and brave, he out maneuvered and outfought the Liberal armies until almost the very end, always being able to rely on the funds of the church as well as on its Te Deums.

With the appeal to arms, Juárez had fled to Querétaro but, his troops unable to stop the advance of the Conservatives, went to Guadalajara with the enemy at his heels. On its outskirts, Conservative troops defeated a Liberal army under General Anastacio Parrodi, a competent soldier but no match for his adversaries. Believing the occasion ripe for betrayal, soldiers, loyal supposedly to the Liberals, mutinied, took Juárez prisoner, and, but for the eloquence of Guillermo Prieto, who came to his defense, would have shot him. Set free, Juárez escaped to Veracruz.

In May 1858, Mexico had two governments, a Liberal one in Veracruz and a Conservative one in Mexico City under Zuloaga. At Veracruz, the Liberals had occupied the country's principal port, the chief source of revenue from foreign trade. Additionally, yellow fever, the local scourge, made Veracruz invulnerable to a long siege by an enemy army. For virtually three years, Juárez, the emblem of the Liberal cause, remained in Veracruz. During 1858 and for much of the next year, Miramón and his cohorts scored victory after victory. The Conservatives, meanwhile, had replaced Zuloaga, naming Miramón their chief, the "young Maccabeus," as he was referred to by friend and foe alike. Miramón, however, could not take Veracruz.

The Guerra de la Reforma was a fratricidal conflict, besmirched by cruelty and killing on both sides. The Liberals started the atrocities by executing captive officers. Their rivals, with Márquez showing how, went them one better, shooting civilians of Liberal stripe, lawyers particularly, whom they judged the mentors of the Reforma. By the middle of 1859, nearly all productive activity had come to a stop: fields lay untilled, commerce stagnated, contraband trade flourished, and bandits infested the countryside. The fortunes of war, nevertheless, were beginning to turn; Juárez and his Liberals were on the path to victory.

In July 1859, the Liberals, trying to stop the church from financing their enemies and wanting to punish it, enacted the Veracruz decrees. Church and state were separated, monastic orders banned, cemeteries secularized, the registration of births and marriages made a civil responsibility, religious holidays reduced in number, and religious processions forbidden. More important, the decrees nationalized not merely the properties of the church but its investment capital, of greater value than its lands. The idea for these final steps came from Miguel Lerdo de Tejada, who, in Veracruz, told Juárez, "If you do not decree the Reforma, it will become a reality without you." Miguel knew of what he spoke, for already in the provinces Vidaurri, Jesús González Ortega, and Pedro Ogazón, with the tacit approval of Degollado, had confiscated church property, closed monasteries, and legislated civil marriage. The decrees attracted into Liberal ranks fresh adherents, among them Mexicans ready to acquire church lands. When it was all over, virtually all of the Liberals—Ignacio Ramírez and a tiny handful being the exceptions—emerged as landlords. The fulmination of the archbishop had discouraged only the timid.

The Veracruz decrees, like the earlier Ley Lerdo, ignored the needs of the poor. For this, one can thank Miguel Lerdo de Tejada and his school of orthodox Liberals and the financial urgency of the moment. Melchor Ocampo, so goes the story, had advocated a gradual nationalization of church lands in order to plan for their subdivision into small parcels, by this method hoping to create small farms. Miguel, by contrast, wanted to nationalize immediately and use proceeds from their sale to finance the war. Practical needs dictated Miguel's decision to sell church property, to cite a Mexican scholar, "at any price to anyone." But, then, Miguel Lerdo de Tejada was a practical politico. In 1853, when asked by the Conservatives to journey to Veracruz to greet Santa Anna on his return from exile, he went gladly. This "theorist of the Liberal bourgeoisie," the tag one pundit pinned on him, had a utilitarian side.

The Ley Lerdo brought about the biggest transfer of property in nineteenth-century Mexico, especially in the provincial cities, which the Liberals controlled by 1860. According to Miguel, his legislation had produced nine thousand additional owners of property, most of it urban homes. However, not all buyers acquired just one house; in the city of Puebla, for example, almost half of them purchased more than one piece of property, which indicated that if not affluent, they were far from poor. In the port city of Veracruz, probably no different from Puebla, the buyers were mostly merchants, lawyers, and public officials. Scores of speculators, especially merchants and foreigners, acquired a goodly number of homes.

By comparison, the results in the countryside were tragic. Because of the failure to subdivide church haciendas, only textile magnates, rich merchants, or hacendados could buy them. Conservative hacendados rarely had harsh words to say about the Ley Lerdo, probably emerging from the Reforma, a Mexican historian argues, "better off than before." Andrés Molina Enríquez, a student of agrarian questions, baptized the well-off buyers of country property the "new criollos." In the countryside, Ocampo's dream of a rural middle class never materialized.

As this came to pass, the international scene was shifting slowly toward the Liberals. The United States had hastened to bestow its blessings on General Zuloaga, but, when he would not sell Washington additional territory, its representative in Mexico went home in a huff. Eventually, Washington replaced him with Robert M. McLane, who arrived in Veracruz with the title of minister, thus conferring American diplomatic recognition on the Juárez government. Unhappily, he also carried instructions to buy Baja California, obtain rights of transit across Mexico, and negotiate a commercial treaty. When the Liberals hesitated, McLane urged Washington to use troops to get what it desired. That proved unnecessary because the Liberals, fearful that Washington might intervene, decided to negotiate. The upshot was the McLane-Ocampo Treaty of December 1859, giving the United States the right of transit across the Isthmus of Tehuantepec and, along the northern border, from the Gulf of Mexico to the Gulf of Baja California. Northern senators in the United States, interpreting the treaty as just one more scheme by southerners to expand their influence, saved the Liberals from their folly, though not before it besmirched the reputations of Ocampo and Juárez.

Washington's diplomatic approval aided the Liberals, for now they could buy military hardware north of the border as well as sell what they produced in American markets. Also, it kept Spanish intervention at bay. By late 1859, the Conservatives, starting to despair of winning, had revived the idea of a Spanish prince for Mexico, thinking that he would save them from defeat and safeguard church property. The Mon-Almonte Treaty of September 1859, which the Conservatives negotiated, acknowledged Spanish tutelage over Mexico. That did not stop Miramón from borrowing money from the Swiss banking house of Jecker, pledging, as a guarantee, one-fifth of all revenues. As it worked out, the Jecker bonds, in return for one million pesos, added fifteen million pesos to Mexico's foreign debt.

As the tide of battle went against the Conservatives, new leaders took charge of the Liberal armies, generals such as Ignacio Zaragoza, Leandro Valle, and Jesús González Ortega, perhaps the ablest of them. At Silao, a town in the Bajío, the armies of Zaragoza, González Ortega, and Doblado slashed to ribbons Miramón's troops, driving them back to Mexico City. González Ortega, the commander in chief of the Liberal forces, then fell on Guadalajara and, with the aid of Valle, captured it after a bloody siege and put to rout Márquez's soldiers, sent to relieve the city's beleaguered defenders. In the south, Porfirio Díaz and Marcos Pérez drove the Conservatives from Oaxaca. Even borrowing 700,000 pesos from the British legation in Mexico City, as Miramón phrased it, failed to prevent his final defeat by González Ortega at Calpulalpan. On Christmas Day, 1860, González Ortega, at the head of a

Liberal army of 25,000 men, marched into Mexico City, its inhabitants greeting them with shouts of joy. A few days afterward, when President Juárez arrived in a black carriage, he rode in virtually unnoticed, overlooked by a populace eager to render homage to conquering warriors. So ended the Guerra de la Reforma.

VI

The flight of Miramón from Mexico City signaled the triumph of the infant, provincial middle class, which unlocked the doors of political power, as Sierra so aptly put it, "to those who had studied in the schools, whose brains were full of dreams, whose hearts were full of ambition, and whose stomachs were full of appetites." From their ranks had come the generals and architects of the Reforma as well as the journalists and intellectuals who glorified it. Campesinos, mestizos mostly, sometimes furnished the cannon fodder for the rival armies, changing sides frequently to fight alongside of their former enemies. By 1860, a majority of Mexicans were partisans of the Liberals; only a tiny coterie of mostly rich clerical or religious fanatics dreamed of a return to the Conservative past. Because of the Reforma, the Mexico of 1860, unlike the disparate Republic that confronted the American invaders, was on the road to becoming a nation.

Hard times, nevertheless, lay ahead. The treasury was empty and the country in ruins, and bureaucrats and soldiers had to be paid, lest the Republic lapse into anarchy. As ill luck would have it, proceeds from the sale of clerical properties proved disappointingly low; what happened to the clerical mortgages inherited by the state is a matter for conjecture. Most likely, they were never collected. Peace, moreover, was not fully achieved, because Márquez still roamed the countryside while Tomás Mejía stayed alive in the mountains of Querétaro. Desiring peace and conciliation, Juárez declared an amnesty, pardoning all but the worst of the enemy generals, though he exiled five of the most recalcitrant bishops and ousted from Mexico the Spanish ambassador, an avowed ally of Miramón. In March, 1861, Juárez won reelection, beating González Ortega, who became chief justice of the Supreme Court. The other candidate, Miguel Lerdo de Tejada, died on the eve of the election. But Juárez faced a sullen Congress, replete with followers of Lerdo, González Ortega, and Doblado, every one of them convinced he could not govern effectively. Tragedy, furthermore, stalked the Liberals. On his hacienda of Pomoca, clerical diehards captained by Márquez killed Ocampo, hanging him from the branches of a pepper tree. That same month, Márquez and his brigands killed Santos Degollado, who had asked for the chance to hunt down Ocampo's assassins. A similar fate befell Leandro Valle. Not until Porfirio Díaz and

Ignacio Mejía, two of Juárez's trusted officers, chased Márquez back into his mountain hideout, was Mexico, for the time being, rid of him. Just when peace seemed a reality and Juárez had settled down to govern the Republic, a fresh danger appeared on the horizon, this time from Europe.

13

THE CROWN OF MEXICO

I

The specter of bankruptcy, the ubiquitous nightmare, would not go away. Profits from the sale of church property fell short of balancing the budget while much of the income from customs duties was mortgaged to European moneylenders. Most of Mexico's debt was owed to England and France, the reigning imperialist powers. Outside of the Federal District, the states controlled local revenues. For Guillermo Prieto, head of the treasury, the way out of the sea of troubles was to reserve for the federal government money from customs duties as well as taxes collected by the states. Prodded by his advice, Congress, in July 1861, gave federal officials authority to collect all revenues and to suspend payments on the foreign debt for two years. By the end of that period, Congress expected, the Republic would have its house in order and be able to renew payments on its international obligations. On the domestic scene, that hope bore fruit; with the suspension of payments (a decree revoked later), there was money for the army, for bureaucrats, and, by implication, for peace and order.

The Europeans, however, were not pleased by this plan. Mexico's financial travails notwithstanding, they wanted their money. For the British, that included money General Miguel Miramón had robbed from their legation in Mexico City. The most vociferous of the imperialists, the French demanded payment in cash for claims totaling twelve million pesos and liquidation of the Jecker bonds. One Frenchman itching to profit off the bonds was the duc de Morny, the fun-loving brother of Napoleon III and a confederate of Jecker, the Swiss banker. The Spaniards, who brought up the rear of this entourage, talked vaguely of their responsibilities under the Mon-Almonte Treaty and retribution for past Mexican sins. To mull over what should be done, the three powers met in October 1861 in London, where they decided to teach Mexico a lesson. By the terms of the London Convention, they agreed to occupy jointly the customhouse in Veracruz unless Mexico resumed regular payments on money owed to them.

In December, Spanish troops under General Juan Prim disembarked at Veracruz, followed by the English and French. Trying to appease them, President Benito Juárez, on their solemn promise to return to Veracruz if fighting broke out, allowed their armies to move inland to escape the danger of yellow fever on the coast. No sooner were the Europeans on Mexican soil than they began to suspect each other's motives. Prim and Sir Charles Wyke, the English commander, saw immediately that Napoleon, the emperor of the French, had more than debts on his schedule, as his ambassador to Mexico, Dubois de Saligny, made clear. As events demonstrated, Saligny was also the errand boy for the duc de Morny, business partner of Jecker and an apostle of Napoleon's dream of empire.

To stave off more trouble, Juárez sent Manuel Doblado, his foreign minister, to negotiate with the intruders. Mexico, promised Doblado, would start repayment on its obligations at the earliest possible moment. Convinced of the sincerity of the Juárez regime, Prim and Wyke urged their governments to withdraw their troops in return for Mexico's pledge to pay. Prim, especially, wanted Spain out of Mexico, above all after seeing the soldiers asked to defend its sovereignty, "some virtually naked and scores without arms," reminding him, Prim wrote, "of the Spanish soldiers who had fought against the other Napoleon." Not so the French, who rejected Doblado's overtures and began planning their march on Mexico City.

II

The France of Napoleon had its eyes set on a Mexican empire. At this time in its history, it was industrializing rapidly, particularly in textiles, buying much of its cotton in the United States. From the perspective of French textile manufacturers, Mexico offered lands for the cultivation of cheap and plentiful cotton, as well as a supply of other raw materials. Eventually, too, Mexico could become a market for French goods. Apart from that, Napoleon dreamed of restoring France to its rightful place at the head of the European powers, as in the days of the first Napoleon, whom he desired to emulate. Civil war in the United States, which had Americans fighting one another, offered the opportunity to get the scheme under way.

Napoleon's court, meanwhile, had become a popular rendezvous for Mexican refugees from the Conservative disaster. Without exception, they were monarchists, proponents of the idea of a foreign prince to save Mexico's soul, as they proclaimed to the Europeans. One of them was José Manuel Hidalgo, the son of an officer who had served Agustín de Iturbide. A salon diplomat, dapper and fond of the ladies, Hidalgo had wangled himself into the good graces of Empress Eugenia de Montijo, Napoleon's Spanish wife, and told her endless tales of how Mexicans pined for a life under a European prince. Her imperial appetite awakened by these stories, Eugenia, more Spanish than French, introduced Hidalgo to Napoleon. Also, Hidalgo had brought more of his Mexican bedfellows to the French court.

A pivotal figure was José Miguel Gutiérrez Estrada, a native of Yucatán and long an advocate of monarchy. Formerly a Liberal, Gutiérrez Estrada, referred to frequently as the "sire" of the Intervention, had been a friend of José María Luis Mora, once urging Mora, who was living in Paris, not to come back to Mexico, because of its turmoil. Married to an Austrian countess and wealthy, Gutiérrez Estrada had abandoned Mexico in 1841, thereafter spending his life in Europe looking for pretenders to the "Mexican throne." He did not return to his native country until 1864.

Juan Nepomuceno Almonte, the bastard son of José María Morelos, was the other prominent monarchist plotter at the French court. A military man by trade, he had been a supporter of Antonio López de Santa Anna, fighting alongside of him in Texas, and Mexico's representative in Washington when Texas was annexed. Of an ingratiating personality, educated and something of a linguist, Almonte was a terribly ambitious man, not unwilling to switch political allegiances if it suited his purpose. Starting out as a Federalist and Yorquino, he was, by the 1850s a prominent Conservative and, on the eve of the Intervention, a trusted confederate of Napoleon, and an adviser to Saligny.

Church prelates, too, soiled their reputations in this monarchical farce, playing leading roles in the plot to topple the Republic. Francisco Javier Miranda, one of them, had been minister of justice and ecclesiastical affairs in the Conservative regime of 1858 and, earlier, had helped entice Santa Anna back from exile, supporting his dictatorship until the end. Pelagio Antonio de Labastida, the bishop of Puebla, also looked fondly on a monarchy, not merely for its own sake but because he believed it offered the only way for the church to recover its property.

The monarchical dream, obviously, had old roots in Mexico, starting with the Plan de Iguala and Iturbide's dream of a Mexican crown for a European prince. When that proved unfeasible, members of the elite, pessimistic about the chances for peace and order, had started to allege that Mexicans could not govern themselves. The first to set down this view in writing was Gutiérrez Estrada, who, in a famous letter of 1837, explained why he thought only a prince could save Mexico. According to him, the political system did not function, no constitution inspired confidence, and Mexicans had not produced anyone able to govern Mexico effectively. Time and schooling, which monarchy would provide, were needed to prepare a future generation of Mexicans to govern themselves. The Republic, he admonished, was a failure because it stood in conflict with three centuries of colonial traditions. Monarchy, once beneficial to Mexico, was more attuned to the colonial experience.

The key to the monarchist scheme was a foreign prince. Only he would be able to overcome domestic factionalism and unite Mexicans of diverse stripes. Similarly, only a prince of a European house, preferably Spanish or French, could, by his family ties, ward off the danger to Mexico from the Republic next door. From the start, Alamán was one of the proponents of this thesis. At the time of his death in 1853, he was negotiating secretly with members of the Spanish Bourbons and corresponding with Gutiérrez Estrada.

Not every Conservative, plainly, believed in this monarchist flight of fancy. More than likely, a majority was indifferent to it, including scores of military chieftains who, unlike Miguel Miramón, Tomás Mejía, and Leonardo Márquez, fervent monarchists, came to terms with the Liberals. Nor were monarchists just Conservatives; to their ultimate shame, scores of Liberals swore fealty to the monarchy imposed by the French. Not every cleric worshiped the idea, some of them being disciples of the Republic and admirers of Juárez.

Unwittingly, perhaps, these Mexican apostles of monarchy played into the hands of Napoleon. As he listened to them, France, he concluded, could launch its empire in the Americas by invitation of the Mexicans themselves; it would be a takeover merely in name. So, for reasons of his own, Napoleon adopted the monarchist designs of Gutiérrez Estrada and his crowd. When French soldiers landed at Veracruz, Mexican expatriates accompanied them; Almonte, one of them, carried in his briefcase Napoleon's endorsement of their monarchist scheme and the title of provisional president of Mexico.

III

The invasion of Mexico, the comte de Lorencez, the French commander, decided, would start from Orizaba, despite his pledge to President Juárez, endorsed by Prim and Wyke, to withdraw to Veracruz if war broke out. The rules of honor did not apply to Mexico. On the eve of the departure from Orizaba, Márquez, the unrepentant Conservative warrior, showed up in the French camp with a band of bedraggled fighters, the first wave of Mexican sympathizers.

Between Orizaba and the capital of the Republic, the city of Puebla stood watch. There, the Mexicans, no longer the disgruntled and apathetic soldiers who fled before Winfield Scott's army in 1847, chose to make a stand. The two armies that confronted each other were entirely different. Some seven thousand strong, the French were professional soldiers, equipped with modern weapons and led by a graduate of a legendary military college. Facing them were the Mexicans, as before, mostly conscripts, ill armed and poorly trained, though veterans of the Guerra de la Reforma, more guerrillas than army. Their leader, Ignacio Zaragoza, a former state militia officer who had earned his spurs fighting Conservatives, was just thirty-three years old. Hardly a strategist, he had, just the same, a blind faith in the Mexican soldier, whose fighting qualities he had come to appreciate.

One of the new breed of Mexican generals, Zaragoza hailed from Nuevo León. A patriot through and through, he never once doubted that victory would fall to his men. Leading an army only slightly bigger than Lorencez's, he ordered part of it to impede the French climb up the central plateau from Orizaba, fighting and losing a battle at Acultzingo, a pass high in the mountains. Meanwhile, he fortified Puebla, throwing up forts on hills above the city to prevent the French artillery from shelling it. Led by Lorencez, a general who belittled the fighting ability of the Mexican soldier, the French attacked on May 5, 1862, flinging their infantry recklessly at the fortified positions, exactly as Zaragoza knew they would. Repeated infantry assaults, the heavy fire of the artillery, and the military savvy of the French officers failed to dislodge the Mexicans from Puebla, who fought as they never had before. At the end of the day of battle, the French, stunned by the Mexican defense, fell back, retreating eventually to Orizaba to await reinforcements. Zaragoza's attempts to drive them out of Orizaba ended in defeat, and so began the stalemate of a year.

The victory at Puebla, since then celebrated as the Cinco de Mayo, thrilled Mexico, inspiring its people to fight on. The lesson was plain: Mexican soldiers, when ably led, could stand up to the finest of Europe. Regardless of the odds, Mexico might yet be saved. However, their defeat at Puebla did not drive the French out of Mexico. Conceding that Mexicans loyal to the Republic would fight, they also believed that more French soldiers and better field marshals could beat them. In this, they were partly correct.

To avenge the embarrassment of Puebla and get on with the job of subjugation, the French shipped 25,000 more soldiers to Mexico, recalled Lorencez, and replaced him with Elie Frédéric Forey and Achille Bazaine, commander at Jalapa, both marshals of the French army. Named commander in chief of the French expeditionary force, Forey, in a decision foretelling the shape of things to come, stripped Almonte of his title of provisional president. Before marching on to Mexico City, Forey, like Lorencez earlier, had to take Puebla. Trying to make his invasion less unpalatable to Mexicans, he proclaimed that France desired merely to "regenerate" their country, not to conquer it.

Forey and his army arrived on the outskirts of Puebla on March 16, 1863. This time the city had a fresh commander; Zaragoza had died of typhoid fever, his responsibility taken over by Jesús González Ortega, one of the stalwarts of the Reforma. His ally in Mexico City was Ignacio Comonfort, just returned from exile to offer his sword to his country. The army defending

Puebla was a motley array of soldiers, mostly from the state militias but, like its predecessor, determined to fight to the last man. That it did, holding out for two months against the French, surrendering only after food and ammunition had run out and a relief column under Comonfort been beaten back. By the time they flew the white flag, the gallant Mexicans, both soldiers and civilians, were eating rats. Among the defenders of Puebla was Porfirio Díaz, who, when captured, managed, along with González Ortega, to escape before the French could ship them to France as prisoners of war. The prelates of Puebla welcomed the French army, "intoning, in the quavering voice of their decrepit dignitaries," to quote a Mexican historian, "impious Te Deums."

The next stop was Mexico City, where the Juárez regime, having lost an army at Puebla, chose not to give battle, although its inhabitants, aware of the heroic struggle at Puebla, wanted to resist. "Everybody begged for arms," remembered Justo Sierra, then a student in the city. Had the Mexicans mounted a battle for their capital, they might have gained time to organize the defense of the countryside. Instead, Juárez packed his bags and transferred the seat of his government to the city of San Luis Potosí.

In June 1863, Forey, preceded by the soldiers of Márquez, made his grand entrance into Mexico City. Old criollo fogies, remnants of the Santa Anna years, stepped out onto the balconies of their palatial homes to applaud their "liberators," while *mochos*, Catholic fanatics, "yelled and waved handkerchiefs." Squat and "pompous like some impersonator of the Romans," Forey "believed that the whole nation was kneeling in gratitude," oblivious to the spectators who watched sullenly from afar.

In a day or two, the celebrants, particularly the clerics, had begun to temper their enthusiasm. Forey arrived bearing bad tidings. France, Napoleon wanted Mexicans to know, would respect the Ley Lerdo and confirm the titles of property seized from the church. Not long after, the Assembly of Notables, picked to decide what kind of government best suited Mexicans, endorsed Napoleon's dictum. This change of heart baffled many a Mexican monarchist. The explanation, however, was simple. Powerful Mexicans, the buyers of ecclesiastical property, sat in the Assembly of Notables; no fewer than four of them had spent over forty thousand pesos each on church real estate, while another eight of them had family ties to buyers in Mexico City. These individuals, and scores of others like them, had no desire to discard what they had just acquired. To the further dismay of the clergy, Napoleon also urged Mexicans to accept the principle of freedom of religion, choking off "hosannas in the sacristies" and sparking mutterings of "shocked indignation."

To govern Mexico provisionally, Saligny chose a committee of malodorous reactionaries to name a regency of three; its choices were Almonte, Pelagio Antonio de Labastida, now archbishop of Mexico, and General

Mariano Salas, a relic of Santa Anna's epoch. It was this committee, too, that picked the Assembly of Notables, which, with Almonte as one of its spokesmen, voted, as expected, for a monarchy under a foreign prince. That individual would be the Austrian archduke Ferdinand Maximilian, the choice of Hidalgo and Gutiérrez Estrada. Before accepting the crown of Mexico, Maximilian asked for a plebiscite of Mexican opinion, compelling the startled Marshal Bazaine, now the substitute for Forey, to manufacture a Mexican vote of confidence in the archduke.

For Benito Juárez, the year had ended on a bleak note. As the French army advanced, Juárez was driven from San Luis Potosí to Saltillo and from there to Monterrey. Thinking the Republic a lost cause, and unwilling to share his fiefdom with Juárez, Santiago Vidaurri, caudillo of Nuevo León, went over to the French. Both Manuel Doblado and González Ortega, two who had recently asked Juárez to resign, thought the better of it and drove Vidaurri into the United States, from where he joined the monarchists in Mexico City. Comonfort, a patriot until the bitter end, had died in battle; in the south, Juan Alvarez, now seventy-four years old, and young Porfirio Díaz were waging a losing struggle; the French army controlled nearly every city. Ominously, Indian Mexico, resentful of Liberal legislation, either stayed out of harm's way or, worse yet, fought against Liberal guerrilla bands. In reprisal, the Liberals burned Indian pueblos to the ground. Unable to fight the French invaders frontally, the Mexicans had reverted to guerrilla warfare.

IV

In April 1864, Ferdinand Maximilian accepted the Mexican throne. Tall and handsome, with big blue eyes, blond hair, and blond beard, he was just thirty-two years of age when he landed in Veracruz. Thanks to the memoirs of José Luis Blasio, his private secretary, we know much about Maximilian's stay in Mexico. An admirer of the archduke, Blasio, whose father faithfully served Félix Zuloaga, kept an account of the activities of Maximilian, his wife, and his coterie of Mexican sycophants. A fastidious dresser, Maximilian wore his clothes to fit the occasion—white, for instance, when he traveled in the hot country. A chain smoker, he was never without a cigarette or, if he could help it, a glass of wine. He loved fine foods, French especially, and brought in chefs from France to satisfy his craving, as well as French wines to go with his food.

Contemplative, profoundly sentimental, and egotistical, Maximilian was the brother of Francis Joseph, the Austrian emperor, and an heir to the Hapsburg throne. An adventurer and an opportunist, he dreamed grandiose plans, seeing himself as the kingmaker in them. He displayed superior qualities, being gracious of manner, a good listener, and a witty and knowledgeable conversationalist. But they were the products of superior circumstance, crown bred, so to speak, never tested by experience; to exacerbate the picture, his will was weak, appearing strong merely because men fawned on him. Maximilian was unstable and frivolous, being most happy, Mexicans suspected, in the company of women.

The subjugation of Mexico, always a political quagmire, called for the talents of superior leadership and strength of character, virtues unknown to the archduke. During his Atlantic crossing, when he should have pondered what to do once he landed, Maximilian spent his time devising a manual of court etiquette and writing a letter to Juárez asking him for his collaboration. A frustrated man, he longed for vindication, seeing himself as a failure, denied recognition by his brother, Francis Joseph, and cowed by his mother. The Mexican crown, which Napoleon dangled before him, offered Maximilian the chance to redeem himself.

His wife, Charlotte, on the other hand, monopolized the common sense in the family. But she, too, was smitten with ambition; like her husband, she wished very much to rule and had visions of herself as a queen. Still in her early twenties, Charlotte was tall and slender, with big, black eyes but nearsighted, with a majestic air about her. She was the daughter of a Protestant, the king of Belgium, while her mother, a princess of the house of Orleans, had imbued in her a "secret loathing" for Napoleon but a love for the French army. She spoke Spanish, Blasio reported, without a trace of an accent. Intelligent and mighty of will, Charlotte dominated her husband. According to Blasio, the two never slept together, rumor had it because Maximilian was impotent.

"I give you a throne on a heap of gold," Napoleon reportedly told Maximilian. But that throne, as Iturbide came to appreciate, had, like the Mexican nopal, a prickly skin. Given his anticlerical bias, encouraged by Charlotte, Maximilian was hardly the man to rescue Conservative chestnuts from the fire. As one Mexican observed, since Maximilian "was neither a politician nor an administrator nor a soldier," he had no business being in Mexico. To his credit, he made valiant attempts to overcome his handicaps, learning to speak a passable Spanish and reading Alamán's *Historia de México.* That one of his goals, according to Blasio, was to persuade Juárez to be his prime minister and, with the French out of the way, to govern Mexico together, spoke volumes about his distorted view of recent Mexican events.

This drama of Maximilian, comical if it had not been so tragic for Mexico, began to unfold at Veracruz, "a tumbledown port with a peeling customhouse." Arriving three days ahead of schedule, Maximilian and Charlotte found neither the French nor their puppet Mexican authorities ready to welcome them. Almonte and his wife, who headed the reception committee, were wating in Orizaba, fearful of succumbing to yellow fever in Veracruz. Having forgotten, when writing to Maximilian and Charlotte in Europe of the warm reception awaiting, to tell them that Mexican patriots might well assault their caravan, Almonte was organizing a military escort for their journey from Veracruz to Mexico City. "On shore, nothing moved," remembered Paula Kolonitz, a lady-in-waiting of Charlotte's, "no one appeared." The European prince so long coveted by the monarchists stood at the door of his empire, but his subjects had gone into hiding. "Nobody wanted to welcome him." Instead of the expected festival on land, Maximilian and Charlotte had to settle for dinner aboard the *Novara,* the ship that had transported them across the Atlantic.

Once they were outside Veracruz, things took a turn for the better. Although Maximilian and Charlotte could not ride the fancy English carriages they had brought with them, because of the bad roads, Almonte made certain that villagers along its route came out to greet "Their Imperial Majesties." In Puebla, the clerics, the sympathizers of monarchy, and the merely curious flocked to cheer the royal couple, lifting the crestfallen spirits of Charlotte. On June 12, 1864, the royal couple made their entrance into Mexico City under hundreds of triumphal arches and showers of flowers; its monarchist ayuntamiento had spent liberally on the decorations. "The populace, into which the police had poured a strong dose of enthusiasm in the pulquerias," reported an eyewitness, "yelled deliriously." Just the same, here and there could be heard the angry shouts of students crying "death to the *mochos,*" voices lost amid the "shouts, bells, cannon shots, and music." For fifteen days, Maximilian and Charlotte, dubbed Carlota by the Mexicans, quaffed imported wines, ate richly and danced into the dawn, attended the opera, and forgot what they had come for.

French rifles, thirty thousand of them, aided by the troops of Márquez, Tomás Mejía, and Miguel Miramón, quickly imposed a peace of sorts. His path swept clean of enemies, Maximilian, just three months after entering Mexico City, made a triumphal tour of its hinterland. Relying on the rhetoric of liberalism and smiling benevolently, Maximilian, to quote a Mexican scholar, seduced the undecided and Mexicans who "had lost hope." In Dolores Hidalgo to celebrate the Sixteenth of September, national Independence day, he bestowed such poignant tribute on the patriot fathers that he convinced even Republicans.

For a while, the monarchists reaped a bountiful harvest. Mexican high society, the dandies and their ladies, enjoyed the delights of royal balls, where French officers danced with their daughters, and which Maximilian and Charlotte, who loved social events, would occasionally attend. For these Mexicans, this was Shangri-la. Everyone who counted, or who thought they should, longed to form part of Mexican royalty, creating, Blasio said, "a veritable fever of aristocracy." Those who could prove ties to the old colonial nobility were blessed from the start; the less fortunate "went about looking frantically for genealogical trees and coats of arms to prove their descent from counts, dukes, or marquis." When Charlotte chose Manuela Gutiérrez Estrada to be a lady of honor at her court, Don José Miguel, her husband, "shed tears of joy for the glory conferred on his family."

Liberals, too, succumbed to Maximilian's spell. One of them was José Fernández Ramírez, once in the cabinet of Valentín Gómez Farías, where he advocated the confiscation of church property to pay for the war against the United States. Knowledgeable but vain, he was merely the first to transfer affiliations; Vidaurri and General José Uraga, an ardent Liberal and hacendado who hosted a dinner in honor of Maximilian during his visit to León, followed in his footsteps, as did Juan de Dios Pesa, the poet, and Manuel Siliceo y López Portillo. Multitudes of office seekers, former adherents of the Liberals, flocked to Maximilian. After his return to the National Palace, Juárez intended to publish a list of everyone who had begged Maximilian for a job but decided not to because, as Sebastián Lerdo de Tejada warned him, "if you do you will not have a Liberal party."

Maximilian's professed benevolence rarely paid political benefits. The French never consulted his backers, running Mexico as they saw fit. Márquez and his soldiers were window dressing, to confer a façade of legitimacy on the Intervention. Not a few Mexican generals in Maximilian's camp were reduced to selling steers to the French army. The poor received nothing from the empire. The Indians of San Juan de Teotihuacán, who sold Maximilian apocryphal pre-Hispanic relics which they manufactured themselves, were just as ragged as ever. His benevolent laws abolishing debt peonage and establishing a German system of public schools remained merely good intentions. To his clerical backers, Maximilian brought a horrendous disillusionment since he refused to rescind the Ley Lerdo for fear of antagonizing prominent Mexicans, the owners of ecclesiastical property. While conceding that Catholicism was the official religion, Maximilian, nevertheless, permitted the worship of other cults.

In addition, Maximilian saddled Mexico with a mountainous debt. By the terms of the Convention of Miramar, French troops were to remain in Mexico until 1867; in return, Maximilian promised to pay for their upkeep and to reimburse France for the cost of the Intervention. He pledged Mexico to pay off its obligations to France, England and Spain, including the Jecker bonds. To cover the cost of the Intervention and the empire, he borrowed money from French bankers, but the lenders kept over a third of it while more was set aside to pay interest on the Mexican debt. By doing this, Maximilian multiplied Mexico's foreign obligations threefold, even mortgaging to the French the silver mines of Sonora. Maximilian had done the bidding of his French masters, upon whom the survival of the empire depended.

On the battlefield, for a while at least, things looked up for the empire.

During the winter of 1864, the French army overran much of Mexico, driving Juárez farther and farther north. General José Uraga, commander of the Liberal army in the west, defected to the French, leaving José María Arteaga to handle the demoralized soldiers. In Jalisco, the French routed them, placing Jalisco and Michoacán under enemy guardians. Trying to avoid capture, Juárez transferred the Republic's capital to Ciudad Chihuahua and from there to El Paso del Norte, a hamlet on the border with Texas. In the south, the French defeated an army led by Porfirio Díaz. Only in the far north, in Juárez himself, did the Republic survive.

Sometime in 1865, the self-assured French predicted, even that tiny flicker of resistance would vanish, enabling them to consolidate the empire and withdraw their army from Mexico. Thinking the battle won, and wishing to rid himself of the guerrillas still holding out, Maximilian, maybe at the instigation of his French allies, declared treasonous all opposition. According to the decree of October 3, 1865, Mexicans caught fighting against the empire would be shot summarily. Maximilian's entire cabinet, Juan de Dios Pesa among other Mexicans, agreed to it. General Arteaga and his men, captured and shot in Michoacán, were the first to forfeit their lives by imperial fiat.

Notwithstanding that, Juárez, the symbol of republican Mexico, held out. Unlike Santa Anna, who quit his country after the capture of Mexico City in 1847, or the delegates at Querétaro who voted to accept the harsh peace terms dictated by Washington, Juárez stuck it out, never forsaking his determination to fight on or his faith in ultimate victory. When his presidency ended in 1865, Juárez, believing himself indispensable, prolonged his stay in office, infuriating González Ortega and Prieto. For all intents and purposes, this converted Juárez into a kind of dictator, but so esteemed was he by then that most Mexicans applauded his decision.

Unbeknownst to Juárez, the tide was starting to turn by 1865. The truth of the imperial venture was filtering into France through letters from soldiers in the expeditionary army. The French public had lost whatever enthusiasm it had summoned for the enterprise. Even Napoleon was troubled by doubts. Next door, Bismarck's Prussia, savoring its victory over Austria at Sadowa, had upset the balance of power in Europe, threatening France itself. French troops in Mexico, Napoleon knew, had to be brought home to save his throne, a decision made in the fall of 1865. The Civil War in the United States had ended with a Northern victory. Almost immediately, Washington, citing the Monroe Doctrine, began pressing the French to pull out of Mexico. Henceforth, Washington did what it could to help the Mexican Republic dislodge the French, selling it arms and ammunition, something it had not done earlier. On January 22, 1866, Napoleon announced he was withdrawing his troops from Mexico, a decision that "struck terror in the Imperial court and in the hearts of monarchists."

Marshal Bazaine conveyed the news to Maximilian and Charlotte. The handwriting was on the wall, he told them; without French troops, the empire would collapse. Bazaine urged Maximilian to abdicate, imploring him to go back to Europe. Maximilian, the evidence indicates, was ready to heed the advice, aware that his crown rested on French bayonets. But, ultimately, he chose to fight on. Realizing that without him they were lost, monarchists, the high clergy, and the puppet generals, as well as sundry opportunists, had goaded him to stay, begging him not to betray them. Maximilian listened to their pleas. Aware that if he were to remain he would require their help, he turned Conservative, ousting from his cabinet his Liberal collaborators.

More ambitious and vain, Charlotte, furthermore, refused to contemplate abdication, terrified by the role of "playing a queen while living on an Austrian pension." So she prevailed upon her husband to fight for his throne while she journeyed to France to hold Napoleon to his word. She departed from Mexico with the words *Adiós Mama Carlota,* from a popular Mexican ditty that poked fun at her, ringing in her ears. In Paris, when she saw Napoleon, he wept tears but told her that he could do nothing. Unwilling to abandon hope, she traveled to Rome to beg aid from the pope, whose secretary informed her that Maximilian, by not restoring the property of the Mexican church, had sealed his own fate. When she finally spoke to the pope, Charlotte could tell him only of her fears of being poisoned. Charlotte, who died in 1927, never regained her sanity.

V

Early in 1866, Juárez had again established his government in Ciudad Chihuahua, from where he watched Mariano Escobedo, one of his new generals, take Matamoros and put a French force to flight at Santa Ysabel. Next Tampico, Monterrey, and Saltillo succumbed to the Mexicans. In Chihuahua, Luis Terrazas and Sóstenes Rocha won out; soon, Durango was once more in republican hands. In the northwest, the French lost Guaymas, the port of Sonora, then the entire state, and finally Mazatlán. The army of the west, under General Ramón Corona, occupied Jalisco while Díaz took back Oaxaca. The French and their Mexican confederates controlled just the central plateau, surrounded by an "advancing wall of fire," armies composed of rancheros, artisans, workers, and, more and more, hacendados. The Red Armies, the color of the Liberal Republic's banners, were on the verge of victory.

In March 1867, Marshal Bazaine and the last of the French soldiers departed from Veracruz, a multitude of monarchist Mexicans, recalled Blasio, at their heels: bureaucrats of the empire, former cabinet ministers, and everyone who feared for his life upon the triumph of Juárez. At Orizaba, Maximilian, still debating what to do, decided to gamble his life on a miracle. For that he counted on the armies of Miramón, Mejía, and Márquez and a sprinkling of Austrian soldiers. Maximilian established his headquarters in the city of Querétaro, where, with Miramón and Mejía and twenty thousand soldiers, he waited for the republican armies, now under General Escobedo. Puebla, in the interim, succumbed to Díaz's army, and, shortly after, an identical fate befell Márquez and his men rushing to defend it. On May 15, 1867, after a siege of seventy-two days, Escobedo, supported by the armies of Corona and Vicente Riva Palacio, took Querétaro. A few days later, Díaz entered Mexico City.

On June 19, on a site known as the Cerro de la Campana (Hill of the Bell), Maximilian, by order of Juárez, met his maker, shot by a firing squad alongside of Miramón and Mejía. He died by his own hand, his death justified partly by the infamous decree of October 1865, by which he had sentenced to death Mexicans bearing arms against him. The frigate *Novara,* which three and a half years earlier had carried Maximilian and Charlotte to Veracruz, transported his remains back to Europe, for burial in the crypt of the Capuchin friars in Vienna, the resting place of the Hapsburgs, his ancestors. Of the principal military plotters who sided with Maximilian, only Márquez escaped, spending the rest of his life running a pawnshop in Cuba.

Once more riding his black carriage, Juárez returned to Mexico City. He came back to govern a country devastated by a decade of war, to mourn the loss of 300,000 Mexicans. This time, he was to govern a country with a soul, a Liberal one, enshrined in the Constitution of 1857. From now on, the future rested in the hands of the Liberals, victors over Conservatives, monarchists, and clericals in the wars of the Reforma and the Intervention. With their triumph, the Liberals planted the seeds of nationhood, in theory, of a bourgeois Republic. The Spanish colony and aspirations to revive its outlines were things of the past. By defeating their rivals once and for all, the Liberals were free to make capitalist doctrines the law of the Republic.

Then there was Juárez, now the symbol of *patria.*

14

PEACE AND ORDER

I

After the Restoration of the Republic (Mexicans refer to it as the República Restaurada) in 1867, another day dawned, calling forth decades of peace and order. At the helm of the ship of state was the middle class, but not alone for long, because the elite fell quickly into step, embracing the values prized by Liberals: money, success, schooling, and science. Urban growth, a signpost of rising middle-class importance, was a mark of the times; the populations of Mexico City, Guadalajara, and León, three of the booming cities, swelled rapidly. More Mexicans lived in cities than ever before. For all that, geographical imbalances remained: six out of ten Mexicans inhabited the region from Mexico City to Guadalajara, yet a mere 3 percent of them were in the Pacific northwest, an area of equal size.

While this was taking form, the Leviathan of industrial capitalism began to alter more and more the old colonial picture. England led the way. Steamships and the construction of railroads in the peripheral countries were tilting the emphasis in the economies of the industrial nations from imports to exports. This change had been going on steadily, but now it was starting to accelerate. From this juncture on, although England and the capitalist West continued to buy raw materials, they dumped more and more cheap manufactures on peripheral markets. Confronted with the flood of imported goods, native crafts fared badly, but the flow of capital to the periphery caused international banking to flower. The establishment of the Banco de Londres y México, the first of the civil banks, was one manifestation of this. During this phase, speculators started to develop lands in the dependent countries for export agriculture, lay out railway grids, and erect infrastructures to handle the export of raw materials and the distribution of factory goods from abroad. In Mexico, with the hunt on for raw materials and markets for exports, investment capital started slowly to multiply, primarily around its metropolis and the mining districts of the northern border states.

Distant countries, virtually self-sufficient before, became spokes in a world economy. Soon, an international division of labor developed: the industrial West manufactured and sold goods, and the rest of the world, the periphery, labored to supply it with cheap raw materials. Much of the earth and its people came to depend, to a greater or lesser degree, on the West. Little of the money exported to the marginal countries found its way into factories, partly because Western capitalist did not want them competing for markets. Native populations awakened to find themselves on the margins. Despite the flow of capital into their countries, the poor went from want to want. Dirt farmers and artisans swelled the ranks of the job seekers, while campesinos who held on to their parcels of land had little money to spend. Designed to supply the needs of the industrial nations, the local economy gave birth to a *burguesía* that blossomed at the cost of its independence.

To share the benefits of the outsiders, upon whom they depended increasingly, Mexican Liberals bid change a hearty welcome, conceding to foreigners power over their economy and politics, aping their culture, and adopting their values, copying initially the French and then their neighbors across the border. A dependent but prosperous economy rested on political stability, so law and order took top priority, as well as the need for a cheap and docile labor force. Out of this concoction of needs and circumstances surfaced a strong and centralized state, which endeavored to rid itself of domestic trade barriers such as the *alcabala* and to institute a standard system of weights and measures.

Trade between Mexico and the industrial West also helps to explain the appearance of political stability, the cherished peace and order. Dependency, that of Mexico on the capitalist nations, offered benefits sufficiently lucrative for better-off Mexicans to end the era of anarchy. The economic pie provided more opportunities. La República Restaurada, the presidencies of Benito Juárez and his successor, Sebastián Lerdo de Tejada (1867–76), laid the foundations for the Liberal transformation of Mexico, what José Mariá Luis Mora and his disciples had advocated since the 1830s.

II

As the victorious caudillo of the Guerra de la Reforma and of the Intervention, Juárez went forth with a moral and political prestige until then never conferred on anyone. The defeats inflicted on the Conservatives, for which he was partly responsible, purged rivals not merely of the Liberals but, no less important, of Juárez. Between 1856, which marked the initiation of the Reforma, and 1867, the empire's debacle, much had changed on the political scene. In the early days, Juárez, after a particularly frustrating experience, had lamented to General Ignacio Mejía, "It is impossible to govern under these circumstances. No one obeys. I can't tell anyone what to do." After the return of the Liberals to Mexico City in 1867, Mejía, then minister of war, could say to Juárez, "Now you will be able to get others to do what they are told, that I promise you." To quote Justo Sierra, "Mexico was never governed until Juárez took over after the fall of the empire."

Juárez, moreover, had altered his behavior. Earlier, he closed his eyes to political differences, willing, at times, to coexist with those of opposite stripe. Now, although he declared a general amnesty, he never forgave those who lent a hand to Maximilian's empire. For him, they were traitors, to be denied government posts and any say in political circles. That attitude also mirrored public opinion, no less convinced that the crime of treason must not be condoned. Given this climate of opinion, many a Conservative was excluded from politics.

Juárez, as Emilio Rabasa pointed out, was now the national caudillo. Branding him a dictator, Ignacio Ramírez even broke with Juárez. Victory was kind and beneficent to Juárez and his Liberals, bestowing on them the National Palace, the state governorships, and an army of sycophants ready to walk in step with them. Death rid Juárez of old rivals: Melchor Ocampo, Manuel Doblado, Miguel Lerdo de Tejada, and Juan Alvarez. Juárez's cohorts were loyalists, men such as Sebastián Lerdo de Tejada, brother of Miguel; José Mariá Iglesias; General Ignacio Mejía; and Matías Romero. Unlike his predecessors, Juárez seldom replaced his ministers: so long as he had confidence in them, they remained in the cabinet.

Unhappy with the Constitution of 1857, which inflated the powers of Congress, Juárez endeavored to strengthen the presidency. Over the vociferous objections of sundry Liberal deputies, he won congressional approval for constitutional amendments conferring on the president virtual veto power over proposed legislation. Although he died before its rebirth, he reestablished the Senate, a step designed to weaken the Chamber of Deputies, the bastion of provincial interests. Juárez, the Federalist of yore, wanted a more centralized Republic, especially power for himself, going so far as to impose "official" candidates for political office. He mastered the art of manipulating the popular vote to suit his own purposes, specifically his "reelections." To gain their support, he worked hand in glove with caciques of diverse types, the local lords; grateful for his indulgence, they became his allies, profiting from the relationship.

III

Before peace and order could reign, the Liberals needed to resolve a host of problems. Old maladies had not gone away with victory. Gangs of robbers, not a few of them former republican or imperial soldiers, infested the countryside, making travel on roads reminiscent of the days of Antonio López de Santa Anna, a condition aptly captured by Manuel Payno in *Los bandidos de Río Frío.* Poorly paid jobs in agriculture, mining, or a textile mill appealed rarely to men accustomed to adventure, pillage, and combat. Political rivalries linked, here and there, to national politics upset the peace of Sonora, Sinaloa, Yucatán, and Puebla, while abortive cuartelazos occurred in San Luis Potosí, Zacatecas, and Jalisco.

Yet cost what it may, peace and order must have their day. To ensure their ecumenicity in the countryside, where robbers mocked the law, a corps of rurales, rural mounted police, had been organized on the eve of the French invasion. In the interlude after victory, rancheros and unemployed soldiers were recruited to fill its ranks; steady wages and colorful uniforms also enticed bandits to forsake their life of crime for law enforcement. Unfortunately for rural Mexicans, scores of *bandoleros* survived the cunning and experience of their former partners in crime.

Of more importance for the stability of the Republic, Juárez cut the army down to size, from 80,000 to 16,000 men, which upset the brass hats. When the Liberals returned to Mexico City, the bloated army had taken up half of the national budget. Cutting it down was no easy feat; other presidents had invited their downfall by doing so, victimized by egotistical military bosses on the prowl for money, power, and laurels. Juárez, amazingly, got his way, replacing the asymmetrical military with an army capable of enforcing the peace. Among the beribboned generals told to go home was Porfirio Díaz, planning already his triumphal climb to the National Palace.

The Reforma, although it turned upside down the political and economic standing of the church, left undisturbed the day-to-day worship of the faithful. The cities of the Republic, from its metropolis to the humblest provincial hub, remained as Catholic as ever, their spiritual climate reeking of incense. The bucolic countryside was no different, lamented Ignacio Manuel Altamirano in his popular novel *La navidad en las montañas.* "Everywhere I traveled I found idolatry so firmly rooted that I felt dismay," he wrote, "being unable to disbelieve that the religion of Jesus of Nazareth was but a fallacious pretext for a cult which bled white the poor" and "blocked the coming of civilization."

This state of affairs, however, was not to the liking of Juárez, who once told Justo Sierra, "I would like to see the Indians converted to Protestantism; they need a religion that will teach them to read and not waste their pennies on candles for the saints." Still, without consulting Congress, Juárez conferred voting rights on the clergy, despite cries of outrage from anticlerical cohorts. Regardless of what Juárez may have thought of him, Archbishop Pelagio Antonio de Labastida, traitor by the president's own definition, was back in Mexico and acting just as important as ever. In 1873, by way of illustration, during the anticlerical administration of Sebastían Lerdo de Tejada, he arrived in his regal finery to bless the inauguration of the railroad from Mexico City to Veracruz.

All the same, Liberal policy failed to mollify the faithful. Incited by Pius IX, a pope who confused the Reforma with the chicanery of the devil, Catholics never truly fell in step with its legislation. When Sebastían Lerdo de Tejada's regime, successor to Juárez's, stepped up enforcement of the anticlerical provisions of the Constitution, a popular hue and cry erupted. Snobbish Catholic women, who just a year earlier had hailed Lerdo de Tejada's rise to the presidency because, unlike Juárez, he was a "respectable gentleman," turned angrily against him, waging a battle of malicious gossip and character assassination in beauty parlors and kitchens. A clerical uprising flared up in Michoacán in 1874, captained by a Conservative guerrilla chieftain still at large. General Mariano Escobedo had to be called upon to put down the bloody rebellion which, momentarily, appeared invincible. A year afterward, when Lerdo de Tejada incorporated the Veracruz decrees into the Constitution, merely a formality, a revolt of Cristeros, or disciples of Christ, upset the peace and quiet of Mexico City.

In their attempt to rebuild the economy, the regimes of Juárez and Lerdo de Tejada had taken on more than they had bargained for. Years of war and domestic strife had left the economy in shambles, a predicament aggravated by the lack of any international credit rating. Needing funds to revive mining and agriculture, Mexico could not borrow them; Europeans revealed no desire to risk their money on a country with such a sorry financial record. Only a miracle would invigorate the economy, and Matías Romero, the new chief of the treasury, was asked to bring it about.

An orthodox Liberal, Romero visualized economics in capitalist terms. A confirmed apostle of free trade, he thought gospel the "law of comparative advantage," selling what one did best. That meant making a virtue of necessity, staying with mining, agriculture, and commerce, the colonial standbys. This conformed to the much talked-about theory of the international division of labor, which held that Mexico could never become an industrial nation, not merely because it lacked business entrepreneurs but because it could not compete with England and France. The raw materials of the Republic, in mines primarily, invited their exploitation. Mining, conversely, attracted foreign capital, which revived the economy.

To restore mining, Mexico had to build a national system of transportation, specifically a railroad network, costly to lay out and, therefore, an enterprise reserved for foreign capital. Its construction, in the opinion of architects of economic policy, opened the door to a better future. By relying on the iron horse to link up with the industrial West, exporting raw materials, mineral ores, and agricultural goods and employing profits from their sale to purchase manufactured articles, Mexico's economy would thrive.

Trying to implement the formula, which antedated the Juárez regime, the Mexicans, in 1837, had made a start on a rail line connecting Mexico City with Veracruz. Work began at both ends, with construction crews meeting eventually at Cumbres de Maltrata, a pass in the Sierra Madre Oriental, in 1872. The railroad was completed during Lerdo de Tejada's administration, but not without a national scandal. This impressive engineering feat, spanning towering mountains and jagged canyons, had languished for years, despite work on it during Maximilian's regime. By 1866, the English company entrusted with the project by Maximilian had gone bankrupt. Anxious to complete the line, Juárez had closed his eyes to legislation punishing collaborators of the monarchy and bailed out the English company. When Congress learned that one of its stockholders was Antonio Escandón, one of the "traitors," a cry of alarm went up, tarnishing reputations.

Despite the completion of the Veracruz railway, the blueprints of Romero and his cohorts failed to revive the economy. The mining doldrums persisted, and, except for minor technological improvements and, once in a while, new machinery, mining remained dormant. Heavily taxed, mining, as during colonial days, consisted almost exclusively of the export of silver and gold. English capitalists, the owners of Real de Monte, a mining emporium in Hidalgo, had gained a stranglehold on the industry, converting their headquarters, a short distance from Pachuca, into an English enclave. Everyone who was anyone was English, "living in English-type houses," the men marrying blond English women and fathering English daughters, so much so that visitors "found themselves in a village of Albion instead of Mexico."

Agriculture, from which much was expected, fared no better. For hacendados, some of whom cultivated cash crops for export, these were depression years of poor harvests and low prices. Rancheros in the Bajío, who produced crops for sale on local markets, enjoyed only marginal success. Except for the henequen hacendados in Yucatán, the cochineal merchants of Oaxaca, and the sugar planters in Morelos and Veracruz, agriculture stagnated.

Industry fared no better. Textiles, the most developed, tottered on the brink of ruin. By disposing of barriers to free trade, the Liberals of the Reforma, to quote one critic, had "sentenced the industry to death." Abolishing measures designed to protect native manufactures, the Liberals left Mexican entrepreneurs to handle as best they could the competition of cheap, imported cloth from England and France.

For workers, the laws of the Reforma were, in the manner of the times, punitive. On the one hand, they swept away the guild system, a preserve for the favored few; on the other, they prohibited labor unions, punished strikers with heavy fines or lengthy prison sentences, and abandoned them to the mercy of their employer, although Juárez, upon hearing of a peon whipped by a hacendado for damaging a plow, abolished, in theory, corporal punishment. With the laws of supply and demand dictating relations between capital and labor, the República Restaurada was no paradise for workers. As Ignacio L. Vallarta, one of its upholders, admitted, employers lowered wages at their whim, relied on debt peonage, and demanded work from dawn to dusk.

By 1872, there were approximately seventy thousand miners and thirty thousand textile workers, more than twice their number at the end of the colony. Having to fend for themselves, they began to organize mutual-aid societies, which largely confined their beneficence to extending legal and material assistance to their members. In 1872, workers in the textile industry banded together in the Gran Círculo de Obreros de México. Its spokesmen, advocating a mixture of Liberal and socialist ideals, organized wildcat strikes, particularly in textiles, at times resulting in higher wages. *El Socialista, La Comuna, El Hijo del Trabajo, El Obrero Internacional,* and *La Huelga,* the labor newspapers of the day, openly advocated the militancy of workers.

Meanwhile, the victorious Liberals, more doctrinaire than compassionate, pushed ahead with the subdivision of the ejidos. During the days of Juárez and Lerdo de Tejada, lands of pueblo after pueblo were turned over as private property to their heads of families. Transformed into the owner of his *parcela,* the Indian, ignorant generally of what private property entailed, became a potential victim of hacendados and rancheros. Usurpation of their lands was a fact of life. Judges sold themselves; venal officials confiscated lands because taxes were not paid promptly; hacendados lent money and then collected in land; and so forth. Made aware of what was going on, Ignacio Ramírez demanded that the subdivision of the ejidos be stopped, but no one heeded him. Instead, when Indians took up arms to defend their ejidos, they were shot, the fate of Manuel Lozada, the cacique of Nayarit.

Colonization was one more Liberal scheme: to entice Europeans to settle in Mexico. The future, architects of national policy proclaimed, lay with hard-working men and women willing to make productive the fertile lands of the Republic. The legislation of 1856 granted foreigners the right to acquire land, and, starting in 1861, the Juárez regime gave subsidies to those who did. The Ley de Terrenos Baldíos (or "idle lands") of 1863 opened public lands to settlement, and, at about the same time, private colonization companies were permitted to sell them. Unhappily for the fathers of these blueprints, Europeans displayed scant interest in Mexico and, when they did, more often than not went into business in the cities.

Moreover, foreign capitalists, whom the Liberals counted on to invest in Mexico, behaved niggardly. Knowing Mexico's record, they took their capital elsewhere. What money filtered into the economy came by way of public works, mainly through the construction of the Veracruz railroad and trade and commerce. Caught between the proverbial abyss and sword, Matías

Romero resurrected time-worn formulas: balance the budget; rid the country of *alcabalas;* entrust the collection of taxes and duties to federal agents; and wipe out graft and corruption. These panaceas, however, lodged more power and responsibility in Mexico City and, inevitably, built up federal payrolls. Necessity had compelled the apostles of provincial rights to adopt Centralist formulas.

Romero's hope for a favorable balance of trade went begging. The Republic's imports outstripped the value of its exports. Precious metals and minted coins, the old colonial staples, still constituted the bulk of sales abroad. Cochineal, vanilla, tobacco, henequen, and sugar made up the rest. Mexico imported cotton and wool cloth, silks, wine, oils, rope, iron and steel, jewels, paper, furniture, wagons, dishes, guns and ammunition, and even raw cotton. Until the seventies, over 60 percent of the Republic's imports were from Europe, mainly England, France, Germany, and Spain. The proclivity of wealthy Mexicans to deposit their money for safekeeping in foreign banks (capital flight) and exports of minted coins made currency scarce and hampered business transactions at home.

As if that were not enough, there was the national debt, over 120 million pesos. Of that total, 80 million was owed to foreigners, nearly a third of it thanks to Maximilian and his Conservative allies. By disavowing their folly, Romero reduced the Republic's debt to 84 million pesos, less frightening but still formidable. However, Washington, blind to Mexico's predicament, continued to press its claims, compelling it to agree to reimburse Americans for damages to their property since the Treaty of Guadalupe of 1848.

Public education, too, held a high priority for the Liberals. Given the sorry neglect of schools, that made sense. At the moment of the Reforma, the Republic had few schools, low enrollments, and more priests than teachers. The church had a firm grip on education, especially for the children of the more affluent, the leaders of the future. That hardly fitted in with the Liberal design of a modern and nationalistic education. Church indoctrination must be supplanted by schools with a Liberal slant, lest youth preserve old values and ideals. A modern school would shatter the hold of the church and introduce Liberal institutions which, their proponents argued, opened paths to progress. As Juárez insisted, schooling assured respect for liberty, the Constitution, and law. So, taking its cue from the blueprints of Gómez Farías, the charter of 1857 legislated the freedom of education, a principle reaffirmed by the República Restaurada; another law, which applied to the Federal District and territories, made primary schooling obligatory and free. To supervise the program, Congress, emulating again the example of the 1830s, revived the Dirección de Instrucción Pública. A scattering of states adopted the federal model.

The rebirth of public education, as the Liberals interpreted it, required a search for compatible philosophical underpinnings, a task which fell into the lap of Gabino Barreda, a medical doctor. A native of Puebla, Barreda had studied medicine and law, then gone off to Paris, where he listened to Auguste Comte, father of positivism, a philosophy he introduced to Mexico when he taught physics and natural history in the school of medicine. Barreda converted the old Jesuit Colegio de San Ildefonso into the Escuela Nacional Preparatoria and, as its director for ten years, made certain that positivism inspired its curriculum. With it, Barreda and his pedagogical allies asserted, students at the Preparatoria, the offspring of the affluent largely, would get the kind of education the country needed. And so the articles of positivism, which sanctified the Liberal creed, sank roots in Mexican soil. Equally pernicious, Barreda had only scorn for technical labor and handicrafts, alleging that every man worth his salt must have a profession. That, of course, was blatant class prejudice.

The enthusiasm for positivism knew no bounds, becoming, one observer remarked, the "hegemonic and official philosophy of the Republic," endorsed by Liberals everywhere. Journals and newspapers enshrined it, *El Monitor Republicano* and *El Siglo XIX* in Mexico City, as well as provincial ones. The more pretentious the journal, the more infected with evangelical positivism, a noteworthy case in point being the *Boletín de la Sociedad Mexicana de Geografía y Estadística.* Both Manuel Orozco y Berra and Joaquín García Icazbalceta, the historians of their era, were positivists, as were the two most popular historical novelists, Altamirano and Manuel Martínez Castro. Not exempt were the poets of the Renacimiento, the nationalistic, artistic, and literary awakening of that time: Manuel Acuña, Juan de Dios Pesa, Manuel M. Flores, and José Rosas Moreno.

The results of the pedagogical juggling, as one may suppose, were mixed. José Díaz Covarrubias, chief of *instrucción pública,* liked to boast that enrollments had doubled by 1875. The gains, however, were distorted. Children of the middle and upper classes received the most benefits, and then just in Mexico City. Rarely did the Preparatoria open its doors to pupils of the working class. In primary education, nothing changed; the new schools, which Díaz Covarrubias loved to talk about, were in Mexico City. Schools for rural folks, in particular Indians, the most illiterate, were noticeably absent. The benefits of the school heralded by Barreda, for which Juárez was often given credit, never trickled down.

The Republic also was striving to learn more about itself. In 1870, the treasury published its monumental *Memoria,* a compilation of statistics on agriculture, mining, industry, and commerce, the first of its kind since Independence. That unique effort dated from 1857, when the government began collecting the information. Until then, the Republic had relied on colonial statistics from 1791.

IV

Positivism failed to spoil the literary awakening, the Renacimiento. The political formula of the Liberals rested on the manipulations of elections, new legislation, the army, and *cultura.* For the first time, government employed culture as an integral part of its political blueprints. Embracing literature, history, the arts, music, and schooling, the official *cultura* exalted Liberalism, nationalism, and *mexicanidad,* pride in things Mexican.

Peace and order made this possible. Mexicans now had the opportunity to confer importance on intellectual and artistic endeavors. Democratic principles such as freedom of thought and press, exclaimed Pedro Santacilia, father-in-law of Juárez, had made possible the Renacimiento. Before, the writing of history and journalism had been used for partisan purposes. With the demise of the conflict between Liberals and Conservatives, intellectual and artistic labors could be utilized to build a national consensus. Helping this along was a government which began to understand that without a change in the mentality of Mexicans the Liberal future it envisaged stood on fragile foundations. Henceforth, there would be no art for the sake of art but, to the contrary, art for the benefit of the Liberal state and for the formation of a national culture.

The Renacimiento, which sprang from the Reforma, started with *veladas literarias* or *tertulias,* meetings of writers and intellectuals to discuss what they were doing, to read each other's works, and to figure out how to get literate Mexicans to buy what they published. Starting in 1867, these *veladas* united writers and thinkers of diverse political opinions, from Ignacio Ramírez to Francisco Pimentel, a poet of standpat views. From them emerged three famous literary societies. The Sociedad Nezahualcóyotl, its name adopted from the legendary Chichimecan poet, tried to stimulate the development of a national literature, enliven drama, and encourage the use of Mexican themes. The Liceo Mexicano, brainchild of the novelist José Tomás Cuéllar, worked also to strengthen the dramatic arts and Mexican literature. The Liceo Hidalgo, the last of the three societies, labored on behalf of Mexican literature and culture. To get their works before the literate public, Altamirano founded *El Renacimiento,* a literary review and the best of some three dozen ones in the Republic.

The Renacimiento signaled the ascendancy of the novel, written for a growing middle class and inspired by the *ambiente Mexicano.* One of its foremost exponents was Altamirano, who, taking time off from writing his own novels, analyzed the state of the Mexican narrative in *La revista literaria de México,* where he chastised authors for neglecting Mexican themes. For him, the desire to imitate blindly the structure of the French novel, which he found "unsuitable for our customs and manner of thinking," had led to mediocrity. Instead, he argued, Mexicans should use the novel as a propaganda tool to affirm the national conscience and *patria* and to educate. It was not enough to want to entertain, for the novel had to inculcate moral, ideological, and patriotic values, using Mexican themes taken from the pre-Hispanic past, three centuries of colonial rule and the Wars for Independence. Altamirano asked Mexicans to write about the typically Mexican. This, clearly, reflected also the influence of the Romantic school in literature, its fascination with landscapes—mountains, forests, and rivers—and native people.

A jack-of-all-trades, Manuel Ignacio Altamirano, a former student of Ignacio Ramírez and like Juárez a "pure-blooded Indian," hailed from Tixtla, a village in Guerrero. Toward Juárez, he was ambivalent, being both critic and admirer. Altamirano was happiest when visiting a rural hamlet, as he reminisced in *La navidad en las montañas,* where he "forgot his troubles." In this popular tale of a visit to a village in the mountains, the climax was midnight mass on Christmas Eve, a time for reflecting on one's life and values. Simple virtues, he concluded, were rarely part of life in the "opulent cities," places of a society "tormented by terrible passions."

Small of stature, of a deeply bronze skin the "color of the Aztecs," and a wide, flat nose, Altamirano was an eloquent teller of tales. Whatever his racial origins, he was a modern man, the upholder of, for instance, European concepts of female beauty: "tall, white, and thin." Versed thoroughly in the classics and an orthodox Liberal, he had a profound faith in the ideals of the French Revolution. As a young man, he had participated in the uprising of Ayutla, serving loyally Juan Alvarez and, as a deputy to Congress, the Reforma. A powerful speaker, he dominated Congress. Beyond that, he was a journalist, then a teacher in the Escuela Nacional Preparatoria, where he taught history and literature, and, last but not least, established the Escuela Nacional de Maestros, the Republic's normal school. Along with *La navidad en las montañas,* Altamirano is remembered for *El Zarco,* a novel of highway bandits, and *Clemencia,* set in the days of the French Intervention.

All the same, it was *Astucia, jefe de los hermanos de la hoja,* a novel by Luis G. Inclán, that exemplified best what Altamirano preached. A story of rancheros, the backbone of the Reforma in the countryside, *Astucia* was read so widely that it eventually eclipsed the popularity of *El periquillo sarniento.* Inclán was a superb storyteller; like Mark Twain, he could "spin a vivid yarn." Born on a rancho, he was the son of José Mariá Inclán, the *administrador* of a hacienda on the outskirts of Mexico City, and Doña Rita Goicochea, a *mulata* from the south. Sent off to study for the priesthood, Inclán, to his father's displeasure, abandoned his studies for the life of the ranchero. Ultimately, like his father, he became the *administrador* of the haciendas of Narvarte, La Teja,

Tepentongo, Santa María, and Chapingo, today the agricultural college. In 1847, when American troops invaded the haciendas, he fled to Mexico City, where he wrote *Astucia.*

From start to finish, *Astucia* was Mexican. Its chief characters were rancheros, prototypes, wrote Inclán, of the "true Mexican character," members of a rural middle class intolerant of "political high jinks." Rustic and simple men, rancheros lived amid the fauna and landscape around them; the sky was their roof. They spoke a vernacular Spanish, the language of the unschooled. They were men of action, strong and resilient and loyal to their fathers, men who knew how to handle their own problems.

A school of history also began to take shape, distinct from that of the generation of Lucas Alamán and José María Luis Mora. It sought to fortify the sense of *patria,* symbolized by its Liberal, republican government. Not simply a hobby of gentlemen or politicos, national history became a subject to be taught from primary schools to the Preparatoria. José María Roa Barcena, Eufemio Mendoza, José María Vigil, Guillermo Prieto, and Justo Sierra, then just embarking on his illustrious career, wrote the Liberal version of the Mexican epic, replete with heroes who exemplified it. The historical novel made its debut, personified by those of Vicente Riva Palacio, general, politico, and journalist, among them *Calvario y Tabor, Monja y casada,* and *Los piratas del golfo.* Equally popular was Juan A. Mateos, also a journalist and politico, whose *Sacerdote y caudillo* retraced the life of Maguel Hidalgo y Costilla, the father of Mexican Independence.

The plastic arts, too, fell into step, now no longer dealing simply with the aesthetic but with what was necessary to strengthen the nationality and well-being of the Republic. Like literature, art must express the national character, describe its boundless grandeur, depict its travails, and encompass the diversity of its people. For Altamirano, Mexican artists, by imitating Hellenic beauty, had lagged behind Europeans who were devising an art of their own. Mexico, wrote Jorge Hammecken y Mejía, a student of Altamirano, had to create an art that was "realistic, Liberal, and progressive." Art "for the sake of art," he added, was a fallacy. Likewise to Miguel Olaguíbel, a critic of art, the time had arrived to discard religious themes and to replace them with a "love for the *patria* . . . our forests . . . coasts . . . rivers."

That this was more than just talk the staid Escuela Nacional de Bellas Artes (formerly the Academia de San Carlos) verified by awarding a prize for the finest painting with a national theme at its art show of 1869. At the Preparatoria, Gabino Barreda, attuned to identical currents, paid Juan Cordero, a well-known Mexican artist, to paint a mural whose theme embodied the new historical epoch. Painters of note, among them Luis Coto, José Jiménez, Javier Alvarez, Gregorio Dumanine, and Salvador Murillo, started to draw Mexican landscapes, scenes recalling the pre-Hispanic past and the Indian heritage. José María Velasco, perhaps the quintessential painter of the nineteenth century, represented most closely the art of this cultural Renacimiento. In 1875, his *Valle de México,* a stunningly beautiful portrait of the color and grandeur of the valley of Mexico, drew raves from his countrymen.

There were cultural ornaments elsewhere, too, although not always in tune with the Renacimiento. In Guadalajara, the Teatro Degollado opened its doors to host opera, ballet, and symphonic music; first-nighters heard Gaetano Donizetti's arias sung by Angela Peralta, a majestic Mexican soprano. The music was not only of Italian vintage but, correspondingly, the inspiration for the design of the arch of the Teatro Degollado: the fourth canto of Dante's *Divine Comedy.* In Mexico City, the National Philharmonic Society listened to the music of Bach, Handel, Haydn, Mozart, Beethoven, Chopin, and Liszt but ignored compositions by Malesio Morales and Cenobio Peralta, author of the opera *Catalina de Guisa.* Despite Altamirano's plea that Mexicans prefer the native, Mexican *burgueses* had chosen to listen to the European. In this, they were faithful to their tastes in economics.

V

In 1872, Juárez, thinking himself indispensable, decided for the fourth time to stay in the National Palace. As Altamirano observed, he should have retired with his laurels intact, but, preferring "power and ambition to republican glory," he allowed a "circle of selfish friends" to prod him to seek reelection. Two rivals challenged him: Sebastián Lerdo de Tejada, chief justice of the Supreme Court, and Díaz, hero of the wars against the French and the Conservatives. When none of them won a majority of the votes, Congress, stacked with Juárez supporters, elected him. An embittered Lerdo de Tejada cried foul, and Díaz, angrier and more egotistical, rebelled in Oaxaca. Sóstenes Rocha, a loyal general of Juárez, crushed the revolt of La Noria, subduing Oaxaca and killing Félix Díaz, its governor and brother of the frustrated candidate. Then, on July 19, 1872, Benito Juárez died suddenly of a heart attack, the roar of artillery telling the citizens of Mexico City of his death.

As chief justice of the Supreme Court, Lerdo de Tejada became acting president, then president in his own right after the elections of October of 1872, which he won easily. Lerdo the "criollo," light of skin and "of aristocratic bearing," had replaced the "Indian" Juárez. Once a student for the priesthood, Lerdo de Tejada possessed a first-rate mind, but, "lordly . . . and authoritarian," he alienated many of his old allies. Still, Lerdo got things done, leaving undisturbed the Liberal edifice erected by the Juaristas.

Then, in 1876, Lerdo de Tejada attempted to reelect himself, counting on his control of the bureaucracy and the army. No sooner were his intentions known than Díaz, once again a candidate, raised the banner of "no reelection," the central plank of his Plan de Tuxtepec, which echoed loudly in every corner of the Republic. Both Ignacio Ramírez and Riva Palacio hailed it. Popular with the military, Díaz mustered an army of ex-soldiers but tasted defeat in Matamoros, a border town, and in Oaxaca. The military of Lerdo de Tejada, in spite of the popularity of Díaz, appeared victorious.

When everything seemed lost, a bit of luck struck Díaz. José María Iglesias, chief justice of the Supreme Court, ruled null and void the election of Lerdo de Tejada, claiming the presidency for himself. Iglesias's meddling split the Lerdistas, allowing Díaz to revive his moribund military campaign. That fall, Díaz and General Manuel González, an ally and friend, beat Lerdo de Tejada's soldiers, chasing both Lerdo de Tejada and Iglesias into exile and leaving the National Palace to Díaz.

15

AND PROGRESS

I

Except for four years, Porfirio Díaz, who stepped onto the presidential stage, stayed in office until 1911. From the start, Lady Luck smiled on him. He arrived at the National Palace at a propitious moment, when Mexicans longed for peace, while the demand for raw materials and minerals from the industrial West made possible a relative prosperity at home. Like much of Latin America, Mexico was being drawn into the vortex of industrial capitalism, first by England, then by France, and, finally, by the United States. Foreign capital, which Liberals had courted for years, began to enter Mexico, at first slowly, then in larger and larger amounts, going mainly into mining, then helping to develop crops for export, and eventually harnessing the petroleum deposits on the Gulf coast to the industrial needs of western Europe and the United States.

The effects were dramatic. Foreign capital built a railway network and brought electricity, the telegraph, telephones, and international banking, part and parcel of its efforts to exploit Mexico's wealth. By the close of the Díaz era, Mexico had nearly thirty major banks. That, plus the political magic of Díaz and his Liberals, pulled the Republic out of the quagmire, transforming it into a copy of Western capitalism.

Conversely, the Mexican economy accelerated its transformation. For decades the Liberal ideal, capitalism became more and more a reality, a Mexican version powerful enough to start to unite local and regional markets into a national one. As this process escalated, it shunted aside primitive forms of production, that of the Indian ejido particularly, and solidified the position of the hacendados. By 1896, the *alcabala,* the ancient barrier to internal trade, had been eliminated.

The formulas responsible for this transformation were hardly novel. Free trade, the panacea of José María Luis Mora and the Constitution of 1857, took center stage. From this time on, theoretically, the tariffs of Lucas Alamán and his cohorts fell into discard, abandoned as illogical for Mexico, the view of Justo Sierra, an apostle of that era. Still, the new industry, also a goal of the day, had to be protected and the federal government needed customs revenues in order to meet its obligations.

In copying the capitalist West, Mexicans paid lip service to the rhetoric of laissez-faire. However, confronted with domestic reality, they pulled back from their axiom, favoring, on occasion, a strong and active state, the stimulator of economic growth, relying on the Ministerio de Fomento, citadel of "developmentalist" officials in Mexico City. The Liberals paid less and less attention to old themes, preferring a centralized state over individual freedoms, medicine Benito Juárez had prescribed for Mexico before his death. As earlier, peace and order were essential ingredients: "Order without progress was impossible, and progress could not exist without order."

The heralded benefits went to the exporters of raw materials; hacendados who produced cash crops for domestic markets; the big merchants who imported articles for resale at home; bankers who financed the transactions; mineowners, mostly foreigners; and, of course, the infant middle class, the bureaucrats, lawyers, engineers, physicians, and shopkeepers who got a slice of the pie. With the exception of foreigners, they made up a dependent *burguesía,* their well-being determined mainly by outsiders.

To implement their doctrines, the Liberals—or Porfiristas, as they came to be known—turned to José Ives Limantour, minister of the treasury, the son of a French immigrant, intelligent and trustworthy, who served Díaz until the bitter end. Assuming office during the international depression of 1893, a time of economic doldrums, Limantour won the plaudits of his countrymen. To pay off the foreign debt, a sacred obligation for him, Limantour tightened the Republic's belt, pruned jobs from the bureaucracy, reduced salaries, and collected revenues. He put the country's finances in order, eliminated or lowered duties on imports, and placed Mexico on the gold standard. When his financial wizardry bore fruit, eulogized Emilio Rabasa, "for the first time . . . a Mexican traveling in Europe . . . heard praise for his country and words of admiration for its government." The traveler, he boasted, had reason "to feel pride in his nationality."

II

It befell Díaz to preside over these decades of "progress." *Befell,* to underline, is the precise term because, given the expansion of Western capitalism and, as the stability and prosperity of Argentina, Uruguay, and Chile testify, what occurred in Mexico, more likely than not, would have taken place no matter who governed. Díaz, to his credit, did everything possible to speed up the transformation and to make the most of it. For his contemporaries, Don Porfirio was a remarkable man. In an age when men apotheosized Herbert Spencer's social Darwinism, Díaz, his admirers proclaimed, exemplified its truths; his amazing accomplishments verified the axiom of the "survival of the fittest."

A mestizo, Díaz was born in the city of Oaxaca, the son of a blacksmith, farrier, and veterinarian for the horse cavalry. His mother's father, an Asturiano, had arrived from Spain, whereas her mother, as if to balance the racial picture, was a Mixtec. Dark of skin, Díaz was of medium height, of broad shoulders, massive chest, and powerful muscles. He wore a military mustache over a mouth neither large nor small. His glance, to quote Rafael de Zayas Enríquez, a friend who knew him intimately, was "firm and a little severe when . . . speaking" and "extraordinarily penetrating" when listening. He ate sparingly, drank moderately, and exercised regularly. A family man, he led a disciplined private life and was a loyal husband to both his wives. He rose early, worked ten to twelve hours a day, and seldom stayed up late.

Gifted with a formidable common sense, he possessed a keen insight into the human character. More shrewd than intelligent, he was hardly an educated man, being the product of a mediocre provincial schooling; he had studied for the priesthood and then dropped out, opting for the law, in which he never obtained a degree. A student of average ability, according to Zayas Enríquez, "he read badly and wrote worse," knowing little about grammar and being a poor speller. He never read books, preferring to learn by listening and observing. During the American War, he enlisted in the militia of Oaxaca and, finding military life to his taste, fought under the banners of the Revolution of Ayutla, rising to the rank of captain in the army and going on to fight against the Conservatives and the French on the side of the Liberals, whose principles he espoused.

When his first wife died in 1880, Díaz, at fifty-one, married Carmen Romero Rubio, just eighteen years of age. Of criollo background, she was the daughter of Manuel Romero Rubio, of Sebastian Lerdo de Tejada's cabinet and something of a social snob. Carmen set about polishing her husband's rustic manners. Socially pretentious, she once attended a ball given by the English minister dressed as Diana the huntress and carrying bow and arrows. A devout Catholic, she loved to officiate at church functions; her husband, on the other hand, was a Mason, a grand commander for life of the national fraternity.

Don Porfirio was a born politico but not a statesman. He governed for the here and now. A military man by vocation, he employed force when necessary and could be ruthless, as he disclosed during his initial administration. *Matalos en caliente,* kill them in cold blood, he wired the governor of Veracruz, who had asked him what to do with captured rebels, a lesson not lost on potential rivals. Distrustful by nature, Díaz never believed fully in the loyalty of anyone, being especially wary of advice bestowed freely. Even Limantour, ally and confidant, thought twice before speaking out of turn. For Díaz, survival in political office required a policy of "divide and rule," inciting suspicions and antagonisms so that his collaborators would not unite against him.

Díaz served his political apprenticeship in the legislature of Oaxaca, as a deputy to Congress, governor of Oaxaca, and cabinet minister. Because of that, according to Zayas Enríquez, he held an unflattering view of men, more than once having witnessed the ugly side of human behavior. He had no use for a free press and feared public discussion of his goals and methods. When necessary, he shackled newspapers or suborned them, as he did with *El Imparcial* of Reyes Spindola, the Republic's major daily. If that failed to yield results, he shut them down.

Don Porfirio's worship of power, a "passion impossible to curb," asserted Rabasa, matched his analysis of Mexico's needs. Mexico, Díaz believed, could not afford the luxury of politics and, at the same time, enjoy economic growth. If it were to "progress," peace and order had to have priority, which explains his famous dictum *Poca política y mucha administración* (Administration before politics). To quote one of his admirers, "the political evolution" of Mexico had to await economic growth. Partly because of this, critics of Díaz baptized him a dictator; that epithet ignores his popularity, a fact of Mexican life until the turn of the century.

In politics, Díaz once asserted, "I neither love nor hate." What he referred to was his policy of conciliation, the cornerstone of his early administrations. For Mexico to have stability, political disagreements must be subordinated and unity assured around the figure of the president. To guarantee this ideal, Díaz opened public office to Juaristas, Lerdistas, old Conservatives, and allies of Maximilian. By pardoning enemies, he declared himself neither a barrier nor a danger to the aspirations of any political faction or individual, in that fashion ensuring that no one saw any advantage in removing him from power. As minister of *gobernación,* he named a general who headed the war office under Iglesias. General Ignacio Mejía, a militant Juarista and once an implacable enemy of the Porfiristas, was allowed to return to Mexico and restored to the good graces of the army. Similar good fortune awaited Romero Rubio, his future father-in-law and a vociferous Juarista. Guillermo Prieto, Ignacio Manuel Altamirano, and Ignacio Ramírez jumped aboard the Porfirista bandwagon. Manuel Payno and Manuel Dublán, both public servants of Maximilian, won forgiveness from Don Porfirio. Juárez, the president against whom he had rebelled, was also treated kindly. Díaz dedicated a stone memorial in his honor, then, in 1887, named a principal artery in Mexico City Avenida Juárez, and, ultimately, erected a national monument to him.

Díaz also made fear one of the pillars of his regime. Scholars still talk of his "military dictatorship." However, the Porfirista army was never a mighty military machine. An avid student of the turmoil of yesteryear, Don Porfirio distrusted generals, wanting, at any cost, to avoid the ubiquitous cuartelazo. He kept the army small, at the height of its glory no more than fourteen thousand men. Its *pelones,* the enlisted men, were recruited by the *leva,* the press gangs, taken from the lowest class of society, illiterate Indians and mestizos from Oaxaca or Guerrero. Poorly paid, they deserted at the first opportunity.

To assure the loyalty of his army, Don Porfirio placated its officers, promoting them on schedule, letting the generals age gracefully, and shutting his eyes to their graft and incompetence. By allowing them access to the public trough, thus making the career of the warrior monetarily attractive, Díaz won their allegiance and subservience. Money for the purchase of military hardware, as well as for the pay of *pelones,* found its way into the pockets of generals and colonels. Phantom regiments existed in the army, an institution, charged one pundit, good merely for "military parades." The rurales, the much acclaimed rural police, numbered only three thousand in 1910, too few to impose on the countryside a peace by the sword.

Conciliation signified coming to terms with the church. In his novel *Guerra de tres años,* Rabasa, a Porfirista to the core, had one of its characters exclaim, "There are no principles. If Juárez were to come back to life, he would want to die immediately." This opinion, voiced by a storekeeper, referred to the demise of the anticlerical legislation of the Reforma, so dear to Liberals. Díaz, who revered no priest, relegated the laws of the Reforma to the archives. His administration closed its eyes to religious processions, priests who wore black cassocks in public, and the emergence of convents, monasteries, and church schools, all banned by the Constitution of 1857.

Díaz never publicly proclaimed a policy of conciliation with the church. He let others do that for him, and the clergy, fully aware of the rules of the game, hailed him. In this manner, Díaz won its support, as countless sermons on his behalf in pulpits across the country illustrated. Even Archbishop Pelagio Antonio de Labastida, the bête noire of the Liberals, made his peace. As though by a miracle, segments of the clergy underwent a partial metamorphosis. Formerly avid defenders of the status quo, priests and prelates began to talk about the deplorable conditions of workers and campesinos. Influenced by the *Rerum Novarum* of Pope Leo XIII in 1891, the church sponsored a series of Catholic congresses which, between 1903 and 1913 endorsed, albeit timidly, the idea of vocational schools, debated problems of rural poverty and debt peonage, urged higher wages for urban workers, demanded a shorter workday, and called for a ban on child labor. At the same time, the Catholic congress of 1906 attributed the rise of urban crime to the "atheistic" lay school.

Occasionally, too, the winds of change blew in the political arena. In 1892, ten young deputies tried to get justices of the Supreme Court appointed for life and the office of vice-president revived. The Chamber voted its approval, but the Senate, more in touch with Díaz's thinking, rejected the legislation. Intelligent and well educated, the Científicos, the nickname bestowed on the reformers, desired, essentially, to limit the powers of the presidency, advocating a limited democracy for the affluent, the design of government in Argentina, Chile, and Uruguay. Not wanting to lose the services of such talented individuals, Díaz frequently relied on them to carry out some especially difficult task. For all intents and purposes, they were his kitchen cabinet.

One of the prominent Científicos was Francisco Bulnes. Brilliant, skeptical, and irascible, he had a political life spanning more than thirty years. Born in Mexico City in 1847, Bulnes, a mining engineer, was also a journalist and historian with a knowledge of Mexican politics second to none, having served in Congress as both a deputy and a senator. Of acerbic wit, he wrote for *La Libertad, El Siglo XIX, México Financiero,* and *La Prensa,* newspapers read widely. Along with Emilio Rabasa and Justo Sierra, two other celebrated Científicos, he thought Mexico unready for democracy, above all because of its Indians, whom he described as dullards and lazy. With *El verdadero Juárez y la verdad sobre la Intervención* and *Juárez y las revoluciones de Ayutla y la Reforma,* he created a public furor with his unrelenting censure of Juárez, whom he portrayed as weak and vacillating. Despite that, he was popular with Mexicans both as author and as speaker.

III

The Díaz era began with the Revolution of Tuxtepec, waged on behalf of the nonreelection of president and state governors. The "revolutionaries," with Díaz at their head, dallied just briefly before discarding their vows. Once the honeymoon was over, they forgot even their promise to eliminate the Senate. From 1876 to 1880, Díaz shared the spoils of office with bedfellows not always to his liking. Most of the governors were military chieftains, convinced usually of their independent right to a provincial post. That changed when Díaz returned to the National Palace in 1884. Though Díaz rarely imposed candidates on the provincial oligarchies, he made certain that they walked hand in glove with him. These oligarchies, as the behavior of the cliques in Sonora and Chihuahua demonstrates, felt no qualms about collaborating with Don Porfirio. Cooperation benefited both parties.

When his initial term of office ended in 1880, Díaz had to step down, memories of the contrived reelections of Juárez and Sebastián Lerdo de Tejada too fresh in the public mind to ignore. But Díaz planned to return to the National Palace. That meant entrusting the presidency to someone who would not plot against him. That excluded Justo Benítez, his logical successor.

A lawyer, intelligent and sophisticated, Benítez was the idol of professional politicians, who believed him to be the brains behind Díaz's first administration. Wary of him, Díaz turned instead to Manuel González, a soldier ally since the battles against the French, who he knew would step down. All the same, Benítez, like González, had served Díaz loyally.

A Liberal and a hacendado, González, ironically, had the bad luck to assume office during a heavy influx of foreign capital, years of wild speculation in commerce and real estate, when many a politico fattened his pocketbook by "lending his influence." Profligate spending drove the country to the brink of bankruptcy, compelling the González administration to reduce salaries of bureaucrats, a response guaranteed to raise the ire of the middle class. Critics say that González profited personally from the economic spree; the evidence, however, suggests that he sinned no more than scores of Liberals, the new rich of society. Still, when he died, he was able to bestow his hacienda Chapingo on a grandson; this, gossip alleged, from a man who before the Tuxtepecazo (Revolution of Textepec) "did not own enough land to fill a flowerpot." When the economic boom subsided, the euphoria vanished. In Mexico City, riots erupted, compelling the use of police to quell them, and with them came the demise of González's popularity. When Díaz returned to the National Palace, the people welcomed him.

So was launched the Porfiriato. From 1884 on, Díaz stamped Mexican politics with his own brand, embellishing his magic every four years. In 1888, Congress had amended the Constitution to permit his reelection for one term; then, in 1902, to allow for his indefinite reelection. In 1904, to ensure oligarchical control over the country's politics, Congress reestablished the office of the vice-president, the plea of the Científicos. For his vice-president, Díaz chose Ramón Corral, a cagey politico from Sonora and a favorite of the Científicos. Both were given six-year terms.

At first, few objected. Only fools and malcontents, according to current propaganda, wished a revival of the turmoil of yesteryear. To quote Sierra, "the dictatorship of a progressive man, provided that he is an honorable and intelligent administrator of the public funds," which described Díaz perfectly, "is generally of great benefit to an immature country because it preserves peace." Without strong rule, Mexicans had only a dismal future. Rule by caudillos, Sierra reflected, "may be abhorrent in theory, but theories belong to the history of political thought and not to political history." Even Altamirano cheered, paying tribute to the arrival of foreign capital which, he boasted, had guarantees.

IV

For Díaz and his Liberals, economic growth required funds and know-how. At the same time, because of Mexico's inability to repay its international obligations, Europe had shut its financial doors. For capital, Mexico had to look toward its northern neighbor, transforming itself rapidly into an economic colossus. As Limantour acknowledged, this decision, which ultimately converted Mexico into a dependency of the Yankee, carried obvious dangers; nonetheless, he helped convince his countrymen, predisposed already to believe him, that the benefits, in the form of railroads, a thriving mining sector, and industries, would contribute to the prosperity of every Mexican. Limantour and like thinkers confidently predicted that when Mexicans were better educated and wealthier they would redeem what had been sold to foreigners. On the assumption of future redemption, the Liberals invited the stranger into their home, with Díaz serving as the bountiful host.

That relationship had a rocky start. In 1876, Díaz had declared null and void concessions issued to foreigners by Lerdo de Tejada's regime, stigmatizing them as mortgages on the country's future. The Lerdistas, he exclaimed, had sold out to foreign capitalists. Fearing meddling from north of the border, his administration had endeavored to meet installments due on money owed the United States. Despite this, Washington had withheld recognition of the Díaz regime for two years.

Complementary needs, nevertheless, nurtured trade and investment. To develop its mines and build railroads, two of its principal priorities, Mexico needed foreign capital, while Americans, in the midst of their industrial revolution, required raw materials, markets, and places to invest surplus profits. By 1911, American investment was more than one billion pesos, over half of the foreign money in Mexico. The value of American investment was twice that of Mexicans and greater than the value of property held by Mexicans and Europeans together. Of the total American stake invested abroad, over a quarter was in Mexico; only Canada had a larger share of American capital. But Americans had only a fraction of their money in industry, another of Mexico's goals; plainly, Mexicans could not count on Americans to build their factories.

The United States, similarly, dominated Mexico's foreign trade; over 75 percent of it was with its northern neighbor. Exports and imports relied mainly on American markets and manufactures; earlier, nearly 60 percent of all Mexican exports had gone to Europe. By the reciprocity treaty of 1880, Mexico had admitted duty free seventy-eight articles from the United States, mostly manufactures; in return, Americans accepted twenty-eight Mexican products, mainly henequen, vanilla, coffee, and leather. The trade balance, once favoring Mexico, now tipped against it. No wonder that foreign capitalists were among Díaz's fondest admirers, some of them banding together in 1900 to urge his fifth reelection.

Foreign capital yielded multiple benefits. For the Liberals, the railroad, the principal one, was a talisman, a magical formula to unite the Republic; build a national market; increase exports; develop agriculture and cattle ranching; and settle idle lands. But, the hope of a national railway grid dropped from sight, replaced by lines that ran from the United States to Mexico City, linking, basically, Mexican mines to industry north of the border. Still, Mexico had 24,717 kilometers of railroads by 1910, the two main lines joining Mexico City to El Paso and Laredo, border towns in Texas. The railroads, whatever their purpose, awakened dormant provincial cities. When the iron horse reached Toluca, capital of Mexico State, over ten thousand people were there to greet it. Among its passengers were Justo Sierra and Vicente Riva Palacio. Toasts were drunk to the future of friendly ties with the United States, whose capitalists had financed the railroad. Similar receptions awaited the iron horse at Hermosillo, Chihuahua, and Durango, three of the jubilant cities. The arrival and departure of the trains evolved into social events, opportunities to flee the tedium of small-town life. Our "journey," said Don Trinidad Ramírez, a character in José Tomás Cuéllar's novel *Los fuereños*, "was simply marvelous. If I had told my mother that I would be able to travel from my home [to Mexico City] in just fourteen hours, she would have laughed in my face."

Nevertheless, unanticipated developments appeared. As the iron horse dominated the countryside, it drove up land prices, exacerbating an already inequitable pattern of land distribution, disrupted the economic and political balance of power in some states, and sharpened the disparity between rural and urban Mexico. It encouraged the geographical mobility of campesinos and, here and there, the release of debt peons from haciendas, and facilitated the movement of people from the less prosperous central and southern states to the north and across the border to the United States. The railroads also restored to merchants in Mexico City their monopolistic role, gone since the Bourbon reforms of the eighteenth century. Their construction squandered public funds because the Porfiristas granted exorbitant subsidies but bore two-thirds of the cost; stimulated speculation; nurtured graft off government contracts; ignited campesino unrest, in Morelos, for example; and fanned the fires of anti-Americanism, since the railroad builders kept the best jobs for themselves. The steam locomotive, in a nutshell, delivered Mexico into the American orbit.

Something similar happened to Mexico's subsoil. Until 1884, the intent of colonial legislation, which declared the subsoil a national reserve, survived the headlong rush of the Liberals to privatize property. Unhappily for Mexico's future, the administration of Manuel González, desirous of attracting foreign investment, conferred ownership of bituminous and other mineral fuels on owners of the surface property. That opened the door to foreigners who wanted to acquire Mexican mines. The law of 1909 reaffirmed that decision, labeling minerals and petroleum in the subsoil the "exclusive property" of the owner. As intended, this legislation aided the revival of mining, in the doldrums since colonial times. While still at the forefront, silver was joined by industrial metals, copper particularly, the beneficiary of the electrical age in the industrial West.

Mining tied the Mexican economy to a kite: the price fluctuations on the international market. Silver, moreover, confronted a somber future because the industrial West had gone on the gold standard. So long as the United States continued to buy silver, all was well; but that situation changed abruptly, bringing an alarming drop in the price of the white metal, the result partly of the international debacle of 1893. With the price of silver down and compelled to meet its international obligations in gold, Mexico could not make ends meet. Recovery came, but just briefly, because of the international crisis of 1900, which shook not only Mexico's economy but the confidence of Mexicans in their government.

The subsoil also denoted petroleum, the black gold to fuel the internal combustion engine of the automobile. Edward Doheny, an American, got the ball rolling in 1900, buying 450,000 acres of land in Ebano, not far from Tampico; for a part of it, he paid one dollar an acre to owners who had no idea that their subsoil hid petroleum. Eventually, Doheny's operations controlled 1.5 million acres. A bit later, the Englishman Weetman Pearson, the architect of ports on the Isthmus of Tehuantepec, discovered oil near Laguna de Tamiahua in Veracruz, marking the start of El Aguila; a cagey entrepreneur, Pearson invited the son of Díaz to sit on its board of directors. El Aguila, which marketed its gasoline under the euphoric names of Excelsior and Aurora, became a pillar of Royal Dutch Shell, while Doheny, in 1925, sold his holdings to the Standard Oil Company. By 1910, Mexico was producing thirteen million barrels of oil, mostly for export.

For a while, the surrender of Mexico's natural resources to foreigners proceeded largely unnoticed; but not for long. Even Sierra, who had earlier defended the rights of foreign capitalists, had misgivings, expressed concisely by Cuéllar in his novel *Los fuereños,* where one of his characters declares that the country had been delivered to foreigners who "will own Mexico while its offspring are left to beg for bread." By 1900, the newspaper *El Hijo de Ahuizote* featured on its front page the epigraph *México para los Mexicanos,* while Díaz's lament "Poor Mexico, so far from God and so near the United States," had become an axiom.

Limantour, likewise, had second thoughts. Troubled by the cost of imports, the drain on the treasury from payments on the foreign debt, and the flow of profits out of Mexico, he took steps to turn the situation around. Seeking to protect domestic industries against outside competition, he lobbied for a higher tariff, which reduced imports, trying, in this manner, to make Mexico less dependent on foreigners. With money from a European loan, he purchased the majority stock of the railroads in 1906, warding off the danger, Limantour affirmed, that Mexico's major transportation arteries might fall into the hands of Standard Oil and foreign banks, which would leave it at the mercy of gigantic American monopolies. However, Limantour left the operation of the railroad in foreign hands.

Between 1890 and 1910, Mexican industrialists erected an edifice of their own. By the dawn of the twentieth century, scores of industrial plants dotted the national landscape. To quote one scholar, the torch of "Mexico's industrial revolution" had been lit. Textile mills, its most significant accomplishment, manufactured cotton and woolen cloth in the corridor from Córdoba to Mexico City, particularly in Puebla and Atlixco, and in Guadalajara, Durango, Saltillo, Chihuahua, and Monterrey. Established in 1900, the Compañía Fundidora de Fierro y Acero de Mexico, a steel conglomerate that employed two thousand workers, could handle daily a thousand tons of ore; equipped with rolling mills, cranes, and locomotives, it produced finished steel. There were paper mills; one of them, the Compañía de las Fábricas de Papel de San Rafael y Anexas, in the state of Mexico, operated its own tree farms, a mechanical wood pulp plant, and railroads and generated its own electricity. The Cervecerías Moctezuma and Cuauhtémoc headed the list of breweries. The Vidriera Monterrey, a glass factory, started out making bottles for the beer industry. The Compañía Industrial Jabonera de la Laguna, with its headquarters in Gómez Palacio, Durango, ranked among the biggest soap factories in the world; its offshoot, the Compañía Nacional Mexicana de Dinamita y Explosivos, turned out dynamite and sundry explosives, including nitroglycerin. El Buen Tono and La Cigarrera Mexicana, the giants of the tobacco industry, produced annually more than six million cigarettes. Cementos Hidalgo, Cementos Cruz Azul, and Cementos Tolteca met the Republic's needs for cement. There were jute mills, meat-packing plants, and manufacturers of henequen twine. Sugar barons in Morelos planted ever larger amounts of cane and mechanized their production.

After 1890, lucrative profits from expanding markets had given merchants money to invest in industry. They were capitalists who believed in the future of the Díaz era. Many of them had been born in Europe, mostly in Spain, France, Germany, and Great Britain. But, in the provinces they were thoroughly Mexican, particularly in Monterrey, where Isaac Garza and Manuel Cantú Treviño set the pace. They organized joint-stock companies to finance and control Mexico's industrial edifice and hired salaried managers to run it. Earlier, Mexican manufacturing, with the exception of textiles, had relied on regional markets; the railroads had changed that. With a threefold increase in the labor force, Mexico had industrial workers with money to spend, which increased the size of the national market, some five million by 1910.

The heralded Industrial Revolution had major flaws. In underdeveloped Mexico, to use a modern term, advanced technology, expensive and mostly imported from Europe and the United States, underlay industrialization. Staffed by foreign technicians, it was capital intensive, a copy of its foreign counterpart, too advanced for the Mexican market and operating at less than capacity. Inefficient production led to high prices, for steel from the Fundidora Monterrey and cement, to name just two. Overproduction was endemic, making economies of scale impossible. Mexican industry proved unable to compete on the home market with imported goods, requiring tariff protection and federal subsidies to stay alive. Tariffs on cotton articles were among the highest in the world, while industrial capitalists, who enjoyed exemptions from taxes from seven to thirty years, could freely import machinery and raw materials. Hampered by high prices and the lack of a national merchant marine, Mexican industrialists were in no position to sell abroad. Compounding the problem was the fact no efforts had been made to build a capital goods industry; all machinery was purchased abroad. Meanwhile, a shortage of skilled workers hampered industry, multiplying the ills of low productivity and pushing up the cost of manufactures.

In response, Mexican entrepreneurs erected monopolies to control the market. No laws barred mergers or consolidations; to the contrary, the influence of industrialists in high government circles kept out competitors, both Mexicans and foreigners. Vertically integrated monopolies cornered the market, among them Fundidora Monterrey, the Compañía de las Fábricas de Papel de San Rafael, Vidriera Monterrey, and the Compañía Industrial Jabonera. Foreign competition, moreover, helped make monopolies almost inevitable; with a head start of half a century or more, European and American industrialists were selling their wares over the entire globe. Trying to expand its monopoly on the world market, United States Steel, for instance, even sold steel at a loss in Mexico. Despite tariffs, Mexican manufacturing was a "risky business," rewarding its patrons with surprisingly "low levels" of profits. "What Mexico built during its industrial revolution," to quote one view, "was underdeveloped industrialization." The depression of 1907, furthermore, which discouraged new investment in plants and equipment, put a stop to Mexico's industrialization.

By 1910, Mexico had an industrial labor force of almost 800,000 men and women. Nearly 18 percent of all workers, this labor bloc could be found, explained Jorge Vera Estañol, one of the sages of the Porfiriato, the length and breadth of the Republic: in the mines of Sonora, Chihuahua, Durango, Guanajuato, and Hidalgo, as well as in the coal fields of Coahuila and in the foundries of Mapimí, Velardeña, Chihuahua, Torreón, Monterrey, Matehuala, Aguascalientes, San Luis Potosí, and Teziutlán; in the fertile Laguna and around cities from Hermosillo, the desert capital of Sonora, to Jalapa, seat of the government of Veracruz; in the petroleum camps of the Huasteca, along the railway routes, and in the commercial entrepôts, especially the ports. The industrial workers, unlike the rural peon, read newspapers, joined mutual-aid societies, and knew how to unite against the employer.

The tinsel and glitter of Mexico's Gilded Age seldom improved the lot of workers. As before, they had to endure a multitude of hardships. The hours of toil were long and the wages poor. Factories opened their doors before the break of day and closed them long after dark. Textile workers, for instance, whose daily schedule was common to most industries, arrived at the mills at five or six in the morning and remained locked up until eight at night. On Saturday, the short day, workers left their job at six in the evening. They had two rest periods, one for breakfast and one for lunch. Management deducted money from their paycheck for the support of the church, for religious services and festivals; levied arbitrary fines as punishment; hired and fired at will; and held workers responsible for worn shuttles and spindles.

Workers earned the highest wages in the mines of the northern provinces, specifically Sonora, and less in the ballyhooed *industrias de transformación,* the factories and mills doing a face-lift on the economy. The invasion of village lands by hacendados, which drove a steady stream of the landless into the cities, resulted in an abundance of cheap labor for the factories and mines. Outside of mining, industrial wages never exceeded, on a national average, 59 centavos per day, just over three pesos a week. Women fared much worse. In the textile mills of the Federal District, they earned as little as 25 centavos a day, while in the mines of Sonora, less than young boys. Many of the women were no more than children, "forsaken girls spending an embittered adolescence in shops and factories." To the anger of workers, management, more likely than not, paid wages in *vales,* chits redeemable at the *tienda de raya* (the company store), notorious for selling low-grade goods at bloated prices.

Men, women, and children, the industrial labor force, spent a good part of their day toiling in sweatshops no better than the colonial *obrajes* or risking life and limb in the mines. Hardened employers showed scant regard for the safety of their workers. One mine in Pachuca suffered over six hundred accidents, a fourth of them fatal. Between 1906 and 1910, according to calculations of *El Imparcial,* five hundred men died in coal mine disasters in Coahuila. Nor did the mining moguls bestir themselves to compensate adequately the victims of accidents. More likely than not, they exhibited a "callous attitude . . . beyond belief." An author of a book on Mexico spoke of a man who had lost both legs in a mine accident; the company covered the costs of his hospitalization and gave him five pesos. Other companies paid ten to fifteen pesos for the loss of an arm or a leg, plus hospital expenses. Yet the mining barons were no more steely than railroad tycoons or textile magnates.

Over and above that, the specter of unemployment haunted the lives of workers. The jobless chart followed the ups and downs of a dependent economy, which the absence of a healthy national market aggravated. The ups and downs of the Victorian Age, the years of the Porfiriato, dealt harshly with Mexico's workers; international economic debacles were the rule, not the exception, starting with the great crash of 1873, followed by that of 1893, the downturn of 1900, and the financial panic of 1907.

Squalid living conditions were the fate of the worker and his family. Housing ranged from the caves described by an American diplomat at Monterrey to flimsy shacks in the mining camps. At Nacozari, a Phelps Dodge operation, Mexican miners resided in huts of wood, mud, or discarded sheet metal, or a combination of all three—sordid, unhygienic, and small. One of the hovels, which caught the eye of an American engineer, was of adobe with a roof of discarded "iron fire doors from an old mine, salvaged from some dump heap," whose owner had fashioned a chimney of "coffee cans telescoped one in another and raised . . . in a haphazard spiral." Openings consisted of a door and two windows, so dirty that one could not see out. At Río Blanco, a textile center, workers and their families shared wooden pavilions under sheet-metal roofs, divided into rectangular rooms each with its door and window. Julio Sesto, a Spanish poet, called the *casas de vecindad*, tenements in Mexico City, "diabolical mansions where hygienic conditions sparkle by their absence." Towns in the petroleum fields were rows of wooden shacks and open sewers, and women drew water from stagnant pools.

Given these dismal conditions, Mexicans got ill and died like flies. Between 1895 and 1911, the death rate for Mexico City was almost double that of the United States, topping that of Cairo and Madras. Workers suffered from tuberculosis, syphilis, and pellagra and from silicosis in the mines. Typhoid fever, smallpox, and intestinal disorders attacked adults and children alike. At Nacozari, health conditions were appalling even "to the most casual humanitarian," reported one American, its inhabitants living "in their own filth, horribly overcrowded," and easy prey "to disease, which would sweep through the camps like wildfire." A never-ending "procession on the road to the graveyard, in which little blue coffins of babies predominated," filled the summer months.

"He that giveth unto the poor shall not lack," runs a biblical proverb, which, sad to say, had scant credibility in the world of Mexican workers. On the contrary, they confronted the hostility not just of management but of government and the courts. Employers united early in order to resist the pleas of labor, while Don Porfirio and his cronies worshiped, in the manner of Europeans and Americans of their time, at the altar of profits; government was simply a gendarme, intervening only when labor got out of hand. Guillermo Prieto, a bellwether of the Liberals, looked upon labor as merchandise subject to the "law of supply and demand," while José López Portillo y Rojas, a leading Catholic writer of the Porfiriato, labeled labor turmoil "criminal."

Workingmen, the rulers of industry declared, could not "take the law into their own hands." Labor strikes were illegal. The *código penal* of 1872, a Liberal landmark, branded private property sacred and levied a fine or a jail sentence on anyone convicted of exerting moral or physical force to modify wages or to impede "the free exercise of industry or labor." A law in Sonora, a haven for Yankee capitalists, punished workers who joined labor unions. Article 4 of the textile codes, symbolic of management's attitude, permitted workers to complain merely in writing to the head of their department.

V

A demographic explosion accompanied progress. When Díaz entered the National Palace, he was one of 8.7 million Mexicans; when he stepped down, Mexico had over 15 million inhabitants. Of that total, one-fifth was "white," mainly of Spanish descent; mestizos made up 43 percent. The rest, 37 percent, was Indian, a figure just slightly smaller than at the close of the colonial era. The census ignored mulattoes, long ago absorbed into the general population. As statistics documented, Mexico was about as rural as always and almost as Indian.

Population growth, much of it the result of landless campesinos looking for jobs, altered the size of the cities. Mexico City grew to 471,000 inhabitants, while Guadalajara, Puebla, Guanajuato, and Querétaro, provincial citadels, enjoyed substantial increases. Along the route of the railroad, cities appeared, Nogales, on the border with Arizona, and Cananea next door, for instance; Torreón, in Coahuila; and also Nuevo Laredo and Tampico, in Tamaulipas, earlier dots on the map. By 1910, Tampico handled a bigger volume of trade than Veracruz, receiving goods from north of the border and from its hinterland for shipment abroad.

The contours of modernity modified the urban façade. After the triumph of Díaz, proclaimed Ignacio Ramírez, a secular trinity demanded fealty; the steam engine, electricity, and the mechanical printing press ushered in a transformation of urban life. From Chapala, a town on a lake in Jalisco, steamboats ferried mail, passengers, and freight to La Barca, while electric lights lit up the Plaza de Armas in Guadalajara. By 1883, Toluca basked in the glow of electricity, an innovation found ultimately in every city of the Republic. On its heels came the telegraph, an invention of unheard of importance, as well as regular mail service between urban enclaves. By 1905, hacendados in the valley of the Río de Sonora spoke to each other by telephone. From the mechanical printing press, a flood of newspapers and journals gushed forth, enlivening gossip and intellectual discourse alike.

As may be expected, Mexico City led the way into the twentieth century. What embellishments Maximilian initiated, the Paseo de la Reforma, for one, the Porfiriato finished; the Paseo, the main thoroughfare of the capital, became a copy of the Champs Elysées, replete with electric lights, trolleys on rails, and theaters and restaurants galore. Residents out for a night on the town listened to Junventino Rosas's "Sobre las olas," a favorite of Don Porfirio and a waltz in the Austrian mood, and laughed at the jokes of Ricardo Bell, an English comic. As the city grew, it engulfed towns on its outskirts such as Mixcoac, subdivided into lots for private sale at fifty-two pesos, two pesos down and the rest in monthly installments.

When the city changed, so did its architecture. Public buildings of a neo-Gothic, French-Italian flair included the Post Office, the Ministry of Communications, the Palacio de Bellas Artes, the Hall of Congress, and the penitentiary. Asphalt pavements appeared, ending the days of mud during the summer rains. In the Colonia Juárez, the rich erected mansions in the French style, especially on Calle Londres, shunting aside the reign of the flat, square, one-story home of colonial origin. To update their buildings, prelates imported Italian architects to modify the design of colonial churches, the cathedral among them. This was also when Genaro Codina composed the stirring march "Zacatecas" and when the *jarabe tapatío* was popular, on the road to becoming Mexico's national dance.

Women, too, started to feel the tides of change, especially because the expanding urban labor market opened doors to them. By 1900, industry employed over 210,000 women, many in the textile mills and cigar factories, where they labored for a third to a half of the wages paid men. Migrants from rural villages made up much of this cheap labor. In the cigar factory El Buen Tono, which produced cigars equal to the finest in Cuba, women workers, called *cigarreras,* had virtually replaced men. Only domestic work and sewing employed more women than the cigar industry.

The daughters of middle-class families found other types of employment. By the turn of the century, women made up 65 percent of all primary school teachers in the Republic, and, as clerks, secretaries, and bookkeepers, almost two thousand of them had jobs in government; only the treasury, where Limantour barred them, was bereft of women employees. Others found jobs in stores. By 1887, a woman had graduated from the medical school, and others, eventually, completed their degrees in law, dentistry, and pharmacy. In 1904, Laura N. Torres, a journalist, founded an organization to fight for the rights of women, while women professionals began publishing *La Mujer Mexicana,* a feminist monthly. Women became labor leaders, among them Carmen Huerta, a prominent workers' spokesman, and others joined mutualist societies and went out on strike alongside of men workers, especially in textiles. Meanwhile, Virginia Fábregas and María Guerrero, acclaimed actresses, performed on the stages of the Teatro Principal, Conservatorio, Arbeau, Hidalgo, Riva Palacio, and Orrin. At the Plaza de Bucareli, Lolita Pedrel and Angelita Pages, bullfighters, drew cheering audiences.

Alongside this drama, an antithetical pageant unfolded. The jobless who flocked to the cities formed a lumpen proletariat, dubbed contemptuously pelados, the inhabitants of the barrios of San Lazaro, Peralvillo, and San Antonio Tomatlán in Mexico City and similar slums in Guadalajara and Puebla. Among the poor, alcoholism ran rampant: the "evil of the century." Mexico City alone had 946 pulquerias (saloons), compared with 34 bakeries and 321 meat markets. In 1910, more than one out of three births were illegitimate, and the malady, up from 22 percent a decade before, was obviously getting worse.

José Tomás Cuéllar left a remarkable portrait of the urban middle class. What began as criollo *letrados*, an embryonic middle class at Independence, bigger and more powerful during the Reforma, blossomed during the Porfiriato. Díaz, never known for panegyrics, referred to the middle class as the bedrock of progress. Economic growth and urbanization sparked its development, converting it into a formidable sector. From it came forth the intellectuals, ever hungry for a larger slice of the national pie.

Even so, although referred to as a middle class, it lacked the credentials of a true class: a strong awareness of itself or a consciousness of its place in society. Defined by the terminology of western Europe, the Mexican middle class had not solidified. Its homage to the Protestant ethic, so characteristic of the middle class in the capitalist West, had a hollow ring. While Díaz spoke of it as the cement of Mexico's democracy and eulogized it for its dedication to hard work, reality only partly upheld his professed convictions. Middle-class Mexicans were more apt to want to rub shoulders with the rich, to copy their dress, to live in the most luxurious home their income could provide, and to emulate the life of the country squire. They lived beyond their means; rather than save for a rainy day, they mortgaged the future. In order to vacation in Acapulco or Veracruz, they went into debt and spent the rest of the year trying to make ends meet.

Mexicans pictured the middle class as a hodgepodge of groups standing between rich and poor. In *La calandria* and *Los parientes ricos,* Rafael Delgado, a provincial schoolmaster, described a middle class of the small cities, *burgueses* ruined by the Reforma on their way down and opportunists who profited from it on their way up. In his classification of the middle class, Antenor Sala, a hacendado of keen intelligence, included skilled workers, rancheros, small-business men, public and private employees, professionals, artists and artisans, small-time mine operators, and the owners of workshops and cargo or fishing boats. He calculated their number, families included, at approximately four million, over one-fourth of the Republic's population. As his definition revealed, the middle class had rural and urban roots, particularly in the northern provinces; in Sonora, made prosperous by the railroad and its mines, the population increased by 40 percent, most of which lived in small urban enclaves of over 2,500 inhabitants.

Belatedly, partisans of the Old Regime, the title conferred on the Porfiriato, set out to update more than technology and machines. For a sprinkling of individuals, wealth widened horizons and the range of concerns. A sense of social responsibility, ever so slight, crept into government circles and infected the society of the *burgueses.* Social Darwinism aside, *indianismo,* an awareness of the Indian and his past reminiscent of the thinking of Carlos de Sigüenza y Góngora and Francisco Javier Clavijero, sprouted roots. Disturbed by the neglect of the Indian and apprehensive for his survival, influential Mexicans sponsored a conference in 1908 to discuss what should be done. After much debate, the delegates, among them Francisco Belmar, chief justice of the Supreme Court, voted to organize the Sociedad Indianista Mexicana. The year before, the government had built a special school for Indians in Tepic, the first of more to come. On the outskirts of Mexico City, archaeologists labored to restore the ancient metropolis of Teotihuacán, site of the great pyramids.

Near the turn of the century, Díaz asked Justo Sierra, a former pupil of Altamirano, to transform the old Dirección de Instrucción Pública into a ministry of cabinet rank. Lamentably, it encompassed schooling merely in the Federal District and the territories. At least 80 percent of Mexico was illiterate, with only a fifth of the children of school age attending class. Figures for the countryside were appalling, with nearly total illiteracy in the Indian regions of such states as Oaxaca, Yucatán, and Chiapas. Under the guidance of Sierra, who built on earlier efforts, the number of urban primary schools more than doubled, while the number of pupils in school rose nearly fivefold. By 1907, Mexico had 9,640 primary schools. Timidly, rural schools, too, began to be built. A few states also took an interest in rural education; Zacatecas, to name one, maintained 251 rural schools and San Luis Potosí 70 of them. In Tabasco and Yucatán, *maestros ambulantes,* traveling teachers, journeyed from village to village teaching the three R's. A few states, Mexico for one, compelled hacendados to establish rural schools for the children of their peons. Both Chihuahua and Sonora, with 35 percent literacy, won national acclaim for their labors. However, the Old Regime favored higher education, spending almost twice as much on it as on primary schooling.

VI

In 1887, Ignacio Ramírez, the loquacious curmudgeon of the Reforma era, died, the burial for him held at the Masonic temple in Mexico City. Not long after, Altamirano, Prieto, Manuel Zarco, and Manuel María Zamacona followed him to the grave. They carried with them the Renacimiento of the República Restaurada, but not entirely. By providing jobs and diplomatic posts for its writers, poets, and intellectuals, the Old Regime proved a bastion of the arts. True, as the architecture of the Palacio de Bellas Artes, a pseudo-replica of Italian Renaissance, confirms, for the Porfiristas, the European, whether in poor taste or not, glittered. The literati read Victor Hugo, George Sand, Lamartine, and Chateaubriand. For Mexican *burgueses,* France, then England, set tastes. To gain the respect of the world, Mexican writers, argued critics like Victoriano Salado Alvarez, must do as the Europeans. So Florencia M. del Castillo became the "Mexican Balzac"; Cuéllar wrote a *Divine Comedy;* López Portillo y Rojas was baptized "Our Dickens"; Federico Gamboa, author of *Santa,* won the sobriquet "Zola of the Americas"; while Rafael Delgado's novels anticipated those of Benito Pérez Galdós, the Spanish genius.

Still, a better novel made its debut, a manifestation of the Porfiriato's cultural vitality. As the middle class grew, a reading public which wanted to be entertained appeared. So was born, critics say, the "true Mexican novel," with ties to such earlier ones as *El periquillo sarniento* and *Astucia,* as well as those of Altamirano and Manuel Payno. The first of them was Delgado's *La calandria.* López Portillo y Rojas, one of these new novelists, rode to fame on *La parcela*, a story describing hacienda life, according to a caustic critic, as a tourist might after a brief visit. Its heroes were the hacendados. One read these novels not as fine literature but for their *mexicanismo.* While such work was not on a par with the best of Europe, Mexicans had reason to hold their heads high. Gamboa's *Santa,* a novel in the realistic vein, went on to become a best-seller. A story of society's ills, *Santa* explored the hypocrisy of moral codes and, to the titillation of its readers, the life of whores in Mexico City. To learn about them, Gamboa, a gentleman of the old school and a diplomat, observed them in the flesh, to bestow on *Santa,* a young lady gone astray, "authenticity."

Under Don Porfirio, who knew nothing of literature, Mexico became a haven for *modernismo,* the first poetic school rooted in Spanish America. Following in the path of Rubén Darío, its Nicaraguan founder, Amado Nervo, Manuel Gutiérrez Nájera, and Salvador Díaz Mirón achieved international fame. The symbols of these effete poets were the ivory tower and the swan. Eventually, poets rejected *modernismo,* abjuring the preoccupation of Nervo with the unknown while ridiculing Gutiérrez Nájera for mourning "the solitude of the soul in pursuit of Alfred de Musset." Enríque González Martínez expressed succinctly the rejection of *modernismo* when he urged poets to "wring the neck of the swan." For intellectuals of this opinion, *modernismo* symbolized the betrayal of political commitments and an accommodation with the Old Regime.

History writing, too, discovered a new niche. An older Manuel Orozco y Berra, Luis González Obregón, and Joaquín Icazbalceta, scholars in the time-tested mold, wrote about colonial history. Vicente Riva Palacio, renowned for his role in the República Restaurada, edited *México a través de los siglos,* the first history of Mexico written from a Liberal perspective; its last volume paid tribute to Juárez. Also the author of *Martín Garatuza,* a novel exalting the Aztecs, Riva Palacio laid the cornerstone for a statue in honor of Cuauhtémoc on Paseo de la Reforma. Relying on Riva Palacio's history, Sierra wrote his famous *México: Su evolución social* and *México: Su evolución política,* in which he made the Indian past an integral part of a mestizo *patria.* In Sierra's history, Cuauhtémoc was the first of Mexico's heroes and worship of him was elevated to a cult.

With the rise of the *burguesía* and the debut of the art gallery, art was transformed into a commodity to be bought and sold. Well-off Mexicans supplied the market, their tastes shaped partly by the dictates of the Escuela Nacional de Bellas Artes, where Bernardo Couto, the art historian, eulogized Greek and Roman art. The buying public desired mainly portraits of family members: father, mother, sons, daughters, and so forth. They were pictures primarily of hacendados, merchants, *jefes políticos* and their children, and, frequently, the parish priest. Art patrons also purchased still lifes.

Just the same, a popular art, labeled primitive by some, bore fruit in the provinces. Its strongholds were Jalisco, Guanajuato, Michoacán, Durango, Puebla, and Veracruz. Cut off from the academic art of the Escuela Nacional de Bellas Artes, "primitives" employed color and form in such a fashion as to instill in their paintings a distinctively Mexican character. For all that, they were not really "primitives," if by that term is meant totally self-taught. Although of an earlier generation, José María Estrada, one of its precursors, studied at the Escuela de Bellas Artes in Guadalajara; Agustín Arrieta, at the Academia de Puebla; and Hermenegildo Bustos, the giant of this group, in the city of León. Nevertheless, many of the anonymous painters among them were surely unschooled. The "primitives" painted in oils, besides portraits and still lifes, religious scenes and retablos of pious miracles. Primarily easel artists, they also painted murals on walls, a sprinkling in pulquerias.

Bustos, who spent his entire life in Purísima del Rincón (now Purísima de Bustos), a small town in Guanajuato, exemplified the *pintura popular* of the era. He fulfilled the dream of every artist to develop a matchless style of his own. The owner of a corner store, where he made ice cream, Bustos was proud of his Indian heritage, signing his name, "I, Hermenegildo Bustos, amateur painter, Indian of this town of Purísima." In the sixteenth century, Purísima had been a *congregación de indios.* Of high cheekbones, wide forehead, long face, and sunken eyes, Bustos wore a droopy mustache and dressed in exotic, oriental clothes. Starting with his splendid self-portrait and then one of his formidable wife, Bustos put on oil and canvas the local *burgueses*, making no concessions to their vanity. He had known most of them since birth. Now they were his customers, the market he catered to; when he painted their portraits, and the retablos and religious scenes, he stamped on canvas, tin, and wall a segment of the history of Mexico.

In Mexico City, too, José María Velasco, a teacher at the Academia de San Carlos, matured into a superb painter of Mexican landscapes. A geologist and botanist, the author of a study of the flora of the Valley of Mexico, Velasco was one of the teachers of Diego Rivera, the famous muralist of the twentieth century. Employing vivid colors, Velasco painted the hinterland of Mexico City, its foliage, volcanic peaks, villages, and scenes of locomotives pulling their cars on the run to Veracruz.

Also, an art renaissance, one of the marvels of the twentieth century, was gestating. Downtown, near the Zócalo, on Calle de Santa Teresa (today Guatemala), José Guadalupe Posada, a graphic artist and master of the burlesque, worked in the print shop of Antonio Venegas. Posada's drawings, his *calaveras* (skulls), above all, encapsulated the foibles of society, dwelling mockingly on the hypocrisy of the *burguesía*. Though hailed by the man on the street, Posada died penniless and ignored by art critics, who dubbed him a cartoonist.

In Jalisco, at the same time, a dynamic school of art had taken root, most of its disciples former students of the Escuela de Bellas Artes de Guadalajara, which dated from 1817. Founded by José María Ugarte, an early painter of note, it had, in the beginning, established for itself a reputation as a center for religious art. One of Ugarte's disciples was José María Estrada, the portrait painter. Later, the Escuela of Guadalajara had broken with academic formality, what characterized the Academia de Bellas Artes in Mexico City, as the work of Estrada and Abundio Rincón, another painter of importance, denotes. Also from the Jalisco group of artists was Gerardo Murillo, a student of Felipe Castro, who painted in the tradition of Estrada and the other *costumbristas*. Murillo went on to study under José María Velasco at the Academia de San Carlos. Among the first artists to ask for walls upon which to paint murals were Murillo, Roberto Montenegro, and Jorge Enciso, all of them from the Escuela Jaliciense, the Jalisco school.

By 1903, meanwhile, Murillo had returned from a European sojourn. In San Pedro Tlaquepaque, a town on the outskirts of Guadalajara, he held an exhibit of his paintings, drawing rave reviews not just for his art but also for his lectures on the murals of the Italian Renaissance in the Sistine Chapel, which he repeated at the Escuela Nacional de Bellas Artes. His message was a simple one: Mexico needed a new art, inspired by what was native and muralist in form. Among those who listened to him were José Clemente Orozco, David Alfaro Siqueiros, and Diego Rivera, who began to look to Murillo for inspiration and guidance.

For the centennial of 1910, the architects of peace, order, and progress planned a year-long celebration to honor their accomplishments. An exhibit of Spanish art was on their agenda but nothing by Mexicans. With Murillo at their head, sixty artists, Orozco among them, went to Sierra, minister of public instruction, to protest their exclusion. Sierra gave them three thousand pesos for an exhibit of their own. "Our showing was an immense, an unexpected success," wrote Orozco. Encouraged by their triumph, Murillo and his brothers in art organized themselves into the Centro Artístico and decided, for their initial project, to paint the walls, if Sierra was willing, of the Escuela Nacional Preparatoria. Sierra approved their request. In November, lamented Orozco, "we were preparing to do the murals. On the twentieth day of that month the Revolution began. There was panic, and our prospects were ruined or postponed." The mural renaissance had to stay in the wings for ten more years.

16

DON PORFIRIO'S TESTAMENT

I

For *burgueses* of the Porfiriato, happiness was, to cite an aphorism of Jean-Jacques Rousseau's, "a good bank account, a good cook, and a good digestion." Unfortunately for them, they did not share their aspirations with everyone, and so, as befalls all things of man, the era of peace, order, and progress came to an end. Its collapse caught by surprise Mexicans and foreigners alike. The causes of this sudden and unexpected volte-face were complex and, at the same time, the logical result of the Porfiriato's successes and failures.

II

The reasons for the Porfiriato's demise begin to unfold, in a manner of speaking, in La Aduana, a mining town in Sonora, whose mayor, late in the nineteenth century, penned an anguished letter to Ramón Corral, the secretary of state in Hermosillo. He wanted money for a bigger jail, with three rooms—two for male drunks and criminals, and a third for prostitutes. If it were not built, he would take no responsibility for the immorality corrupting the town and the jail. On weekends, he complained, miners with money to spend, whores, gamblers, and criminals of varying hues came to La Aduana, to get drunk, fight with each other, fleece the unwary, and generally raise hell. The mayor's letter, a quintessential document for its time, voiced a deep concern with the changes taking place around him. The revival of mining on a grand scale in the late nineteenth century, one key to progress, unleashed disruptive forces that were turning society upside down. The mayor of La Aduana, in his own way, was responding to the breakup of a mode of life.

III

Progress, capitalist by design and surely welcomed, had, indeed, laid its hand upon the tiller. To quote Francisco I. Madero, the man destined to drive Don Porfirio into exile, "Our economic, industrial, commercial, and mining progress is undeniable." But that progress, viewed in hindsight, was, at best, ambivalent; it was not the same to all men or, worse still, a faithful lover. And rebellions, which toppled Díaz, as sages throughout the ages have admonished their disciples, originate not in the souls of people crippled by hunger and want but, to the contrary, with those who have tasted the fruits of change. The dashed hopes of a beneficent future or their abrupt loss plants its seeds. Such was the condition of Mexicans as a new century replaced the old. "In every corner of the Republic reigned prosperity and an enviable peace," reported the steel magnate Andrew Carnegie after a visit to Mexico.

Economic growth, despite its rewards, exacted a price. Its repercussions were felt even in rural Mexico. With the building of railroads, the advent of industrialization, and the trappings of a capitalist economy, the traditional way of life clashed with new ambitions and needs and, likewise, as the mayor of La Aduana's letter testified, fed fears for the future. Similarly, if industry were to prosper, a domestic market would have to grow apace or foreign markets be found; but signs indicated that the buying power of the consumer had failed to stay abreast of the ability of the manufacturer to produce, while foreign buyers did not rush to buy the goods of Mexican industry. Yet, as Andrés Molina Enríquez pointed out in his eloquent analysis of Mexico's ills, *Los grandes problemas nacionales,* only industries turning out exports profited. Two examples were tobacco and henequen. Those relying on the domestic market faltered upon arriving at a certain stage in their development. To the manufacturer, the only way to circumvent this barrier was to sell abroad. Failure to do so meant stagnation, since it was impossible to build industry on the buying power of the masses.

To make matters worse, the cyclical fluctuations of foreign markets, a result of economic currents outside the control of Mexico, made reliance on exports hazardous. This was the nature of dependency. During the bonanza years of henequen, to retell a story of Julio Sesto, the Spanish tourist and poet, a clerk counting money in a store in Mérida dropped a quarter accidentally and, seeing a janitor standing nearby, asked him to pick it up. "Bah! I don't stoop for a *pinche* quarter," he replied. After the bottom fell out of the export market for henequen, that same janitor, if he was lucky enough to have a job, labored from dawn to dusk for less than a quarter. The uneven nature of economic growth, characteristic of the society of that time, helped bring about its downfall. Reliance on the vagaries of the export market, the failure to enlarge the consumer market, and the fickleness of social change undermined the foundations of the old structure.

The regions of Mexico which enjoyed the most economic growth were its most troubled. By 1910, they had become the seedbeds of discontent and rebellion. Being swallowed into the international capitalist vortex, for the most part into the economy of the United States, split society more and exacerbated old divisions. A dependent *burguesía,* more powerful and numerous than before, was the chief beneficiary of ties with outside markets and capital but also, to some extent, industrial labor. Of like importance, the dependency relationship spurred the expansion of the middle class, part and parcel of the *burguesía* but with an agenda of its own.

Most of all, links with international markets and capital transformed the border states of the north, the focus of much anti-Díaz sentiment. The repercussions were noteworthy in Sonora, only less so in Chihuahua and Coahuila. For Sonora, where the malcontents of 1910 found eager listeners, the arrival of American capital molded a Western colonial society out of tune with its Spanish roots. It was no less colonial, just different. As Sonora's rich silver veins, bedrock of the Spanish mining economy, petered out, the old system fell apart, replaced by something different. As Eric Hobsbawm put it in his study of an earlier era, "old colonialism did not grow into new colonialism; it collapsed and was replaced by it." That description fits Sonora, where a rudimentary, silver-mining structure barely survived the first years of Independence, to be supplanted by a dynamic mining economy, mostly of industrial metals, financed and controlled by Yankee capitalists.

In Sonora, as elsewhere in the Republic, the railroad ushered in the transformation. Appearing first in 1882, it ran the length of the state by 1910, connecting the mining towns of the north with Arizona and spurring commerce. As its economy prospered, so did merchants, artisans, professionals, and rancheros. Since Sonora attracted a colony of Americans, a clash inevitably arose between them and affluent Mexicans, who gave voice to local interests.

The mining boom made Sonora the richest and most prosperous state in the Republic. Americans played the leading role in the drama, controlling an investment of $45 million, largely in mining. The axis of the ore empire was the copper bastion of Cananea. In 1910, Sonora exported ores worth 26 million pesos, three-fifths of it copper. During the boom, the population of the mining towns multiplied; Cananea led the way, growing from barely 900 inhabitants in 1900 to 25,000 in 1906. By then it was the largest city in Sonora.

The railroads also paved the way for commercial agriculture. In the farming district of southern Alamos, the population had multiplied from 43,346 in 1891 to nearly 60,000 in 1910; Navojoa, its hub on the Mayo River, had 1,334 people in 1884 and nearly 11,000 after the arrival of the Southern Pacific Railroad. On lands watered by the Mayo, hacendados planted garbanzos for export, sold to the Spanish merchants of Mazatlán, Hermosillo, and Alamos for consumption in Spain.

The American colony, a factor in Sonora's rise from rags to riches, started to grow rapidly after 1900. One of the newcomers was the Richardson Company, which, after surveying *terrenos baldíos* in the Yaqui Valley, acquired 76,000 hectares, subdividing and selling them to colonists from California. With the backing of the state's oligarchy, Mexico City granted the Richardson Company extensive water rights to the Yaqui River. The concession plunged the company and the American farmers, who cultivated fruits and vegetables, into a conflict with Mexican interests.

The ebullience of individual enterprise spilled over into the public domain. Corral and the kingpins of Sonora built roads, constructed public buildings, developed the port of Guaymas, and poured money into education. The schools offered teaching jobs to scores of future rebels, including Alvaro Obregón and Plutarco Elías Calles. Francisco C. Aguilar, though chastised for holding office for two decades, won fame for his encouragement of public schooling. In their support of education, Corral and Aguilar exceeded the call of duty; few of their companions in office acted with similar concern for education. As a result, over a third of Sonora's population could read and write, as compared with a national average of less than 15 percent.

The Yaqui question, tied intimately to the land issue, added one more twist to the tangled web of events which eventually cost Díaz his office. Through the 1870s, the Yaquis, a hardworking tribe, had cultivated the lands of their ancestors, providing also most of the workers in agriculture, as well as in mining and in the construction of the railroads. In the 1880s, their fertile lands in the Yaqui Valley drew the attention of speculators. By opening up the valleys of the Yaqui and Mayo, home of the Mayo Indians, to farmers, the railroad had added impetus to the desire to acquire their lands. Mexicans and Americans, individually or in association with surveying companies, rushed to stake their claims. By 1881, a Mexican general observed wryly, these claims, if honored, would "deprive the unfortunate Yaquis of even the means to feed themselves." To the despair of the Yaquis, the rulers of Sonora, with the connivance of Mexico City, honored these claims. As a result, a long and bloody war broke out between the Yaquis and their voracious enemies.

Quixotically, some Yaquis, the *mansos,* or domesticated ones, continued to provide most of the labor of the hacendados. Without it, their lands would have lain fallow. All the same, other Yaquis, the *broncos,* or unconquered ones, harassed the haciendas, attacking towns and destroying property. Often the same Yaquis who tilled the fields belonged to the marauding guerrillas, or lent them moral support and provided them with guns and food. Because of their tenacity, it was impossible to eliminate the guerrillas. Only the return of the lands to their rightful owners, a plea rejected by the masters of Sonora, would have restored peace.

To settle the matter once and for all, Governor Rafael Izábel launched a full-scale attack against the Yaqui in the years between 1903 and 1907. With the backing of Díaz and Corral, then in Mexico City, he brought federal troops into battle and started to deport Yaquis to the henequen plantations of Yucatán. His formula backfired; rather than bring peace, it exacerbated political rivalries in Sonora. Threatened with the loss of their workers, hacendados and American miners, who had earlier complained of Yaqui depredations, opposed Izábel's policy, charging that authorities deported both *mansos* and *broncos.* But vested interests in Hermosillo, with whom Izábal had close ties, urged him to push on, alienating, in the process, the merchants of Guaymas, gateway for the planters of the Yaqui and Mayo. Guaymas had already been hurt by the railroad, which, by destroying the monopoly of its port, favored Hermosillo, a commercial and financial depot linked with Tucson. Earlier, Yaquis had fought whites; now the campaign to exterminate them split the rulers of Sonora into warring camps.

Because Corral and Díaz stood by Izábal, his scheme ignited a clash between business and agricultural interests in Sonora and politicians in Mexico City. The Yaqui issue shattered the fragile unity of Sonora. One of the hacendados hurt by Izábal's tactics was Ramón Maytorena, sentenced to sixteen months in jail for harboring Yaquis. Not surprisingly, a member of the Maytorena family had a role in the downfall of the Díaz regime in Sonora. The hacendados had no stomach for a policy which, at their expense, provided the planters of Yucatán with cheap labor. The Yaqui wars, wrote Francisco Bulnes, cost the regime dearly, bleeding Sonora, damaging its economy, dividing its inhabitants into antagonistic camps, and driving the Yaquis and their employers into rebellion.

Chihuahua, also a hotbed of malcontents by 1910, shared a similar "progress" after the arrival of the railroad. Its prosperity, Sesto, the peripatetic Spaniard, recalled, had "astonished the natives of Mexico City who accompanied Díaz on his journey to El Paso . . . for his meeting with President Taft." From 1895 to 1909, Chihuahua enjoyed the sixth-largest rate of population increase in the country, the highest in the northern provinces. An intelligent and hardworking people inhabited the small but thriving capital city of almost forty thousand. *El Imparcial* claimed euphorically for Chihuahua "one of the brightest futures in all of the Republic."

Indeed, if official statistics merit study, Chihuahua had vaulted over the threshold of progress. The value of its mineral production had multiplied, from less than 7 million pesos in 1899 to over 23 million pesos ten years later. Its livestock industry sold annually 70,000 cattle to American buyers, and its affluent citizens consumed 2.5 million pesos worth of beef a year. Between 1902 and 1908, the value of local commerce went from 8.2 million to nearly 13 million pesos. According to tax rolls, notorious for their low assessments, private and public property in 1908 was worth almost 20 million pesos, compared with 7 million pesos in 1877. Mining production in 1898 had a value of 6.9 million pesos, and ten years later over 23 million pesos. The Guggenheim Corporation had an iron plant on the outskirts of the capital, while smaller enterprises manufactured cube sugar (*piloncillo*) and leather articles. Both Talamantes and Dolores had textile mills. The Banco Minero of Chihuahua was one of the leading provincial banks.

In Chihuahua, the elite welcomed foreign capital. As in Sonora, the lure of mining profits drew the bulk of it, either American or Anglo-American. Until approximately 1870, Mexicans controlled mining; after that, the picture changed, as more and more of the old mining camps came under foreign domination. After 1884, when the government abolished the colonial mining codes which banned the acquisition of subsoil rights, the invasion of Chihuahua accelerated. By 1910, the foreign mining barons, mostly Americans, had staked out empires. For the protection of their extraterritorial rights from Mexican intruders, they put up miles of barbwire fences and hired rifle-toting guards to patrol them, while their stores purchased and sold goods with company currency. With few exceptions, the foreign monopolists kept the door shut to Mexicans.

The mining boom attracted other entrepreneurs, almost always from north of the border. The arrival of William C. Greene, of Cananea fame, began the exploitation of the forests of the Sierra Madre Occidental. More foreigners entered Chihuahua when Governor Enrique Creel granted additional lucrative concessions. Foreigners owned the metallurgical plants of Aquiles Serdán, Parral, Villa Escobedo, San Martín, and Jiménez; the hydraulic plant on the Río Conchos; the cement factory of Ciudad Juárez; the railroads; and the natural gas plants in Chihuahua City and Ciudad Juárez. As the numbers of foreigners multiplied, so did their privileges. Four groups of American entrepreneurs acquired land kingdoms in Chihuahua: William Randolph Hearst, 3.1 million acres; the Corralitos Cattle Company and the Palomas Company, 5 million acres; and the T. O. Ranch, 2.47 million acres. Of the nearly three hundred concessions granted between 1879 and 1910, almost every one bestowed on foreigners, over two-thirds dated from the final six years.

The edifice sat on a bed of sand: its dependency on American capital and markets. Moods and economic realities on the other side of the border dictated Chihuahua's fate. During the "financial panic" of 1907 in the United States, Chihuahua was hard hit. Inhabitants of its western rim, a mining and lumbering center, bore the brunt of the crisis. Much of their fate rested with Greene, who, in Galeana and Guerrero, built sawmills, a paper manufacturing plant, and a furniture factory, invested in banking, and brought the Ferrocarril Noroeste de México to Madera, the heart of his kingdom. To develop his mining stake, the Green Gold Silver Company, he cut a road through mountains judged impenetrable to the isolated towns of Cocheño and Ocampo. The crisis of 1907 struck Greene's empire with devastating blows, leaving a shattered economy in its wake. Merchants lost their shirts while over two thousand jobless workers and their families faced starvation. To quell the cries of protest, authorities dispatched rurales.

The arrival of the railroad also upset the balance of power in Chihuahua. Until then, the inhabitants of the western district of Guerrero, rancheros and small merchants, had, more or less, run local politics. By linking the central flatlands to El Paso, the railroad opened the way for a profitable cattle industry, to the benefit of Luis Terrazas and his clan. The economic shift occurred at the expense of Ciudad Guerrero, which had lost its political leadership by 1894. With its headquarters in Ciudad Chihuahua, Terrazas and his allies, cattlemen and hacendados, sat in the driver's seat. Among the ambitions stymied was that of Abraham González, scion of a prominent family of Guerrero and, along with Pascual Orozco, who ran wagon trains between the western mining camps, one of the first to challenge Don Porfirio.

Coahuila, too, basked in the sunlight of progress, mainly thanks to the ubiquitous iron horse. The Central and the Internacional, which met at Torreón, transformed that sleepy town into a commercial entrepôt of 35,000 inhabitants. To capitalize on the cotton cultivated nearby, entrepreneurs built a textile mill and the Compañía Industrial Jabonera to produce soap and oil from its seed. Others erected a brewery and a soft-drink plant. At Río Sabinas, Americans operated the biggest coal mine in Mexico. Guayule, a bush that grew wild on the arid plains, produced rubber for markets in England, Germany, and the United States. Plants to process it sprang up, some costing as much as 500,000 pesos. Around Parras, hacendados cultivated grapes and bottled wines, which they sold in Mexico City.

The progress had a familiar ring. The American presence was ubiquitous. Of the manufactured goods purchased locally, nine out of ten came from across the border, while exports went mostly to American buyers. One company, United States Rubber, controlled the guayule industry, after cotton the second in the state. The Carbonífera del Norte, an American enterprise, owned the major coal mines; other Americans owned the railroads, the biggest investment in Coahuila. Large tracts of land were in American hands; Piedra Blanca, one of the holdings, embraced 1.2 million hectares; San José de Piedras, 460,000 hectares.

The railroad paved the road for the export of cotton to the United States and for sale to textile mills in Veracruz. That transformed the Laguna, the fertile lands watered by the Nazas, into a huge cotton plantation. In 1887, Díaz had granted the Compañía Tlahualilo, a Mexican syndicate, a concession to plant cotton and sell lands on the Nazas. When the Mexicans went bankrupt, English stockholders took over the operation. The initial success of the Tlahualilo syndicate, nonetheless, attracted scores of Mexican planters, among them Francisco Madero, father of the rebel leader of 1910. Lively quarrels over water rights soon broke out between upstream and downstream planters, with the Compañía Tlahualilo in the middle of them. The solution of Díaz, to whom the planter appealed, satisfied no one, including Madero.

IV

The Porfirista edifice had started to crumble for other reasons. A major one, ironically, was the growth of the middle class, some 8 to 10 percent of the population, 70 percent of it on the government payroll and chafing at the bit by 1900. In Sonora, for instance, middle-class dissidents attempted unsuccessfully to wrest control of the mayorship of Hermosillo from Ramón Corral's father-in-law, endorsing the son of a big landowner. As one writer phrased it, his backers represented the *clase media decente,* the middle class with proper credentials; for their campaign, they adopted the color green, immortalized by Rodolfo Campodónico in "Club Verde," a waltz which rivaled in popularity "Sobre las Olas." Barring mavericks such as Ricardo Flores Magón and his disciples, whose crusade for social justice went mostly unheeded, the middle class cared little for unorthodox formulas. The restrictions on upward mobility and the political monopoly reserved for the elite had alienated the more ambitious. Not one of the *gente decente* wanted to drop out of a middle class that had cost them so much sweat and toil to join, a fear exacerbated by the economic debacle of 1907.

Only late in the Porfiriato, when the economy had taken a downward turn, did the so-called middle class unfurl the flag of protest. Still, it wanted no truck with the radical Partido Liberal of the Flores Magón. It focused its anger not on the octogenarian Díaz but on his confederates. "Nobody," reported Rafael de Zayas Enríquez, "dreamed of the presidency, aspired to it, or conspired against it." The angry held Don Porfirio accountable for keeping in office a gang of sycophants. As late as 1909, confessed Francisco Vázquez Gómez, once personal physician to Díaz, "nobody envisaged a thorough housecleaning, merely a transitional government," dwelling rarely on "social and economic evils."

For those who vented their ire on the coterie around Díaz, the ills lay not in the system but in its administration. During three decades, a select few had shared the spoils of office and the fruits of business. Fresh blood seldom infiltrated the inner circles. In Díaz's cabinet, Ignacio Mariscal handled foreign relations for twenty years; Manuel González Cosío managed the war office for nineteen years; for nearly two decades Leandro Fernández presided over communications; and Limantour had no peers in hacienda for seventeen years. Some of the governors established records of longevity: both Francisco Cosío, in Querétaro, and Próspero Cahuantzi, of Tlaxcala, enjoyed office for twenty-six years; Alejandro Vázquez del Mercado, in Aguascalientes, and Aristeo Mercado, of Michoacán, for twenty-four years; for eighteen of them, Mucio P. Martínez and Teodoro Dehesa governed Puebla and Veracruz. Two clans, the Terrazas in Chihuahua and the triumvirate of Luis E. Torres in Sonora, monopolized politics for virtually the entire length of the Porfiriato. Yet the Mafia in power was not homogeneous: between Governor Cahuantzi, swarthy of complexion and of Indian background, and Eduardo Pankurst of Zacatecas, a light-skinned criollo type, there was a world of difference.

The political octopus had long tentacles. Between 1879 and 1911, the people of Sonora, for example, "elected" sixteen state legislatures but only infrequently new deputies to them. Vacancies occurred mainly as a result of death or promotion to higher office or, once in a lifetime, because a maverick bit the hand that fed him. The local deputies represented with equal aplomb the nine districts of the state, regardless of their place of residence. Just seventy-four individuals in thirty-two years occupied the 208 seats available in the thirteen-member legislature, elected every two years. To top that, four of the collaborators of Torres served as deputies in ten or more legislatures; eight others held the post from five to nine times; and twenty-five were "reelected" on two, three, or four occasions. Just twenty-seven deputies failed to be "reelected." During its days of mercantile and financial glory, deputies from Hermosillo dominated the legislature. Nepotism flourished. The "reelected" deputies included the brothers, cousins, and *compadres* ("godfathers") of Torres and, beyond that, his in-laws, also related to Rafael Izábel (one of the triumvirate); the in-laws of Ramón Corral (the third of the triumvirate); and cousins of Izábel.

The tentacles dug deep, gripping tightly the office of prefect, the omnipotent *jefe político* of the districts. Again, Sonora epitomized what went on. In Alamos District, it was the clan of the Salidos—Bartolome in the 1880s and later Francisco A.—who stayed in the prefect's office, more or less, from 1897 to 1909. If a Salido was not the prefect, an Almada was; Angel Almada, for example, surrendered to the victorious rebels in 1911. Vincent A. Almada was prefect of Magdalena District. Francisco M. Espino, an ally of Torres, was prefect of Magdalena from 1881 to 1883 and again in 1889, of Hermosillo in 1887, of Arizpe in 1891, and of Guaymas in 1879, 1885, and 1893–1900. He died in office. Francisco C. Aguilar, prefect of Ures, turned the post into a lifetime job, serving for twenty-one years. He died in 1906, a year after Governor Izábal replaced him; rumor had it that the cause of his death was the shame of losing his job. The next prefect, Francisco J. Telles, incidentally, relinquished the office in Ures to another Aguilar, the son of the old prefect. In Hermosillo, Francisco M. Aguilar wielded power for years; in Arizpe, Ignacio E. Elias, offspring of a noted clan, held office from 1902 to 1910.

These prefects not only enforced the peace, serving often as allies of foreign speculators, but used their office to become entrepreneurs themselves. Francisco A. Aguilar, related to the wealthy Aguilars of Guaymas, owned the biggest general stores in Ures and Hermosillo, and wheat fields and mines. So well off was he that he lent money to his district, going long periods without being repaid. Ignacio E. Elias had a flour mill, a cattle ranch, and haciendas in Arizpe. A prefect with an eye for profit, Leonardo Gámez once held a contract to supply firewood to the Creston Colorado Mining Company, an American operation, and also sold land for the railway to Estación Torres. Jacinto Padilla, a physician turned politician, bottled and sold soft drinks, while Antonio A. Martínez, prefect of Magdalena and a crony of Torres, had cattle ranches and haciendas. One prefect of Hermosillo served as the legal representative of the Hullen Mining Company.

Peace and order implied permanence for the *presidentes municipales,* the mayors. The prefects, with the approval of officials in Hermosillo, the state capital, named them though, theoretically, the people "elected" them. The *presidentes municipales* had a facility for staying on. The same names, which constituted a sort of "plutocratic royalty," surfaced again and again: Don Vicente V. Escalante in Hermosillo; Don Ignacio Almada in Alamos; Don Matias Tamayo in Ures; Doctor Prisciliano Figueroa and Don Arturo Morales in Guaymas; and José Tiburcio Otero in Huatabampo. With the exception of Morales, these gentlemen were each "reelected" ten to fifteen times. None of these luminaries lived off his salary; all had business ties.

By 1910, Mexico was governed by old men. Of the twenty-four governors, only one was under fifty years of age, and sixteen had celebrated their sixtieth birthday. The chief justice of the Supreme Court was eighty-three, and six out of ten of the Republic's judges were over seventy years of age. Men eighty and ninety years old sat in the Chamber of Deputies, while the Senate, to quote Bulnes, "housed a collection of senile mummies in a state of lingering stupor."

Bulnes aside, what galled the middle class was the absence of access to public office and, therefore, to lucrative business ventures. The evil was cliquish control of politics. The rotation of the same men in office, the denial of opportunity to others—not age—was what the ambitious resented. Writing under the pseudonym of Sancho Bola, Rabasa depicted artfully the sophistry of politics resented by the middle class, which he knew from firsthand experience. Born in 1856, he was a native of Chiapas, by trade a lawyer but by avocation a politico, serving his state in the legislature, as governor and as a senator. Arriving in Mexico City in 1886, he founded, in collaboration with

Reyes Spindola, *El Imparcial,* spokesman for the Porfiriato. In *La guerra de tres años,* Rabasa wrote about the vices and vicissitudes of provincial politicians. Employing an acerbic wit, he held up for reproach the *jefe político,* doltish and voracious; rapped the knuckles of insolent military louts; and berated the pursuit of money at the expense of everything else. He was hard on provincial venality, the world of swindlers masquerading as lawyers, irresponsible and libelous journalists, and so forth. Don Santos Camacho, the *jefe político* of Salado, wrote Rabasa in *Guerra,* "made much ado about his job," visualizing himself as the cacique of his *jefatura* (district), with "the right to call the tune and compel everyone to obey," unable to conceive of authority in any other way. "But, just the same, he was a Liberal, par excellence."

To the ultimate sorrow of Don Porfirio, the upsurge of the economy failed to match the numerical explosion as well as the aspirations of the *gente de medio pelo,* a pejorative term for the middle class. The drain on the federal budget occasioned by salaries of public employees compelled Limantour to limit their number and, eventually, to reduce their paycheck. These austerity measures aggravated the discontent of the middle class, made more acute by the financial debacle of 1907. To complicate the situation, there was almost no turnover in jobs, because, in the absence of any retirement system, the aged and the infirm held on till death.

The list of job hunters took in the ubiquitous *licenciado* (lawyer), engineers, architects, agronomists, physicians, writers, and poets. Schoolteachers, whose ranks multiplied dramatically during the early years of the twentieth century, were an especially troubled lot. Poorly paid, they eked out a paltry existence. With the possible exception of *licenciados,* no other group contributed a bigger number of rebel chieftains and designers of a *plan*, the justification for shouldering arms. When the Díaz regime put learning at the disposal of the lower middle class, but denied it commensurate rewards and opportunities for advancement, it signed its death warrant.

Especially worrisome were the privileges showered on foreigners. Nationalism, a telling factor in the rebellion of 1910, contained a logical but striking paradox. Mexico won acclaim in the Western world, as Bulnes warned cogently, because of foreign investments and markets. Eventually, Mexicans denied a place at the banquet table came to place the blame for their exclusion on their guests. Their bitterness sparked a wave of xenophobia which colored the twilight years of the Old Regime and set the stage for rebellion. Nationalist firebrands, predominantly from the middle class, accused Díaz of betraying Mexico to foreigners, most of them Americans, the ugly neighbor next door.

From the cherished dream of ridding the country of alien potentates surfaced a strident cry of *México para los Mexicanos*. Although a twentieth-century crusade, it was an old gospel. In its origins, the rebellion of 1910, wrote Bulnes, "had a markedly Boxer character . . . directed primarily against the influence, prestige, and interests of the United States." Political attacks on the Old Regime implied censure of its investment policies for foreigners. The rejection of Díaz, to paraphrase Luis Cabrera, a politico from the middle class, embodied an angry denunciation of the system of privileges, the juiciest and best reserved for foreigners. From the beginning, the battle against the Old Regime and that against foreign domination were one and the same.

The outcry against Yankees and other foreigners gained wide popularity. The man in the street, who gave an enthusiastic hearing to condemnations of Uncle Sam, had seldom echoed the elite's adulation of the foreigner. For too long, in his opinion, official favors had fallen on intimates of Díaz and on outsiders. As one observer commented on the nature of Yankees, "At the start, they were few and useful; but, when they came in droves, with every honest one of them, a trainload of rascals arrived boasting of talent and money and claiming to speak for big investors but who, in the long run, were just scoundrels in frock coats." As Ignacio Bonillas, the sole Mexican mining engineer in Sonora, put it, "Their word must be taken with a grain of salt." By 1910, according to *El Tiempo*, the middle class was "solidly anti-American."

Unquestionably, Don Porfirio lived to regret whatever faith he conferred on American capitalists. Stung by the charges of treason hurled at him by nationalists, the old warrior endeavored until his death to vindicate himself. "I was never," he told an Argentine reporter who interviewed him in exile, "a darling of the Yankee." To the contrary, his policies had cut short the desire by Americans to dominate Mexico. "That desire," he continued, "is more than enough to justify fears for the future of my country."

V

Labor, too, had a hand in the downfall of the Porfiriato. Until 1900, industrial workers benefited from a slight increase in real wages. However, between 1891 and 1908, food prices rose alarmingly, with markups for corn, beans, and wheat, staples of the diet. That, plus the drop in the value of silver and the crisis of 1907, wiped out their gains.

By the turn of the century, labor had started to fend for itself. Mutual-aid societies, which "buried the dead and cured the sick," met with considerable success. Sadly, the Gran Círculo de Obreros, the first of the labor organizations, which appeared in the textile industry, split into warring camps, with one answering the siren call of Díaz. Two of its messiahs and the editors of *El Socialista*, a labor journal, allowed themselves to be "elected" to Congress, setting an odious precedent for the future. However, other labor groups, to the shock of the Liberals, adopted anarchist slogans and doctrines.

Anarchism infiltrated labor's ranks by way of the French thinker, Pierre Joseph Proudhon, whose book *What Is Property?* Mexicans read avidly. Also from France appeared the work of Elisée Reclus, *Evolution, Revolution, and the Anarchist Ideal*, followed by the writings of Pyotr A. Kropotkin, the Russian revolutionary, and Mikhail Bakunin, the Russian anarchist. From their wisdom, Mexicans learned that man is by nature good; but institutions, primarily the state and private property, corrupted, while industrial civilization blocked man's aspirations and converted him into a slave of the machine.

Unexpectedly, Americans, too, planted the seeds of the labor union in Mexico. The railroads employed American workers affiliated with labor organizations across the border, specifically the Knights of Labor and the Industrial Workers of the World. Imitating the Americans, Mexicans began to organize brotherhoods. Their initial effort, the Sociedad de Ferrocarrileros Mexicanos, took root in 1887 in Nuevo Laredo, a border town. One year later, the Orden Suprema de Empleados del Ferrocarril, an early victim of Porfirista cupidity, appeared; then followed the Confederación de Sociedades Ferrocarrileras de la República Mexicana, while workers in Puebla founded the Unión de Mecánicos Mexicanos. As these efforts testify, Mexican workers were developing what Marx baptized a class conscience.

The tug-of-war between Mexican workers and their foreign bosses intensified the sense of "class struggle." Responding to reductions in jobs and the lowering of wages, Mexicans unfurled the banner of the wildcat strike. As early as 1889, they had walked off the job at Trinidad, an isolated mining camp in the mountains of southern Sonora run by Englishmen; in 1894, unemployed workers, victims of international hard times, rioted in Torreón, compelling the ayuntamiento to provide temporary jobs. Strikes flared in San Luis Potosí in 1903, and then in Nuevo León. In 1906, in the railway shops of Aguascalientes, Mexicans left their jobs to vent their anger at the dismissal of one of their leaders and the inflated pay of Americans. That same year, three hundred workers went on strike in the shops of the Ferrocarril Central Mexicano in Chihuahua over the issue of equal pay for Mexicans and recognition of the Unión de Mecánicos y Maquinistas. The strike paralyzed the cities of San Luis Potosí, Torreón, Monterrey, and Aguascalientes. The year before, in Cárdenas, a railway hub in San Luis Potosí, a pitched battle between American and Mexican railroad workers left eighteen dead. Also, workers on the railroads had organized the Gran Liga de Ferricarrileros Mexicanos, demanding that Mexicans run the railroads; fifteen thousand railroad workers had joined it by 1908.

Other Mexicans had emulated the railroaders. In Guadalajara, the printers formed a union. The textile workers of Puebla, Veracruz, and Tlaxcala, after establishing labor cells in each of the states, got together in the Gran Círculo de Obreros Libres, a name chosen out of a desire to identify with the earlier labor body; branches were organized in Oaxaca, Querétaro, Jalisco, Hidalgo, and Puebla. The Liga Obrera made its headquarters in Mexico City, while the miners of Coahuila formed the Unión Minera Mexicana and the workers of Torreón the Confederación del Trabajo.

Not to be outdone, the Catholic church developed an interest in labor matters, encouraged by the papal encyclical of 1891. The Obreros Guadalupanos, Catholic laymen, set out to organize Catholic unions in the textile mills, while priests attempted to unite workers in the Unión de Obreros Católicos. By 1911, the Confederación Católica Obrera claimed forty-six *círculos obreros* with over twelve thousand members. According to prelates, the Catholic unions shielded workers from the pitfalls of socialism and the dangers of radical trade unions and taught them the error of class conflict.

Management, just the same, refused to deal with any labor union, Catholic or not. To retaliate, workers employed the wildcat strike, approximately 250 times from 1881 to 1911. Of the sundry strikes, three set the stage for the downfall of Díaz. The north hosted two: the violence at Cananea, Sonora's copper kingdom, in 1906 and the railroad walkout of 1908. The other occurred at the textile mills at Río Blanco, in Veracruz. The disputes reveal much about the nature of labor unrest and the industrial sector of the economy. At Cananea, the strike halted operations in the biggest mining hub of the Republic; at Río Blanco, the strike closed the doors on the largest textile center; the railroads, the stage for the third of them, were the key to the Republic's economic well-being.

The strikes had common threads. Declining exports linked two of them. Copper and the railroad running from San Luis Potosí to Texas, where the strike erupted, needed foreign customers. The financial debacle of 1907, felt earlier in Mexico, hurt copper and the transport industry. On the railroads, the lag in business kept wages low in the face of the spiraling cost of living and increased competition for jobs between Mexicans and foreigners. Fear and envy of foreigners also played a role. Price gouging by the French owner of the *tienda de raya* lit the fuse at Río Blanco, mills owned by Frenchmen who paid foreign workers higher wages. Foreign control of the best jobs as well as better wages applied the torch on the railroads. At Cananea, Greene paid his compatriots five gold pesos for a day's labor but Mexicans less than half of that. The Mexicans asked for equal wages, access to better jobs, an eight-hour day, and the dismissal of two arbitrary American foremen. Before the strike subsided, half a dozen Americans died, while rurales, with the aid of Arizona rangers from across the border who arrived at the behest of Governor Izábal, killed thirty Mexican miners, an act that raised a public furor in the Republic. At Río Blanco, where soldiers also shot strikers, Díaz, at the request of the textile workers, who mistakenly looked to him for help, arbitrated the dispute. His dictum, which favored management, offered merely skimpy concessions to labor. Political dissidents uncovered fertile soil to exploit in labor's ranks.

The middle class led the movement to dump Díaz, but, as one prominent rebel acknowledged, it inherited its strength from labor.

VI

On agrarian questions, the Liberals of Juárez and Díaz thought alike. Their tonic for agriculture was to "privatize" the land. Rhetoric about preference for small farmers aside, they prized efficiency and productivity, though that helped concentrate the lands in the hands of a minority. This attitude was hardly novel, dating from the dismantling of colonial legislation safeguarding the Indian ejido from rapacious hacendados and rancheros. The land rulings of the Reforma merely confirmed this trend. By 1900, the hacendados, their numbers fortified by foreigners, were a bulwark of the Porfiriato. Americans, alone, owned a hundred million acres of valuable agricultural, timber, cattle, and mining real estate; the newspaper publisher William Randolph Hearst, one of them, had title to eight million acres of land.

All of this, according to contemporary wisdom, was in the name of progress. The Indian had not held up his end of the bargain. His nature, specifically his attachment to the communal ejido, as Rabasa maintained, blocked individualism and personal ambitions, the bedrock of the Liberal creed, making the Indian lazy and little inclined to cultivate his parcel of land. The Indian must not be allowed to stifle the development of agriculture.

Equally axiomatic, Mexico had to attract colonists from Europe, as one Científico pontificated, "so as to obtain a cross with the indigenous race." Only European blood, he insisted, could "raise the level of civilization" or keep it "from sinking." What he meant, of course, was that Mexico must "whiten" its skin, become more European and less Indian, lest progress be shut out. To lure European colonists, as well as encourage hardworking and ambitious mestizos to take up farming, Mexico had to hold out the promise of land, whatever the cost to the Indian ejido.

Putting their views into practice, the Liberals, in December 1893, approved the Ley de Terrenos Baldíos, updating the legislation of 1863. To attract European in-migrants and open lands to Mexicans, the law encouraged individuals to denounce idle lands. Merchants, hacendados, politicos, real estate speculators, and foreign mining prospectors formed surveying companies mainly because the law allowed them to keep one-third of the land mapped out. The government, in theory, sold the rest to private buyers. Legislation passed in 1894 reinforced this policy.

Whatever the intent of the lawmakers, the results, as before, were lamentable. Few Europeans arrived, and those who did settled in the cities, usually as merchants. To the delight of the architects of the legislation, however, private individuals gobbled up the idle lands. And, because of the bad faith of the surveyors and the shoddy methods employed, the idle lands included countless ejidos, although their exact number remains terra incognita. In less than a decade, over 38 million hectares were mapped out; of that total, the government kept for sale slightly more than 12 million hectares; private individuals kept the rest. As a result, the Indian ejido was reduced mostly to marginal lands unfit for agriculture, usually in central Mexico or confined to states such as Oaxaca where, for reasons of soil and economics, the big hacienda stayed on the fringes. By 1910, the Porfiristas had largely accomplished what criollo hacendados and mestizo rancheros had attempted to do with the ejido after Independence and during the Reforma.

Of the seven states most exploited by the surveying companies, five were in the north, none with big Indian populations. More than 3 million hectares were given away or sold for a pittance in Chihuahua and Sonora; Sinaloa lost almost 2 million hectares; while a tiny clique acquired over 1.3 million hectares in Coahuila and Durango. In Chihuahua, nineteen latifundios encompassed over 100,000 hectares, while twelve ranged in size from 40,000 to 100,000 hectares. Seventeen hacendados owned over two-fifths of Chihuahua, virtually all of the land useful for agriculture or cattle. Luis Terrazas, the mogul of the landlords, had two sons, Juan and Alberto, who owned haciendas of over 200,000 hectares. Enríque Creel, who married into the Terrazas family, was master of over 433,000 hectares. By 1900, perhaps 82 percent of the country's campesinos lacked land; on the other hand, 1 percent of the population owned 97 percent of the fertile land. Alongside of them were 400,000 rancheros or small farmers, almost always lacking tools, water, and fertilizers to plant their marginal lands.

The peon, who supplied the hacienda labor, eked out a Spartan existence. Whether in a free village or *acasillado* on hacienda lands, he was low man on the totem pole. His exploitation was as manifest as the scandalous absence of justice for him in the courts. In the valley of Toluca, for example, a peon earned a *real y medio*, less than twenty-five centavos, for a day's work, not enough to sustain him and his family. At times, wages were higher, especially in the north, but never good. At the end of the week, Gregorio López y Fuentes alleged in his novel, *El indio*, the wages earned did not buy "unbleached muslin to make pants and shirts." Here and there, a remorseful public official endeavored to make amends; on two occasions, Celso Vicencio, governor of Mexico State, purchased lands from the hacienda El Mayorazgo for resale at cost in small parcels. All the same, rural Mexicans, by and large, were badly paid, poorly fed, ill housed, and condemned to an early death because of disease and malnutrition.

The exploitation of campesinos, as well as the growth of private property, modernized only here and there (the valley of the Río Sonora, for instance) the traditional hacienda. In much of the countryside, machinery and new techniques made their appearance belatedly. Despite an increase in the population, Mexico harvested more corn and beans in 1867 than in 1910. Although overwhelmingly rural, Mexico had to import food. Population growth, moreover, had intensified the struggle for land.

Not surprisingly, the history of the Porfiriato includes a record of rural rebellions. Revolts flared in 1879, 1882, and 1905 in San Luis Potosí. The theft of pueblo lands sparked uprisings in Quintana Roo in 1891 and 1892 and in Veracruz in 1906. Yaquis and Mayos of Sonora and the Maya of Yucatán died fighting for their lands. The novelist Heriberto Frías left for posterity the gallant story of Tomóchic in Chihuahua, a struggle pitting the poor against Díaz's soldiers. An army lieutenant, he was ordered north to help quell the uprising, then was cashiered from the army for publishing *Tomóchic*, a novel sympathetic to the underdogs.

A wide gulf, all the same, separated the traditional hacienda from the commercial ones. Far-reaching steps had been taken to encourage the cultivation of crops for export, mostly for industrial processing, peanuts, flax, sesame, and cotton, for example, for the manufacture of oils or soap. The production of cotton in La Laguna had doubled, while Mexico ranked among the major exporters of henequen. Sugar, too, enjoyed a bonanza in Morelos, and prospered in Veracruz and Michoacán. Tobacco and coffee were sold abroad, as well as guayule, a native rubber plant, principally from Coahuila, Chihuahua, Durango, and Zacatecas. Hacendados in the Mayo Valley of Sonora shipped garbanzos to Spain and stockmen from Chihuahua and Sonora cattle across the border. Their sale rewarded hacendados handsomely, but, at the same time, their cultivation in place of corn, rice, and beans, far less profitable, exacerbated food shortages. No balanced assessment of the hacienda can ignore this side.

Most attempts to explain why Mexicans rebelled in 1910 point an accusing finger at the "agrarian question." The landless and their champions, the enemies of the octopus-like hacienda, kindled the armed protest. However, as an embittered but sagacious Limantour recalled from exile in Paris, the character of the notorious "agrarian question" underwent a transformation in retrospect. The old Porfirista had ample reason to complain. To credit the discontent of the landless for the rebellion simplifies, if not distorts, the nature of the problem. As Limantour observed, to argue from hindsight that "popular agitation for land and water ignited the revolution . . . falsifies intentionally the facts on behalf of a cause that either did not exist or had begun to take shape only vaguely." Bulnes phrased it succinctly. Long before Madero challenged Don Porfirio, apostles of agrarian reform had called the country to arms; yet its proponents, the Magonistas, only got themselves jailed in the United States. The landless of Coahuila and Chihuahua failed to answer their call. A few months later, nonetheless, Madero, no arch-enemy of hacendados, uncovered fervent rebels in the northern provinces. If the hunger for land had put the match to the tinderbox, asked Bulnes, why had northerners not rushed to enlist in the ranks of the Magonistas? Similarly, the tragic course of the rebellion records the death of apostles of agrarian reform at the hands of their companions in arms.

Novelists, artists, and historians have depicted vividly the plight of the campesino. Still, it is risky to conclude that rural neglect and the exploitation of the poor spawned the rebellion. That they encouraged discontent requires no documentation. But at what point and for what reason they encouraged campesinos to take up arms is another matter. Despite their earlier protests, the most persecuted, the campesinos of rural Mexico, neither plotted nor spearheaded the rebellion. Quite the contrary, the rebellion fared poorly where the peon was most exploited: in the Valle Nacional of Oaxaca, Tabasco, Campeche, Yucatán, and Chiapas. Only in Yucatán did rebels uncover somewhat fertile soil. In Chiapas, with one of the most abominable records of man's inhumanity to man, rebel propaganda fell mostly on deaf ears.

In central Mexico, for instance, a region with vast populations of peons, no early outburst of rebel activity occurred—outside of tiny Morelos, southern Puebla, the state of Mexico, and a slice of Hidalgo. This region took in the largest number of ejidos, as well as the biggest share of the Republic's haciendas, suggesting that campesinos tilling both their land and that of the neighboring hacienda had come to terms with the modus vivendi. In some instances, *peones acasillados* even took up arms to defend haciendas from rebel attacks. Nor did regions with large numbers of rancheros—Jalisco, Michoacán, and Guanajuato, for example—rush to forsake the Porfiristas. That honor befell Coahuila, Chihuahua, and Sonora, none with large numbers of hacienda peons or rural wage workers.

To many scholars, the numerical multiplication of the haciendas from 1877 to 1910 verifies the relationship between agrarian unrest and the coming of the rebellion. In that time span, they increased from 5,869 to 8,431. Nevertheless, their numerical importance, compared with the growth of other rural units, declined from 21 percent to 12 percent of the total. Similarly, ranchos increased from 14,705 to 48,633. While the hacienda and its expansion figure among the causes of the rebellion, they do not alone explain its coming.

Rural maladies, which statistics easily document, were endemic and complex; the Porfirista epoch exacerbated them but did not introduce them. What, then, brought the "agrarian question" to a head? The evidence, to begin, does not support the theory of a troubled conscience. Not until late 1914 did the future leaders of Mexico embrace the doctrine of land reform. Before that, only José Wistano Orozco, who published in 1895 his monumental *Legislación y jurisprudencia sobre terrenos baldíos*, and his disciple Andrés Molina Enríquez, author of the classic *Los grandes problemas nacionales,* which saw the light of day years later, as well as three church *congresos agrícolas*, which bemoaned the plight of campesinos, especially Indians, took the trouble to probe the social implications of rural problems. Both authors were lawyers and small-town magistrates, while Molina Enríquez was a positivist and an admirer of Herbert Spencer. Orozco called attention to the inefficiency of the haciendas and to the fact that they exploited the poor, and he spoke optimistically of small property, which he believed more productive. The initial Plan del Partido Liberal, published in 1906, urged merely the recovery of uncultivated lands and an end to the alienation of the public domain.

More than likely, the snowballing awareness of rural problems developed from a concern with the low productivity of agriculture. For twenty years, Mexico had imported corn and wheat from Argentina and the United States. From the perspective of Bulnes and the Centíficos, this fact documented the inability of Mexico to feed itself; others placed the blame on the hacienda system. Reliance on imports, moreover, worsened during the final years of the Díaz regime, bringing about rising public expenditures on food. Clearly, something was wrong with the agricultural system.

That debate heated up in 1907, well nigh by accident. Tláloc, the flighty deity, forgot to water the lands of his worshipers. Droughts, which had already damaged the crops of two previous years, struck with devastating fury and continued to wreak havoc in the countryside until 1910. One of the regions hardest hit was the Bajío, the Republic's breadbasket; by 1909, the droughts, exacerbated by cold weather, had driven authorities in the Bajío to buy corn for sale to the starving poor.

The disaster did not spare the northern provinces. In Chihuahua, the last plentiful rains fell in 1906; by May of the next year, *El Imparcial* had begun to report news of an "alarming drought with terrible consequences in nearly the entire state." The drought lingered on through 1908 and into 1909, damaging severely the wheat crop and "leaving the countryside parched and dry, without a blade of grass for the cattle to feed on." By April, the livestock industry, a leading source of Chihuahua's wealth, confronted a "crisis of major proportions." One apocryphal story sums up the severity of the situation. In Miñaca, a town in the district of Guerrero, saloons, faced with a grave shortage of water, put up the following sign: "whiskey *solo*, twenty centavos; *con agua*, fifty centavos."

The fickle hand of Mother Nature punished unevenly. The droughts crippled mostly rancheros, tenant farmers, and sharecroppers, who depended on Tláloc to water their fields. Few of them cultivated irrigated lands. Rancheros and *medieros,* the tenant farmers or sharecroppers, blamed their plight on the hacendados who denied them irrigated lands. Shortages of corn and wheat reflected the predicament of *medieros* and rancheros. By 1910, as Molina Enríquez explained, they harvested the bulk of the grains for sale on local markets, though the haciendas occupied nine-tenths of the fertile lands. Grain shortages, therefore, occurred at the expense of dirt farmers; without irrigated lands, they had to gamble on the weather. The droughts penalized them, not the hacendados who relied on irrigation to cultivate their lands. To the contrary, hacendados profited during years of scarcity, selling their crops at inflated prices.

Harvests in short supply meant bad news for consumers. The sharp rise in the cost of foodstuffs, moreover, coincided with the financial collapse of 1907. By closing down markets abroad for Mexican ores, the crisis cut national revenue and reduced the buying power of the peso. The disparity between income and the cost of living, aggravated by the agricultural debacle, brought loud complaints from cities and towns, from Hermosillo and Guaymas in the northwest, across the expanse of the border communities, and south to Mexico City. Everyone suffered, but some more than others, with the middle class and the industrial workers carrying the brunt of the burden. Much of the middle class, to cite *El Imparcial*, had not enjoyed a raise in salary for twenty years.

Approximately 3.1 million Mexicans made their living from the land. *Peones acasillados* spent their entire lives under the tutelage of the hacendado who, in one way or another, took care of them, with varying degrees of benevolence. Other campesinos tilled small plots of their own, or those of their pueblo. Not infrequently, both scratched out a meager existence; to feed their families, they needed jobs on the neighboring hacienda for at least a part of each year. At the same time, the hacienda's monopoly of the land, plus the increase in the rural population, multiplied the landless proletariat, employed seasonally by the hacendado. The hacendado, however, could not provide either jobs for the entire year or decent wages. On the average, he paid twenty-five centavos for a day's work, but only for approximately half of the year. At best, he employed workers for two months to plant the crop, for another two to thin and weed it, and perhaps for an additional two to harvest it. The landless in rural Mexico, therefore, had limited alternatives.

The focus of the protest in the countryside did not arise from *peones acasillados*, often thought to be the worst off. On the contrary, it came from landless workers but, for all that, the more able and aggressive of the rural sector, the tens of thousands unwilling to spend their lives on haciendas. This sector, rural wageworkers, often jobless and without alternatives, grew dramatically before 1910. From this sector came the men who, after the call to arms, enlisted in the rebel armies. The *peones acasillados* often watched the rebellion unfold from afar.

Just the same, no one denies that alienation of the land spurred the gestation of rebellion, as the example of Morelos, a tiny state victimized by voracious sugar planters, documents. Isolated from central Mexico by towering mountains, Morelos, home of sugar since colonial times, had for centuries scarcely changed. With only a small market to supply, the planters had worked out a fragile peace with neighboring villages. Although not forgotten, the theft of village lands was a matter of historical record. Scores of villages still farmed their own land. The arrival of the railroad in Cuautla and Yautepec upset that truce. For the first time, planters dreamed of a national market for their sugar, even of foreign customers. When the Spanish-American War disrupted the Cuban sugar industry, which partially supplied the Mexican home market, the planters of Morelos rushed to acquire its customers. They built huge mills and equipped them with the latest machinery. Hungry mills and bigger markets called for additional lands on which to plant cane, for more irrigation water, and for fresh supplies of cheap labor. The "race was on to grab land, water, and labor."

Land thefts became a major business. As villages succumbed to the hacendados, they became, for all intents and purposes, company towns. As in the mining camps of Sonora, their owners ruled the lives of their inhabitants, gave the *tienda de raya* a monopoly, and meted out justice as they saw fit. The haphazard exploitation of former years turned into the systematic oppression of the Gilded Age factory. With the help of authorities in Mexico City, and the complicity of local judges, the planters made themselves masters of Morelos.

More and more villages lost their lands, transforming their inhabitants into wageworkers on plantations. Wages kept low by the demands of cheap sugar and the proclivities of planters for bigger profits exacerbated the predicament of the workers. It mattered little that big agriculture had brought to Morelos labor-saving machinery, a profitable trade, and even a cultural renaissance. In 1909, the planters elected Pablo Escandón, one of their own, governor of Morelos. Patricio Leyva, the defeated candidate, according to *El Imparcial*, had promised to return the stolen lands to their rightful owners.

VII

One event, as so often happens, ignited the fuse of rebellion. The financial crisis of 1907, which marked the swan song of prosperity, revealed flaws in Mexico's economic and social fabric and became the watershed of rebellion. Until the depression paralyzed mining, commerce, and industry, the people paid homage to the Mexican success story; with its onset, even disciples of the Old Regime began to listen to the disciples of change.

For the beneficiaries of the years of progress, the depression dashed hopes of greater things to come, lowering expectations and shutting down the gates to upward social mobility. The middle class was hardest hit. *Licenciados*, physicians, engineers, bureaucrats, teachers, and small merchants saw their dreams vanish in the wake of the disaster. Unemployment, poor wages, and a sharp rise in the cost of living aggravated the already difficult plight of workers in mines, railroads, and industry. Foreign-owned corporations cut wages and jobs; small merchants went out of business. *El Imparcial*, previously renowned for its panegyrics on the Mexican miracle, increasingly featured stories on the bankruptcies of commercial houses. Ironically, the tide of rebellion swept Díaz out of office as the depression receded; Mexico had a healthier balance of trade in 1911 than a year earlier.

The disaster had no single cause. Multiple ills had sapped the economy of its vigor. The financial panic of 1907 headed the list because, for all intents and purposes, the United States determined the welfare of the Mexican economy. Proximity to the northern neighbor, helped along by the railroad network and, above all, heavy investments of American capital, had transformed Mexico into a tributary of the United States. The crisis, Don Porfirio informed Congress, by reducing the value of Mexico's exports, had rocked the foundations of its prosperity.

His message had special relevance in the northern provinces, since their economies depended entirely on their customers across the border. The railroad carried coppper northward from Sonora for the industrial northeast; cattle from Chihuahua for the Kansas City stockyards, and ores too; and cotton and guayule from Coahuila. Falling prices hurt large sectors of these northern states. The drop in the price of cotton, for instance, cut into the income of planters in Coahuila, among them the Maderos, and left unemployment in its wake. Plummeting prices for mineral ores hurt the national economy. The misfortunes of silver, Mexico's venerable export, antedated the depression of 1907; the specter of low prices for the white metal haunted the Díaz regime. When the bottom dropped out of the copper market, the mining industry suffered a staggering blow. As Greene shut down his mines in Cananea, the jobless filled its streets. Once the biggest city in Sonora, Cananea lost two-fifths of its inhabitants.

To rub salt into the wound, the depression touched off a banking panic. Prior to 1907, upward of fifty million pesos entered Mexico annually. When the financial debacle engulfed the United States, the principal source for outside funds, Mexico had no one to turn to for money to shore up its economy. With their capital tied up in long-term loans, usually to hacendados, Mexican banks could not come to the rescue of merchants, businessmen, shopkeepers, rancheros, and the hacendados themselves. Debtors who, having borrowed large sums of money from the banks, could not repay it were partly responsible for the banking crisis. The shortage of loans punished chiefly the small entrepreneur. On the heels of this came an epidemic of bank failures, most of them accompanied by charges of mismanagement and wrongdoing. Even the

Banco Nacional de México, according to Bulnes, had "water in its wine barrels."

Such a fate befell Yucatán, home of the henequen tycoons. In the summer of 1907, Mexicans, to their astonishment, learned that the financial house of Eusebio Escalante Peón, Yucatán's leading business, was bankrupt. Behind the debacle lay the story of henequen, the lifeblood of the province. From 1898 to 1902, the ancient land of the Maya had enjoyed a boom of which not even the boldest of planters had dared to dream. But a slow decline set in; by 1910, the planters, though able to produce over 30,000 more bales of henequen than in 1902, sold them for less than half of their value nearly a decade before. When Díaz fled Mexico, 170,000 unsold bales lay rotting in the port of Progreso because American buyers had no need for them.

The prosperity of Yucatán had rested mostly on credit. The buying and selling, the imports of machinery as well as luxury articles, the expansion of commerce, and the bank loans presupposed ever widening markets abroad for henequen. It was an era of frenzied speculation in haciendas and urban real estate at inflated prices. To increase their profits, bank directors gambled their reserves on spurious investments and rode the crest of the wave of speculation. By 1907, the landed barons of Yucatán, as well as the merchants and bankers who depended on them for their well-being, were spending more than they earned. When the henequen market shrank as a result of the crisis of 1907, and from the competition of manila hemp from the Philippines, the speculative prosperity disintegrated. With money no longer available to fill their empty coffers, banks started to foreclose on their loans to merchants and planters. The banks that survived the storm had to occupy bankrupt properties. The incapacity of planters, the principal beneficiaries of the bankers' largess, to meet payments on their mortgages touched off widespread banking failures.

To hardly anyone's surprise, the campaign to reelect Don Porfirio in 1910 encountered a frigid reception in Yucatán. Instead, the "violence of political agitators," to quote *El Imparcial*, "knew no limits." When Madero made Mérida, capital of Yucatán, one of the stops in his presidential campaign, local admirers gave him a rousing welcome.

17

THE GREAT REBELLION

I

By 1910, few Mexicans, according to Emilio Rabasa, wanted Porfirio Díaz to prolong his stay in office; yet they revealed no desire to rely on rifles to oust him. An opposition, nonetheless, was beginning to form. Early on, the Flores Magón brothers, at their helm Ricardo, had started to publish *Regeneración*, a journal sympathetic to Camilo Arriaga's Liberal Clubs, symbol of a resurgent anticlericalism. Driven across the border, the Flores Magón, accompanied by Arriaga, organized a revolutionary junta in, of all places, St. Louis, Missouri, which, in 1906, published its Plan Liberal, calling, in the fashion of the day, for political reform but, more significantly, for labor laws and, timidly, for a dose of agrarian justice. By 1910, the Plan del Partido Liberal, now the platform of a militant party, had taken in socialist concepts and held aloft the ideal of land redistribution. Still, although influential in labor circles, the Plan Liberal went mostly unnoticed while Ricardo, the firebrand, died in a Kansas jail.

A rival political bloc garnered adherents of a different opinion. In 1908, Don Porfirio had told James Creelman, an American journalist, that he wanted to retire, saying that at the end of his term in office he would not serve again. "I welcome," he added, "an opposition party in the Mexican Republic." Partly convinced, General Bernardo Reyes, the caudillo of Nuevo León, decided to test the political waters, his proselytes hailing him as the right man to fill Díaz's shoes. His adversaries, one of them José Ives Limantour, asked Díaz, who required no prodding, to run for reelection with Ramón Corral, the politico from Sonora. When the army, upon which he counted, remained loyal to Díaz, Reyes sailed off to Europe.

In Coahuila, in the interval, Francisco I. Madero had published, with money provided by Reyes, *La sucesión presidencial en 1910*, an analysis of political ills which eulogized municipal autonomy, so dear to the hearts of the provincial middle class. Like Reyes, Madero was looking to be on a ticket with

Díaz in the upcoming elections. When Don Porfirio declined, Madero, unlike Reyes, started to organize an anti-reelection movement, to the plaudits of former Reyistas, their idol having disappointed them.

To Díaz's amazement, Madero set out on a political tour of cities, visiting Monterrey, Torreón, Veracruz, Campeche, Mérida, and Progreso, and then proceeding to Sonora and Chihuahua, where he gained the adherence of Abraham González, president of the Centro Anti-reeleccionista Benito Juárez. At the convention of the anti-reelectionists, which met in Mexico City in April 1910, with old Reyistas in attendance, González persuaded the delegates to back Madero for the presidency and Francisco Vásquez Gómez as his running mate. Their platform hailed the ideals of the Constitution of 1857, spoke of free and honest elections, and banged the drums for municipal autonomy. On social issues, it was silent but talked of improving the "material, intellectual, and moral condition" of the worker, dwelt on the need to curb his drinking and gambling, and labeled public education a cure-all for public evils.

The old man in Mexico City had not meant for Madero to take seriously his conversation with Creelman. Disturbed by Madero's attacks on his administration, he had him arrested in Monterrey on the trumped-up charge of aiding and abetting a fugitive from justice. With Madero in jail, Díaz and Corral were elected "overwhelmingly." Don Porfirio went back to the National Palace for the eighth time, just months away from his eightieth birthday, while Mexicans blew trumpets in honor of a century of Independence, extolling the heroic deeds of Miguel Hidalgo y Costilla and, by implication, three decades of progress. Díaz, nevertheless, had misjudged Madero. Released on bail in the city of San Luis Potosí, he escaped to Texas and made public his Plan de San Luis Potosí, declaring the election of Díaz null and void and setting the date of November 20 for the start of a rebellion.

This drama unfolded as dissidents, liberals with a small *l*, challenged the status quo in the Western Hemisphere. At its southern cone, the Radical party, captained by Hipólito Yrigoyen, wrested control of Argentine politics from the Conservatives, enshrined middle-class principles, and bowed temporarily to labor demands. Next door, José Batlle y Ordóñez, a remarkable politico, was trying to inject social justice into the laissez-faire doctrines of tiny Uruguay, installing public schooling and adopting higher tariffs to protect national industry. In the north, Woodrow Wilson and the Democrats captured the White House and pushed through Congress "progressive" legislation. The Great Rebellion, which Madero ignited, occurred within this context. Except for the issue of land reform, which neither Batlle y Ordóñez nor the Radicals of Argentina tackled, the Great Rebellion had brotherly links to the reform currents sweeping the Western Hemisphere.

II

The debut of Madero the rebel was less than auspicious. When he slipped across the border into Coahuila but found merely a handful of bedfellows awaiting him, he thought the better of it and marched back into Texas. Nonetheless, one family, now a pillar of Mexican history, chose to obey Madero's call to arms. In Puebla City, Aquiles, Maximo, Carmen, and Natalia, offspring of the Serdáns, once wealthy landowners but down on their luck, had sympathized with Madero from the start. After Aquiles swore allegiance to the Maderistas, Carmen and the others followed him. When Madero fled to Texas, Aquiles accompanied him while Carmen traveled to Monterrey to collect money to buy arms and ammunition. On November 20, the date Madero set for the uprising, the Serdáns rebelled in Puebla, where both brothers lost their lives.

Despite the initial setback, fate smiled on Madero because his allies had better luck. In western Chihuahua, Abraham González, their spokesman, recruited Pascual Orozco, who, inclined to read the journal *Regeneración* of the Flores Magón, required no encouragement. With modest funds and rifles supplied by González, Orozco won minor skirmishes and a name for himself. Soon Francisco Villa, a cattle thief, sided with him. So well did the fighting go for Orozco and his confederates that, by January 1911, they had defeated federal troops sent to subdue them. Taking heart from that, Madero arrived in Chihuahua, as he pontificated, to assume military and political command of the revolution. Unfortunately for him, federal soldiers routed Madero and his followers at Casas Grandes, a town in Chihuahua. Henceforth, Madero left the fighting to Orozco and Villa.

In Morelos, too, the fires of rebellion flared, where Emiliano Zapata, a native of Anenecuilco, thumbed his nose at state authorities. Slight but sinewy, with a face the color of the bronze earth, he was just thirty-four when he stood up to be counted. Unlike his campesino neighbors, who spent their lives within the confines of their villages, Zapata had seen the outside world, having lived in Puebla and Mexico City. To his neighbors, Zapata was a man of substance, the owner of a solid house built of adobe and stone, who tilled his piece of land and raised livestock, adding to his income by running a pack train of mules through the villages in the vicinity and sharecropping the lands of a nearby hacienda. A dapper dresser, Zapata admired fine horses, and nothing pleased him more than to ride through town in his Sunday best. When he married, he chose for his wife Josefa Espejo, the daughter of a not-too-poor livestock dealer from Ayala. In 1909, the elders of Anenecuilco, a village of four hundred inhabitants, picked Zapata to speak for them, a singular honor and token of the high esteem he commanded.

From the perspective of his worshipers today, Zapata was a simple man ready to purge Morelos of tyrants who robbed the people of their lands and took the bread from their lips. The truth, as always, was more complicated. No man, and Zapata least of all, is born a revolutionary. Zapata became one almost against his will, victimized by the hostility of his enemies and a conscience that would not let him quit until the wrongs had been righted. For a while, Zapata even seemed willing to go along with the slow pace of political reform, determined to sign a truce and to lay down his arms. From this background evolved the dogmatic rebel, the conscience of militant reformers. Drafted in the language of the dirt farmer, his Plan de Ayala, signed on November 25, 1911, made land reform synonymous with social justice. As Zapata verbalized his battle, "we fight so that the people will have lands, forests, and water."

Stolen lands, the Plan de Ayala proclaimed, would be restored to their former owners through the expropriation of one-third of the property of each hacienda; recalcitrant hacendados would lose their entire lands. Yet not even the paltry one-third, swore the patrons of Ayala, would be seized without prior indemnification. Haciendas and land-owning villages would live side by side in the society envisaged by the Zapatistas. By leaving two-thirds of the real estate in the hands of its owners, and by asking payment for lands taken, the Plan de Ayala hardly robbed the rich of their wealth and income.

III

On May 10, 1911, Ciudad Juárez succumbed to the men of Orozco and Villa. Ill-trained fighters had defeated soldiers of a professional army. All of this, by the way, occurred over the protests of Madero, who, fearful that bullets from battle straying into El Paso, just across the Río Bravo, might invite American retaliation, advised retreat. Less cautious, Orozco, with Villa's concurrence, ignored Madero, the erstwhile leader of the "revolution," as it was referred to. But the petulant Madero got even. When he appointed his cabinet, Orozco's name was nowhere on it.

Don Porfirio, suffering from a terrible toothache, decided to negotiate. At Ciudad Juárez, on a "table illuminated by the headlights of automobiles," his representatives signed an agreement with the rebels. After that, Madero, to the anger of Orozco and Villa, handled the defeated enemy as an equal, asking that the "reasonable and wise be consulted" in the selection of the new government. To get that advice, he turned to the "best moral and intellectual segments" of society. Díaz and Corral were told to pack their bags, the victors would name fourteen governors and four cabinet ministers; and federal troops must evacuate Chihuahua, Coahuila, and Sonora, rebel strongholds. As for "political, social, and administrative reforms," reminisced Limantour, the peace said "nothing, absolutely nothing," which left intact the edifice of the Old Regime.

Pending elections, Francisco León de la Barra, minister of foreign relations under Díaz and a smooth-talking lawyer-diplomat with aristocratic airs, would be president. Madero felt comfortable with De la Barra because of his "legalistic spirit, so accentuated that it made him feel a deep repugnance for the role of the victorious revolutionary." By endorsing De la Barra, the constitutional successor to Díaz as foreign minister, Madero wiped from the record the stigma of illegality, his military victory. So succumbed Don Porfirio, either too old to fight or, perhaps, too good a politician not to know that the game was up.

A malignancy that sooner or later would plague Madero survived the Treaty of Ciudad Juárez. Much to his later sorrow, he permitted the old army to keep its weapons, believing that the plethora of aging generals who had stood up for Díaz would do the same for him. But the army brass refused to recognize as equals any of the rebel chieftains, willing only to give them ranks in the corps of rurales in Sonora and Chihuahua. With the signing of the Juárez accord, Madero, furthermore, disbanded the rebel forces. When Emilio Vázquez Gómez, then interim minister of *gobernación*, attempted to keep them together, De la Barra, with Madero's concurrence, dismissed him. Díaz had fallen, but his conquerors had made their peace with his military. This dimmed the prospects for reform, because the army, a consort of Porfirista society, could not be expected to sit idly by while the rebels dismantled it.

With old Porfiristas in control of Congress, the state legislatures, half of the governorships, and the army, Madero went off on a triumphal tour of the Republic. In August, when his supporters met in Mexico City to acclaim him their candidate, Madero, no longer willing to tolerate the energetic Francisco Vázquez Gómez, who, in the opinion of some, had plans of his own, chose José María Pino Suárez, a lawyer-journalist from Yucatán, for his vice-president. In the National Palace, León de la Barra presided over national affairs. Madero won the elections and, on November 6, 1911, became president of Mexico.

IV

Without revolutionary theory, to quote Vladimir Ilyich Lenin, on this subject a man of impeccable credentials, there can be no Revolution. By this rule of thumb, Madero and his successors were woefully unprepared to lead an authentic Revolution (spelled with a capital *R*), social change designed to dismantle the class structure. Madero's credentials, like those of his middle-class backers, lacked authenticity. A son of the elite of Coahuila, Madero was born with a silver spoon in his mouth. Fate, nevertheless, picked this quixotic figure, a spiritualist who spent countless hours contemplating the mysteries of the unknown, to head a rebellion that overthrew the most entrenched regime in Mexican history. Not only did he ignite the tinderbox, but his ideals survived his death and, despite modifications, set the tone for much of what transpired in the years ahead. In Madero, so to speak, lies a clue to the nature of the Great Rebellion.

The son of the master of the hacienda del Rosario, Madero was only thirty-seven years old when he confronted Don Porfirio. Short and fair of skin, he spoke in a high-pitched voice. His wealthy family had a stake in the cotton plantations of La Laguna, banks, textile mills, coal and silver mines, the wine and grape industry, and guayule. When he was twelve years old, his parents sent him to study at the Jesuit Colegio de San Juan in Saltillo, and later to schools in France; he was also briefly a student at the University of California at Berkeley. At no time during his educational career did Madero reveal an abiding interest in study.

Madero and his family had strong links to the Porfiristas. Neither made any attempt to hide their admiration for Díaz. You "honor me," Madero told Don Porfirio, "when you think of me as a friend." His political gambit gained momentum only when efforts to install General Bernardo Reyes as Díaz's running mate in the election of 1910 faltered. Had Díaz substituted Reyes for Corral, Madero would probably not have disturbed the status quo. To Bulnes, the abortive effort of Reyes and the Madero rebellion were cut from the same cloth.

Madero had carved out for himself a reputation as a moderate reformer. As a candidate for the ayuntamiento of San Pedro, a town in La Laguna, he had asked neighboring hacendados to establish schools for the children of their workers. He was an advocate of public education, a defender of individual liberties, and an enemy of one-man rule, urging Mexicans to work for "the progress of humanity," which required "strengthening individual morality by combating vices and developing virtue." The people of this world, he informed his cabinet, "must march forward"; but, he cautioned, "we cannot in the short time that I am president expect to transform the Republic; we can just lay the foundations for future greatness." Madero, to quote Francisco Vázquez Gómez, counseled a prudent, evolutionary approach that, although slow to work, "gave better and more lasting results."

Madero thought in political terms reminiscent of those of early-nineteenth-century Liberals. First and foremost, he abhorred autocratic rule by Díaz and his state governors, the servility of Congress, and the corruption of justices. He wanted to rid Mexico of the *carro completo*, the nefarious practice of distributing public jobs to those in the inner circle. In the opinion of one Mexican author, Madero represented "the Porfirista wing that rebelled not to defend popular rights but to gain public office." "The poverty of the people, their plight in the cities and villages," commented another, "did not appear to be a weighty concern of dissident politicians."

Similarly, Madero distrusted revolutionaries, the Magonistas especially. He was willing to believe that the tyranny of caciques had emboldened them to attempt the capture of Viesca, a small town in Coahuila, in 1908; but, "whatever the reason," he explained, "I believe that these [abortive] military schemes demonstrate that the people no longer welcome revolutions." Once, when the Magonistas questioned his intentions, he had them disarmed, although on his way to lay siege to Ciudad Juárez and, with victory in hand, his forces attacked them at at Galeana and Ahumada. To Madero, the Magonistas symbolized the violence he detested and the destruction of the society he knew.

He dealt with Zapata in like fashion. Madero never stopped thinking as a hacendado and judged Zapata's banner of agrarian reform from that perspective. He loathed the campesino uprising in Morelos. In a speech to Congress, he harped on the "impatience" and the "amorphous agrarian socialism" of the people of Morelos, attitudes "peculiar to the vulgar minds" of campesinos, branding their actions a "perverse vandalism." Díaz had dispatched troops under General Victoriano Huerta to battle Zapata in Morelos; De la Barra, with Madero's approval, kept them there; and Madero, for his part, relied on Huerta again.

Madero wanted Zapata to disarm his campesinos and to stop pillaging the sugar plantations, judging "hostile acts against them as tantamount to an act of war." This sorry chronicle occurred with Madero aware of Zapata's popularity among the dirt farmers of Morelos, "almost always obstinately Zapatistas," as Huerta acknowledged in a speech to the Jockey Club in Mexico City. But Madero wanted no truck with the truth. By December 1911, Zapata had tagged Madero "the most fickle and most vacillating man" he had ever known. Nothing would give him greater pleasure than to hang "him from one of the biggest trees."

In the Plan de San Luis Potosí, Madero's platform for rebellion, only one article, which condemned the loss of village lands under the Leyes de Tierras Baldías, and urged their return when "legally possible," touched on nonpolitical issues. By no stretch of the imagination did this plan rank with the great blueprints for land reform in Mexican history. Its silence on the land question signaled tacit acceptance of the sacredness of private property by the Maderistas. With this attitude, land reform would be difficult if not impossible.

From this ideological posture, Madero deviated only slightly. In June 1912, angered by accusations that he had betrayed his commitments, he set the record straight, denying categorically that he had promised to distribute land to the poor or to subdivide the latifundios. While he believed in creating small property, he did not intend to do it "by stripping any landlord of his property." It was "one thing to create small property by dint of hard work and another to redistribute large landholdings, something I have never thought of doing." To quell Zapatista demands, the Maderistas established the National Agrarian Commission to look into the land issue and talked of restoring stolen ejido lands, but placed the burden on the petitioners, thereby assuring that nothing disturbed the rural status quo. When Pascual Orozco, then considering an invitation to be governor of Chihuahua, urged the expropriation of the uncultivated lands of the haciendas, Madero ignored him. The Maderista formula for industrial labor, too, had a familiar ring. The workers, Madero believed, would not be satisfied "until they enjoy a meaningful liberty." Strikes in the textile industry, he admitted, were brought on by the injustices of long hours of toil and poor pay. While the "nation sympathized with the workers," they must not forget that management could not pay higher wages. Instead, it must be encouraged to provide decent housing, equitable *tiendas de raya*, and schools for the children of their workers. He had not traveled to Orizaba, he told incredulous textile workers, to "incite passions" by telling them that government had a moral duty "to raise wages or to reduce hours" of toil, "because that is not what you want; you want liberty . . . for liberty will give you bread." Bulnes, with his acerbic wit, discovered in Madero's fondness for moral homilies a "national rival of the Virgen de Guadalupe."

Labor, however, quickly tested the Maderistas. The "Romantic Honeymoon of the Proletariat," so were the years 1911–12 baptized by Rosendo Salazar, printer and author of the monumental *Pugnas de la gleba*. Bold men set out to erect a just labor structure: radicals such as Juan Sarabia, Paulino Martínez, and Antonio I. Villarreal; socialists such as Fredesvindo Elvira Alonzo and Antonio P. de Araujo; the syndicalists Luis Méndez and Pedro Junco, a native of Spain; and the anarchists Juan Francisco Moncaleano, a primary-school teacher from Spain, and Ricardo Flores Magón and his brothers. From Mexico City, the militant *tipógrafos*, or printers, banded together in the Confederación Tipográfica de México and carried their efforts to the provinces, their success inspiring masons, cobblers, tailors, bakers, carpenters, and musicians to organize, while their journal, *El Tipógrafo Mexicano*, circulated in Sonora, Tamaulipas, Sinaloa, and Yucatán. By 1912, the Unión Minera Mexicana, a combative northern group, claimed sixteen mining affiliates, while Lázaro Gutiérrez de Lara labored to unite workers and campesinos in Zacatecas. The Partido Socialista flourished briefly, as workers in Mexico City celebrated May 1 as labor day in 1912.

Mexico City became a haven for ideologues of the labor movement. From their reunions emerged the Casa del Obrero Mundial, headquarters for the labor leadership that blossomed. At the start, the Casa, relying for its support on workers in Mexico City, represented a small segment of labor but, gradually, established ties with workers in Veracruz, Jalisco, Nuevo León, and San

Luis Potosí. Its goal was to promulgate advanced labor doctrines and to get workers to organize labor unions and to employ strikes and boycotts to improve their lot. With its second goal, the Casa drew upon itself the hostility of government, then, as in the days of Díaz, unfriendly to the idea of labor unions.

When a rash of strikes erupted in the textile industry, which endangered political stability, the Maderistas, like it or not, had to respond to the demands of labor. It became readily apparent that Madero's administration had neither abandoned sacrosanct principles nor committed itself to new ones. But deal with labor it must, for the wave of strikes ruled out a hands-off approach. Compelled to act, the Maderistas embarked upon a tortuous road that in the decades ahead led to a system of government-controlled unions.

The rejection of neutrality augured no philosophical metamorphosis. The Porfiristas had never kept their distance in industrial disputes, and no one in government urged the adoption of remedies giving preference to labor over business. Private enterprise, the offspring of free competition, required government benevolence, whether owned by Mexicans or by foreigners. Property rights claimed no nationality. Strikes must be handled rapidly and firmly, for labor "must not forget that the laws of supply and demand fixed wages." Under the Maderistas, policy held labor leaders responsible for the country's industrial problems. Workers should emulate the wisdom and prudence of businessmen and "forsake the stupid and pernicious custom of relying on strikes to settle labor conflicts."

To handle labor, the Maderistas hit upon a policy of the carrot and the stick. When miners refused to work—for example, in Coahuila, Madero's home state—soldiers silenced their protest. Reliance on the stick, however, was merely a first step; less inflexible than the Old Regime, the Maderistas knew that repression alone was merely a Band-Aid. Labor must be courted, if necessary some of its demands satisfied, and, more significantly, its leadership controlled by government. To give voice to the policy, the Maderistas established, initially for the textile industry, the Departamento de Trabajo, a labor office in the Ministerio de Fomento, which was assigned the task of preventing work stoppages, solving them when they occurred and keeping the budding labor movement under control. With no authority of its own, the department mediated disputes between labor and management solely on a voluntary basis, with the goal of encouraging "harmonious relations between capital and labor." For its head, the Maderistas chose a former Díaz congressman who believed in the responsibilities of citizenship and in respect for authority. Hostile to workers, he rarely overlooked the interests of businessmen, upon whom he lavished praise for their patience and prudence. According to *El Ahuizote*, a labor journal, the "much publicized Departamento del Trabajo was of no earthly use."

The Maderistas lasted just slightly over fifteen months in office, before the reality of Mexico's political situation overwhelmed them. The reasons for their brief tenure lie in the nature of the Maderistas. The popularity of Madero, their leader, had a narrow base, for he appealed largely to urbanites, the middle class of the cities and towns. His program, in essence the restoration of the Constitution of 1857, especially the principle of no reelection, was aimed at them. Beyond middle-class political virtues, the Maderistas had no program. Their appeal was of interest to a middle class that made up no more than a fraction of the population. That middle class had no intention of renovating the economic edifice; it had its mind set on political reform, wanting to secure its place in society and move upward, either through public jobs or by gaining entrance into the echelons of business and commerce, at that juncture the domain of foreigners.

The Maderistas attracted few followers at both the top and the bottom of the social ladder. The wealthy, the old Porfiristas, desired to preserve the status quo, fearful of any change that jeopardized it. Most army brass hats shared that opinion. Similarly, campesinos, whether on ejidos, *peones acasillados*, or day laborers, had no ties to the Maderistas. Largely illiterate, they had, most likely, seldom heard of Madero and, if they had, gave scant credence to his political rhetoric. The unhappy ones among them wanted jobs or better-paying ones and land to till. The Maderistas offered none of that. While they attracted more of a following among urban workers, their rank and file were not ready to fight to keep them in office. Madero and his allies, by turning their backs on men such as Pascual Orozco, who had elevated them to power, isolated themselves even more. When they embraced the old bureaucracy, left intact the military, and recruited advisers, cabinet ministers, and governors from among the Porfiristas, they sealed their doom.

The jilted did not go away. In November 1911, just as Madero entered the National Palace, Emiliano Zapata promulgated his Plan de Ayala. Fighting erupted not merely in Morelos but in Tlaxcala, Guerrero, Puebla, Mexico State, and the Federal District. The Zapatistas burned sugar plantations, captured towns, blew up railroad bridges, and cut telegraph wires.

Frightened by the inability of the Maderistas to defeat the Zapatistas and to quell labor strife, the old elite rebelled. In December 1911, General Bernardo Reyes crossed into Mexico from the United States but, discovering no disciples, surrendered to local authorities, who sent him off to await trial for treason in a jail in Mexico City. Then, a month later, Emilio Vázquez Gómez, still smoldering over how the Maderistas had replaced his brother with Pino Suárez, rebelled and captured Ciudad Juárez. To Madero's good fortune, Pascual Orozco, much admired by the Vazquiztas, talked the rebel soldiers into surrendering their arms.

In March 1912, Orozco himself rebelled, aided and abetted by the powerful

Terrazas clan of Chihuahua. In his Plan de la Empacadora, Orozco endorsed political and economic reform, including a shorter workday, better working conditions, the employment of Mexicans on the railroads, and, most significantly, the return to the villages of lands illegally seized. At first, destiny smiled on Orozco, who, with money to burn, recruited a large fighting force and defeated an army commanded by General José González Sala, Madero's minister of war, who, embarrassed by his defeat, committed suicide. Seeking to head off Orozco's soldiers, Madero asked General Victoriano Huerta, back from battling Zapata, to halt their advance. In May, Huerta, a much better soldier than González Sala, dealt Orozco a staggering blow at Bachimba, ending temporarily his ambitions. Huerta returned to Mexico City a hero, his military reputation much revered.

Another rebellion broke out four months later, this time in Veracruz, led by Félix Díaz, nephew of Don Porfirio. Like Reyes, he courted the army but, though he won its backing in Veracruz, failed to win over the rest of it. Loyal soldiers squashed the uprising, taking Díaz captive. Although an army court-martial sentenced Díaz to death for treason, Madero, perhaps remembering his admiration for Don Porfirio, revoked the sentence and ordered Díaz jailed in Mexico City. Before long, Félix Díaz and Reyes were plotting, with the help of army generals, the overthrow of Madero's government from their respective jail cells.

On February 9, 1912, General Manuel Mondragón, at the head of soldiers and cadets from the Colegio Militar, set free Bernardo Reyes and Félix Díaz. Then, with Reyes at their head, they marched on the National Palace; when Reyes led their charge, soldiers loyal to Madero killed him. Félix Díaz, now in command, pulled back to the Ciudadela, an old army barracks, while Madero placed Huerta at the head of his troops. So began the Decena Trágica, the Tragic Ten Days, when rival bands of soldiers lobbed artillery shells across Mexico City, inflicting heavy civilian casualties and destroying buildings. On February 18, Huerta, who went over to the enemy, ordered the arrest of Madero and Pino Suárez. Three days later, on the evening of February 21, soldiers, under orders of an officer of the rurales, killed Madero and Pino Suárez, shot for "trying to escape," according to the official version.

For Huerta's betrayal, much of the responsibility lies on the shoulders of Henry Lane Wilson, the ambassador of the United States. From the start, Wilson, hard drinking, arrogant, and associated closely with the Guggenheim interests in Mexico, had no use for the Maderistas' political reforms, alleging they invited unrest, which affected adversely United States holdings in Mexico. The rebel plots of Félix Díaz, Reyes, and Orozco, as well as the failure of the Maderistas to subdue the Zapatistas, multiplied his fears. As early as January 1912, Wilson had told Washington that Mexico seethed "with discontent." Moreover, Wilson did not enjoy watching nationalist sentiment explode in

Mexico, objecting, for example, to Maderista demands that foreigners hired by the railroads be able to speak and write Spanish. For Wilson, the administration's tax of twenty centavos on each ton of crude petroleum was but the "camel's nose under the tent." The Maderistas, nonetheless, had never once thought of reversing the Díaz policy of welcoming foreign capital into Mexico.

Wilson, all the same, plotted with the concurrence of Washington. The Taft administration made clear to Madero that it would not sit idly and watch Mexico jeopardize foreign investments, a threat it backed up by ordering warships to Mexican waters and stationing more troops along the border. In March 1912, it advised Americans to leave Mexican northern states, where their lives and property were supposedly in danger. In August 1912, Wilson labeled Mexico's government "apathetic, inefficient, cynically indifferent or stupidly optimistic," and Washington sent a note accusing the Maderistas of failing to offer Americans adequate protection, of sanctioning "frivolous" legal actions against them, and of discriminating against United States companies, referring specifically to the tax on petroleum. Should Mexico not mend its ways, Washington would take whatever steps were necessary. None of this helped the Maderistas consolidate their regime.

For the United States, for which Wilson spoke, as well as for Europeans with investments in Mexico, the cuartelazo occurred at just the right time. To them, to quote a Mexican scholar, "the alternative to Huerta was anarchy." Encouraged by his European colleagues, Wilson worked hard to bring about the cuartelazo. With Washington's approval, he threatened to disembark American troops if the lives of Americans in Mexico City were not safeguarded. When that failed to appease him, he told Madero to resign. When Madero refused, Wilson asked Félix Díaz and Huerta to confer with him at the American embassy. From that meeting, the notorious Pact of the Embassy, Huerta left to betray Madero, promising to wield power only until Félix Díaz, his coconspirator, could be elected president of Mexico. For that pact, Wilson took full credit; "Generals Díaz and Huerta," he wrote, "are united in opposing all efforts to restore [Madero] . . . to power." A "wicked despotism" had fallen. When Huerta, after jailing Madero, asked Wilson whether to exile him or lock him up in an "insane asylum," Wilson replied, "Do whatever you think is best for the country." Earlier, he had told Madero's sobbing wife, who came to plead with Wilson to ask Huerta to spare his life, that he could "not interfere."

In retrospect, Madero had run his government as he had promised in the Plan de San Luis Potosí. His admirers were the discontented members of the old elite who, with the middle class, decried the cliquish control of politics and the privileges of the minority. Maderista policy embraced capitalism, attempted to update it, and sought to rescue the economy from the doldrums.

The accomplishments of the Maderistas, declared an editorial in *El Microbio*, disturbed little the plight in which Díaz had left the Mexican people. Madero died abandoned by tens of thousands of his early supporters. Only two of his governors, José María Maytorena, in Sonora, and Venustiano Carranza, in Coahuila, rejected Huerta's tutelage. Maytorena had so little faith in armed opposition to Huerta that he relinquished his job and fled across the border.

V

The Pact of the Embassy notwithstanding, Huerta did not vacate the presidential office. The Old Regime, with a military man in the driver's seat, had weathered the storm. For all that, Huerta survived merely from February 1913 to July 1914, months of political turmoil, meddling by the United States, and military warfare. Huerta, the official history insists, set the clock back. He did no such thing. The son of a Huichol Indian mother and a mestizo father, Huerta was from a village in Jalisco; though a mediocre student, he graduated from the Colegio Militar. By the time of his promotion to brigadier general, he had fought against the Yaquis in Sonora as well as the Maya of Yucatán, earning the description as a "fine and loyal soldier" from Porfiristas. That did not rid him of his gluttonous taste for brandy, which he drank day and night.

For whatever reason, this soldier, crude of manners and bloodthirsty, stacked his cabinet with men of impeccable credentials, a number of them intellectuals. Tagged neo-Porfirista by its enemies, his regime proved no more hostile to labor than Madero's, adopting its reforms, promoting labor legislation, and, occasionally, tolerating labor unions. Nonetheless, Huerta and his allies had not seized the National Palace to espouse the cause of labor, nor did they have any sympathy for radicals. They closed down the Casa del Obrero Mundial but, oddly, appointed Andrés Molina Enríquez and Rafael Sierra, able reformers, to head the Departmento de Trabajo, which received a bigger budget. In their willingness to mildly tolerate labor unions, Huerta's "conservatives" broke with Porfirista politics that the Maderistas had left undisturbed. The Departmento de Trabajo maintained amicable relations with the Partido Obrero Popular, a labor bloc, urged Congress to approve legislation covering industrial accidents, and endorsed the wage scales for the textile industry adopted by the Maderistas. However, military turmoil, which brought inflation and reduced the number of jobs, led the unhappy to swell the ranks of Huerta's foes.

In education, the Huertistas exceeded the limits of the Maderistas. Nemesio García Naranjo, Huerta's minister of education and a former Científico, broke ranks with positivism and embraced Henri Bergson's antithetical philosophy. Additionally, he conferred his blessings on the "rudimentary school" program, which taught Indian campesinos to read and write Spanish and the basics of arithmetic. Aureliano Urrutia, minister of *gobernación* and, like Huerta, of Indian background, sent "experts" into the countryside to organize community projects. The Huertistas, moreover, began to restore the land stolen from the ejidos of the Yaquis and Mayo Indians of Sonora and, as a bellwether for future policy, converted the National Agrarian Commission into a ministry with cabinet status.

But militarily, the Huertistas had more than they could handle. The Maderistas had no intention of allowing the Huertistas to savor their ill-gotten laurels, finding their champion in Venustiano Carranza, governor of Coahuila. Refusing to recognize the Huerta regime, Carranza, with the backing of Francisco Villa in Chihuahua and Alvaro Obregón, a garbanzo planter turned rebel in Sonora, declared he would not rest until Huerta was out of the National Palace. The Plan de Guadalupe, the Carrancista platform, just the same, said nary a word about social reform, calling merely for the defeat of Huerta and naming Carranza Primer Jefe, or First Chief, of the Constitutionalists, the name they adopted and a reference to their pledge of allegiance to the Liberal charter of 1857. In Obregón and Villa, the Constitutionalists, "legal revolutionaries," found talented military leaders.

In Morelos, meanwhile, Huerta found Zapata no less hostile than Madero. Zapata did not confront the Huertistas to restore Maderistas to office or deliver the National Palace to Constitutionalists. Remembering Huerta's campaign in Morelos, Zapata had no faith in his agrarian "promises." At the same time, he kept his distance from the Constitutionalists, distrusting their allegiance to land reform. Huerta was caught between two pincers, Constitutionalists in the north and, to his rear, Zapatistas, the dirt farmers of Morelos.

The war between the Huertistas and their enemies left chaos in its wake, the destruction of property and the loss of lives. To pacify the country, Huerta resorted to the *leva*, multiplying the size of his army twelve times. The Constitutionalists, too, built up their armies, with Obregón and Villa in the forefront of the recruiting drives. Most of their soldiers, the privates, corporals, and sergeants, were of humble background, but rarely campesinos of the type fighting alongside of Zapata, because the northern provinces had few of them. Wageworkers of diverse types, whether miners, rural *jornaleros*, cowboys, railroad laborers, or the like, made up the majority. By contrast, the officers derived generally from a higher social class: rancheros, schoolteachers, sharecroppers, clerks in drugstores, labor bosses in mines, trainmen, police, craftsmen, trolley conductors, or traveling salesmen, "without taking into account the rustics and ne'er-do-wells." In Sonora, Obregón, for example, recruited Yaquis as privates but his officers from the "white . . . and partly educated and politically aware."

"If they are going to kill me tomorrow, let them kill me now," runs one stanza of "La Valentina," a popular ballad of the Constitutionalists. Still, Mexicans neither volunteered freely to fight nor risked death eagerly. Barring exceptions, the military chieftains had to lure Mexicans with more than rhetoric, which meant offering "good wages" to compensate for the risks taken, paying their soldiers more than they would earn by staying home. The ravages of war, the destruction of jobs in mines, industry, and agriculture, depriving thousands of their wages, drove the jobless to join rebel armies. But the idealistic and selfless constituted a minority.

From Chihuahua, Villa, baptized the Centaur of the North, advanced south and, with his capture of the city of Zacatecas in 1914, doomed the Huertistas to defeat. Obregón, a skillful warrior, pushed off from Hermosillo, taking Mazatlán, León, and Guadalajara. Southern Mexico, specifically Chiapas and Oaxaca, despite sporadic outbursts of fighting, stayed largely out of the fray. Indian Mexico, apparently, had little cause to take on Huerta, though campesinos in Puebla and Guerrero joined Zapata's ragtag guerrillas.

Washington added to Huerta's woes. Believing Henry Lane Wilson, Huerta looked to the Republic next door to extend a friendly hand. But Taft, though probably sympathetic to the views of his ambassador, left the recognition of Huerta in the lap of his successor, the capitalist moralist Woodrow Wilson. The Puritan in the White House, as he came to be known, dismissed Wilson the ambassador, then, to the consternation of Great Britain, which had recognized Huerta's government, refused to follow suit, deciding, instead, to depose it. Huerta, by entering the National Palace through a military coup, had committed an "unconstitutional act."

Huerta, however, was not eliminated easily. Confronted by Washington's hostility, he looked to Europe for arms and credit, finding a friendly response among London bankers. However, in return for special privileges in the Panama Canal from Washington, Great Britain withdrew its support of Huerta. When Mexican soldiers, early in April 1914, jailed sailors from the U.S.S. *Dolphin*, an American ship anchored in Tampico harbor, for going ashore without permission, marines occupied the port city of Veracruz, to prevent, Washington alleged, the landing of arms for the Huertistas by a German ship. That blatant bit of military meddling killed hundreds of Mexican men, women, and children, but, ironically, failed to stop the Germans from landing the arms at the port of Coatzacoalcos. At the same time, Washington allowed the Constitutionalists to buy arms in the United States. The military triumphs of Villa and Obregón, as well as the hostility of Woodrow Wilson's Washington, led the Huertistas to call it quits.

VI

With their victory over Huerta, the rebels had defeated the federal army, one tentacle of the Old Regime. Tragically, that feat failed to bring peace, because the rebel factions were soon at each other's throats. Not peace but turbulence, a falling peso, and inflation, hunger, and epidemics of disease, especially in Mexico City, befell Mexicans. Why?

First, goals and aspirations, reflecting class interests, set the rebel chieftains apart. In one camp, virtually alone, stood Emiliano Zapata, the torchbearer for rebels of more radical bent. Clashing personalities and hunger for glory also split the rebels into factions, each, so to speak, loyal to its *jefe*. Though Villa and Carranza both hailed from the north, they were, by personality and upbringing, as different as day and night. Ideologically, on the other hand, despite public declarations to the contrary, they were, though not like peas in a pod, not at loggerheads. To the contrary; Villa, anathema to Mexican *burgueses*, fits, nevertheless, into the ideological framework established by Madero and embellished by Carranza and his lieutenant, Alvaro Obregón.

Villa was born on July 7, 1878, as Doroteo Arango in La Coyotada, a hamlet in Durango, to a family of sharecroppers. By 1892, he had earned his spurs as a petty thief, joining eventually a gang of bandits led by Francisco Villa, from whom he took his eponym. A decade later, he moved to Parral, the mining town in Chihuahua, and added cattle rustling to his list of clandestine escapades; by 1908, he captained his own band of rustlers. One man, whose family knew Villa, writes that Villa included murder among his crimes. In 1910, Villa, the cattle thief wanted for murder, joined Pascual Orozco and Madero for their assault on Ciudad Juárez.

No one knows precisely why he did. In *El hombre y sus armas*, Martín Luís Guzmán, who had the ear of Villa, attributed the metamorphosis to Abraham González, the disciple of Madero and a cattle buyer. According to this interpretation, González persuaded Villa to identify his battle against legal authorities with the plight of the poor and exploited. By espousing their cause, Villa no longer would be simply a *bandolero*, a highwayman, and a purloiner of cattle. In his classic *El águila y la serpiente*, Guzmán explored the fascinating and bewildering complexities of Villa, at one and the same time cruel and lovable, a man who was capable of butchering in cold blood scores of defenseless Chinese in Torreón and who chose for his *compadres* killers devoid of mercy.

What Villa's "metamorphosis" really signified remains shrouded in controversy. Only with difficulty can one deduce from the evidence that Villa truly embraced the crusade for social justice. For example: in 1914, Villa and Obregón, in a joint declaration of principles, recommended the holding of elections, a purge of the judicial system and a political housecleaning. Of their nine points, only one, the last on their list, touched on social maladies, urging state governors to appoint special committees to study the agrarian question. From this statement derived Carranza's call for a "convention" of military leaders in Mexico City to consolidate the Constitutionalist movement. When

Villa refused to journey to Carranza's lair, the convention met in Aguascalientes.

If Guzmán's version can be trusted, Villa believed in an "organized revolution, captained by a leader who behaved prudently, with men who loved order, respected property, and upheld the rights of others." Carranza taunted his rival by accusing him of defending the status quo because of his "desire to install a constitutional system of government before the Revolution had time to enact the social reforms demanded by the Nation." Villa, according to Carranza, wanted the adoption of "radical and social reforms" postponed until a constitutional government could study, discuss, and resolve them. To Carranza, who conveniently forgot that he, too, defended the identical formula, "only enemies of the Revolution" could endorse such a plan. By 1915, Obregón and Lucio Blanco, a reformer of impeccable credentials, had jointly published a manifesto calling Villa "the conservative of today."

On the cardinal question of agrarian reform, the Villistas' stance was, at best, ambiguous. According to Francisco Vázquez Gómez, a politico out of favor with the Constitutionalists, Villa never intended to subdivide the great estates, nor did lands change hands in Chihuahua between 1912 and 1915, years of Villista ascendancy. For that time, at least, the Villistas had shelved the idea of land reform. The decree of May 24, 1915, promulgated by Villa as commander of the army of the Aguascalientes Convention, authorized the division of haciendas in order to create small private property; the beneficiaries, for all that, had to buy their parcels. The hacendado was to be paid for his lands before they were either subdivided or occupied by their new owners. Except for sanctioning expropriation, the decree copied most of what Madero had suggested. After the split with the Constitutionalists, the Villistas promised to uphold the property guarantees in the charter of 1857. Later, the defeated Villa condemned Article 27 of the Constitution of 1917, key to the land issue, claiming that it invited intervention by the United States and fanned the fires of conflict in Mexico.

Nor did Villa disregard the benefits of pecuniary gain. He displayed a sharp eye for profit; as a rebel, he was also an entrepreneur. For helping his brother take Ciudad Juárez, Gustavo Madero gave Villa ten thousand pesos for a meat-packing plant, a business venture he kept out of the public eye by registering it in the name of one of his sundry wives. In Parral, Villa owned the Hotel Hidalgo, the best and finest, and, in Ciudad Juárez, ran the gambling casinos. On El Fresno, a hacienda he owned on the outskirts of Chihuahua City, Villa lived like a country squire, as he later did on his hacienda Canutillo, given to him in 1920 in return for his pledge to give up his marauding life.

Venustiano Carranza, a criollo type, "white, very white," wrote Vicente Blasco Ibáñez, the Spanish intellectual, was a different kettle of fish. At the dinner table in Nogales, Martín Luis Guzmán recalled in *El águila y la serpiente*, Don Venustiano rode herd on the conversation with a firm hand. His guests, invariably lawyers, physicians, engineers, journalists, and other city dandies dressed correctly in coat and tie, listened attentively while the First Chief, Madero's successor, spiced his remarks with "historical allusions" to the Reforma, his cherished topic. His views never went much beyond the ideals of Benito Juárez, over half a century old when the Constitutionalists launched their crusade.

Don Venustiano was a native of Coahuila. Born in 1859 on a hacienda near the villa of Cuatro Ciénegas, he was nearly sixty years of age when he took up the rebel cause. His father, an army officer who had fought in the Indian wars of Coahuila and Chihuahua, had served Juárez against the Conservatives and the French. As a boy, Carranza attended school in Saltillo, the capital of Coahuila, and graduated from the Escuela Nacional Preparatoria in Mexico City. Upon his return home, he became a successful hacendado and, finally, the patriarch of Cuatro Ciénegas.

Like Madero, Carranza could not claim that he was an outsider in the days of Porfirio Díaz. His father, a prosperous hacendado, enjoyed the esteem of the rulers in Mexico City. Carranza had been *presidente municipal* of Cuatro Ciénegas, and served in the state legislature and then as deputy and senator to Congress from Coahuila for seventeen years. In 1908, he became interim governor of Coahuila and appeared likely to be confirmed in that office by the coming elections. His espousal of the political ambitions of Bernardo Reyes incurred the wrath of rivals, particularly José Yves Limantour. Critics say that Carranza was an enthusiastic ally of the Old Regime so long as he had entrance to political office.

Of "gentlemanly bearing," Carranza was a man of principle, refusing to compromise for the sake of expediency or personal profit. While *carrancismo*, the movement he headed acquired notoriety for theft and plunder, the First Chief, well-off when he challenged Huerta, died a hacendado of modest means. Urbane but provincial, he prized learning and held Western culture in high esteem. He read widely if not thoroughly, thought of himself as a historian, and kept a copy of Plutarch by his bedside. Above all, Carranza knew intimately the twists and turns of Mexican politics, accepting as inevitable the crass opportunism of his rebel colleagues. Loyalty he viewed as a fleeting hope. He loathed rivals, hating Villa not so much because of his cruelty but because he was a strong, exuberant opponent.

Carranza's ideological convictions were those of a Liberal, essentially those of Juárez and José María Luis Mora, but shaped to fit the mold of a northern hacendado. A conservative, he believed in law and order, and in firm and vigorous leadership, thinking that only the strong could govern Mexico. He wanted men of his own ilk around him; extremists of the left never won his confidence. Given his choice, he picked moderates and conservatives to work with him. Luis Cabrera, a lawyer of abiding faith in private property, best represented the men of Carranza. His famous speech of September 1913, before an audience in Hermosillo, rated the loss of "liberty" the worst of Díaz's crimes and demanded "the return of constitutional order." Without respect for life, liberty, and property, he told Congress in 1917, morality and individual rights, the substance of order, withered and died.

Carranza lived by the tenets of capitalist doctrine. He believed that a healthy society thrived on competition, and he bewailed the "immoral monopolies of businessmen who for centuries had sucked dry the public coffers of the Republic." While condemning the acquisition of wealth by the few and deploring the poverty of the "masses," he insisted that these evils were divorced from the ideal of private property. Carranza had matured amid the language of free trade and eulogies to Herbert Spencer. To him, the "protected industry, rather than an asset, is a burden" because, assured of an easy profit, it grew fat and flabby. Competition hardened muscles and strengthened industry. Some Mexican industries might well fall by the wayside; but the unsuccessful would have been of negligible benefit anyway.

Carranza's version of agrarian reform left Zapata cold. At no time did the patriarch from Coahuila sympathize with the plea to redistribute the land. While he was not above using the rhetoric of land reform, he sat on his haunches when it came time to implement slogans. José Vasconcelos, one of the young intellectuals of that time, remembered Carranza saying frequently that he "could not understand the constant harping on the agrarian problem, because it was not the main issue in Mexico." When General Lucio Blanco divided the lands of a hacienda among its peons, Carranza punished him. Blanco had overstepped the boundaries of the Plan de Guadalupe. Common sense, Carranza pontificated, made mandatory a policy that would "not alarm landlords, industrialists, and capitalists."

Nationalistic considerations, for all that, tempered admiration for classical dogma. A fervent nationalist, Carranza waited for the day when Mexicans would own their industries. So out of necessity as well as conviction, he embraced the tariffs advocated by protectionists. The subsoil, he believed with all of his soul, belonged to Mexico, specifically the petroleum underground. For Woodrow Wilson's meddling, Carranza, forever the champion of Mexican sovereignty, displayed anger and disdain, wanting no part of Washington's efforts to overthrow Huerta.

Factional strife, simmering already between Villa and Carranza, broke out openly at the Convention called together by the military warlords at Aguascalientes in October 1914. Carranza had wanted them to meet in Mexico City, where he could keep tabs on them. Villa, however, refused to venture south, so, in a compromise, the military bosses met at Aguascalientes, to decide who would be the interim president of the Republic until elections could be held, a job Carranza had already allotted to himself. Obregón and other Constitutionalists did not tarry long, once it became evident that Villa, who controlled Aguascalientes, opposed Carranza. For Obregón and his allies, Carranza, whatever his quirks, was the logical choice to follow Madero. With their departure from Aguascalientes, Villa, with the concurrence of the Zapatistas, picked General Eulalio Gutiérrez to head the Convention government.

Even in the absence of the Constitutionalists, the delegates at Aguascalientes hardly behaved in radical fashion on land reform, one of the planks endorsed. The generals (Zapata did not attend) stepped gingerly around the issue. Manuel Palafox, a Zapatista named minister of agriculture, for example, while urging the breakup of the large estates, asked for expropriation with prior indemnification. Not until the Convention government, then on its last legs, moved to Cuernavaca, where Zapata had the upper hand, did it take a militant stance on the land issue.

For their part, the Carrancistas confronted a debacle since Villa, with a mightier army, drove them out of Mexico City, compelling them to seek refuge in the port of Veracruz, then occupied by American marines. Villa's *dorados* ruled the key regions of the Republic. To triumph, the Carrancistas had to win over or neutralize the campesinos, firmly in Zapata's camp. So, largely out of necessity, Carranza gave his blessings to the decree of January 6, 1915. The brainchild of Luis Cabrera, the decree, which represented the thinking of Andrés Molina Enríquez, author of *Los grandes problemas nacionales*, nullified the theft of lands, water, and forests of pueblos, rancherias, *congregaciones*, or *comunidades* sanctioned by the law of June 25, 1856; ruled invalid concessions or sales of lands, water, and forests made by officials since 1876 that had led to the illegal occupation of ejidos or other lands; and declared null and void land surveys or demarcations of property that alienated their lands, water, and forests.

To restore lands to the villages, the decree of 1915 adopted restitution and dotation. Villages that could prove title to property lost could petition for its restitution; eligible villages without proof of ownership had to rely on dotation. Governors and, in certain cases, military commanders were authorized to review petitions. Federal and state agrarian commissions were to judge the validity of the requests and decide the amount of land to be granted. A favorable ruling gave villages provisional title and the right to farm the land. The final decision, conferring ownership, was up to the National Agrarian Commission and the president of the Republic. No confiscation of property was intended; lands seized had to be paid for. The decree only partly met the hopes of the land hungry. Expropriation applied merely to haciendas on the edges of villages with the right to ask for land. Nothing defined the amount or character of the lands subject to expropriation. Initial possession was provisional.

Given the limited number of categories, a host of rural communities and individuals were excluded from the right to ask for land, among them agricultural workers not living in villages adjacent to haciendas, sharecroppers, and tenant farmers. The decree placed *peones acasillados,* the workers on the haciendas, in this category, the only ones with a valid claim to the lands they tilled. The decree, for all intents and purposes, safeguarded haciendas from expropriation, while benefiting a small segment of the rural population, nearly always Indians. Though the grant went to the villages, the intent was to make individuals the owners of the plots of land.

As one may have expected, the Carrancista decree failed to win over Zapata. Moreover, Villa, at a meeting in Xochimilco, endorsed the Plan de Ayala, swearing to join hands with Zapata to crush Carranza. Once out of Xochimilco, he promptly went his own way. The Constitutionalists, on the one hand, and the Villistas and Zapatistas, on the other, stood at loggerheads. The factional strife between them lasted until the defeat of Villa's army by Obregón in Celaya, a city in Querétaro, in April 1915. Even then, sporadic fighting dragged on for years.

Inadvertently, the United States and the European war that erupted in 1914, assured the triumph of the Constitutionalists. At first, Washington refused to take sides in the factional quarrel, proclaiming its right to decide what was best for American interests. Woodrow Wilson, who dispatched agents to inform him of what was going on in Mexico, toyed with the idea of backing Villa, who promised guarantees for American investments. Even after the Battle of Celaya; a mortal blow for the Villistas, Wilson warned that if the quarreling factions could not come to terms, he would take steps "to help Mexico save itself." When Carranza ignored the warning, Wilson asked Argentina, Brazil, Chile, Uruguay, Bolivia, and Guatemala to find, in cooperation with Washington, a solution for Mexico's problems. While Villistas and Zapatistas declared their willingness to confer with the "mediators," Carranza refused. Deciding that a bit of wisdom was necessary, Washington found it expedient to confer de facto recognition on Carranza's regime, mainly because Germany, the enemy of England and France in Europe, wanted factional strife on the doorsteps of the United States. Opening the American border to purchases of arms tipped the scales in favor of the Constitutionalists.

Villa, however, nearly upset the applecart. Miffed by Washington's recognition of Carranza, Villistas, at Santa Isabel, in Sonora, killed sixteen American mine employees; then, on March 9, 1916, they crossed the border and attacked Columbus, New Mexico, again killing Americans. Carranza ordered Villa arrested, but Washington, little mollified, sent an army into Chihuahua in pursuit of Villa. General John J. Pershing's "punitive expedition" failed to capture Villa; at El Carrizal, moreover, Carrancista soldiers stopped its southward advance. However, before Washington would recall Pershing, it demanded that Mexico respect the life and property of foreigners. Carranza rejected this demand, telling Washington that Mexico would not compromise its sovereignty just to get Pershing to withdraw. The conflict in Europe eventually compelled Washington to pull its troops out of Mexico.

VII

With Villa out of the way, Zapata bottled up in Morelos, and Carranza at the helm, the Constitutionalists, in the winter of 1916, sat down in Querétaro to write a national charter. When they convened, only the moderate wing of the rebel factions answered the roll call. The Constitutionalists at Querétaro, an urban middle class mainly, stamped their ideological seal on the Mexico of the future. They were, above all, lawyers, but also generals, schoolteachers, engineers, journalists, poets, writers, physicians, store clerks, and salesmen. The Constitution of 1917, which these architects designed, signaled the victory of the new middle class, offspring of the Porfiriato. After weeks of debate, the delegates hammered out a blueprint often at odds with the dreams of their First Chief, who wanted just to update the charter of 1857; but, despite the revolutionary rhetoric and the revisions adopted, many of the ideals of nineteenth-century liberalism survived. The statutes on land, labor, and public education document the amorphous and contradictory nature of the legislation adopted.

For a majority at Querétaro, turbulence and unrest in the countryside, unleashed by the war against Huerta, would disappear only by a resolution of the agrarian question. But, in drafting their legislation, the Constitutionalists were more orthodox than not. Even the radical Francisco Múgica, who led the forces of change, shared Carranza's belief in private property; both looked upon it as the pillar of society. For most Constitutionalists, as Molina Enríquez pointed out, the objective was to "defend, develop, and multiply small property," which would be the nucleus of "a big and strong middle class." They consigned the ejido, the one exception to private ownership of property, to a secondary role, viewing it as a legacy of the past. Only a radical fringe demanded the expropriation of the lands of the hacendados and foreign landlords in order to distribute their holdings among the poor. To Múgica as well as Carranza, the right to private property usually took precedence over the public need. Nearly every one of the delegates at Querétaro agreed on the necessity to pay for property taken. The delegates, moreover, had to bear in mind that any tinkering with the structure of private property jeopardized agricultural production, hurt sorely by years of war and turmoil.

Article 27, which encapsulated the land reform provisions, reflected a hodgepodge of ambiguities and contradictions. To safeguard the public interests, the state had the authority to regulate private property and the use of natural resources, as well as the responsibility to guarantee the equitable distribution of the national wealth and its conservation. Article 27 called for the subdivision but not the total disappearance of large property. Since landowners would be paid for lands lost, buyers bore the cost. The need to redistribute wealth and income was glossed over. The states determined the maximum size of private property; hacendados had to divest themselves of the excess lands. The buyer, for his part, could not sell his lands for twenty years. Certain types of landless communities, or with insufficient lands, had the right to ask for lands to be taken from adjoining haciendas. If the hacendado refused to sell his excess lands, state authorities would expropriate them. Sellers had to accept government bonds as payment for their lands, their value to be determined by tax assessments, notoriously low during the Porfiriato. Congress and the state legislatures were to enact laws, *leyes reglamentarias,* setting up guidelines for the subdivision of large property. No wonder, then, that, given the political clout of the hacendados at the provincial level, the first of the *leyes reglamentarias* was not adopted until 1923. Section 6 of Article 27, which dealt with the ejidos, embodied the decree of January 6, 1915.

Article 27 marched in tune with the slogan *México para los mexicanos.* Both the land and the subsoil belonged to the Mexican nation. Foreigners had to obey Mexican laws, while government had the authority to review contracts and concessions made since 1876 that gave individuals or corporations monopolies of land, water, or natural resources and to nullify them when in conflict with the public interest. Only Mexicans by birth or citizenship and national corporations had the right to acquire mines or water or to exploit the subsoil. The state, nonetheless, had the power to grant concessions to foreigners who agreed to abide by Mexican legislation.

Article 123 was the labor code. Although a response to labor's demands, workers had no voice in its drafting; at Querétaro, the Constitutionalists embraced just two of them. To rub salt into the wound, in the elections of the Twenty-seventh Congress, the first to operate under the new Constitution, every candidate of the labor movement lost his bid for office. The Carrancistas revealed no desire to share political power with militant workers. The nationalistic provisions of the labor code, nevertheless, allowed them to utilize their demands to limit the influence of foreigners.

Article 123 included an eight-hour day, limited the type of labor to be done by women and children, set aside Sundays for rest, called for a minimum wage based on local living costs and health and accident insurance, and required special company schools for the children of the workers. To settle industrial disputes, Article 123 set up boards of arbitration and conciliation and gave labor the right to organize and to join unions, recognizing explicitly its right to strike. It placed Mexican and foreign workers on an equal footing, stating bluntly, "For equal work, equal pay, regardless of sex or nationality." Nothing in Article 123, nonetheless, dangled a socialist paradise before the worker. Rather, it sought to establish an equilibrium between labor and capital. The state, the new Leviathan, had the authority to supervise and control relations between them and to decide what was in the public interest. Article 123 did not do away with classes, or the poor, but simply made the state the protector of the worker, who, presumably, would be better off, although still a worker in a capitalist world. Theoretically, laissez-faire no longer held sway. Management, nevertheless, had the right to shut down plants when overproduction cut into reasonable profits. The labor code, like Article 27, left the formulation of *leyes reglamentarias* to the states; in formulating these, some states adopted less liberal measures.

For public education, the delegates gave birth to a truncated measure. At Querétaro many demanded federal school legislation; at stake was primary education, particularly for rural Mexico. What emerged was a setback for reform and the first of sundry mistakes in school policy. Article 3 provided merely that "primary instruction in public institutions shall be free." Nothing guaranteed a national network of public primary schools or, incredibly, obligatory school attendance. To have done so, critics argued, would have compelled the states and the federal government to provide schools; the delegates were unwilling to shoulder this burden. Worse yet, Justo Sierra's justly famous Ministry of Public Instruction, an innovation of the Porfiristas, was disbanded. Supporting a concoction of centralized authority and regional autonomy, the Carrancistas placed the implementation of Article 3 in the hands of states and municipalities, the least able or willing to carry it out.

To complicate matters, the question of church schools monopolized debate. Most of the discussions on Article 3 focused on the right of the church to have schools, with "conservatives," under the guise of liberty of thought, advocating their legality, and "radicals" opposed to them. Ultimately, a compromise was reached; the church could have secondary schools but had to stay out of primary education.

The "liberals" of 1917, as the debate of Article 3 revealed, were no less anticlerical than their mentors of 1857. The church, for its sin of coexisting with Don Porfirio's regime, got its comeuppance; Article 130 reaffirmed the earlier principles of faith and added some of its own, denying churches, for example, juridical personality and declaring priests to be members of a profession. States were given authority to regulate the number of priests who were required to have been born in Mexico. The church, according to the Constitution of 1917, was subordinate to civil authority. Freedom of worship, however, was guaranteed.

The middle-class delegates, despite all their talk about the federal responsibility for the welfare of workers and campesinos, had not assembled at Querétaro to dismantle Mexican capitalism. True, as "liberals" of the twentieth century, they no longer worshiped at the shrine of laissez-faire, whether theory or fact. On the contrary, they wanted an activist state, ready and able to encourage a measure of social change. Even legalistically, however, they tinkered with more than transformed the structure they inherited. For example, they conferred on industrial entrepreneurs the freedoms and privileges they enjoyed in Western capitalist nations. Private enterprise was, generally speaking, permitted to go its own way. Cabrera, economic guru of Carranza, put the matter well; the rebels, he wrote, *querian revolución pero no mucha* (wanted revolution, but not very much).

VIII

The Constitution of 1917, a copy partly of the Liberal charter of the century before, was the climax of the Great Rebellion. With blueprints for reform in hand, the victors set out to govern "revolutionary" Mexico, in theory markedly at odds with the Porfiriato. Venustiano Carranza, elected president in May 1917, was the first to try.

18

THE RELUCTANT SAMARITANS

I

With the despot out to pasture and a charter adopted, Mexicans, in 1917, looked forward to a benevolent future. Sadly, their expectations languished, by and large. Regardless of their rhetoric, their redeemers, it became crystal clear, did not intend to overhaul the Republic's structure completely. Tinker with it, yes; replace it with one of radical bent, as the slogans proclaimed, never.

Rhetoric could not evade international realities. Whatever its nationalist expectations, Mexico was a dependency of the United States. The "Revolution," as the uprising against the Old Regime was officially called, for all of its bombastic nationalism, had done nothing to alter that picture. Every Yankee illness, no matter how fleeting, put Mexico in the hospital for the gravely sick. By the same token, a healthy economy across the border, generally, though not always, meant better times for better-off Mexicans.

II

Venustiano Carranza inherited a troubled economy. Paper currency, most of it not worth the paper it was printed on, some of Carrancista manufacture, flooded the country. That, plus a banking system in distress, had hurt the financial edifice, making a shambles of Mexico's international credit rating. Huge debts had piled up, the results partly of damages claimed by foreigners, mainly Americans, who demanded repayment. Mining production had dropped—copper, for instance, by 65 percent. Wages were down and unemployment rampant in the industrial centers, and shortages of food, part of the crisis in agriculture, drove prices skyward. Caught in the spiral of inflation, city dwellers never knew from one day to the next if they could make ends meet. The railroads, which carried the country's goods, lay destroyed, testimony to the ability of rival armies to blow up bridges, tear up tracks, and wreck locomotives and rolling stock. Only revenues from exports of oil and henequen, both required by the United States and its allies in their struggle with Germany, remained high.

The European war, to the despair of Mexicans, ended in 1918. Sales of henequen toppled, and only oil exports stayed up. Then an upturn in the economies of the United States and western Europe helped Mexico to overcome its slump. Good times, however, proved fleeting; by 1926, Mexico had again fallen on hard times, the winds of the approaching Great Depression felt already. In July, the price of silver plummeted, along with exports of petroleum. To add to the drab scene, Tláloc forgot to water the crops, converting 1929 into a terrible year for agriculture; one-fourth of the lands planted never yielded harvests. Frightened capitalists sent their money to foreign banks, bringing on a wave of capital flight and a monetary crisis.

III

During the interval, Mexican politics shifted gears ever so slightly. In the National Palace, Carranza, now president, oversaw the Republic's business. Díaz had told Congress how to vote, and so did Don Venustiano; rarely did senators and deputies speak their mind. It could not be otherwise, because the centralized political structure weathered the collapse of the Old Regime, as did the exalted role of the chief executive. Given the absence of state and local autonomy, which testified to the lack of political organization at the grass roots, power was in the hands of the president, who wielded it so long as he did not antagonize unduly the interests of subordinate caciques and their bedfellows. Below the president sat the sundry power brokers, beholden to him but also his constituents, without whom he could not rule.

Still, politics had taken on a slightly different hue. Channels of communication had opened between government and the people. True, the people had little say, their opinions being usually ignored by the powerful. Yet government no longer saw the people simply as an inert mass; having learned a lesson from the pratfall of the Old Regime, the new rulers recognized that their survival required concessions to the people. In theory, they talked of a government by and for the people, of a "revolution" waged to correct past sins, a kind of Mexican populism.

From that, it followed, according to the official version, that government was "revolutionary," the offspring of a *Revolución,* baptized unique in Mexican annals, earlier ones, not excepting La Reforma and the Wars for Independence, relegated to lesser categories. The official jargon, however, neglected to define what was meant by *Revolución,* beyond speaking of an uprising of hungry campesinos and angry workers led by noble leaders against an evil empire of rapacious hacendados, a greedy *burguesía,* and "imperialistic foreigners." As a term, *Revolución* was left in a state of flux, used to justify and explain government policy—*revolutionary* meaning, as the occasion demanded, "*verdadero,*" or authentic, "nationalistic," "Mexican," "virile," and "modern." Ideologically, the propaganda pronounced the "revolutionary" regimes not to be *burgués,* without explaining what that signified, especially since the capitalist trappings of the Old Regime survived. As Manuel Gómez Morín, the founder of the Partido de Acción Nacional (PAN), would say, that left the door open for any bandit to wrap himself in the revolutionary mantle. From the "revolutionary" perspective of the power brokers, the "reactionaries," as the French were wont to say of their eighteenth-century foes, were the enemy.

Rhetoric aside, there was an Emiliano Zapata to deal with, a radical who swore never to lay down his arms until his people had land and workers social justice. While Zapata, alone, could not defeat the Carrancistas, like a burr on a horse's back, he would not allow them to sit comfortably in the saddle. Plainly, he must be eliminated. To silence him, the Carrancistas, in 1919, killed him in cold blood, promoting the author of the crime, a sleazy colonel, to general. The tragic end was inevitable. For the victors, the men in the forefront of the battle against Victoriano Huerta, Zapata's crusade was much too radical. As one admirer lamented to Carranza, "to our sorrow," Zapata was "confused mistakenly with the revolution."

IV

In 1920, the law stipulated, Don Venustiano must step down; unfortunately for him, he attempted to dictate the choice of his successor, forgetting he owed his authority to subordinates, among them Alvaro Obregón, who coveted the presidency. No friend of the "revolutionary" army or of the ambitious Obregón, Carranza thought otherwise, bestowing his benediction on Ignacio Bonillas, a little-known mining engineer and politico from Sonora. Obregón and his companions, to belittle Bonillas, who was identified closely with Yankee mining speculators, went about saying that he had been either a Protestant minister in Texas or a sheriff in Arizona.

The military brass being Obregonista almost to a man, the plot against Carranza was not long in hatching. One of those who sided with Obregón was Pablo González, a mediocre general who owed his career to Don Venustiano. The Plan de Agua Prieta, a blueprint for rebellion bereft of reform fervor, denounced Carranza's shenanigans; shorn of an army to defend him, Carranza took flight to Veracruz, from where he planned to regroup his forces. Instead, at the village of Tlaxcalantongo, he met his maker, shot to death by soldiers, probably obeying orders from Obregón, shouting, "Come out, you cowardly old man. Here is your *padre* [father]."

To complete Carranza's unexpired term, the Obregonistas, henceforth the kingpins of politics, picked Adolfo de la Huerta, a former bank clerk and singer from Guaymas, the port city of Sonora. De la Huerta, who held office until Obregón got himself elected, pacified Francisco Villa, the old nemesis, by giving him a hacienda in Durango. A gentle man, De la Huerta also got the Yaquis to the peace table and ran national affairs honestly and competently. It was about this time, too, that General Benjamin Hill, cousin and crony of Obregón, but like him with eyes on the National Palace, died; at his postmortem, physicians discovered arsenic poison in his stomach.

Alvaro Obregón was from Huatabampo, a town in the delta of the Río Mayo of southern Sonora. A garbanzo planter, he had not lifted a finger against the Old Regime; to the contrary, he boasted of his friendship with Luis Emeterio Torres, one of Sonora's *jefes.* With the aid of a brother, the local cacique, he became *presidente municipal* of Huatabampo in the days of Madero and then rose to fame as a general in the battle to oust Victoriano Huerta. At the constitutional Convention of 1917, delegates claiming to speak for him substantially modified Carranza's tepid outlines. When Obregón took office in 1920, many expected a sharp break with the politics of Don Venustiano; they were mistaken. No substantial change of policy occurred.

Despite his reputation as a reformer, Obregón was a politician with whom bankers and men of business could sympathize. His ideals were in tune with the rhetoric of the self-proclaimed practical men. Like Madero and Carranza before him, he was light of skin, so "white," recalled Vicente Blasco Ibáñez, "that it is impossible to tell whether he has a drop of Indian blood." The offspring of Francisco Obregón and Cenobia Salido, he belonged to one of Sonora's mightiest clans. Along with the Almadas and Elías, the Salidos, an old Alamos family, reigned over the social register. A self-taught man, Obregón was born to be a military chieftain as well as a politician. His ambition for high public office had early beginnings. "General," so goes an apocryphal story, "you have excellent eyesight." It is so good, replied Obregón, "that I could see the presidency from Huatabampo." His unwillingness to tolerate rivals drove Salvador Alvarado and Lucio Blanco, reformers of note, into the enemy camp.

When he occupied the National Palace, Obregón was on his way to joining the multimillionaires' club. No one disputed that Obregón loved money. As he boasted, he had not turned rebel to "satisfy mundane wants." The men who walked by his side, he exclaimed, were of the same background, "men of work, well known and respected in their communities." Obregón, the self-made man, had amassed his wealth not just by tilling the soil but by dabbling in sundry enterprises. By 1925, no longer in the National Palace, Obregón, from his home in Cajeme, ran Sonora's banks, controlled its food canneries, oversaw its flour mills, monopolized the harvest of garbanzos, reaped profits from the sale of land in Navajoa and Cajeme, and had the final say on the distribution of irrigation water. Named a member of the exclusive Casino Unión de Navolato, Obregón, as president, accepted membership with alacrity, joining, he admitted, many of his "old and dear friends."

Obregón was a man of the soil. Despite his military feats and his political triumphs, he never lost touch with the lands of his native Sonora. Unlike a legion of other "revolutionaries," he was never seduced by the bright lights of Mexico City. Until his death, he remained a loyal son of the countryside, a twentieth-century hacendado and Sonorense to the core. In Mexico City, his cook had to make him flour tortillas, big and thin, Sonora style, and, like Plutarco Elías Calles, his successor, he thrived on *menudo,* beef tripe soup. As president, he spent vacations on the haciendas of friends, whether old planters or "revolutionaries" who had acquired estates of their own.

A cautious politician, Obregón judged patience a virtue. All the same, his administration was the first to enforce articles of the national charter but, for all that, timidly. What was lacking in revolutionary fervor was made up for in official bombast. More exuberant than in the days of Carranza, it filled the air with talk of socialism, government by the proletariat, class struggle, and anti-imperialism. Former Zapatistas were allowed into the ranks, but their ideals were placed on the back burner. The Obregonistas, like their leader, acquired fortunes and, little by little, identified with the status quo, ending up, to cite a Mexican scholar, not by destroying what was left of the Porfirista edifice but by joining it.

Obregón, a capitalist ideologue, was a man of his era. As late as 1915, the artist Gerardo Murillo recalled, neither socialist doctrines nor radical panacea had beclouded Obregón's mind. While expressing sympathy for the underdog, he believed in the gospel of the survival of the fittest. To update Mexican capitalism, that was his goal. In its pursuit, he welcomed industrialists, bankers, merchants, and hacendados into the "revolutionary" family. He looked upon Mexico and its neighbor across the Rio Grande as sister nations. Like most Yankees, he believed in private enterprise and the sacredness of property. José María Maytorena, his old rival from Sonora, never tired of castigating Obregón for his defense of foreigners and their property in Mexico. Carranza, to some extent, refused to back Obregón's presidential ambitions because of his lukewarm defense of Mexican interests.

That attitude got Obregón into trouble in 1923, when he endorsed the Bucareli Agreements, an accord with Washington that declared Article 27 nonretroactive; that, as well as his determination to elevate Plutarco Elías Calles, a disliked ally, into the presidential chair. Nationalists and political rivals were soon up in arms. More than half of the military, stalwart enemies of Carranza's Bonillas scheme, turned on Obregón for his imposition of Calles. The rebel list included allies from Obregón's past: Manuel Diéguez, a hero of the Cananea strike of 1906; Salvador Alvarado, formerly governor of Yucatán; Fortunato Maycotte, who once saved Obregón's life; Manuel Chao, schoolteacher and ex-governor of Chihuahua; and Raul Madero, brother of the apostle. The military rebellion also counted on labor groups, which deemed Obregón's policies unfriendly. The generals and their allies found their leader in Adolfo de la Huerta, a suitor with presidential dreams jilted by Obregón.

The uprising failed, mainly because Washington embraced Obregón, the upshot of the Bucareli Agreements. With diplomatic recognition, the Obregonistas had guns and bullets. Obregón, for his part, vowed to shoot every captured rebel leader, a promise he kept. Before the fighting ended, some seven thousand had died, including Alvarado, Diéguez, Chao, and, not to be forgotten, Francisco Villa, shot dead on the eve of the rebellion by those who feared he might join it. In Yucatán, meanwhile, hacendados murdered Felipe Carrillo Puerto, its reform governor.

Don Plutarco, born of a family of *notables,* had deep roots in Sonora. The original patriarch, Francisco Elías González de Zayas, a native of La Rioja in Spain, had settled in Alamos in 1729. Calles, as he was known throughout his life, was born in Guaymas, the son of Plutarco Elías and Doña Jesús Campuzano. A bastard child, he was raised by Juan B. Calles, a saloonkeeper in Hermosillo. A grateful Calles adopted his name but, as he grew older, rebuilt his bridges to the Elías clan. At twenty-five, he married Natalia Chacon, daughter of Don Andrés, chief of the harbor guard of Guaymas, a job of some prestige. Tall and outwardly robust, he was, in fact, sickly. Whenever a crisis arose, Calles took to bed. In office, he aged rapidly, so much so that, when he was fifty, people referred to him as El Viejo, the Old Man. Calles, who refused to side with Madero in 1910, joined the rebellion against Huerta, rising to the rank of general as the faithful crony of Obregón. While eventually a wealthy man, he was never "too rich," nor, unlike Obregón, did he take pleasure in killing his enemies, although it did not disturb him greatly.

Frequently compared to Kemal Atatürk, the Turkish leader, Calles, in spite of his leftist reputation, was not a radical. Back home, he had been a schoolteacher, hotelkeeper, government bureaucrat, mayordomo of an Elías rancho, and partner of an American entrepreneur. As president, he tagged pernicious any revolutionary movement that attacked capitalism, welcoming foreign investors to Mexico. Barely in office, he ordered in-migration officials to bar the doors to "foreign leftists and communists," in 1929 severing diplomatic relations, established by Obregón, with the Soviet Union. Not always a strong leader and totally lacking in charisma, Calles, during the years 1926 and

1927, had to govern by executive decree, largely because the Senate blocked his plans.

The Callistas endeavored to promote capitalist growth. Their goal was to put the nation's finances back on their feet, to repair its credit standing, and to expand its infrastructure. That required integrating Mexico by way of highways, schools, a controlled press and radio, and a program of *mexicanidad*, urging Mexicans to be Mexican, as well as, initially, a modicum of agrarian reform. What emerged, especially as the Callistas lost their dubious fondness for change, was a plan to spur mining and agricultural exports, the old Porfirista policy. It was an economy of dependency, relying on foreigners. To increase farm exports and help private farmers, the government established the Banco de Crédito Agrícola and started to build dams.

The Callistas, like the Old Regime, also dreamed of fostering industry. The Great Rebellion had left undisturbed the old factories; moreover, it did not break up the industrial monopolies or make them more efficient. Quite the contrary: "the Revolution," writes one sage, "rather than tearing down the industrial structure of the Porfiriato, reinforced it." Recovery came quickly; soon industrial output had climbed back to the old levels. From 1918 to 1925, industrialists made big profits, roughly twice those of earlier years. Until the onset of the Great Depression, the industrial barons, though unwilling to reinvest in their factories, simply went on being rich and powerful. To aid industrialization, the Callistas, in 1934, organized the Nacional Financiera, modeled after a lending agency of the United States. Earlier, to stabilize the financial structure, they had established the Banco de México, a central bank, with the government owning over half of its shares.

By the will of Obregón, Calles had become president. That, so to speak, was also how he governed. In Mexico City, the chief executive occupied the National Palace, but Cajeme, to cite a popular refrain, was "the seat of power." Off cultivating his garbanzos, Obregón, nevertheless, had the final say. Astute politicos traveled to Cajeme, the more so after Obregón told them he wanted to return to the National Palace. A dutiful Congress, prodded by Calles, rewrote the Constitution, ruled reelection valid, and added two years to the presidential term. Porfirio Díaz, dead for over a decade, must surely have let out a hearty guffaw in his grave.

Aspiring politicians, nonetheless, were not delighted, among them Generals Arnulfo Gómez and Francisco Serrano. Both Sonorenses, they had early joined the *bola*, the tumult and fighting. Obregón, gossip had it, looked upon Serrano, known more for his debaucheries than for his fighting record, as "a son," while Gómez, notorious for his cruelty and corruption, and Calles were friends of long standing. All the same, when they made known their presidential hopes, Obregón ordered them shot. The death of Serrano occurred on the highway between Cuernavaca and Mexico City on the night of October 2, 1927, the infamous Noche de Huitzilac; Claudio Fox, the general in charge of the bloody massacre and once a student at the University of Arizona, confessed afterward he felt only nausea for the horrible crime entrusted to him. But not Obregón. When told of Serrano's death, Obregón reportedly exclaimed, "Well, Gentlemen, *a esa rebelión se la llevo la chingada* [so much for the fucking rebellion]." Gómez was sick on the day of his death; soldiers had to prop him up against a wall so that he could be shot. Before the purported rebellion ended, twenty-seven generals died by the firing squad, none given their day in court. In *La sombra del caudillo,* a novel of striking power, Martín Luis Guzmán recorded brilliantly for posterity the sordid episode.

Obregón went on to win the election of 1928. Unhappily for him, he never took office. He escaped the first attempt on his life; Segura Vilchis, a Catholic engineer in league, supposedly, with Father Agustín Pro, tried to kill him on the streets of Mexico City. At their execution, Roberto Cruz, the general commanding the firing squad, smoked a cigar while his soldiers riddled Pro and Vilchis with bullets. On the next attempt, Obregón was not so lucky. At La Bombilla, a restaurant in San Angel, a suburb of Mexico City, José de León Torral, a Catholic fanatic under the influence of a nun known as Madre Conchita and friend of the Pro family, shot Obregón, who was attending a banquet in his honor.

The death of the caudillo, as Guzman dubbed him, rocked politics. Everyone thought it was a Callista plot. Well aware that Obregonistas held him responsible for the death of their chief, Calles, to prove his innocence, fired Luis Morones, his able secretary (the term *minister* was no longer used) of industry, commerce, and labor, and an enemy of Obregón. With presidential aspirations of his own, Morones had opposed Obregón's reelection. That sacrifice, however, failed to stifle the cries of betrayal of Obregonistas, abruptly denied access to the public trough by these events, a bitter pill described jocularly by Jorge Ibargüengoitia in *Los relámpagos de agosto.* "Our chief is dead," one character "nearly in tears" tells another: Obregón, the author goes on to say, "had promised to name him secretary of agriculture." That aside, Calles, in a moment of political wisdom, swore to step down once his term was over, *presidencialismo* to be replaced by a Partido Nacional Revolucionario, or PNR. However, angry Obregonistas led by Gonzalo Escobar, a general with unkindly thoughts about agrarian reform, rebelled in 1929. No one seconded the Plan de Hermosillo, and the beaten Escobar had to flee for his life.

Long under the shadow of the caudillo, Calles, during his farewell to Congress in 1928, announced that henceforth Mexico would be governed by "institutions" and not by "caudillos." To set an example for others to emulate, he pledged never again to seek the presidency. At last, Mexican politicos, fascinated always by the Porfirista formula, had found a way to duplicate its success. As the Porfiristas had done, the PNR united the power brokers, baptized the "revolutionary family," who, behind closed doors, decided the course of politics. Discussion, compromise, and the peaceful settlement of family disputes eliminated the cuartelazo. Calles, nevertheless, ran affairs from the wings.

The PNR, a confederation of political interests, represented military chieftains, regional caciques, and state political organizations, as well as their subordinate workers and campesinos. The PNR made it possible for them to continue in control and, in so doing, avoid anarchy. During the years of turmoil, furthermore, their numbers had multiplied endlessly, central authorities being powerless to check their proliferation. It took more than a decade to get army chiefs, either as regional commanders or as governors, to obey, and then only moderately so. The caciques were often men of renown, such as Saturnino Cedillo, in San Luis Potosí; in Tamaulipas, Emilio Portes Gil; José Guadalupe Zuno and Margarito Ramírez, in Jalisco; and Manuel Pérez Treviño, of Coahuila.

In spite of its "revolutionary" slogans, the PNR was a bundle of contradictions, offering, at one and the same time, guarantees to capitalists, labor, and campesinos. Its principal role was to run and win elections. Heading the PNR was a national committee in Mexico City, which, under the guidance of a party head, supervised national operations. Next in line were the state committees, chosen theoretically by their municipal delegates but, in reality, by political bosses beholden to the strongmen. At the bottom stood the local committees, elected supposedly by members of the PNR in the *municipios*.

Since the death of Obregón, the non-reelection of the president had become a fact of political life—but not for governors, senators, and deputies. Since 1925, a small coterie of Callistas had monopolized these posts, as well as those in the state legislatures, which duplicated the *carro completo* of the Porfiriato. Aware of the swelling discontent among the ambitious, Calles prevailed upon Congress to ban the reelection of the president and, for good measure, that of governors, senators, and deputies. Congress complied but lengthened the terms of senators from four to six years and for deputies from two to three. This restored political mobility. Additionally, the Callistas decreed membership in the PNR an individual matter, thus undercutting regional parties, which lost their vote. That change, nonetheless, failed to strip regional bosses of their power; on their way to the top, they had forged close ties with labor and campesino organizations, which they manipulated. The caciques were indispensable to the administration of the local political structure, upon which the national edifice rested.

Military reform was also on the Callista agenda. From the Great Rebellion had come a bloated army; thousands had gone off to do battle at the beck and call of generals with flabby commitments to social change. Countless heroes of the fighting had become hacendados. When public works became the vogue, they appeared in government offices posing as contractors, ready to bid on the construction of roads and dams. Others built hotels, racetracks, and gambling casinos, not infrequently with government funds. Obregón had squelched the abortive cuartelazo of 1923, but not before pinning the eagle of the general on sundry officers. Nor did he reduce the size of the army. When the fighting ended, it was alive and well, with 14,000 officers for 78,000 enlisted men. In 1928, they ate up 40 percent of the national budget.

To modernize the army, Calles called on General Joaquín Amaro, the son of an Indian peon. Referred to as *el indio,* Amaro was from Zacatecas, a man shorn of compassion but intelligent and disciplined. Self-taught, he played polo and had studied science, military tactics, and, to acquire a veneer of polish, French, which he spoke fluently. While he became wealthy, he was always anticlerical and "antigringo." Amaro reduced the size of the army, weeded out the worst of its officers, instilled discipline, and raised morale among the troops. He tolerated no *cacicazgos;* the generals obeyed Amaro, secretary of war. To train his officers, he reopened the Colegio Militar, shut down since its cadets sided with Huerta's coup.

That activity, however, stopped short of transforming the army. As before, the army chiefs spent military funds on themselves and acquired lands of their own. Of the soldiers, only half were volunteers; the rest, as in the days of Don Porfirio, the *leva* recruited, mostly from the Indian villages of Oaxaca, where the Old Regime had found its soldiers. Soldaderas, as Indian as their men, fed and took care of them. Recruited by force, the *juanes,* the enlisted men, deserted in droves, up to 45 percent of them each year. More than ever, generals meddled in politics. Under Díaz, they had stayed in the barracks; the Great Rebellion let them out. Madero gave 15 percent of the high government posts to the brass hats; Carranza, 28 percent; and Obregón 58 percent, where Calles left it. All told, they controlled half of the cabinet ministries and governorships, while one of them, Calles, ran national affairs. Four generals, moreover, coveted the presidency in 1933.

Obregón's death left Calles the undisputed boss of Mexican politics. In 1929, Luis L. León, editor of *El Nacional,* the official newspaper, bestowed on him the title of Jefe Máximo, a sobriquet that stuck. From that date on, Mexicans spoke of the Maximato. To recall graffiti on the walls of the presidential home:

> Here lives the president
> but the boss
> resides in the house across the way

Choosing a successor to Obregón required time, so the man who lived "across the street," with the aid of the PNR, named Emilio Portes Gil, his secretary of *gobernación,* interim president. A conciliator, Portes Gil had organized agrarian leagues in Tamaulipas, which gave him something of the reputation of a reformer. Above all, he was loyal. Calles, in the meantime, traveled to Europe, leaving Portes Gil to mind the store while Mexicans elected a president. So began the era of the *gobiernos peleles,* the puppet presidencies of the Jefe Máximo.

The choice of the Callistas fell on Pascual Ortiz Rubio, a native of Michoacán and an engineer by profession. A Maderista, he had joined the Constitutionalists, risen to the rank of general, then as governor of Michoacán backed the Plan de Agua Prieta, Obregón's leap to the presidency. After serving briefly as secretary of public works, he became a diplomat; he had been out of the country for six years when told he was the candidate of the PNR. His designation shunted aside Aaron Sáenz, governor of Nuevo León, wealthy, conservative, and leader of what was left of the Obregonistas.

Ortiz Rubio, the "official candidate," had one obstacle to overcome. José Vasconcelos, Obregón's flamboyant secretary of public education, had decided to seek the presidency as spokesman for the Partido Nacional Antireelectionista, primarily middle-class urbanites. No less conservative than the PNR, the Vasconcelistas decried the despotism of Calles, lamented corruption, and spoke glowingly of individual rights. When forty thousand of them turned out to hear Vasconcelos in Mexico City, politicos of the PNR called out gangs of thugs to harass them and, on election day, put soldiers to watch over the polls. Official vigilance made certain that ballot boxes were stuffed, that the dead voted, and that the final count favored Ortiz Rubio.

If Ortiz Rubio contemplated governing on his own, he forgot that quickly. On inauguration day, a rifle bullet struck him in the face; from then on, he rarely appeared in public and, without protest, accepted a cabinet of Callistas, among them Portes Gil, one of his enemies. Most of the time, Ortiz Rubio bowed to Calles's wishes, earning the sobriquet Nopalito—a *don nadie,* or nobody. When he tried to act on his own, it cost him his job; after only two years, he abandoned the National Palace, his letter of resignation, dated September 1932, written by José Manuel Puig Casauranc, a notorious Calles sycophant.

To replace him, Calles, with the approval of the PNR, selected Abelardo Rodríguez, like him a general from Sonora and his obedient servant. A native of Guaymas, Rodríguez had worked for the Cananea Consolidated Copper Company and, in 1913, had enlisted in the uprising against Huerta; after signing the Plan de Agua Prieta, he eventually became a general. After a short stint in Mexico City, Calles dispatched him to Baja California, where, off and on, he served as chief of military operations and governor until 1932. There, he also became a millionaire. On the day that he took the presidential oath of office, he traveled to Cuernavaca to pay his respects to Calles, for whom he felt a deep "affection." A self-made man, so he boasted in his memoirs, he admired Henry Ford, being, to quote a Mexican writer, an illustrious exponent of "private revolutionary enterprise." As president, he did the administrative chores and left questions of policy to the Jefe Máximo.

V

Mexico's leaders had to deal with a truculent Uncle Sam. From Carranza to Abelardo Rodríguez, Washington watched Mexico like a hawk, seeing to it that nothing disturbed foreign investments. Any attack on international capitalism, Woodrow Wilson told Carranza, "was no less than an attack on democracy and on civilization itself." Carranza would be well advised not to attempt to enforce the Constitution of 1917, an anticapitalist doctrine.

The Carrancistas, though uninterested in basic reforms, were nevertheless nationalists. Foreigners, Don Venustiano insisted, could not expect preferential treatment but had to share good and bad times with Mexicans. Washington, London, and Paris, however, had a different interpretation of international law, claiming the right to intervene on behalf of their nationals regardless of what the Mexican Constitution said. Phrased in terms of glowing principles, the quarrel was actually over Mexico's petroleum deposits. Given this scenario, Mexicans, whatever their politics, had to temper their behavior.

With few exceptions, ironically, the men who steered Mexico down the path of rebellion had no quarrel with the principle of foreign investment. Like the Porfiristas, they coveted outside capital. At no time did they ask Americans, the principal capitalists, to leave or to stop investing their money in Mexico. Madero pledged to honor "obligations" and spoke of the respect for the rights of foreigners and their property. Carranza acknowledged the right of foreigners to sue for damages; ordered his army chieftains to punish the theft of their goods; and promised to "protect their lives, liberty, and the enjoyment of their legitimate property." Nevertheless, the Carrancistas, voicing rising nationalist sentiment, started to step on the toes of foreigners.

That drama unfolded on the petroleum stage. To defeat their rivals, the Constitutionalists needed funds. While bottled up in Veracruz, they raised the tax, dating from the days of Madero, on petroleum. But timidly, to merely a fourth of what the oil companies paid in the United States; a subsequent hike in 1917 made it clear that Mexico had ended Díaz's exemption for petroleum producers. That the black gold should be singled out for taxes was both logical and necessary, because it was Mexico's major source of revenue, representing a third of its national budget. On top of that, the Carrancistas were bankrupt, while the petroleum giants, American and British, were having banner years. The gasoline engine had revolutionized the petroleum industry, and, on its heels, had come World War I, the "first major fueled" conflict; of the crude petroleum imported by the United States, Mexico supplied 95 percent, much of it shipped to Britain for use by its wartime navy. When the war came to a close in 1918, the oil boom survived. Between 1911 and 1921, the golden age of Mexican oil, only the United States produced more.

The Carrancistas, however, had more than revenue taxes on their agenda. They declared that petroleum deposits belonged to Mexico, no matter what rights individuals had to them. But Washington rejected this interpretation, refusing to exchange, as the Carrancistas demanded, titles to petroleum properties for state concessions. When Uncle Sam labeled Mexico's decision confiscation, the Carrancistas, fearful of armed intervention, left their edict unenforced. They had ample cause to hesitate. In 1917, Washington had threatened to invade Mexico if the Carrancistas gave trouble to the oil companies and, to put teeth into its warning, sent four warships to the coasts of Tamaulipas. On their own, the oil companies encouraged Manuel Peláez, a renegade Mexican general, to rebel against his government, paying him to defend their properties, while Washington, to twist the knife more, told the Carrancistas not to trifle with Peláez. Not until 1920, when Peláez made peace with Obregón, did Mexican troops occupy the petroleum zone.

Washington did not shed tears over Carranza's death; but neither did it embrace the Sonorenses, as Obregón and his clique were referred to. It saw them as less dogmatic, but wanted, echoing the cries of American investors, formal guarantees for property in Mexico. From its perspective, this made good sense because the value of American investments in Mexico, due mostly to petroleum, had risen between 1910 and 1920. While Mexicans battled each other, oil production had increased from 3.6 million barrels in 1910 to 157.1 million. That bonanza spelled trouble for Mexico because, as petroleum revenues spiraled upward, so did national dependency on the industry. Any decline in the oil boom translated into doom for Mexico; oil revenues, Mexicans knew, placed their country at the mercy of the petroleum barons. In Washington, in the meantime, Albert Fall, a senator with his fingers in the oil pot, led jingoists' demands that Mexico nullify Articles 3, 27, 33, and 130 of the charter of 1917. Unless this was forthcoming, Washington was not to recognize Carranza's successor.

Washington, first under Woodrow Wilson and then under Calvin Coolidge, heeded that advice. Cowed by Washington's behavior, the Sonorenses capitulated but said that they would accede to the demands only after receiving formal diplomatic recognition. The Americans rejected the compromise, leaving the Sonorenses in a quandary; lacking Washington's blessings, they saw their enemies operate freely in the United States and ship arms to their allies in Mexico, and, more tellingly, they could not establish Mexico's credit on the international money market. Without it, their government had merely a ghost of a chance of surviving. On the other hand, to bow to Washington's demands in the face of Mexican nationalist fervor would mean, most likely, the end of the Sonorenses.

President Adolfo de la Huerta and Obregón, therefore, had to walk a tightrope. The clan from Sonora, pragmatist to the bone, had to assure the United States "through sovereign acts that its acquired rights would be respected" and, thus, convince it that no need existed for a formal treaty, anathema to Mexican nationalists. To triumph, the Sonorenses had to resolve the petroleum impasse and the problem of Mexico's international debt, owed mainly to American banks. Obregón's *mano suave,* or policy of concessions, rested on a *nacionalismo moderado,* a temperate machismo. The Obregonistas were not dealing from strength, especially because of the rocky economy of the early twenties, which reduced exports of silver, copper, and henequen and placed the revenue burden on petroleum.

The Obregonistas picked the Mexican Supreme Court to unveil their conciliatory policy. In the autumn of 1921, the court ruled invalid, in response to an appeal from the Texas oil company, the Carrancista decrees of 1918 and declared Article 27 nonretroactive. Seeking to preserve a semblance of Mexican sovereignty, the court dictated that this ruling applied only to lands where the companies had undertaken "positive acts" to exploit the oil reserves prior to 1917; lands left untouched were under the provisions of Article 27. The ruling, which confirmed foreign ownership, failed to convince the petroleum companies; despite their victory, they still opposed Washington's recognition of Obregón's government.

Failing to win over the stubborn oil barons, the Obregonistas started to court American bankers and merchants, dangling markets and a pledge of repayment before them. By the terms of the De la Huerta–Lamont Agreements, of June 1922, Mexico acknowledged an obligation of $500 million and promised to pay $30 million annually for four years, almost a fourth of the yearly national income, and to pay more after that. The pledge cut deeply into money for social reform. The Obregonistas, many of them landlords, among them Obregón, had not assigned agrarian reform a high priority anyway.

The Obregonistas, despite the concession, did not achieve United States recognition. Prodded by American investors in Mexico, Washington held out for a formal treaty. The Obregonistas, for their part, had to go one step further; Obregón's presidency was approaching its end, and a successor had to be found. If Plutarco Elías Calles was the choice, his enemies, among them De la Huerta, would be tempted to rebel. In that case, the rebels must not be allowed to buy weapons across the border; but Washington would not enforce its ban without a treaty.

By the Bucareli Agreements of 1923, the Obregonistas, as was mentioned earlier, declared Article 27 to be nonretroactive when the owners of the oil fields had undertaken positive acts before 1917. That confirmed the ruling of the Mexican Supreme Court in the Texas Company case. The Obregonistas also acknowledged the validity of American claims against Mexico dating from 1868. As a concession, Washington let stand Mexico's insistence that titles to oil properties be exchanged for almost indefinite concessions. That done, Uncle Sam conferred diplomatic recognition on Obregón, but at the cost of subverting Mexican sovereignty and undermining reform. When De la Huerta and the Mexican military revolted, alleging that Obregón had betrayed Mexico at Bucareli, the United States allowed Obregón to buy what he needed to put out the fire. To placate nationalists, the Obregonistas, in an outburst of political patriotism, recognized the Soviet Union, then ostracized by the capitalist West.

The embrace of the Yankee lasted only briefly. Petroleum output had begun to decline in 1922, and, when it took a nosedive after 1925, President Calles and his confederates blamed the oil barons, believing that the companies, unhappy with Mexican nationalists, had decided to punish them by shifting the focus of their activities to Venezuela, in that way telling them to make additional concessions or face the consequences. In response, the Callistas, initially more nationalistic than their predecessors, defiantly declared Mexico's ownership of the subsoil "inalienable" and limited concessions to fifty years.

Hardly had the ink dried on the proclamation when the oil companies began to voice strident objections. In Washington, President Coolidge, extolling nostalgically the peace of the Porfiriato, lamented the revival of "disorder" in Mexico, while his ambassador, James R. Sheffield, called Calles a "thief and an assassin," asserting that only military force would compel him to toe the line. Taking his cue from Sheffield, Frank B. Kellogg, speaking for the State Department, told Calles to respect American property or face an armed invasion. But Calles, defying Kellogg, shipped arms and supplies to the Sandinistas in Nicaragua, then trying to unseat a puppet regime of Washington's. Public opinion in the United States stopped Kellogg and like thinkers from carrying out their threat.

Unable to get its way, the wolf turned sly fox. If the belligerent Sheffield antagonized the Callistas, why not send a soft-talking gentleman to Mexico? Dwight Morrow, the man chosen by Coolidge, was no less a defender of capitalist rights but, just the same, a diplomat; he would get his way by using sweet talk. Morrow was a banker, a partner of J. P. Morgan of Wall Street, not an advocate of oil companies. As a banker, he wanted Mexico to pay its debts and to shelve talk of social reform at the expense of foreign capitalists. Oil was not uppermost on his mind; on that issue, he could be flexible.

Morrow arrived in Mexico near the end of 1927, carrying instructions to cool the quarrel. Bankers in the United States, Coolidge was informed, believed that threats of armed intervention jeopardized Mexico's repayment of its international obligations, a promise the Callistas had ratified once again in the Pani-Lamont Agreements of 1925. Facing a rebellion of Catholic Cristeros, Calles, moreover, had his back up against the wall. Morrow, by displaying none of the arrogance of Sheffield, who referred to Mexico as a "non-white" society, got his way. In 1928, the Mexican Supreme Court, upholding an appeal from the oil companies, ruled Article 27 nonretroactive and unlawful limits on property concessions. Morrow had won out; he went on to persuade the Callistas to downplay nationalist legislation, open wide the doors to foreign investment, curb labor demands, balance the budget, and pay off Mexico's international debts. This relegated social reform to limbo.

Morrow was not yet finished. To assure financial policies in accord with American blueprints, he took Luis Montes de Oca, Mexico's secretary of the treasury, under his wing in order to teach him the wisdom of capitalist finance. When the Great Depression cut into Mexico's revenues, and the cost of putting down the Escobar revolt of 1929 drove it to the edge of bankruptcy, which jeopardized repayment of its debt, Morrow, with the aid of Wall Street bankers, worked out a new agreement. For forty-five years, Mexico would make annual payments of $12.5 million, at from 2 to 5 percent interest.

Thanks partly to Morrow, relations between Mexico and the United States took a turn for the better. So improved were they that Herbert Hoover, a businessman's president, likened them to the friendly ties of the days of Don Porfirio. Even the Estrada Doctrine, by which Mexico denounced the withholding of recognition by a foreign power, failed to ruffle the calm. By 1930, foreigners, with Americans at their forefront, had more money invested in Mexico than in 1910, the bulk of it in petroleum, mining, the railroads, and electricity. Yet there were signs of a decline in the importance of foreign investment; by 1930, Mexican capital had a bigger role to play, mainly because the Great Depression had reduced the flow of outside capital.

In 1926, a conflict pitting the church against the state erupted, and soon armed campesinos, shouting "Viva Cristo Rey" (Long live Christ King), were swarming over Jalisco, Colima, Michoacán, and neighboring Zacatecas and Nayarit. At its height, the Cristero Rebellion had fifty thousand campesinos fighting the Mexican army and more than holding their own. Both sides dealt harshly with each other, asking no quarter and committing atrocities of sundry types. In April 1927, to mention just one, Cristeros led by a priest dynamited the Guadalajara–Mexico City train at El Limón, a hamlet in Jalisco; every soldier in the military escort and over a hundred passengers died, including women and children. The butchery at El Limón was not unique. Before the uprising subsided, soldiers killed priests, raped nuns, and looted churches, while Cristeros, not to be outdone, tortured and killed "atheistic" schoolteachers. Some eighty thousand Mexicans died in this holy war.

The clash, of course, antedated Calles's stay in the National Palace, going back to the Bourbon reforms of the eighteenth century, to Valentín Gómez Farías and his Liberals and to the Reforma. The Porfiristas had worked out a truce, but the delegates at Querétaro, fathers of the charter of 1917, fanned again the anticlerical flames. With ample cause, the church saw itself persecuted. The CROM, the official labor confederation, had, from its beginning, attacked Catholic labor unions, destroying them eventually. With the enthusiastic collaboration of Luis Morones, boss of the CROM, Calles had even attempted to establish an independent Catholic church, free of papal control.

The church, likewise, had challenged the legislation of Querétaro. Events in Jalisco, heavily Catholic, bear that out. There, in 1917, the clergy had refused to hold services in protest against the anticlerical articles in the Constitution. To avoid a confrontation, which might have led to violence, Carranza, more pragmatist than ideologue, left Articles 3 and 130 unenforced. Although no admirer of priests, Obregón did not tinker with the status quo.

The events of 1926 shattered the truce. No one knows who threw the first stone. In January 1926, Calles decided to enforce the inflammatory articles or, his apologists say, responded to a dictum of Archbishop José Mora y del Río nullifying them. Whatever the truth, Calles, infuriated by Mora y del Río's defiance, ordered priests to register with state authorities. The archbishop, equally stubborn, had chosen a poor time to challenge Calles, then confronted with threats from a hostile Washington and the petroleum companies. In his opinion, the church had joined his enemies. When Callistas in Jalisco, Colima, and Hidalgo enforced the Constitution, the clergy, in retaliation, abandoned the churches but, so as not to antagonize Catholics, continued to say mass and offer the sacraments in private homes. In retaliation, the Callistas banned private services.

The Cristero uprising, for all the meddling of the hierarchy, flared up not in the cities but in the countryside. Its causes were multiple. Rhetoric notwithstanding, the "revolutionaries" had dragged their feet. As one author writes, between 1913 and 1926, except for *ejidatarios,* most campesinos had "merely won for themselves added burdens, bigger risks, and dashed hopes." Military bosses, some fanatical anticlericals, had looted at will, killed the defenseless, and seized land for themselves. The chicanery of state and national politicos was no less brazen. The hammer blows of hard times, which inflated jobless rolls in the countryside, exacerbated the plight of the poor. The "violence," writes one historian, "sprang from the anger felt daily but repressed until then, which the Callista assault on the faith unleashed." The closing of the churches was the straw that broke the camel's back.

Eventually the fighting ended. Hungry for peace, Catholic *burgueses,* the city faithful of middle-class background or rich, wished for their churches to reopen. The high clergy, too, wanted its jobs back, while the Vatican, which had opposed the closing of churches from the start, urged a compromise. The

Callistas, confronted with the cost of the war, the Great Depression, and, additionally, the Vasconcelos campaign of 1929, which daily attracted more of the middle class, had lost their stomach for the fighting. Also, Washington, fearing chaos in Mexico, labored mightily to bring the conflict to a close, with Morrow, its ambassador, playing a key role. Peace came, but at the expense of the campesinos, who were, so to speak, left on their own. From that time on, they got no help from Catholic *burgueses,* who, earlier, had supplied rifles and bullets. The victory went to the government; but the Callistas, less belligerent, abandoned attempts to enforce the anticlerical stipulations of the charter of 1917.

VI

The hacienda, meanwhile, outlived the Great Rebellion. Its survival was neither ironic nor unpredictable; the victors in the bloody civil strife had rarely disguised their dislike of radical reforms. Ridding Mexico of the hacienda, which exercised a monopoly over the land, tempted only the boldest. Still, like it or not, the dirt farmers of the countryside, their aspirations given voice by Zapata and his brothers in arms, started to cry for land of their own.

Had Article 27, the bill of rights of land reform, been honored fully, the scenario would have been different. However, the Carrancistas, like the Maderistas, worshiped mundane goals. The years of warfare, which hampered cultivation of the soil, particularly in the Bajío, cut deeply into the food supply of the Republic. Feeding Mexicans, therefore, took precedence over schemes to divide haciendas. Awareness of the need for land reform by the Constitutionalists, who talked glibly of legal niceties, matured slowly, largely in response to a rising popular clamor, especially after the promulgation of Article 27, which awakened the hopes of the landless.

Pledge and performance, for all that, were not one and the same. By 1917, the National Agrarian Commission, established to implement the distribution of land, had solemnly announced that, thereafter, villages seeking to acquire it by dotation, of far more importance than restitution, would have to buy it. If one had not lost lands, or could not prove title to them, one had to buy them. If this was not done, the government would be unable to pay hacendados for their lands. Agrarian reform was put on a pay-as-you-go basis. In 1920, Congress approved legislation for an agrarian public debt, promising to indemnify owners for land taken. Nonetheless, hacendados in Coahuila, Carranza's bailiwick, as well as in Sonora and Chihuahua, home to the conquerors of Huerta, kept their lands. By 1919, just 111,065 hectares had been redistributed by dotation; the lands changing hands represented about 0.5 percent. A goodly slice of the lands expropriated often belonged to political enemies.

The Plan de Agua Prieta, a summons to rebellion remarkable for its silence on the land issue, swung open the doors to the clan from Sonora. Since the days of Governor José María Maytorena, a hacendado and kindred soul of Madero, the Sonorenses had exhibited little desire to trifle with property rights. They saw agrarian reform not as a solution for the agrarian problem but, instead, as a tool for dealing with a political question. Obregonistas and Callistas employed land reform as a pacification gimmick, as a means to avert rebellions. The solution to Mexico's ills, they believed, was the modernization of agriculture: mechanize farming; build dams; and diversify crops, always with an eye on export markets. Hoping to push that along, the Calles administration established the Banco de Crédito Agrícola, a bank for private farmers; poured money into irrigation projects; organized agricultural schools; and built roads linking farms to markets.

The goal, according to official propaganda, was to multiply the number of small, private farms. The path ahead, for all that, was long and labyrinthine. "I am an advocate of the small farm," Obregón explained, "because I believe in helping those who want to help themselves rise above their penurious condition." But, he added, "I do not believe that the hacienda should be broken up before the advent of small property." Obregón never spelled out how he would create small farms without taking fertile lands away from hacendados. No Sonorense, by the same logic, lifted a finger to rectify the glaring omission in Article 27 denying *peones acasillados* the right to petition for the lands they tilled. Until this was done, most haciendas would survive.

Land reform and politics walked arm in arm. For the period 1920–21, when the Sonorenses needed popular support, statistics show an upswing in the pace of land distribution. With the consolidation of their political control, a decline set in. The De la Huerta revolt of 1923 jarred the Obregonistas out of their complacency; Obregón's report to Congress in 1924, the last of his messages, confirmed that more lands had been given out; 140,000 Mexicans had benefited. Wanting to pacify Zapata's old followers, Obregón took special care to redistribute lands in Morelos. Likewise, in Yucatán, Felipe Carrillo Puerto, a disciple of Alvarado, established ejidos but, tellingly, left undisturbed the henequen plantations. Francisco Múgica and Lázaro Cárdenas, in Michoacán, as well as Emilio Portes Gil, in Tamaulipas, also distributed lands. At the national level, the Callistas doubled the pace of land reform until 1926, years of consolidation after the abortive De la Huerta uprising. Once they were firmly in the saddle, land reform was virtually no more. Of the puppet presidents, only Portes Gil endorsed land reform.

Official statistics, moreover, can mislead. One example is the purchase for upwards of five million dollars, in 1923, of nearly one million hectares lying along the border from Chihuahua to Sonora of the Paloma Land and Cattle Company, ostensibly for redistribution to landless campesino. The reality was something else. While official rhetoric proclaimed that the goal was to create *pequeñas colonias agrícolas,* small farms, most of the land of the Paloma barons ended up in the arms of the wealthy and powerful, among them high politicos. The best lands, sometimes in 100,000-hectare plots, fell into their lap. When accused of hoarding, their owners "sold" them off to family relatives or faithful friends, in that fashion circumventing the intent of the law. As the years went by, even Americans once more became owners of some of the lands.

The Sonorenses, additionally, did not always pacify by bowing to demands for land. When the Yaquis started to fight for the return of their fields, Obregón dispatched General Manuel Diéguez to Sonora; to placate the Yaquis, he pontificated, would be to "sanction . . . the survival of barbarism and to relinquish control of lands now blessed by civilization." Calles, then Obregón's sidekick, even revived briefly the deportation policy of the Old Regime. When the Yaquis took up arms for the last time in 1926, Obregón got Calles to buy up the lands of the Richardson Company, the principal latifundista in the Yaqui Valley; but most of the lands were acquired by private individuals. Campesino demands for lands in the Mexicali Valley of Baja California, the domain of the Colorado River Land Company, led to jail sentences for their leaders. The Partido Nacional Agrarista, a political tool of the Obregonistas designed to win campesino support, dropped from sight under Calles, its demands for land no longer welcomed. Not by chance, "Cuatro Milpas," a song on everyone's lips in the 1920s, which, between *ayes de dolor,* dwelt on the ruin of the countryside, deplored untilled corn patches.

For rural peoples, says a Mexican scholar, the Mexico of Don Porfirio and that of Plutarco Elías Calles differed little. As in 1910, a tiny coterie of Mexicans owned the fertile lands. The owners of the big estates, some thirteen thousand of them, earmarked their harvests for the export market. Just 2.2 percent of the rural estates, all over one thousand hectares, monopolized 84 percent of the agricultural lands; rancheros mostly and *ejidatarios* tilled what was left of the farmlands. Nearly 87 percent of the agricultural lands were private property.

Approximately 670,000 *ejidatarios* cultivated merely a small fraction of the Republic's soil. With few exceptions, Veracruz for one, most of the new ejidos had been carved out of poor lands, nearly always *terrenos baldíos.* Only here and there had haciendas succumbed to ejidal demands. The ejido, as conceived by the *norteños,* or northerners, was simply a means to liberate the Indian campesino from his total dependence on the hacendado, and permit him to sell his labor on the free market. Inhabitants of communal pueblos would supplement their incomes by working for wages on neighboring haciendas and, additionally, have lands of their own to fall back on when jobs dried up. The framers of the Constitution, as the Sonorenses knew, never contemplated replacing private property with a communal system of landownership.

Given this picture, Mexico failed to shake off the legacy of the landless. Of the 3.5 million who, in one way or another, tilled the land, 2.5 million had not a spadeful. The census of 1930 classified them as agricultural workers, a rural proletariat, but neglected to point out that thousands of them went begging for jobs for weeks and months on end. No less exploited were 500,000 *minifundistas,* dirt farmers with minuscule plots of scrubby land. While the hacendados, who monopolized the fertile and irrigated lands, produced two or more crops a year, the *minifundistas* harvested, at best, one crop.

In 1930, Don Plutarco returned from a trip to Europe, convinced that agrarian reform had been an error. It was time to call a halt to the nonsense; such was the message conveyed to Pascual Ortiz Rubio, recently elected president of Mexico. With that pronouncement, the reforms of Portes Gil, who had taken advantage of Calles's absence to distribute land, ended. As of this juncture, the question was how to increase the productivity of commercial farms, no matter what their size. In 1934, despite the so-called agrarian revolution, Mexico had a higher concentration of land in the hands of the few than did sister republics in Spanish America.

VII

Labor, by and large, fared better under the *norteños.* Yet its blessings were a mixed bag. The struggle to unseat Huerta had worsened labor's difficulties, while the factional fighting left more misery behind. Moreover, many Constitutionalists, like the Maderistas, viewed suspiciously efforts to organize an independent labor movement. Yet the Constitutionalists had to court labor. The Huertistas, to repeat, had been no more "unfriendly" to labor than the Maderistas had. In addition, the battle to defeat Villa's armies, then occupying Mexico City, compelled the Constitutionalists to share their fate with the Casa del Obrero Mundial, practical politics making bedmates of them. The alliance, signed in February 1915, occurred none too soon, for already Antonio Díaz Soto y Gama and Luis Méndez, two regulars of the Casa, had embraced Zapata, Villa's ally.

The merger shattered the neutrality of labor, which, until then, had kept its distance from the quarreling factions. By embracing the Constitutionalists, the Casa, led, ironically, by white-collar thinkers, assured itself of government meddling in its affairs. Worse yet, the marriage destroyed hopes for solidarity among workers, pitting industrial labor against campesinos in Zapata's army. By backing the Carrancistas, industrial workers of the Casa had come to the aid of politicians hostile to campesinos. "Red Battalions" of armed workers, in the pay of the Carrancistas, helped defeat Zapata.

Although the Carrancistas welcomed the Red Battalions, they had no intention of allowing the Casa to alter their blueprints. Carranza wanted no rivals, especially left-wingers or labor revolutionaries. To his anger, the Casa, with Villa and Zapata defeated, started to build a labor network in the Republic. Labor unions, some affiliated with the Casa, blossomed in nearly every industry, encouraged by the revolutionary euphoria. Strikes against industry, latent since the fall of Huerta, broke out again. When a general strike erupted in Mexico City in the summer of 1916, which paralyzed its public utilities, the Carrancistas jailed the leaders of the Casa and closed its doors, then persecuted its affiliates in the provinces. By 1916, they had dealt a mortal blow to the independent labor movement.

Between 1916 and 1918, the Carrancistas evolved a formula for handling labor. At Querétaro, Article 123 had bestowed on labor the right to organize and to bargain collectively. The pledge, furthermore, had revived the drive to organize unions, while strikes sanctioned by it disrupted the economy. Caught between the need for industrial peace, the necessity to court labor, and fear of an independent labor bloc, the Carrancistas chose to build a captive labor organization.

The Confederación Regional Obrera Mexicana, or CROM, emerged from a meeting in Saltillo, capital of Coahuila, convoked by its governor, a crony of Carranza. Luis Morones, chief of the CROM until the 1930s, had collaborated earlier with the American Federation of Labor and opposed the general strike of 1916 in Mexico City. The birth of the CROM, a confederation with intimate links to government, ended the "romantic, idealistic period in the Mexican labor movement." In spite of its leftist rhetoric, the CROM worked for an "equilibrium between capital and labor." Opportunistic and pragmatic, its leaders, with Morones at the helm, accommodated themselves to capitalism and learned to collaborate with employers unfriendly to labor. Their success set the stage for the manipulation of labor and its subservience to government. Morones, the crown prince of the CROM, according to one source, lost no time in gaining notoriety for "the extravagant revelry at [his] . . . weekend parties and his ostentatious display of automobiles and diamonds."

When the cuartelazo of Agua Prieta took place, the lot of labor had hardly gotten better; still prevalent were low wages, long hours of toil, squalid working conditions, and arbitrary decisions by management. Little had been done to enforce Article 123. The CROM, nonetheless, backed Obregón's bid for the presidency. The Partido Laborista Mexicano, an offshoot of the CROM, worked for his candidacy. As a reward, the Obregonistas set aside half of the seats on the ayuntamiento of Mexico City for the Partido Laborista and named mayor one of the CROM's bosses, while Morones received an important government post. Yet the Partido Laborista, born to bring the Obregonistas to power, quarreled incessantly with the Partido Nacional Agrarista, likewise a tool to win campesino backing for the Sonorenses.

The 1920s were the "age of the CROM," when its bosses, in return for monetary and political rewards, manipulated labor for the benefit of government and business, while the Sonorenses took advantage of the industrial peace to fortify capitalist development. The triumph of Morones and his henchmen, which undercut the autonomy of labor, encouraged the development of captive unions. One result was a marked decline in the number of strikes while recalcitrant labor groups fared badly.

Still, dissidents challenged the supremacy of the CROM, among them the textile and streetcar workers, who established the Confederación General del Trabajo (CGT) in 1921. It fought hard to organize campesinos and workers under one banner and, more alarming to the Sonorenses, to collectivize the means of production. The CGT, its influence felt mostly in the Bajío, enjoyed the support of anarcho-syndicalists and the Communist party, which dated from 1919. David Siqueiros, the muralist, was one of the militants of the CGT. From their headquarters in Guadalajara, Siqueiros and his allies helped workers organize strikes against industries allied with the CROM and foreign mining companies, which usually had federal soldiers guarding their properties. Siqueiros and the Communists also encouraged women to join the Centro Evolucionista de Mujeres, a labor union for women in Jalisco.

The church, too, founded a short-lived rival to the CROM, the Confederación Católica de Trabajo, which, primarily in the textile industry, clashed head on with the CROM and the CGT. Although endorsing Article 123, the Confederación had nothing good to say about agrarian reform, labeling expropriation theft of private property. The Catholics tasted limited success; in the textile industry, for example, they failed to win control of a single mill. Unfortunately, too, the Catholic challenge weakened the influence of the CGT, particularly in Puebla.

Whether the Sonorenses, as critics often write, converted the CROM's bosses into puppets is debatable. At times, Morones and his companions displayed an alarming degree of independence, not being above playing their own game. Although at the beck and call of politicos in Mexico City and, similarly, willing to embrace the tycoons of industry, the stalwarts of the CROM also coveted power for themselves. The workers, therefore, gained sporadic benefits. Affiliates of the CROM, for instance, won a majority of their industrial disputes in the years between 1920 and 1924.

Under the Callistas, the CROM briefly won added laurels. Morones, for one, became head of a cabinet ministry, a novelty in the Mexico of that day. The rolls of the CROM swelled with new memberships. By 1927, the CROM had 200,000 members. The Catholic unions, the next-largest, had no more than 40,000, twice that of the CGT. The CROM controlled two-thirds of the Republic's organized workers, most of them in foreign-owned industries.

The splendor of the CROM was over in less than a decade. By 1927, Morones had broken with Obregón, one reason for the discord being their mutual aspiration to the presidency. As a result, Calles blocked the CROM's control of the ayuntamiento in Mexico City and severed his ties to Morones. For interim president, moreover, he picked Emilio Portes Gil, the CROM's biggest enemy, who lost no time going after "communists" in labor, even jailing Siqueiros. When Morones and his companions refused to help Calles establish the Partido Nacional Revolucionario in 1929, the break was complete. Thereafter, Morones and the Partido Laborista Mexicano, the political arm of the CROM, lost their clout.

The demise of the CROM had multiple causes. The Great Depression, which upended the Mexican economy, brought unemployment in industry. By 1929, the Callistas were protecting industry and curbing labor, part and parcel of their decision to curtail agrarian reform. Still, the CROM was not entirely blameless for its misfortunes; the unwillingness of its leaders to stand up and be counted hurt them with the rank and file. Without a word of dissent, Morones and his henchmen had allowed politicos in Mexico City, through the recently established Juntas de Conciliación y Arbitraje (labor boards), to rule on the legality of strikes and labor unions.

From the downfall of the CROM emerged rival labor bosses. First to leave Morones, who at this stage of his life resembled, Mexicans say, "a fat opera singer," were the *cinco lobitos* (five little wolves), one of them Fidel Velázquez. In 1932, Vicente Lombardo Toledano and his cohorts, powerful in Veracruz, Puebla, Coahuila, Chihuahua, Zacatecas, and the Federal District, escaped the sanctity of the CROM. Claiming to represent the "real" CROM, Lombardo Toledano wooed Velázquez over to his side.

VIII

On the subject of women, the "revolutionaries" of 1910 were ambivalent. Labor won the right to organize; campesinos, a chance at some land; but women, though loved as mothers, wives, and daughters, were denied the vote. The "radicals" at Querétaro swore to bar women from voting, whereas, paradoxically, "conservatives," allies of Carranza, did not. What split them, of course, was the church issue and, denials to the contrary, machismo, men's belief that women could not think for themselves. Delegates of leftist bent, Francisco Múgica, for one, believed that priests told women how to vote. If Mexico was to change, women had to be kept out of politics. Mexican legislation, however, embraced divorce, with Carranza one of its champions. Abandonment was made the sole grounds for divorce: a woman's one night away from home gave a man the right to sue for divorce; women had to prove that their husbands had been gone for thirty days.

Women, for all that, did not sit back and wait for men to legislate on their behalf. In 1916, women of reform convictions met in Mérida, capital of Yucatán, then under the tutelage of Salvador Alvarado, where they dealt with questions of suffrage, literacy, and education. Again in Yucatán, this time in the days of Governor Felipe Carrillo Puerto, women gained the right to vote and to hold public office, winning three seats in the state legislature in 1923, one for Elvia Carrillo Puerto, the governor's sister and a militant crusader. Believing large families a barrier to a better life for the poor, the women of Yucatán established a birth-control program and distributed the literature of Margaret Sanger. In an attempt to get women to participate in community affairs, women reformers organized *ligas feministas,* spoke out against demon drink, fanaticism, and superstition, and sponsored literacy programs. The murder of Carrillo Puerto in 1923 aborted the feminist crusade in Yucatán. Under his "revolutionary" successors, women even lost the right to vote.

19

THE JUMBLED HARVEST

I

Whatever the importance of politics, the trials and, ultimately, failure of the quest for agrarian justice, or the ramifications of the international oil dispute, the singularity of the years from 1917 to 1935 lies elsewhere. The most lasting legacy, what captured the spotlight of world attention for Mexico, was the Great Rebellion as a cultural event, the epic of a people searching for its soul. It was in mural art, a form largely ignored since the days of the Italian masters of the sixteenth century, where Mexicans saw visions and dreamed dreams and, by doing so, gave meaning and substance to the upheaval of 1910. Literature, too, although on a less grand scale, built castles in the air, leaving a rich bequest, Mexican to the core. Quixotically, the arts surfaced in a society that, though changing, still sat on traditional pillars, as the tribulations of rural education documented vividly.

II

Overwhelmingly powerful and, both in color and theme, Mexican, the muralist renaissance, as it was baptized, did not just spring out of nowhere. Nor, claims to the contrary, was it merely the offspring of the "Revolution." In spite of its uniquely Mexican character, it was hardly an isolated phenomenon but, rather, part and parcel of European artistic renovations at the turn of the century yet, at the same time, a rejection of foreign tutelage. The innovation in Mexican art, it must not be forgotten, stepped out of the framework of European Impressionism. Though poles apart in themes and colors, José Clemente Orozco's stoic figures had ties to Edouard Manet's painting of a French courtesan with dirty feet lying naked on a couch and to the revolt of Paul Cézanne and Vincent van Gogh, who wanted to rely on colors to depict emotions. Until the 1940s, mural art dominated the Mexican artistic scene.

Mural art, the soul of Mexico's artistic renaissance, had its heyday in the time of Michelangelo. The murals in the Sistine Chapel testify to his genius. Then, as in the Mexico of the 1920s, it was conceived as a popular art, for a people, to cite Diego Rivera, untrained in looking at objects of art. The artist had to provide an understandable art, interesting at first sight. Besides being an art for the people, it was also an epic art, which dealt with momentous themes and controversial topics. Orozco, Rivera, and David Siqueiros, the "Big Three," were its masters.

Why the art renaissance? The question, first off, is misleading because it implies that Mexico had no art of any consequences before the 1920s. To quote one critic of this opinion, Mexico, during the Porfiriato, was the "original home of the Coca Cola school of art." Nowhere "in the world," he went on to allege, "not even in Victorian England, had bad taste in art . . . been so carefully nurtured."

But it was Gerardo Murillo, the artist most responsible for the muralist outburst, who offered the classic answer, thus winning for himself a niche in "revolutionary" circles. For Murillo, or Dr. Atl, as he titled himself, the Revolution held the secret to the renaissance. Before 1910, art had been both Spanish and Christian, an architectural art basically, orphaned by the culture that produced it. Imitation was the result. To overcome the cycle of mediocre art, a sharp break with the past was necessary; that rupture, said Atl, must be Mexican and pagan. The Revolution, to Atl, made that possible. It was, to start, an anticlerical crusade which acquired a religion of its own, becoming a facsimile of the Counter-Reformation, the mother, as Atl rightly pointed out, of Spanish art. The Revolution symbolized the struggle for social justice; from it, a spiritual rebirth took shape, conferring importance on the common people, as well as rediscovering the Indian and the pre-Hispanic heritage. *Indianismo,* its philosophical foundation, recognized that the ancients had carved out mighty civilizations where art enjoyed center stage. Unlike Europe, ancient Mexico had "no art for the sake of art," no artistic elite. Quite the opposite: everyone was an artist, while the useful and the beautiful were one and the same. Additionally, folk art, which survived the tastes of Porfiristas, left behind examples for others to emulate, for instance in the murals of the pulquerias, where the poor went to drink; in the retablos of churches, artistic testimonials to miracles; and in the lithographs, namely, the drawings of José Guadalupe Posada. Then, there was the inspiration of the popular arts, revived in the 1920s when tourists started to visit Mexico, more and more on the lookout for blankets from Toluca and sarapes from Saltillo; black pottery from Oaxaca; and colorful baskets and huaraches. All of this, Atl concluded, explained the renaissance.

Atl forgot to add that Mexico, even during the balmiest days of the Porfiriato, had produced exciting art; witness the legacy of the Primitives, of painters such as Hermenegildo Bustos, an artist deeply rooted in his native Purísima. The Porfiristas, moreover, had more than just Posada and Bustos to boast about. José María Velasco, the painter of Mexican landscapes, was a pillar of the Old Regime, which also had its intelligent art patrons. For example: the governor of Veracruz, a dyed-in-the-wool Porfirista, recognizing genius in the young Diego Rivera, had sent him off to Europe to study painting, while Justo Sierra's Ministry of Public Instruction had sponsored an exhibit of Mexican artists, Orozco among them, in 1910.

For all of its worship of the "revolutionary," Atl's theory only partly explained the birth of the renaissance. Actually, Bertram D. Wolfe, one of the biographers of Rivera, provided a more plausible answer. For Wolfe, the Revolution, so exalted by Atl, was an "aborted and tragic one." Moreover, an art renaissance had never taken shape from a social upheaval, such as the French and the Russian, to name two. For Wolfe, the explanation lay in the official patronage of mural art. When talented painters like Orozco and Rivera did not have to depend for their livelihood on the sale of their art to *burgueses,* channels previously closed were opened to them. No longer captives of the tastes of private buyers, artists were free to experiment, to paint in novel fashion. Not dependent on the goodwill of the rich, they could refuse to paint a wealthy Mexican's wife or mistress, the horizons of their art liberated from the dictates of critics in the European mold.

Over and beyond that, Wolfe might also have mentioned the pragmatic politicians of the twenties. Having risen to power partly on their revolutionary rhetoric, they had to make good on it. Since they had little inclination to do so, they had to offer something on account, a promise of better things in the future. If contemporary Mexico had changed just so slightly, tomorrow, politicians swore, would be different. Mural art, which spoke of nationalistic aspirations, hailed the Bronze Man of Mexico, took comfort in the fall of tyrants and pictured, in the drawings of Rivera, happy campesinos tilling land of their own, filled that need. If the people were patient, they would have their banquet. Walls for the muralists to paint on, similarly, beckoned everywhere, on the buildings of government ministries, the National Palace, schools, and open-air *mercados.* By encouraging artists to cover the walls of public buildings, the government, by association, gained for itself the veneer of "revolutionary" and nationalist. For Obregonistas and Callistas, the murals were tools of propaganda. Claims notwithstanding, government officials, however, rarely worshiped either the artists or their works. From the start, they paid badly, to quote Rivera, barely enough for artists to keep body and soul together. Nor did José Vasconcelos, who as secretary of public education never tired of assuming credit for the murals, think highly of them, once confessing he "abhorred Orozco's caricatures."

Still, artists had radical ideas on their minds. As early as 1917, Siqueiros, already conversant with socialist theories, had met in Guadalajara with artists of similar views to define, as they phrased it, the "social purpose of art." By 1923, after they had walls to paint on, their thinking had jelled. The *manifiesto* of the Syndicate of Painters and Sculptors, founded by Siqueiros, Orozco, and Rivera, among others, called on "soldiers, workers, campesinos, and intellectuals," to quote Orozco, to "socialize art, to destroy bourgeois individualism, and to repudiate easel painting and any other art that emanated from ultra-intellectual and aristocratic circles." The *manifiesto* asked artists "to produce only monumental works for the public domain," demanding, "at this historic moment of transition from a decrepit order to a new one, . . . a rich art for the people instead of an expression of individual pleasure." Beauty had to suggest and encourage class struggle. Many artists came to believe that pre-Columbian art was their "true heritage," even talking of a "renaissance of indigenous art." To broadcast its views, the Syndicate of Painters and Sculptors started to publish *El Machete,* a journal of political and artistic opinion. The themes, as outlined in the *manifiesto,* appeared in paint in the murals of Rivera in the Secretariat of Public Education; the year was 1923.

III

The muralists were a heterogeneous lot. Mercurial and bombastic, Siqueiros, short, curly-haired, and "aggressively virile," was from Chihuahua, the son of a very Catholic, wealthy family. As a student at the Escuela Nacional de Bellas Artes, he was jailed in 1910 for participating in a strike against the art taught there, the first of many stays in Mexican prisons. An agitator and drawer of manifestos, Siqueiros, at the age of sixteen, joined the *bola,* rising to the rank of captain in the army of General Manuel Diéguez, arch-enemy of Francisco Villa. After the triumph of the Carrancistas, he visited Europe, serving as military attaché and attending the meetings of Communist workers in Argenteuil, in France. In Paris, Rivera introduced Siqueiros to the circle of French artists, but, fortunately for Mexican art, Vasconcelos enticed him home before he was seduced. In 1922, side by side with Orozco and Rivera, he participated in the initial attempts at fresco painting at the Preparatoria, the old Colegio de San Ildefonso. But Siqueiros, for all of his leftist bombast, was a painter who despised *indigenista* themes in art.

The best-known of the muralists was Diego Rivera, whose father worshiped the memory of Benito Juárez. Born in the city of Guanajuato, Rivera spent most of his life in Mexico City. Big and fat with bulging eyes like those of a frog but with tiny hands, Rivera was an intellectual of brilliant mind. A picturesque character who craved public acclaim, he painted on a scaffold with a pistol at his waist, "to orient the critics," he was fond of saying. Educated in Catholic schools, Rivera was never an orthodox pupil, once shocking the nuns by questioning the truth of the Immaculate Conception. At the age of ten, he enrolled at the Escuela Nacional de Bellas Artes; one of his teachers was José María Velasco. There, Rivera heard Gerardo Murillo talk of the murals at the Sistine Chapel. In Mexico City, too, he met José Guadalupe Posada, when he would stop to watch him at work; Posada left a strong imprint on him. In 1907, Rivera departed for Europe, his study financed by Governor Teodoro Dehesa of Veracruz; there he spent fifteen years, initially in Spain and then in Paris, earning fame as a Cubist painter but then abandoning it, looking for inspiration to Renoir, Matisse, Cézanne, and Juan Gris.

An artist who read and pondered, Rivera, during his travels in Europe, started to wonder why artists separated themselves from the community and to study the history of art, trying to discover how this had come about. Until the European Renaissance, he concluded, the artist was not isolated from society but a craftsman among fellow craftsmen, who taught his neighbors the importance of art and beauty. That was also true for pre-Hispanic artists. The rupture with society occurred during the Renaissance, a break prolonged by the commercial and industrial revolutions, birthplaces of capitalism. At this juncture, easel art, the prerogative of wealthy patrons, came to dominate, when artists catered to the whims of their buyers and became outcasts in society, the pawns of the rich.

Rivera's Italian visit, when he saw the murals of Michelangelo and Bonozzo Gozzoli, provided answers to these questions. To integrate the artist into society, Rivera deduced, art, like that of the ancient masters, must be for the people and in union with architecture. As he saw it, the Russian revolution, which had brought the Communists to power, had ended the era of "modern Christian art," which dated from the French Revolution. Socialist Russia opened up a new era, a Marxist world asking artists to give birth to a social art, accessible to the people, nourishing and reforming their tastes. Art must serve the interests of workers and not of *burgueses.*

Rivera, for all that, had not come home to paint in the manner of Gozzoli, whom he admired most. Determined to be a Mexican artist, he made the Indian the centerpiece of his art. Everything of value in Mexico, he insisted, had Indian roots; without the inspiration of the Indian, "we cannot be authentic." Show me, he declared, "one original Hispanic-American . . . idea and I will . . . beg forgiveness from the Virgen de Guadalupe." An ideologue who scoffed at the "neutrality of art," Rivera believed "all of it to be propaganda" and, as a fervent nationalist, scorned the *burguesía* of Latin America, labeling it *malinchista,* a class fawning on foreigners, the victim of a colonial inferiority complex, warning, time and again, against imitating "whites and blonds," saying it led to feelings of shame for the native. By the middle of the 1920s, moreover, Rivera, a disciple of social change saddened by events at home, had labeled "petty bourgeois" the Mexican upheaval of 1910.

For his initial efforts, Rivera persuaded Vasconcelos, whom he had known previously, to allow him to paint the walls of the old chapel in the Preparatoria. His *Creation,* as this mural was called, however, did not satisfy him. His allegorical figures, some twelve feet high, were too abstract, too Italian and insufficiently Mexican, despite allusions to pre-Hispanic peoples. Then, in 1923, he started to paint murals in the Secretariat of Public Education, a task completed in three years. In a herculean effort, Rivera painted 124 murals on the walls of corridors of a courtyard three stories tall and a city block long. The murals confirmed the birth of the Mexican art renaissance. For Rivera, the people were the heroes of his murals, campesinos fighting for land and workers for their rights, where before angels, kings, military lords, and battles held center stage. Where he painted, by the same token, children appeared; "we have discovered," wrote one critic, "in the soul of this big and corpulent painter the ingenuousness and tenderness of a child."

A prodigious worker, Rivera in 1926–27 moved on to paint the murals in the old chapel of the Agricultural College of Chapingo; art connoisseurs rate his *Fecund Earth,* whose theme emblazons the agrarian ideals of Zapata, his finest. In 1929, Rivera finished his murals at Cortés's palace in Cuernavaca, paid for by, of all people, Dwight Morrow, the American ambassador. They reveal Rivera's anticlerical biases at their strongest. As always, Rivera depicted priests as brutal men, lashing Indians and gathering gold. When Morrow, so goes the story, learned what Rivera was up to, he went, thoroughly alarmed, to talk to the artist, for he had no desire to fan the fires of the religious conflict raging in Mexico. Diego was on the scaffolding, brush in hand. Always the diplomat, Morrow praised the unfinished fresco, then said, "Don Diego, these are pretty mean-looking priests."

"Mm," grumbled Diego, without laying down his brush or turning around.

"Don't you think you could paint a nice-looking priest for a change?"

"Mm," growled Diego.

But Morrow persisted. "Haven't you ever seen one?"

"Nope," grumbled Diego. "Never."

On the following day, however, Diego appeared at the Morrow house in Cuernavaca.

"I've just read of one," he told Morrow excitedly.

So, "Diego changed his plans." On "one of the doorway panels he painted a picture of the famous Bartolomé de las Casas, who spent his life laboring in behalf of the Indians." On the opposite panel, "Diego put the fires of the Inquisition."

Between 1929 and 1935, Rivera painted murals in the National Palace, one of his most ambitious projects and perhaps his most controversial. Covering walls facing and flanking a monumental staircase, the murals, revolutionary paintings inspired by Marxism, tell the history of Mexico from pre-Hispanic days down to the Maximato, interpreted, in Hegelian fashion, as thesis and antithesis, a dialogue between exploited and oppressor. The murals, a cacophony of colors and striking figures, among them a beautiful Indian prostitute, are a landmark in Mexican historiography. At the top of the mural on the staircase to the next floor, Marx, with arms outstretched, points the way.

International fame befell Orozco, the last of the trio, relatively late. Not until past his fortieth birthday was he known widely. He was, in the opinion of experts, the finest of the masters. His powerful murals at the Hospicio Cabañas, the Promethean Hidalgo at the State Government Palace as well as at the university, all in Guadalajara, display Orozco's majesty and eloquence as an artist. With "a scale, a power, and an intensity" that, by comparison, "make a large portion of contemporary art seem decorative," they furnish ample evidence, wrote an American art critic, "for considering Orozco the major artist of the twentieth century."

This "Goya" of Mexico, as Mexicans refer to him, was born in 1883 in Ciudad Guzmán, a city in Jalisco, but, like Rivera, spent most of his life in Mexico City. Of medium height, slender, dark of skin, and with thining hair, he was the son of an entrepreneur who manufactured soap and a mother who painted, played the piano, and sang. He lost the use of his left hand in an accident in a chemistry laboratory, was nearsighted and, by nature, sullen, preferring his own company. He had few friends, shunned conversation, and rarely spoke in public, his life so related to his work that he had no time for small talk; but he was eloquent with brush and paint. For Wolfe, Orozco "seemed to paint out of a penumbra of gloom which surrounded him." Whatever the truth, he took up painting early, enrolling at the Escuela Nacional de Bellas Artes after being a student at the Agricultural School in Chapingo and at the Preparatoria. Unlike Rivera and Siqueiros, Orozco barely knew the outside world, only twice spending time in the United States and once visiting Europe.

Orozco found the atmosphere of the Escuela Nacional stifling. Its director, Antonio Fabrés, a Spanish painter hired by Justo Sierra, demanded "photographic exactness" in design and had no interest in things Mexican. Fabrés looked upon Mexicans as colonial servants, asking them to paint in the style of Spanish art. "It was inconceivable that a wretched Mexican," Orozco recalled in his *Autobiografía,* "should dream of vying with the world abroad." So the Mexican journeyed abroad to study art, "and if he ever afterward gave a thought to the backward country in which he was born it was only to beg for help in time of need." Fortunately, at the Escuela Nacional, Orozco also met Dr. Atl, praising to the heavens Michelangelo and "drawing muscular giants in the violent attitudes of the Sistine." Listening to Atl, Orozco confessed, "we began to suspect that the whole colonial situation was nothing but a swindle foisted on us by international traders." Mexicans, too, had talent: "We would learn what the ancients and foreigners could teach us, but we could do as much as they, or more." For the first time, Orozco boasted, Mexican artists "took stock of the country they lived in."

Before entering the hallowed Escuela Nacional, Orozco had stumbled upon José Guadalupe Posada's work. It "was the push that first set my imagination in motion," he said, impelling "me to cover paper with my earliest little figures." This was his introduction to the world of painting. Watching Posada decorate his engravings, "I received my first lessons in the use of color." The engravings of the "Master Posada" had "many imitators" but never any equals.

Working for the Maderistas, Orozco drew caricatures for the newspaper *El Ahuizote* while, with money from his paycheck, he rented a studio in Illescas Street in the red-light district. Not illogically, his paintings dealt with bordellos, with gentlemen and their ladies. The "most radiant goddesses frequented my studio," he remembered, prostitutes he employed as models and who loved to see themselves in his paintings. When Francisco Villa drove the Carrancistas to Veracruz, Orozco joined them; there, under the tutelage of Dr. Atl, he drew propaganda caricatures and posters.

For many who have studied the Mexican artists, Orozco was merely an anarchist, unlike Rivera and Siqueiros, both ideologues. This view misinterprets Orozco. Though not an ideologue, Orozco was a man of passionate convictions, of likes and dislikes, a "supremely political animal," one of the most highly politicized of Mexican artists. For Impressionists, he gave nary a damn, refusing "to paint as birds sing," what Claude Monet advocated. He scoffed at Mexicans who imitated French Impressionists, painting "sunlight in the field and the sun itself . . . forgetting objects in an effort to capture the wavering play of light on water."

Orozco's art is a striking paradox. Known as the "painter of the Revolution," he was hardly its defender. Quite the reverse: he thought poorly of Madero, describing his stay in office as "sheer confusion and senselessness" and likening the Revolution to "the gayest and most diverting of carnivals." His easel paintings of 1916, pictures of fat and cruel campesino generals, the rape of women by their "revolutionary saviors," and so on, reveal no admiration for events in Mexico. For him, sycophants and political hangers-on, which he associated with the Revolution, were the bane of Mexico. One of his paintings depicts drunken army officers celebrating victory in battle surrounded by whores; the spoils of war, which the warriors hold aloft proudly, are a harlot's stocking and a bishop's hat. The upheaval of 1910, he believed, had hurt the poor. Still, Orozco was a relentless critic of bourgeois society, taking special aim at "ladies who wore their piety as a self-righteous garment."

While sympathetic to the poor, whether worker or campesino, he rejected the cult of the Indian. For him, *indianismo,* the rediscovery of the Indian, split Mexican society into rival camps; he was unwilling to discuss Mexicans as Spaniards, mestizos, or Indians, wanting the Indian "considered as a man, the equal of any other." If Mexicans continue to classify themselves "as Indians, criollos, and mestizos, following bloodlines only, as if we were discussing race horses," wrote Orozco, it will "divide us into implacable partisan groups, as Hispanists and *indigenistas,* " and foment racial antagonism. To achieve unity and harmony, he insisted, racial questions must be dismissed "for good and all. No more talk of Indians, Spaniards, and mestizos." As Orozco saw it, the art of the New World could stand neither on the traditions of the Old World nor on pre-Hispanic ruins. Just the same, Orozco, whose heroic figures stood tall and bronze of color, made the Conquest a favorite topic, displaying prominently his sympathies for the vanquished.

For the church hierarchy, he had nothing but contempt. He wanted to "desanctify" the religious. On the walls of the Preparatoria, he painted a grotesque *Dios Padre* (God the Father), surrounded by bureaucratic nuns and clerics who symbolized the intolerance of the church. Just the same, he believed in the proverb of the camel and the needle's eye, enshrining in his murals at the Preparatoria the Franciscan ideal of the poor friar: universal love, habitual wantlessness, and sacrifice, a social philosophy of service and abnegation and key to the salvation of Mexico. Juxtaposed to the *Dios Padre,* he painted three scenes of monks and Indians; the monks, bent over to embrace the Indian (the poor, the crippled, and the suffering), personified strength, pity, and compassion. The hero-savior whom Orozco drew in his murals was a composite of Moses, Quetzalcóatl, and Cortés, who might yet destroy the forces of evil and redeem mankind. He upheld the Christian doctrine of rebirth, of man reborn through misery and suffering: the greater the sacrifice, the greater the purification of man's soul—the message of Orozco's Christ at Dartmouth College.

Orozco preached no national gospels, fearing systematic formulas, which, he thought, imposed hardships on simple people. His heroes were solitary beings and his masses multiples of nonentities, nudes devoid of any intellectual baggage or material goods. The emphasis, as the murals at the Hospicio Cabañas demonstrate, was on the dynamics of movement. Not a patriotic painter, he repudiated the curse of war, painted with angry brushstrokes military brass hats, and fulminated against colonialism, which the imperialists imposed on the weak, belittling patriotic holidays and the rhetoric of politicians who hid behind flags.

The Big Three, of course, were not alone. Others, muralists and easel artists alike, helped spur the renaissance. Atl not only unlocked gates to fresh artistic horizons but painted landscapes and, especially, volcanoes. A native of Zacatecas, Francisco Goitia, a genius who lived the life of a hermit in Xochimilco, painted morbid incidents of Mexican life; his *Tata Cristo,* an oil on canvas, springs from this mold. Carlos Mérida, an abstract artist, celebrated Maya motifs in his easel paintings, while Xavier Guerrero, a political ally of Siqueiros and Rivera, won acclaim for his murals in Chile. The *Dance of the Chalma* in the Preparatoria in Mexico City, one of his many murals, embodied the best artistry of Fernando Leal. Jean Charlot, a Frenchman who arrived in Mexico as a young man, stayed to temper "our crude youth," to quote Orozco; his alliance with mural art dated from the days of the Preparatoria. Even Rufino Tamayo, an easel artist, dabbled in murals, decorating the walls of the Secretaría de Bienes Nacionales with dark figures singing and playing musical instruments. Leopoldo Méndez, whose caricatures appeared in *El Machete,* though a muralist of note, was primarily a graphic artist, an engraver in the tradition of Posada. Pablo O'Higgins, who, along with Rivera, painted murals at Chapingo, became known as a "painter of the Mexican people," filling his scenes with workers clad in overalls.

The murals at the Preparatoria, the initial outburst of the renaissance, did not go unnoticed. Quite the contrary: they ignited a heated public debate, much of it critical, mainly from traditional Mexicans, among them university students, who lampooned the murals, poking fun at them and going so far as to demand their removal. When Vasconcelos resigned in 1924, the outcry grew by leaps and bounds. The anger at Orozco's murals was especially brutal. Vandals defaced them, threw rocks at them, and pasted paper over them. The attack on Orozco should not have surprised anyone. As early as 1916, art galleries had refused to exhibit his work, lest their business suffer. One hostile pundit of that time called his drawings of prostitutes the work of a "young man with the soul of an old man." In 1917, when Orozco attempted to carry paintings of his into the United States, customs agents at Laredo, a border crossing in Texas, hacked to bits sixty of them, claiming that American laws prohibited the entry of "immoral" materials.

The attacks on their works, rather than frighten the artists, made them more militant and their themes more radical. In response, too, the muralists went on the offensive in *El Machete.* Yet so vicious was the criticism of the murals that the Callistas, unsympathetic and afraid of public violence, halted work on them. Not until later, when the Callistas relented, did Orozco finish his murals, painting the "revolutionary trinity," a soldier, campesino, and worker, their eyes blinded by a flag, which depicts the betrayal of the Revolution by false leaders, a theme common in his later art. Rivera's murals in the Secretariat of Public Education lit once more the public uproar, with *burgueses* demanding their destruction and encouraging another round of vandalism. By then, Vasconcelos was publicly critical. The vilification ended, in true *malinche* style, when critics from Paris and New York started to praise the murals.

IV

A transformation in thought was also gestating. In 1907, young writers and intellectuals, born in the decade of the 1880s, had resurrected the *tertulias* of the Reforma generation to discuss the latest European intellectual trends. Among those in attendance were José Vasconcelos; Antonio Caso, who taught philosophy; Alfonso Reyes, a budding poet and son of the caudillo of Nuevo León; and Pedro Enríquez Ureña, a literary critic from the Dominican Republic. Endeavoring to reinvigorate the Mexican academic world, they organized themselves into a *sociedad de conferencias,* where they read and discussed the works of writers ignored by the curriculum of the Preparatoria. Justo Sierra, minister of public instruction, conferred his blessings, and gave them entrance into the National University and the Escuela de Altos Estudios, the School of Advanced Studies.

During the centennial celebration of 1910, this group of young intellectuals, calling themselves the Ateneo de la Juventud, held a series of lectures; one by Vasconcelos branded positivism outmoded. For members of the Ateneo, *modernismo,* the literary school ignited by Rubén Darío, and highly popular during the Porfiriato, had one foot in the grave. No longer worshiping Darío, they categorized as *cursi,* pretentious, and shoddy the ivory tower of *modernismo.* In 1912, the Ateneo established the Universidad Popular Mexicana, an extension school for adults which conferred no degree, did not pay its professors, and banned the discussion of political topics. Its director was Alberto J. Pani, a famous economist during the twenties. The Ateneo survived until 1914; one reason for its demise, a commentary on the nature of intellectuals, was that many accepted posts in Victoriano Huerta's administration, one being Nemesio García Naranjo, its minister of public instruction. Not a few had to flee Mexico. That turn of events, by and large, boded ill. As in the days of Don Porfirio, when poets became ambassadors, intellectuals tarnished their integrity. Then, with the end of factional hostilities, "eggheads" by the dozen, "more actors than writers," to quote a cynical Octavio Paz, began to collaborate with the "revolutionary" regimes, becoming advisers, either privately or publicly, of illiterate generals, campesino prophets, labor union bosses, or caudillos. But, by accepting the carrot, they sold their souls, turning into servants, if not sycophants, of the men in power. Such a fate befell the Siete Sabios, the famous seven sages, among them Manuel Gómez Morín, father of the Partido de Acción Nacional, and Vicente Lombardo Toledano, militant labor boss of the thirties. The hunger for jobs and recognition seduced them, just as it had under Díaz. With that, liberty of thought, the right to voice openly what was on one's mind, disappeared. From then on, intellectuals beholden to government upheld the "official" truth.

The publication, in 1922, of Manuel Gamio's monumental *La población del valle de Teotihuacán,* about the site of an ancient civilization, invited anthropologists, formerly merely interested in the pre-Hispanic, to study the contemporary Indian. In law, Narciso Bassols, grandson of Sebastián Lerdo de Tejada, broke with old juridical principles and turned to socialist ideals for inspiration. When "revolutionary" intellectuals, as they titled themselves, became pragmatists, Samuel Ramos, philosopher and student of Antonio Caso, ridiculed the idea that Mexico's salvation lay with men indifferent to ideas. The practical and the theoretical, he argued, were one and the same, labeling "idiots" those who thought they could labor without thinking. In *Perfil del hombre y la cultura en México,* Ramos, seldom one to duck controversy, explored why, as he wrote, Mexicans believed themselves to be "inferior," relying on history to verify his thesis. To quote Ramos, manifestations of the Mexican character compensated for "an unconscious sense of inferiority." His book stoked a fiery public debate.

Vasconcelos, meanwhile, embittered by his defeat in the elections of 1929, began to write his memoirs, in which he recalled bitter episodes, rekindled resentments, and revealed embarrassing secrets long hidden from public view. He spoke of his youth in Oaxaca, his ties to Francisco I. Madero, the era of factional disputes when he sided against Venustiano Carranza, and his days at the helm of the Secretariat of Public Education. Earlier, in *La raza cósmica,* Vasconcelos had speculated on the effects of racial miscegenation, accepting the "superiority of whites but not their arrogance," alleging that Mexicans would not be mighty and strong till they felt themselves "to be as Spanish as the offspring of Spain." The Indian, he exclaimed, had no other door to the future than "that of Latin civilization." In his *Breve historia de México,* he lampooned Joel R. Poinsett and labeled dupes and traitors the Liberals who listened to him.

V

It was literature, not the cognitive designs of intellectuals, however, that mirrored more closely the artistic ferment. Like mural art, it enjoyed, for better or worse, the patronage of government. In December 1924, José Manuel Puig Casauranc, a physician and politico who supplanted Vasconcelos in the Secretariat of Public Education, had dangled a carrot before writers. If they accepted certain literary premises, he implied, the secretariat would find jobs for them. For Puig, who thought of himself as a writer, literature must be shorn of affectation and sham, both replaced by a somber and austere style, faithful "to our way of life." He wanted fiction to portray anguish, selfless and sincere grief, but not that of the melancholic poets of *modernismo.* He urged writers to spotlight despair and link it to "our terrible social situation, thus lifting the curtains that hide from sight the misery of the damned." Literature had to "humanize, to make us more compassionate," and to "encourage us to seek the collective welfare of society."

The "literature of the Revolution," so labeled by Puig, led, as may be expected, to confusion. Some regarded "revolutionary" as calling simply for an affinity with the people and a sympathy for the deeds and ideals of the decade of 1910, a literature written in prose untainted by embellishments characteristic of Porfirista snobs. Others conceived of "revolutionary" fiction as a radical change in form as well as content, which defined national and traditional values, integrating the old into the modern. Like art, literature had to be written for the people and march in step with "revolutionary culture." Besides that, literature had to embody the "popular soul" so as to be authentic and nationalistic, deal with Mexican themes, and be part of the Mexican heritage but, concurrently, introduce the proletariat to Marx, Lenin, and Tolstoy. Above all, it had to stand shoulder to shoulder with the Revolution, while voicing the will of the people as well as its sentiments, the foundations of a robust literature nourished "by the blood and flesh . . . of our race."

Most authors accepted the benevolence of the state. The reason, obviously, was the poverty and illiteracy of society; just a select circle read books, short stories, or poetry and, worse still, purchased them. Given this reality, only government jobs nourished literary endeavors, which was both a plus and a minus. Not till the 1940s, furthermore, did Mexico have more than just a handful of publishers. The book merchants, who printed and sold the efforts of authors, were few.

The new literature, called the "novel of the Mexican Revolution," made its bow in 1925, when the soothsayers eulogized Mariano Azuela's *Los de abajo,* published initially in 1915 in El Paso, Texas. Few had read Azuela's other novels, starting with *María Luisa,* his first, which dated from 1907. An admirer of Emile Zola, Azuela, in *María Luisa,* a novel about the misfortunes that befall a girl gone wrong, dealt with alcoholism, prostitution, illness, and tragic death. No one doubted that it was a "bourgeois novel written for the bourgeoisie." But in *Los de abajo,* Azuela broke with European naturalism and realism, the formulas until then. A tale of the Revolution, *Los de abajo* told of "brutal acts," to quote a Mexican savant, in "brutal style." With the rediscovery of Azuela in 1925, old literary formulas lost their popularity. Like easel art, they had gone out of style.

Los de abajo, nevertheless, had been ignored by critics and readers alike for more than a decade. After its initial publication, the novel had been reprinted in small editions in 1916 and 1920, but, as before, a veil of silence shielded it from public acclaim. After its publication in 1925, however, the novel rose to the top of the best-seller list, especially after Francisco Monterde, a renowned pundit, used it to demonstrate that Mexican literature was both "virile" and nationalistic. Those "who want to know what our recent revolutions were all about," wrote Monterde, must read *Los de abajo.*

Ironically, Azuela, a physician with Francisco Villa's armies, had not written a sympathetic account of the "Revolution." About "underdogs," it told of waiters, barbers, and thieves as well as of campesinos who had turned warriors. He scoffed at the idea of a social revolution, describing its antiheroes not merely as cruel and grasping but as not knowing why they fought. As one baffled Mexican reviewer confessed in 1925, "this is not a revolutionary novel because it detests the Revolution" nor, paradoxically, "is it reactionary because it reveals no zest for the past." For that interpretation, Azuela, once the idol of revolutionaries, was ultimately castigated for his "reactionary" views. Still, his fiction met the demands of Puig; in *Los de abajo,* one found Mexican life portrayed in somber colors, depicting, in a style that packed a wallop, the agony of the poor. More to the point, the novel was anchored firmly in the Revolution.

Azuela unlocked the gates. In 1928, Martín Luis Guzmán published *El águila y la serpiente,* both fiction and historical memoir. A journalist by trade, Guzmán, who lost no love for Carranza and Alvaro Obregón, wrote about the caudillos of the upheaval of 1910, depicting the confrontation of Villa and Carranza. His chapter on Rodolfo Fierro, the sadistic lieutenant of Villa, which he titled "Feast of the Bullets," is a chilling portrait of cruelty, lust for blood, and man's inhumanity to man. For sycophants and hangers-on, the entourage of caudillos, Guzmán showed no mercy. *La sombra del caudillo* was his unsympathetic portrait of Obregón, the national boss, and the merciless killing of Francisco Serrano. No one who reads this novel forgets how Obregón, without batting an eye, ordered the murder of Serrano, an ally of long standing. Yet, as early as 1915, this "revolutionary" novelist shed no tears for the Indian, who, he claimed, lacked "pride in his race," judging him, because of "an irritating docility," a "weight and burden" on Mexico.

Then, in 1931, Rafael F. Muñoz published *Se llevaron el cañón para Bachimba,* one of his many novels about the Revolution. That same year, Francisco L. Urquizo wrote *Tropa vieja.* It was followed by *Tierra grande,* by Mauricio Magdaleno; *Cartucho,* by Nellie Campobello; and *Campamento,* by Gregorio López y Fuentes. All of them adopted the story-telling techniques of Azuela and dealt with episodes of the Revolution, told in colorful detail, tales of individual heroics and the tragedy of men. José Rubén Romero, a native of Santa Clara del Cobre, a town in Michoacán, in *Mi caballo, mi perro y mi rifle,* wrote of a revolutionary soldier who comes home to find that little has changed although he has lost everything. In *La vida inútil de Pito Pérez,* his best work. Romero revived the picaresque style. His fictional Pito, also a native of Santa Clara del Cobre, was wise to the devious ways of society but, all the same, a *picaro,* a man who lived by his wits and drank himself to sleep.

The adventures of Pito Pérez were the saga of a man embittered by the false values of a society he rejects. When he strayed from the straight and narrow path, it was to escape from social hypocrisy.

Meanwhile, Carlos Chávez won international acclaim for his *Sinfonía India* and *El Sol.* A disciple of Manuel M. Ponce, he founded the Orquesta Sinfónica de Mexico and, as a composer, rescued from oblivion Mexico's aboriginal music and strongly influenced the music of Silvestre Revueltas and Blas Galindo, two noted composers. Popular music, too, had its day in the sun, especially because of María Gréver, a composer and singer whose "Júrame" swept Mexico like a brushfire. Others who helped to revive it were the songwriters Guty Cárdenas, Luis Martínez Serrano, Alfonso Esparza Oteo, and José Sabre Marroquín, as well as Alfonso Ortíz Tirado, a physician from Sonora who sang both operatic airs and romantic ballads.

VI

Education, too, particularly in rural Mexico, savored the emotion and excitement of a gospel revival meeting. Unwilling and unable to carry out radical change, the Sonorenses and their allies invoked palliatives. Education was their panacea. To get schooling under way, Congress in 1920 gave the federal government the green light to build a national system of primary schools, restoring Justo Sierra's proud design, now titled the Secretaría de Educación Publica. States and municipalities, nevertheless, retained the right to operate schools, leading, in scores of cases, to local neglect of rural education, to duplication and waste, to a wide range of standards and goals, and to conflicts between school officials. To head the Secretaría, Obregón named José Vasconcelos.

A native of Oaxaca, Vasconcelos was a man of ideas, thinking of himself as the Ulises Criollo of Mexico, a facsimile of the ancient hero of Greek mythology. A traditionalist at heart, Vasconcelos trusted in the bourgeoisie and his Catholic faith. His social gospel was democracy, not that of the United States but that of the Latin world, a society along the lines drawn by José Ortega y Gasset, which recognized the superiority of an aristocracy of learning. His idol was Domingo Faustino Sarmiento, the conservative Argentine politico of the nineteenth century, seeing, in his attacks on the gaucho, the basis for Argentina's leadership of Hispanic America.

This strange hybrid of moralist and planner was not a pedagogue, nor had his ideas prepared him for Mexican reality. For him, education was a moral crusade, upholding Platonic ideas, stressing the three R's, and scorning American Deweyites. The classics represented the flower of literature. So Vasconcelos had printed the works of Dante, Homer, Cervantes, Pérez Galdós, Rolland, and Tolstoy. But the masters had not written for Mexican campesinos, a fact illustrated by the following story. Obregón and his party, among whom was Vasconcelos, had lost their way in a remote region. After riding all day, the party sighted a tiny hut in the distance. When the party rode up, an old Indian was standing by the door.

"Compadre," Obregón hailed the man. "Can you tell us where we are?"

The man shook his head.

"But what place is this? What town are we near?"

Again the man did not know.

"Were you born here?" Obregón asked.

"Yes."

"And your wife also?"

"Yes."

"So you were born here, your wife was born here. You've both lived out your lives on this spot, and yet you don't know where you are?"

"No," the Indian replied indifferently.

"José," said Obregón, turning to Vasconcelos, "make a note of this man so that you can send him a complete edition of the classics you've just edited."

The classics were in keeping with Vasconcelos's rejection of what he called the Robinson Crusoe approach of Anglo-Saxons. Education might have a place for statistics, work techniques, and science, but it must be crowned by ethics and aesthetics. Education was first and foremost a defense of culture, a school to further Mexico's own brand, essentially Spanish and Latin-European. His scale of values excluded the Indian contribution.

For all that, there was another side, inspired by the labors of the early colonial friars. Vasco de Quiroga and his cohorts had emphasized the practical, teaching the Indian not only the catechism but European skills. From these holy men, Vasconcelos adopted what relevant ideas he had on rural education, which others developed into specific programs. This was the inspiration for the famous cultural missions, peripatetic groups which, traveling from village to village to carry the school gospel, emulated the missionaries of the Conquest. Two remarkable pedagogues, Moisés Sáenz and Rafael Ramírez, gave form and substance to Vasconcelos's dream. The Mexican rural school, what John Dewey called Mexico's "educational renaissance," owed its origins to a trio of architects. Sáenz and Ramírez converted Vasconcelos's moral crusade into a down-to-earth attempt to do something about everyday problems of rural Mexicans.

Under secretary of education from 1925 to 1930, Sáenz, a native of Nuevo León, was a graduate of the normal school of Jalapa, with a doctorate from Columbia University. An intellectual, he wrote books and essays that ranged widely, the majority on rural questions. While no radical, he recognized that Mexico's Achilles' heel was the poverty of its countryside. Education could not ignore economic problems but had to contribute to their solution. Sáenz had a keen appreciation of Indians, whom he prized as individuals and as a people. He wanted the Indian to be an integral part of society, but, unlike his old boss, who wanted to strip the Indian of his culture, Sáenz sought to conserve its strong features and to combine them with the values and customs of the modern world. The Indian was not a ward to shelter or a beast of burden to exploit; he was a human being with a citizen's rights to share the fruits of Mexican life and to help shape national culture. Translated into pedagogy, this meant the "incorporation of the Indian into civilization," but a civilization formed by merging the European contribution with the Indian's.

A native of Veracruz and, like Sáenz, a graduate of the normal school at Jalapa, Ramírez had started teaching in 1906, entering rural education by way of the cultural missions, which he helped to organize. A man of profound moral convictions, he "swept from the temple that he built the faithless who dared profane it with their shameless presence." In 1927, he became chief of cultural missions and later head of rural schools, a job he held until 1935. Like Sáenz, he was a prolific writer on rural education. A moderate reformer in the twenties, he became a militant apostle of change. His dream was a rural school to free campesinos of their shackles; "to educate is to redeem," he said. The three R's were not enough. He wanted a school concerned with social and economic betterment, at first in terms of the individual, essentially what moderates had in mind. But, in time, he became an enthusiastic advocate of schooling for the group or community.

The *casa del pueblo,* which is what Vasconcelos called his rural school, was for everyone, children and adults alike, on the premise that education must minister to all, lest the neglect of adults hinder the learning of the child. Children came during the day, the adults in the evening, after the day's work was done. Rural poverty and scarce federal funds limited schooling to four years and usually less. Since life was a struggle for survival, the parents could not afford to send children to school, needing them at home to help with the work. Constrained by time and money, the curriculum had no place for frills; every hour counted. Learning to read and write the Spanish language, simple arithmetic, a few fundamentals of geography and national history—this was the school curriculum. The vocational was no less elementary.

By 1932, the apparatus of a modern educational system was in place. The results were often praiseworthy. Between 1921 and 1931, national expenditures on education had risen from 4 percent to 13 percent of the national budget; almost a third of it was spent on rural schools. There were only a handful of rural schools in 1921; ten years afterward, there were 6,796 of them, with nearly 600,000 students, children and adults. An army of teachers, dedicated young adults, was being trained in normal schools, some in rural Mexico.

Statistics, however, told a negative story too: 81 percent of the 72,000 communities of fewer than 4,000 people lacked schools. Nor were schools always satisfactory. Buildings varied according to the resources of the communities, which built them; but, since most communities were poor, most schools were one-room adobe huts. Less than a third of the children of school age in rural communities enrolled in school. From 1920 to 1930, all but 2 percent of them abandoned school, usually during the first two years. Teachers were badly trained, overworked, and underpaid. More frightening, the selfless enthusiasm of the early days of the school crusade had started to fizzle out, a symptom, one Mexican noted, of the survival of the latifundio and of old patterns of exploitation.

Whatever the prognosis for the future, the educational crusade had injected new life into the age-old question of the Indian's place in society. Arrayed against each other were Hispanists, who believed that the culture of Mexico had been shaped by three centuries of Spanish rule, and the Indianists, firm believers in what they labeled their "native" roots. The views of Moisés Sáenz went hand in glove with *indianismo* or *indigenismo,* the "rediscovery" in the 1920s of Indian "culture." For *indigenistas,* whether artists such as Diego Rivera or pedagogues like Sáenz, the Indian was not "uncivilized"; to the contrary, he represented rich and diverse cultures, the equal of those of the Western world. The issue was not which was the superior one; the point was merely that they were different.

This was in keeping with the views of anthropologists who, since the days of Franz Boas, had devised their own definition of the term *culture,* thereby rejecting the old "humanist" concept, which was "absolutistic and knew perfection." Anthropological "culture" was "relativistic"; instead of starting with an "inherited scale of values," it assumed "that every society through its culture seeks and in some measure finds values." Traditional humanist usage distinguished between degrees of "culture," while for anthropologists all men were equally "cultured." That Sáenz and Manuel Gamio, Mexico's leading anthropologist and a noted *indigenista,* should accept this interpretation was surely no accident. Both had studied at Columbia University, where Boas held forth, and Gamio had been his student.

VII

These were also the days long awaited by middle-class Mexicans, scions of Porfirio Díaz's benevolence. By opening doors previously closed, the Great Rebellion invited them to sit down at the banquet table. The more fortunate of them found a niche in the charmed circles of the rich and powerful. They married up, so to speak, like Artemio Cruz, an opportunistic rebel in Carlos Fuente's novel *La muerte de Artemio Cruz,* who took for his wife the daughter of Don Gamaliel Bernal, a hacendado of Puebla. By his marriage, Artemio, a "revolutionary" of nebulous ancestry, entered high society.

All the same, Porfirista aristocrats did not disappear from view or fall from grace; they simply discovered their ranks infiltrated by the "revolutionary family." In Mexico City, the *colonias* of Anzures, Lomas de Chapultepec, and Polanco, where the newly anointed dwelt, grew alarmingly. Their homes adopted the blueprints of the newly rich of California, built, bemoaned Diego Rivera, "for Yankees of poor taste," a style baptized "colonial" California. "When I returned from exile," recalled Jorge Prieto Lauren, a politico who lost out, "to my surprise I found many of my former companions," once inhabitants of modest apartments in the most humble *colonias* of Mexico City, "the owners of palatial castles in the Lomas de Chapultepec."

The upheaval of 1910, obviously, did not push an entire class upward. Most of it stayed put, caught between the rich and the poor and mainly urban. When finances permitted, the middle class emulated the rich, buying homes in the once prestigious *colonias* of yesteryear, dreamed of having bathrooms in the American mold, which it equated with happiness, and patronized restaurants and theaters frequented by the better off. Eating at Prendes, a Porfirista restaurant in Mexico City, was a badge of honor. In Mexico City, Guadalajara, Puebla, Hermosillo, and other urban enclaves, fashionable *colonias* sprang up, home to the more affluent, their architecture, like that of Lomas de Chapultepec, with a distinctly California air.

But the breakup of the old society, nonetheless, left the ancient edifice standing. The poor had not replaced the rich at the top of the social pyramid; with exceptions, they remained at the bottom, still poor, exploited, and neglected. Every city had its barrios, where the poor and their families struggled to make ends meet. Their homes, sometimes where their parents had lived, had not changed for the better. The identical pulquerías sold their beverages to the same customers. Some barrios in Puebla had as many as three pulquerías every thirty paces. In 1934, Mexicans, mostly the poor, drank 60 million liters of pulque, 8 million of mescal, and 1.2 million of tequila. The alcoholism of the slums inflicted suffering on entire families and claimed untold victims. An occasional health clinic, a visiting nurse or physician, a school or a mural on the wall of an open-air market, testifying to Mexico's entry into the twentieth century, rarely bettered the lot of the urban poor. Nor had Obregonistas and Callistas rid the Republic of the huge gap separating city from countryside. Life in the villages of Mexico, hamlets lacking electricity, running water, and toilets, had changed nary a bit.

These were also the "roaring twenties," when the newly rich aped the dress and life-styles of Hollywood stars, worshiped Lupe Vélez, the "Mexican bombshell," and women wore skirts above the knee. From north of the border, an invasion was under way. For three colonial centuries, Mexico had been shut off from the world; the nineteenth century, despite the coming of the railroad, had not shattered the old isolation. However, by the 1920s, tourists, more and more from the United States, made their appearance, lured by low prices and exotic scenes. Not long after, petates, clay ollas, huaraches, and rebozos filled Mexico's markets. Taxco and Cuernavaca, in the hinterlands of Mexico City, enjoyed tourist booms. The Yankee cultural invasion had started; first to feel its effects was the Spanish language, as Mexicans began to use *okay*, *chance*, *pichel*, and sundry other English words. *Mexicanidad*, the slogan of the Callistas, was dealt a mortal blow, Vasconcelos raged, by a "second-rate *burguesía* of *pochos* and *apochados*," toadies of American ways, which groveled unabashedly before the "sermons of Rotarians." Their ideal, he alleged, was to send offspring to study in the United States "so that they might become lackeys of its imperialism."

Whether exaggerated or not, the Mexican veneer had an ugly side. Prodded by the Great Depression, racial bigotry had its day in the sun, this time against the Chinese. Brought in during the late nineteenth century, mostly to lay railroad track and work in the mines, the Chinese had tarried only briefly in those jobs. When the Maderistas took office, most of them were in business and commerce for themselves, the owners of laundries and stores selling groceries, vegetables, clothing, shoes, and diverse other items. Usually they were in competition with Mexicans. They took Mexican women for their wives, and raised boys and girls with the faces of two races. This led Sonora in 1923 to bar marriages between Mexicans and Chinese and, two years later, to confine the Chinese to their own barrios. Those who broke the law were fined, sent to jail, or deported. Ghettos for Chinese, also decreed by law, could be found virtually the length and breadth of the border and, to the south, in Zacatecas, Sinaloa, and Michoacán; even Chiapas and Oaxaca, heavily Indian states, followed that pattern. For all that, this failed to satisfy the bigots who, in the early 1930s, ran the Chinese out of Sonora and Sinaloa, headquarters of the agitators, and Chihuahua. One of their principal leaders was Rodolfo Elías Calles, son of the Jefe Máximo and governor of Sonora. Francisco Villa had earlier shot and killed Chinese in Torreón, a rail hub in Coahuila. In towns such as Cananea, mobs fell upon the hapless Chinese, beating them and looting their stores. Altogether, eleven thousand Chinese had to flee northern Mexico.

Graft and corruption, too, survived the winds of change. Among the biggest culprits were the "revolutionary" military and their political allies; to quote Governor Celestino Llaca of Querétaro, an example of what was sleazy, "If I don't profit now when I can, I will never do it." Lamented Alvaro Obregón, "How sad to see the most distinguished men, civilians and soldiers, convert the revolutionary movement into a butt for ridicule by devoting heart and soul to the pursuit of the almight peso." Obregón had put his finger on a cancer that outlived Don Porfirio and his bevy of docile millionaires. The appetites of the neophyte rulers, for so long denied the pleasures of the rich, knew no bounds; this was no time to obey moral laws but, instead, to make up for lost time. So "revolutionaries" feasted at the public trough, called *el hueso* by Mexicans, or acquired millions in shady business deals. Politics resembled the ancient profession: first you did it for love; then you did it for a few friends; and then you did it for money.

Miraculously, remarked one cynic, the Revolution had awakened, where least expected, "a passion for agriculture." He was referring to the acquisition of haciendas and ranchos by generals. How many fell into their laps, one can merely speculate; but many, undoubtedly, did. Rare were the generals, and often colonels and majors, who died without land of their own, at the least a *ranchito.* The list of landowners included generals from Obregón and Calles on down. Equally galling, they converted the Banco de Crédito Agrícola, the bank established to aid small farmers, into a private treasury. When in need of money to exploit their lands, the generals and politicos turned farmers hurried to the bank; none were denied. Calles and Obregón were among the first to receive a loan, called a *préstamo de favor,* money lent to friends. So that General Joaquín Amaro might buy the hacienda Ojo de Agua, the bank lent him 100,000 pesos; at about the same time, it assumed the home mortgage of Luis L. León, a fervent Callista and politico. When the bank lent more and more money to Calles for his haciendas in El Mante, a sugar enclave in San Luis Potosí, Manuel Gómez Morín, its founder and head, resigned in disgust. The bank, he said, "had become a whorehouse."

From 1919 to 1933, the United States embarked on a crusade to rid itself of alcohol and drunks. But prohibition merely drove thirsty Yankees to Mexico's border towns, where their compatriots, with an eye for profits, opened saloons, whorehouses, and gambling casinos. Wealthy Mexicans, too, joined in the merrymaking. One of them was Abelardo Rodríguez, future president of Mexico. Sent north to calm Baja California, this balding general had become the "richest man in the Republic" by the age of forty-three. Of a keen business sense, Rodríguez built his fortune, critics say, by investing in the "pleasures of the flesh," whether drink, women, or games of chance, mainly for fun-loving Yankee tourists. At the Casino de la Selva in Cuernavaca and the Foreign Clubs of Mexico City and Tijuana, which he owned, the well-off played roulette, drank highballs, and had a good time. When Narciso Bassols, the secretary of *gobernación,* endeavored to shut down the Casino de la Selva and the Foreign Club in Mexico, Rodríguez, with the blessings of Calles, fired him.

Tijuana, notable for its Casino de Agua Caliente, its whorehouses, including the resplendent Molino Rojo (Red Mill), and its many cantinas, almost every one of them owned by Americans, won for itself a reputation for wickedness. In *Tijuana In,* Hernán de la Roca, a novelist in the mold of Federico Gamboa, portrayed the plight of young girls led astray by the lure of cabaret life. For all that, Tijuana was not unique among border towns. Ciudad Juárez, across from El Paso, and sister cities welcomed similar evils, if catering to the joys of the flesh was, indeed, sinful. For Tampico, the oil port on the Gulf of Mexico, the Golden Twenties brought a bevy of nightclubs patronized by gamblers and prostitutes, where petroleum workers, in a matter of hours, squandered wages from a week's hard labor. Of the casinos, the Playa Miramar was the gaudiest; its boss was a Mexican half Cuban with ties to the Mafia bosses of Havana.

Meanwhile, the hunt for public jobs, *empleomanía,* went on unabated. The uncertainty of the times, the ups and down of the economy, and the possibilities for public office worsened the ancient malady. The hunt for sinecures, whether in the cabinet, Congress, or the bureaucracy, helped to sabotage reform, as ideals sank deeper into the muck of the Mexican past. Every Mexican leader had to fend off a horde of applicants for government posts. To write the national caudillo, and to claim to speak honestly and forthrightly since "I covet no post or harbor political ambitions," to quote a letter to Venustiano Carranza, was a mark of singular distinction.

The quest for public office rendered ideology meaningless. The hungry supplicant, like a chameleon, adjusted to any set of principles and to any leader. To cite a complaint from Ixhuatlán, a small town in Veracruz, its caciques had "been Porfiristas and timid Magonistas; cautious Maderistas; exalted Vazquistas; dedicated Orozquistas; enthusiastic Felicistas, Huertistas, and Carrancistas"—and now were "Villistas and Zapatistas." A decade later, most assuredly, they were Obregonistas and Callistas. Endurance and survival, the bricks and mortar of the successful politico, demanded adaptability or *servilismo,* being a lackey to the boss. When Calles, the Jefe Máximo, entered the halls of Congress, one deputy, for example, shouted, "¡Papacito!" For his contribution, Puig Casauranc, a devoted Callista, introduced to politics the custom of speaking on and on and not saying anything. No politico, if he valued his job and his future, moreover, dared speak ill of his companions.

20

A PLEDGE REVIVED

I

In the charter of 1917, the triumphant rebels swore to redistribute the land, defend labor's rights, build schools, and obey the popular will. For all that, despite a bit of land reform, a CROM that, on occasion, spoke for workers and a school crusade, demagoguery rather than social justice won the day. Then, to the astonishment of Mexicans, different circumstances and the appearance of Lázaro Cárdenas, a caudillo with a vivid memory of Querétaro, revived the pledge.

II

The Great Depression, a malady of the capitalist West, shook Mexico, turning topsy-turvy an economy already reeling from years of strife. Exports plummeted, with petroleum and mining suffering the heaviest losses; not until 1933 did they show signs of recovery. A similar catastrophe struck the exports of agricultural goods—cotton and henequen, to single out two. As exports dropped, so did national income, by a quarter between 1929 and 1933 and, consequently, the value of the peso.

For the poor, the results were catastrophic. At Cananea, the copper emporium of the Republic, half of the miners were unemployed. At Nacozari and Pilares, two camps in Sonora, all the miners lost their jobs when the Moctezuma Copper Company shut them down. When life got tough, the unemployed of Cananea, on more than one occasion, resorted to stealing in order to feed their families. Elsewhere, factories closed their doors, leaving the jobless to fend for themselves. In Toluca, capital of the state of Mexico, to cite one case, the Toluca y México brewery went out of business, as well as the textile mills María de Otzolopec, San Ildefonso de Nicolás Romero, and San Pedro de Zinacatepec. In Jalisco, armies of jobless men begged for work, while the return of Mexicans expelled from the United States exacerbated their plight. Facing a budget deficit, authorities in Jalisco reduced salaries of bureaucrats, adding to middle-class unhappiness. The ranks of the jobless tripled between 1930 and 1932. The poor were not merely worse off than before but more numerous.

To complicate the picture, the harvests of Mexico's two basic crops stumbled upon hard times. In 1933, Mexico produced 30 percent less corn and 22 percent fewer beans than in 1907, the last of the good agricultural years of the Porfiriato. Per capita consumption of corn, the mainstay of the popular diet, dropped from 136 kilograms in 1928 to 88 in 1930. Meanwhile, commercial agriculture had taken a fall. With the end of the war in Europe, demands for cotton and henequen petered out. As their markets shrunk, so did lands under cultivation. When textile mills slashed production and let workers go, cotton planters reduced the size of their crops and cut their labor force, a formula also adopted by henequen hacendados, their difficulties augmented by competing fibers from Africa.

The brunt of all this fell on the back of labor. Since nearly 70 percent of the rural population lacked land and survived on wages, it felt the cutbacks severely. The hardest hit were the commercial agricultural zones, which provided the bulk of jobs. Difficult times encouraged labor unrest. Workers in the cotton belt of the Laguna in Coahuila, for instance, began to heed the exhortations of "agitators." Even so, the Callistas, politicos less and less enthusiastic about reform, saw the crisis as an opportunity to discipline labor. That occurred in Jalisco, where politicos, in league with employers, ran roughshod over the remnants of the independent labor movement. As expected, strikes dropped dramatically; only thirteen of them disturbed the tranquillity of the entire Republic in 1932.

That condition did not endure for long. With labor unrest on the rise, strikes flared anew, despite the unhappiness of Callistas and business tycoons. Abelardo Rodríguez, a president who blamed strikes on Communists, had to deal with 202 of them in 1934. In Mexico State, a skip and jump from the National Palace, for example, workers, risking the ire of politicos and business, went on strike while campesinos occupied lands of hacendados. These confrontations erupted as the first signs of recovery from the crisis surfaced.

III

It was at this juncture that Lázaro Cárdenas walked onto the national stage. History remembers him as the best of the social reformers of Mexico, though, as one cynic remarked, that was like being the tallest building in Zapotepec or any other forlorn village in the countryside. Mexican social reform is one of those national oxymorons like Italian Protestantism or British cooking, of which nothing much is expected. But, somehow, once in a while the threadbare tradition of Mexican reform finds a spokesman who reaches out beyond the narrow confines of his adherents to strike a chord in the larger society. Such a man was Lázaro Cárdenas, called upon to fulfill the oath of Querétaro.

A man who loved horses, plants, and water, Cárdenas was something of a puritan. Neither tall nor short, nor light nor dark of skin, he neither smoked nor attended bullfights, dressed simply, and, unless on a political tour, ate breakfast and dinner with his family. He hailed from Jiquilpan, a town in Michoacán not too far from Lake Chapala. Its a name signifying "a place of flowers" in Tarascan, Jiquilpan lived off the manufacture of rebozos (shawls) in blue and black colors for women, tightly knit woolen sarapes, leather saddles, and the tanning of hides. For miles around, Jiquilpan was famous for the milk from its cows and its delicious round cheese and for its *trancas,* egg bread. It was a town living in poverty; many of its one thousand inhabitants farmed nearby lands as sharecroppers or cultivated tiny parcels of rocky soil. The people of Jiquilpan, like most natives of Michoacán, including the mother of Lázaro Cárdenas, were Catholics to the core.

Up the road from Jiquilpan, on the way to Chapala and Guadalajara, was the hacienda of Guaracha, the property of Don Diego Moreno. One of the richest in Mexico, Guaracha dated from colonial times, when African slaves planted sugarcane on its lands. On its outskirts lay the haciendas of Cerro Pelón, Platanal, Cerrito Colorado, Guarachita, San Antonio, Las Arquillas, El Sabino, Guadalupe, Las Ordeñas, and Capadero—all, more or less, part of Guaracha. So big was it that, according to its neighbors, Don Diego did not know exactly how much land he owned. His property included a sugar mill, twenty thousand head of cattle, horses, mules, and sheep. Sharecroppers largely, Don Diego's labor force, cultivated sugarcane for the manufacture of sugar and alcohol, and wheat, corn, and alfalfa for the markets of Guadalajara and Mexico City. Don Diego and, afterward, his son spent little time on their hacienda, preferring Guadalajara and Europe.

On March 25, 1895, Cárdenas was born into this world. His father, Dámaso, was the son of a soldier in the armies of Benito Juárez, a native of Jalisco who married a girl from Jiquilpan and stayed there, at first making his livelihood as a campesino and weaver of rebozos. In time, however, Dámaso went on to become the proprietor of La Reunión de Amigos, a small store, and, because he could read, a *curandero,* or quack. By then, Dámaso had married and sired a family, the eldest being Lázaro. The family resided on San Francisco, the main street in Jiquilpan, in one of the biggest houses in town, the bequest of a well-off godmother and distant aunt of Felicitas del Río, mother of the Cárdenas clan and native of Guarachita.

At the age of six, Lázaro enrolled in a private school; after two years, he transferred to the public school in Jiquilpan. Its teacher, Don Hilario de Jesús Fajardo, worshiped José María Morelos and Benito Juárez and talked of heroes who fought against the clergy and the French invaders of Mexico. To Fajardo's school came the sons of the artisans, merchants, and rancheros of Jiquilpan, the better off. Shy and little inclined to converse with others, a demeanor that earned him the sobriquet Sphinx of Jiquilpan, young Cárdenas, when not in class, preferred the company of old men who whiled away their time seated on the benches of the Plaza Zaragoza, the town square, or the friends of his father. One of them, Esteban Arteaga, spoke to him about history and botany and lent him books to read, novels such as those of Victor Hugo and Antonio Plaza. During school vacations, Cárdenas visited his grandfather, a dirt farmer, cutting weeds with a hoe, helping harvest the corn, or bringing in the squash. As he grew older, he found a job in the tax collector's office in Jiquilpan, which required that he wear a coat and tie. After the death of his father in 1911, he became the assistant to the secretary of the prefect, the political boss of the district, and spent his spare time as an apprentice in the local printshop, where he learned to bind books.

In June 1913, Cárdenas, then sixteen years old, went off to fight Victoriano Huerta, joining the guerrillas of Guillermo García Aragón, killed eventually by Emiliano Zapata, one of Cárdenas's heroes. Cárdenas had a long and distinguished military career, fighting under Generals Manuel M. Diéguez, Arnulfo R. Gómez, and, fortunately for him, Plutarco Elías Calles. Along the way, he was a Carrancista, and Obregonista, and a Callista, battling, alongside of them, Francisco Villa, Zapata, and the Yaquis of Sonora. On his way up the military ladder, and as a politico, Cárdenas rode the coattails of Calles, who considered him one of his most loyal generals. Obregón, on the contrary, judged him "trustworthy but incompetent."

Obregón's opinion notwithstanding, Cárdenas had few peers as a politico. He always knew which way the winds were blowing. In the best sense of the term, he was a *político a la mexicana;* when necessary, he bent with the wind, looked the other way when his colleagues dipped into the public coffer, and never questioned the wisdom of his superiors. Knowing intimately the jungle of Mexican politics, he kept his guard up and spoke only when spoken to. Cárdenas, the people who knew him say, was *desconfiado,* wary and distrustful, a man who wanted to control his own decisions. All the same, he felt profoundly the poverty and exploitation of the poor; the condition of campesinos, above all, disturbed him. His policies as governor of Michoacán, a term he began in 1928, provide an insight into this complex man.

When Cárdenas arrived in Morelia, capital of the state, he confronted formidable obstacles. Although he could count on the support of reformers, he faced the united opposition of hacendados, clergy, and Cristeros. To deal with them and bring his allies under one roof, Cárdenas organized the Confederación Regional Michoacana del Trabajo, or CRMDT. Made up mainly of campesinos, the CRMDT included a scattering of workers (Michoacán had little industry), public employees, university students, and teachers. By 1932, Cárdenas's last year as governor, the CRMDT, the most powerful political body in the state, had 100,000 members plus four thousand agrarian committees; beyond that, Cárdenas had organized the ejidos, many the result of his land reform program, into rural defense units and given them rifles. With less success, he and his cohorts, as part of the effort of the CRMDT, organized the Feminist Federation of Michoacán, which, aside from its crusade against alcoholism and religious fanaticism, undertook to ready women to defend their ejidos if something happened to their husbands. The platform of the CRMDT called for agrarian reform, an eight-hour day, a minimum wage, and, to avoid conflict with labor chieftains in Mexico City, cooperation with the CROM.

But Cárdenas kept political power to himself. Members of the CRMDT's central committee, the ruling authority, could not be reelected; no strong or independent voice emerged from its ranks. Cárdenas saw to it that its former members lost their public posts. As "honorary president," he presided over the meetings of the Confederación and helped to finance it. Both profited: Cárdenas won a popular base of support in Michoacán which he could use against Mexico City; and the members of the Confederación had agrarian and labor reform. In reality, Cárdenas co-opted the leaders of the Confederación. In return for their backing, they became members of the state legislature or national Congress, regidores of ayuntamientos, or *presidentes municipales* and, on occasion, sat on courts. The backing of the Confederación converted Cárdenas into one of the provincial caudillos to be reckoned with in an era when rifles often determined political status. With the Confederación behind him, Cárdenas climbed the political ladder to the head of the Partido Nacional Revolucionario and then to the post of secretary of war, becoming, by 1932, one of that select body of individuals who, with Calles, governed Mexico.

The legacy of the Confederación was a mixed one. By winning undisputed sway over the politics of Michoacán, Cárdenas compelled the local oligarchy to relinquish its monopoly over public jobs. Unfortunately, it kept control of the economic structure. The result was a kind of stalemate: some reform but not much. Hacendados lost some of their lands; but not enough to alleviate the poverty of most campesinos. Parts of Guaracha, to illustrate, became an ejido for eight hundred families. During his four years as governor, Cárdenas distributed nearly 142,000 hectares of land to 191 villages, more than had been given out before, at a time when Calles, the Jefe Máximo, was labeling land reform a mistake. Yet not once did Cárdenas overstep the legal boundaries set down by Mexico City, and most of the big haciendas of Michoacán outlived Cárdenas and his Confederación.

With the concurrence of Mexico City, Cárdenas turned over the governorship to a conservative in 1932, according to critics because he did not want to bequeath the Confederación to a popular individual who might undermine his base of power in Michoacán. General Benigno Serrato, the military chief of Nuevo León, fell quickly under the influence of hacendados and clergy and, with the blessings of President Abelardo Rodríguez, started to dismantle the political structure erected by Cárdenas, who kept his silence. Silence, the mark of a loyal party man, helped Cárdenas become the PNR's candidate; his presidency was no blessing to the Confederación in Michoacán. To govern Michoacán, Cárdenas imposed Gildardo Magaña, an outsider who, by encouraging local campesinos and workers to join the recently organized CTM and CNC, the national organizations, dealt a mortal blow to the Confederación. Now more concerned with forming a national power base, Cárdenas saw no need for an independent bloc that might challenge his authority. By 1937, the Confederación had outlived its usefulness; born of Cárdenas's needs, it died by his hands when he no longer required its support.

Cárdenas won the presidency with an eclectic band of believers. Despite his reform credentials, he had antagonized no major rival on the political scene. An early supporter of Pascual Ortiz Rubio, he won the respect of his successor, Abelardo Rodríguez. As a soldier, he was a Callista with strong ties to the army, one reason for his being named secretary of war. He had the backing of key caudillos, among them Saturnino Cedillo, boss of San Luis Potosí. Thanks to him, Cárdenas's quest for the presidency received the seal of approval of the Confederación Campesina Mexicana, organized in San Luis Potosí in 1933 and the most important of its kind in Mexico. Among its godparents were Cedillo, Emilio Portes Gil, and Graciano Sánchez, big names in agrarian politics. The Confederación Campesina, with strong support in San Luis Potosí, Tamaulipas, Michoacán, and Chihuahua, wrote its platform with Cárdenas in mind.

Within the PNR, three generals coveted its blessings. Aside from Cárdenas, Manuel Pérez Treviño, and Carlos Riva Palacio had their eyes on the National Palace. Riva Palacio never had a chance, but the ambitions of Cárdenas and Perez Treviño split the PNR. At this juncture, Calles, so goes the political gossip, wavered, not yet having made up his mind. Pérez Treviño, it was clear, counted on the well-wishes of the "right wing" of the PNR, while Cárdenas counted on those of its "left," an assortment of governors, deputies to Congress, military chiefs, and agrarian and labor spokesmen. When Cárdenas became the popular favorite, Calles chose to back him. At that point, Cárdenas, without having waged a public campaign, had won the presidency. His election was a foregone conclusion; the PNR ruled, not the people.

Not in the opinion of Cárdenas, who, with the election assured, traveled to the four corners of the Republic, the first Mexican politico to do so. In total, he covered 27,709 kilometers, 475 of them on horseback. His journeys took him to cities and towns and to countless villages off the beaten path, on occasion to pueblos whose inhabitants knew no Spanish. His acceptance speech, which dwelt on agricultural issues, campesinos, and labor, concluded on this note: "I have been elected president and I intend to be president." But Calles had other ideas, as Cárdenas learned. Already elected head of the Republic, Cárdenas went to see Calles, then visiting Navolato, site of his haciendas in Sonora. When he arrived, the Jefe Máximo was playing cards with two generals. Told by a colonel that Cárdenas awaited him, Calles, the story goes, replied, "Entertain him while I finish my game." Cárdenas, obviously, still had a long way to go before becoming, to quote his acceptance speech, "president."

IV

Stability, the attribute acclaimed by Porfirio Díaz, was absent from the Mexico inherited by Cárdenas. Not only was the economy ailing, but one had to deal with the conservative Callistas. Catholics were restless once again. For their anger, they had ample cause; the anticlerical Calles, judged by his public utterances, had forgotten nothing. In Cárdenas's cabinet, partly as a result of Calles's doings, sat Tomás Garrido Canábal, cacique of Tabasco and known, for good reason, as the "executioner of priests." Secretary of agriculture, he was, nonetheless, an hacendado who, to heap ridicule on the clergy, had named one of his bulls El Obispo (The Bishop) and a donkey El Papa (The Pope). His Red Shirts, armed thugs under his command, committed atrocities daily against priests who ventured into Tabasco. Garrido Canábal was a loyal fan of Calles.

Reformers, all the same, had captured control of the convention of the PNR in Querétaro in 1934. Unhappy with the lagging economy and the conservative stance of the Jefe Máximo and his disciples, the dissidents mapped out a Plan Sexenal, or Six-Year Plan, for the incoming administration, at odds with the thinking of the Callistas. By then, Calles had sided with foreign capital, spoke of the sanctity of private property, employed puppets to manipulate labor, and believed capitalism the tonic for Mexico's ills. The Plan Sexenal, at one and the same time a promise for the future and a confession of failure, pledged the federal government to spur and regulate the economy.

Under its guidance, Mexico would have land reform, recognize the importance of the ejido, provide agricultural credit, and build systems of irrigation—this as well as guarantees for "authentic small property." The Plan sexenal urged the transformation of the National Agrarian Commission, a legacy of the Carrancistas, into a Departamento Agrario and, of tremendous import for the future, the extension to *peones acasillados* of the right to petition for land. The plan asked for compliance with Article 123, upholding labor's right to organize and to strike. Highly nationalistic, it demanded enforcement of legislation dealing with the subsoil, specifically petroleum and mining. In the next six years, it promised, twelve thousand rural schools would be built. Cárdenas embraced the Plan Sexenal as gospel. Confronted with rising unrest because of the Great Depression, Calles had no choice but to bow to the wishes of the plan's architects. He did so believing that Cárdenas could not implement it without his help, which he had no intention of bestowing.

The plan had also called for the reform of Article 3. Henceforth, schooling would be "socialistic," a tacit acceptance of the materialistic interpretation that man's lot depends on his ability to support himself—that economics lies at the core of his problems. Utilitarian in character and emphasizing technical training, socialist education, as it was baptized, banned religious teachings, substituting for them true, scientific, and rational knowledge which provided an "exact concept of the world and society." Narciso Bassols, secretary of education under Abelardo Rodríguez, also decided, early in 1934, to implement sexual education in the public schools.

Sex and the socialist school, particularly after the reform of Article 3, stirred a hornet's nest. With their elevation to national gospel, a public outcry was heard. The clergy, charging heresy and blasphemy, jumped into the fray, joined by the Padres de Familia, a kind of Mexican PTA and, as expected, the press. Parents in the cities withdrew their children from school, denounced sex education as immoral, and branded the socialist school evil. So great was the furor that Bassols had to postpone momentarily the attempt to teach boys and girls about "the birds and the bees."

The socialist school, however, weathered Bassols's troubles, becoming a bone of contention, particularly in the provinces where Callista governors gleefully persecuted the clergy. Adalberto Tejeda, one of them, limited the number of priests in Veracruz to one for every one thousand inhabitants, and Garrido Canábal's Red Shirts burned religious images in the streets of Tabasco. By 1935, the Republic had only 308 priests; incredibly, seventeen states had none. Without priests, hundreds of churches closed.

From the persecution of the clergy and the defiant attitude of the Vatican, which earlier had labeled Mexico's government "tyrannical and hostile to the church," plus the irritant of the socialist school, surfaced a second Cristiada, with adherents in fifteen states, where eight thousand of the faithful had taken up arms. Unlike the Cristero Rebellion of the 1920s, overwhelmingly campesino, this protest was led by the middle class of the cities and towns; mass rallies against the socialist school were organized in Michoacán, Morelos, Zacatecas, Puebla, and Jalisco, where police and soldiers wounded and killed the faithful.

Labor unrest, moreover, broke out. Strikes multiplied, reaching 650 during 1935, three times that of Rodríguez's final year. The economic doldrums and fears that conservative Callistas might undercut labor's gains led unions outside of the CROM, mainly the electricians, railroaders, and mining and petroleum workers, to become more militant. And with good reason. The Callistas, aided by the effects of the Great Depression, had dismissed nearly 10,500 of the men toiling on the railroads. None of the independent unions backed the candidacy of Cárdenas, believing him a stooge of Calles. Only the CROM offered backing, which Cárdenas refused to accept.

At this juncture, Cárdenas came to the National Palace. He did nothing to deter the wave of strikes. When asked to comment on them, he replied that he saw them as the normal adjustment of wages to profits. In the strikes, the recently established Department of Labor, which arbitrated industrial disputes, ruled in favor of employers on only eight occasions. That, in the view of Calles and businessmen, was heresy. When Calles warned that such behavior would lead to a repetition of the Ortiz Rubio "abdication" of 1932, independent labor rallied to Cárdenas's defense. The electrical workers, small numerically but renowned for their independence, joined hands with the railroad men and miners. By disavowing Calles and honoring labor's right to strike, Cárdenas began not only to unite labor but, significantly, to win its loyalty for his approaching battle with Calles. Independent labor, moreover, had taken cover under the government umbrella, something it had refused to do until then.

With labor in his camp, Cárdenas, preparing for his confrontation with the Callistas, rid himself of all but three governors and military zone commanders, then dismissed the cabinet picked for him, replacing Garrido Canábal with Saturnino Cedillo, and named Emilio Portes Gil head of the PNR. Neither had sworn fealty to Calles. When Calles's puppets went off to Cuernavaca to complain to the Jefe Máximo, labor groups under the tutelage of Vicente Lombardo Toledano, boss of the Confederación General de Obreros y Campesinos de México, sided with Cárdenas. If the Callistas attempted to unseat him, warned Lombardo Toledano, the workers would organize a general strike. Seeing the handwriting on the wall, Calles, on June 19, declaring that he had "retired from politics," took a plane for the United States. A few days before, ninety-nine deputies to Congress and forty-five senators had sworn eternal loyalty to him; after his flight, just twenty-six of them kept their vows. When Calles, in December of 1935, returned home to meddle again in the Republic's affairs, some eighty thousand workers marched in Mexico City while the PNR, now Cardenista, purged itself of the Jefe Máximo and his friends. When Calles kept on plotting, Cárdenas put him on board a plane bound for Brownsville, Texas.

The final rupture with the old politics occurred in Monterrey, the northern citadel of industry, in February 1936. A strike had broken out in the Republic's biggest glass factory, the Vidriera of the Garza-Sada clan, the leaders of the conservative business magnates who ran local industry, organized and supremely confident. In 1929, these *regiomontanos,* as the inhabitants of Monterrey were referred to, had come together to form COPARMEX, an employers' association, mightier than the chambers of industry and the chambers of commerce organized under government auspices between 1917 and 1918. When the workers struck the Vidriera, the Garza-Sadas and their allies mounted antilabor demonstrations, their propaganda labeling Communist both labor and Cardenistas. The factory owners, clasping hands with the Garza-Sadas, locked out their workers, despite a Department of Labor ruling.

Upon learning what had happened, Cárdenas took a special train to Monterrey. The challenge went beyond the rights of labor, striking at the heart of the Cardenista formula. When he confronted the businessmen of Monterrey, Cárdenas informed them that if they were "tired of the social struggle they could hand over their factories to the workers or to the government." That, he added, "would be patriotic, but not lockouts." Out of this confrontation, a Pyrrhic victory for the Cardenistas, was born the Confederación de Trabajadores de México, or CTM, until today Mexico's national labor confederation.

Vicente Lombardo Toledano, its architect, was partly of Italian ancestry. He was born in 1894 in Teziutlán, a town in Puebla, to parents who owned a house in Mexico and oil stocks and boasted of being friends of Porfirio Díaz. By 1917, the family had lost its fortune and moved to Mexico City, where Lombardo Toledano blossomed into a prize student at the exclusive Internado Internacional, won the praise of Antonio Caso, his teacher at the National University, and became a lawyer. Lombardo Toledano found politics more to his liking, siding early with labor and, in 1918, attending the convention in Saltillo that founded the CROM. Also, he had turned Marxist, the first graduate of the National University to do so. He did not, however, join the Communist party.

In 1936, the CTM had 350,000 workers. Its pillars were the industrial unions, chiefly miners and metallurgical workers, stevedores, sugar and textile hands, teachers, and, of course, the electricians, plus regional federations, usually small and disunited, claiming 400,000 in their ranks. The unity of the CTM survived barely one year. When Lombardo Toledano and his allies claimed that a strike by one was a strike by all, the electricians, always jealous of their prerogatives, dropped out, joined by the miners and metallurgical workers. Fidel Velázquez, with his attacks on the Communist party, further jeopardized the fragile alliance. Cárdenas, however, wanted labor unity. Relying on the aid of Lombardo Toledano, he enticed back into the CTM some of the deserters. Just the same, Cárdenas had not helped to reunite labor in order to build an independent political body beyond the government's control. The new unity cost the Communists their bastions of power in labor's ranks; Cárdenas, additionally, made certain that the CTM had no role to play in organizing campesinos; the government, he declared, would do that, a task already under way in commercial agriculture. Likewise, he left the CROM and the CGT, the old labor confederations, undisturbed.

While this drama was unfolding, the Cardenistas made peace with the church. During 1936, Cárdenas had gone out of his way to acknowledge the right of Mexicans to worship freely, telling them that he had no quarrel with any religion and that his government had no plans for antireligious campaigns or, he added, in reference to the socialist school, for propaganda in the classroom. The socialist school would be "rational and science minded" but, regardless of that, not tamper with religious beliefs. Sex education, by the same token, vanished from the curriculum. Anticlerical legislation had become a dead letter. Priests reopened churches, Catholics won peace for their souls, and the Cristeros, disavowed by their supporters, laid down their arms. By the spring of 1936, the church conflict had largely ended. However, in the following year, Catholic fanatics founded the Unión Nacional Sinarquista, troublemakers of the future.

The times had taken on a rosy hue for the Cardenistas; sales of cash crops for export rose, the GNP climbed upward, and the economy improved. With his triumph over the Callistas, Cárdenas now sat in the driver's seat. *Presidencialismo,* a national politics in which the primordial role is played by the chief executive, was a fact of life. No Jefe Máximo manipulated politics; nor did Mexicans speak of *gobiernos peleles,* government by lackeys. Cárdenas had his own cabinet, men of his choosing; even Cedillo, the replacement for Garrido Canábal, had departed. At the same time, the system of *cacicazgos,* state bosses, had mainly come to an end. Only Cedillo in San Luis Potosí still held out.

V

Under the Cardenistas, big government made its entrance. The days of laissez-faire, in both theory and fact, were but a distant memory. The idea of government intervention in the economy, nevertheless, was not entirely novel, as the Constitution of 1917 testified; only a strongly centralized and activist state could have enforced it. Similarly, the Callistas, with their Banco de México, agricultural banks, irrigation projects, and highways, had modified the traditional interpretation of laissez-faire. The Great Depression, as it did everywhere else, invited government intervention to restore the economy; the Republic's maladies, its helmsmen believed, exceeded the therapeutic powers of the private sector. The failure to comply with the ideals of 1917, as the Six-Year Plan documented, required government action, a view shared by reformers unhappy with the capitalist model, who wanted to revive stipulations in Article 27 for Mexican ownership of natural resources.

The Cardenistas were not socialists. Though some of them upheld socialist goals, their patron did not. Cárdenas, according to his friend Francisco

Múgica, one of the fathers of the charter of 1917, had read neither Marx nor Lenin and had no inkling of revolutionary theory or of social orders beyond what he had witnessed firsthand. Like most of the generals of the Great Rebellion, he was self-taught, a pragmatist but, for all that, a reformer with a nagging social conscience. The future, Cárdenas affirmed, would be capitalistic but with a soul.

First and foremost, the Cardenistas set out to revive the agrarian promises of 1917. Come what may, they were going to redistribute the land, to give campesinos a plot of soil. Although they blessed the ejido, a first in the history of Mexico, they had no intention of breaking up the small, private farm. In this campaign, the Cardenistas were aided by the Código Agrario of 1934, the blueprint of agrarian reform of the Plan Sexenal, which, as legislation, allowed *peones acasillados* to petition for the hacienda lands they cultivated. The Código Agrario, which updated existing laws, had already mildly revived the pace of land redistribution. Until 1934, however, the government had paid hacendados for lands taken with bonds but, reeling from the ills of the depression, had stopped issuing them.

Late in 1935, with the Callistas on the run, Cárdenas gave the green light to agrarian reform. The ejido became its cornerstone, a departure from the formula of 1917. Hacienda lands, the best of them, Cárdenas pledged, would be given to the poorest campesinos. To support the ejido, the Cardenistas organized the Banco Nacional de Crédito Ejidal, a bank to lend money to *ejidatarios.* Planning for the political organization of campesinos, what became the Confederación Nacional Campesina (CNC) in 1938, got under way. The goal was to unite campesinos (in the pattern of the Michoacán Confederación), to gain their support and bring peace to the countryside by eliminating rival bands. The Cardenistas had in mind the Ligas de Agrónomos Socialistas, affiliates of the CROM, the Partido Nacional Agrarista, the Liga Nacional Campesina, and politicos of the PNR (the Confederación Nacional Campesina Mexicana of Portes Gil, for one), all competing for the loyalty of dirt farmers. None, in the opinion of the Cardenistas, could be trusted to be loyal to their regime.

Land reform started in the Laguna, a cotton belt lying largely in Coahuila. In this hot and arid region, two rivers, the Nazas principally and the Aguanaval, watered the rich alluvial soil, ideal for the planting of cotton. The Tlahualilo and Rapp-Sommer y Purcell companies were the biggest of the conglomerates in the Laguna. "Revolutionary" generals had also acquired haciendas, among them Manuel Pérez Treviño, a rival of Cárdenas for the presidency, and Eulogio Ortiz, who, after being stripped of his lands, uttered the much quoted statement "The Revolution gave me my lands and the Revolution took them away." Aside from Torreón, two more cities straddled the Laguna: San Pedro, once home to Francisco I. Madero, and Gómez Palacio;

together, they had 125,000 inhabitants, nearly all, in one way or another, linked to the cotton industry. The hacendados employed, in about equal numbers, both wageworkers, many of whom lived in the nearby cities, and *peones acasillados.* The time was ripe for change because the Great Depression and a prolonged drought had created unrest in the Laguna. With the rise in unemployment, workers had gone on strike, threatening the harvests of cotton. In response, the hacendados imported *esquiroles* (scabs) and, to alleviate the unrest, established a few ejidos on the outskirts of Gómez Palacio, but to no avail. Given the poor soil and the lack of water, the ejidos merely led their campesinos to join neighbors in demands for work and higher wages.

Seldom nostalgic for Mexico City, Cárdenas spent the autumn of 1936 in Torreón, supervising the expropriation of the haciendas. When it was over, more than 34,000 campesinos had land; 73 percent of the irrigated lands had been given to them. The rest, about 70,000 hectares, were subdivided into plots of 150 hectares for distribution among dispossessed hacendados, sharecroppers, or *colonos.*

The Cardenistas did not simply carve the Laguna up into village ejidos. Instead, they organized it into a giant collective ejido; the goal was to redistribute the lands of the hacendados but leave intact their productive capacity, keeping alive their economies of scale, part and parcel of big, capitalist enterprise. Campesinos in the communities of the Laguna received an ejidal parcel to till; tractors, plows, and other implements, seeds, fertilizers, and insecticides were owned collectively. Profits from the sale of the harvest were then split up among the *ejidatarios* on the basis of their contribution to it. The Banco Ejidal provided credit, offered technical assistance, and oversaw the operation. After a rocky start, most of the ejidos showed a profit, permitting them to pay back loans from the Banco Ejidal. The collective ejido of the Laguna became the forerunner of similar ones, "islands of socialism floating in a sea of capitalism."

Yucatán's turn came next. Henequen, once Yucatán's golden crop, was in the doldrums; with markets closing and prices falling, its production had plummeted. Not illogically, private investors, both Mexicans and foreigners, showed no interest in Yucatán, to the sorrow of its 300,000 inhabitants, a multitude of them jobless and hungry. To alleviate discontent, state authorities had redistributed 30 percent of the henequen lands in 1935. Cárdenas arrived in Progreso almost two years later, accompanied by engineers, surveyors, and bureaucrats. Before the end of 1937, in the single biggest act of agrarian reform in the history of Mexico, Cárdenas gave the campesinos 40 percent more of the *henequenales,* as the fields were called. The disenfranchised planters kept the rest of the land, but in parcels of 300 hectares, half in cultivated land. The old henequen haciendas had been banished from the face of Yucatán, replaced, in the manner of the Laguna, by 272 collective ejidos. The *desfibradoras,* the rasping machines that shredded henequen into fiber, went with them. To maintain the unity of henequen production, the Cardenistas established a henequen "trust" run by campesinos and "small farmers," the former hacendados.

Cárdenas was not through altering the Republic's landownership map. In Sonora, he returned to the Yaquis 17,000 hectares of irrigated land, the right bank of the Río Yaqui; the noble act, even so, restored merely a fraction of the stolen lands. In Mexicali, capital of Baja California, Cárdenas expropriated the cotton plantation of the Colorado River Land Company, converting it into ejidos. In 1937, too, El Mante and Santa Barbara, the haciendas of Calles in Tamaulipas, went to their workers. Then the ax fell on the hacendados of Los Mochis, the rich Fuerte River valley of Sinaloa. In 1938, the Dante Cusi family, originally from Italy, lost Nueva Lombardía and Nueva Italia, haciendas growing rice and citrus fruits in Michoacán; according to local natives, they were richer and more productive than Guaracha, the former fiefdom of Diego Moreno, also the victim of Cardenista agrarian reform. Both Nueva Lombardía and Nueva Italia became collective ejidos. In 1939, some of the coffee planters of Chiapas, notorious for their ill treatment of their Indian workers, lost their lands.

On balance, the accomplishments loomed large. Unbelievably, Cárdenas had kept his word. When he entered the National Palace, just 6 percent of the Republic's land had been redistributed; in just six years, he added another 12 percent, a good part of it fertile. Virtually by his own hand, Cárdenas had distributed nearly 18.4 million hectares of land to over one million campesino families, by any standard a formidable achievement.

Annual Land Distribution
(Millions of Hectares)

1935	1.9
1936	3.9
1937	5.4
1938	3.2
1939	2.0
1940	1.3

By 1940, over 1.5 million *ejidatarios*, the owners of 47 percent of the arable land, constituted nearly 42 percent of the agricultural population.

A qualitative difference, furthermore, set apart the Cárdenas epoch from that of the years before. Of the parcels distributed prior to Cárdenas, 40 percent were smaller than two hectares; 30 percent, from two to four; 25 percent, between four and ten; and only 5 percent, over ten. In contrast, lands distributed from 1935 to 1937, the bonanza years, averaged seventeen hectares; few parcels had less than four. Earlier, parcels distributed were not merely tiny but of poor quality, not infrequently dependent on rainfall to water their crops. More often than not, the Cardenistas distributed irrigated lands. *Ejidatarios* who sold their crops had more to spend, thus stimulating the demand for manufactured goods.

Still, not everything had gone well. Nearly half of the Republic's hacendados survived the Cardenista onslaught. Despite the hectic pace of reformers, over two million campesino families lacked fertile lands in 1940; to meet their needs, they had to be given not only lands but, equally important, loans, irrigation works, and roads. The cupboard of the Banco Ejidal, however, was bare. To make matters worse, rainfall fell off from 1936 to 1938; that, plus problems of readjustment, led to a decline in agricultural production and to a rise in the price of food. Many *ejidatarios,* additionally, had too little land or farmed, despite efforts to the contrary, poor land, compelling them to sell a part of their labor to others or to rent their lands and go off to the city to find work.

On the collective ejidos, mistakes of a different stripe hampered them. Haste had led to unexpected problems. On more than one occasion, hacendados had kept large plots, circumventing the limit of 300 hectares by establishing the legal right of offspring and relatives to a share of the land. In Yucatán, no rational criteria dictated how haciendas were carved up, leading to "crazy quilt" land patterns. Some ejidos received henequen plants about to bear; others, with plants years from maturity, were born without any sources of income. Now and then, city dandies from Progreso and Mérida who knew influential Cardenistas, received lands at the expense of campesinos. Many ejidos had no access to *desfibradoras,* rendering impossible the stripping of the henequen leaf in the required twenty-four hours. Many *ejidatarios* complained that the Banco Ejidal, entrusted with marketing and production decisions, had simply replaced the hacendado; the worker had exchanged an old master for an impersonal bureaucracy controlled from Mexico City. This litany of complaints, especially about the role of the Banco Ejidal, rang a familiar bell in the Laguna and elsewhere.

Unexpectedly, agrarian reform inflated the size of the middle class. From the days of the Maximato, when the first steps were taken to spur economic growth, its management required cadres of bureaucrats and professionals. The government's role, magnified manyfold by the needs of the revised agrarian structure of the Cardenistas and, after 1938, the management of the nationalized petroleum industry, added to the federal payroll more agronomists, engineers, architects, physicians, clerks, and secretaries. Intellectuals, never ones to reject public jobs, seldom failed to proffer their wisdom in return for one of them. Some of the recipients of land went on to swell the ranks of the rural middle class. Not since the days of the Porfiriato had aspirants to middle-class status enjoyed such bountiful days.

In the Cardenista blueprint, industry, though important, was low man on the totem pole. No one, nevertheless, spoke of nationalizing industry; if its magnates handled labor fairly, they were free to go their own way. Industry, moreover, was a reality, nearly all of it dating from the Porfiriato; more recently, Ford and Palmolive, American corporations, had made their debut, while Du Pont had acquired the Compañía Nacional Mexicana de Dinamita, the first of many to fall to outsiders. The interest of foreign investors testified to the recovery of Mexican markets from the blows of the Great Depression, the result of the rise in value and volume of exports of gold, silver, and oil. By 1939, manufacturing was the most dynamic sector of the economy, with sales of steel and cement booming because of government spending on the infrastructure. With profits soaring, Mexican industrialists began to update their factories, while recent immigrants from Europe started new plants for the manufacture of silk, rayon, cotton knitwear, and hosiery, to name four.

Dirt farmers, according to an axiom of the Cardenistas, needed schools in order to cultivate their soil wisely. So rural education again became a priority. Narcisco Bassols, chief of public education between 1931 and 1934, had planted the seeds for its revival. Young, short, and suffering from nearsightedness, a condition he overcame by wearing dark, horn-rimmed glasses, Bassols was keenly interested in rural education. An economic determinist, he believed that man's life revolved around economics. Satisfying the material necessities of rural dwellers, not the "incorporation" of Indians into society, ranked at the top of his priorities. The issue for Bassols and Rafael Ramírez, still head of rural schools, was "a concrete one: a hungry Indian cannot be turned into a good scholar, and studies of him have value only if they help to transform his economic life."

More sensitive to cultural values and long disturbed by the deplorable plight of the Indian, Cárdenas revived the Indianist program, neglected since the glory days of Moisés Sáenz. The Cardenistas inherited a troubled school program, with 6,000 out of 22,000 teachers jobless. Campesino parents, once enamored of schooling, had started to question its efficacy. In the isolated rancherias, children either dropped out early from school or stayed at home to help with the chores. Besides, children had appetities, an old Indian told the teacher in Gregorio López y Fuentes's *El Indio;* time was "wasted going back and forth to school." When "there is not enough to eat, schools are a luxury." Determined to change that, Cárdenas had given land to the poor, then watched closely over their schools, taking time to visit them. For him, the rural schoolteacher was one of the most important cogs in the mechanism for change in Mexico.

Reformers in the thirties believed that the rural school waged an uphill battle, an opinion shared by Sáenz, one of its architects. "I am," he wrote in *Carapan: Bosquejo de una experiencia,* "convinced of the futility of the countless sporadic and puerile activities of our so-called School of Action." Critics, he acknowledged, referred to the ill-equipped and poorly led schools as schools of reading, writing, and arithmetic, rarely as institutions for social change. Countless rural schools were simply out of touch with reality, as one school inspector learned. During one of the periodic anti-alcohol campaigns, he had stopped at a village notorious for its pulque drinkers, where he lectured its inhabitants on the pitfalls of alcohol, urging them to drink water instead. His audience listened attentively, saying nothing. After he had finished, the villagers asked him to stay and eat with them. At the table, he noticed that his glass held rancid water. Surprised and angered, the inspector demanded an explanation. *Maestro,* they replied, "this is what you have asked us to drink." For miles around, there was nothing to drink but water from stagnant pools. The people drank pulque instead.

To get at these shortcomings, the Cardenistas reverted to Manuel Gamio's cherished concept of "integral education." Seeking to formulate a practical blueprint, which reflected community needs, planners called for coordinated, large-scale reforms, asking every federal agency to play a role. Unless they worked as one, the entire effort would fail. Without roads and water, without the electrification of villages that night cut off from the world of books, as well as rural credit, the schools waged a fruitless battle. Nor could they remain mere centers of learning, divorced from the day-to-day activity of village life.

Given these objectives, traditional pedagogical methods received less attention. For the socialist school, learning, productive work, and social action were one and the same. Community needs were emphasized over individual demands. Entire regions were mapped out for the combined efforts of federal agencies, among them the Yaqui in Sonora and the Mezquital of Hidalgo, home of the destitute Otomí. The initial step was to provide the inhabitants with land; after that was done, other agencies stepped in. That of communications built roads; irrigation dammed streams and dug canals; agriculture supplied seeds and fertilizers, technical assistance, tools, and draft animals; education and health authorities brought schools and teachers, a clinic, doctors, and nurses.

Wherever federal banners flew, the cooperative made its appearance. Conceived initially as a means of employing collective action to obtain help for the school, the collective had its scope enlarged to cover the solution of community problems. By 1940, over eight hundred cooperative societies had been organized, which led to a bitter clash between schoolmaster and *acaparador,* the local middleman, who purchased village products for next to nothing and resold them for profit. When the teacher, by relying on the cooperative, attempted to upset the monopoly of the *acaparador,* frequently the local bigwig, he incurred the wrath of the most powerful figure in rural Mexico. Without prominent friends upon whom to rely and isolated from authorities in Mexico City, the teacher usually tasted defeat.

Indoctrination in the ideals of the "Revolution," in theory long characteristic of the rural school, became a pivotal part of education. A barrage of propaganda, oral and written, descended upon students and parents. There were pamphlets on the socialist school, articles on the classless society that came with state planning, and leaflets on every subject deemed worthy of study. What was left undone by the written word, the teacher filled in. The school had become a political weapon to use against the status quo.

By 1936, the Cardenistas had established the Department of Indian Affairs. Advocated by Gamio as far back as 1916, the department reflected public recognition of the wrongs committed against the Indian. The goal was to promote, unify, and supervise the activities of federal and state governments on behalf of the Indian by relying on systematic studies of his problems and the formulation of programs to meet them. The department had multiple duties. Representing the Indian on matters dealing with land, taxes, and labor rights, it offered legal advice. It endeavored to improve the living conditions of the Indian communities, urging branches of government to build clinics, roads, dams, and schools. It organized cooperative societies and sponsored programs to teach the Indian to speak Spanish. Also, it sponsored eight Indian congresses, where Indians met to discuss their problems. Cárdenas never missed these meetings, listening patiently to complaints and pleas for help. From them came projects of benefit to specific Indian groups, such as the Otomí, Yaquis, Tarahumaras of Chihuahua, and Chamulas of Chiapas. Additionally, the department managed special schools for Indians, called Escuelas Vocacionales para Indígenas, offshoots of the Centros de Educación Indígena of the 1920s. Vocational schools mainly, they taught agricultural techniques to boys and homemaking to girls. Located in the heart of Indian zones, they were agencies for the incorporation of the people into the surrounding communities.

VI

As promised by the Plan Sexenal, the Cardenistas revived Mexican nationalism, long dormant. The more militant the Cardenistas, the more hostile Washington's architects, but less so than Kellogg and his ilk during the 1920s. Washington, after all, had to wrestle with its own Great Depression; sympathy for Mexico's aims was not entirely lacking. That was especially true of Josephus Daniels, named ambassador to Mexico in 1933, who thought well of the Cardenista reforms, interpreting them to Washington as an effort to improve the purchasing power of Mexicans, which, ultimately, would convert

Mexico into a country with more customers for the United States.

The Cardenistas, all the same, wanted a sovereign Mexico. To establish its independence in foreign affairs, Cárdenas, in 1937, for example, offered asylum to Leon Trotsky, the dissident Russian Communist, to the anguish of Washington. That year, too, Mexico, at the League of Nations, castigated the West for refusing to come to the aid of Republican Spain, then fighting off Francisco Franco and his Fascist allies from Germany and Italy. When the West turned a deaf ear, Cárdenas shipped food, clothing, and guns to the Republicans. Then, to help rid Mexico of foreign domination, the Cardenistas completed the nationalization of the railroads, buying out foreign shareholders. At last, Mexico owned and controlled its railroads. Wishing to rid Mexico of gambling and related vices, the Cardenistas shut down the casinos, despite cries of anger from their American owners and Abelardo Rodríguez and his friends. None of this upset amicable relations between Mexico City and Washington; the redistribution of land in the Yaqui Valley, some at the expense of American owners, did, but not beyond the dispatching of nasty diplomatic notes by Washington demanding prompt payment for property taken. Still, it was a poor omen for future relations between the rich uncle and his poor relative.

The veneer of good feelings vanished in March 1938 when Cárdenas, to the surprise of the world, expropriated the properties of the foreign oil companies. That decision should not have been unexpected. The Morrow-Calles pact of the late twenties had papered over differences, which a decline in oil production magnified gradually. In the opinion of many Mexicans, the oil barons, while shoring up production in Venezuela, had neglected their properties in Mexico, in that way putting pressure on it to behave. The Mexicans were partly correct. Deposits were neglected and new explorations for oil not carried out. But, additionally, known oil reserves, which the companies controlled, were drying up. To get around the foot-dragging of the petroleum lords, the Mexicans, in 1934, organized Petróleos de Mexico, with shares to be owned by both Mexican capitalists and the government; when no Mexicans showed any willingness to risk their money, Petromex, as it was known, became a government monopoly. In comparison to the petroleum cartels, Petromex was a mere toddler.

The foreign oilmen had reaped great profits, perhaps the highest in the world. Between 1901 and 1938, on an investment of $100 million, profits may have been as much as $5 billion. High profits had not translated into equitable wages for workers. In response, strikes had broken out against El Aguila and La Huasteca Oil companies in 1934. The eighteen thousand workers in the oil industry, on the other hand, were not united, belonging to nineteen different unions or to none at all. Seeking to unify them, the Cardenistas brought them into the Sindicato de Trabajadores Petroleros de la República Mexicana

(STPRM) and then incorporated them into the CTM, the national labor confederation. Soon after, the STPRM started to negotiate its first collective labor contract, asking for higher wages and benefits totaling 65 million pesos. The petroleum magnates, claiming they could not afford it, offered a package worth 14 million pesos. Government mediation failed to bring the two parties together.

The strike of May 1937 led to the final confrontation. After an exhaustive study of labor's demands, the government judged them valid and asked the companies to increase their offer to 26 million pesos. The oilmen refused to budge; the conflict now pitted the government against the oil companies. However, the Cardenistas, so it seemed to most observers, merely intended to bend the oil lords to the will of Mexican nationalism. No one believed that the confrontation would lead to expropriation—least of all the petroleum moguls, convinced that Mexico possessed neither the technical know-how nor the money to run the industry.

When the Mexican Supreme Court ruled against them, early in March 1938, the oilmen, now frightened by the turn of events, found funds to pay the 26 million pesos but, to their later regret, quibbled over labor policy. By then, it was too late. On March 18, Cárdenas, no longer willing to allow "national sovereignty to be at the mercy of foreign capital," expropriated virtually all the oil properties held by foreigners in Mexico. By a stroke of the pen, the Bucareli and the Calles-Morrow accords, as well as the properties of Royal Dutch Shell and Standard Oil, were no more. For the first time, the nationalist vows of Article 27 had carried the day. Cárdenas offered to pay compensation within ten years, after both parties fixed a value on the property taken, and preferably in oil. With Standard Oil labeling expropriation "robbery under the law," the oil magnates rejected Mexico's solution. So defiant were the British, along with the Dutch capitalists who owned El Aguila, that Mexico severed diplomatic relations with them.

Washington was no less angry than the British. Fortunately for the Cardenistas, Washington found itself caught in a dilemma of its own making. By the Good Neighbor Policy, the pledge given at the Pan American Conference of 1933, Washington had rejected intervention, the big stick of yesteryear. With Germany, Italy, and Japan on the warpath, this was no time to jeopardize access to raw materials in Latin America, a possibility if marines were sent. Cárdenas, moreover, had vowed to blow up the oil fields if marines were landed on Mexican soil. That compelled Washington, which thought Communists infested the Mexican government, to be less bellicose.

Even so, Washington and the oil barons took their pound of flesh. They did what they could to prevent the sale of Mexican petroleum to Latin America and stopped the purchase of Mexican silver by the Treasury Department. Washington intervened also to stop independent American oilmen from selling Mexican petroleum in Europe, as well as to curtail the lending of money, public or private, to the Mexican government or the Mexican businessmen. Standard Oil, Royal Dutch Shell, and, for a time, Sinclair Oil boycotted Mexican petroleum, keeping it out of the world market. Both England and France stopped buying Mexican petroleum. The oil moguls, with the cooperation of Washington, made it impossible for Mexico to buy machinery and replacement parts for PEMEX, the Mexican oil monopoly. In 1937, Mexico had exported nearly 25 million barrels of oil; the boycott reduced that figure to 14.5 million barrels. Most probably, too, the oil magnates financed the abortive uprising of Saturnino Cedillo in 1938. As a result of the barrage of propaganda against Mexico, financed partly by the oil companies, fewer tourists visited Mexico. Not until 1942 was the boycott lifted. To market their oil, Mexicans were driven to selling it to Germany, Italy, and Japan, enemies of the United States. Expropriation, nevertheless, reduced the amount of foreign investment in Mexico from $1 billion to $300 by 1940, to the Cardenistas a sign of independence.

Finally, the Cardenistas, in 1938, altered the nature of official politics. By then, the Partido Nacional Revolucionario had outlived its usefulness. The reforms of the Cardenistas, specifically for labor and campesinos, had made it obsolete. Equally true, reform had made certain sectors restless. The middle class was openly hostile, while the Sinarquistas, religious fanatics, claimed one million adherents. Juan Andreu Almazán, a conservative general with presidential ambitions, had influential backers among the rich, especially in places such as Monterrey, citadel of industry, and the army. In order for reform to survive, a different party structure was necessary.

So emerged the Partido Revolucionario Mexicano, or PRM. No longer reflecting the Mexico of "revolutionary" generals, the PRM was a corporate body. To defend what had been accomplished, the Cardenistas built a party base of workers and campesinos, incorporating the CTM, the CROM, and CGT, the labor confederations, and the CNC and Ligas de Comunidades Agrarias, their equivalent in the countryside. On the model of the Michoacán Confederación, Cárdenas kept workers and campesinos apart. The Cardenistas also invited the military and the urban middle class—the public bureaucracy, essentially—to join. This was labeled the popular sector.

The PRM, the government in reality, controlled the leadership of the CTM, the CNC, and the military. Only the public sector stood on its own feet. Aside from bureaucrats, it took in university students, organizations of women, professionals, and small merchants. Without government tutelage, the CNC, the largest of the units, would have fallen apart; a government creation, it took orders from Mexico City. Factional strife, meanwhile, had weakened the CTM. The fight to oust Communists from the CTM, which drove out the most militant and most politicized, left labor at the beck and call of Fidel Velázquez and his pragmatic politicos. Partly because of that, the number of strikes declined sharply during the last years of the Cardenistas. The entire apparatus of the PRM depended on the whims of the political power brokers. With Cárdenas in office, labor and campesinos had little to fear; under conservative leadership, the popular sector and its allies would get the upper hand.

VII

The tide of reform peaked in 1938, then receded precipitously. The expropriation of the petroleum properties, applauded as the culmination of the Revolution, turned Cardenista policy around. Bankers, industrialists, and merchants, frightened by Cárdenas's defiance of the powerful Yankees, wanted to call a halt to reform. Monterrey industrialists, the Garza-Sadas among the most vociferous of them, had opposed the oil expropriation, fearing its consequences. Nor did all the generals in the army hail it. For them, as well as for much of the middle class, the interventionist role of government was alarming, in the opinion of some a Communist plot. Additionally, Mexico was unprepared to operate the oil industry; only a few Mexicans had held managerial or technical posts under Standard Oil and Royal Dutch Shell. Mexico lacked tankers for the export of its oil, a limitation aggravated by the boycott of the petroleum cartel and the hostility of Washington. As a result, oil revenues dropped off, drying up a principal source of money for the national budget. There was less money to spend on reforms, including wages for oil workers. The wealthy, for their part, began to withdraw money from Mexican banks for safekeeping in the United States, causing a flight of capital.

The economy, too, took a turn for the worse; for that, the oil crisis was only marginally responsible. More responsible was the resurgence of depression in the United States; markets for Mexican exports stagnated while foreign investors, frightened by the oil expropriation, kept their money at home. Inflation, likewise, engulfed the economy. Reform had cost money, hurting the national budget and driving the Cardenistas to print more money, which drove inflation to higher and higher levels. As prices of food, clothes, and housing rose, the buying power of wages and salaries dropped, to the detriment of Mexicans on fixed incomes, the middle class mainly. As if that were not enough, the value of the peso fell, making imported articles more expensive.

When prices of food shot up, inhabitants of Mexico City and the provincial redoubts blamed the Cardenistas. Already up in arms over the socialist school, the middle class was especially angry, as were intellectuals of the traditional mold. One of them was Dr. Atl, his hostile views echoed by José Vasconcelos. A few rushed to the defense of the embattled hacendados; others, such as Luis Cabrera, the old Carrancista, labeled the ejido of the Cardenistas a betrayal of the small-property ideal of the Revolution and the reason for the decline in agricultural productivity. The Banco Ejidal, he charged, had taken on the role of agitator of campesinos and the teacher of socialist dribble. Landownership, lamented López y Fuentes in *El Indio,* a novel about Indians, "isn't everything." "Tribes," he had a schoolteacher say, "had held their land for centuries, yet they continued in poverty and ignorance." Mexican newspapers and journals, nearly always organs of the rich and conservative, gave banner headlines to such opinions.

By 1938, Europe had split into rival camps, with the Fascists of Germany and Italy threatening the old order of England and France. In the Far East, Japan had invaded China, jeopardizing the Open Door Policy of the West. At home, reform, particularly land redistribution and oil expropriation, both at the expense of property rights dear to conservatives, menaced, in their opinion, political stability. To voice the fears of conservatives, Manuel Gómez Morin, an economist, native of Chihuahua and former Callista, founded the Partido de Acción Nacional (PAN), a political body embraced by Catholics. Gómez Morin and his Panistas, as they came to be known, denounced the "ideological confusion" of the times as well as politicians "bedazzled by Communist doctrines." The PAN drew enthusiastic support from urban women. The Sinarquistas, who trumpeted the virtues of Francisco Franco's Spain, also made their bow, standing at the opposite pole from the Cardenistas.

With the enemy at their front door, the Cardenistas took a step backward. Politicos such as Lombardo Toledano, a Marxist but pragmatic, shed their enthusiasm for change, advocating, instead, conciliation. With the world on the brink of war, and a clash between left and right in Mexico looming ahead, it was time to consolidate gains. This led the Cardenistas, their chief among them, to court, more and more, the private sector and to manipulate, through their control of the PRM, workers and campesinos. The oil expropriation, paradoxically, had translated into a victory for Mexicans opposed to modifications of the economic model followed since the days of Venustiano Carranza.

This scenario helps to explain why Cárdenas accepted a conservative as his successor. Francisco Múgica, hero of the reformers, never had a chance, the more so because a majority of governors opposed him. Before the PRM met, supposedly to pick its candidate, Múgica withdrew his candidacy. The blessings descended on Manuel Avila Camacho, a general as conservative as Juan Andreu Almazán, the anti-Cardenista candidate. At the PRM convention, leaders of the CTM and CNC, dutiful to their political role, backed him as Washington smiled benevolently.

The new Plan Sexenal spoke of the PRM's duty to protect democracy, reminded Mexicans that social injustices lingered on, and favored the ejido but left the door ajar for the dismantling of the collective ejidos. Urging guarantees for private property, the plan held aloft the ideal of the "union" of all Mexicans, appealed to "private enterprise," and called for the reform of Article 3.

The PRM, especially in the cities, probably lost the election of 1940. Almazán, a savvy politico, millionaire general, and charismatic, had accumulated much of his fortune off profits from government contracts in the days of Abelardo Rodríguez. An influential figure in the army, Almazán led the foes of Cárdenas. For the election, he had the support of the CROM, while speaking of honest politics, the sanctity of private property and home, and women's rights. Orthodox Catholics, as well as businessmen, adored him. On the day of the election, forty-seven Mexicans died, thirty of them in Mexico City. Violence aside, Avila Camacho carried the day, aided, Mariano Azuela recalled in *Nueva burguesía,* by carloads of campesinos decked out in tattered clothes and huaraches and trucked in to vote for the candidate of the PRM.

21

THE FALSE MIRACLE

I

Many of the reforms of the Cardenistas, under heavy fire since the expropriation of the foreign oil giants, fell by the wayside after 1940, dismantled before they could bear fruit. From this time on, conservatives, more and more, called the tune. Just the same, euphoric Mexicans, mainly the rich and the middle class, had a fiesta. For the first time, bureaucrats, university professors, storekeepers, and the like could buy automobiles, acquire homes of their own, and take vacations in Acapulco, the mecca of the affluent. The architects of this prosperity, the magnates of industry and their allies in politics, labeled it a "miracle."

II

For this drama, World War II set the stage. With the United States off fighting, Mexicans were left to themselves. Since Hollywood, for example, was turning out war movies, Mexican cinema enjoyed a golden age, becoming, in the space of a brief interval, one of the salient industries of the Republic. Mexicans went to see their own films, with their own movie stars: Jorge Negrete, dashing and romantic; Pedro Armendáriz, who sported a big mustache; the brothers Soler; Sara García, the *madre sufrida,* symbol of motherhood and *patria;* Gloria Marín, always beautiful; and Dolores del Río, back from a sojourn in Hollywood. In their films, women were either saints or sinners, the archetypes of the men who ran the industry. During the war years, popular music, too, enjoyed a heyday, with Mexicans dancing to Afro-Cuban rhumbas and danzones and traditional pasos dobles. But, above all, it was the bolero, a seductive rhythm and darling of the *burgués.* The melodies of Agustín Lara, the "musical poet," Gonzalo Curiel, Pepe Guízar, Manuel Esperón, and fellow composers filled the airwaves and played to packed houses in nightclubs from Mexico City to Tijuana. Even today, Mexicans still recall nostalgically the melodies of "Hilos de Plata," "Mala Noche," and "Perfidia," which Toña la Negra, a sultry chanteuse from Veracruz, sang to the delight of rich and poor alike. The golden age of film and popular music, for the enjoyment mainly of urbanites, testified to a shift away from populist reforms of benefit to the countryside and toward blueprints favoring industry, commerce, and big agriculture. How did it occur?

III

The whys and wherefores are complex. Mexicans hostile to the Cardenista formula had triumphed, their ranks swollen by the inhabitants of booming cities and a thriving middle class. World War II, furthermore, conferred a bonanza on Mexico, which joined the fray after German U-boats sank two of its oil tankers on the high seas. For its contribution to the war effort, Mexico dispatched a squadron of fighter planes to fight the Japanese in the Philippines and braceros to labor in the United States. More important, Mexico sold tons of copper, lead, graphite, cadmium, and mercury to American war industries, as well as cotton and coffee.

The war cut off Mexico from manufactures formerly imported. Unable to spend on consumer goods, Mexicans had money to invest. So was born a blueprint for industrialization based on import substitution, resting, logically, on the industrial edifice erected by the Porfiristas. Without it, no manufacturing revolution would have been possible, because the necessary capital goods were unattainable. Industrial growth was largely, says one expert, "the running of the nation's already installed plant night and day." As the years went by, this policy brought to center stage a manufacturing sector of big, capital-intensive, monopolistic firms relying on cheap labor to produce goods for captive, mostly middle-class consumers.

The end of World War II did not alter policy. On the contrary, efforts were redoubled to spur industrialization. To get wealthy Mexicans to invest in factories, government dangled inducements before their eyes, which included import licenses, protective tariffs, tax breaks, and loans at low interest rates through the Nacional Financiera. Foreign investors were invited to the banquet table to further whet the palate of Mexican capitalists. The door to Mexico, for all that, was not entirely unlocked, since foreigners, according to national legislation, were barred from the film industry, radio broadcasting, land and air transportation, commercial fishing, and publishing.

Additionally, the network of highways was expanded and plants were built to provide electricity, cement, steel, and sundry items at low cost to industry, baptized *paraestatales* and subsidized, at public expense, for the benefit of private capitalists. A commercial agriculture for export, designed to earn dollars to pay for the erection of the industrial edifice, received similar blessings. Encouraged by the incentives and the absence of competing imports, Mexican factories multiplied, especially in the Federal District, Guadalajara, and Monterrey. By the 1950s, the GNP was averaging 6 percent or better. All the same, the end of the war left Mexico more than ever at the mercy of markets north of the border; by 1944, over 90 percent of its foreign trade was with the United States.

With industrialization, the dream of a bucolic, agrarian, and self-sufficient Mexico flew out the window. Instead of a "socialist paradise," Mexico would be capitalistic, offering freedom for private enterprise and the laws of supply and demand. The "trickle-down" theory held sway. Inevitably, businessmen were part and parcel of the government entourage. As early as 1942, COPARMEX joined the parade, when industrialists from Monterrey, headed by the Garza-Sada clan, made their pilgrimage to Mexico City, where the nation's authorities no longer adhered to the labor policies of the Cardenistas.

Thus began an era of government largess for the private sector, when Mexican leaders proclaimed, tongue-in-cheek, allegiance to the adage "The less government, the better." Bankers and business tycoons applauded the annual reports of sympathetic governors. For their part, the industrialists born of import substitution banded together in the Confederación Nacional de la Industria de Transformacion, or CONACINTRA, to defend their interests and stand apart from the older COPARMEX. Businessmen won entrance into the presidential cabinet, their influence enhanced through COPARMEX and CONACINTRA, by personal ties to public officials, by their importance in the economy, and because they came to own the press, radio, and television. It was a rosy era for the *burguesía,* when domestic and foreign admirers saw Mexican capitalism "at the cutting edge of the battle against hunger."

All the same, the road was often rocky. World War II unleashed an inflationary spiral when foreign money poured into Mexico to compete for scarce goods; hoarding and speculation were rife. The price of food, clothing, and housing shot up. Price gouging on rents was so rampant in Mexico City that rent controls had to be installed. Shortages of *masa* for the tortilla led women in the barrios of the capital to take it forcibly from stores; others marched in the streets to protest against speculation in food prices. To cool the fires of inflation and keep pesos at home, officials devalued the national currency in 1948, to 6 pesos to the dollar and, when that failed to achieve results, to 8.65 pesos two years afterward. Consumerism by the rich and the middle class, nonetheless, became the vogue, and hungry campesinos started again to trek into the cities. Protected by tariffs, Mexican businessmen grew "accustomed to quick profits and low taxes." Yet the domestic market expanded ever so slowly, partly because industrialists targeted production to the buying habits of the middle class, kept wages of workers down, and seldom looked for customers among campesinos. For urbanites, the middle class and the rich, times were good, as new industries sprang up and old ones expanded, textiles particularly, while plants producing chemicals, cement, and beer and processing foods had banner years. The production of both pig iron and steel rose, and electrical output soared.

Corruption, too, took on fresh vigor, with one president acquiring real estate in Acapulco and erecting a business empire that included *Novedades,* a national newspaper, and Televisa, the country's television network. Businessmen gained fortunes overnight while governors, cabinet officers, and military lords used their posts for personal gain. Even teachers exacted bribes from parents waiting to enter their children in overcrowded urban schools. Ill-gotten gains were as Mexican as the tortilla, but they had been condemned in the past; now efforts were made to justify them on the grounds that tribute had to be paid to the almsgivers. "We laid the basis for Mexican capitalism," Carlos Fuentes had the banker Federico Robles say in *La región más transparente.* "What if we did get our percentage from . . . every contract?" Would you, he asked, "prefer that in order to avoid these evils we had done nothing at all? I repeat, because of what we went through we are entitled to everything. Because we were born in dirt-floor shacks, we have the right now to live in mansions with high ceilings and stone walls, with a Rolls-Royce at the door." A man had to take advantage of his opportunities. "And if I hadn't," Robles continued, "someone else would have seized what I have seized, stand where I stand, do what I do."

In 1950, just when Robles's boast started to sound hollow, the Korean War, which saw American troops in battle again, revived the economy, faltering from the effects of Europe's recovery from World War II. Along with that, a horde of Yankee tourists brought welcome dollars, especially to Tijuana and sister towns; their visits to buy curios, drink, eat, and be merry started to transform the dusty border. Affluent politicos and their allies in business sank millions of pesos into Acapulco, the first of the international resorts, which paved the way for Cancún, Ixtapa-Zihuatanejo, Puerto Vallarta, and Mazatlán. Until 1964, braceros, their ranks swollen by "wetbacks," sent their checks home and added more dollars.

When the Korean War ended and a recession struck the United States, the boom sputtered, as the price of lead, zinc, and cotton plummeted. Restrictions by the Congress of the United States on lead and zinc imports sent Mexico's mining industry into a tailspin. Most alarming, Europe no longer needed Mexican raw materials, because of the development of synthetic fibers and the availability of manufacturers from the United States. In addition, Washington's protectionist policies, which curtailed Mexican exports, damaged the economy; 75 percent of them were sold north of the border. The competition of Americans in the international market added another burden. During the

1940s, Mexican officials had encouraged the production of cotton, investing millions in irrigation projects, mostly in northern Mexico. By 1956, cotton exports represented 33 percent of all sales abroad. When the United States dumped surplus cotton on the world market for a pittance, Mexican planters lost their shirts. The decline of agricultural exports compelled Mexicans to cut back on their investments, thus deepening the economic doldrums. As the national budget tumbled, federal spending on public projects, designed to stimulate growth, slackened. Worried *burgueses,* likewise, started to deposit their money in foreign banks. To top off the list of misfortunes, droughts disrupted the harvests in the farm belts and Mexico had to import corn and beans.

By 1952, the growth of the GNP had started to lag, and Mexico had a crisis on its hands. Victimized by the previous spending spree, the treasury was empty, while nothing had been done to balance the Republic's budget. Policymakers had to shift gears. Henceforth, the platform would be austerity, required to clean up the financial mess and curtail inflation. But austerity, which reduced government spending, as well as the recession north of the border, led to economic stagnation. Among those unhappy with this turn of events were influential Mexicans in business, commerce, and industry who had gotten rich off government largess. Policy planners had to dump austerity and return to previous practice. The battle to balance the budget and curb inflation was put on the shelf. Trying to hold down the spiraling cost of food, federal officials established the Compañía Exportadora e Importadora (CEIMSA) to sell it at low prices to consumers, bureaucrats on fixed salaries hurt by inflation primarily. However, merchants, egged on by CONCANACO, the Republic's chamber of commerce, started to complain that CEIMSA endangered private enterprise. Then the government devalued the peso once more in 1954, which encouraged more capital flight.

Eventually, the recession in the United States ended, which restored a semblance of prosperity to Mexico. But the upturn was fleeting. Exports of cotton climbed, but soon their value, as well as that of coffee and mineral ores, dropped. Between 1956 and 1966, as the volume of exports declined, government revenues felt the pinch. Mexico, manifestly, could not count on foreign buyers to sustain economic growth. Devaluation, moreover, had fueled the inflationary fires. While exporters benefited from the devaluation of the peso, the poor had suffered the brunt of its blows.

Until the early 1950s, wages had been kept in check; for all intents and purposes, labor had been asked to subsidize the cost of industrialization. But labor could not be kept at bay indefinitely. So wage increases were granted; not to have done so would have torn apart the Republic's social fabric, a dilemma complicated by the need to keep inflation under control and maintain the pace of industrialization. The old policy of import substitution, furthermore, was reaching the end of its usefulness. To produce intermediate and capital goods, it was necessary to go beyond the manufacture of articles once imported. This required bigger plants, more machines, and costly technology, which exceeded the ability of Mexican private enterprise to finance. If Mexico was to industrialize fully, government had to shoulder a larger share of the burden.

Although turning their backs on austerity, Mexican officials, nevertheless, had no wish to revive inflationary spending. Another freeze on industrial wages was out of the question. To raise income taxes or to undertake fiscal reforms, likewise, would antagonize the *burguesía.* Strangely, no thought was given to the increasing of consumer demand, specifically by raising incomes of rural Mexicans. Business and government, more and more brothers in arms, believed that they could erect an industrial edifice by expanding the urban markets.

The solution adopted opened wider Mexico's doors to foreign capital. Outside money, it was thought, would finance the industrialization effort. Between 1955 and 1958, direct foreign investment rose by over $400 million, most of it going into industry. Industries did not all profit equally; targeted for special favors were those which produced machinery, heavy equipment, and vehicles required for the industrial and agricultural needs of the Republic. As before, government offered diverse incentives. Industries in the categories thought vital enjoyed virtual monopolies, thriving on captive buyers but unable to compete on the international scene. The industries most favored were the new ones, employing, by and large, the latest technology and nearly always branches of foreign corporations. As a consequence, foreigners widened their beachhead in manufacturing. These highly capitalized industries were a paradox in a country full of cheap labor. Giant industry gobbled up small plants which, earlier, had destroyed the livelihood of artisans.

The men who set policy in the 1950s also began to borrow from foreigners. These funds, they said, were "indispensable," a view which ignored the advise of Lázaro Cárdenas, who, more than once, warned of the pitfalls that awaited Mexico were it to incur a foreign debt. Until 1950, Mexicans had been unable to obtain loans from international lending agencies, which, under the tutelage of Washington, urged one and all to seek private capital. Between 1940 and 1950, capital for "economic development," as it was dubbed, was raised internally, by means of inflationary policies, duties on exports and imports, hidden taxes, and profits from the state-owned industries, the *paraestatales.* However, in the 1950s, the International Bank for Reconstruction and Development, as well as the Export-Import Bank, reflecting Washington's fear of Communist infiltration in Latin America, started to lend money. By 1952, Mexico had borrowed $206 million; with the arrival of this money in the form of loans or investment capital began the era of "stabilized development," the "miracle" long anticipated.

Stability accompanied by economic growth, which required Mexico's willingness to plunge into debt, had specific goals. One was to rely on outside capital to keep the lid on prices; it was no longer fashionable to finance economic "development" by asking the Banco de México to print pesos. Outside funds, too, were needed to keep the prices of the *paraestatales* low; much of the money borrowed was employed to make up the losses of the *paraestatales*, which frequently ran a deficit in order to aid private enterprise. Duties on exports and imports were either reduced or eliminated, at the expense of national revenue; foreign loans made up the loss. More and more of the cost of industrialization was being borne by foreign capital. Since its credit standing received rave ratings from Washington, Mexico borrowed freely, approximately $626 million by 1958, three times its foreign debt of 1950.

Washington's shift in its lending politics, for which the Cuban revolution's threat to its hegemony in Latin America was also responsible, helped stoke the fires of Mexican borrowing. When international lending agencies cooled their ardor, private banks in the United States took up the slack. In 1960, to illustrate, the Prudential Insurance Company lent Mexico $100 million, not once asking how it would be spent. Direct investment in Mexico, at the same time, jumped from just over $900 million in 1959 to nearly $1.3 billion by 1964. On behalf of economic growth, Mexico was becoming increasingly dependent on the United States.

By 1955, priming the pump with foreign capital, like the earlier deficit spending, had produced bountiful days, aided by the rebirth of Yankee prosperity. The Mexican economy sparkled as private capitalists, foreigners and natives alike, invested more money. With the exception of ores, exports did well, coffee and cotton above all. Also, by 1955, a lid had been placed on inflation, most likely because of an increase in industrial productivity. For the first time, urban Mexicans had a plentiful supply of goods. But that turnabout rested on pump priming, which meant a continued reliance on foreign bankers. Despite that, 1955 was a banner year, mainly thanks to rising exports, a development encouraged by the devaluation of the peso in 1954.

"God's plenty" lasted only briefly. By 1958, exports of coffee, cattle, lead, and petroleum had started to decline. Economic troubles had surfaced across the border; Americans were not buying. No less ominous, the cost of imports had exceeded the value of exports, because industrialization required costly machinery, equipment, tools, and technology. To complicate the picture, more and more speculative capital had entered Mexico, attracted by the promise of easy profits and ready to flee at a moment's notice. The flight of capital became, if not a daily occurrence, a constant menace. In 1958, when the GNP tottered, droves of foreign speculators fled the country, taking their money with them and worsening the financial picture.

For the first time, Mexican economists began to wonder if reliance on exports could get the job done. With another worldwide recession under way, Mexico, in order to export, had to keep prices down; but at that juncture the benefits of the 1954 peso devaluation had evaporated and prices gone up again. At the same time, the devaluation of 1954, as well as the rise in prices, which reduced the buying power of workers, had once more planted the seeds of unrest in their ranks. Not unreasonably, their unions began to ask for wage adjustments. National policy had brought this on itself; since little was done to stimulate the production of food crops, their price had moved upward. Because of the wish to bring money into Mexico, efforts had gone into cash crops for export; commercial agriculture, carried on by the big farmers, had received the lion's share of benefits, at the expense of rancheros and others who harvested much of the food Mexicans ate. For a while, few in official circles worried, since, as the population multiplied, big farmers, the "new hacendados," had huge pools of cheap labor, which made it easier for them to sell their harvests on foreign markets. But, starting in 1956, exports of agricultural products entered a long period of decline.

As farm exports took a nosedive, jobs vanished and wages dropped in the countryside, further deflating the puny buying power of rural Mexicans, hampering the development of a dynamic internal market, which the relaxation of controls over the wages of industrial workers failed to offset. Mexican-owned industries of consumer goods suffered the most. The rate of growth of manufacturing, though remaining at acceptable levels, dropped below that of the forties. Imports of corn and wheat multiplied rapidly after 1957, placing another burden on the national exchequer. As this occurred, more campesinos abandoned the countryside for the cities, further depleting the harvests of corn and beans, just as the rush to build capital-intensive industries inflated the jobless rolls.

Economic planning, likewise, was too often done from one day to the next. Government had intervened in the economy to shore it up, maintain industrialization on track, and preserve political stability. Long-range requirements, the need to upgrade the life of campesinos, a must if domestic markets were to expand, or to control both native and foreign capitalists for the sake of the national priorities, were ignored. The process of industrialization lacked blueprints, developing haphazardly, without reference to the social needs of a majority of the population. Foreign borrowing had been employed to avoid fiscal reform. No one, furthermore, saw to it that the *paraestatales* operated efficiently. The success of pump priming, too, invariably coincided with cycles of prosperity in the United States. What had saved the day was an accident—specifically, the wars of the United States, the last one in Vietnam a tonic for the Mexican economy from 1965 to 1972.

IV

The results of this era of "stabilized development," as the miracle was defined, were markedly uneven. On the positive side, economic growth was sustained, and prices, though exorbitant at times, were more or less stable during the 1960s, and, after the devaluation of 1954, so was the value of the peso. With subsidized equipment, technology, and cheap raw materials, Mexican industry continued to prosper. Even a semblance of long-range planning made its bow; more attention was lavished on the *paraestatales,* primarily in steel and petrochemicals. When the foreign conglomerate which produced electricity for the nation started to lose money and offered to sell, Mexico "nationalized" it, paying a seller's price.

Private entrepreneurs, regardless of nationality, reaped big rewards. So lucrative was the sale of consumer articles that Mexicans had no incentive to invest in the manufacture of capital goods. Workers and the poor, on the other hand, fared badly; by the end of the 1960s, the inequality in the distribution of income and wealth was alarming, ranking among the worst in Latin America. For the pacification of the urban restless, social services, lagging since 1940, were given some additional money, which was spent on urban schools, health care, and social security, a system which dated from 1943.

Mexicans, in retrospect, had forged an industrial plant integrated into the capitalist economies by offering guarantees to foreign investors. Whatever else it might be, it was dependent on the United States. Scores of industries were offshoots of transnational parents established in Mexico to circumvent trade restrictions. Industrialization, ironically, had reinforced Mexico's legendary dependency on its northern neighbor. By welcoming American capital, too, policy planners had aggravated the disequilibrium in the domestic structure.

Reliance on imported technology, a characteristic of the era after 1960, had tied more Mexican industry to the developed capitalist economies and, simultaneously, magnified the national financial burden. Technology, to underline, cost money. Yet the degree of technology and not market demand determined rates of profit; the better the technology, the more competitive the industry and the bigger the profits. Labor costs played a marginal role. Likewise, ties to American industry had nullified attempts to integrate the domestic economy.

Mexican industrialization, nevertheless, had taken off by 1970. Economic and political stability was a fact of life. In the eyes of foreign observers, as well as in those of native sympathizers, a "miracle" had occurred, which they attributed mistakenly to Mexico's political institutions. These offspring of the Revolution, they claimed, "harmonized" the interests of diverse sectors in society. In reality, the "miracle," a version of the old "trickle-down" theory, had come at the expense of social justice. It had taken place despite unplanned economic growth, often shoddy goods, and high prices. Official rhetoric notwithstanding, foreigners, mainly Americans, had controlled this drama. Closing their eyes to legislation restricting foreign investment to 49 percent of the capital, Mexicans had allowed transnational corporations to establish wholly owned subsidiaries. Much of Mexican industry, perhaps its most impressive sector, was not Mexican.

Nevertheless, "modernization," the offspring of industrialization had, theoretically, altered the character of Mexico. Infant mortality was reduced, life spans were extended, and, consequently, a population explosion was engendered. With a population of under twenty million in 1940, Mexico had only five million more inhabitants than in 1910, when the curtain dropped on the drama of the Porfiriato. By 1970, with the population multiplying rapidly, Mexico had nearly seventy million people, over half of them living in cities and towns. Urban growth, a child of the forties, had mushroomed after 1950; by then, half of the migrants from the countryside, victims of rural neglect, were heading for the Republic's metropolis.

More significant, perhaps 20 percent of the Republic's inhabitants were middle class. Mexico had one of the biggest middle classes in Latin America. Like the industrial edifice, it was no stranger to American ways, preferring clothes, automobiles, and electrical gadgets of American manufacture. The Colonia Pitic, on the edge of Hermosillo, and the Colonia del Valle, in Monterrey, the "Pittsburgh of Mexico," testified that American-style homes had captured the hearts of the affluent. More and more of them traveled to the United States to admire its efficiency, cleanliness, and wealth, rarely wondering why Mexico should be so poor. To its Mexican critics, the middle class, by and large, had succumbed to *malinchismo,* the colonial mentality so harshly condemned by Samuel Ramos in *Perfil del hombre y de la cultura en México.*

V

With a conservative *burguesía* in the saddle, relations with Washington improved. The more Mexicans discarded Cardenista formulas, the closer the ties. World War II, moreover, had driven the United States, which coveted raw materials for its fighting men and a Western Hemisphere safe from Axis sabotage, to come to terms with Mexico. Oil ranked at the top of the differences. To start the ball rolling, Mexico told Washington that it stood ready to negotiate. As a result, talks began almost immediately, leading to the appointment of a joint committee to "fix the value of the expropriated property" and suggest "terms of payment." Its report of 1941 put a value of $24 million on the oil property and added $5 million for interest. The oil barons, who wanted millions more, rejected it. At this juncture, Washington, with a war on two fronts, broke ranks with the oil companies and accepted the verdict of the joint committee. Left to fight their own battles, the oil magnates decided to negotiate, accepting a settlement of $30 million.

Mexico City and Washington, on top of that, labored to settle the debt issue. Since 1930, the Mexicans had defaulted on their payments to American bankers; now both parties desired to end this dispute. In 1942, Mexico agreed to pay nearly $50 million, approximately 10 percent of the original debt; four years later, it started to pay another $50 million to retire the debt from the nationalization of the railroads. By 1946, Mexico had wiped clean the slate of its reputation for malingering on its debt obligations, and, henceforth, its international credit rating improved dramatically.

During World War II, Mexicans had trekked north to work on the farms, on the railroads, and in the industries of the United States. The military draft in the United States had depleted its work force, and so Mexicans were imported to take up the slack. This was the bracero program, signed by Mexico City and Washington in 1942 and, despite modifications, not ended until 1964. By its terms, the United States Department of Agriculture recruited Mexicans to work for private employers and agreed to shield them from discriminatory practices, help them during times of unemployment, and pay their transportation. Over 300,000 braceros, usually for paltry wages, labored north of the border during World War II. The money they sent home nourished the national economy.

For all that, not everything smelled of roses. After the defeat of the Axis powers, few American businessmen had applauded Mexico's drive to industrialize, labeling the goal "artificial" and "utopian" and at odds with the "international division of labor" dictated by the "law of comparative advantage." Mexico would be wiser to produce raw materials to exchange for American manufactured goods. Not until Mexico unlocked its gates to American investors did this attitude wane.

This was also the era of the cold war, when Washington demanded complete obedience to its drive against the Soviet Union and anything hinting of communism, socialism, or radical change. The Truman Doctrine, of 1947, the trumpet call of the cold warriors, had immediate repercussions in Mexico. At the behest of Washington, and obeying their own inclinations, the lords of Mexican politics and business repudiated, to cite one of their proclamations, "communism and all other forms of totalitarianism." All it took to rid oneself of a rival in public office was to "accuse him of being Communist," wrote Angeles Mastretta in *Arráncame la vida,* a best-selling novel about the Mexico of that day. After all, "we didn't fight a Revolution," she had one of her characters say, "just so that the Russians could take it away." Amid that climate of official opinion, the witch-hunt thrived. In 1954, for example, a distinguished intellectual was fired from his job as head of the Instituto Nacional de Bellas Artes for allowing the audience to sing the Internationale at the wake of Frida Kahlo in the Palace of Fine Arts.

No matter; Mexico and the United States, by mutual consent, were drawing closer together. For Mexicans, it was a "kind of geographic fatalism": with the United States, the richest and mightiest nation in the world, on the opposite side of a border two thousand miles long, it was unrealistic for Mexicans to think they could escape its embrace. That view of destiny was not entirely defeatist; Mexicans of this school were not just "building castles in the air." On the contrary, they believed that Mexico could profit from its proximity, winning, in the process, preferential treatment for its exports, a haven for its unemployed, and capital for its development.

That view embodied a skewed sense of psychological dependency. Without Washington's embrace, its advocates declared, progress was impossible. The courtship of American politicos, diplomats, and businessmen, therefore, became the rule of the game. During World War II, for instance, Ezequiel Padilla, the foreign secretary and a man of presidential ambitions, worked incessantly to build close ties with Washington, so much so that Mexicans came to see him as its lackey. For his part, Miguel Alemán, Padilla's rival, made known his presidential ambitions to the American embassy in Mexico City, trying to woo its approval. After taking office, he assured the embassy that Communists would not serve in his government, nor would allies of Vicente Lombaro Toledano, the labor leader out of favor in Washington. Mexico would turn for advice and consent to businessmen and bankers north of the border. Given this political climate, there was no place for the anti-imperialist thinking of yesteryear which, dating from the Texas imbroglio of 1836, cautioned Mexicans to keep Americans at arm's length.

Even so, nationalist rhetoric, an intergral part of politics, endured, the more so when the Mexican establishment clamped down on reform. An "independent foreign policy," by which Mexico departed from Washington's embrace, would document that "revolutionary" Mexico was alive and well, refuting, its architects were wont to say, the widely held view of a conservative tilt to politics. Mexicans could rest assured that their country remained faithful to the ideals of the "revolutionary" fathers. One of them, of course, was the Estrada Doctrine of 1929, which raised aloft the ideal of national self-determination and rejected the right of intervention by outside powers in the internal affairs of sovereign nations. That, plainly, meant the United States, the only country ready and able to intervene in Mexico and sister Latin American republics.

Rhetoric and reality were horses of a different color. In time, the wide gap between them became readily apparent, as the tragedy of Guatemala in 1954 made clear. When nationalists in that country launched a mild program of agrarian reform, at the expense of the United Fruit Company, an American corporation, Washington labeled them Communists and, at the Inter-American conference at Caracas, called for their condemnation. Along with Argentina, Mexico balked but said nary a word when Washington overthrew the reformers. Again in 1961, Mexico remained silent when Washington, at the Bay of Pigs, attempted to oust Fidel Castro's regime in Cuba.

Mexican diplomatic slogans, not illogically, failed to alarm American investors. Quite the opposite: after 1950, dollars entered Mexico in larger and larger amounts, and an increase in the Mexican tariff, ostensibly designed to protect national industry, led to an influx of transnational corporations, which, by building branches in Mexico, circumvented it. Mexico had transformed itself into a citadel for foreign capitalists, the best in Latin America. So profitable was it that many Americans recovered their initial investment in one or two years and earned money besides. Sears, Roebuck, one of those ventures, established its initial store in 1947 and in ten years had seventeen branches, nine of them inaugurated in 1955 alone. With their credit cards, a novel phenomenon in Mexico, the Sears stores introduced middle-class customers to a veritable marketing metamorphosis; for the first time, they could buy to their heart's content, like their neighbors across the border going into debt buying stoves, refrigerators, washers, and clothes.

Whatever their benefits, the transnationals undercut their Mexican competitors. With improved technology and far-flung marketing networks, they set the pace, controlling the character of industrialization and creating a new laboring segment, better off usually than workers in native industries. CONCANACO and CONCAMIN, organizations with strong ties to foreign capital, cheered, but CONACINTRA, Mexican industrialists in competition with outsiders, had doubts. And well they might. By 1960, nearly 55 percent of the foreign investment had gone into manufacturing and had begun to dominate the consumer-goods industry, the most profitable. Ford, General Motors, Chrysler, Kellogg, Campbell Soup, H. J. Heinz, Proctor & Gamble, Colgate-Palmolive, Bristol-Meyer, and similar giants controlled the market for autos, rubber tires, electrical appliances, chemicals, pharmaceuticals, and packaged foods. The American Chamber of Commerce in Mexico was the biggest of its kind in the world, a spokesman for transnationals and smaller fry. By 1970, Americans had invested $2.8 billion in Mexico. European and Japanese rivals did not start to challenge their supremacy until the 1960s. The value of foreign capital invested in manufacturing, regardless of its nationality, climbed from $147 million in 1950 to more than $2 billion by 1970. With profits high, remittances on investments reached $2.99 billion during the 1960s, leaving Mexico with a net loss of $931 million. Of the profits taken out, $838 million went to Americans.

VI

Early in 1946, the politicos discarded the PRM, substituting for it the Partido Revolucionario Institucional (PRI). The PRI mirrored the ascendancy of politicos sympathetic to the magnates of industry and big agriculture, the architects of the economic transformation shaping up. From the start, conservatives chartered its course. Paying lip service to the Revolution, the PRI eulogized economic growth and gave token homage to agrarian reform. While still a "corporate" body, it no longer sheltered the military and, far more important, included the Confederación Nacional de Organizaciones Populares (CNOP), the old popular sector, reorganized in 1943 to blunt the power of labor and campesinos. Increasingly, both the CTM and the CNC took a backseat to the CNOP within the PRI.

Nothing, however, was done to tamper with the political pyramid. The heads of the CTM, the pragmatic Fidel Velázquez by 1946, and of the CNC, both Samsons shorn of their locks, marched in cadence with the lords of politics, industry, and agriculture. For all intents and purposes, they did the bidding of the PRI bosses. The democratic slogans of the PRI were of dubious validity, given its highly centralized structure and, ominously, greater role in its affairs for the Secretaría de Gobernación. The PRI, in actuality, was fast becoming the voice of the *burguesía,* the political organ by which the president, the national guru, transmitted its wishes to the people and, simultaneously, manipulated them.

In ascendancy was the CNOP, the voice, it was claimed, of the budding middle class; mostly urban, it included merchants, artisans, professionals, intellectuals, bureaucrats, women's groups, university students, and small private farmers. Its political clout matured "rapidly, controlling eventually a larger bloc of deputies to Congress than either the CTM or the CNC. Soon it had a loud voice in the PRI. The CNOP enjoyed a remarkable measure of autonomy under the PRI, its membership, literate and affluent, electing its spokesmen. PRI politicos had to court them. Well-informed and ably guided, the CNOP enjoyed the lion's share of the spoils, including jobs in the PRI and Congress and, in so doing, a pipeline to the presidents, whose decisions it influenced.

All of this marched in step with the growth of the private sector. Merely the tail in the days of the Cardenistas, it now began to wag the dog, manipulating the PRI, largely because it accounted for 90 percent of the Republic's GNP. CONCANACO (chambers of commerce), CONCAMIN (chambers of industry), and CONACINTRA helped mold legislation, even modifying presidential decisions. Their members owned the Republic's newspapers, nearly all of its journals, the radio networks, and the television channels. The *burguesía,* linked invariably to American capital and markets, had come to have the most influence in government.

The "revolutionary family," the inner circle, had experienced a transformation. The *burguesía,* the "reactionaries" against whom the rebels of 1910 fought, had crashed the gates of the official family, where it joined hands with the governors of the richest states, the mayor of Mexico City, the chiefs of the army, the directors of the Banco de México, the principal cabinet ministers, and, to quote cynics, the ambassador from the United States to run Mexico. Every six years, they also selected its president.

Over this apparatus presided the president, according to political folklore virtually sovereign. This interpretation, in the light of the foregoing, strains one's credulity. How can a president elected for six years dictate when the powerful and wealthy have the upper hand? The answer is that he cannot. With the exception of Manuel Avila Camacho, more than likely picked by Cárdenas, presidential candidates rose from the ranks of the PRI. Until 1970, they were politicos who had filled a variety of jobs, from deputies and senators to governors and cabinet officers. Above everything else, they had accepted the rules of the game. Unorthodox players dropped by the roadside. The politicos who became presidents were trained to keep the ship of state on course. A president "picked" his successor, but only after consulting with the "official family."

Once in office, the president undoubtedly wielded impressive authority. His powers, nonetheless, were political mainly; he could remove governors, discipline labor bosses, appoint the "spokesmen" for campesinos, and, always, appear to speak for the nation. All of this, nonetheless, within reason, so as not to endanger the status quo. Presidents had to live with their underlings, even governors elevated to office by rivals. In the universe of economics and high finance, the president's power was limited; he could prod the moguls of industry and big agriculture but had to consult his "official family" first. If the winds blew cold, he dropped the subject. Loyal politicos had not been promoted to the presidential office to become mavericks, advocating, for instance, taxes on the rich.

To hide reality from public scrutiny, rule by the wealthy and powerful required that presidents appear omnipotent and, at the same time, govern for everyone. Never identified with any one sector and, according to political legend, above class interests, the president, who swore allegiance to the "Revolution," had the welfare of all Mexicans in mind. Similarly, it was necessary that he be seen as formulating policy so that if it were to prove unpopular he would be blamed, and not the affluent who, more and more, managed Mexico.

When labor was disciplined or campesinos were punished, he was responsible, not the economic structure, which weathered every presidential term. Every six years, with the advent of a new president, there was hope for change. Never mind that presidents were the offspring of the same ideological family, reared to respect vested interests. Basic policies never changed. There were fresh faces in office but all of like opinion. The sin of the old Porfiristas was not that they had stayed in office too long but that their *carro completo* had shut the door to outsiders. More sophisticated, the PRI let more people in, but on the condition that they not tinker with the national formula.

Urban women were especially welcome. Acceptance, just the same, came slowly. In 1947, Congress, an integral cog of the PRI machine, granted women the right to vote and hold public office in the municipalities. Then, seeking to further consolidate the political system, the PRI started to recruit women into its ranks, claiming 1.2 million of them by the early fifties. In 1953, women got the right to vote in national elections.

Opening the gates to women signaled no rush toward democracy. Quite the opposite: the evidence shows that the political system became less flexible, more tightly in the hands of PRI bosses. As earlier, municipal officials, the most loyal of the Priístas, managed voting booths, named election judges, and printed the voting lists. Having done this, they controlled the vote. The PRI oligarchy, in the meantime, chose the candidates. In Congress, deputies and senators voted the government line, taking orders from their leaders and seldom voicing personal opinions. The Senate was practically useless, lacking political influence. To speak ill of one's party or of one's political companions meant the end of a political career. Priístas, said the wags, "spoke no evil, saw none, and heard none" of fellow Priístas. Being *servil*—toadying, that is—had a fieldday. Martín Luis Guzmán, an aging senator in 1969, said the Republic owed to President Gustavo Díaz Ordaz its "liberty, tranquillity, peace, order, and progress." So well oiled was the political machinery of the PRI that it faced only token opposition. Many Mexicans, having lost faith in the system, had simply stopped voting.

That proved embarrassing. Having crushed the opposition, the power brokers had to create one, or else be accused of dictatorial behavior. Authoritarianism, the legacy of the PRI, ironically, demanded the appearance of democracy. Above all, the give and take of a "democratic" Congress, what PRI rhetoric talked about, required discordant voices. To deal with the embarrassment of an all-PRI Chamber of Deputies, the Priístas in 1963, introduced elections based on proportional representation. A political party winning 2.5 percent of the vote recieved one deputy for 0.5 percent of its vote, up to a maximum of twenty seats. The reform, hailed as unlocking the doors to democracy, conferred benefits on the Partido de Acción Nacional (PAN), the Partido Popular Socialista, friendly to the PRI, and the Partido Auténtico de la Revolución Mexicana, conservative old-timers who but for the reform would have vanished from the political stage. Nothing changed; the overwhelming majority of the PRI carried every vote in Congress.

Of the three ostensible opposition parties, only the PAN enjoyed a measure of legitimacy. Dating from 1939, it had initially spoken for enemies of the Cardenistas. Conservative and pro-Catholic, its leadership proclaimed the virtues of private property and individual rights. The Priístas, ideologues of similar stripe, later co-opted key Panistas, giving bankers, industrialists, and big farmers, who held the PAN together, a role in government. Given this, the well-off and powerful joined the PRI, leaving the PAN to grow slowly. Not until 1952 did it nominate a candidate for the presidency. The reforms of 1963 resurrected the PAN, and gave the PRI the opportunity to pose as the "revolutionary" ally of campesinos and workers against the "reactionary" PAN. A whipping boy for the PRI, the PAN garnered the protest votes, especially those of the middle class.

Reformers only once challenged the reign of the PRI. During the elections of 1952, Miguel Henríquez Guzmán, a wealthy general and friend of Cárdenas, made a run for the presidency, winning campesino and labor support. His platform, mainly that of the Cardenistas, lamented rural neglect, promised labor reform, castigated malfeasance in public office, and urged a return to the ideals of the Revolution. Cárdenas, however, stayed out of the fray. Henríquez Guzmán never had a chance against the monopoly of the PRI.

With business and industry in the saddle, the presidents of Mexico were neither radicals nor reformers. They were conservatives, believers in the capitalist ethic. Only one, Manuel Avila Camacho, had ties with the Revolution. A polo-playing general, Avila Camacho had seen almost no combat but spent his time as a staff officer, rising through the ranks as a plodding subordinate. His father was a landowner, "not very rich, not very poor," a political bigwig in Puebla, and a spokesman for its Catholic *burguesía.* Not very bright, Avila Camacho was a bureaucrat's bureaucrat, who entrusted policy-making to his cabinet, where his brother, Maximino, once a salesman for Singer sewing machines but now the cacique of Puebla and a millionaire, reigned supreme. Upon taking office, Avila Camacho confessed he believed in God, thus leaving the way clear for the revival of church schools. He was buried in consecrated ground.

Miguel Alemán, the next in line, was the harbinger of the industrial age. Smooth, alert, and a party fixer, he had been governor of Veracruz and head of the Secretaría de Gobernación under Avila Camacho. Once a disciple of the Cardenistas, he proclaimed that "what was good for business was good for Mexico." The first truly civilian president, he was a lawyer by profession. By 1952, he was also a multimillionaire, the owner of much real estate and an intimate of the international jet set. During his sojourn, public and private corruption had sundry opportunities; cabinet officers, in cahoots with businessmen, made millions. While speaking reverently of the "Revolution," Alemán purged public office of reformers, radicals, and Communists. Nor did he have time for campesinos. To govern, he relied on technocrats, bureaucrats with a university degree, primarily in economics. So popular was Alemán with politicos and the rich that he dreamed of reelection. Others, either more prudent or equally ambitious, thought poorly of the idea. So Alemán retired from political office, enjoying, nonetheless, enourmous political influence until his death.

Aldofo Ruiz Cortines, who followed Alemán into the National Palace, also hailed from Veracruz. Chief of Gobernación and a former governor of Veracruz, he was old for a Mexican president. Modest and austere in habits and behavior, he was a pencil pusher rather than a glamorous personality; his pastime was playing dominoes. Honest and conservative, he kept his hands out of the public till, dying without having accumulated a fortune. For his rectitude, as well as for his politics, he earned the plaudits of stand-pat intellectuals, among them Samuel Ramos and the novelist Agustín Yáñez.

A native of Mexico State, Adolfo López Mateos, next to occupy the National Palace, had served as a senator and then as minister of labor under Ruiz Cortines. Known for his tough stance on labor matters, he counted among his backers Emilio Azcárraga and Manuel Espinosa Yglesias, wealthy and powerful business tycoons. He did not disappoint them, gaining notoriety for his law of *disolución social,* by which he jailed labor leaders and the painter David Siqueiros. Petty and mediocre, he toured the world, as he asid, looking for markets for Mexican exports. The victim of severe migraine headaches, he left the management of government to his subordinates during the last two years in office.

Gustavo Díaz Ordaz, the last of these politicos, almost brought down the house upon himself and his sponsors. The occasion was the student protest of 1968. To quell it, Díaz Ordaz, with the consent of his cabinet, dispatched police and soldiers to kill students. The massacre of the night of October 2, 1968, which occurred in the Plaza de Tlatelolco in Mexico City, closed the curtain on the drama of the "miracle," laying bare its ugly side. A keen scholar of Mexican politics, Díaz Ordaz was a native of Puebla, a disciple of Maximino Avila Camacho. Like other successful Priístas, he had risen through the ranks, from a deputy to Congress to *secretario de gobernación* under López Mateos. Taciturn and a puritan by habits, he neither drank nor smoked, watched carefully what he ate but, for all that, was a bundle of nerves. Of brownish, yellowish skin, he was, as he admitted, not a handsome man. A fan of boxing matches, soccer, and baseball, he played golf and swam and wore monographed silk shirts imported from London. Tough and outspoken, he never hesitated to employ profanity. *Chingar* and *chingada,* expletives made famous by the pelado, were two of his favorites. A firm believer in private enterprise, which he saw as the key to Mexico's salvation, he was the most anti-Communist of the Mexican presidents since the days of Abelardo Rodríguez. Yet he had no love for the United States, once remarking that "every Mexican worth his salt dreamed of gaining revenge for the wrongs done to Mexico."

Student protests antedated Díaz Ordaz. As early as 1934, the governor of Jalisco had employed soldiers to squelch a strike of students at the University of Guadalajara, and his colleague in the state house of Durango relied on soldiers to douse the ire of students at the normal school. During the days of the Alemanistas, student disruptions had ousted a governor of Michoacán who dared raise university fees. Alemán himself had known the ire of students when, on more than one occasion, they toppled a statue of him on the campus of the National University. In 1958, students had taken to the streets of Mexico City to protest an increase in bus fares, and soldiers had occupied the campus of the National Polytechnic Institute.

Middle-class students instigated the troubles of 1968. At the National University, one site of the uproar, less than 3 percent of its students were of campesino origins and no more than 15 percent from workers' families. Before ending, the protest of 1968 had involved students from the National University, the Polytechnic Institute, the Agricultural College of Chapingo, normal schools, the *preparatorias,* and secondary schools, as well as professors, intellectuals, and parents. On one march in late August, 500,000 students and sympathizers gathered in the Zócalo in Mexico City.

The student conflagration which, as Elena Poniatowska wrote in *La noche de Tlatelolco,* shook the fabric of Priísta society, had multiple causes. They included student resentment of official hypocrisy and of corruption and cooptation, a tool employed by Priístas to keep people in line. The economy, while healthy on the surface, had stopped opening doors to university graduates. Few jobs beckoned in the fields for which students had trained. Young economists, for instance, could be found in low-paying bureaucratic jobs.

The demands of the students were hardly radical. What they wanted was the release of political prisoners, students and railroad leaders to name two; the repeal of the law of *disolución social;* an end to the *granaderos* (riot police); the departure of the police from school and university campuses; and compensation for harm done by government thugs to students and their families. The students were asking Díaz Ordaz and his cronies to abide by constitutional guarantees. Their demands, just the same, called attention to skewed national priorities, pervasive poverty, the gap between rich and poor, and the myth of the "miracle." By publicly giving vent to their discontent, they had ridiculed the rhetoric of the "institutionalized" Revolution. "We want a revolution, not Olympic Games," they shouted.

That, precisely, was the problem. Earlier, Díaz Ordaz and his business friends had pledged to sponsor the Olympic Games in Mexico City, the site of the uproar. Student protests endangered not merely the peace of the PRI but the prestige of its leaders. Repression was swift and harsh. Countless students died, according to one estimate as many as five hundred of them. Some fifteen hundred were locked up in jails, beaten, and tortured by the police. Notwithstanding that, Priístas, among them Fidel Velázquez, applauded, while television and newspaper luminaries called Díaz Ordaz a "patriot"; the students, they claimed, had brought it upon themselves.

22

THE STEPCHILDREN

I

What was sauce for the goose was not sauce for the gander. Unlike industry and big agriculture, which reaped a bountiful reward, the miracle yielded puny, if any, benefits for the lower class. Claims notwithstanding, for the millions of Mexicans at the bottom of society, the stepchildren of the miracle, the recipe was a hoax. Even industrial labor, the least exploited, savored only the leftovers. After Mexico's entrance into the war in 1942, government, taking advantage of the "emergency," compelled workers to agree to a "solidarity pact"—an act of patriotism, it was dubbed. The labor federations promised not to strike during the emergency and to accept arbitration in their disputes with employers. When workers overlooked the pledge given by their leaders, government, siding with management, handled their strikes harshly. By this pact, labor, as was mentioned earlier, was asked to shoulder the cost of industrialization. Policy, however, did not just rely on the stick; there was also a carrot. Along with a curb on labor's demands, workers were offered a social security system. In return for forsaking the "class struggle," they would have health care, an idea, incidentally, dating from the days of the Cardenistas.

Wartime policies, if not the "solidarity pact," survived the coming of peace, but there was a new leadership for labor. Fidel Velázquez, a bedfellow of the Alemanistas, pliant and anti-Communist, ousted Vicente Lombardo Toledano, the feisty chieftain, as head of the CTM. Ambitious and practical, he went along with the gospel of trickle-down economic growth. What was left of the CROM and the CGT fell into line. The triumph of Velázquez transformed the CTM, bestowing a more powerful voice on the big urban industrial unions, most of them in Mexico City, at the expense of smaller provincial ones.

Just the same, Velázquez, a cagey veteran of labor's battles since his days as a dairy worker in the 1920s, had not climbed aboard the bandwagon merely at the whim of the politicos. True, he had wooed them. But he was in good standing with the labor bureaucracy; his tough pragmatism had won him its support. To ignore him, the politicos believed, might well disrupt the labor unity they so ardently desired. Of similar importance, Velázquez, a leader who did not relish rocking the boat, had the support of labor organizations in the United States, specifically the American Federation of Labor; he represented the kind of anti-Communist boss its chieftains admired. His good standing with them helped endear him to Mexican industrialists. However, Velázquez could, from time to time, be counted on by labor's rank and file to deliver benefits. He knew how to wangle concessions from government and business.

Mexico's oracles, believers in the wonders of private enterprise, had their eyes set on economic growth. Government in league with capitalists would bring it about. That depended on high profits for investors, which meant wages must be kept low, lest margins of profits decline. So the right to strike, in a mood reminiscent of the war era, tumbled into disrepute, while officials of the Labor Department meddled in the affairs of unions, splitting workers into warring factions and relying on venal bosses to control them. In 1953, to illustrate, only sixteen strikes were allowed to take place; by 1960, only one-third of the industrial workers were unionized. Company unions, particularly in such cities as Monterrey, flourished.

Dissident labor, nonetheless, did not surrender without a struggle. In 1948, the miners and petroleum and railroad workers, representing 185,000 men and women, had defied the government, while workers in the cotton belt of the Laguna had severed their ties to the CTM, vowing to fight for the independence of labor. The spark that lit the fuse of this unrest was the peso devaluation of 1948, which set off a wave of inflation that undercut wages. Officials in Mexico City emplyed troops to crush the strikes. When they imposed Jesús Díaz de León, known as El Charro, on the petroleum workers, his nickname became synonymous with kept labor bosses. Before long, *charros* ran the unions; only the electrical workers held out.

The labor truce failed to endure. The peso devaluation of 1954 upset the applecart. Rises in the price of food, clothing, and rent brought vociferous demands for wage hikes, and with ample cause. By 1954, real wages lagged behind those of 1936. Since the government desired peace, it had to allow the big unions a pay increase of 10 percent, a concession to labor but not enough to match the cost of living. Industrial labor, nonetheless, had made clear to government that it would no longer alone bear the cost of industrialization.

Once more, to the dismay of its architects, peace proved brittle, mainly because of economic doldrums north of the border. To complicate the picture, Mexican authorities, at that juncture in 1959, were negotiating an agreement with the Treasury Department of the United States and the Export-Import

Bank. Mexico would have access to $621 million; but, in return, Washington insisted on measures to curb the inflationary winds, while in Mexico, Antonio Ortiz Mena, secretary of finance, was blaming them on the wage adjustments recently granted. At the same time, railroad and petroleum workers, as well as teachers and telephone operators, had taken it upon themselves to "democratize" their unions, which meant replacing the *charros* with leaders of their own choosing. The stage was set for a confrontation.

The challenge to the *charros* dated from 1956, when primary school teachers in Mexico City, Section 9 of the Sindicato Nacional de Trabajadores de la Educación (SNTE), had rebelled against their *charros,* labeling them "saints abroad and devils at home." Under the leadership of Othón Salazar, a young teacher, they had organized themselves into the Movimiento Revolucionario del Magisterio (MRM), a widely popular union. When police fell upon their protest march in Mexico City in 1958, they shut down its primary schools. While the *charros* of the SNTE, the official teachers' union, vilified the strikers, officials, faced with mounting public sympathy for the poorly paid teachers and an upcoming presidential election, decided to grant a salary boost but, ominously, withheld recognition of Salazar and his MRM. The election over, the new regime immediately jailed Salazar and, ultimately, destroyed the MRM.

The teachers were not the only mavericks. In January 1959, a strike of operators threatened to close down the telephones of the Republic. The operators wanted more money, the right to pick their own leaders, and the rehiring of sixteen of their spokesmen recently fired. It took the government, which immediately branded the strike illegal, just four hours to send scabs and police to put it down. Like Salazar, its leaders were locked up behind bars.

The biggest of the labor disputes was yet to occur. The railroad strike of February 1959 nearly tore asunder the political framework of the Republic. The grievances of the railroad men had prior roots, dating from at least ten years before, when authorities in Mexico City imposed a *charro* on them and jailed Valentín Campa, their spokesman. By 1954, the devaluation of the peso and the decline of real wages had, once more, stirred trouble on the railroads and, again, led to jail sentences for labor spokesmen, on the charge of fomenting *disolución social,* endangering political stability. This time, repression failed to quiet the discontent; government squelched the strikes of 1955 but ignored their underlying cause: poor wages as well as a decline in the quality of medical care, retirement benefits, and housing. The *charros* had shut their ears to the pleas for help. In 1957, government officials, confronted by rising unrest, conceded a pay raise and improved benefits, but not enough to satisfy the railroad workers, especially because *charros* managed their unions.

In 1958, therefore, the workers, on their own, chose Demetrio Vallejo, a veteran of the railroad wars, to voice their demands for higher wages, more benefits, and an end to the *charros.* That summer, Vallejo, with almost every one of the sixty thousand railroad workers behind him, led a series of national work stoppages, the last of ten hours, all tellingly effective. Confronted by transportation bottlenecks and complaints by shippers, government granted one more pay increase, but smaller than what the workers had asked for. That merely whetted the appetite of Vallejo and the workers for more. Now they demanded that their *charro* boss be removed, calling him a *lambiscón,* a toady of politicos. Aware that he had outlived his usefulness, officials in Mexico City replaced him with another *charro,* brushing aside Vallejo's legitimate claims to the job. In a display of support, the workers stopped the trains from running, and the government, to pacify angry shippers, sent soldiers to take over the railroads, threatening to put the strikers in jail if they did not return to work. To its chagrin, the strike continued, forcing the government to call for new union elections. This was no time to haggle; teachers in Mexico City were up in arms, and this was an election year. The results, therefore, favored Vallejo overwhelmingly: 59,759 to 9.

Backed by his *comité ejecutivo,* Vallejo started to clean out the *charros.* As he did this, the press, always at the government's beck and call, labeled Vallejo a Communist, especially after he brought back Valentín Campa, the defeated spokesman of 1948. The success of the railroad workers, to exacerbate affairs, spurred other workers to defy employers and politicos; faced with a challenge to its authority, the regime chose to confront Vallejo and the railroad men.

Confident of their strength, the railroad unions, meanwhile, had voted to ask for a wage hike, telling government that it could find the money for it in higher shipping fees. Unwilling to antagonize foreign investors, the mine operators particularly, the government rejected the demand and set out to undermine Vallejo with the help of Fidel Velázquez, boss of the CTM. When a strike erupted in February 1959, government officials, half an hour after it had started, declared it "illegal." Playing for time, they granted a wage increase but, weeks later, when they felt more sure of themselves, fired thirteen thousand railroad workers, gave their jobs to scabs, and jailed Vallejo and his *comité ejecutivo,* both accused of the crime of *disolución social.*

The government's triumph accomplished by a reliance on army and police, left the unemployed and their families to fend for themselves. New *charros* replaced Vallejo and his men. With labor disciplined, "stabilized development," the gist of the "miracle," was now firmly under way. From then on, only a strike by physicians in Mexico City in 1964 disrupted the peace. For all intents and purposes, the independent labor movement was dead, replaced, in 1966, by the Congreso del Trabajo, a government-sponsored labor umbrella. Coincidentally, the military budget began to climb, from 112 million pesos in 1961 to nearly 164 million by 1967.

II

Policy for agriculture, too, made an about-face. Everything must be done to increase the harvests of crops for export, proclaimed current slogans. Inherent in them was a disbelief in the adequacy of the ejido as a tool of production, as well as a blind faith in the private farm. Even news of high yields from some ejidos failed to shake that disbelief. Before long, the ejido was relegated to the sidelines, replaced by the private farm, large or small.

That shift went hand in glove with the dual goals of rapid economic growth and full steam ahead with industrialization, which called for an agricultural system capable of providing cheap raw materials for industry as well as revenue for government through cash crops for export. Only the private sector, it was alleged, could do this. There was nothing unique about this policy: its roots went back to José María Luis Mora and his Liberals of the nineteenth century, a gospel embraced by Porfiristas and the Sonorenses. With that decision, the agricultural credit went increasingly to private farmers, and little found its way into the hands of *ejidatarios,* a turnabout that almost assured their failure. Policy required the *parcelamiento* of ejidos; henceforth, every *ejidatario* would receive title to his own plot of land, although he was still barred from selling it. As statistics reveal, land reform, too, slowed down rapidly. Many of the lands listed in official statistics as distributed merely confirmed provisional titles granted by the Cardenistas. Lands actually distributed were often poor, leading, on diverse occasions, to rejection by their recipients.

Annual Land Distribution
(Millions of Hectares)

1941	1.1
1942	0.9
1943	0.5
1944	0.3
1945	0.04

Officials in the 1940s spoke of a "march to the sea" as a means of distributing land. The coastal plains on the Gulf of Mexico would be opened to agriculture. No one explained how that would be done, since most of the available lands were of poor quality, lacked water, or had no access to markets. The scheme required uprooting the landless from their homes and families. A revised agrarian code, meanwhile, set aside more land free from the threat of expropriation: up to 300 hectares for the cultivation of coconuts, rubber trees, grapes, olives, vanilla, henequen, and cinchona. The legislation also exempted lands required to pasture two hundred head of cattle. Just the same, the agrarian code still recognized the existence of *peones acasillados.*

Land reform confronted obstacles of a different stripe, too; again federal bureaucrats, their nose to the shifting winds, delayed or failed to expedite petitions for land, or sided with the landlords, permitting them to "divide up" their holdings into small plots, each, of course, owned by a relative in the family. By relying on *prestanombres,* persons who lent their names, the *latifundistas* kept their lands safe from expropriation. When that ploy failed, more than one owner hired gangs of armed thugs, *guardias blancas,* to frighten campesinos from petitioning for land or from accepting it if granted. Puebla, Veracruz, Guanajuato, and Sinaloa earned notoriety for their thugs. On other occasions, *latifundistas* bribed federal, state, and municipal authorities. Governors, too, soiled their reputations in this squalid game, among them Gildardo Magaña, the ex-Zapatista, and Maximino Avila Camacho, brother of a president; both acquired huge estates. Federal law, moreover, allowed state legislatures, where *latifundistas* often had a powerful say, to fix the limits of landownership. Not surprisingly, the amounts varied, from 50,000 hectares in Coahuila and 40,000 in Chihuahua to 200 in Veracruz.

The best-laid plans of mice and men, nonetheless, often go awry. The gifts showered on big private farmers encouraged them to plant crops for sale across the border and to neglect the needs of the domestic market. As food grew scarce, its price rose. The resulting inflation cut into the pocketbooks of millions of Mexicans, not the least of them urban consumers. The lack of credit to *ejidatarios* who sold their corn and beans on local markets reduced their harvests while encouraging the activities of private moneylenders who relied on usury to fatten their profits. Lacking funds or credit, *ejidatarios* started to abandon their lands, aggravating the food picture. Conservatives put the blame for the "debacle" on land reform and the ejido, which they dubbed antediluvian.

The critics, increasingly, got a sympathetic hearing in official circles. In spite of an oath to distribute the lands of the new irrigation districts to *ejidatarios,* officials permitted them to fall into the lap of private farmers, in the Yaqui Valley for instance. "Nylon" farmers made their bow, land speculators who could not tell a plow from a harrow. One of them was the comedian Roberto Soto, El Panzón (the Fat One), who abandoned the theater to get rich off lands given him by the Secretariat of Agriculture in the irrigation district of Mexicali, in Baja California. Under the pretext of multiplying the yields of henequen fiber, the policy architects also returned the *desfibradoras* (rasping machines) to the hacendados of Yucatán, leaving the *ejidatarios* at their mercy.

In 1947, politicos in the National Palace pushed through a compliant Congress a reform of Article 27, broadening the right of the *amparo,* an injunction in defense of the family latifundios of the "revolutionary rich." Not long afterward, they expanded the limits of small property to include 100 hectares of irrigated land, 200 of *tierras temporales* (seasonal), 300 of orchards, 400 of pasture, 800 of scrub plants, and, in arid zones, enough to feed five hundred head of cattle—50,000 acres. In some regions, *latifundistas,* in league with local authorities, occupied the lands of Indian communities, while *ejidatarios,* unable to cultivate their lands, rented them out to private farmers and then went to work for them, tilling their own soil as day laborers. In this fashion, 80 percent of the campesinos given lands had lost control of them by the 1970s. As this was happening, the population of rural Mexico was multiplying, leaving in its wake larger numbers of landless campesinos. This turn of events delighted industrialists, who saw the landless flocking to Mexico City to provide cheap labor for their factories.

The apostles of the era also wished to modernize agriculture, relying for their model on the mechanized farms of the United States. The "Green Revolution," so labeled by its advocates, opened up the Mayo and Yaqui valleys of Sonora and the delta of the Río Fuerte in Sinaloa to private entrepreneurs who tilled cotton or winter vegetables for sale north of the border or, more and more, for processing in Mexico by American corporations such as Anderson Clayton, Nestlé, Ralston Purina, United Brands, and Carnation, busily setting up plants in Mexico.

The giant collective ejidos, the darlings of the Cardenistas, were abandoned, sabotaged by hostile politicos and entrepreneurs, who called them socialistic. Mistakes by the Cardenistas, too, brought on their demise. Unwilling to leave the hacendado landless, the Cardenistas allowed him to retain 150 hectares of his choice. Naturally, he kept the most fertile lands, plus his manor house, sheds, wells, and irrigation canals, "the heart and hub of the hacienda," to the detriment of the *ejidatarios.* Many a hacendado set himself up in business in a nearby town—Torreón, in the Laguna, to name one—where he became the local moneylender as well as the salesman for agricultural machinery, fertilizers, and insecticides, the bread and butter of the ejidos. Once more *ejidatarios* found themselves beholden, although in a different manner, to their old boss or to his offspring.

For a while, despite the harm that befell campesinos, the fathers of agricultural policy had cause for jubilation. The new irrigation districts, where huge amounts of capital were invested, as well as high prices for agricultural products on the international market, had indeed multiplied the size of national harvests. In the decade between 1940 and 1950, production rose by 71 percent, something unheard of until then. Peace reigned in the countryside, and food production matched demand even for beans, though just barely so.

Yet agrarian unrest, the likes of which had not been seen in years, broke out late in 1958. That the trouble came as a surprise was no fault of campesinos, millions of them landless, paid miserable wages when employed or, when jobless, fleeing to the United States to find work. Along with labor, campesinos had borne much of the burden of economic stability; their low wages made possible bountiful harvests of cash crops for sale abroad of *latifundistas* and, indirectly, industrialization.

Trouble appeared initially in Sinaloa. Wanting soil of their own to till, campesinos occupied lands of neighboring *latifundistas,* who, predictably, blamed campesino leaders, specifically Jacinto López and Félix Rubio. The small property, which the *latifundistas* declared had been invaded by López and his followers, was, all the same, big property. To buy off the unrest, officials in Mexico City granted a bit of land to López and his campesinos, but that merely ignited trouble in the Laguna of Coahuila, where the jobless occupied cotton fields. Then demands for land broke out in Nayarit, Colima, and Sonora, where the government had acquired the vast holdings of the Cananea Cattle Company. As these events developed, López went to jail. However, politicos in Mexico City had learned that the clenched fist alone would not quell unrest. So it was decided to add the carrot to the stick to maintain peace in the countryside. The sop was the distribution of three million hectares of land, much of it poor, while the stick, in the guise of soldiers, squashed campesino protests, killing, among others, Rubén Jaramillo, the noted agrarian chieftain, and his entire family.

The problems of agriculture, plainly, were far from being resolved. Until 1965, agricultural exports had paid for nearly one-third of the cost of imports, mostly for industry, helping, in this manner, to keep a balance of payments. Starting in 1956, the value of agricultural exports had begun to decline, mainly because farmers were being asked to produce raw materials for industry. As this occurred, imports of wheat, corn, and other grains grew. Thereafter, things merely got worse for the campesinos, leading them to take, more and more, flight to the cities, where they formed a lumpen proletariat. A story about a visit of Lázaro Cárdenas to the Yaqui Valley, thirty years after he gave its inhabitants land, captures succinctly the campesino's tragedy. Living in poverty, an old Yaqui asked Cárdenas, "Is this the Revolution?" Cárdenas, it was said, "could not hold back his tears."

III

For nearly two decades, policy architects had labored to better rural education. After 1940, their successors, who worshiped business and industry, started to favor urban schools and secondary and technical education, doing everything to make learning a part of the industrial effort, a decision made easy by public indifference to rural problems. The pursuit of peace in the countryside lowered the curtain on the era of the militant teacher, whose usefulness declined after the oil expropriation of 1938. Legal and public sanction was extended to old enemies of secular education, including the church, in the midst of a revival. When it built schools, authorities looked the other way. Surplus funds were channeled into the construction of a university campus in Mexico City for the benefit of half a dozen cities, whose graduates seldom bothered with campesinos. By 1950, public welfare got only 20 percent of the national budget; of that, public education had less than 2 percent.

Given this ideological climate, the socialist school stuck out like a sore thumb. The challenge of education, the new pedagogues explained, was a moral one. There was no room for the socialist reform of Article 3, which had spawned "a historic materialism companion to communism." Evolution, not revolution, was the way out. The campaign against the socialist school, which started with the presidential campaign of 1940, split teachers and public alike. Manuel Avila Camacho, the new president and no fan of the socialist school, paradoxically, had run on a platform endorsing it but, once in office, discarded it, in defense of what was baptized "freedom to teach and learn." But what critics of the socialist school really had in mind was to revise Article 3 in order to permit the church to sponsor schools. Not only was the socialist school at stake but so were tenents of secular education.

That the political winds blew from that direction was made obvious by the attack on coeducation, for the fault-finding originated in the same quarter. Schools for both sexes had appeared under José Vasconcelos, and their numbers multiplied after Moisés Sáenz assumed command under Calles. During the twenties, coeducation was limited to the primary grades; in the thirties, Narciso Bassols, secretary of education, had raised a storm of protest by including secondary schools. Early in the forties, coeducation was abolished, over the cries of alarm of teachers and thousands of parents who pointed out that this step came at a time when the entire world was marching in the opposite direction. Hardest hit by the nonsense were the women of Mexico, who, once more, found themselves classified as second-class citizens. They were saved from the full impact of the blow by the inability to change over completely to a dual system for lack of funds to duplicate facilities.

Having attempted to scuttle coeducation, and almost succeeded, conservatives went after the socialist school. With the support of affluent businessmen and the church, and with the middle class rallying to their cause, they won the battle. In Congress, the sole opposition to the reform of Article 3 came from ten votes cast by the spokesmen for the CTM. As of 1945, the "rational" concepts of the socialist school disappeared, their place taken by a schooling designed to "develop harmoniously the faculties of the human spirit and, at the same time, inculcate a love of country." Nothing was said of the class struggle.

Less controversial, although equally meaningful as a commentary on the state of opinion, was the question of a curriculum for the primary schools. Were country and city to have an identical one? For the men and women who took over for the Cardenistas, the answer was yes. Every Mexican youngster would have the same education. That view reversed the advice of men such as Moisés Sáenz and Rafael Ramírez who had stressed that the needs of rural life differed markedly from those of the city. They had advocated a school program designed to meet the educational needs of the inhabitants of rural villages. "When I visit a village," lamented Ramírez in 1945, "hoping to find our rural school, to stop and speak with it, it is difficult to locate it." If he asked the neighbors about it, he was told, "Ah yes, you are speaking of the school that the people built themselves in order to learn from it how to live better. It has been a long time since we have seen it, but now that you remind us of it, we can tell you that it was wonderful and good." The inability of officials in Mexico City to implement their policy once more left remnants of the old rural school program intact. In 1960, officials introduced "free and compulsory" textbooks, which, while undoubtedly aiding the poor, also imposed more uniformity on education.

To rulers after Cárdenas, the inability to read and write lay at the bottom of Mexico's educational problems. To remedy this, they launched campaigns to teach the ABC's to illiterate Mexicans. The idea was hardly novel. Vasconcelos had sponsored a national literacy campaign; the Cardenistas, too, had flirted briefly with one. It remained for the spokesmen of the post–World War II era, however, to enshrine the panacea. But how to carry it out? Since there were only so many schools and teachers, the solution was to employ literate Mexicans to teach their neighbors to read and write. In this way, Angeles Mastretta recalled sarcastically in her novel, "overnight there would not be a single Indian unable to write his name, that of his country and, of course, that of his well-deserving president."

Whatever the merits of the idea, its results proved fleeting. Public enthusiasm waned quickly after the novelty wore off. From the start, the campaign focused on urban communities; almost nothing was done in the villages, which had the highest illiteracy rates. What complicated the problem was that many of their inhabitants spoke only an Indian tongue. The chief barrier, all the same, was poverty, which literacy could not eliminate. Unless steps were taken to correct economic conditions that produced illiteracy, being able to read and write was of little value. Illiteracy was not a pedagogical ill but a symptom of deep-seated social maladies. In 1958, despite the drum-beating of the illiteracy campaign, seventeen million Mexicans could not read or write, a number larger than that of any other era in the history of Mexico.

Indigenismo, the gospel of Sáenz and the Cardenistas, also dropped from favor. For their successors, the Indian did not merit special attention. Someday in the future, according to their blueprints, when industry and business thrived, their benefits would "trickle down," altering the life of the Indian and transforming him into a Mexican. Although the Department of Indian Affairs lived on briefly, it was eventually disbanded, its place taken by the Instituto Nacional Indigenista. Shorn of cabinet rank and with less money than the government spent "on the capital's fountains," its activities reached only a tiny fraction of the Indian population. *Indigenismo,* obviously, had died.

For teachers, too, the Cardenista years marked a watershed. To safeguard their interests and win salary boosts, schoolteachers, starting in the 1920s, had organized themselves into unions. By 1930, every schoolteacher belonged to one of them. Union organization brought benefits but also intrigue and factional squabbles, bogging down the Secretariat of Education in a morass of politics. In his letter of resignation, Narciso Bassols had censured teachers who opposed his efforts to establish a system of tenure and promotions based on ability, training, and performance. Under Cárdenas, the teachers became a major political bloc, while the political turmoil survived him and the problem was inherited by his successors. By 1940, the STERM (Union of Workers in Education of the Mexican Republic), teachers sympathetic to the socialist school, had won the upper hand, but not for long.

Under the politics of the forties, the STERM fell from its pinnacle of power. Encouraged by the Secretariat of Education, conservative organizations of teachers made their appearance, labeling the STERM Communist and unpatriotic. From the disarray, which government officials manipulated, emerged the SNTE, a syndicate of teachers led by anti-Communist *charros.* Poor and corrupt leadership had repercussions in the countryside, where untold numbers of teachers joined the ranks of those who lived by exploiting campesinos. There were villages where the schoolmasters controlled the pulque trade, served as middlemen who bought and sold at a profit local products, or lived in neighboring towns, arriving to teach on Tuesday and departing on Thursday, leaving the school unattended for the better part of the week. Censurable as were these teachers, the fault was not entirely theirs. The corruption of the times and a public hostile or indifferent to the plight of the Republic's teachers were equally responsible. Much of the trouble could be traced to salaries; by 1960, rural schoolteachers were earning half as much as in 1936 and less than factory workers.

IV

Urbanization and an expanding middle class, the accoutrements of industrialization, gave birth to a different artistic and literary mood, at odds with that of the muralists and novelists of the Revolution. From it emerged a literary boom unmatched in Mexican history. During the 1940s, Mexicans, like other Latin Americans, had started to experiment with fresh techniques, among them the stream of consciousness, unusual time sequences, and complex structures. Their work focused on the imagination and used a vibrant, rich language. Setting aside realism, so much a part of the older novels, José Reveltas and Agustín Yáñez had led the way, finding new paths to explore old revolutionary themes. For his book *El luto humano,* Revueltas had relied on the stream of consciousness to tell tales about troubled campesinos, while Yáñez, in *Al filo del agua,* added symbolism and multiple viewpoints to write about a small town on the eve of the Revolution. Earlier, Rodolfo Usigli, a dramatist, had written *El gesticulador,* a play about the "big lie," a Mexico of people who believed either everything or nothing at all. The principal character, the *gesticulador,* impersonates a dead revolutionary general but, even though eventually confessing his deception, is disbelieved because, said Usigli, Mexicans "prefer myth to reality."

It remained for Juan Rulfo, native of Jalisco, and Carlos Fuentes to achieve international acclaim for the Mexican novel. Along with Gabriel García Márquez, the author from Colombia, and Mario Vargas Llosa, from Peru, these two writers placed the Latin American novel at the top of the Western world's literature. In *El llano en llamas,* a collection of short stories, Rulfo pictured a government indifferent to the needs of campesinos, with the power to "kill or let live," distributing worthless parcels of land. His *Pedro Páramo,* perhaps the best of Mexico's novels, spoke of a young man who inherited a hacienda, married well, and died a wealthy chief of revolutionaries. But, from the first, Pedro Páramo, the hacendado, was dead, as were all of the people he knew. Juan Preciado, the son sent out to search for Pedro, his father, dies without finding him. The dead of Mexico, the novel seems to say, linger on and on and, more important, the myths about them, too. Nor did Rulfo place much faith in campesino revolutionaries, preferring to believe that they took up arms not to fight for goals but to defend what they had.

For all that, Fuentes best personified the contemporary urban novel. With *La región más transparente,* a story about people in Mexico City, Fuentes laid the foundations for this genre of the future and substitute for the tales of the Revolution. His city people included a host of types, from campesinos become plutocrats to aristocrats despoiled of their lands by the upheaval of 1910 yet still atop society. Whatever their importance, it was the middle class that drew the author's attention, the mother of selfish politicos who, according to Fuentes, betrayed the Revolution. The backdrop for the drama was Mexico City, a place of slums, gaudy suburbs for the rich, and cafés where business tycoons hatched deals. Fuentes went on to write another novel about the Revolution betrayed, titled *La muerte de Artemio Cruz,* about an illegitimate boy who grew up to fight in the Revolution, then betrayed it, became rich and powerful, but died a lonely and embittered old man. For these novels, Fuentes drew heavily on the thinking of Samuel Ramos and Octavio Paz, author of the

Laberinto de la soledad, essays probing the psyche, and Mexico's finest poet.

After 1968, the urban novel spoke of the massacre of Tlatelolco, increasingly omnipotent in Mexican literature. Of the accounts, Elena Poniatowska's *La noche de Tlatelolco,* a collection of remembrances by participants in the tragedy, was read most widely. A documentary with an artistic flavor, *La noche de Tlatelolco* gave life to witnesses who, in the course of their testimony, took on the role of characters in a novel. *Con el, conmigo, con nosotros tres,* a novel by María Luisa Mendoza, explored the night of the massacre of Tlatelolco and its aftermath as witnessed by a family from the provinces.

For art, the 1940s and 1950s represented a rupture with the past. Mural painting dropped from favor. Once again, urban Mexicans took to vilifying José Clemente Orozco, this time his murals in the Supreme Court, which were labeled a "travesty," art "out of touch with the tastes of the Mexican people." When Orozco died in 1949, during the days of a cold war he detested, few came to his burial, least of all Miguel Alemán, then president of the Republic, although Pablo Neruda, the Chilean poet, who read the eulogy, reminded the mourners that Orozco's art had never lost touch with the people. Diego Rivera, though still painting murals, also made money with portraits of Ramón Beteta, *secretario de hacienda* under Alemán and a new millionaire, and María Félix, the movie queen from Sonora. Rivera died in 1957.

A distinct art current had crept into Mexico, alien, to quoté José Luis Cuevas, its most notable exponent, to the "cactus curtain," the Mexican school of mural art. An abstract painter, Cuevas, nonetheless, did not wish to imitate the art of foreigners, certainly not that of "Pollock, Kline, Motherwell, and De Kooning," or to accept "the dictates fo the Museum of Modern Art in New York City." For all that, he acknowledged that most of his contemporaries merely copied what was done elsewhere. Yet Cuevas did not labor alone. Siqueiros, when not in jail, still worked on his murals, his clothes splattered from head to toe, remembered one observer, "with the colors of his paints."

At the same time, Frida Kahlo, a distinguished painter, earned international fame for her surrealistic interpretations. Crippled by a trafic accident when young, Kahlo endured physical pain all of her life. Raised to be very Catholic and very conservative by her parents, she later became a militant political ideologue and a member of the Communist party, an artist who urged aspiring young painters to read Marxist literature and keep alive *el realismo mexicanista* and not be seduced by modern European easel art. Blessed with a social conscience, she remained until her death at the age of forty-seven a loyal admirer of the ideals of Emiliano Zapata, a friend of campesinos, an *indigenista,* and a feminist. Kahlo was a paradox. Although she admired Grünewald, Piero della Francesca, Bosch, Blake, and Klee and was enchanted by the "primitivism" and "fantasy" of Gauguin and Rousseau, her art mimicked the

Mexican popular tradition. For example, when she painted *La venadita*, picturing herself as a deer, she identified herself with all animals, a concept inherent in Aztec culture.

In music, the 1950s similarly saw a shift away from the "nationalist" compositions of Carlos Chavez, Silvestre Revueltas, and Manuel Ponce. It was no longer fashionable to think of a classical music "distinctly Mexican." The times, instead, called for a return to the music of Europe and the United States.

23

DEBACLE

I

The axiom of the Mexico of the 1970s was dependency, reliance on the neighbor next door for markets, manufactures, and money. This was not a novel development; Mexico, after all, had historic ties with the United States. For all that, the new dependency, unhappy Mexican dissidents alleged, had virtually converted Mexico "into a colony of the Yankee." As José Agustín, author of *Ciudades desiertas,* a celebrated novel, put it, "regardless of what politicians might say, we have put the motherland in hock."

II

What Augustín referred to stood in bold relief. Approximately 70 percent of what Mexicans sold on the world market traveled north, while more of what they imported had an American label. That relationship promoted an unfavorable balance of payments. From 1975 to 1980, trade had tripled between the two neighbors, transforming Mexico into the third-best customer of the United States. Americans controlled 70 percent of the foreign investment in Mexico, and much of its foreign debt, second in size only to Brazil's, was owed to American creditors. Foreign investment, however, had not greatly expanded the industrial base, the bulk of it going into the purchase of existing industries, especially food processing, electronics, and machinery. As a result, Mexican industry had become increasingly denationalized. Of the one hundred biggest firms, nearly half were foreign; of the capital goods industries, over half. Foreigners controlled the most dynamic industries and the most essential to economic growth.

The foreign companies that arrived in Mexico were rarely independent ones, but mostly branches of transnational corporations. Mexico had more of them than any other country in Latin America, ranking fifth in the world in the number of transnationals. Virtually every major American corporation had a branch in Mexico. By 1987, the transnationals produced over a third of the Republic's industrial output and, at times, 60 percent of the consumer items and 40 percent of the capital goods. A few, favored Mexicans had profited alongside of the foreign giants, among them Miguel Alemán Velasco, son of a former president and head of Aluminio, S.A., allegedly a Mexican firm but actually a branch of Alcoa.

The transnationals, according to their Mexican critics, often behaved arrogantly, riding roughshod over local needs. In Michoacán, for instance, Celanesa Mexicana, a transnational offshoot, had arrived in Zacapu in 1948, converting the sleepy town into an industrial depot. During its prosperous days, the company employed over two thousand workers, natives mostly of Michoacán. So powerful was it that governors and military commanders intervened on its behalf in labor disputes. When bad times crippled the economy, Celanesa Mexicana had fired all but two hundred of its workers. The plant, moreover, with its belching smokestacks and its dumping of waste in the Río Angulo, the source for water for farmers, had polluted the lands of Zacapu and the surrounding countryside. In Sahagún, a city in Hidalgo, Renault shut down its factory without notifying either the governor or the federal authorities, although both had asked it to continue operations in order to limit unemployment.

The transnationals, nevertheless, weathered the ups and downs of the economy, so characteristic of the seventies. The peso devaluations, the paucity of credit, inflated interest rates, shrinking markets, and declines in production, which cut into profits, hurt the small companies, mostly Mexican. As Mexican companies went out of business, the transnationals more and more dominated local industry. By depositing their profits in banks back home, they exacerbated the flight of capital from Mexico, tilting more its negative balance of payments.

On the northern border, Americans and, by the 1980s, the Japanese, too, had established over one thousand *maquiladoras*, a third of them in Tijuana, Mexicali, and Ensenada. Assembly plants, they hired young women to piece together television sets, radios, electronic gadgets, computer hardware, athletic supporters, and so forth for sale on the American market. Mexicans provided the cheap labor; everything else, from plant managers to cloth, arrived invariably from north of the border. From this enterprise, Mexican border towns reaped the money from wages but had to provide the water, sewers, schools, and diverse social services required by the workers and their families, almost always from far away.

Most alarmingly, a handful of companies had a corner on Mexican industry. Just 1 percent of the industries accounted for 66 percent of the value of production and investment and employed one-third of the industrial labor force. This was textbook monopoly capitalism, the concentration of economic power in an elite of industrialists and bankers, foreigners usually. Whatever their nationality, they rigged prices, virtually eliminating competition, and were inclined to diversify their production rather than welcome rivals. When marketing their wares, they sold to the identical constituency, basically the urban middle class. Little was done to enlarge the home market.

The small national market suffered from distorted geographical contours. Consuming and producing enclaves were one and the same. Regions of high buying capacity also had many industries, specifically the Federal District, Jalisco, Veracruz, Puebla, and the border states. The Federal District, Mexico City fundamentally, took in approximately one-fifth of all consumers, who purchased half of the machinery, half of the scientific and technical equipment, half of the hardware, nearly 43 percent of the cars, trucks, radios, and television sets, and over 35 percent of the sugar, beer, soft drinks, soap, medicine, cosmetics, and cigarettes. Similarly, the Federal District, with the highest per capita income in the Republic and 55 percent of its industry, was the preeminent industrial bastion. The entire system functioned, more or less, for the benefit of an Americanized minority, the rich and the middle class, ever eager to ape Yankees.

The dependency model, as was outlined earlier, relied on exports to the United States, mostly raw materials, mineral ores, and agricultural commodities. Despite sales of winter vegetables from the Fuerte and Yaqui valleys, the terms of trade seldom favored Mexico, because profits, more and more, lagged behind the price of manufactured articles. International capitalist cycles, primarily the vicissitudes of the American economy, made reliance on exports a gamble. Shorn of export markets, the Mexican economy teetered, in spite of high profits for industrialists. Reliance on exports went hand in glove with giving foreigners inducements to invest in Mexico, keeping down wages, and borrowing money in order to pump life into the economy.

III

Part and parcel of this edifice was the PRI. Rather than a political party, it was an arm of the state, the mouthpiece and tool of the oligarchy in power. So successful was it that politics, as in the Porfiriato, had only marginal significance. The opinions of voters, who seldom visited the polls, were usually ignored. The Mexican political system, like a modern corporation, required able management, not a politician at its head. Rather than a populist paragon, the president was a glorified manager. After the departure of Gustavo Díaz Ordaz, the men promoted to the presidency had not even won their spurs in politics. None had held elective office. Starting with Luis Echeverría in 1970, they were bureaucrats, an apt description for José López Portillo and Miguel de la Madrid, his successors. Their primary loyalty was to those who had seated them in the presidency and to the political system. For that reason alone, they could not transform the PRI or accept the triumph of carpetbaggers which, should it occur, invited the demise of the system entrusted to them for safekeeping. For these bureaucrats, referred to as "technocrats" in the current jargon, the PRI, to cite one view, was no more than a "ministry of elections" to be trotted out every six years and ignored in the interim.

That the chiefs of state differed in personality goes without saying. No less certain, they had their political proclivities, some being less conservative than others, although Priístas to the bone. They were, just the same, asked to perform particular roles—the "reformer," for instance, followed on the heels of the "hard-liner," or the "moralist" who cleaned up the mess of his predecessor. Like actors, they had scripts to read, though, occasionally, when unexpected events disrupted their performance, they improvised. Still, in the face of superficial differences, they were loyal bureaucrats, doing the task assigned to them, "their authority circumscribed carefully by its nature."

Echeverría, a lawyer, had mastered dutifully the rules of the political game. In the conservative and anti-Communist era of the Alemanistas, he was the private secretary of General Rodolfo Sánchez Toboada, head of the PRI, then director of its propaganda arm, and finally *secretario de gobernación* under Díaz Ordaz. A man devoid of intellectual pretensions but intelligent, he played golf and courted higher-ups. When Díaz Ordaz, then president, invited Echeverría to join him for a round of golf the next morning, he arrived at dawn, before his host had gotten out of bed. With the physical stamina of an athlete, he was usually on the run, never, apparently, fatigued. "Rarely," it was whispered about, "did he go to the toilet," which led malicious tongues to say that "he never urinated if he did not want to." Earlier a coat-and-tie man, he tossed them to the four winds upon entering the National Palace, adopting the *guayabera,* the coat shirt from Yucatán, and, by doing it, turning upside down the dress code of ambitious politicos. Cautious on the way up, Echeverría was a doer in the presidential chair. His wife, Ester Zuno, daughter of a former governor and caudillo of Jalisco, called him by his last name, with "passion and pride." Herself a populist in behavior, she addressed women as *compañeras* (comrades), employing the informal *tu* form, and spent her days as the first lady rushing here and there, to quote Julio Scherer, editor of *Excélsior,* "as though granted just so much time to save her country."

Entrusted with rescuing the system from the public ridicule heaped upon it by Díaz Ordaz's brutal handling of the students, Echeverría, who quickly mastered populist rhetoric, became a "reform" president. Though a defender of Mexican capitalists, he never tired of reminding them that their excessive wealth was acquired at the expense of the poor. Rhetoric and reality, however, did not always match. Equity for Echeverría, at times, had a hollow ring, in

1968, for example, when, as *secretario de gobernación,* he went along with the assault on the defenseless students and, again in the summer of 1971, when armed thugs, called *halcones,* or hawks, beat, wounded, and killed student demonstrators in Mexico City. Echeverría, who promised to punish the guilty, failed to do so, because he either could not, as some allege, or was unwilling to jail fellow Priístas. Whatever the truth, the culprits escaped unpunished despite a public outcry.

José López Portillo, scion of the venerable clan from Jalisco, was clay of a different sort. Charismatic and outgoing, he was a bon vivant by inclination. A lawyer, too, he had been under secretary of the Patrimonio Nacional and chief of the Comimisión Federal de Electricidad, from where he jumped to the post of secretary of finance under Echeverría. A bureaucrat with literary talents, López Portillo had published two books, *Don Q* and *Génesis y teoría del Estado,* a somber analysis of government. A "peacock who enjoyed displaying his feathers," he lived life to the full. On the day of his anointment, he arrived for a luncheon with Julio Scherer driving an old Borgward, so nervous that he barely ate. Upon taking office in 1976, he assured Scherer that he needed just "three years to pull the country out of its tailspin."

Told to save the Republic from the folly of Echeverría, López Portillo played the savior for three years. He was seldom late for appointments, kept a rigorous schedule, was lively and attentive, sure that he had the answers, and bubbled with good humor. These were the years of his triumph, when the oil boom showered gifts and he predicted euphorically that Mexico would be a middling world power "like France." Then, he altered his style, embracing the fast life and joining arms with the likes of Arturo Durazo, a cheap thug indicted afterward in the United States for drug trafficking, whom he named chief of security for Mexico City, and Carlos Hank González, a politico notorious for his unexplained wealth. When he left office, López Portillo was no longer, according to his former admirers, "the bold conservative" who stacked his cabinet with pragmatic, "qualified" technocrats," what Americans had admired.

Miguel de la Madrid, who relieved the defrocked idol, was from head to foot a bureaucrat. Also a lawyer, he was short but sat tall, "with his back so stiff and straight that he gave the impression of posing for a sculptor." Endeavoring to appear taller, he wore elevated heels and combed his hair straight back. A career public servant, he lived by the rules of the game, as *subsecretario de programación y presupuesto*—to illustrate, naming José Ramón, son of López Portillo, to a good post. The rules of ambition took in nepotism and favoritism. A conservative, De la Madrid filled his cabinet with men of similar mold, mostly from the Banco de México or the Secretariat of Finance, usually his friends. Of the fourteen closest to him, just three had not spent an apprenticeship in the financial world, the citadel of influence during his sojourn in the

National Palace. Two of them had degrees from universities in the United States.

Assuming office in 1982, the year of Mexico's bankruptcy, De la Madrid earned accolades from Washington for his "tough policies of austerity," for his willingness to slash public spending, to add to the jobless rolls, and to prevent widespread public unrest. Although vowing to bring order out of chaos and clean up public corruption, he left things more or less as he found them. That included the severe economic depression. Ultimately, Mexicans disenchanted by his policies took a dim view of him. At a soccer match in Mexico City he attended, they booed him, an act unheard of until then.

Industrialization, the urban explosion, and the omnipotent presence of the middle class had not altered the nature of politics. Although changing, politics still ran, so to speak, true to Mexican form. As during the days of Porfirio Díaz, to cite the testimony of Heberto Castillo, a pundit and renowned maverick, the government, through its manipulation of the PRI, called the tune. Mexican democracy, hailed constantly by Priístas, was still the sham of the Porfiristas, only more sophisticated.

By the charter of 1917, thirty-one states, claiming an autonomy of their own, as well as statutes of individual liberties, composed the Republic. Every six years, Mexicans elected a president, a Senate, and the governors of the states; every three years, they went to the polls to select deputies to Congress and municipal officers. Opposition candidates had the right openly to challenge their PRI foes. Yet all Mexicans, even the poorest campesino, knew this was a charade because the PRI had never lost an election for president, governor, or senator. When deciding on its presidential flag bearer, the PRI, as a matter of fact, seldom consulted public opinion. The choice of the *tapado,* the hidden one, baffled the man on the street. Governors, likewise, were chosen mainly because of their loyalty to the system. Barred from seeking reelection, deputies could never pursue independent political careers. In the Chamber of Deputies, mammoth PRI majorities silenced the so-called opposition. The Supreme Court, the highest judicial body in the Republic, always sided with key government decisions.

The PRI relied on repression and co-optation to stay in power, buying off rivals with juicy government posts or the chance to fill one's wallet. When women won the right to vote and hold national office, the PRI opened its doors to them, almost always from the urban middle class. Once co-opted, they became deputies, senators, and governors of Colima and Tlaxcala, sat on the Supreme Court, and held posts in the PRI hierarchy. All were faithful Priístas, no less so than their menfolk. Occasionally, a maverick appeared, such as Rosario Ibarra de Piedra, housewife, mother, middle class, and native of Monterrey. Angered by the death of her son, who was the victim of police brutality, she organized the National Committee to Defend Political Prisoners and, in the election of 1982, was the presidential candidate of the Partido Revolucionario de los Trabajadores, a Trotskyist group.

The Ibarras were the exception to the rule. With bulging coffers and plenty of disciples, the PRI set the tone for politics, not only buying off the ambitious but blocking the formation of rival bands. Controlling a pliant Congress, it dictated electoral laws, counted the votes, ruled on contested elections, and, when necessary, gerrymandered districts to defuse middle-class discontent. Refusing to heed appeals from residents of the Federal District, the PRI denied them self-rule, fearing a confrontation with a literate electorate. On rare occasions when their foes won an election for *presidente municipal* of a provincial city, Priístas controlled the purse strings in the statehouse. In the 1980s, the Panista mayor of Hermosillo was even denied money to fill in the potholes of the streets of his city.

The reforms of the Echeverristas, which lowered the voting age and gave the opposition a bigger share of congressional seats, was merely a face-lift of politics. During the reign of his successor, legislation expanded the Chamber of Deputies to four hundred, one-fourth of them reserved for the opposition. Government, which financed the Priístas, would pay its salaries. Opposition parties, therefore, were more political theater than anything else. Even if they were to unite, they could not win a vote in Congress. The PRI majority saw to that; at best, they were a thorn in the side of the body politic. Moreover, by paying their salaries, government could manipulate oppostion deputies and suborn, to quote Heberto Castillo, their "submissive parties." Rival parties now existed, but they carried little weight, appearing only at election time, conferring on Priístas the opportunity to speak of a *sistema pluripartidista,* a multiparty system.

Party was a poor title for these political bands. With the exception of the PAN, none merited the name, being mainly ploys of ambitious politicos kept in business by federal funds. Three were simply satellites of the PRI: the Partido Auténtico de la Revolución Mexicana (PARM), a collection of aging conservatives; the Partido Popular Socialista (PPS), once the kingdom of Vicente Lombardo Toledano; and the Partido Socialista de los Trabajadores (PST). On the political "right," so claimed official propaganda, was the PAN, its spirits revived by the collapse of the economy in 1982. In the elections of that year, Panistas, voicing middle-class discontent, won the *presidencias municipales* of Hermosillo, Durango, Ciudad Chihuahua, and Ciudad Juárez, San Luis Potosí, and Monclova, in Coahuila. For all that, the PAN had a fragile political organization and, until 1988, lacked charismatic leadership. Wielding little clout as a party, Panistas, instead, infiltrated the government, influencing decisions by the back door. Alongside of the PAN was the Partido Democrático Mexicano, an offshoot of the Unión Nacional Sinarquista, home to fanatical Catholics, whose principal appeal was regional, and to campesinos.

The "left," for its part, was split into tiny bands, best known for ideological wrangling and quarreling personalities. Each traveled its own route, more intent on preserving its subsidy from government than in forming a united front against the PRI. The most important of the leftist parties, the Partido Socialista Unido Mexicano (PSUM), born out of the merger of four others, had gone its separate way, but helped form the Partido Mexicano Socialista. Whatever their ideological proclivities, the "leftist" parties, in contact rarely with labor and campesinos, attracted mainly university students and urbanites of reform inclination.

The "loyal opposition" had a circumscribed role to perform. Knowingly or not, it legitimized the system, conferring a thin veneer of democracy on politics, mainly for foreign consumption. To quote Mario Moya Palencia, once *secretario de gobernación*, "a vote against the PRI is a vote for the system." Foreigners, among them American scholars, were fooled; Mexicans, a cynical lot, were not. A study of public opinion published in 1987 revealed that nearly 80 percent of all Mexicans had no faith in either the chief executive or the Congress; almost half of them distrusted the courts, judges, and, in a capsule, the whole legal network. Equally telling, less than a third of them had any faith in private enterprise.

To Mexicans, the causes of the *desconfianza*, an absence of trust bordering on cynicism, were as plain as the nose on one's face. In government, to come back to Castillo, a politico who spoke his mind, "there was obvious dishonesty, as much as or more so than in the private sector—which is to say a lot." Government openly flaunted the popular will. Or, to cite the jaundiced testimony of an American reporter, the system fed on corruption, which provided "the oil that makes the wheels of the bureaucratic machine turn and the glue that seals political alliance." The *mordida* was the tip of the iceberg.

Political fraud was the name of the game. Win elections, that was the watchword of the PRI. In the countryside, where political trickery was commonplace, Priístas bused campesinos to the voting booths in nearby towns, their vote assured by drink, food, or money. Election day was a fiesta. The national budget, which Priístas controlled, paid for the mariachis who provided the music, the singers, and the dancers. And win elections the PRI did. In 1982, it walked away with 71 percent of the popular vote, won all sixty-four Senate seats, and lost merely one election for deputy. In 1976, José López Portillo, running unopposed, swept the popular vote. During the elections of 1986 in heavily Panista Chihuahua, Priísta bosses brazenly informed its inhabitants that PAN candidates had captured only one *presidencia municipal* out of sixty-eight, while losing the governorship and every race for the state legislature. In Juchitán, a small city in Oaxaca, whose citizens had the temerity to vote their conscience, Priístas, between 1974 and 1986, voided every political victory of COCEI, a coalition of labor, campesino, and leftist voters.

IV

Despite Tlatelolco, the 1970s opened auspiciously for Mexico. With the war still raging in Vietnam, exports to the northern neighbor thrived. But, in 1975, the conflict ended, sending the American economy into a tailspin and with it Mexico's. The value of its exports declined, a situation aggravated by an earlier drop in tourism, the increasing instability of the dollar, and worldwide inflationary trends. When profits tumbled, investors, both natives and foreigners, withdrew their capital from Mexico. As production declined, inflation flared anew, while the trade deficit with the United States, a goodly share of it to pay for imported foodstuffs, ballooned. Shortages encouraged a rise in food prices, above all for corn, beans, and tortillas, while the increasing cost of manufactured articles outstripped wage gains. Per capita income dropped, and the GNP stagnated, reflecting maladies in industry and agriculture. Intensifying the doldrums, the United States legislated a 10 percent surcharge on imports, which, in 1977 alone, cost Mexico $200 million in foreign exchange.

When private investment proved unable to keep the economy humming, government spending took up the slack. The *paraestatales* had multiplied from 84 in 1970 to 845 by 1976. The Echeverristas were especially fond of big state projects, financed inevitably from abroad, among them tourist resorts—Cancún and Ixtapa-Zihuatanejo, to name two—and the Sicartsa steel plant on the coast of Michoacán. To cover deficits and, simultaneously, make up losses caused by capital flight, the government borrowed from foreign banks. When Hugo Margaín, the finance secretary, announced that the cupboard was empty, Echeverría, so goes the gossip, fired him, saying, "I'll name someone who can find the money." That job went to López Portillo, who discovered the solution in foreign banks. By 1975, Mexico's foreign debt, excluding money borrowed by private enterprise, totaled nearly $20 billion.

Unwillingness to devalue the peso, meanwhile, kept Mexican exports uncompetitive on the international market, and borrowing from abroad fueled inflation as well as foreign indebtedness. This reflected the neglect of fiscal reform which the Echeverristas, to their credit, had attempted to rectify but, confronted by the opposition of the wealthy and influential, had abandoned. As Echeverría explained, hostile interest groups were too powerful.

On the eve of their departure from office, the Echeverristas, totally discredited, had gone in desperation to the International Monetary Fund. In August 1976, they signed a letter of intent; for a cash bailout, they embraced the monetarist panacea: stable growth assured by control of the money supply to match the capacity for expansion of productivity. From now on, Mexico would abide by the whims of the marketplace, encourage foreign investment, relegate the solution of social problems to the future, and stop spending more than it earned. Austerity, the IMF formula, also meant letting the peso float until "it reached its own rate of exchange with world currencies," a decision adopted late in 1976; soon its value plummeted from 12.5 pesos to the dollar to 29 pesos. This exacerbated Mexico's balance of payments problem and hastened capital flight. The monetarists omitted to explain that their tonic, whatever its healing remedies, stifled the growth of the internal market, mainly as a result of low wages and salaries.

Recovery came swiftly, but not because of the IMF formula. López Portillo's slogan of an "alliance for profits," by which he swore to permit business and industry to enjoy their rewards, may have encouraged Mexican capitalists to bank their money at home and Americans to invest in Mexico. Inflation, moreover, along with public spending, subsided momentarily. For all that, it was oil that revived the economy and, ironically, foreign borrowing. By 1978, the Mexican economy, ablaze with oil, had acquired fresh vigor.

Large deposits of petroleum had been discovered in Campeche, Tabasco, Chiapas, and Veracruz, states on the southern rim of the Gulf of Mexico, and in Tamaulipas, next door to Texas. The experts calculated that Mexico had 300 million barrels of oil buried underground. Oil, nevertheless, had a seamy history. Petroleum-rich countries had seldom employed their petropesos wisely; Venezuela, a sister republic, offered a glaring example of how not to exploit the black gold. Instead of alleviating poverty and inequality, Venezuela mishandled its oil reserves and exacerbated old ills. Knowing that, Mexicans were of diverse minds on how to handle their sudden good fortune. The wise among them warned of the harm it might produce; fearful of the consequences and not wanting to deplete rapidly the oil reserve, they advocated modest development and conservation. On the opposite side of the fence were those who wanted to pump as much oil as possible, sell it at high prices, and use profits to get on with Mexico's development. A disciple of this opinion was Jorge Díaz Serrano, director of PEMEX, the national oil monopoly. "For the first time since the mining glory of the colonial years," he was wont to say, "Mexico, because of its oil, could plot its own destiny."

Briefly, the conservationists appeared to predominate. Mexico, the official slogans proclaimed, would pump just enough petroleum to satisfy national needs, extracting daily a mere 1.1 million barrels. Revenues from petroleum would be used to promote an export-oriented industrial economy to substitute for the old import-substitution one, mostly unworkable, it was acknowledged, because of the high cost of machinery and technology. Eventually, Mexico would export manufactured goods and petrochemical products and thus avoid reliance on sales of unrefined oil. When the benefits of the oil boom and the resulting industrialization "trickled down" to workers and campesinos, an internal market would develop.

Facts, however, are stubborn things, and they have to be reckoned with. The euphoria of the oil bonanza quickly cast a pall on the celebration of the conservationists. Between 1977 and 1981, exports of petroleum multiplied fourteenfold. The explanation for the flip-flop was labyrinthine. Given its high price on the world market, oil was profitable to peddle. The rich, industrial nations clamored for it; the United States, for instance, saw Mexican oil as a means to reduce its dependency on OPEC and the unpredictable Arabs. But drilling oil, as well as storing and transporting it to foreign markets, required expensive equipment and technology, generally from the United States, calling for payments in dollars. To pay for updating and expanding the oil industry, so that it might produce more, to cite the convoluted logic, it was necessary to sell oil in order to finance its production. Naturally, PEMEX started to buy expensive equipment, its cost overrunning profits from exports of crude oil, a dilemma worsened by the requirements of industrialization. To make up the deficit, Mexico borrowed from foreign bankers, who were eager to lend money on the asumption that oil-rich Mexico was a sound investment. When the bankers fell over each other in their haste to extend loans, the austerity formula of the IMF was shelved. Not quite $30 billion in 1977, Mexico's foreign indebtedness had risen to $72 billion by 1981.

Still, with money pouring in and oil exports on the rise, Mexico enjoyed prosperity. The rate of growth of the GNP climbed to a fantastic 8.2 percent. The bonanza, in the words of a reporter for the *New York Times,* unveiled a "fiesta of borrowing and spending," with PEMEX alone running up a bill of $15.7 billion in 1981. Some of the money was used to construct a natural-gas pipeline to the north, oil refineries, and petrochemical plants, which pumped life into the moribund steel industry and brought ecstasy to the souls of salesmen of heavy equipment. Foreign funds, only partly repaid with oil profits, rejuvenated the country's electrical output, added roads and airports, and inaugurated chichi tourist meccas in Yucatán and on the Pacific. In an endeavor to make Mexico self-sufficient in grains, primarily corn and wheat, billions of pesos were plowed into an agricultural program known by its acronym, SAM.

Capitalists, both Mexicans and foreigners, jumped on the bandwagon. With Ford, General Motors, and Chrysler in the forefront, they expanded their operations. Foreign investment, amounting to $3.7 billion in 1970, was $10.7 billion by 1982. When Mexican capitalists exhausted their money, they, too, rushed to foreign bankers, ready to bestow loans on factory owners with booming sales and rising profits. Alfa, the huge conglomerate in Monterrey, which had been organized in 1947, went on a buying spree, acquiring HYLSA steel, plants manufacturing electrical appliances and auto parts and processing food, as well as tourist spots and urban real estate. Spending money lent by foreigners, Alfa mushroomed into the biggest private corporation in Latin

America. Bernardo Garza Sada, scion of the venerable Monterrey clan and lord of Alfa, flew his executives about, often graduates of Caltech and MIT, in private jets, paid them handsomely, and had "a direct line to the president of the Republic." The bonanza, claimed Garza Sada, was here to stay.

Clouds, nevertheless, darkened the horizon. Rather than loosen Mexico's ties to the United States, oil cemented them more; to pump its oil, Mexico turned for help to its neighbor, buying from it the bulk of its equipment and, ominously, selling it 80 percent of its oil and 94 percent of it natural gas. More disturbing, oil sales represented 75 percent of all exports by 1982, which testified to the failure of manufacturing and agriculture to keep pace. As this occurred, massive imports of manufacturing articles and food followed, dictating further foreign borrowing to pay for them. While the value of exports reached $19.4 billion in 1981, the cost of imports was $23.9 billion. To plug the gap in the balance of trade and to pay the interest and principal on the burgeoning foreign debt required additional exports of oil. No one in government gave any thought to augmenting taxes on the rich in order to reduce the deficit.

Instead, trying to spur the oil boom, officials spent money Mexico did not have, borrowing and printing paper pesos. With scarce goods and food but plenty of money to go around, prices leaped upward, firing inflation again. Growth at any cost, the motto of the establishment, once more undercut the value of the peso and, consequently, its buying power. Meanwhile, PEMEX, in its eagerness to drill wells, lay out pipelines, and build storage tanks, upset the ecology of Tabasco, to the anger of thousands of campesinos who saw fertile lands rendered useless.

Graft and corruption, as may be expected, lived high on the hog in both government and business. The *mordida,* or bribe, was an exalted national institution, the size of its bite fixed by what had to be done and the nature of the government or business employee one dealt with. Corruption, to quote one reporter, was "an ingredient of doing business." Though vocally critical of corruption in politics, those in the private sector, too, evaded paying taxes, practiced price gouging, speculated freely, and hoarded. To reap big profits, factory owners sold shoddy goods and bribed government inspectors to "overlook violations of health, labor, and environmental standards." To Manuel Buendía, a crusading journalist of note, one of the nests of skulduggery was PEMEX, whose chief, Díaz Serrano, absconded with $34 million, his share from the purchase of two oil tankers. Buendía was shot to death on the streets of Mexico City, a fate shared by over thirty newspaper reporters during the regime of De la Madrid.

Then, suddenly, in 1982, catastrophe struck. A world depression, the likes of which had not been seen since the great crash of 1929, set in, turning upside down the capitalist economies of the United States and Western Europe. The crisis reduced demand for Mexican exports, cutting the price of raw materials and mineral ores. Exports dropped off while rampant inflation rode majestically in the saddle. As this developed, Mexico's foreign debt multiplied eightfold, far beyond its capacity to pay.

An oil glut was partialy responsible for the world depression. With less demand for oil, its price collapsed, leading to a loss of billions of dollars in revenue for Mexico. Fighting to protect its share of the American market, Mexico lowered the price of its oil, violating the silent accord with OPEC producers. That bit of opportunism soiled Mexico's honor. When revenues from oil sales and exports shriveled up, and Mexico could not meet its payments on the foreign debt, the collapse of confidence in its economy led to drastic cutbacks in investments, both foreign and Mexican, and to more capital flight. The Mexican rich either stored their money in foreign banks or purchased real estate, usually in the sunbelt across the border. In Texas, alone, Mexicans invested in real estate or bank savings $24.4 billion between 1976 and 1981. Politicians, from cabinet dignitaries to state governors, as well as bankers, did this. Billions more ended up in dollar currency accounts at home. Compounding the disaster were the spending habits of the middle class, which squandered its money on autos, television sets, and stereos, often as a hedge against inflation.

To reduce the deficit and to increase exports of oil, a step required by its drop in price, and to pay for imports of grains, needed to provide basic staples at lower prices, the government spent what little money it had in reserve, obtained, ironically, from banks abroad. The lenders, in the meantime, frightened by the Mexican debacle, stopped offering loans or raised interest rates. As money fled Mexico, authorities devalued the peso again in February 1982, despite a public oath by López Portillo to defend it "like a dog." After the devaluation, the peso plummeted from 26 to 45 to the dollar, a development that sparked more inflation. When this occurred, industrial labor demanded more money, and employers, to compensate for the added cost of higher wages and imported machinery, as well as to maintain profits, doubled the prices of their manufacturers. Big industry, much of it foreign, survived the devaluation crisis, but countless smaller Mexican firms went under. Devaluation hurt even big Mexican corporations—Alfa for one, which, unable to pay its foreign creditors, had to sell off half of its assets, mainly to foreigners, and to dismiss one-fifth of its workers.

That was just the tip of the iceberg. Overnight the foreign debt, measured in pesos, almost doubled, multiplying the expense of paying it off. By the summer of 1982, Mexico was bankrupt. Searching for a way out of its predicament, Jesús Silva Herzog, secretary of finance, journeyed to Washington and New York, hat in hand. After much haggling, the International Monetary Fund put together a rescue package of $4 billion, and the opportunity for

Mexicans to negotiate $4 billion more. Private banks conceded Mexico a three months' reprieve from paying on the principal of the money owed to them. The Mexicans, in return, agreed to sell, at "favorable prices," the bulk of their oil and natural gas to Americans.

Mexico was not yet out of the woods. Frightened by the dimensions of the debacle, well-heeled Mexicans again rushed to put their money in foreign banks. The resulting capital flight threatened to sabotage efforts to overcome the crisis. Clearly, dramatic measures were called for. So, just three months before departing from the National Palace, López Portillo nationalized the Republic's banks, setting up two exchange rates for the peso—one for the purchase of imported goods by business and another, less favorable, for the public. By this decree, the politicos had endeavored to assert a measure of control over private capital but, as subsequent decisions revealed, only temporarily.

For all the spectacular headlines, the recipes prescribed for Mexico's ills were palliatives. None got to the heart of the problems. Capitalist Mexico, it was clear, would be denied balanced economic growth until it developed a vigorous productive capacity and, similarly, a national market sufficiently big to encourage investment. The inability to meet obligations on the foreign debt merely highlighted industry's failure to compete with imported manufactures and agriculture's doldrums, which led to dependency on foreign funds to shore up the economy and assure political stability.

However, market economics, which establishment Mexicans endorsed and the IMF formula prescribed, had not been discarded by the bank nationalization. Authorities evinced no wish to run the banks or to acquire private firms mortgaged to them. The austerity imposed by the IMF was more in keeping with official opinion and the proclivities of businessmen, powerful in political circles. In the initial months of De la Madrid's regime, officials, troubled by doubts, sold off 34 percent of the shares of the banks to private buyers, some of them foreigners. Included in the sale were 339 out of the 467 enterprises held by the banks. In 1990, the political gurus in Mexico City put the country's banks on the market; the most likely buyers included the families that had controlled them before their nationalization, along with powerful industrial conglomerates, brokerage houses, and insurance firms. Authorities had also loosened foreign-exchange controls, accepting one floating rate for the peso, and discarded price controls on 4,700 items thought nonessential.

That done, Mexican officials went back again to the IMF. By the terms of this accord, which the IMF dictated, Mexico renegotiated its financial burden, which put off temporarily the obligation to start repayment immediately of $23 billion. At this juncture, the payment on interest alone was consuming over two-thirds of Mexico's oil revenue. Once more, government spending would be curbed drastically and a 15 percent sales tax (IVA) levied—but, tellingly, just 20 percent on luxury items. Wages would be held in check but price controls abandoned, on the assumption that market forces would prevent them from rising exorbitantly.

But the "hard times," which De la Madrid warned lay ahead, led promptly to increases in the price of gasoline, electricity, telephones, water, and, worse yet, tortillas, beans, eggs, milk, sugar, and soap. Buffeted by inflation, the per capita income of the poor dropped by over 50 percent, the burden of "belt tightening" falling mainly on them. In the countryside, the shortage of government funds for credit, seldom bountiful since the days of the Cardenistas, cut into the harvests of campesinos and, similarly, led to the liquidation of SAM, the agricultural program. The urban middle class, too, caught between frozen salaries and rising prices, increasingly felt the economic pinch.

In the meantime, officials set about modifying priorities. Disciples of neoliberal economics, they had little use for state-funded enterprises, such as the steel *paraestatal,* formerly justified under the then popular theory of the need for import substitution. No longer was it necessary to rely on state intervention to build up fledgling industries and to protect them from foreign competition. From then on, government had to balance the budget, encourage exports, invite the latest technology, and improve productivity. The oligarchy, too, was counting on foreign investment and access to international markets to end the economic crisis, a free-enterprise approach which entailed asking Mexico to offer cheap labor, raw materials, services, and tourism in exchange for capital goods, manufactured articles, grains, credit, and dollars.

Above all, contemporary Mexican regimes were staking, as never before, their fate on the economic and political support of the United States, subordinating Mexico's national interests to North American preferences. This was so even when compared with the behavior of the Callistas during the late 1920s. Heady flows of American public and private capital, according to the accepted wisdom, would keep the Mexican political ship afloat, giving officials in Mexico time to neutralize popular rumblings of discontent and to buy off the country's middle class, which seldom spent much time worrying about the plight of the poor.

On that assumption, officials put on sale multiple *paraestatales,* among them steel, airlines, telephones, and the mines of Cananea, where, before dawn on August 2, 1989, soldiers evicted the night shift at gunpoint and occupied the copper bastion, a national symbol of the Revolution of 1910. More than half of the 1,115 *paraestatales* had been sold by 1990; most of them, such as Teléfonos de México, had been showing a profit. They were the only ones private investors would buy. Henceforth, the ability of Mexican industries to compete on the international market would determine whether they survived or perished. The devaluation of the peso, which sought to make Mexican exports more attractive on world markets, would hold down imports of consumer goods by putting their price out of reach of the middle class.

Somehow forgotten by these high priests of "privatization," the current term for the old slogan "The best government is the one that governs least," was that state intervention in Mexico, certainly until now, had been the sole formula which had paved the way for the development of an infrastructure, for industrialization, an export agriculture, and whatever had been done to lessen the terrible maldistribution of income and wealth. This had been true since the days of Porfirio Díaz, when the developmentalist state, albeit timidly, started to play a role. That, too, was what the so-called Revolution of 1910 was all about. In a society as diverse, skewed, and complex as Mexico's, the only unifying force was the state. The issue, therefore, was not whether to weaken the state but, to cite one Mexican observer, how to make its intervention in the economy, politics, and social matters "truly democratic. It cannot, and should not be, shrunk into oblivion." To do so would cripple the economy and leave the majority of the nation at the mercy of a *burguesía* that had yet to demonstrate that its leadership could be of benefit to everyone.

Facts and expectations, moreover, are not always identical. By 1990, for example, the floating peso, which devaluation entailed, stood at over 2,800 to the dollar but imports had skyrocketed; purchases abroad rose 57 percent in 1988 and nearly 30 percent in 1989, while the economy vegetated. By contrast, exports increased by a mere 15 percent in 1989, and half of that growth represented a temporary rise in oil prices; exports of nonpetroleum products rose by only 8 percent. At the end of 1989, the trade deficit was $3.5 billion, the highest since 1981. For nearly a decade, the internal market had been either stagnating or shrinking. Clearly, reliance on exports, a formula as old as the Republic, had drawbacks. Not only had the Western nations erected barriers to shield their industries, but, at the same time, the entire Third World competed for a slice of the pie, convinced, as Mexico was, that exports implied salvation. That led to glutted world markets and the lowest commodity prices in half a century.

Nothing had been done, moreover, to encourage investment in the infrastructure, or in capital goods and retooling, which proved disappointingly low. Despite the neoliberal tonic, foreign investment stayed home, the net flow during much of 1989 down 45 percent from the previous year. With Eastern Europe rushing to enter the international capitalist economy in 1990, the prospects for greater foreign investments in Mexico appeared even dimmer.

Yet, earlier, to stimulate foreign investment, officials in Mexico City, complying with the demands of the IMF, had waived the 51 percent requirement for Mexican majority rule in thirty-four priority sectors, formerly closed to foreigners. They included telecommunications, computers, advanced technological equipment, industrial machinery, and hotels, which played into the hands of the transnational cartels and strengthened bonds between the Mexican economy and the highly industrialized nations, the suppliers of costly technology. Even so, little was done to develop the dilatory capital-goods industry. For this and other reasons, industrial output barely grew.

Perennial headaches, for all that, did not vanish. The foreign debt topped the list. The rescue package of 1982 merely saved Mexico from going over the brink. Debt renegotiation, for the same reasons, became the watchword, new agreements being signed in 1983, 1984, and 1985. The debt now stood at $102 billion, and yearly payments ran from $12 billion to $16 billion, down, incidentally, from $20 billion during the era of petroleum. Mexico was spending over half of its national budget on debt interest. To no one's astonishment, Mexico, in the fall of 1988, welcomed yet another $3.5 billion from Washington, earmarked to pay the interest on money due banks.

Austerity cost Mexico dearly. At the behest of the IMF, spending on social services, already among the lowest in Latin America, was slashed and food subsidies eliminated. Malnutrition, disease, and illiteracy were widespread. The draconian measures, however, brought inflation under control. The goal was to right Mexico's balance of payments and stabilize the economy, not the welfare of the indigent. Still, as the value of the peso declined, the well-off, in their customary manner, shipped their money out of Mexico, worsening its payment deficit. No less real were the skewed prices for food, clothing, and other staples, the results of free-market blueprints and the lagging output of industry and agriculture.

Just the same, nothing was done to change the "fast buck" mentality of Mexico's business community. Hiding behind the federal umbrella, it looked for easy profits from the captive domestic market, while fostering a chronic trade deficit with its imports of machinery, technology, and raw materials. So long as the giant transnationals did not cut into their share of the market, Mexican businessmen were willing to live and let live. Antagonistic to any form of government regulation, they, nevertheless, lobbied constantly for subsidies, special tariffs, loans, and the like. The top industrial, financial, and commercial magnates, the soul of the Businessmen's Council, had a pipeline to high Mexican officials, the president being one of them.

Dependency on foreign capital was also a trait of private enterprise. The Grupo Alfa, referred to often as an example of successful national capital, had, all the same, ended up bankrupt. In October 1986, Mexicans learned that foreign banks, mostly American, had acquired virtually half of Alfa. Bernardo Garza Sada, whose family patriarchs had defied Lázaro Cárdenas, acknowledged that Alfa "owed more than it was worth," having spent, in its haste to expand, more than it should have by borrowing from foreign bankers. With the crash of 1982, and the failure of the Mexican stock market, Alfa collapsed, owing more than $2.3 billion. When government loans failed to prop it up, the value of its shares dropped from 300 pesos to 25 pesos.

V

Given this somber scene, labor, too, fared poorly. Briefly, however, the early 1970s augured well. With prices, more or less, holding firm, real wages stayed even and job openings grew by 3.2 percent. That started to change with the economic downturn of the early 1970s when the cost of raw materials went up, reducing profits of industrialists. Unable to increase productivity, they raised prices, and labor, lacking bargaining clout, could merely look on.

The flurry of prosperity of the late seventies did not improve labor's lot. The oil boom fed the fires of inflation, and workers bore the brunt of it. Between 1976 and 1989, wages dropped by 60 percent; the bottom of the labor pyramid had less than 40 percent of its buying power in 1939. The average factory wage was among the lowest in the world, below that of Singapore, South Korea, and Hong Kong. The much hailed "solidarity pacts," the first of them in December 1987, which were designed to freeze wages and prices and which were signed by the big labor unions and business, yielded political dividends but punished workers. There was more of a freeze on wages than on prices.

After the debacle of 1982, and the shrinkage of the urban, middle-class market, industry cut production or shut its doors, and unemployment got worse. Most of the one million new workers who each year appeared on the labor scene found no jobs; by 1989, over eight million workers were idle or underemployed, statistics placing Mexico among the countries of the world with the most appalling rates of unemployment. Among the cities hardest hit were Mexico City and Monterrey, citadels of industry. Especially victimized were those who were twenty to thirty years of age. Calloused politicos and profit-hungry businessmen came to accept high rates of the jobless as inevitable.

The marvels of science, which the sins of monopoly complicated, aggravated the plight of the worker. Technology, upon which the big industries relied, added to the jobless rolls. By 1986, to illustrate, the automobile industry, a monopoly of the transnationals, had laid off 25,000 workers; steel, also in the throes of modernization, dismissed another 20,000. The giants, about 5 percent of the total, which monopolized 80 percent of the sales, employed only 40 percent of the workers. As the buying power of labor slid downward, its standard of living, to cite the economist Efigenia Martínez, had declined by 40 percent.

The labor unions, in the meantime, languished in disrepute. Fidel Velázquez, the leader who had backed every PRI candidate, was almost a puppet of government and industry. The chief of the Congreso del Trabajo, the national umbrella for labor, was named by Velázquez, who picked him from among his *charros.* In exchange for their loyalty, the government backed Fidel and his unions, conceding, occasionally, wage hikes, never, however, sufficient to match the cost of living. The beneficiaries were in the industrial world, about a third of the work force of twenty million. In gratitude, Velázquez and his "aristocracy of labor" conferred tranquillity on the industrial scene. If perchance a labor leader proved recalcitrant, employers bought him off, preferring that to granting a wage increase to the rank and file.

Corruption afflicted the labor pyramid from top to bottom. In the Sindicato de Petroleros, the labor union of PEMEX, the caciques cheated and swindled. Outlasting presidents and directors of PEMEX, they bought politicos who blocked their path or, if necessary, had them killed. PRI officials, on the other hand, counted on them to keep the workers in line. Chief among the labor bosses was La Quiña, Joaquín Hernández Galicia, son of an oil worker and former welder who, with the benediction of Adolfo López Mateos, became the *charro* of Local 1 and secretary general of the Sindicato in 1962. Hernández Galicia also spent millions of pesos on housing and medical care and subsidized food stores for PEMEX workers. When politicos in Mexico City finally ousted him in 1989, they replaced him with an obedient *charro.*

VI

The marginalization of agriculture, a phenomenon of the years since the fifties, had taken its toll. Outside of the Yaqui Valley, the Fuerte in Sinaloa, and one or two other entrepôts, agriculture atrophied. The annual growth in production, which lagged behind the population explosion, was less than 1 percent by 1990, while the value of its yield declined precipitously. Aside from tomatoes from the northwest and frozen broccoli and cauliflower from the central zone, the saga of export agriculture was a sorry one.

Land reform, the promise of the charter of 1917, was no more. All but 15 percent of the land distributed between 1952 and 1982 was either "too dry, too rocky, or too eroded for farming." Even then, little correlation existed between statistics for land distribution and the reality; the regimes of López Mateos and Gustavo Díaz Ordaz, for instance, claimed to have handed out 25.3 million hectares of land but, actually, delivered less than 7 million, most of it unsuitable for farming. The Echeverristas, dedicated to restoring a semblance of social justice, did better, distributing 6.5 million hectares. About 36,000 were in the Yaqui Valley, lands seized just eleven days before Echeverría left office. The López Portillo regime restored most of them to their old owners.

The Echeverristas, however, were hardly agrarian revolutionaries. What they proffered with one hand, they took back with the other, dealing with rural unrest in the time-honored fashion. Soldiers with rifles killed Genaro Vázquez Rojas and Lucio Cabañas, schoolteachers turned land reformers. When necessary, "family and friends were captured, tortured, and killed"; by 1978, four hundred people, campesinos and their sympathizers, had vanished.

The administrations of López Portillo and De la Madrid, neither a crusader for social justice, laid to rest the agrarian ideal. López Portillo also wanted to wipe clean the slate of pending executive decrees; so he gave away 15.7 million hectares of land, nearly all unfit for farming. De la Madrid's administration, which called a halt to land reform, proclaimed there was no more left to subdivide and its faith in the sanctity of private property. Congress, furthermore, amended the Republic's agrarian legislation in 1983, leaving responsibility for land reform in the laps of state governors. Though millions of campesinos still begged for land, the legislation sailed through Congress in just one day.

Over seventy years after the installation of the charter of 1917, statistics scarcely bore out Mexico's claim to have undergone a revolution for agrarian justice. Its irrigated lands were mostly in private hands, yielding over 70 percent of the national harvest. The rest of the farmlands, what campesinos tilled, produced mainly corn and beans for consumption by the people who lived on them. With few exceptions, the thirty million campesinos, twice the population of the Republic in 1910, lived in abject poverty. Some 3 percent of the land barons owned 84 percent of all rural property, land safe from expropriation.

Campesinos confronted a bleak future. Landless or, at best, living on poor lands, they survived by their wits. *Minifundistas,* campesinos with plots of land of five hectares or less, represented approximately 86 percent of the rural units. In Chiapas, an extreme case, where just 1 percent of the landlords possessed 45 percent of the land, over a third of its farmers owned a mere 1 percent of its soil. Chamulas and Tzotziles, Indian *jornaleros* who labored on the coffee and cotton plantations of Chiapas, earned less than the equivalent of one dollar per day. Maya campesinos in Yucatán eked out a living by tilling their milpas of corn or harvesting henequen for sale to the government. Of the five million *jornaleros* in the Republic's countryside, about three-fourths labored for under the minimum wage ($4 a day), denied the benefits of Article 123. In the state of Mexico, a not untypical case, campesinos lived on $200 a year, hiring their labor out when the opportunity presented itself. Corn occupied nearly 80 percent of the land planted, yet its campesinos could count on just one crop each year, never knowing when a cold spell might destroy it. More and more campesinos fled the countryside, flocking to the cities and, the more daring, to the United States.

The plight of the *ejidatario* was perhaps worse. Of the 28,000 ejidos, over

83 percent had only marginal, largely unproductive lands, rarely sufficient for them to keep body and soul together. Faced with this reality, ejidatarios abandoned them in droves. For instance, in Jojutla, Morelos, a place on the map not far from Anenecuilco, birthplace of Emiliano Zapata, only five of its forty-five *ejidatarios* remained; the others had gone off to the United States, to quote one of those who stayed behind, "in search of food." In Zamora, Michoacán, the strawberry capital of Mexico, 85 percent of the crop was grown on ejido lands, but only 15 percent of the *ejidatarios* cultivated their own *parcelas;* the others rented them out to American corporations. Under 40 percent of the ejidos had access to credit from the Banco de Crédito Rural (Banrural), the new bank run by a bloated bureaucracy of 38,000 employees.

Shortages of corn and wheat, too, afflicted Mexico. A perennial feature of Mexican life, shortages had grown acute during the 1980s. Increasingly, Mexico imported its food staples. One reason for this alarming development was that bigger profits awaited producers of sorghum and sunflower seeds, to mention just two. The implications of this turn of events were disastrous; in Jalisco, which produced 30 percent of the Republic's corn, shortages were commonplace, as less and less of the land was planted to it. Even for *ejidatarios* in Jalisco, who formerly cultivated corn, selling sorghum to Anderson Clayton, one of the transnationals, which transformed it into animal feed, was more profitable, a change spurred by the rising demand of the well-off for meat, bacon, ham, milk, and cheese.

VII

Nor were these fruitful days for Mexico's much extolled, "independent" foreign policy, what with a gross national product just 3.7 percent that of its next-door neighbor. A pygmy sat on the steps of the giant. Yearly, millions of its citizens trekked north in quest of work, mostly to the American southwest; by 1989, perhaps six million of them had illegally entered the United States, baptized "undocumented workers" by their fellow countrymen. An attempt by Mexico to regulate foreign investment in 1973 survived only briefly. Between 1910 and 1942, Mexican presidents had met with their American counterparts two times. After that, visits became commonplace. Survival, Mexican officials declared, required close ties with the United States. An independent foreign policy was one of the victims.

For domestic consumption, official Mexico put on a brave front. Until 1970, little upset the friendly relations between Mexico and the United States. Mexican poverty, unemployment, and social inequality, after all, worried Washington not a bit. The Echeverristas, who embarked on a mild program of reforms, temporarily modified the nature of Mexican foreign policy. Trying to expand commercial markets, Mexican architects, in time-honored tradition, also wanted to distract "public opinion from domestic troubles." This, however, occurred only after Washington rebuffed Mexican efforts to exempt their goods from the 10 percent surtax on imports. While making certain not to upset the applecart with the colossus next door, the Echeverristas started courting other foreign countries, with the president visiting thirty-six of them. The goal, wrote one scholar, was "to diversify Mexico's commercial ... partners in order to stimulate its industry and lessen its dependence on the United States."

The results were mixed. On the one hand, Mexico failed to alter its commercial dependency on the United States; to the contrary, it got worse. By 1975, Mexico had a trade deficit of one billion dollars. That was probably inevitable, since Mexico's commercial welfare rested on markets to the north. Yet trade between the two countries was but 5 percent of the total of United States's foreign commerce. However, the Echeverristas, collaborating with Venezuela, gained Latin American endorsement for the Latin American Economic System and later won agreements from the European Economic Community. Mexico even submitted to the United Nations the Charter of Economic Rights and Duties of States, which its General Assembly approved but Washington ignored.

Mexico also sought to distance itself from Washington's diplomacy. In 1973, when Washington backed a military coup against Salvador Allende's reform regime in Chile, Mexico balked, offering refuge to its ousted politicians and intellectuals. A year later, nonetheless, Mexico had to eat crow, promising to reopen diplomatic relations with Chile. Another embarrassment followed when Mexico, voting with the majority in the United Nations, approved a resolution defining Zionism as racism. The resulting outcry of American Jews and their tourist boycott of Mexico compelled it to retract its vote. For all that, President Echeverría dared to visit Cuba and give Fidel Castro, anathema to Washington, an *abrazo.* In 1978, Castro visited Mexico, but a wary López Portillo, fearful of the popular acclaim the Cuban might receive in Mexico City, saw him in Cozumel, an island off the coast of Yucatán.

Afterward, Mexico turned its attention to Central America, where dissidents menaced a status quo dear to Washington. In 1978, during the oil boom, Mexico broke relations with Anastasio Somoza's dictatorship in Nicaragua, conferring its blessings on the Sandinista rebels. When they toppled the tyrant, Mexico, partly to nullify Cuban influence, offered them economic and technical assistance, including the sale of oil at reduced prices. For a time, Mexico toyed with the idea of thwarting Washington's aims in El Salvador, joining hands with France in 1981 to denounce human rights violations by the military, intent upon squashing a popular uprising. A year later, President López Portillo paid a visit to Nicaragua, where, to the applause of its populace, he compared its revolution to Mexico's.

The economic calamity of 1982 changed that. After all, how could a bankrupt Mexico oppose Washington's designs? Yet, for a time, Mexico, now a partner of Contadora, a coalition with Venezuela, Colombia, and Panama, attempted to promote an end to the fighting in Central America. The United States, nevertheless, while lauding publicly the plan, sabotaged it, organizing and equipping mercenaries, mostly former Somocistas, to overthrow the Sandinistas, simultaneously converting Honduras into a base of military operations and siding with the right-wing regime in El Salvador. Mexico's independent foreign policy, a goal of the Great Rebellion, had died on the rocks of hard times, opportunism, and Yankee intransigence. In 1986, De la Madrid's annual *informe* to Congress said not a word about United States intervention in Central America.

Nothing better illustrates Mexico's diplomatic fortunes than its about-face on GATT. During the bonanza era, Mexico, rejecting pressure from Washington, had refused steadfastly to join GATT, a trade accord sponsored by ninety-one countries under the leadership of the United States. Saying that GATT, which called for the elimination of tariff barriers, would damage national industry and jeopardize jobs, Mexico had gone its own way. By 1986, however, Mexican officials whistled a different tune and embraced GATT (General Agreement on Trade and Tariffs), bowing to the wishes of the International Monetary Fund and opening wider the door to imports. Additionally, by 1990, plans were afoot for Mexico to join the common market of the United States and Canada, which, according to one caustic Mexican dissenter, was "the deal to give away the store." Mexican industries, which relied on protected markets to survive, would have to learn to swim or sink.

24

EPILOGUE

I

Marx wrote that history tends to repeat itself, coming the first time as tragedy and the second time as farce. That, perhaps, best describes the trajectory of Mexico since Independence, particularly with the unmitigated return to fashion of Porfirista economic dogmas, now baptized neoliberal. Certainly, it evokes the contorted thinking of officials in the United States who deal in foreign aid and refer to the world's poor, the condition of most Mexicans, as living in a "developing" country, an Orwellian term employed to describe a global spread of diverse nations united by a common history of dependency and dashed hopes.

In Mexico, nonetheless, after decades of loose talk about miracles and "takeoffs" just around the corner into the industrial prosperity of a free-market economy, poverty, as in the rest of the "developing" world, is just as pervasive as ever. Between the "wretched of this earth," the reality of Mexico, and the well-off, the distribution of wealth is more unequal now than before. In some circles of affluent foreigners, according to one American pundit, it is now fashionable to write off countries like Mexico as "basket cases."

Whether or not that is a figment of their imagination, some truths are clear. "Developing," as applied to Mexico by orthodox economists, is a fairy tale. Dependent capitalism, a formula as old as the Republic, is bankrupt. No matter what its apostles may say, it has failed to provide the Mexican masses with a decorous and just standard of living. Social justice is a stranger in today's Mexico. What this old panacea of the nineteenth century has accomplished is to to place the majority of Mexicans at the beck and call of an opportunistic few, both natives and foreigners. Class divisions are ubiquitous.

Still, the Mexico on the brink of the twenty-first century is a far cry from the country that embarked on its Independence. Unlike the disparate array of people of Agustín de Iturbide's empire, modern Mexico is a nation. Although paying lip service to local loyalties and idiosyncrasies, its citizens know they are Mexicans and they exhibit a growing pride in that. Mostly mestizos, they form a racial melting pot, no longer either Indian or Spanish. For all that, the top of the pyramid is far lighter of color than its base.

However, the Indian, the symbolic descendant of the pre-Columbian inhabitants of ancient Anáhuac, both as a cultural phenomenon and as a person, lives on; there are now more of them, in fact, than there were at the time of Father Miguel Hidalgo's Grito de Dolores. Though a much smaller fraction of the total population, as many as twelve million Indians dwelt in the land of their ancient ancestors, including Nahuas (kin of the Aztecs), Maya, Yaquis, Mixtecs, and Zapotecs, who, as in Oaxaca and Yucatán, stamped their imprint on whole regions. Representing over fifty ethnic groups, they spoke more than a hundred languages and dialects. Laws inscribed on the statute books by Spanish bureaucrats in 1770, which banned the use of Indian languages, had simply failed. Marginalized, living in dire poverty, and cut off from the other Mexico, the Indian, as always, relied on his native tongues, his family and community, to defend himself from the exploiter. Since the days of Lázaro Cárdenas, *indigenismo,* the glorification of the Indian and his past, had wasted away, despite a short-lived revival during the 1970s. Views on what constituted the national heritage had shifted, so much so that José López Portillo, enthralled with ancestor worship, took special pride in his Spanish forebears, once making a pilgrimage to their native village in Spain.

Mexico's population had exploded. In 1990, Mexico had close to ninety million inhabitants. Better health care, especially massive vaccination campaigns against smallpox and sundry diseases, were mostly responsible for this upward surge. The Catholic church's stance against the use of artificial birth control methods exacerbated the problem. Over half of all Mexicans were under twenty years of age. The demographic explosion, the experts predicted, augured ill, if the Republic's architects took its consequences seriously. There were more people to feed, clothe, and educate and to find jobs for.

One of the features of modern Mexico was rapid urbanization. Mexico City, the biggest metropolis in the world, alone accounted for nineteen million *chilangos,* so baptized by their sisters and brothers in the rest of the Republic, their numbers swelled daily by the influx of countless campesinos who, destitute and hungry, traded villages for urban living. Guadalajara and Monterrey, a jump behind, had four million residents apiece, while Tijuana and Ciudad Juárez, once small, dusty border towns, had each over a million inhabitants. Mexico City was a megalopolis polluted by 35,000 industrial installations, the big ones owned by foreigners, and three million automobiles belching 5.5 million tons of poison into the air, rendering breathing difficult and the survival of foliage doubtful. Half of all infants had unacceptable toxic levels in their blood, which, medical researchers warned, would reduce IQs by as much as 10 percent. When that occurred, one-fifth of the city's dwellers would have IQs below eighty, a mental retardation of sorts.

Mexico was a land of contrasts. More Mexicans could read and write than formerly; over 60 percent of all Mexicans were literate; just 15 percent of them completely illiterate. Yet the reverse was also true; there were more illiterates than ever before. Many Mexicans were better off; but the gap between rich and poor widened every day. Along with Brazil, Mexico had enjoyed the highest rates of economic growth in Latin America; both, nonetheless, had the most skewed distribution of income and wealth. The top 20 percent of Mexicans monopolized nearly 55 percent of the national income; the wealthiest 5 percent, 36 percent; the bottom 50 percent had to make do with just 16 percent. The upper and middle classes shared 73 percent of Mexico's income.

Life for the poor was niggardly. In the cities, they lived in slums, cut off from the splendors of the affluent *colonias;* when lucky, they occupied tiny apartments or, if not, huts and shacks just off the highway. In Mexico City, the worst off lived in caves; in Tijuana, in tin and plyboard shacks clinging to barren hillsides. Jacales in the villages had not changed in centuries. Nationally, two out of three Mexicans endured "blatantly unsatisfactory" housing. López Portillo had put the plight of the poor well. "If I could make an appeal to the dispossessed and marginalized," he told his listeners, "it would be for forgiveness for not lifting them out of their misery."

The miracle, so lauded by its admirers, had not shielded millions of Mexicans from the ravages of malnutrition. The diet of two-thirds of all Mexicans stopped short of the required minimum 2,000 calories per day; a mere one-fifth of all Mexicans ate well. Nearly five million youngsters under the age of fifteen had never tasted milk. By 1989, according to a poll of the *Los Angeles Times,* 69 percent of the children of the poor endured hunger sometimes. At the same time, more and more Mexicans, victimized by cheap and misleading advertising, preferred to buy packaged foods sold by the transnationals, much of it "junk food." After Americans, Mexicans drank more Coca-Cola and Pepsi-Cola than any other people in the world. However, just one-fourth of the rural children four years old or less, and just 40 percent of them in cities, were of normal height and weight.

The so-called safety net for society, never extensive, had gaping holes. While better than the notion of private charity, so dear to the hearts of Porfiristas, the federal effort lagged. Only twenty-two million Mexicans were covered by social security, the vast majority of them urbanites. Medical care, plainly, had excluded millions from its benefits, especially in the countryside. CONASUPO (Basic Foods Corporation), established in 1961, subsidized food and clothing for the poor; austerity had cut its budget dramatically. In the 1970s, INFONAVIT had helped pay for housing for unionized workers, while COPLAMAR briefly endeavored to aid the marginalized. For the three million bureaucrats, there were job security, yearly bonuses, and stores selling underpriced food, clothes, and other items. All the same, these programs took in a minority of the population.

More Mexicans lived in cities than in the countryside. Similarly, Mexico had a substantial middle class, the inhabitants of the cities, who could be found from Tijuana to Mérida, a city in Yucatán known for its hot sun and glistening white walls. Urbanites in the Latin American manner, they were, at one and the same time, profoundly traditional. Not all was sweetness and light for urbanites; crime, for one, was on the rise, because hard times had left millions jobless. For university graduates, the debacle of the eighties had reduced employment opportunities. More than three thousand agronomists, for instance, were unemployed, while physicians, facing dismal prospects, were working at other jobs, particularly in states such as Sonora, glutted by medical doctors. Ironically, though physicians failed to find employment in their chosen profession, 113,000 communities of fewer than five hundred people lacked medical care of any type. The poverty of the rural community, as well as its isolation and cultural backwardness, rarely encouraged doctors to minister to its needs. Each year millions of Mexicans, to escape poverty at home, braved the perils of illegal entry into the United States, willing to endure racial discrimination in exchange for low-paying jobs.

The north, from Tijuana to Matamoros, nevertheless, basked in the glow of an economic boom, with *maquiladoras* a fixture of the economy of nearly every border city. The northern states generated 22 percent of the Republic's gross national product. At the other extreme were Oaxaca, Chiapas, and the southern provinces. The north, however, had become a haven for drug merchants who got rich off markets for marijuana, cocaine, and heroin across the border.

The woes of education were no less dramatic. All but a few students in rural schools dropped out before completing the third grade. On a national average, 54 percent of the children entering primary school never finished. A tiny percentage went on to secondary schools. At the higher echelons, most of the students at the National University were from families with good incomes. Just the same, the Priístas spent proportionately six times less of the federal budget on schooling than had been spent on it in the days of Lázaro Cárdenas. Most of their efforts had gone into transferring responsibility for primary education and teacher training to state governments, mainly to break the hold of the SNTE, the official teachers' union. In the meantime, urban children, many truants from school, either loitered in the streets or sat in front of television sets, over half of them for more than two hours daily; the poorer the families, the more time spent watching, making for, to cite the testimony of Mexican pedagogues, "mental malnutrition."

Another tragedy was playing in the national theater. Its theme, as Daniel

Cosío Villegas, the historian and politco, explained, was the indifference of the *burguesía* toward the poor. Superficially prudent and punctilious but rarely unwilling to boast of its accomplishments, the *burguesía,* said Cosío, had an ugly side. An aficionado of conspicuous consumption, which Thorstein Veblen had berated, it prattled on about the vices of the poor yet rarely raised a finger on their behalf. For these gentlemen and ladies, to cite the opinion of the monarchs of Monterrey, "only individual hard work" generated "well-being." Nor was hypocrisy alien to them; to quote a millionaire governor of Puebla: "yes," he was a rich man but of a "progressive and revolutionary mentality." Mexico's social profile, in short, differed not a bit from that of countries with no claim to a social revolution.

Blessed with money, the *burguesía* converted its lack of a social conscience into a fetish. What women of this class cared about, wrote Guadalupe Loaeza in *Las reinas de Polanco,* was their own pleasure, whether they ate at the Café 58, because it was "in," or met for cocktails in the Zona Rosa of Mexico City. If they could not buy their dresses in Paris or New York, they flew to La Jolla. What mattered, said Loaeza, "was the present, the moment, today, and, above everything else, now." Thinking themselves stylish, these modern "juniors" drank Coca-Cola, Orange Crush, and Seven-Up and avoided, at all cost, having to drive Volkswagen cars. From the ranks of this *burguesía* emerged bankers, industrialists, and politicos, as well as the boyfriends and husbands of the princesses of Polanco.

Just the same, these darlings of Polanco, who could be found in every city of the Republic, were a minority of the women. By and large, Mexican women were a hardworking lot, either in their homes, their traditional site, or, in larger and larger numbers, the marketplace. Perhaps as many as a fourth of them had jobs of one kind or another, a reflection of changing values and, not unimportant, the need for a second income to keep family together during difficult times. For Mexican women, a job also meant independence from a domineering husband, a not uncommon phenomenon in Mexico. One of them expressed it as follows: "Now that I get my own money, I feel better, less short of it because I know how much I have for everything." Before, "I used to ask him for everything." While women still had to marry by twenty years of age or face the likelihood of spinsterhood, more and more of them left their husbands, either by divorce or, if Catholic to the bone, by separation.

Urban life, as the above documents, was altering the lives of urban women. The meek and mild wife and daughter of the middle class was becoming a relic of yesteryear. In Ciudad Chihuahua, for instance, a beauty contest to choose Señorita México for 1987 was canceled abruptly because women, labeling it a "degrading spectacle," organized mass rallies against it. While the Mexican penal code barred abortions except in the case of rape or if the mother's life was in jeopardy, women, particularly of the middle class, not only had them but agitated for a change in the law. In a country where birth control was legalized just in 1973, and where church and machismo ruled the roost, women writers, intellectuals, artists, and politicians were calling for abortion reform. To them, it was a health issue, not a moral one. Secular authorities, argued Amalia García, a *deputy* to Congress from the Partido Socialista Mexicano, rather than "impose a religious point of view" on everyone, should "guarantee the right of women to follow their own conscience."

More women were attending school. On a percentage basis, more women than men completed twelve years of schooling, the *preparatoria* or equivalent. From that point on, however, women lagged; only 1.4 percent of them, compared with 14.3 percent of the men, had sixteen years or more of education. Women seldom wandered far from the traditional roles in education; in teacher-training institutions, to illustrate, they made up 40 percent of the advanced students but less than 1 percent of the enrollments in the professional schools of the universities. At the National University, women were just 12.5 percent of the faculty but nearly 90 percent of the teachers in the primary schools. Women in the provinces fared less well, though they had other escapes. The debacle of 1982 had driven countless young women, many arrived recently from the countryside, into prostitution, a "profession" they employed to feed themselves and their families.

II

Of the ancient institutions, the church lived on and thrived. Elegant churches were still being erected, convents and monasteries existed, and the rich still donated alms. Nothing had been done to jettison the anticlerical legislation on the statute books; in practice church and state ignored it, part and parcel of the modus vivendi. The church had the backing of the Padres de Familia, Familias Cristianas, and Acción Católica. Invariably, PAN and the Partido Democrático Mexicano, as well as Opus Dei, lent their support. The technocrats in government, moreover, rarely displayed any anticlerical feelings; José López Portillo, for one, installed a chapel in Los Pinos, the residence of presidents, while the wife of Miguel de la Madrid, a Catholic faithful, never missed mass and, according to gossip, walked arm and arm with Opus Dei. When prelates turned thumbs down on a proposal to legalize abortion in 1983, it became moot. Earlier, the government had paid for the new basilica of Nuestra Señora de Guadalupe, the shrine of the national Virgen. In 1990, President Carlos Salinas had dispatched a personal representative to the Vatican, thus ending a century of political tradition.

Despite Article 3 of the Constitution of 1917, which banned church involvement, clerics and nuns, living in monasteries and convents prohibited by law, ran schools. Of the 13,000 private schools in Mexico, from kindergarten to college, 30 percent were controlled by the clergy; with 2.6 million students, they had 10 percent of all school enrollments. Most had chapels or religious images, while their priests said mass and taught catechism classes. The wealthy and influential enrolled their children in them, and the middle class, when it could afford to, followed suit. Many of the technocrats had attended church schools; De la Madrid, to name one, had gone to the Colegio Colón of the Lasallistas.

Everything, nonetheless, was not well with the holy fathers. Mexican Catholics were not always loyal, as the case of Jalisco revealed. Although 97.6 percent of its inhabitants were baptized Catholics, less than half of them attended mass on Sundays. Religious apathy, a report alleged, reigned in Catholic Guadalajara, the capital of Jalisco, a city hampered by a lack of priests and beset by the activity of militant Protestant sects. With 4.3 million Catholics, the diocese of Guadalajara had fewer than one thousand priests. In Jalisco, on the average, there was one priest for every 7,000 Catholics, compared with one for every 3,000 in the 1950s. For the countryside, the ideal ratio of priests to their flock, the savants maintained, was one to 2,000 Catholics; the reality was one for 10,000 to 12,000 of the faithful. Up to 40 percent of the students in seminaries dropped out before becoming priests.

The clergy, furthermore, was not of one mind. The hierarchy, as in the past, was conservative, as were most priests. For them, the choice of school had to be made by parents, not secular officials. But, there were notable exceptions. Until he retired in 1983, Sergio Méndez Arceo, bishop of Cuernavaca, had consistently sided with reformers, as had Arturo Lomo of Tehuantepec, friendly to COCEI, the leftist political coalition. In San Cristóbal de las Casas, an urban hub of Chiapas, Bishop Samuel Ruiz García shared similar sentiments, as did his colleague in Guerrero, a mountain diocese in Chihuahua. Méndez Arceo had visited Cuba, where Fidel decorated him with the Orden de la Solidaridad, bestowed for "merit in the struggle against imperialism, fascism, colonialism, neocolonialism, and other forms of exploitation." Referring to him as a friend, Méndez Arceo thought Fidel a "model leader." For Méndez Arceo and his followers, Mexico's economic model spawned false hopes at the expense of the poor. Bishops and priests of dissimilar opinion, surely the majority, upheld the banners of the PRI or, more likely, the PAN. More and more, however, bishops and priests, whatever their political persuasion, were asking government to honor its pledge to hold honest elections, especially after the PRI manipulated voting tallies in Chihuahua and Durango in 1986, both PAN redoubts.

The military, the other historical legacy, enjoyed a nebulous existence. Though visible everywhere, its generals, outside of patriotic utterances on the Sixteenth of September, rarely spoke out, at least for the public to hear. Since 1929, when the Obregonistas rebelled, no military coup had upset the quiet of the Republic. Dabblers in politics claimed that the army had been depoliticized, a view not shared by cynical Mexicans. True, the generals had stayed out of politics; a mere handful had gone on to become governors of states, and only one had headed the PRI.

That behavior, just the same, was an illusion. The PRI bosses and the army brass, in actuality, were cut from the same cloth, men of identical values and attitudes. Taking its cue from Priístas, much of the older officer corps was corrupt, with ties to business and the drug traffic. The government, knowing on what side its bread was buttered, ruled off-limits any criticism of the military, even when generals were implicated in the drug trade. Of the freedoms of expression, López Portillo once said, just one was off-limits: flaying the military. "Of me, say what you will, but utter not one word against the army." When the novelist Juan Rulfo, on an official visit to Argentina, had the temerity to say that corruption was employed to keep the generals in line, López Portillo, a friend of the author, ordered him home immediately.

For all that, the military, some seventy thousand strong by 1989, was not necessarily monolithic. Generally of conservative inclinations, the army bosses marched alongside of the PRI, applauding, for example, its forceful handling of election protest in Chihuahua in 1986. Like Priístas, the brass hats had gotten their eagles by obeying orders. Under their command, the army helped train men for the Contras in Nicaragua, mercenaries in the pay of the United States. Next in line were middle-rank officers, loyal to their superiors but mindful of shifts in the political winds; not a few, it was rumored, had agendas of their own. At the bottom of the ladder were the younger officers, many of them wishing to modernize the army, to adopt the latest technology, and ready, so it was said, to sponsor change. What the fighting qualities of the military were, one could merely speculate. Like the old Porfirista military, it was a police force, employed to keep order and to squelch political dissent, rather than an army for the defense of the *patria*.

In Mexico, to quote one wag, people enjoyed full freedom of thought, relative freedom of expression, and no freedom of action. That, more or less, summed up reality. Freedom of expression, however, was more myth than truth. When it came to speaking or writing the truth, said the bishop of Ciudad Juárez, referring to the elections of 1986, "silence prevailed, plus misinformation, as well as the violent distortion of the facts." He asserted that both television and radio had parroted official propaganda, while newspapers and journals were only slightly less dishonest.

Control of the media had old antecedents. Don Porfirio, never fond of critics, had muzzled newspapers and journals, while the rebels of 1910, after a brief fling with freedom of the press, had clamped tight controls on it. By the 1920s, both *El Universal* and *Excélsior*, the two national newspapers, had been made to toe the line. Things got worse after 1944, when Miguel Alemán, then *secretario de gobernación,* had gone after the owner of *Novedades,* a newspaper he wanted to acquire for his forthcoming presidential campaign. A strike, engineered by the Alemanistas, shut down the newspaper, and, after its owner was murdered, *Novedades* became Alemán's.

Other tools, too, were used to muzzle the media. Until recently, the importation and sale of newsprint was controlled by the government. Newspapers and journals had to ask PIPSA, a government agency, for their supply. For lack of sufficient private business, the press depended on government for much of its advertising, which it withheld if newsmen were critical. Badly paid reporters were given bribes, referred to as *el chayote,* to write favorable stories. When Julio Scherer, editor of *Excélsior,* tried to give it an independent slant in the 1970s, bankers, industrialists, and merchants, frightened by what they labeled its "leftist" orientation, stopped advertising. A bit later, President Luis Echeverría, stung by *Excélsior*'s criticism of his regime, manipulated the ouster of Scherer.

Radio and television, too, danced to the oligarchical tune, but for slightly different reasons. After a sojourn in Los Angeles, Raul Azcárraga, of the Monterrey clans, had founded the Casa de la Radio in Mexico, largely as a branch of the Radio Corporation of America (RCA). From that time on, radio in Mexico had close links with networks north of the border. In 1950, Azcárraga, along with Miguel Alemán, established Televisa, a private television network allied with government and hostile to strikes, leftist opinion, Cuba and the Soviet Union, socialist and Communist "ideas" and friendly to Washington's version of the universe. Imevision, the public television chain, was a distant second to Televisa and, though running, from time to time, laudable programs, echoed PRI propaganda.

III

In *Los relámpagos de agosto,* published in 1965, Jorge Ibargüengoitia deftly captured the transformation of Mexican life. Writing at a time when the Mexican novel was devoid of humor, Ibargüengoitia employed it to parody the era of the Revolution, that venerable episode of Mexican mythology. In *Los relámpagos,* a novel about the military uprising of 1929, the heroes were absurd and outrageous and the deeds ludicrous anecdotes. In the course of the story, the rhetoric of the Revolution was unveiled as the empty talk of opportunistic and bungling fools. Ibargüengoitia's novels laid to rest the heroic themes of the novel of the Revolution.

For the generation of Ibargüengoitia, Tlatelolco, that bloody night in October, had untold consequences, as he demonstrated in *Maten el león,* a satire of the Spanish-American dictator whose brutality, by implication, spawned the tragedy of 1968. Tlatelolco also conferred fresh stature on José

Revueltas, author of *El luto humano.* Jailed for his role in the student protest, Reveultas wrote *El apando,* his last novel, in 1969, a scathing indictment of life behind bars. An early Communist who dropped out of the party, he rejoined it after the death of Joseph Stalin, dying an admirer of the Cuban revolution.

Along with the search for identity, heart and soul of Carlos Fuentes's first novels, the city, more and more, became the focus of contemporary literature. Although still writing, Fuentes was no longer in Mexico; his novels, by the same token, had acquired an international flavor. Once an avid critic of the United States, he now taught and wrote there. The search for identity, but in an urban setting, was the theme of *Morirás lejos,* a novel by José Emilio Pacheco, a master of the technique of self-analysis in prose, a style also adopted by Salvador Elizondo in *El hipogeo secreto* and by Julieta Campos in *Tiene los cabellos rojizos y se llama Sabina.*

Nostalgia, the longing for a safer, more comfortable past, was one more pillar of the contemporary novel. The metamorphosis of Mexico City into a giant metropolis left many Mexicans uncertain about their future, an obsession mirrored in the novel. One example of it was Pacheco's *Las batallas en el desierto,* where he recalled the *colonia* (suburb) of his youth in the days of the Alemanistas. Arturo Azuela, in *Un tal Salomé,* evoked memories of people now dead, while María Luisa Mendoza, in *El perro de la escribana,* explored the house she had lived in.

The publication of *La tumba* by José Agustín in 1964 lifted the curtain on the *novela de la onda,* a literary assault on society, traditional customs, and the contemporary generation. In *Se está hacienda tarde,* he told of urbanites who looked for happiness in Acapulco, relying on drugs and sex to find it. Given the nature of Mexico, where the police preyed on you and corruption was ubiquitous and misery and poverty constant companions, it was best to look to the past for guidance. Bad as it may have been, one at least knew what it was; the future was menacing and unknown. For Agustín, in *Cerca del fuego,* Mexicans, in order to survive, had learned to shut their eyes to the catastrophe of their country. Only when Mexicans had reached rock bottom, Agustín seemed to say, was salvation possible; only then would they take steps to destroy the horrible fiasco around them.

Art had also undergone a transformation. With the mural masters dead, the "cactus curtain," so baptized by José Luis Cuevas, was gone. Mexican painters had opened their souls to outside models. Rufino Tamayo, the ancient of the contemporary masters, still painted. Eleven years of age when he arrived in Mexico City from his native Oaxaca, Tamayo had been an acolyte in the Catholic church. Mexico City, half colonial and half French, as he remembered, had "made me change completely. It made me forget about religion . . . and that's when I started to make drawings." In the 1960s, after thirty years in Paris and New York, Tamayo, in appearance more Indian than

Spaniard, returned home. Wealthy and the pampered artist of rich foreigners and natives alike, Tamayo, always a conservative, delighted in attacking David Alfaro Siqueiros for being a Communist. Yet Tamayo's work extolled pre-Columbian art, adopting its forms, themes, and colors. For Tamayo, the "Mexican tradition" was "pre-Hispanic." Something of an international celebrity and a disciple of modern art, Cuevas lived in Paris and New York, having rejected the realistic style of the muralists, which he referred to as "pictorial *indigenismo.*" Still, to quote him, he painted "sweat-stained masses of businessmen, priests, clerks, prostitutes, bank cashiers, and pregnant women who go their own way without realizing that they are seeking oblivion."

For the theater, playwrights still wrote dramas that caught the public's eye, one being Vicente Leñero's much lauded *Nadie Sabe Nada,* an angry spoof on Mexican politics. Poking fun at Priístas, the play focused on government immorality, bribes to newspaper reporters, and cops who engaged in perverted sex acts in public toilets. Officials in Mexico City, where the drama had its showing, shut it down, until Leñero agreed to delete, according to the Instituto de Bellas Artes, "references of questionable taste to persons and institutions that deserve our consideration and respect." Leñero replied that since the "drama speaks of political and press corruption . . . it cannot be considered slanderous."

The film industry, meanwhile, had taken a turn for the worse. Emilio Fernández, Roberto Gavaldón, and Mauricio Magdaleno, three of the great directors, had died, leaving picture making in the hands of producers interested primarily in profits. Banality characterized their productions. Only Paul Leduc's version of John Reed's *Insurgent Mexico* and a handful of other films broke with that pattern. Offering a fresh interpretation of the Revolution, the film *México Insurgente* portrayed it as a "chaotic conflict between bands rather than an epic struggle between good and evil." Most Mexicans paid to see Hollywood movies, one reason for the decline of the Mexican film industry.

Mexicans, if young at heart, listened to music popularized in the United States, from rock and roll played by steel guitar bands to salsa and rock. The poor in the countryside and in the urban barrios continued to listen to mariachis, trumpet sounds, once absent, now a steady din. The lyrics of this "country" music recalled heroes of bygone days, usually of the "Revolución," hailed the deeds of macho males and lamented loves spurned.

IV

Unbelievably, the PRI machine, the oligarchy's voice, finally faltered. Confident that they would get their usual victories during the presidential elections of 1988, its bosses chose a colorless bureaucrat to carry its banners. In doing so, they shut their eyes to widespread discontent, preferring to rely on shopworn remedies rather than strike a balance. But hard times, which daily nibbled away at the living standards of workers, campesinos, and middle class, had turned politics upside down. By ignoring this, the Priístas courted disaster.

Carlos Salinas de Gortari, the candidate, was just thirty-nine years old. A crony of Miguel de la Madrid, he had never held elective office. Possessor of a doctor's degree in political economy from Harvard, he was *secretario de programación y presupuesto,* the former job of De la Madrid, and, as its head, influential in charting policy. Mexicans knew what he stood for; once in office, he declared obsolete the Mexican Revolution and its welfare state. Like his companions in politics and business, Salinas, a neoliberal reminiscent of the days of the Porfiriato, believed in sacrificing a generation in order to save the next; it was necessary to impose "short-term suffering" in exchange for more comfortable days to follow. Thin, partly bald, and a dull public speaker, he was everything but charismatic. As a national symbol of hope in a time of crisis, he was a poor choice.

The Priístas had counted on their customary rivals, mainly the PAN and candidates of the splintered leftist parties. For their standard-bearer, the Panistas postulated Manuel Clouthier, a wealthy businessman from Sinaloa, charismatic and an eloquent speaker. There was hardly a "dime's worth of difference" between him and Salinas. Clouthier claimed simply that he would do a better job, be honest and more efficient. From the start, many *norteños* supported him, primarily in Chihuahua and Sonora and, farther south, in Jalisco, as did much of the clerical hierarchy and many of the old-line conservatives.

What the PRI had not reckoned with was an independent, popular, left-of-center candidate, precisely what it confronted in the summer of 1988. Almost by default, dissident Priístas, unhappy with the autocratic rule of their party and the coloration of its blueprints, took it upon themselves to jump ship and put up a candidate of their own. The mantle fell on Cuauhtémoc Cárdenas. A former governor of Michoacán, Cuauhtémoc, a bookish engineer, was the least likely candidate to rally the people behind him. But he did, despite being "somber, restrained, and unexcitable." Cárdenas, unlike run-of-the-mill Priístas, projected sincerity, decency, and, no less significant, a sense of caring for the marginalized. He was also the son of Don Lázaro, Mexico's popular reform president; to quote a truck driver in Tijuana, Cuauhtémoc "was of good stock."

To challenge the PRI, Cárdenas, who proved an inspiring and forceful leader, organized, with the help of his cohorts, the Frente Democrático Nacional (FDN), a coalition that took in the Partido Socialista Mexicano. Its appeal was a populist one, beyond parties, aimed directly at the people, demanding respect for the Constitution and promising to revive the spirit of social justice. Instead of austerity, Cárdenas talked about money for education, public health, and programs of benefit to campesinos and small farmers. For labor, he asked for just wages and unions free of *charros;* to the middle class, he pledged honest elections, independent political parties, democracy, and legislation to protect "authentic" Mexican industry. Payments on the foreign debt, which he likened to a yoke on Mexico's neck, he thought misguided, calling for a postponement as well as a cancellation of part of it. Upholding a nationalistic stance on foreign affairs, he denounced Washington's meddling in Central America.

As expected, the PRI claimed victory but, surprisingly, with just 50.36 percent of the popular vote, the lowest ever for a presidential candidate. Cárdenas, the PRI acknowledged, had captured the Federal District and the cities of Tijuana and Mexicali in Baja California Norte. For all that, only Priístas knew actually how people had voted because the stench of fraud hung over the land. The election, most Mexicans believed, had been stolen from Cárdenas. To assure their triumph, the Priístas, in December of 1986, had revised the electoral code, allotting to themselves an absolute majority on the Federal Electoral Commission, the final arbiter. During the campaign, two of Cárdenas's aides in Michoacán were killed by thugs. On the day of the election, opposition poll watchers were driven off, ballot boxes stuffed, unfriendly voters turned asway, and ballots burned. In the Federal District, one-fifth of the voters were either dead, among them Miguel Alemán, underage, or figments of Priísta imagination. As election results started coming in, mostly negative to Salinas, the national computerized vote tabulation system unexpectedly broke down. Delayed results, with nearly 25,000 out of 55,000 precincts missing, showed that Salinas had won.

What the election results meant for the future was difficult to say. Many Mexicans, among them pundits of repute, believed that politics would never be the same again. The PRI, according to this interpretation, had lost its stranglehold on Mexican politics. This view overlooked the reality of the PRI, its access to the national treasury, the size of its bureaucratic network, and its friends in Washington. Relying on the International Monetary Fund and the World Bank, Washington, to document this, had by April 1989 propped up the Salinas regime with loans of $7.5 billion. This was, nevertheless, a paper rescue, for Mexico would have to pay much of it back.

The bailout did not prevent the PAN from winning the governorship of Baja California Norte, a first in Mexico, in the midterm elections of July 1989. So overwhelming was its victory that the PRI leadership chose to make its peace with the old rival. As political wags pointed out, the PAN triumph did not jeopardize the hold of the oligarchy on Mexico; the PRI and the PAN were like two peas in a pod. On the other hand, in Michoacán, the Partido de la Revolución Democrática (PRD), the new Cardenista vehicle, met a different fate. Although the Cardenistas won a majority of the seats in the state legislature, the Priístas denied them victory, turning a deaf ear to the opinion of a review of election results by an independent tribunal of respected citizens who cried foul. Unlike the PAN, the PRD, which in Michoacán had heavy campesino support, challenged not just the political control of the PRI but the economic formula of the power brokers. By January 1990, some fifty-six members of the opposition Partido de la Revolución Democrática had been killed in political violence since Cárdenas, its leader, had challenged the PRI's dominance.

Later, to shore up Salinas and the PRI, Washington formulated one more rescue scheme, by which Mexico committed itself to purchase about $3 billion of United States treasury bonds, to be paid for by loans from the IMF, the World Bank, and Japan, in return for a savings, if all went well, of up to $11 billion from the $53 billion owed banks, 11 percent of the Republic's $100 billion foreign debt. Although a substantial concession to Mexico, the agreement brought far less than the amount of money required to get the economy back on its feet. When that debt-relief agreement faltered, Washington, in January 1990, again answered Mexico's pleas for help, this time selling special bonds at discount prices. Nonetheless, 68 percent of Mexico's total expenditures would have to be set aside to service its foreign and domestic debt.

Washington's largess, which Salinas described as a glowing victory for Mexico, won the hearts of his visible supporters, among them the three hundred or so wealthiest families, the Catholic hierarchy, much of the middle class, United States officials, and investors in accord with the government's drive to privatize the economy. The hyperbole of Salinas received enthusiastic endorsements from big business and industry, one sure sign of who benefited from the financial accords. That applause, too, reminded one of the days of Don Porfirio, whose policies incurred the wrath of the rebels of 1910.

V

This, then, is the saga of the Mexican people, a story of sporadic triumphs played out on a stage of tragic drama. Like the Othello of Shakespeare, Mexicans have witnessed the worst and best of their time: "machinations, hollowness, treachery, and all ruinous disorders" which "follow us disquietly to our grave." But then, too, they had a Lázaro Cárdenas, an apostle of the downtrodden, and a José Clemente Orozco, one of the major artists of the twentieth century, one of that handful of titans who have made our century one of the most creative in history.

BOOKS AND MORE BOOKS

This is a far cry from being an exhaustive bibliography; I simply entered some of the books I found handy in the writing of this *History of the Mexican People* and added others. Obviously, I have overlooked a multitude of articles, which one must read if one is to have a solid grasp of Mexico's past. I apologize to all of those worthy colleagues I have neglected. The books are listed by author, title, and date of publication; when available, translations are given. Bear in mind, too, that some books go through more than one edition.

The Forefathers

Early versions of the pre-Columbian era, told with a Spanish slant, are Francisco Javier Clavijero, *Historia antigua de Nueva España* (1787); Fernando de Alva Ixtlilxóchitl, *Historia Chichimeca* (1892), scholarship of "mestizo" vintage; Jerónimo de Mendieta, *Historia ecclesiástica indiana* (1870); Toribio de Motolinía, *Historia de los Indios de Nueva España* (1914); Bernardino de Sahagún, *Historia de las cosas de Nueva España* (1829); and Juan de Torquemada, *Monarquía indiana* (1613–15). Among recent publications of note are Richard Adams, *The Origins of Maya Civilization* (1977); Ignacio Bernal, *Mexico before Cortez: Art, History, and Legend* (1975), small but delightfully written; Alfonso Caso, *The Aztecs: People of the Sun* (1958); a cherished opus is Miguel Covarrubias, *Indian Art of Mexico and Central America* (1957); Nigel Davis, *The Ancient Kingdoms of Mexico* (1982); George Kubler, *The Art and Architecture of Ancient America* (1962), solid and highly informative; Salvador Toscano, *Arte precolombino de México y de la América Central* (1944), for artistic currents; Sylvanus G. Morley, *The Ancient Maya* (1965), the version of the "peaceful" Maya; Linda Schele and David Freidel, *A Forest of Kings: The Untold Story of the Ancient Maya* (1990), the warrior interpretation; J. Eric Thompson, *The Rise and Fall of Maya Civilization* (1985); George Vaillant, *The Aztecs of Mexico* (1941), vintage but excellent.

For medieval Spain, read Rafael Altamira, *A History of Spain* (1949), a traditional but important rendering; Trevor R. Davis, *The Golden Century of Spain, 1501–1621* (1961); a sympathetic and well-done account is John H. Elliott, *Imperial Spain, 1469–*

1716 (1962); Jaime Vicens Vives, *Aproximación a la historia de España* (1952), is a splendid diagnosis by an economic historian; and Rodolfo Puiggros, *La España que conquistó el Nuevo Mundo* (1965), looks at "mother" Spain from a Marxist point of view.

The Colonial Centuries

The literature of the Conquest, when the colonial drama unfolds, begins with two mighty accounts: Hernán Cortés, *Letters from Mexico* (1971), and Bernal Díaz del Castillo's much quoted *True History of the Conquest of New Spain* (1966). Not as well known but also famous is Francisco López de Gómara's *The Life of the Conqueror by His Secretary* (1964). For the "Indian" version see Miguel León Portilla, ed., *Visión de los vencidos* (1971). Also worthy of reading are Ramón Iglesia, *El hombre Colón y otros ensayos* (1944), beautifully written; Salvador Madariaga, *Hernán Cortés, Conqueror of Mexico* (1955), hero-worship by a Spanish historian; William H. Prescott's justly famous *History of the Conquest of Mexico* (1967), a Protestant eulogy to Cortés dating from 1843; and Silvio Zavala, *La filosofía política en la conquista de América* (1947).

The study of three centuries of colonial tutelage spawned a vast literature; to do it justice would require a voluminous essay. Among the tomes that merit attention are Peter J. Bakewell, *Silver Mining and Society in Colonial Mexico: Zacatecas, 1546–1700* (1971); Woodrow Wilson Borah, *New Spain's Century of Depression* (1951), a disputed version of the seventeenth-century economy; Marcelo Carmagnani, *El regreso de los dioses* (1988); François Chevalier, *Land and Society in Colonial Mexico: The Great Hacienda* (1963); Jesús Estrada, *Música y músicos de la época virreinal* (1973), a rare look at colonial music; Nancy M. Farris, *Maya Society under Colonial Rule: The Collective Enterprise of Survival* (1984); Thomas Gage, *Travels in the New World* (1969), an English friar's insular view of life in the Spanish colonies; Charles Gibson, *The Aztecs under Spanish Rule: A History of the Valley of Mexico, 1521–1810,* a pillar of scholarship; Richard E. Greenleaf, *The Mexican Inquisition of the Sixteenth Century* (1969); Lewis Hanke, *The Spanish Struggle for Justice in the Conquest of America* (1949); J. I. Israel, *Race, Class and Politics in Colonial Mexico* (1975), a perceptive inquiry into this forgotten topic; Wigberto Jiménez Moreno, *Estudios de historia colonial* (1958); George Kubler, *Mexican Architecture of the Sixteenth Century* (1948), much more than simply a study of buildings; Irving R. Leonard, *Baroque Times in Old Mexico* (1971) and *Books of the Brave* (1949), forays into literary and cultural history; Robert Ricard, *The Spiritual Conquest of Mexico* (1966); Richard C. Salvucci, *Textiles and Capitalism in Colonial Mexico: An Economic History of the Obrajes, 1690–1840* (1986); a Marxist explanation is offered by Enrique Semo's *Historia del capitalismo en México: Los origines* (1973); Lesley B. Simpson, *The Encomienda in New Spain* (1960); Robert Stevenson, *Music in Mexico: A Historical Survey* (1971), one of the few books in English on this subject; William B. Taylor, *Landlord and Peasant in Colonial Oaxaca* (1972) and *Drinking, Homicide and Rebellion in Colonial Mexico* (1979), the latter an innovative look at Indian resistance under Spanish tutelage; Guillermo Tovar de Teresa, *México Barroco* (1981); and Manuel Toussaint, *Arte colonial en México* (1974), the masterwork by the best of the colonial art historians.

Era of Independence

An eyewitness account, where research must start, is Lucas Alamán's *Historia de México desde los primeros movimientos que prepararon su independencia en el año de 1808, hasta la época presente* (1849–52), a massive, five-volume work by one of Mexico's most famous historians; no less important is José María Luis Mora's *México y sus revoluciones* (1836), the Liberal argument in three volumes. In that same category is Carlos María de Bustamente's *Cuadro histórico de la revolución de la América mexicana* (1823–32), a study in six volumes by a lawyer of the period. A milestone is Justo Sierra's *The Political Evolution of the Mexican People* (1969), published initially in 1902.

The days of New Spain are also described in Silvia M. Arrom, *The Women of Mexico City, 1790–1857* (1985), a pioneering inquiry into the role of gender; David A. Brading, *Miners and Merchants in Bourbon Mexico, 1763–1810* (1971) and *The Origins of Mexican Nationalism* (1985); Luis Castillo Ledón, *Hidalgo: La vida del héroe* (1960), the "patriotic" version; must reading is Enrique Florescano's *Precios de maíz y crisis agrícola en México, 1708–1810* (1969); Alexander von Humboldt, *Political Essay on the Kingdom of New Spain* (1972), a historical gem; for a controversial portrait of Miguel Hidalgo, see Jorge Ibargüengoitia, *Los pasos de López* (1981), a fascinating novel; Doris M. Ladd, *The Mexican Nobility at Independence* (1976); Ernesto Lemoine Villicaña, *Morelos: Su vida revolucionaria a través de sus escritos y de otros testimonios de la época* (1965); Colin M. MacLachlan, *Spain's Empire in the New World* (1988); and Herbert I. Priestley, *José de Gálvez, Visitor-General of New Spain, 1765–1771* (1916), an oldie that merits attention. On the era of conflict, the following are useful: Hugh Hamill, *The Hidalgo Revolt: Prelude to Mexican Independence* (1966), and Ernesto de la Torre Villar, *La constitución de Apatzingán y los creadores del estado mexicano* (1964); and, of course, Luis Villoro's intriguing *El proceso ideológico de la Revolución de Independencia* (1953), an unorthodox interpretation of ideas and events.

Early National

Once again, the basic "texts" are Alamán, Mora, and Bustamante, now joined by Lorenzo Zavala's *Ensayo histórico de las revoluciones de México desde 1808 hasta 1830* (1931–32), a study of that era in two volumes by a participant. In a category by itself is Madame Calderón de la Barca's *Life in Mexico* (1843). Also helpful are José Fuentes Mares, *Santa Anna: Aurora y ocaso de un comediante* (1956); Moisés González Navarro, *El pensamiento político de Lucas Alamán* (1952); Charles A. Hale, *Mexican Liberalism in the Age of Mora, 1821–1853* (1968); Nelson Reed, an anthropologist who tells the saga of the Maya revolt in *The Caste War of Yucatán* (1964); Julio Jiménez Rueda, *Letras mexicanas en el siglo xix* (1944); Jesús Reyes Heroles, *El liberalismo mexicano* (1957); José M. Roa Barcena, *Recuerdos de la invasión norteamericana, 1846–48* (1947), a firsthand view of the War of 1846; Anne Staples, *La iglesia en la primera república federal mexicana (1824–1835)* (1976); José C. Valadés, *Santa Anna y la guerra de Texas* (1936), a portrait of the caudillo by a novelist; and Josefina Vázquez de Knauth, *Mexicanos y norteamericanos ante la guerra del 47* (1960).

The Middle Years

The most complete chronicle of the era is Justo Sierra's *Juárez: Su obra y su tiempo* (1905–06). No one can claim familiarity with the Reforma generation who slights Ignacio Altamirano's *Navidad en las montañas* (1957), a moving *cuento* (story) of Christmas in rural Mexico, or Guillermo Prieto's *Memorias de mis tiempos* (1969). To fill out the picture, read Jan Bazant, *Los bienes de la iglesia en México, 1856–1875* (1971), which deals with church wealth; José Luis Blasio, *Maximiliano intimo: El emperador Maximiliano y su corte* (1960), the private secretary's opinions on Maximilian; Francisco Bulnes, *Juárez y las revoluciones de Ayutla y de la Reforma* (1905), a jaundiced interpretation of Juárez; Egon C. Corti, *Maximilian and Carlota* (1944), a flattering picture of the emperor; Luis González y González, *La vida social,* in Daniel Cosío Villegas, ed., *Historia moderna de México* (1957); on rancheros of the Reforma period, there is Luis G. Inclán, *Astucia* (1984), a novel about *charros;* Paula Kolonitz, *Un viaje a México en 1864* (1976), an Austrian woman's thoughts on Mexicans and their women; Matías Romero, *Diario personal, 1855–1865* (1960), the memoirs of a leading politico and diplomat of that time; and Francisco Zarco, *Historia del Congreso Constituyente Extraordinario de 1856–1857* (1956), a narrative of the assembly that drew up the charter of 1857.

Porfiriato

The most complete, if uneven, account of these years is the *Historia moderna de México* (1955–74), in ten volumes, edited by Daniel Cosío Villegas; he wrote the last two. On Díaz, consult Franciso Bulnes, *El verdadero Díaz y la Revolución* (1967), and Rafael de Zayas Enríquez, *Porfirio Díaz* (1908), a provocative analysis of the strongman by a firend and collaborator. To that add Mariano Azuela, *Cien años de novela mexicana* (1947), an assessment of the nineteenth-century novel; John H. Coatsworth, *Crecimiento contra desarrollo: El Impacto económico de los ferrocarriles en el porfiriato* (1976); Charles M. Flandrau, *Viva Mexico* (1908), a delightful tour of Don Porfirio's Mexico; Stephen H. Haber, in *Industry and Underdevelopment: The Industrialization of Mexico* (1989), believes Mexico turned the industrial corner under Porfirio Díaz; Gilbert M. Joseph, in *Revolution from Without: Yucatán, Mexico and the United States, 1880–1924* (1982), sheds light on the empire of henequen; Ramón Prida, *De la dictadura a la anarquía* (1914), a view of events by a disappointed aspirant to public office; William C. Raat, *El positivismo durante el porfiriato (1876–1910)* (1975); Emilio Rabasa, *La evolución histórica de México* (1920), one of the "bibles" of the Porfiristas by a politico; Ramón Eduardo Ruiz, *The People of Sonora and Yankee Capitalists* (1988), examines the impact of foreign investment on a Mexican province; Raquel Tibol, *Hermenegildo Bustos, pintor de pueble* (1981), a short but lively portrait of this legendary "primitive" painter; John Kenneth Turner, *Barbarous Mexico* (1910), an indictment of the Porfiriato; and José M. Valadés, *El porfirismo: Historia de un régimen* (1941–47), by a rival historian of Daniel Cosío Villagas.

The Great Rebellion

A fascinating narrative of Francisco Madero's travails in northwest Mexico is Hector Aguilar Camín's *La Frontera nómada: Sonora y la Revolución mexicana* (1977); from that, jump to Mariano Azuela's epic *Los de abajo,* an unflattering picture of the Revolution; valuable, too, are Martín Luis Guzmán, *El águila y la serpiente* (1928), part fiction and part memoir; read, too, his novel *La sombra del caudillo* (1929), for a harsh verdict of Alvaro Obregón; Manuel Calero, *Un decenio de política mexicana* (1920), an evaluation by an opportunistic and ambitious politico; Barry Carr, *El movimiento obrero y la política en México, 1910–1929* (1976); John M. Hart, *Revolutionary Mexico: The Coming and Process of the Mexican Revolution* (1987); Friedrich Katz, *The Secret War in Mexico* (1981), the story of foreign plotting against change in Mexico; Gildardo Magaña, *Emiliano Zapata y el agrarismo en México* (1934–52), a defense of Zapata's ideals by a general who later collaborated with his enemies; Manuel Márquez Sterling, *Los últimos días del Presidente Madero* (1958), a diplomat on the scene laments the tragic death of Madero; Michael C. Meyer, *Huerta: A Political Portrait* (1972), a dissenting view of the "Usurper"; Ramón Eduardo Ruiz, *Labor and the Ambivalent Revolutionaries: Mexico, 1911–1923* (1973) and *The Great Rebellion: Mexico, 1905–1924* (1980), which rejects the thesis of a "social revolution" in Mexico; Rosendo Salazar, *Las pugnas de la gleba, 1907–1922* (1923), labor memoirs recalled with gusto; Jesús Sotelo Inclán, *Raíz y razón de Zapata* (1970); and John Womack, *Zapata and the Mexican Revolution* (1970).

Only Yesterday

Luis Cabrera, an economist and politico under Venustiano Carranza, tells his side of events in *Obras completas* (1921), while Lázaro Cárdenas gives disappointingly few in his *Ideario político* (1972). See also Aflredo Cardona Peña, *Conversaciones con Diego Rivera* (1986); Arnaldo Córdova, *La ideolgía de la Revolución mexicana* (1973); for art history, Justino Fernández, *El arte moderno en México* (1937); on the agrarian question, Marte R. Gómez, *La reforma agraria de México: Su crisis duarante el periodo 1928–1934* (1964), an analysis by an expert; Pablo González Casanova, *La democracia en México* (1965), a negative judgment of contemporary policy: Manuel González Ramírez, *La revolución social de México* (1960–66); Judith Adler Hellman, *Mexico in Crisis* (1983), offers good insights into what is wrong with today's Mexico; an intimate biography of Frida Kahlo is Hayden Herrera, *Frida: A Biography of Frida Kahlo* (1983); Jean Meyer, *La Cristiada: El conflicto entre la inglesia y el estado, 1926–1929* (1973), deals with the Cristero uprising; the oil question is discussed by Lorenzo Meyer in *México y Estado Unidos en el conflicto petrolero (1917–1942)* (1968); Olga Pellicer de Brody and Esteban L. Mancilla, *Historia de la Revolución mexicana: Periodo 1952–1960* (1978), offer a logical explanation of the economic planning of that decade; Elena Poniatowska, *La noche de Tlatelolco: Testimonios de historia oral* (1971), is required reading on the student massacre of 1968; in Emilio Portes Gil, *Quince años de política mexicana* (1941), an ex-president cautiously speaks his mind; David R. Raby, *Educación y revolución social en México, 1921–1940* (1974); a famous polemic is Samuel Ramos, *Profile of Man and Culture in Mexico* (1962); Alan Riding, a journalist dissects contemporary Mexico in *Distant*

Neighbors: A Portrait of the Mexicans (1985); Guadalupe Rivera Marín, daughter of Diego Rivera, recalls his life in *Un Río, dos Riveras: Vida de Diego Rivera (1886–1929)* (1989); Ramón Eduardo Ruiz, *The Challenge of Poverty and Illiteracy in Mexico* (1973); Alex M. Saragoza, *The Monterrey Elite and the Mexican State, 1880–1940* (1988), a good business history; on presidents, ponder Julio Scherer García, *Los presidentes* (1986); Peter D. Smith, *Labryinths of Power: Political Recruitment in Twentieth-Century Mexico* (1979), examines the political structure; Raquel Tibol, *Historia general del arte mexicano: Epoca moderna y contemporanea* (1964), a book by a fine art historian, and her acclaimed *José Clemente Orozco: Una vida para el arte* (1984); José Vasconcelos, *Obras completas* (1957–61), four volumes of opinions by an unhappy and bitter former politico and intellectual; Mary Kay Vaughn, *The State, Education and Social Class in Mexico, 1880–1928* (1982); Nathaniel and Sylvia Weyl, *The Reconquest of Mexico: The Years of Lazaro Cardenas* (1939), a positive appraisal of *Cardenismo;* and, finally, Bertram D. Wolfe's *The Life and Times of Diego Rivera* (1939), an engrossing sketch of the artist and and his Mexico.

INDEX